ARCTIC   OCEAN

Svalbard
(Norway)

Franz Josef Land
(Rus. Fed.)

FINLAND

SWEDEN   ESTONIA
          LATVIA
          LITHUANIA

POLAND   BELARUS

CZ REP.
          UKRAINE

HUNGARY
          ROMANIA

          BULGARIA

RUSSIAN   FEDERATION

KAZAKHSTAN

KYRGYZSTAN

UZBEKISTAN

TURKMENISTAN

TAJIKISTAN

MONGOLIA

CHINA

GREECE   TURKEY

Aleppo
Cherry kebabs
  ○ *p172*

LEBANON   SYRIA

ISRAEL

Beirut
Kibbeh Nayyeh
p176

Tehran
Polo
p178

IRAQ

AFGHANISTAN

IRAN

Isfahan
Khoresh-e Fesenjan
p164

PAKISTAN

Delhi
Tandoori
p250

NEPAL

Beijing
Peking duck
p220

NORTH
KOREA

Seoul
Royal banquets
p226

SOUTH
KOREA

Kyoto
Kaiseki
p196

Tokyo
Sushi
p246

JAPAN

Dujiangyan
Gong bao chicken
  p248

Chengdu
Teahouses
p206

Hangzhou
West Lake fish
p190

Fukuoka
Ramen
p208

Osaka
Okonomiyaki
p234

Okinawa
Goya chanpuru
p218

LIBYA

Cairo
Falafel, p162
Stuffed pigeon, p184

EGYPT

KUWAIT

SAUDI
ARABIA

U.A.E.

OMAN

INDIA

BANGLADESH

MYANMAR

Hanoi
Pho
p238

Hong Kong
Dim Sum
p200

PACIFIC
OCEAN

Mumbai
Chaat
p192

Vientiane
Laap
p236

VIETNAM

CHAD   SUDAN

ERITREA   YEMEN

Socotra
(Yemen)

Lalibela
Injera
p180

DJIBOUTI

ETHIOPIA

CENTRAL
AFRICAN REP.

Kerala
Fish curry
p228

MALDIVES

Tamil Nadu
Thali
p210

SRI
LANKA

Bangkok
Tom yam
p244

THAILAND

CAMBODIA

Hoi An
Street food
p212

Phnom Penh
Amok
p224

PHILIPPINES

Phuket
Green curry
p252

CONGO

DEM. REP.
CONGO

UGANDA
          KENYA

RWANDA
BURUNDI
          TANZANIA

SEYCHELLES

Penang
Asam laksa
p204

SINGAPORE

BRUNEI

MALAYSIA

MICRONESIA

Zanzibar
Swahili curry
p170

INDONESIA

ANGOLA   ZAMBIA   MALAWI

MOZAMBIQUE

MADAGASCAR

MAURITIUS

Réunion
(France)

INDIAN

OCEAN

Yogyakarta
Nasi goreng
p222

Bali
Satay
p198

EAST
TIMOR

PAPUA NEW
GUINEA

SOLOMON
ISLANDS

NAMIBIA

BOTSWANA

ZIMBABWE

VANUATU   FIJI

New Caledonia
(France)

Maputo
Chicken piri-piri
p182

SWAZILAND

AUSTRALIA

SOUTH
AFRICA

LESOTHO

Town
obotie
p166

Margaret River
Venison
p194

Sydney
Balmain Bugs
p216

Melbourne
Pan-Asian fusion
p232

NEW
ZEALAND

South Island
Bluff oysters
p240

ULTIMATE
FOOD JOURNEYS

ULTIMATE
FOOD JOURNEYS

THE WORLD'S BEST DISHES & WHERE TO EAT THEM

DK

LONDON, NEW YORK, MELBOURNE,
MUNICH, AND DELHI

LIST MANAGER Christine Stroyan
MANAGING EDITOR Julie Oughton
SENIOR EDITOR Sadie Smith
DESIGN MANAGER Mabel Chan
DESIGNER Tracy Smith
SENIOR DTP DESIGNER Jason Little

SENIOR CARTOGRAPHER Casper Morris
PRODUCTION CONTROLLER Sophie Argyris

PUBLISHER Vivien Antwi

Produced for Dorling Kindersley by

cobaltid

The Stables, Wood Farm, Deopham Road,
Attleborough, Norfolk NR17 1AJ
www.cobaltid.co.uk

EDITORS Louise Abbott, Sarah Tomley,
Marek Walisiewicz

DESIGN AND PICTURE RESEARCH
Paul Reid, Darren Bland

Printed and bound in Singapore by Tien Wah Press

First American Edition, 2011

11 12 13 10 9 8 7 6 5 4 3 2 1

Published in the United States by DK Publishing,
375 Hudson Street, New York, New York 10014

Copyright © 2011 Dorling Kindersley Limited, London
A Penguin Company

ISBN 978-0-7566-8600-0

Every effort has been made to ensure that this book is as up-to-date as
possible at the time of going to press. Some details, however, such as
telephone numbers, opening hours, prices, and travel information are liable
to change. The publishers cannot accept responsibility for any consequences
arising from the use of this book, nor for any material on third-party websites,
and cannot guarantee that any website address in this book will be a suitable
source of travel information. We value the views and suggestions of our readers
very highly. Please write to: Publisher, DK Travel Guides, Dorling Kindersley,
80 Strand, London, WC2R 0RL, or email travelguides@uk.dk.com.

www.traveldk.com

MAIN COVER IMAGE: Floating market, Damnoen Saduak, Thailand
HALF TITLE PAGE IMAGE: Grilling sardines, Algarve, Portugal
TITLE PAGE IMAGE: Outdoor market, Kota Bharu, Malaysia

Contents

Left to right A colorful fruit stand at a Mexican market; fresh-caught mackerel, Maine, USA; South African white wine on the Cape Town waterfront; a dim sum window menu in Hong Kong

Introduction

Somewhere in the world, it is always time for dinner. That happy fact is one of the joys of travel, as much a part of the vacation experience as visiting a destination's top sights. Rome offers the thrill of walking in the footsteps of the Caesars inside the Roman Forum and gazing heavenward at the Biblical tales that Michelangelo splashed across the ceiling of the Sistine Chapel. Yet the cuisine of the Eternal City is equally unforgettable. After a day of sightseeing, earthy fried artichokes – *carciofi alla giudia* – await in a neighborhood trattoria where the white-shirted waiter balances plates over his head as he weaves between tightly packed tables. There is no better way of finding out what makes a nation tick than through its culinary traditions.

> *Food does more than satisfy hunger – it awakens the senses and becomes the touchstone of memory.*

Food does so much more than satisfy hunger – it awakens the senses and becomes the touchstone of memory. Anyone who has ever visited Marrakech associates the lemony tang of a Moroccan chicken tagine with the phantasmagorical scene of evening dining on Jemaa el-Fna, the medina's central square. One nibble and it all floods back: the scent of wood smoke, calls to prayer rising from surrounding mosques, the nasal flutes of snake charmers, the deepening color of the sky as it arches from dusky rose to inky blue. Even months later, a single bite can summon up happy memories of an entire vacation.

But food is more than memory's trigger: it also recalls the deep history of a place. Long after people change their language, their dress, and even their religion, they continue cooking like their ancestors. Fresh food markets, many of which are featured in these pages, are tangible links between past and present. Winding mountainside streets and elaborate Spanish Baroque churches make Ecuador's Quito the best-preserved colonial city in the Americas. Yet its market stands brimming with potatoes speak of an era when Andean peasants first domesticated the humble spud, centuries before the conquistadors or even the Incas. Hungry travelers who tuck into a hearty bowl of the Ecuadoran potato stew, *locro de papa*, savor history one bite at a time.

In contrast to the epic sweep of the centuries, family traditions are often inextricably tied to the simple act of dining. A traveler in the right place at the right time might feel like a member of the extended clan. For many families in Rio de Janeiro, Sunday would be incomplete without a swim in the gentle surf and a romp on the sands of Ipanema Beach, immortalized in the bossa nova tune "The Girl from Ipanema." Equally important is the afternoon gathering at an Ipanema restaurant to share a large casserole

Below (left and center) A luxury chocolate shop in Brussels, Belgium; women selling vegetables at a street market in Jaisalmer, Rajasthan, India of the black-bean-and-sausage stew called *feijoada*. Food sets the rhythm of the day in the land of the samba – and around the world.

This book explores more than 125 destinations around the globe, with itineraries that pinpoint must-see attractions, from the dimly lit tango halls of Buenos Aires to the mirrored walls of the Jain Temple on Mumbai's Malabar Hill. Because taste and place are often inseparable, the book also identifies signature dishes and dining experiences for each destination. Riding the Star Ferry across Victoria Harbour and haggling over carvings in the Jade Market are don't-miss experiences for every traveler to Hong Kong. So is eating dim sum in a crowded restaurant – summoning the rolling carts of steamed delights until finally tasting the perfect *har gau* (shrimp dumpling).

The hundreds of restaurant recommendations have been hand-picked by the authors for unsurpassed versions of a destination's signature dish. They also identify other places to find the dishes in the region (where you can sometimes try interesting regional variations) and even around the world. The dining spots range from cozy one-room *bouchons* in Lyon to a theatrical 900-seat duck restaurant in Beijing, from brightly lit 24-hour taco stands in Mexico City to lobster shacks on floating docks along the craggy Maine coast. They share a single characteristic: authenticity.

Encountering a familiar food in its birthplace is one pleasure of any journey. From a hillside vista, a traveler can drink in the sweep of Naples: its red-tile rooftops cascading down to the crescent harbor, the ominous volcanic peak of Vesuvius on the horizon, the garden isles of Capri and Ischia bobbing in the bay. Down in the pulsing heart of the city, a tangle of Vespas stands outside every pizzeria as their riders wait for bubbling pies to emerge from wood-fired beehive ovens.

Travel can also unveil surprising culinary experiences and new flavors. Mozambique's capital Maputo, for example, fuses African heart and Mediterranean style. At every turn it is as spicy and exotic as the piquant chili-based piri-piri sauce ladled over barbecued chicken and shrimp at the city's finest restaurants and casual roadside stands. Whatever your destination, this book offers the promise of a good meal and convivial surroundings at the end of the day.

Encountering a familiar food in its birthplace is one pleasure of any journey.

Nearly two centuries ago, French epicure Jean Anthelme Brillat-Savarin wrote, "Tell me what you eat, and I will tell you who you are." The food experiences presented in this book will certainly leave you fulfilled, both in body and in spirit.

Below right Open-air food stand vendor serving spicy tea and snacks in Jemaa el-Fna, Marrakech, Morocco

VENTE
EN
CORNETS
DE GLACE
BERTHILLON

SPECIALITE
DE
TARTES CHAUDES
SALEES
A TOUTE HEURE

Above A traditional neighborhood restaurant in Paris, France, offering bistro fare, patisserie, and ice creams

POM'CANNELLE

RESTAURANT
SALON DE THE
PATISSERIES
GLACES

DEGUSTATION
DE GLACES
ET SORBETS
DE LA MAISON
BERTHILLON

Europe

The Flavors of
Europe

From the Silk Road gateway of Tbilisi, Georgia, and the rolling plains of Portugal's Alentejo to the volcanic islands of Sicily and the chill highlands of Scotland, the European continent is a complex patchwork of landscapes, cultures, and cuisines. The tale of its tables is a celebration of local products augmented by the spoils of empire, the fruits of trade, and the enthusiastic embrace of meats, vegetables, and cooking techniques from North Africa, Asia Minor, and the Americas.

Certain flavors pale when uprooted. The rich-tasting Greek fava bean becomes a plain-Jane legume in other soils. Shavings of Italian black truffles lend an earthy musk to pastas and risottos wherever they're used, but never with such piquancy as in the dishes of Umbria. The exquisite Roman artichoke anywhere else is just another globe thistle, while the distinctive basil and olive oil of Genoa combine to make Ligurian pesto the green queen of pasta cuisines.

Warm water or cold, sweet or salt – the oceans, lakes, and rivers of Europe are the starting point for many iconic dishes, from steamed mussels in Brussels to fried fish on Whitby's North Sea strand. The crystalline Adriatic waters of Croatia teem with succulent scampi – all the better cooked with tomato, garlic, and white wine. In the Caspian Sea, armor-plated sturgeon produce delicious, rich caviar, while the pink-fleshed salmon from the mouths of icy Norwegian rivers are salt-cured to create the pungent delicacy called gravadlax.

> *Salmon from the mouths of icy Norwegian rivers are salt-cured to create the pungent delicacy gravadlax.*

Across Europe, cooks make fish stews that are virtual census counts of their harbors. Marseille bubbles with bouillabaisse spiked with a garlicky *rouille*, while Barcelona sings the light opera of fish known as *zarzuela*. Far to the north, the white fish of Belgian rivers form the toothy basis of Ghent's creamy *waterzooi*. All three fish stews rely on the ethereal but haunting overtones of saffron, the crocus spice brought to Europe in the North African conquest of Iberia. The Moors left an even more indelible stamp on European cuisine by introducing the short-grained rices essential to Valencia's seafood-studded paellas and Italy's unctuous, saffron-scented *risotto milanese*. Masters of metallurgy, the Moors also introduced the clamshell-shaped steaming vessel that became the Portuguese *cataplana*, though it took the Portuguese Christians to concoct the nation's signature dish of pork and clams.

New World Ingredients

Iberian seafarers revolutionized European cuisine with their New World culinary finds. Potatoes swiftly took hold in central Europe, forming the basis of the Swiss rösti, the *Reiberknödel* dumpling of

Right The vineyards of Burgundy, France, play an important role in the area's cuisine
Below Alfresco dining in Istanbul, Turkey, opposite the 17th-century Blue Mosque

Munich, and the *patatnik* pie of Bulgaria's Rhodope mountains. Seville's refreshing cold salad soup, gazpacho, was born with the landing of New World peppers and sweet tomatoes. Few New World plants had the transformative impact of the tomato, so perfectly matched to mozzarella cheese, fragrant basil, and fulsome olive oil in Capri's *insalata caprese*. Mount the same ingredients on a thin bread crust – but with the tomato strained and lightly cooked – and the combination becomes Naples' pizza Margherita, a dish that now graces tables across the globe.

Changing Traditions

Many culinary traditions of Europe embrace the same informality as pizza. Spanish tapas are often eaten with the fingers or skewered with a toothpick. The bite-sized meze of Istanbul reprise the old Ottoman empire, from the stuffed vine leaves called dolmades (shared with the cuisine of Greece) to the eggplant salads, little meatballs, white cheese, and sliced melons of the far reaches of Asia Minor. The twin themes of bounty and hospitality underpin such a feast – concepts echoed far to the north with the Swedish smorgasbord buffet and its dishes of herring, eel, meatballs, potato casseroles, sliced meats, and fat sausages.

Traditionally, Europeans are the world's great meat-eaters. Feasts can be as rustic as a Toulouse cassoulet of pork, sausages, and beans or Burgundy's braised beef stew, or as ceremonial as the roast haunch of beef with all the trimmings that's key to the identity of the English. Similarly, few Greeks would give up their roast Easter lamb – nor the *Madrileños* their mixed *cocido* hotpot, the Berliners their hearty braised pork knuckle, or the Alsatians the tangy pickled vegetables and rich sausages of their *choucroute garnie*. No German worth his or her salt would pass up the spicy pot roast known as sauerbraten, while any Scot worth a tartan feasts on haggis every Burns Night.

The master chefs of Spain's San Sebastián married inventive genius with Basque traditions.

But Europeans also love to turn tradition on its head. English pub cooks have transformed the leaden repasts of yesteryear into the bright, fresh-ingredient cooking of the gastropubs. The master chefs of Spain's San Sebastián married inventive genius with Basque traditions to revolutionize fine dining in Spain – and, by example, across Europe and the Americas.

Creative genius applies to European sweets as well, from pistachio and honey confections like Anatolian baklava to the elaborate torten of Salzburg, from the simple cream-filled *pasteis de nata* of Lisbon to the textural perfection and simple grace of a Parisian *macaron* delicately filled with a chocolate ganache. In Europe, the French say it best: *Bon appétit!*

Left Cakes and pastries were raised to the level of an art form in the patisseries of France
Below A restaurant terrace in Vernazza on the Cinque Terre coastline of Italy

LISBON PORTUGAL

Creamy Custard Tarts in Lisbon

The Tagus River meets the sea at Lisbon, and it was from the city's historic riverside district, Belém, that Portuguese explorers set sail, their discoveries creating an empire for Portugal. The most famous of all, Vasco da Gama, set his course for India here, and his fame is perhaps matched by a pastry first produced in Belém in 1837, and now the country's favorite treat.

Belém is an essential visit on any trip to Lisbon; its great monuments and buildings still shimmer with the wealth and glory of Portugal's Golden Age in the 16th century. Riches poured into the country through the discoveries of bold Portuguese explorers, who can be seen commemorated in the famous Monument to the Discoveries. The period gave birth to a magnificent architectural style known as Manueline (after the king, Dom Manuel I), and two defining examples are the highlights of any visit to Belém – the Torre de Belém and the Mosteiro dos Jerónimos, the stupendously decorated monastery that graces the riverside here. Elaborate sculpted detail virtually drips from its columns, vaults, and window frames, with naturalistic and maritime motifs to the fore, from twisted ropes and seashells to entwined leaves and branches.

The monastery, museums, cultural center, royal palace, and botanic gardens at Belém add up to a great day out from the Portuguese capital. But for many visitors, the first stop is a pastry shop, to sample a small *pastel de nata* served warm from the oven, its flaky pastry slightly crunchy to the bite, the creamy custard blistered by the heat. Three or four bites and it's gone, but it's a fleeting taste that will conjure fond memories of Portugal long after you've returned home.

The Portuguese take on the custard tart is actually one of its more restrained confections – other pastry and pudding recipes commonly use a dozen eggs, mounds of sugar, and lots of cream, but the *pastel de nata* is simple and rather elegant, calling for nothing more than well-made puff pastry and a modest, if rich, cream-custard filling. Like many traditional Portuguese tarts and desserts, it owes its origins to an unsung pastry chef in a religious order, in this case from Belém's Jerónimos monastery. Selling pastries to supplement church income was once a common sideline, and since 1837 the custard tarts have been inextricably linked with one particular pastry shop and café near the monastery, the Antiga Confeitaria de Belém, which remains in business today. This is why in Lisbon the tart is known as a *pastel de Belém* – but everywhere else in the country, you need only ask for a *pastel de nata*, or even simply a *nata*, to sample this sweet favorite.

Above The Torre de Belém *(far right in picture)* was built as a defense and ceremonial gateway to Lisbon by Portugal's king João II, sponsor of great explorers

What Else to Eat

Fish and shellfish are Lisbon specialties, and there's an entire central street – **Rua das Portas de Santo Antão** – devoted to seafood restaurants. The painted Portuguese tiles known as *azulejos* are another typical feature of the city, and the two come together in Lisbon's traditional *cervejarias*, or beer halls, which are often elaborately tiled and serve great seafood. **Cervejaria Trindade** *(www.cervejariatrindade.pt)* is the oldest in the city and magnificently decorated with Masonic imagery. Lisbon is also home to populations of immigrants from Portugal's former colonies of Brazil, Angola, Mozambique, and Goa, and they have endowed the city with some great ethnic eateries – try **Comida de Santo** *(www.comidadesanto.pt)* for spicy Brazilian dishes and punchy cocktails.

A Day in Belém

Central Lisbon spreads across various distinct neighborhoods, from the medieval castle area to the 18th-century center known as the Baixa. Belém is a small district lying around 4 miles (7 km) from downtown Lisbon, and its historic sights and monuments make a visit here a must.

MORNING If you're staying in Lisbon, take the tram along the **Rio Tejo** (Tagus River) to **Belém** (around 20 minutes), getting off near the **Mosteiro dos Jerónimos**. Explore the grandiose monastery and its exquisite cloister before strolling along the landscaped riverfront, past the striking **Monument to the Discoveries** to the fanciful **Torre de Belém** (Belém Tower).

AFTERNOON Visit the engaging **Museu dos Coches** (carriage museum), then walk through the leafy pathways of the **Jardins do Ultramar** to reach the **Palácio Nacional da Ajuda**, an opulent 19th-century royal residence.

EVENING For drinks with a river view, and to sample something from a rich cultural program spanning jazz to opera, visit the striking **Centro Cultural de Belém** (Belém Cultural Center), situated opposite the monastery.

Essentials

GETTING THERE
Fly to Lisbon's international **airport**, Aeroporto de Lisboa, then take the **bus**, **train**, or a **taxi** downtown. The **tram** to Belém departs from Praça do Comércio in Lisbon's Baixa neighborhood.

WHERE TO STAY
Oasis (inexpensive) is a stylish downtown backpackers' hostel. *www.hostelsoasis.com*
As Janelas Verdes (moderate) has lovely rooms in an intimate 18th-century town house. *www.heritage.pt*
Solar dos Mouros (expensive) is a boutique hotel five minutes from the center of the city with wonderful views. *www.solardosmouros.com*

TOURIST INFORMATION
Rua do Arsenal 15, Lisbon; *www.visitlisboa.com*

The Best Places to Eat Pasteis de Nata

Antiga Confeitaria de Belém
moderate

Despite the charms of the riverside in Belém, it's hard not to make a beeline for the Antiga Confeitaria, the "old pastry shop," but you can reassure yourself that it's just as much a cultural highlight as the nearby monastery and other attractions. The busy, traffic-choked street outside gives way to a typically Portuguese tiled and polished interior, the vaulted rooms lined with antique *azulejo* tiles. There's a bustling carry-out counter and café tables inside, and while a score of different cakes and pastries vie for attention, there's only one real choice for aficionados – a *pastel de Belém* (ask for *pasteis de Belém* if you want several), made to the same recipe since the shop first opened in 1837. They're sprinkled with ground cinnamon in the traditional manner (not all cafés serve them this way), and while most Portuguese people would take one with an espresso coffee (known here as a *bica*), it's also perfectly in order to have a pot of tea.

Rua de Belém 84–92, Belém, Lisbon; open Jun–Sep: 8 AM–midnight daily; Oct–May: 8 AM–11 PM daily; www.pasteisdebelem.pt

Also in Lisbon

To enjoy a custard tart with a view, try the elegant if slightly touristy cafés on central Lisbon's main square, the Rossio, or the stately **Confeitaria Nacional** *(www. confeitarianacional.com; moderate)* on the adjacent Praça da Figueira. Other famous cafés in the capital, each with tantalizing cakes and pastries, include **Martinho da Arcada** *(+351 218 879 259; moderate)*, an old literary haunt under the arches on Praça do Comércio, and the uptown and very ornate **Café Versailles** *(+351 213 546 340; moderate)*.

Also in Portugal

There are traditional cafés in every town and city that serve an excellent *pastel de nata*. In Porto, try the beautifully decorated **Café Majestic** *(+351 22 200 3887; moderate)*. In the medieval university city of Coimbra, the **Café Santa Cruz** *(www.cafesantacruz.com; inexpensive)* serves delicious *pasteis de nata* in the vaulted rooms of a former monastery.

Around the World

In any city with a large Portuguese population, from London to Luanda, you're sure to find a *pastel de nata*. It's a different matter just across the border in Spain, however, which has its own, very different, pastry-making heritage. But in Barcelona's excellent **A Casa Portuguesa** *(www.acasaportuguesa.com; moderate)*, a deli/café in the hip suburb of Gràcia, they serve a *pastel de nata* every bit as good as those made in Portugal.

Above *Pasteis de nata* are traditionally served warm, often with a generous sprinkling of cinnamon

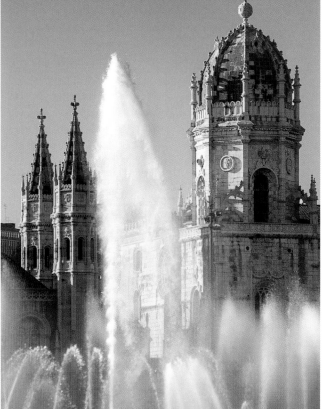

Right Home of the *pastel de nata*, the Mosteiro dos Jerónimos in Belém is a much more elaborate confection, in Portuguese late-Gothic style

BEAUNE FRANCE

Tender Beef in Wine Country

Almost every French province has its own version of a beef stew, but vine-rich Burgundy's boeuf bourguignon has to be the most famous, and nowhere is it better made than in its birthplace. Perched in the center of the Côte d'Or wine region, the pretty town of Beaune is the perfect base for exploring the vineyards and cuisine of this exceptional part of France.

Burgundy has more than its share of legendary, grape-related names: Pommard, Romanée-Conti, Nuits-Saint-George, Montrachet. The red wines of this region are made from Pinot Noir grapes, the whites from Chardonnay. The greatest Burgundies hail from the celebrated Côte d'Or, which is divided into the Côte de Nuits and the Côte de Beaune – and the latter begins just north of the town of Beaune. Each village in the Burgundy region is like a small realm in the empire of wine, and majestic Beaune is its proud capital.

Historic buildings with multicolored tiled roofs line the cobbled streets of Beaune. Two of the most outstanding are the Hôtel des Ducs, now a wine museum, and the Hôtel Dieu des Hospices de Beaune, a masterpiece of medieval architecture built in 1443 as a hospital for the poor, dubbed the "Palace of the Poor" because of its Gothic grandeur. Now a museum, each November it throws open its doors for a charity wine auction, at which wines from vineyards gifted to the Hospice go under the hammer. The auction dates back to 1859 and a portion of the money raised still goes toward helping the sick, these days via the modern Beaune Hospital.

Beaune's streets are filled with palate-tempting restaurants and shops selling homemade jams, chocolates, cakes, aniseed candy, and fruit liqueurs. The twice-weekly market in the center of the old town is always a hive of activity, and the place to gather ingredients for a picnic lunch among the vines: *cabrion* (a goat cheese ripened in grape husks), farm-fresh terrines and pâtés, or a just-roasted Bresse chicken with crispy baby potatoes.

Local cooking is, unsurprisingly, awash with wine. "A la Bourguignon" denotes a dish made with plenty of wine, little white onions, a few mushrooms, and bacon – such as boeuf bourguignon, or *oeufs à la bourguignonne* (eggs poached in red wine). Burgundy's boeuf bourguignon isn't just a pot of stewed beef; this perennial wintry favorite must be made with Charolais beef, France's most tender and the region's best, doused in nothing else but a Burgundy red. The meat is braised with the wine, stock, onions, bacon, and mushrooms, so that as the sauce reduces, the flavor intensifies. In days gone by, before it morphed into a highbrow classic, boeuf bourguignon was simple farmers' food, and the long, slow cooking process evolved to tenderize tough cuts of meat. Even today, this is not a dish in a hurry.

A Day in Beaune

Beaune, an important cultural center in the Middle Ages, is a medieval city rich in history and tradition as well as a great place for food, wine-tasting, and shopping.

MORNING Soak up the past at **Hôtel Dieu des Hospices de Beaune**, pausing at red-curtained cubicles lining the "Room of the Poor" where the sick once languished, before stepping into the courtyard to see the dazzling glazed tile roof. Visit the 12th-century **Basilique Collégiale Notre Dame** for a glimpse of Gothic Beaune.

AFTERNOON Explore food and wine shops in **rue Carnot** and **rue Monge**. Join a mustard-tasting tour at **La Moutarderie Fallot**, a family mustard mill in operation since 1840, or visit a wine cellar in town, such as **Bouchard Père & Fils**. This has one of the greatest collections of Burgundy vintages and is housed in the glorious 15th-century **Château de Beaune**; the underground cellars have 23-ft- (7-m-) thick walls.

EVENING Stroll the **old town** to see the antique tiles and facades of buildings lit up against the night sky. Cozy up on a terrace with a velvety Burgundy.

Essentials

GETTING THERE
Aéroport Dijon Bourgogne is 18 miles (30 km) from Beaune. **High-speed trains** operate from Paris, Lyon, and Dijon.

WHERE TO STAY
Les Jardins de Loïs (inexpensive) is a serene and smart B&B. *www.jardinsdelois.com*
Via Mokis (moderate) is a modern hotel in the heart of the old town. *www.viamokis.com*
Hôtel de la Poste (expensive) is Beaune's oldest hotel; its stylish rooms feature French fabrics. *www.hoteldelapostebeaune.com*

TOURIST INFORMATION
1 rue de l'Hôtel-Dieu; *www.ot-beaune.fr*

Above The Hôtel Dieu des Hospices de Beaune was built at the end of the Hundred Years War, when Burgundy suffered both poverty and famine

Left The vineyards of the Hautes-Côtes de Beaune spill down the long slopes of the Côte d'Or escarpment, seen here in fall

Above A great boeuf bourguignon depends on the integrity of its ingredients, specifically Charolais beef and red Burgundy wine

The Best Places to Eat Boeuf Bourguignon

Ma Cuisine inexpensive

Tucked down a side street off the Place Carnot, this cozy restaurant run by husband-and-wife team Pierre and Fabienne has amassed thousands of fans over the years, not just for the well-cooked regional specialties they turn out but equally for the wine list (featuring more than 700 bottles) – this is Burgundy, after all. Ma Cuisine is resolutely, unrepentantly old-fashioned, and that's exactly why people keep coming back. If you crave waistline-friendly, edgy food, give this rustic roost a wide berth. The entreés sound a roll call for old rural France: *jambon persillé* (cubed ham with parsley in aspic), Burgundy's famed *escargots* (snails) served in their shells brimming with parsley butter, and wobbly *oeufs en meurette* (eggs poached in red wine). Main courses run from roasted whole pigeon to soul-warming favorites such as *coq au vin* (chicken in – of course – red wine) and plush, dark, meltingly tender boeuf bourguignon. To finish, try a fresh fruit tart or an eggy *crème brûlée*.

Passage Sainte-Hélène, Beaune; open for lunch and dinner Mon, Tue, Thu & Fri; +33 380 223 022

Also in Beaune

The cool contemporary decor of Bruno Monnoir's **Le Benaton** *(www.lebenaton.com; expensive)* is typified by the tan ostrich-leather chairs. It is advance warning that there are no fusty old classics here; instead, you can expect a sophisticated and inventive reworking of Burgundy's culinary traditions. Monnoir's highly refined take on boeuf bourguignon features "nuts" of beef cheek confited in red wine.

Also in France

Those old-world Paris bistros with proper linen tablecloths and food that deserves a return visit seem to be a disappearing breed, but **Josephine Chez Dumonet** *(+33 1 4548 5240; moderate),* in the city's 6th arrondissement, is valiantly fighting the trend – and winning. French classics dominate this menu: steak tartare, crispy-skin *confit de canard*, omelet with truffles (in season, of course), and spoon-tender boeuf bourguignon. This restaurant is reason enough for a Paris stopover.

Around the World

Bustling **Brasserie Les Halles** *(www.leshalles. net/brasserie; inexpensive)* is a typical Parisian restaurant serving up a host of French classics – except it's doing it in New York. The kitchen home of chef, author, and straight-talking television host Anthony Bourdain, the restaurant takes its name from Paris's once-thriving, now defunct, market district Les Halles. It's open from noon to midnight, so you can slake a craving for rib-sticking boeuf bourguignon almost any time of day.

Cookery Classes

A cooking class at **The Cook's Atelier** *(www. thecooksatelier.com)* kicks off in style with a glass of chilled *crémant*, Burgundy's bubbly. Marjorie Taylor's menu pays homage to the small artisan producers of the region. **La Terre d'Or** *(www.laterredor.com)* will arrange a session at the stove of a Michelin-starred restaurant with a winemaker on hand to discuss the best partner wines. Learn how to visually recognize, smell, and taste regional wines in a three-hour crash course at **Ecole des Vins de Bourgogne** *(www.ecoledesvins-bourgogne.com)*. Longer sessions are also available.

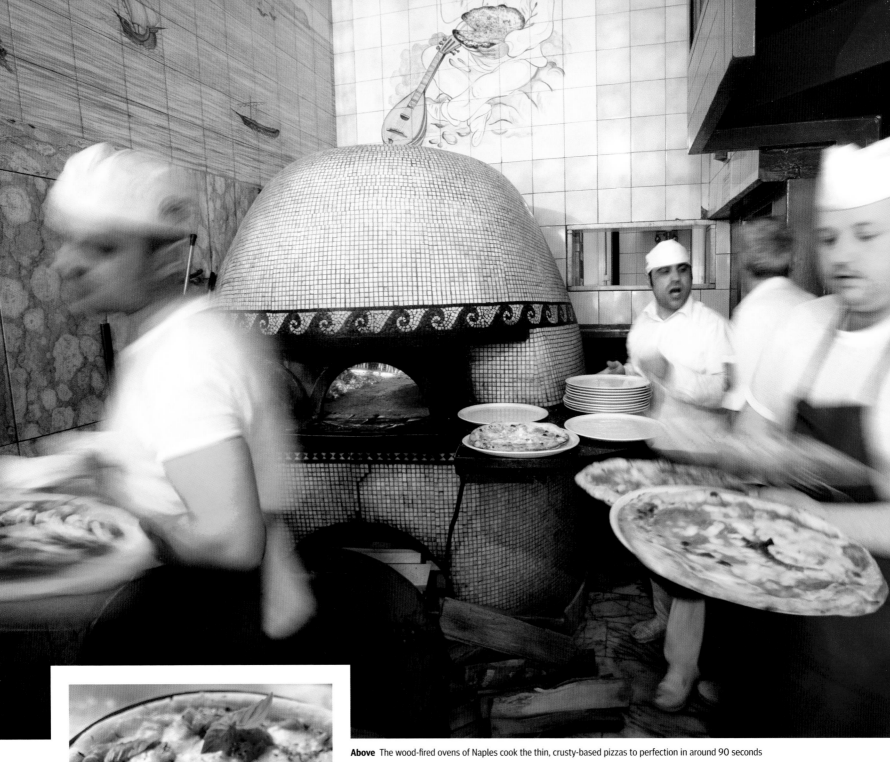

Above The wood-fired ovens of Naples cook the thin, crusty-based pizzas to perfection in around 90 seconds

Above Local San Marzano tomatoes, *mozzarella di bufala*, and basil raise the humble Margherita pizza from fast food to gourmet delight

A Day in Naples

Naples has superb and easy-to-reach art galleries, museums, and city sights, with plenty for the discerning visitor.

MORNING Start in the lively district of **Spaccanapoli**. Its **Via San Gregorio Armeno** has a concentration of artisans' shops producing painstakingly handcrafted figures, furniture, and accessories for the traditional *presepi* – Christmas Nativity scenes. Visit the impressive **Museo Nazionale Archeologico** in the **Piazza** to see the treasures – especially the mosaics and frescoes – unearthed at Pompeii.

AFTERNOON If you go to only one of Naples' numerous churches, make it the ornate **Duomo**. Then visit the impressive **Palazzo Reale**, home to the Spanish, Bourbon, and French rulers.

EVENING Take a relaxing ride uphill on one of the famous **funicular railways**, inspiration for the 1880s song "Funiculì Funiculà." Essential for transporting hundreds of people on a day-to-day basis, they have all been modernized and now whisk passengers to their homes, and travelers to high spots with great views over the twinkling city lights.

Essentials

GETTING THERE
Naples' **Capodichino International Airport** has frequent **buses** to the downtown. Fast **trains** from many European cities pull in at Napoli Centrale station. The rapid **metro** lines, local **buses**, and the historic **funicular railways** are all good ways to get around.

WHERE TO STAY
La Casa della Nonna (inexpensive) is simple and central. *www.lacasadellanonna.it*
Donna Regina B&B (moderate) has charming rooms in a centrally located, converted historic convent. *www.discovernaples.net*
Grand Hotel Parker's (expensive), a sumptuous 1870s hotel, has a superb terrace overlooking the Bay of Naples. *www.grandhotelparkers.it*

TOURIST INFORMATION
Via Santa Lucia 107; *www.inaples.it*

NAPLES ITALY

Perfect Pizza in Buzzing Naples

The bustling southern Italian city of Naples may at first seem chaotic, but visitors quickly fall under the spell of this underappreciated gem and its rich artistic heritage. Naples is quintessential Mediterranean Italy, and as a region it's famous for its delicious tomatoes and outstanding mozzarella cheese, so it's not surprising that it's also the undisputed "home of the pizza."

A sprawling city of dramatic contrasts, Naples displays its regal past in the shape of impressive castles and magnificent palaces erected by Spanish and Bourbon rulers from the 16th to the 19th centuries. But the city is best known for a more ancient event – the eruption of Vesuvius in AD 79. Still visible across the waters of the Bay of Naples, the volcano submerged the neighboring Roman city of Pompeii in yards of ash and debris, wiping out its entire population.

Amazingly, the narrow streets of the historic heart of modern-day Naples still correspond to an ancient Greek-Roman grid. In this maze, life spills out into the public domain – people call to each other from windows, scooters zoom along doing their best to dodge pedestrians, and minuscule shops, neighborhood churches, and cafés juggle for precious space. Just as in centuries past, a lot of eating takes place outside, with food bought from open-air stands and glass-fronted kiosks displaying tempting wares. The vast array of "fast" street food includes sweet and savory treats, from sugary doughnuts and crispy chunks of potato to fried *arancini* rice balls stuffed with minced meat. There's even fried wrap-over pizza, though this oil-drenched snack is not to everyone's liking.

Originally fare for the poor, pizza has long been the flagship of Italian cuisine across the world. There are countless fanciful international toppings, but the most famous pizza of all is the classic Margherita. Invented by Neapolitan chef Raffaello Esposito in 1889 to honor a visiting Italian queen and the recently unified nation, it features the colors of the nation's flag: white (cheese), red (locally grown San Marzano tomatoes), and green (basil). Today, pizza marinara is a close favorite, its anchovies jostling for attention among black olives, garlic, and sometimes capers.

Without a doubt, the best place to enjoy a pizza is at one of the numerous family-run pizzerias in Naples, which fill the air with an irresistible fragrance of sizzling mozzarella and fresh San Marzano tomatoes bubbling under a drizzle of Campania olive oil and a sprinkling of native oregano. Whatever the topping, there is complete agreement on how the pizza is to be consumed – immediately and on the spot.

Above Naples is spread out along the Bay of Naples, overlooked by Vesuvius

What Else to Eat

Naples is also famous for its rich cakes and heavenly desserts, and the city has a mouthwatering choice of *pasticceria*, where freshly baked sweet delights are showcased in glass-topped counters. **Sfogliatelle** are shell-shaped, layered pastries flavored with vanilla and filled with a mixture of delicate ricotta cheese and morsels of candied orange. The epitome of sugar heaven is a **babà al rhum**, a mushroom-shaped sponge cake drenched in rum syrup and smothered in whipped cream. Probably introduced to Naples by the French cooks at court, it was created by an 18th-century Polish king, who named it after Ali Baba and the Forty Thieves, stories about whom he adored. Another special treat is a slice of **pastiera napoletana**, a celebratory Easter pie baked with ricotta cheese, candied citrus fruits, and spices.

The Best Places to Eat Pizza

Antica Pizzeria Da Michele
inexpensive

The bare marble table tops and stark tiled walls don't put off the constant stream of diners who flock to this highly popular and long-standing Neapolitan establishment. Neither do the long lines. Everyone knows it's well worth the wait, and there's a mouthwatering aroma to keep you company in the street. When your number is called, you're given a table amid jovial groups of families and friends. The choice of liquid refreshment is limited to soft drinks, water, or beer, all served in plastic cups. And ordering your meal doesn't take long either, as it's a simple choice between just two pizzas: the Marinara or the Margherita. Both are spread with *passato* (puréed) San Marzano tomatoes from the nearby Sarno Valley and topped with a fresh, smooth *fior di latte* cow's milk mozzarella from Agerola on the Amalfi coast. The huge, soft pizzas are served steaming straight from the oven, for delicious, immediate consumption.
Via Cesare Sersale, Naples; open 10 AM–11 PM Mon–Sat; www.damichele.net

Also in Naples

Antica Pizzeria de Borgo Orefici *(+39 81 552 0996; moderate)* is a simple, family-run establishment tucked away down a narrow street that was once the heart of the goldsmiths' district. It has many faithful diners and the place can get busy. Toppings are generous and pizzas include *miseria e nobiltà*: a catch-all pizza that's half marinara and half Margherita.

Also in Italy

Muro Frari *(www.murovinoecucina.it; moderate)* at San Polo 2604 in Venice is a modern restaurant offering gourmet pizzas with all manner of treats, such as porcini mushrooms, fresh buffalo mozzarella, and smoked swordfish and tuna. Don't miss the delicious apéritifs with seasonal fresh fruit and sparkling Prosecco, which can be enjoyed outside in summer.

Around the World

Long lines form outside **Grimaldi's Pizzeria** *(www.grimaldis.com; inexpensive)* at the foot of the Brooklyn Bridge in New York. Regulars rub shoulders with celebrities among the trademark red-and-white check tablecloths. It's the coal-brick oven here that gives the pizzas their sought-after crisp crust and smoky flavor. A long list of toppings allows you to invent your very own pizza with your favorite flavors. In the UK, **Santoré** *(www.santorerestaurant.co.uk; inexpensive)* in London serves outstandingly good, authentic Neapolitan pizzas in lively Exmouth Market.

ALICANTE SPAIN

The Thousand Tastes of Spain

Straining toward the sea as it hunkers beneath a castle-topped mountain, Alicante is fishing port, yacht haven, and beach resort in one. Called the "City of Light" for the bright wash of sun on its ancient streets, Alicante – like so many Spanish cities – comes most alive in the evening, when locals and vacationers gather around drinks and the savory delights known as tapas.

Capital of the Costa Blanca, Alicante retains far more of its historic identity than nearby mega-resorts. The romance of its high and lonely Moorish castle contrasts with the elegance of Baroque buildings wedged into steep medieval streets. Ultimately, Alicante is defined by the sea – trade route to Africa, boundless well of fish, and rhythmic source of waves lapping pale, sandy beaches.

Once the vacationers have come down from the castle ramparts, or ambled back from Postiguet and Sant Joan beaches, Alicante gets its sea legs for the evening. As a cool ocean breeze stirs, people promenade down palm-lined Explanada de Espanya, the wide esplanade separating ancient city from modern seafront, paved with 6.6 million marble tiles laid in wave patterns. A sudden urge to drink and snack overwhelms the city. It is time for tapas.

No-one knows when the tapas tradition began, but the practice of placing a small dish atop a glass to keep out the flies has evolved into Spain's most generous act of hospitality. An ingrained part of Spanish culture, tapas sampling lets visitors socialize elbow-to-elbow with fellow drinkers and diners at the bar. Although

many tapas – from Jabugo mountain ham to La Mancha's ewe's-milk cheeses and the ubiquitous potato omelet – can be found across the country, each region also boasts its own specialties. To see what will be on the bars of Alicante at night, one need only visit the Mercado Central by day. The great slabs of red tuna and the clenched blue shells of mussels displayed on ice will become delicate tartares, seared bites, or pink morsels in a tangy vinegar sauce. Few drinks better suit these explosively briny tidbits than Fondillón, Alicante's unique, long-aged wine, with overtones of almonds, ginger, dates, and dark dried fruits.

So superb are the tapas at Alicante's bars that it's tempting to stay put once you have found a rail to lean on. But inertia violates the unwritten rules of a night of tapas-hopping. Each establishment on the esplanade or in the narrow streets of the medieval quarter has a treat it does better than anyone else – so staying in one means missing the others. Eating tapas can be a means to stave off hunger until a typically late Spanish dinner (always after 10:00 PM), or it can become dinner and the evening's entertainment all in one – in which case, it is perhaps wisest not to look down at the swirling, wave-patterned pavement on the way home.

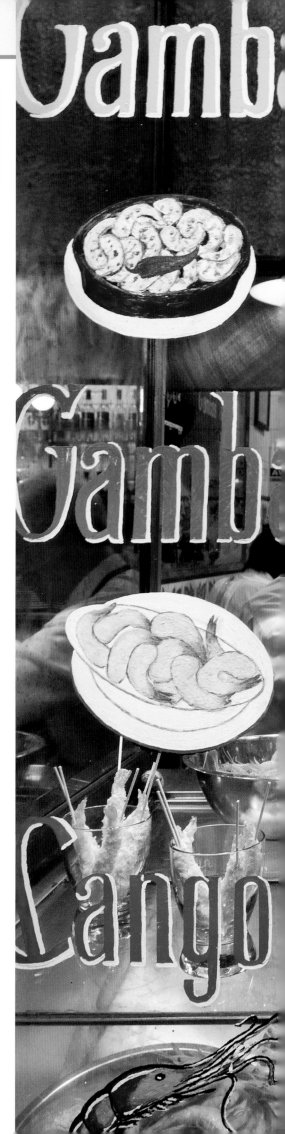

A Day in Alicante

Alicante is one of Spain's major cities on the east coast and has a much more "Spanish" feel than many of the surrounding Costa Blanca resort areas. The historic port, beautiful beaches, ideal climate, and fabulous gastronomy have much to offer visitors.

MORNING Take the elevator from Postiguet Beach through Benacantil mountain to the **Castell de Santa Bárbara**, expanded from a 9th-century Moorish castle, for panoramic views of the city and the coast.

AFTERNOON Visit the Baroque **Concatedral de San Nicolás de Bari** with its lovely images of saints painted on wooden panels. Try to decipher the Bible stories on the Baroque facade of **Santa María** church, and don't miss the twisted-barleycorn columns of the **Town Hall**. Leave time to relax on **Sant Joan beach**, easily reached by tram.

EVENING Immerse yourself in one of Spain's best tapas scenes. The splashiest bars are on the **Explanada de Espanya**, but seek out gastronomic heaven on narrow interior streets like Villegas and César Elguezábal.

Essentials

GETTING THERE
European and Spanish carriers fly to **Alicante airport**. Get around the city on foot or by **tram**.

WHERE TO STAY
Hostal Monges Palace (inexpensive) is family-run, with stylish small rooms in the historic downtown. www.lesmonges.es
Melia Alicante (moderate) offers resort hotel amenities near the esplanade. www.solmelia.com
Hotel Spa Porta Maris & Suites del Mar (moderate) combines two luxury hotels on a downtown pier. www.hotelspaportamaris.com

TOURIST INFORMATION
www.alicanteturismo.com

Above Super-fresh ingredients of immaculate provenance and an eye for presentation put Alicante's tapas among Spain's finest

Left Fish and seafood such as *gambas* (shrimp) and *langostinos* (langoustines) are specialties in this coastal fishing port

Below An extraordinary elevator bored through the rock will take you to the Castell de Santa Bárbara, perched high above Alicante

Below Bars groaning with tapas dishes welcome workers at the end of the day all over Spain **Bottom left** Air-dried *jamón serrano*, one of Spain's finest delicacies, is often hung from the ceiling

Right (top to bottom) *Gambas* (shrimp) from the grill with, in the background, marinated artichokes; tapas are always best shared, preferably with good red wine; a modern tapas bar in London

Tapas Around the World

Tapas distill all of Spanish cuisine into perfect little snacks, making the nibbling of small savories while drinking into a casual feast. The Spanish penchant for two-bite dining and its associated conviviality has swept the world, bringing Iberian dishes along for the ride.

ALICANTE

El Cisne de Oro inexpensive
Calle César Elguezábal 23; www.elcisnedeoro.com
This tile-encrusted traditional bar with hams hanging overhead captures the tastes of both land and sea — slices of mountain ham sit alongside plates of white anchovies in olive oil. The kitchen's own pungent aïoli enlivens both the potato salad and small rolls stuffed with pork and mushrooms.

Nou Manolín Restaurante & Bar moderate
Calle Villegas 3; www.noumanolin.com
One of the quintessential tapas spots, not just in Alicante but in all of Spain, Nou Manolín offers more than 50 different tapas every day in the ground-level bar. All the classics are available, as are dishes with a modern twist, from shrimp in a spicy garlic sauce to sushi-grade slices of fresh red tuna.

La Taberna del Gourmet expensive
Calle San Fernando 10; www.latabernadelgourmet.com
The owners of this pioneer gastrobar are fanatical about sourcing the best fish, vegetables, fruits, and meats and playing up the perfection of the produce. Excellent tapas choices include a fresh tomato salad with tuna belly or tempura-fried baby squid.

GRANADA

Granada's restaurants and bars offer Spain's most generous free tapas, making tapas-hopping an inexpensive way to dine. Dishes might escalate from potato salad to a small dish of stew as customers keep ordering drinks.

Bar Casa Julio inexpensive
Calle Hermosa, just off Plaza Nueva (no telephone)
There's no telling just how old Casa Julio might be, but the jam-packed bar looks little changed from the days before the Spanish Civil War. Specialty tapas here include several variations on octopus and squid — always best with red wine.

On the Menu

Albóndigas Meatballs that combine bread crumbs with pork, veal, lamb, or some combination of meats. They are served in either a brown sauce or a tomato sauce.

Almejas Clams served in the shells, often steamed with wine, herbs, and vegetables.

Anchoas The small Spanish white anchovies, usually lightly poached and preserved in olive oil.

Berenjenas rebozadas A dish with North African origins, consisting of eggplant that is salted, breaded, and fried in olive oil.

Boquerones Anchovies, either canned in vinegar or fresh and deep-fried.

Chorizo A distinctive Spanish sausage with many regional variations. It usually contains pieces of cured ham as well as ground pork and is always strongly flavored with Spanish paprika.

Croquetas These take many forms but most often feature minced cured ham or poached tuna. In both cases, the filling is blended with béchamel sauce, rolled in fine crumbs, and deep-fried in olive oil.

Gambas Shrimp or prawns (species can vary by season): served *a la plancha*, they are grilled whole with the heads on; *gambas al ajillo* are peeled shrimp that are fried in olive oil with copious quantities of fresh garlic.

Jamón serrano The air-dried mountain hams seen hanging from the ceilings of tapas bars, so concentrated and intense that servings are sliced paper-thin.

Morcilla A blood sausage or black pudding. As a tapa, it is usually sliced, fried in olive oil, and served with toothpicks.

In northern Spain, it is filled with pork fat, rice, and onions, but in central and southern Spain the filler usually includes bread crumbs and almonds.

Patatas bravas Named for the Madrid bar that invented them, fried potatoes served with a dip of paprika-laced aïoli (a very garlicky, mayonnaise-like sauce).

Pimientos rellenos Stuffed peppers: there are a number of varieties, the most common being small triangular peppers from the north (either green or red) filled with salt cod and whipped potato.

Queso manchego The famous aged sheep's milk cheese of La Mancha, usually sliced very thin and served in triangles.

Tortilla española Perhaps the most universal dish in Spain, a masterful combination of fried potatoes baked into a thick omelet, sliced and often eaten cold.

Taberna Salinas inexpensive
Calle de Elvira 13; www.tabernassalinas.com
Widely known for offering high quality at low prices, Salinas proffers tapas that are scaled-down versions of full recipe dishes: scrambled eggs with ham and fried potatoes, broad beans simmered with little pieces of ham, or beef braised with sweet peppers.

Cunini Restaurante & Marisquería moderate
Plaza de Pescadería 14; +34 958 250 777
Appropriately for its location on the fishmongers' square, Cunini serves the best seafood tapas in Granada. Salt cod dishes or calamari are common first offerings – it could take three drinks before they bring out the shrimp or crisply fried mullet.

NEW YORK CITY
Following the Spanish Civil War, thousands of Spaniards fled to New York, and many made their homes in Manhattan's Chelsea neighborhood. Few restaurants from that era remain, but New York has blossomed with contemporary tapas restaurants.

Boqueria moderate
53 West 19th Street; www.boquerianyc.com
Named for the famous Barcelona market, Boqueria ranges across Spain for its tapas, from the classic potato omelet to bacon-wrapped dates stuffed with almonds and blue cheese and a Catalan sauté of spinach, garbanzos, pine nuts, garlic, and raisins.

Txikito moderate
240 Ninth Avenue; www.txikitonyc.com
Serving mostly Basque wines with its *pintxos* (as the Basques call tapas), Txikito pays homage to Spanish Basque cookery with dishes such as blistered peppers with sea salt, or a salad of Basque anchovies and bonito tuna on butter lettuce.

LONDON, UK
The English love affair with vacations in sunny Spain has translated into a boom in Spanish restaurants, especially in London's Soho and Bloomsbury areas. Most offer extensive tapas menus and a strong list of Spanish wines.

Navarro's inexpensive
67 Charlotte Street, W1; www.navarros.co.uk
With a menu (and wine list) more redolent of northern than southern Spain, the tapas at Navarro's are rib-sticking and satisfying – like the Galician tuna *empanada* (stuffed pastry), braised oxtail, and lentil stew with chorizo. Its red wine choices are splendid.

Barrafina moderate
54 Frith Street, W1; www.barrafina.co.uk
An intimate room with about two dozen stools around a counter, Barrafina has the crowd density to claim Spanish authenticity and the menu to match, from grilled bread smeared with tomato and olive oil to grilled quail with aïoli.

Tapas Brindisa moderate
18–20 Southwark Street, SE1; www.brindisa.com
The south London tapas bar of a famous Spanish food importer, Brindisa always has just the ingredients on hand for top-notch, authentic tapas like thin slices of *jamón ibérico*, intensely spicy Léon chorizo, and the incomparable canned anchovies of Galicia.

SYDNEY, AUSTRALIA
Although the expansion of Chinatown has nearly absorbed the old Spanish Quarter along Liverpool Street in central Sydney, Spanish tapas restaurants and bars are sprouting up all over the city as dining-by-the-nibble catches on.

Bodega inexpensive
216 Commonwealth Street, Surry Hills; www.bodegatapas.com
With a tapas menu that travels beyond Spain to embrace Latin America, Bodega serves authentic Spanish dishes like salt-cod-stuffed *piquillo* peppers and Argentine plates like beef *empanadas* with *criolla* sauce. The short, sweet dessert list is also a big hit.

Kika moderate
247 Victoria Street, Darlinghurst; www.kika.com.au
The color splashes of this dynamic tapas bar could have been lifted from an early Pedro Almodóvar film, but dishes like deep-fried eggplant in parsley batter or barbecued pork fillets with blue cheese come straight from rustic Spanish cuisine.

El Toro Loco expensive
49–53 North Steyne, Manly; www.eltoroloco.com.au
The Crazy Bull is as bold as its name, bringing authentic Spanish cooking to Manly Beach with tapas like Jerez-style duck pâté, Madrid-style *cocido*, and Castilian lamb cutlets char-grilled with rosemary. Wines are a great mix of Spanish and Australian.

Above The Dugald Stewart monument on Calton Hill overlooking the city of Edinburgh

A Day in Edinburgh

The Scottish capital runs over seven hills, so there are plenty of places to get a good overview of the city and its glorious surroundings.

MORNING Immerse yourself in 1,500 years of Scottish history at **Edinburgh Castle** on its towering rock above **Princes Street Gardens**. Other high points are **Calton Hill**, with its smattering of monuments, and **Arthur's Seat**, which looks down on Holyrood Palace and the modern architecture of the Scottish Parliament.

AFTERNOON Enjoy modern art in imposing 18th-century surrounds at the **Dean Gallery** and **Scottish National Gallery of Modern Art**, which face each other across sculpture-dotted parkland. Then take a peaceful walk through the **Royal Botanic Garden**. This verdant paradise includes the largest collection of Chinese plants outside Asia, a highland Heath Garden, and a towering 19th-century Palm House.

EVENING See Edinburgh's dark past at **The Real Mary King's Close**, a subterranean warren of 17th-century streets where actors bring long-dead former citizens back to life.

Essentials

GETTING THERE
Edinburgh's **international airport** has flights from European cities; Glasgow Airport, 60 miles (96 km) away, has flights from long-haul departure points. There are **taxis** and a **bus** shuttle service to downtown Edinburgh.

WHERE TO STAY
Albyn Town House (inexpensive) is a graceful Victorian house with hearty Scottish breakfasts. *www.albyntownhouse.co.uk*
Hotel Du Vin (moderate) in the Old Town is a former asylum turned into a calm haven, with a whiskey snug. *www.hotelduvin.com*
The Witchery (expensive) is a 16th-century gem by Edinburgh Castle with opulently theatrical suites. *www.thewitchery.com*

TOURIST INFORMATION
www.visitscotland.com

Above The Edinburgh International Festival runs alongside its famous younger brother – the Fringe Festival – for three weeks in late summer

EDINBURGH

EDINBURGH SCOTLAND

Hearty Haggis in Edinburgh

Legendary Scottish bard Robert Burns celebrated his majestic capital Edinburgh as "Scotia's darling seat." The city's evocative history and grand architecture complement a deep love of ideas and culture, epitomized in its world-famous summer arts festival – but the Scots also prize the wild and rugged in life, and it's to this older, less rarified Scotland that haggis belongs.

Set back from the rugged shores of the wide Firth of Forth, Scotland's capital is cradled by hills and crags. The city combines the historic with the chic – grand architecture woven with ancient lanes lined with desirable boutiques. Overseen by its majestic castle, it is a place so old that even the "New Town" is made up of 200-year-old sweeping Georgian crescents.

In the 18th century the Edinburgh edition of Robbie Burns's *Poems* was published, including his ode "Address to a Haggis." Burns saw haggis as a symbol of Scottish life during those harsher times when it was essential to use as much as possible of a slain animal: for food, clothing, and even something to write on. While other cuts could be dried for preservation, internal organs were far more perishable. So they were stuffed into the natural casing of the animal's stomach – forming "haggis" – and cooked on the spot.

Traditionally, haggis takes the minced "pluck" of a sheep (heart, liver, and lungs), mixes it with onion, oatmeal, suet, spices, salt, and stock, then stuffs it into a casing – today usually synthetic – to be simmered for around three hours. Its ingredients may not sound appealing, but the end result is richly meaty, with a nutty texture and delicious spicy savoriness.

On Burns Night, January 25, the national dish is served with accompaniments of neeps (boiled turnips or rutabagas) and tatties (mashed potato) – plus Scotch whiskey, of course. But with the growth of nationalist pride in recent years, haggis has become increasingly popular year-round in Scotland, often with intriguing twists. Scotland's abundance of deer underpins a surge in venison haggis, while the country's significant Indian population has inspired haggis pakora, spiced with ginger, cumin seeds, coriander seeds, turmeric, and garam masala.

Haggis was a hearty, portable meal for those on the move: whiskey-makers transporting their liquid gold across majestic Highland hills; merchants shipping wares across the choppy channels from the dramatically beautiful islands of Orkney and the Hebrides; and drovers taking animals from the heather-clad moors to the hungry cities. Eating haggis is to join the company of these intrepid travelers – an honor indeed.

The Best Places to Eat Haggis

The Kitchin expensive

Opened in 2006 by husband and wife team Tom and Michaela Kitchin on Edinburgh's hip Leith waterfront, it took just six months for The Kitchin to gain a Michelin star. The restaurant showcases the best of Scotland's superb pantry with inventive cooking that nods to fusion without ever overreaching. When haggis appears here, it is transformed from its humble beginnings to a rare dish indeed, served with accompaniments of pickled turnips, foie gras, and crispy potato galette. The range of daily menus provides varied themes and different price levels, from an expansive "Land And Sea Surprise Tasting Menu" or "Celebration Of The Season" to a set lunch hailed by critics as one of the best gourmet deals in Britain.

Seafood temptations might include "spoots" (a Scottish term for razor clams) served with chorizo and lemon *confit*, or perhaps ravioli of Scrabster squid in a langoustine bisque, or escabeche of Shetland halibut with fennel, orange, and sea buckthorn.

78 Commercial Quay, Leith, Edinburgh; open 12:15–2 PM and 6:30–10 PM Tue–Sat (closes at 10:30 PM Fri–Sat); www.thekitchin.com

Also in Edinburgh

Oloroso *(www.oloroso.co.uk; expensive)* combines a glamorous Edinburgh rooftop setting with simple cooking by Tony Singh, who insists on local sourcing. Singh treats the rich earthiness of haggis to a global makeover with dishes such as haggis wonton with plum and whiskey sauce, haggis tortellini with spiked salsa verde, and haggis pakora with whiskey-tinged *chaat* mayonnaise. The duo serving classic Scottish dishes at the **Urban Angel** *(www.urban-angel.co.uk; inexpensive)* tweak the classic haggis accompaniments by serving theirs with clapshot mash (potatoes, rutabagas, and chives).

Also in Scotland

The house haggis – venison or vegetarian – is a hearty perennial on the menu at Glasgow's **Ubiquitous Chip** *(www.ubiquitouschip.co.uk; moderate)*, in its fifth decade in the city's trendy West End. Other Scottish classics include peat-smoked Finnan haddie (haddock), Rothesay black pudding, Ayrshire halibut, and Perthshire wood pigeon.

Also in the UK

London-based haggis-lovers head for **Boisdale** *(www.boisdale.co.uk; expensive)*, an upmarket outpost of Caledonian cooking with two spaces: an elegant Regency town house in chic Belgravia and an intimate basement in the heart of the City financial district. The Scottish menu is complemented by a superb whiskey list.

Above Haggis with "tatties and bashit neeps" – mashed potatoes and turnips

What Else to Eat

Fish underpins Caledonian classics such as **Arbroath smokies** (salted haddock smoked over beech and oak), which in turn can become part of **cullen skink** (a soup of smoked haddock, potatoes, and onion). Other seafood enticements include diver-caught **scallops**, **Loch Etive mussels**, **turbot** and **lobster** from Scrabster, **oysters** from Skye, and some of the world's best **salmon**. There's also superb meat, such as **Aberdeen Angus beef**, seaweed-fed **Orkney lamb**, game birds – like **grouse** – and superb **venison** from Scotland's rugged uplands. The sweet-toothed can enjoy **Tipsy Laird** (a Scottish sherry trifle) or **cranachan** (whipped cream, whiskey, honey, raspberries, and toasted oatmeal). **Scottish cheeses**, such as Arran Brie, whiskey-coated Bishop Kennedy, Gruth Dhu (soft crowdie cheese), and Dunsyre Blue are a delight.

RHODOPES

RHODOPES BULGARIA

Patatnik in the Rhodopes

Along the vast green undulations of the Rhodope Mountains, shepherds rely on fearsome Karakachan dogs to guard their flocks against wolves, and farmers use oxen to plow the fields. Rural life here is simple, satisfying, and healthy, and the cuisine reflects this lifestyle, with a series of delicious, wholesome dishes such as *patatnik*, a golden-crusted potato pie.

Straddling Greece and Bulgaria, the thickly forested Rhodopes spread over more than 4,000 square miles (10,000 km²), and they are dotted with picturesque villages where life has changed little for centuries. Home to an abundance of wildlife, the mountains are renowned for their stunning limestone gorges, deep caverns, and pristine lakes. Hikers can follow a wealth of well-marked trails linked by simple mountain huts, and skiers fill the snow-covered slopes at Pamporovo, one of Bulgaria's premier ski resorts.

A good base for touring is Smolyan, a town near Pamporovo that's also close to the Smolyan Lakes and the towering Orpheus Rocks. The legendary Orpheus is said to have been born in the Rhodopes, later entering the underworld to search for his wife at the breathtaking gorge of "The Devil's Throat" near Trigrad. In Zlatograd, a bit farther south, there's a chance to see – and stay in – perfectly preserved traditional houses and workshops, now protected as part of an ethnographic complex.

The region has been populated for millennia, but it wasn't until the mid-19th century that potatoes were introduced here. Initially rejected as "devil's apples" by superstitious elders, potatoes eventually proved successful as they thrived at high altitude in the rich Rhodopean soil. Canny villagers were quick to recognize their potential and, having boiled, baked, roasted, and fried the hardy new vegetable, began to experiment with a potato version of *banitsa*, a traditional Bulgarian pastry. This ultimately evolved into *patatnik*, a subtle blend of grated potato, white cheese, egg, onion, and mint cooked slowly in a pan over a wood stove.

During the economic upheaval that followed the collapse of Socialism in the 1990s, the then prime minister Ivan Kostov famously exhorted Rhodopeans to profit from their potato expertise and "Make patatnik!" Locals took heed and started to promote the dish as a culinary tourist attraction to be eaten in cozy traditional pubs *(mehanas)*. Today *patatnik* is firmly established as the region's classic dish, and every *mehana* serves its own version – some add tomatoes and red pepper, while others bake it in an oven rather than cook it on a stove, but all use a few crushed mint leaves to enhance the distinctive *patatnik* flavor. The hour-plus cooking time isn't really a problem, because it's easily spent beside a crackling log fire in a hospitable *mehana*, sampling some freshly baked bread and nursing a fine glass of *rakia*, a spirit distilled from mountain plums.

Above The cheesy onion and potato *patatnik* evolved from the *banitsa*, a Bulgarian savory filled pastry

Right The village of Shiroka Luka has been declared an Architectural Reserve, with many authentic Rhodopean buildings dating back to the early 19th century

Below Away from the cities, up in the mountains, many people still travel simply with a donkey and cart

Three Days in the Rhodope Mountains

The best way to experience the Rhodopes is to spend weeks walking through them, but if time is short, you can easily experience the highlights on a driving tour.

DAY ONE Though blighted by some unappealing Socialist-era buildings, **Smolyan's** mountainous setting is still wondrously dramatic. Visit the **Historical Museum**, then head for the tiny nearby village of **Momchilovtsi**, high in the mountains.

DAY TWO Visit **Zlatograd**, a small ex-mining town 35 miles (55 km) southeast of Smolyan. This has a wonderful **Museum Quarter** where you can watch artisans at work, sip coffee in a 19th-century café, sample Rhodopean delights in a traditional *mehana*, and even stay – it offers atmospheric accommodations in period mansions.

DAY THREE Travel northwest past the well-developed ski resort of **Pamporovo** to **Shiroka Luka**, a delightful village of old stone houses tucked away in the mountains. Lunch at the excellent **Pri Slavchev** *mehana* before continuing west to the spectacular **Trigrad Gorge**, where you can visit the **Devil's Throat** cavern.

Essentials

GETTING THERE
Fly to **Sofia Airport**, from which it's a five-hour **bus** journey to Smolyan.

WHERE TO STAY
Trite Eli (inexpensive) in Smolyan has spotless rooms and hiking information. *+359 3018 1028*
Pachilovska Kushta (moderate) in the Museum Quarter at Zlatograd is bursting with period charm. *www.eac-zlatograd.com*
Arena di Serdica (expensive) in Sofia offers five-star comforts. *www.arenadiserdica.com*

TOURIST INFORMATION
Smolyan: Mladeshki Dom; Zlatograd: *www.eac-zlatograd.com*

What Else to Eat

The scrumptious *banitsa* (pastry) known as **klin** is a Rhodopean staple that's cooked slowly on both sides, in much the same way as *patatnik*. The filling is made from rice, eggs, white cheese, and butter, and flavored with nettles or spinach. It's delicious served hot with a dollop of yogurt. Another favorite, **bob chorba**, is a thick, hearty soup that is popular throughout Bulgaria. It contains beans, peppers, tomatoes, celery, and carrots, flavored with mint or parsley. Traditionally prepared in a large earthenware pot, the Rhodopean version is made with white beans from Smolyan. For dessert, try **marudnik**, a kind of pancake with gently cooked wild berries. Buy some strawberry honey to take home.

The Best Places to Eat Patatnik

Alexandrovi Kushti inexpensive

Located in Zlatograd's old Museum Quarter, Alexandrovi Kushti occupies a wonderfully restored 19th-century building with a wood-paneled interior featuring ornate carvings by local craftsmen. As you'd expect from a restaurant that has published its own cookbook of regional delights, the *patatnik* here is superb – cooked slowly over a stove and turned midway through, as the crust develops, according to the traditional recipe.

Bulgarian cuisine is renowned for its broad variety of salads and this is also a great place to sample a classic *shopska* salad of tomatoes, cucumbers, onion, and white cheese accompanied by a complimentary glass of *rakia*. Carnivores can choose from a staggering array of meat dishes that range from fried chicken hearts to a whole baked lamb; vegetarians are equally well catered to, with enticing options such as *chushky burek* (stuffed peppers) and *sarmi* (vine leaves filled with rice). Save room for a dessert of sticky baklava or sweet *banitsa* filled with Turkish delight and sit back to enjoy a live performance of Bulgarian folk music.

Museum Quarter, Zlatograd; open for lunch and dinner daily; +359 3071 4166

Also in the Rhodope Mountains

Patatnik, *klin*, roast lamb, and sweet *banitsa* are among the specialties served up at **Mehana Pri Slavchev** *(+359 3030 675; inexpensive)*. This traditional *mehana* is in Shiroka Luka, a pretty village of sturdy stone houses famous for its annual bagpipe festival. In Smolyan, **Trite Eli** *(+359 301 81028; inexpensive)*, also known as Three Fir-Tree House, is run by a wonderfully hospitable English-speaking tour guide. This small *pension* has a tiny dining room where guests are served a mind-boggling array of mouthwatering Rhodopean dishes, cooked by the owner using the freshest of ingredients.

Also in Bulgaria

Hidden deep within Sofia's densely forested Borisova Garden, **Veselo Selo** *(www. veseloselo.com; moderate)* is one of the few places that serves *patatnik* in Sofia. The enchanting restaurant complex resembles a country *mehana* – once inside, it's easy to forget that you're close to the heart of the capital.

Around the World

One of several Bulgarian restaurants in London, **Arda 2** *(+44 20 7263 5902; moderate)* serves all manner of traditional dishes and, although it doesn't specialize in Rhodopean cuisine, the chef will accept advance orders for *patatnik*. Live folk performances add extra flavor.

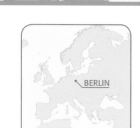

BERLIN GERMANY

Prussian Pork in Berlin

Berlin's outward-looking dynamism, nonconformism, and hip self-confidence have transformed it into one of Europe's most exciting cities. Many world cuisines flourish here, but in the city's corner pubs, earthy traditional favorites such as *Eisbein* still survive. This tender pork knuckle dish allows a rare taste of the flavors of Berlin in its heyday, as the capital of Prussia.

Berlin had a famously eventful 20th century, to say the least. The Nazi era and the city's subsequent near-obliteration in World War II, followed by its division by opposing ideologies and the Berlin Wall, all left the city deeply scarred. With points of interest that are often somber and include bombed-out churches, remains of the Wall, and dozens of memorials to almost unimaginable horrors, it's not really a place for light-hearted sightseeing, yet exploring its layers of history quickly becomes a compelling activity.

But it's not all gravitas in Berlin. Reunification and an almost constant rebuilding process have fostered a creative atmosphere that encourages the lively and offbeat, evident in the city's many festivals, its thriving arts scene, and its intense nightlife. The rebuilding has left the city with a showcase of cutting-edge architecture and its museums have a wealth of treasures to rival any national collection.

Berlin is also inventive in its food and restaurants, which include places where food is served in the dark by blind waiters, or where you pay according to how wealthy you feel. Yet its traditional foods speak of a simpler and earthier time, ruled by calorific dishes like *Eisbein*, which was a particular favorite of both philosopher Immanuel Kant and singer and actress Marlene Dietrich. The enduring popularity of the dish has something to do with Germany's love of pork – the country eats more of it than all other meats and poultry combined. This love affair dates back to Roman times, when wild boar was the meat of choice at feasts. Fresh, pickled, or smoked pork became the basis for hundreds of specialties, and there's a recipe in traditional German cuisine for every part of the animal.

Eisbein is a heavily fat-marbled cut of cured pork clinging to a large bone; it frequently unsettles unwary and squeamish visitors, but remains a firm favorite among Berliners. The pork is cured and sometimes smoked before it is soaked overnight in brine or rubbed with salt, pepper, garlic, and caraway seeds. Its extreme tenderness comes from hours of slow simmering, after which it is served with simple vegetables, such as sauerkraut, puréed peas, and boiled potatoes. First mentioned in a Berlin cookbook in 1638, *Eisbein* is a genuine taste of the past.

Above Berlin embraces the old and the new, from its magnificent cathedral to its high-tech telecom tower

Cooking Courses

Berliners have developed a healthy interest in world food, and most courses at cooking schools reflect this. But you can also find instruction on mastering the basics of German cuisine together with cooking modern and traditional German recipes. **Kochetage** *(www.kochetage.de)* is a highly rated Berlin school whose range of courses include instruction on preparing meat, game dishes, and German sauces. **Kochschule Berlin** *(www.kochschule-berlin.de)* offers a huge number of courses, including those on the basics of German cooking and its traditional dishes. **Kochatelier Berlin** *(www.kochatelier-berlin.de)* offers a broad range of courses, including "Oma's Küche" (grandmother's kitchen) and the "Berlin-Brandenburg," lessons on traditional cooking using local ingredients.

A Day in Berlin

Central Berlin gathers around the city's pivotal grand avenue, Unter den Linden, and is compact enough to be explored on foot.

MORNING Begin at the west end of **Unter den Linden**, at the **Brandenburg Gate**. Then ascend the impressive cupola of the neighboring **Reichstag**, Germany's parliament, for city views. Afterward visit the giant **Holocaust Memorial** on the other side of the Brandenburg Gate and wander through **Tiergarten Park** to the impressive modern architecture of **Potsdamer Platz**.

AFTERNOON Follow the former course of the **Berlin Wall**, passing a preserved section en route to **Checkpoint Charlie**, the famous former Iron Curtain checkpoint. Then walk north through the **Gendarmenmarkt**, Berlin's most elegant plaza, to **Bebelplatz**, a square surrounded by stately Neo-Classical buildings, before exploring the adjacent **Museum Island**, the location of Berlin's greatest museums.

EVENING Pass through the **Nikolaiviertel**, a rebuilt version of old Berlin, on the way to the distinctive **Fernsehturm Television Tower** for night views of city. Afterward, explore **Hackescher Markt** nightlife area to the northwest.

Essentials

GETTING THERE
Berlin's **Schoenefeld Airport** is being expanded to become Berlin Brandenburg International (BBI) in 2012. The city has an excellent network of **metro trains, buses**, and **trams**.

WHERE TO STAY
Circus Hotel (inexpensive) is a youthful and central hotel with classy, colorful rooms and a beer garden. *www.circus-berlin.de*
Luise Kunsthotel (moderate) is an eccentric and attractive art hotel in an 1820s building near the Brandenburg Gate. *www.luise-berlin.com*
Adlon (expensive) is the *grande dame* of Berlin's hotels, with an elegant 1920s feel and first-class service and amenities. *www.hotel-adlon.de*

TOURIST INFORMATION
www.tourist.visitberlin.de

The Best Places to Eat Eisbein

Zur Letzten Instanz expensive

Berlin's oldest restaurant has a real sense of history. There's been an inn on this spot since 1621, when a schnapps bar opened; it was still going strong when a conquering Napoleon Bonaparte visited in 1806. The present business dates back to 1924, when it was a popular stop on the way to the nearby courthouse. In honor of this, all the dishes here have been given legal-themed names like *Zeugen-Aussage* ("Eyewitness Account"), but it's the wood-clad interior and classic tiled oven that really preserve the historic feel. This, and its superb execution of Berlin's traditional dishes, make the place so authentic and so well known that foreign heads of state have often been brought here, including former Soviet statesman Mikhail Gorbachev and former French president Jacques Chirac. *Eisbein* is the most popular dish, but if you want something lighter, try a *boulette* – a ground meat and herb burger that's also a Berlin specialty and is done here to perfection.

Waisenstrasse 14–16, Berlin; open noon–11 PM Mon–Sat, noon–9 PM Sun; www.zurletzteninstanz.de

Also in Berlin

The plastic and Formica decor of **Schusterjunge** *(+49 30 442 7654; inexpensive)* reminds visitors of life in former East Germany, but this old-fashioned Berlin corner pub has built up a cult following for its mountainous portions of no-nonsense Berlin food, including *Eisbein*.

Also in Germany

Outside Berlin, genuine *Eisbein* is hard to find and pork knuckles are more commonly prepared as roasted *Schweinshaxe*, with mustard, horseradish, and pickled chili peppers. However, **Max Walloschke** *(www.max-walloschke.de; inexpensive)*, a friendly 1950s-style urban pub in Hanover, and the lovely old-fashioned **Restaurant Eisbeinhaus** *(+49 20 2251 4670; moderate)* in Wuppertal both serve wonderfully tender *Eisbein*, with giant portions of sauerkraut and mashed potatoes.

Around the World

Elsewhere in the world, authentic *Eisbein* is almost impossible to come by. However, in the US, **Mark's East Side** *(www.markseastside. com; moderate)* in Appleton, WI, is extremely competent at cooking German food and will serve *Eisbein* simmered, rather than roasted, if requested. Meanwhile, the slight inauthenticity of *Eisbein* in **Bar do Alemão** *(www. bardoalemaocuritiba.com.br; moderate)* in Curitiba, Brazil, can be forgiven once tasted; the addition of herbs and pickled salads gives this dish some South American flair and color.

Above Restaurant Zur Letzten Instanz ("To the Last Judgment") has counted Napoleon and Beethoven among its customers

Left The traditional German dish *Eisbein*, a slow-cooked knuckle of pork, is usually served with an accompaniment of sauerkraut

GAZIANTEP TURKEY

Fresh-Baked Baklava in Turkey

Gaziantep, gateway to southeastern Anatolia, claims to be the historic homeland of Turkey's most famous pastry. Among the evocative ruins of past powers, bazaars, and museums, nearly 200 pastry shops compete to bake the best version of baklava – and with excellent restaurants and coffee and tea houses, too, Gaziantep has become something of a culinary capital.

Capital of Turkey's Gaziantep province and the country's sixth-largest city, Gaziantep is also one of the oldest continuously inhabited towns in the world. Lying on a valuable caravan route connecting Mesopotamia, Egypt, and Anatolia, the town saw many powers, including the Assyrians, Babylonians, Persians, Greeks, and Romans pass through its portals. The ghosts of these transient rulers can sometimes be felt in the evocative and melancholy old ruins that dot the modern city.

Gaziantep is an important center of traditional and modern industry. Around the town, coppersmiths can be seen, smelled, and above all heard as they hammer away at glinting pots and pans. But this is also one of Turkey's most productive agricultural regions, and Gaziantep is the epicenter of the region's famous *fıstık* (pistachio) cultivation, the fundamental ingredient for the town's famous pastry, baklava. A local saying has it that you are never more than five minutes' walk from one of the town's innumerable pastry shops, and both Turkish and foreign tourists alike flock to the town to satisfy a sweet tooth and a growling stomach.

The baklava, with its countless layers of crisp filo pastry filled with chopped nuts that ooze syrup or honey, is found all over Turkey. The word "baklava" may stem from a Mongolian-Turkic word meaning "to pile up," and local tradition has it that the pastry was developed in the imperial kitchens of the Topkapı Palace in Istanbul as a way of pleasing and placating the Sultan. The dessert later became fashionable throughout the Ottoman empire. Gaziantep's acclaimed version is always made with pistachios and is judged to be the best not just in Turkey, but in the world.

The city's top baklava chefs claim the secret lies in selecting the finest and freshest local ingredients: carefully sourced and organically grown pistachio nuts, olive oil, and honey. Gaziantep's soil is believed to infuse the ingredients with a special flavor and aroma, and its top chefs use pastry skills and recipes often closely guarded within a family for generations.

According to local connoisseurs, the perfect pastry should be light in the hand, sweet (but not overly syrupy) in the mouth, and, above all, crisp to the bite. A Gaziantep baklava fresh out of the oven, served with a cup of thick, dark Turkish coffee, is an eating experience never forgotten. It's no wonder that so many visitors to Gaziantep come away with a copper Turkish coffee pot tucked under one arm and a box of baklava under the other.

A Day in Gaziantep

Most of the sights, pastry shops, cafés, and restaurants can be found within strolling distance of the square still popularly known as **Hükümet Konağı** (Government House).

MORNING Climb up to the Roman-built, Seljuk-restored **Kale** (citadel) for a great view of the city. Then visit the **bazaar**, where you can wander the stands, alleyways, and workshops and shop for pistachios. Stop for coffee and baklava at **Tahmis** *kahvehane* (coffeehouse) or **Tütün Hanı** teahouse, set in an atmospheric former caravanserai – a fortified inn built to protect and house travelers on the Silk Road.

AFTERNOON Head for the **Gaziantep Museum** and the **Zeugma Kültür ve Müze Merkezi** on İstasyon Caddesi, with its stunning collection of Roman mosaics. Picnic in the lovely **100 Yıl Atatürk Kültür Parkı**, then explore the **Hasan Süzer Ethnography Museum** just off Atatürk Caddesi, in a 200-year-old traditional Gaziantep house.

EVENING Take in the 19th-century **Kurtuluş Camii mosque** and the **Alaüddevle Camii**, near the coppersmith market, where you can pick up that copper coffee pot.

Essentials

GETTING THERE
Domestic flights from Istanbul serve **Oguzeli Airport**, a short **taxi** or **bus** ride from downtown.

WHERE TO STAY
Has Hotel (inexpensive) is centrally located, with plain but well-furnished, spotless rooms. email: info@hotelhas.com
Anadolu Evleri (moderate) is a traditional stone house near the bazaar. www.anadoluevleri.com
Dayı Ahmet Ağa Konağı (moderate–expensive) offers central, boutique-style rooms in a *konak* (mansion). www.dayiahmetagakonagi.com

TOURIST INFORMATION
100 Yıl Atatürk Kültür Parkı; +90 342 230 5969

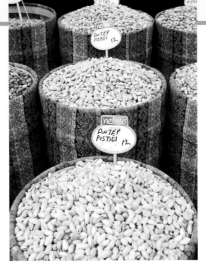

Above Carefully graded pistachios grown locally fill the bazaars in Gaziantep

Left A pastry counter in Gaziantep, with fresh-baked baklava in the foreground; the sweet may contain up to 70 layers of pastry

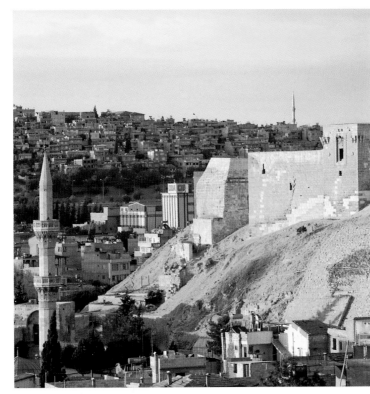

Above The ancient Kale, or walled citadel, was in use as a defensive structure until the end of the Ottoman empire in the early 20th century

The Best Places to Eat Baklava

İmam Çağdaş
moderate–expensive

Family-run İmam Çağdaş is arguably Gaziantep's best *baklavacı* (baklava shop). The eponymous owner, **Burhan Çağdaş**, grandson of **İmam Dede** who founded the pastry shop in 1887, exports his little boxes of baklava daily all across the country and abroad too, including, it is rumored, to Turkey's premier himself, President Abdullah Gül. Burhan sustains his success and high standards by using only high-quality, organic ingredients hand-selected from carefully sourced local producers. Though the recently relocated pastry shop itself is unremarkable, decorated in a plain, contemporary style, it is on the excellence of his pastries that Burhan has continued the Çağdaş family reputation. According to Burhan, his baklava should be eaten not with the knife and fork supplied but with the thumb and index finger, placing the baklava in the top of the mouth and then biting down. The *baklavacı* is open all day, serving pastries with coffee and preparing parcels of baklava for its customers to take away.

Eski Hal Civarı, Uzun Çarşı 47, Şahinbey, Gaziantep; +90 342 231 2678

Also in Gaziantep

Çavuşoğlu *(+90 342 231 3069; moderate)* has a good reputation as both a *baklavacı* and a *kebapçı* (kebab house) and is a good choice for a complete Turkish meal. Food is fresh, well-prepared, and well-priced and the baklava are legendary. Other famous Gaziantep *baklavacıs* well worth visiting include **Baclava Ünlüler** *(+90 342 232 2043; inexpensive–moderate)*, and **Fıstıkzade** *(+90 342 336 0020; inexpensive–moderate)*, both in the center of town.

Also in Turkey

Karaköy Güllüoğlu *(+90 212 293 0910; moderate–expensive)* opened in Istanbul in 1949, the first in a series of famous *baklavacıs* owned by the Güllü family. From the tantalizing pastry counter, customers can choose a *porsiyon* (portion) of whatever baklava takes their fancy, including *cevizli* (the walnut variety), *fıstıklı* (pistachio), or *sade* (plain).

Around the World

Güllüoğlu *(718 645 1822; expensive)* in Brooklyn, New York, is the first American branch of the famous Turkish chain founded by the Güllü family *(see above)*. The bakers are trained in Istanbul and ingredients are flown in daily from Turkey.

Other Sweet Treats

An old and oft-quoted Turkish saying goes "Eat sweet; talk sweet," and **tatlılar** (candy and desserts) play a vital role in Turkish cultural life, accompanying many of life's major events. At engagements and weddings, **baklava** is the traditional gift; **lokma** (fried dough balls in syrup) and **helva** (halva) are associated with funerals, as well as New Year, and a piece of **Turkish delight** wrapped in muslin is traditionally placed between the lips of a newborn child. Modern Turkish cookbooks list up to 300 sweet recipes, many bearing evocative names including **hoşmerim** (meaning "Something nice for my brave man").

A Day in Milan

Milan has some superb cultural and architectural sights, but leave time for a round of clothes-shopping at the many fashion outlets.

MORNING Take a tram or the metro to **Piazza del Duomo** and the fantastic Gothic cathedral. Take the elevator or the winding stairs to its roof terraces for bird's-eye views over the city and north to the Alps. Then stroll through the grandiose **Galleria Vittorio Emanuele II** shopping arcade to reach the world-famous **La Scala** opera house. Continuing in the same direction, you'll reach the **Pinacoteca di Brera**, a cavernous palazzo housing a rich collection of Italian art.

AFTERNOON Head to **Piazza Santa Maria delle Grazie** to gaze on one of the world's masterpieces in a more modest setting – Leonardo da Vinci's *Last Supper* is painted on the walls of the convent's refectory. Relaxing time out can be spent exploring the vast Renaissance brick **Castello Sforzesco** and its adjacent park.

EVENING Wander along the **Navigli canals** and enjoy a drink or meal at the waterside bars and restaurants.

Essentials

GETTING THERE
Milan has two **airports**; Malpensa has frequent **trains** and **buses** to the city, while Linate has only a **bus** link. International and domestic **trains** run into Milano Centrale station, to connect with the **metro, tram**, and **bus** network.

WHERE TO STAY
Hotel Bernina (inexpensive) is a businesslike hotel that's a bargain and handy for the train station. *www.hotelbernina.com*
Antica Locanda Leonardo (moderate) is a charming, 19th-century boutique hotel near Santa Maria delle Grazie. *www.leoloc.com*
Bulgari (expensive) offers stylish modern suites and a relaxing garden. *www.bulgarihotels.com*

TOURIST INFORMATION
Piazza Castello 1; *http://turismo.provincia. milano.it/turismo_en*

Right The rice is stirred as it absorbs ladleful after ladleful of stock until just the right consistency is achieved

Below Milan's Duomo is a 14th-century masterpiece of Gothic architecture, built under the reign of the Visconti family

MILAN ITALY

Risotto in Fashionable Milan

The fashion and finance capital of Italy, Milan is a calm, cool, and collected city where traffic flows in an orderly manner and trams rumble along carefully paved streets. Innovation is part of the lifestyle, but thankfully culinary classics such as risotto never change radically. A rich and refined dish, *risotto alla milanese* uses bounty from the fertile plains and hills of Lombardy.

Standing on a street in Milan, you could be forgiven for thinking you're in Switzerland rather than northern Italy, as efficiency and business are obviously paramount. Milan lies at a providential crossroads of transalpine trade routes, and boasts a remarkable heritage of art and architecture from the 14th and 15th centuries, when it was ruled by powerful families such as the Viscontis and Sforzas. Money and art continue to fascinate today, and the city is home to both the Italian stock exchange and many of the world's leading fashion houses.

However, culinary traditions have not been sacrificed for business, and at lunch time a stream of office workers put down their technological tools and head out onto the street in search of sustenance. Rediscovering the healthy custom of a sit-down meal from bygone days when workers went home for a full three courses, Milan's citizens now take a break to dine in eateries that range from glamorous greenhouses to traditional family trattorias.

Milan's long-standing dishes still shine strong. Thanks to the extensive wet fields to the west and south of the city, where the country's best rice varieties, such as *vialone nano* and *carnaroli*, are successfully cultivated, risotto is a constant on city menus – especially *risotto alla milanese*. The cooking process is drawn out, like the eating. It begins with a slow *soffritto*, where an onion is gently sweated in olive oil. The rice is added and stirred, and then the heat is turned up, and a rich, meaty broth is added, in small ladlefuls – one containing a pinch of saffron – until the rice is just tender. Finally, butter and grated *parmigiano* cheese are beaten in, giving the rice a creamy texture and satin finish. The dish is also known as *risotto giallo* (yellow) for its saffron-bestowed golden sheen.

Saffron is the dried filaments of a type of crocus grown in limited quantities in Abruzzo in southern Italy, as well as in Spain, but it originated in Persia, as did its name. The pretty lilac flowers are painstakingly harvested to produce the most expensive spice in the world, lending Milan's version of this most Italian of dishes the warm yellow of a gentle Italian sun.

What Else to Eat

One of Milan's tasty staples is **osso bucco**, rich and succulent braised veal shank. This is often twinned with *risotto alla milanese* to great effect, as the sauce blends perfectly with the rice. Another meat treat is **cotoletta alla milanese**, a slice of veal layered with ham and cheese, then breaded and fried. Around the beginning of December each year, the windows and counters of the city's leading *pasticceria* (pastry shops) start filling up with huge, festively wrapped packages. **Panettone**, literally "big bread," is a fragrant, soft, yeasty cake baked with dried fruit such as raisins and candied orange peel. It is traditionally consumed during Christmas celebrations with a glass of sparkling wine, but cooks have begun to play with this age-old recipe, adding fillings or sauces such as ice cream or layers of melted chocolate.

Above The wet fields west of Milan provide the perfect rice for *risotto alla milanese*

The Best Places to Eat Risotto

Trattoria Milanese moderate

Reservations are highly recommended here, especially for evening dining, as this bustling restaurant is immensely popular with the Milanese for its traditional cuisine. But don't expect a romantic candlelit atmosphere – this time-tested trattoria has been a serious eating place since 1933, and diners here want to see their meal. Guests are welcomed at the door and ushered into a dining room infused with mouthwatering smells and lined with shelves crammed with precariously balanced bottles and platters of freshly prepared vegetables and sweets. Tables are often shared, encouraging friendly banter and discussion of meal choices. The uniformed waiters never tire of explaining the menu of the day, though most people come here for the signature dish, *risotto alla milanese*. Served piping hot at half-hour intervals, the delicately yellow rice comes out of the kitchen on a flat plate, which allows it to spread to the edges and cool uniformly. On request it can be dished up with osso bucco on top.

Via Santa Marta 11, Milan; open noon–2:45 PM and 7 PM–12:45 AM Mon–Fri; +39 2 41 8645 1991

Also in Milan

Going strong since 1921, **Trattoria Masuelli San Marco** *(www.masuelli-trattoria.com; expensive)* has crisp white tablecloths, immaculate service, and an affable owner who offers you a personal elucidation of the day's dishes. Here the *risotto alla milanese* is proudly prepared with fresh saffron pistils and is exceptionally fragrant. Meats fresh and cured from the family property include *cotechino*, a flavorsome sausage served with fondue.

Also in Italy

La Risotteria Melotti *(www.melotti.it; moderate)* in Isola della Scala, just outside Verona in the Veneto, has 24 creamy risottos on the menu. Each is masterfully created using the *vialone nano veronese* rice grown locally on the family property. One house specialty, *risotto all'isolana*, is a justifiable favorite for its unusual match of veal and pork with fresh rosemary and cinnamon, while the *risotto con zafferano e finferli* with saffron and wild mushrooms is delicate and heavenly.

Around the World

As its name suggests, **RisOTTO** *(www.ris-otto. de; inexpensive)* in Berlin serves only risotto. Guests can perch on stools and watch the chef at work, creating imaginative variations such as pea and lime or zucchini and cinnamon risotto. Open for lunch and early-evening meals, this is a great casual stop.

THESSALONIKI GREECE

Dolmades in Thessaloniki

As a rule, Greek food is for purists and traditionalists, but Thessaloniki, the capital of Macedonia, is an exhilarating exception to the rule. Bridging East and West, Greece's second city has adapted to its cosmopolitan population over the centuries to develop a fusion of Middle Eastern and Balkan cuisine. Its signature dishes – such as dolmades (stuffed vine leaves) – are full of surprises.

Lying on the ancient trade route linking the Adriatic with Istanbul, Thessaloniki has long been a confluence of cultures. Echoes of its former occupants crop up all over the city, in Roman ruins, Ottoman baths, crumbling synagogues, and Byzantine chapels. The city's eclectic cuisine also bears the hallmarks of all its past residents. But the most pervasive flavors are those left by the Ottoman empire, whose rule of Macedonia extended to 1913, almost a century after the rest of Greece was liberated.

Centuries of Ottoman occupation are most obvious today in the ramshackle Turkish quarter of Kastra, which is a 19th-century time warp. Minarets poke out among apartment buildings; former hammams (Turkish baths) are now cultural centers, movie theaters, or flower stands. Even the city's most prominent landmark, the White Tower (which isn't white at all), was built by the Ottomans as a fortress, before becoming a notorious prison. The tower is an evocative monument to the city's diversity, and has a fascinating virtual tour of its culinary history on the top floor.

Thessaloniki's thriving meze culture owes much to the influence of Asia Minor (the area that now encompasses most of modern-day Turkey). Convivial meals consist of a succession of small dishes designed to be shared, usually accompanied by a glass of ouzo or *tsipouro*, spirits distilled from the vine. Grape leaves are also used to make one of the city's most popular meze dishes, dolmades, whose name reveals its origin: *dolma* is the Turkish word for "stuffed." These glossy little parcels are also known as *yaprakia*, from the Turkish *yaprak*, or leaf. The cooks of Thessaloniki have access to tender vine leaves from the fertile mountains of Macedonia, the source of northern Greece's robust red wines. The leaves are picked in late spring, blanched and preserved in brine, then rolled by hand.

Eating a dolma is like opening a gift – you never quite know what's inside until the first bite. Tightly wrapped into dainty bundles, they might be filled with minced lamb, currants, and pine nuts, spiced with cloves, cumin, or cinnamon, speckled with mint, dill, or parsley, or bursting at the seams with sardines, fennel, and onions. *Yalantzi* (Turkish for "fake") are meatless dolma; *sarmadakia* uses pickled cabbage leaves stuffed with minced lamb and smothered in *avgolemono*, a tangy egg and lemon sauce that is almost as tricky to perfect as mayonnaise. The variations are endless, and always delicious.

A Day in Thessaloniki

Layers of history intersect in Thessaloniki, Greece's most alluring city. With its high density of museums, waterfront bars, restaurants, and hip hotels, Thessaloniki also has a vibrant modern identity.

MORNING Visit the **Archaeological Museum**, a thrilling modernist building with an extraordinary collection of artifacts. Then wander along the boardwalk to the **Photography and Cinema museums**, formerly shipping warehouses. Head to the **Teloglion Foundation of Art**, a museum in a hilltop park with a great café, Art 02.

AFTERNOON Get lost in the twisting alleys of the old Turkish Quarter, ringed by Byzantine walls. Old-time *ouzeri* (meze bars) with overgrown courtyards are tucked among the timber-framed houses. Meals here are often accompanied by spontaneous renditions of *rembetika* – the Greek blues.

EVENING The party gets started around midnight; follow the crowds outside the bars on **Valaoritou Street** and around the splendid **Malakopi** arcade.

Essentials

GETTING THERE
Fly to **Macedonia International Airport**, then take **Bus 78** into town. Intercity **trains** from Athens's Larissis station take about 5 hours.

WHERE TO STAY
The Met (inexpensive) is a glossy newcomer with a destination Asian restaurant, spa, and rooftop pool. *www.themethotel.gr*
Excelsior (moderate) is a restored 1920s property with a fun bistro. *www.excelsiorhotel.gr*
Daios (expensive) offers modern minimalism on the waterfront. *www.daioshotels.com*

TOURIST INFORMATION
136 Tsimiski Street; *www.saloniki.org*

Above The streets of Thessaloniki are lined with high-quality restaurants and tempting *ouzeri*

Left Thessaloniki, also known as Salonika, sits around a spacious harbor built by the Romans

Above Dolmades are cigar-shaped, stuffed vine leaves bursting with flavor; a subtle scent of lemon tantalizes the taste buds

The Modiano Market

The glass-domed Modiano, built in 1922, is Thessaloniki's best and biggest food market. It's a celebration of the city's culinary diversity: stands are heaped with glistening olives, sticky pastries, delicate rosebuds, pickled peppers, fragrant mounds of saffron, and briny buckets of vine leaves. There are several places to sample meze inside the market, which echoes day and night with the banter of bargain-hunters and *bon viveurs*. Gypsy minstrels weave among tightly packed tables, where shoppers dig in to tiny plates of grilled sardines or smoky eggplant purée. The beauty of these shared feasts is their spontaneity – and the fact that they can go on indefinitely.

The Best Places to Eat Dolmades

Aristotelous moderate

This classic *ouzeri* is a throwback to another era. Situated in a plant-filled arcade decorated with checkerboard tiles and retro posters of Greece, it offers calm respite from the hustle of Aristotelous Square. Writers and artists, lawyers and lovers squeeze around the marble-topped tables while genteel waiters ply them with a parade of little dishes. You must, of course, try the dolmades. But it's also a good place to dip into the vast repertoire of meze dishes – red peppers stuffed with spicy feta, shrimp sautéed with garlic and tomato, squid oozing cheese sauce, and lightly battered zucchini. With live Greek music most evenings, the experience is as much about the atmosphere as the food. Tourists have discovered its charms, so you often have to wait for a table and prices are a little steep. Yet the appeal of this former Turkish coffeehouse, which miraculously survived the great fire that ravaged Thessaloniki in 1917, is as enduring as ever.

Aristotelous 8, Thessaloniki; open 10 AM–2 AM Mon–Sat, 11 AM–6 PM Sun; +30 2310 233 195

Also in Thessaloniki

Aglaia's Kitchen *(+30 2310 280 044; inexpensive)* is a tiny restaurant with a menu straight out of Asia Minor, situated in the heart of the flower market. Dishes of the day depend on what Aglaia finds in nearby Modiano market, but if you're lucky the day's menu will include her legendary *sarmadakia*, smothered in *avgolemono*. The sophisticated bistro **B** *(www.brestaurant.gr; moderate)* is also known as **Vyzantino**, after its location in the Byzantine Museum. It serves tasty dolmades with minted yogurt, and you can enjoy a tour of the museum's frescoes, mosaics, and icons as a marvelous *digestif*.

Also in Greece

The far-flung isle of Kasos in the Dodecanese is renowned for its tiny dolmades (or *dourmaes*, as they are called in the local dialect). The best place to try them is **Emborios** *(www.emborios. com; inexpensive)*, a lively, family-run taverna, which serves addictive meze accompanied by fantastically fresh fish and improvised singalongs to a lyre and lute.

Around the World

Melbourne, Australia, has the largest Greek community outside Greece, so it's not surprising that it has several excellent Greek restaurants. **Philhellene** *(www.philhellene.com.au; moderate)* is like eating at home with the garrulous Rerakis family, whose beef and cumin dolmades are wrapped in silverbeet leaves grown in their own garden. Don't miss their wonderful stuffed zucchini flowers, only featured when in season.

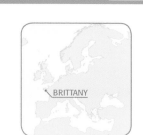

BRITTANY FRANCE

Crêpes in Cornouaille

Reaching out into the wild Atlantic and dotted with prehistoric megaliths, the granite peninsula of Brittany has an elemental mystery. In the ancient Celtic region of Cornouaille, residents take as much pride in its distinct culture as in its signature dish – the *crêpe*. The Bretons have elevated these simple golden disks, filled with seafood or smeared with honey or lemon, into an art form.

The humble pancake occupies a revered place in Brittany, where delicate, wafer-thin *crêpes* have been a way of life and an essential ingredient of gatherings since medieval times. *Crêpes* certainly rule in Quimper, Brittany's oldest city and the capital of Cornouaille, an historic region that was first settled in the Middle Ages by Welsh and Cornish Celts fleeing from the Anglo-Saxon invasion of Britain. They named this region in the southwest of Brittany "Cornouaille", the same as one of the places they had left – Cornwall.

Brittany became part of France in 1532, but Quimper still has much to show of its Breton history. Cobbled streets lined with 14th-century timber houses still bear the names of the trades that once thrived there: rue Kèrèon was full of shoemakers, rue des Boucheries housed butchers, and the Place au Beurre was the place to buy butter. In July every year the town celebrates its Breton culture and heritage in the Festival de Cornouaille, drawing musicians, dancers, and visitors from Celtic communities around the world.

Beyond Quimper, Cornouaille's coast of dramatic cliffs, sheltered bays, and sandy beaches beckons fans of watersports along with walkers and cyclists. The region has long been a favorite of painters escaping Paris in summer, and in the 1860s a cosmopolitan colony of artists sprang up in Pont Aven, a coastal village southeast of Quimper. It included the celebrated Post-Impressionist artist Paul Gauguin, who immortalized the Bretons in his paintings. The Inn of Marie Henri in neighboring Le Pouldu still features walls covered in works by the artist and his followers.

Crêpes provide the perfect counterpoint to any activity in Cornouaille, functioning as a snack, meal, or dessert according to the size and filling. There are two main varieties: true *crêpes*, which are made from white wheat flour, milk, and eggs; and *galettes*, made from buckwheat flour, salt, and water. Some insist the batter be beaten with a wooden spoon, while others add local Breton cider and skip the milk, but everyone agrees on the need for a tiny wooden rake (a *rozell*, or *rouable*) to spread the batter onto a hotplate, and a spatula (*spanell* or *viroué*) to flip it. Traditionally, *galettes* are savory – a classic is topped with ham, grated cheese, and a softly fried egg nestling in the middle – while *crêpes* are usually vehicles for sweet treats, such as hazelnut cream or strawberry jam. But the joy of these pancakes is their endless variety, which allows modern tastes to play with a 15th-century classic.

Three Days in Cornouaille

Wild surfing beaches, sandy seaside resorts, lively markets, and fishing villages with wonderfully fresh seafood vie for attention with walled towns and the Breton interior with its fascinating Celtic heritage.

DAY ONE Ramble around **Quimper's** charming old town, taking in the twin-spired **St. Corentin Cathedral**. Visit the **Breton Museum** to learn how Celtic and Breton folklores intertwine. Anyone with a penchant for pottery will love the **Musèe de la Faïence**, with its 2,000-strong collection of centuries-old ceramics.

DAY TWO Drive or catch a bus to **Locronan**, one of France's most beautiful villages. Sacred to the Celts, it was a sail-making hub in the 16th century and its granite houses have inspired many a movie director, including Roman Polanski, who filmed *Tess* (based on Thomas Hardy's novel *Tess of the d'Urbervilles*) here in 1979.

DAY THREE Follow the **Painters' Trail** (using guides from the tourist office in Quimper) to see how and where the artists lived and what inspired them.

Essentials

GETTING THERE
Regular **trains** run from Paris to Quimper.
Car rental is essential to explore the region.

WHERE TO STAY
Hôtel Gradlon (inexpensive) offers cozy rooms near downtown Quimper. *www.hotel-gradlon.fr*
Les Sables Blancs (moderate) is a stylish hotel perched on the Bay of Concarneau. *www.hotel-les-sables-blancs.com*
Domaine de Kerbastic (expensive) is a boutique hotel in a pretty château 40 minutes from Quimper. *www.domaine-de-kerbastic.com*

TOURIST INFORMATION
www.quimper-tourisme.com

Above Camembert and chives provide a savory *crêpe* filling, ideally washed down with some chilled Breton cider

Left Quimper's recently restored granite cathedral, with its distinctive twin spires, towers over the city's half-timbered houses

Above Women wearing traditional headdresses, the strikingly shaped *coiffe bigoudène*, as part of a Breton religious procession

Crêpe Festivals

Fête de la Crêpe On the last weekend in July, the *crêpe* takes pride of place in the village of Gourin, in Morbihan. Breton dancing, pipe bands, Celtic singers, exhibitions by local artists, and, of course, fresh *crêpes* provide entertainment for all.
Rennes festival In May and June, *crêperies* in the city of Rennes compete to win the title of best *galette* and best *crêpe*. Pancake eaters are spoiled for choice, with everyone vying for accolades.
Fête de la Galette On the last Sunday in September, Pipriac, in Ille-et-Vilaine, hosts its *galette* festival. Expect a *galette*-making competition, buckwheat exhibitions, and Celtic concerts.

The Best Places to Eat Crêpes

Crêperie An Diskuiz inexpensive

Billing itself as a *crêperie gourmande*, this establishment is serious about what it puts on a plate – only 100 percent quality buckwheat and wheat *crêpes*. Settle into the tiny stone-walled room with its wooden beams and tables splashed with red, yellow, and pale green cloths, order a house cocktail (kir with chestnut cream in winter, or morello cherries and sparkling apple juice in summer) and study the menu. Savory *crêpe* offerings include *Cabri,* filled with goat cheese, bacon, walnuts, and cream; *La Dahouet,* stuffed with scallops from Saint Brieuc and leek fondue; and *Côte d'Emeraude* – a creamy melange of scallops, mushrooms, bacon, and parsley. Dessert *crêpes* feature local products such as jellies from Vergers du Cap Coz and de Fouesnant honey, with combinations including orange marmalade with chocolate enveloped in a black wheat *crêpe*, and one bursting with seasonal fruit. Wash it down with farmhouse cider or, better still, apple brandy.

12 rue Elie Fréron, Quimper; open noon–2 PM Mon–Sat, 7–10 PM Mon–Tue, Thu–Sat; +33 2 9895 5570

Also in Quimper

Sainte Catherine *(+33 2 9853 2824; inexpensive),* in the shadow of Quimper's cathedral, dishes up *crêpes* bursting with local goodness. Seafood fanciers will fall for the buckwheat pancake with mussels, scallops, shrimp, and mushrooms in a saffron sauce, while meat-eaters can opt for hearty black pudding and pan-fried apples. Sweet treats include an oozy salted caramel *crêpe.*

Also in France

Crêperies are a common sight in Paris, but they're rarely the real Breton deal. For that, you need to head to the rue du Montparnasse in the 14th arrondissement. The reason? Montparnasse station, the hub for trains to and from Brittany, is close by. Two popular *crêpe* crusaders in the street are **Crêperie de Josselin** *(+33 1 4320 9350; inexpensive)* at number 67 and **Crêperie Saint-Malo** *(+33 1 4320 8719; inexpensive)* at number 53. The flambéed apple and maple syrup *crêpe* here will crank up lagging sugar levels.

Around the World

French expat Sylvie Lemer is responsible for bringing some Breton flavor to San Francisco's funky Mission district. At **Ti Couz** *(415-252-7373; moderate),* she cooks up thin buckwheat *galettes* embracing fat scallops in a buttery sauce or classic ham and cheese, and sweet *crêpes* like the decadent white chocolate and Chantilly cream.

SALZBURG AUSTRIA

Creamy Torten in Salzburg

Rich cakes, or *torten*, are as much a product of Austria's Baroque era as its classical music or architecture, and all three of these remain wonderfully preserved in today's Salzburg. Deliciously creamy *torten* beckon from gleaming café counters, ready to be served by tuxedoed waiters to diners sitting in the very same chandeliered coffeehouses that Mozart once frequented.

Austria claims to have invented coffeehouses after the 1693 siege of Vienna, when it captured coffee from Turkish troops. Unlike the Ottomans, the drink took the city by storm. The local elite loved it, and cafés soon sprouted up everywhere; fashionable Salzburg opened its first café – the Tomaselli – in 1705. Cake was immediately recognized as coffee's natural partner, and before long there were expert pastry chefs in every good café. Their rich and creamy embellishment of traditional cakes created *torten*, a culinary form that has obsessed central Europe ever since.

Most of modern Vienna has tended to move on, but Salzburg's love of tradition has allowed the Tomaselli to thrive, and it is now Austria's oldest café. The main reason for Salzburg's affection for the 18th century is that this was its cultural heyday, as the hometown of its most famous son, Wolfgang Amadeus Mozart. Many city attractions still relate to the great composer: the house of his birth and his family residence have both

become first-class museums to his life and times, while the city's main square is named after him and dominated by his huge statue. A visit to the medieval Hohensalzburg castle above the city affords a great view onto the square and the city's wonderfully scenic Alpine location, already familiar to those who have watched the classic 1965 movie *The Sound of Music*.

Salzburg's time-warp café culture is so authentic that visitors often find themselves sharing the experience with gossiping elderly ladies tending spoiled dogs on their laps, rumpled writers penning verses over coffee, and the occasional Hungarian fiddler pouring out his heart. Aloof waiters usher in coffee on a silver plate, with a glass of water and a small piece of chocolate, or – best of all – a *torte*. Based on eggs, sugar, and ground nuts, *torten* are defined by their decorative icing and creamy layers, which routinely contain buttercream, vanilla, cocoa, coffee, fresh or candied fruits, jellies, marzipan, and even liqueurs. These are the creations of masterly pastry chefs – and Salzburg attracts some of Europe's best.

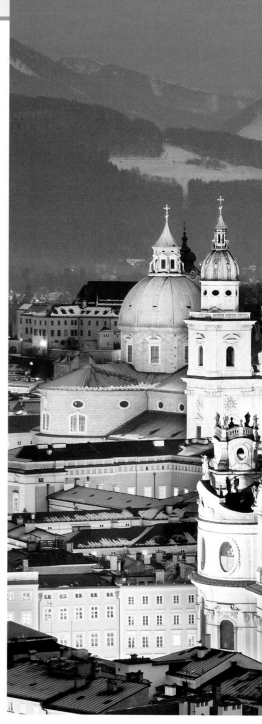

A Day in Salzburg

Salzburg's compact Old Town centers on several graceful Baroque squares. It straddles the Salzach River and sits below Hohensalzburg Castle.

MORNING Orient yourself with a trip to the battlements of the medieval **Hohensalzburg** castle, by using Austria's oldest **funicular railway** or walking up its steep cobbled drive. Later, explore the two focal squares near the funicular's base. Elegant Baroque **Mozartplatz** is flanked by the regal living quarters of Salzburg's archbishops and home to a 17th-century Glockenspiel, a musical clock that chimes three times a day. **Domplatz** contains the **Franziskanerkirche**, Salzburg's cavernous Renaissance cathedral, which has dazzling ceiling frescoes.

AFTERNOON Head into the network of atmospheric alleys and streets just north of the cathedral to find the evocative **Mozarts Geburtshaus**, where the composer was born in 1756. Then cross the river to seek out **Mozarts Wohnhaus**, Mozart's home from 1773 to 1787, which is now a first-rate multimedia museum dedicated to his life.

EVENING Seek out the jovial **Augustiner Bräu** beer gardens to discover why the city is regionally famous for its beer.

Essentials
GETTING THERE
Salzburg **airport** has regular flights from large European cities, and is a half-hour **bus** ride from downtown. Austria's **fast train**, Railjet, runs between Munich, Salzburg, and Vienna.

WHERE TO STAY
Sandwirt (inexpensive) is a basic but clean and friendly *pension* near the station. +43 662 874 351
Haus Wartenberg (moderate) is a relaxed, family-run B&B in a 350-year-old downtown house. www.hauswartenberg.com
Hotel Goldener Hirsch (expensive) offers elegant, traditional Austrian comforts in the center of Salzburg's Old Town. www.goldenerhirschsalzburg.com

TOURIST INFORMATION
www.salzburg.info/en

Left Café Tomaselli, the oldest café in Austria, serves a wide range of luscious *torten*

Above The Baroque buildings of Salzburg's Old Town are dominated by Hohensalzburg Castle

Below The busy, upmarket shopping street of Getreidegasse, where Mozart was born

Patisserie Around the World

Throughout German-speaking lands, afternoon *Kaffee und Kuchen* (coffee and cake) has become a sophisticated social ritual that demands lavish surroundings and ornate *torten*.

SALZBURG

Café Tomaselli
Alter Markt 9; www.tomaselli.at

Austria's oldest coffeehouse, founded in 1705, was once the haunt of Mozart and prides itself on barely having changed since then. The *torten* are outstanding, but the place prides itself on its *Guglhupf*, a simple marble cake.

Café Fürst
Brodgasse 13; www.original-mozartkugel.com

The upmarket coffeehouse opposite Café Tomaselli invented the ubiquitous marzipan "Mozart Ball" in 1890. It has many delicious *torten* and some lovely outdoor seating on the square outside.

Fingerlos
Franz Josef Strasse 9; +43 662 874 213

This is the locals' choice for coffee and cake: a little off the beaten path, but well worth the effort for its broad selection of freshly made, high-quality *torten* and the lively and contemporary atmosphere.

Konditorei Zauner
Pfarrgasse 7, Bad Ischl; www.zauner.at

Located in Salzburg's hinterland spa town of Bad Ischl, the glittering chandeliers, marble floors, and fantastical confectionery of this patisserie are a draw for the entire region. It began life in the early 19th century as a supplier to the Austrian royal family.

VIENNA, AUSTRIA

The Viennese claim that they invented the notion of afternoon coffee and cake, and they certainly have enough venerable cafés and patisseries, or *Konditoreien*, to help prove it.

Hotel Sacher
Schwarzstrasse 5–7 and Philharmonikerstrasse 4; www.sacher.com

The Sacher hotel chain is a legacy of the pastry chef who invented the Sacher Torte, and it has branches in Salzburg and Vienna. Both have slightly snooty cafés with deep-red upholstery, liveried tableware, and arguably the best Sacher Torte in the world.

Café Central
Corner of Strauchgasse/Herrengasse; www.cafecentral-wien.at

The favorite coffeehouse of Sigmund Freud and Leon Trotsky (in exile) is still steeped in Viennese tradition with tuxedoed waiters, extravagant chandeliers, and locals poring over newspapers. The setting, ambience, and unique *torten* often make it very busy, but it's spacious enough to cope.

Demel
Kohlmarkt 14; www.demel.at

A fine, long-standing Viennese coffee house that opened as an aristocrats' playground in 1786. It is best known for its Sacher Torte, which was first made here by Eduard Sacher (son of Franz, its inventor), sparking a legal contest within the family. The café today is more exceptional for its many coffees and extraordinary multicolored *torten*, which have included waxwork-style recreations of celebrities. It also has branches in Salzburg and New York.

Konditorei Heiner
Wollzeile 9; www.heiner.co.at

A popular local café chain with several Viennese branches, including this cozy wood-paneled one on Wollzeile. Reasonable prices belie the superb quality and the pedigree of this bakery, which once supplied the Austrian court. The succulent poppy-seed *torte* is in a league of its own.

BLACK FOREST, GERMANY

The namesake of the famous Black Forest cake, this region of southwest Germany loves to celebrate fine foods and its heritage, be it in the form of cuckoo clocks, traditional dress, wooden farmhouses, or delicious *torten*.

Café König
Lichtentaler Strasse 12, Baden-Baden; www.chocolatier.de

This is a stylish throwback to Baden-Baden's 18th-century heyday, as depicted in the black-and-white prints that line the café walls. Elderly ladies in extravagant hats adore its famously delicate Black Forest cake; the fruit *torten* are also superb.

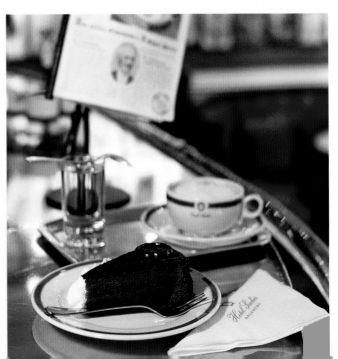

Left (top to bottom) Café Tomaselli, Austria's oldest "Viennese coffee house"; Schwarzwälder Kirschtorte, or Black Forest gâteau; coffee and the classic Sacher Torte.

Below (top to bottom) A tempting display of *torten* in a Viennese café with, far right, the tall, ring-shaped *Guglhupf*; afternoon coffee and cake in Café Gerbeaud in Budapest

Café Adler

Hauptstrasse 52, Triberg; www.hotel-cafe-adler.de

An understated café and patisserie with some of the best cakes in the region, which can be enjoyed in its pastel interiors or outside in a lovely little courtyard. They have a tremendous line in decorative confectionery items that make perfect gifts.

Café Decker

Hauptstrasse 70, Staufen; www.cafe-decker.de

The star café of the southwestern Black Forest region has a lovely riverside outdoor terrace and around 40 stunning fresh *torten* every day. It is also a first-class chocolatier and ice-cream maker, but beware: it gets packed at peak times.

ZURICH, SWITZERLAND

Chocolate and confectionery are a major export for the Swiss, so it's no surprise that they take great pride in their cakes too. There is a touch of the French *pâtissier* in their smaller and more delicate confections.

Confiserie Sprüngli

Bahnhofstrasse 21; www.spruengli.ch

This is run by a world-famous confectioner who's famed for *Luxemburgerli*, a sugar-based cookie much like a French *macaron*. But there are plenty of *torten* to choose from too and everything is lovingly handmade using the best ingredients – though some might gripe about the high prices.

Café Bauer

Badenerstrasse 355; www.cafe-bauer.ch

This has been a local institution since the 1920s, thanks to its great selection of freshly made *torten* as well as a fine range of French-style patisserie. It also has delicious versions of everyday bakery products, such as pretzels and croissants.

BUDAPEST, HUNGARY

As the joint capital of the Austro-Hungarian empire, Budapest shared much of Vienna's culture, and the "coffee and cake" tradition took root here at about the same time. The results are almost as venerable.

Café Gerbeaud

Vörösmarty tér 7–8; www.gerbeaud.hu

A large and noble coffeehouse where hanging drapes and extraordinary chandeliers dominate interiors that have barely changed since its foundation in 1858. Despite seating over 300 people, a relaxed atmosphere prevails and the *torten* are impeccable.

Konditorei Ruszwurm

Szentháromság utca. 7; www.ruszwurm.hu

This tiny and charmingly well-preserved 1820s coffeehouse sits on Budapest's Castle Hill and has a superb cake selection, including traditional Hungarian favorites such as the *Dobos* and the walnut *Esterházy* with its succulent marbled icing.

On the Menu

Torten are rarely labeled and it's often simply a case of picking something that catches the eye. Even so, it's worth bearing the classics in mind and seeking them out.

Dobos Torte Simple but elegant five-layered Hungarian chocolate buttercream sponge cake from the 1880s. Often coated with ground nuts and topped with an angled wedge of caramel.

Frankfurter Kranz (Frankfurt wreath) Classic rum-flavored cake with layers of buttercream filling and a single layer of jelly.

Herrentorte (Gentlemen's cake) A term used for a range of cakes made with large amounts of dark chocolate, particularly in their icing.

Linzer Torte A Christmas favorite from the 17th century with a latticework top and chopped almonds around the edge. The pastry is a crumbly combination of lemon, cinnamon, and ground nuts, and its most common filling is red-currant jelly.

Obsttorte (Fruit *torte*) Usually the simplest-looking *torte*, this fruit tart generally uses glazed fruits (often strawberries) and is sometimes decorated with toasted nuts.

Prinzregententorte (Prince Regent Cake) A layered *torte* with chocolate buttercream and apricot preserve, often dubbed the "Sacher Torte of Bavaria," where it's particularly popular.

Sacher Torte This classic, dark chocolate cake with a layer of apricot jelly was invented by 16-year-old apprentice pastry chef Franz Sacher in 1832; the recipe remains a closely guarded secret.

Schwarzwälder Kirschtorte (Black Forest cherry cake) This is probably the most famous cake. Layers of whipped cream and Kirsch-flavored chocolate cake studded with maraschino cherries are topped with dark chocolate curls.

Zuger Kirschtorte (Zug cherry cake) Swiss *torte* made from ground almonds and hazelnuts, filled with Kirsch and buttercream and topped with a dusting of icing sugar.

TBILISI GEORGIA

Satsivi in Medieval Tbilisi

Perched on the slopes above the Kura River, and sprinkled with medieval churches and old wooden houses, the capital of Georgia is one of the most atmospheric cities you could hope to visit. It is also one of the few places in Georgia where you are likely to find *satsivi*, one of the most famous and memorable dishes in a country renowned for its cuisine.

The Georgian capital, Tbilisi, has an almost kaleidoscopic range of architecture, from ancient stone churches to grand Soviet constructions, and traditional wooden houses to modern high-rise buildings. The city is around ten times the size of any other city in Georgia, yet it is small enough to get around the main sites on foot. It was founded in the 5th century by the Georgian king Vakhtang Gorgasali, whose fortress stood on the site of the present Metekhi church above the Kura River; there is a statue of the ruler next to the church.

Among the city's narrow lanes and along its broad avenues you'll stumble upon everything from cafés to carpet shops and thermal baths, and some first-rate theaters and museums, together with a wider choice of restaurants than anywhere else in the country. *Satsivi* is one of Georgia's most luxurious dishes, and this classic concoction is often served on festive occasions. Appearing deceptively simple, *satsivi* is essentially a whole portioned turkey, or sometimes chicken, bathed in a thick walnut sauce – and therein lies the secret. The sauce is a mix of ground walnuts and a distinctive blend of spices that incorporates coriander, cinnamon, cloves, paprika, a sprinkling of chili pepper flakes,

and a touch of saffron or ground marigold petals. A similar, ready-made spice mix called *khmeli-suneli* is sometimes used. The turkey (or chicken) is poached, then roasted, and finally combined with a sauce made from the poaching liquid and the ground walnuts, onions, garlic, and spices. The *satsivi* is not served piping hot – the dish is allowed to stand for a period before serving, its sauce thickening as it cools to room temperature. Any extra sauce is eagerly scooped up with bread or *gomi* (polenta-like cornmeal porridge). The Georgians even have a summer version of *satsivi* called *bazhe*, another nut-based sauce dish that uses chicken or turkey, but fewer spices.

Georgian feasts are legendary, and eating out in Georgia is a genuinely memorable experience. As well as dishes such as *satsivi* and *chakapuli* (lamb with fresh tarragon and other herbs), there is a wide range of delicious appetizers, including more unusual ones such as *khachapuri*, a delicious cheese-filled bread. No self-respecting Georgian table would be complete without a plate of *khinkali* – fig-shaped, meat-filled dumplings eaten with plenty of freshly ground black pepper. The challenge lies in holding these by the "stem" and catching the flood of juice that runs out with the first bite.

A Day in Tbilisi

A walking tour of Tbilisi is the best way to see its historic churches and explore the warren of streets that run through the old town and up to the hilltop fort.

MORNING Start at **Rustaveli Avenue**, then head downhill past the State and Rustaveli theaters and the **Kashveti church**, to **Freedom Square** and the historic **Sioni Cathedral**. Continue to the Kura River, crossing the Metekhi bridge to the **Metekhi church** and the statue of the founder of Tbilisi, Vakhtang Gorgasali.

AFTERNOON Return to the southern side of the river and head up through the warren of old streets of the old town (with their bathhouses) to the **Narikala fortress** and the **botanical gardens**. From here walk west to the huge statue of **Kartlis Deda**, Mother of Kartli (the central region of Georgia), who – in true Georgian fashion – wields an enormous sword in one hand while the other holds a bowl of wine.

EVENING Wander back down through the old town for dinner – and wine – on the terrace at Hotel Kopala.

Essentials

GETTING THERE
Tbilisi's **international airport,** around 9 miles (15 km) outside town, is connected to the city by **bus**, **train**, and **taxi**.

WHERE TO STAY
Irine's Place (inexpensive) is a hugely popular guesthouse. *www.irinesplace.com*
Hotel Villa Mtiebi (moderate) has stylish, Art Nouveau-decorated rooms, set around a plant-filled atrium. *www.hotelmtiebi.ge*
The British House (moderate) has sumptuous old-style rooms. *www.british-house.ge*

TOURIST INFORMATION
www.info-tbilisi.com

Above The walnut sauce of *satsivi* is a favorite at winter festivities in Tbilisi, along with the juicy dumplings known as *khinkali* (top left)

Left Tbilisi has been the capital of Georgia almost continuously since its founding in the 5th century

Above Georgia's thriving wine industry can draw on more than 500 varieties of grapes, and most — 90 percent — are Georgian varieties

Georgian Wines

Relatively little-known outside the Caucasus and Russia, Georgian wine is superb, and Georgia may be the oldest area of wine production in the world – dating back to around 4000 BC, when locals buried it in the ground in clay jars to ferment. The main area for wine production is the **Kakheti region** in the east, in particular **Telavi**. Among the most distinctive of Georgian wines are semisweet reds such as **Pirosmani** or **Khvanchkara**. The country has an elaborate wine toasting tradition, which includes a *tamada* or toastmaster whose duty it is to propose suitable toasts throughout the course of a feast, and make sure no guest runs short of *gvino* (wine).

The Best Places to Eat Satsivi

Hotel Kopala moderate

With a terrace overlooking the old town, the Hotel Kopala is a great place to stay, and its restaurant – one of the finest in Tbilisi – has an excellent range of traditional Georgian dishes. Starched white tablecloths indoors give way to pretty wrought-iron tables and chairs on the lovely open terrace, where customers dine at a relaxed pace. This vantage point has unbeatable views of the Metekhi church and across the river to the Narikala fort, rising above the atmospheric streets and houses of the old town. Inside the restaurant, large floor-to-ceiling windows share the same view (as do most of the rooms in the hotel). The menu includes either *satsivi* or *bazhe*, together with other favorites such as juicy *shashlik* (kebabs) and various specials, such as stuffed mushrooms. Both *satsivi* and *bazhe* are served with warming, homey *gomi* – the preferred earthy accompaniment to these thick, fragrant sauces. Pick a wine from the extensive Georgian wine list, and enjoy a delicious dining experience with an unforgettable view.

8–10 Chekhov Street, Tbilisi; open noon–11 PM daily; www.kopala.ge

Also in Tbilisi

The large **Kolkheti** restaurant *(+995 32 357153; moderate)*, on the bank of the Kura River, has long tables with comfortable wood and leather chairs, and a wide range of traditional dishes including *satsivi* made – unusually – with sturgeon and other fish. **Ortachala** *(+995 32 788050; moderate)* is another good choice in the Georgian capital. For an indulgence in *khinkali*, head for **Khinklis Sakhli** *(www.khinklissakhli.info-tbilisi.com; inexpensive)* on Rustaveli Avenue, which specializes in *khinkali* in all their guises, along with other Georgian dishes.

Also in Georgia

There is no guarantee of finding *satsivi* on the menu in restaurants outside the Georgian capital, but one of the better bets if you're in Telavi is the **Hotel Rcheuli Marani** *(www. rcheuli.ge; moderate)*, which has its own cellar restaurant, the Old Marani.

Around the World

The excellent (and appropriately named) **Tbilisi** *(+44 20 7607 2536; moderate)* restaurant on London's Holloway Road serves a delicious *satsivi*, among other Georgian dishes, including some mouthwateringly good entrée platters and super *khinkali*. They also serve Georgian wines such as the heady Pirosmani. **Little Georgia** *(+44 20 7739 8154; moderate)* and **Mimino** *(www.mimino.co.uk; moderate)* are two more excellent choices in London that both have regularly changing specials.

Right The regular line outside the famous Magpie Café fish-and-chips restaurant in Whitby, North Yorkshire

Below Crisply battered cod and piping-hot chips are accompanied by the traditional northern garnish, mushy peas

A Day in Whitby

Most visits to Whitby are divided between the cobbled old town and the beach. It's only a small place (population around 15,000), but it makes a great base for exploring the nearby smugglers' villages and coastal cliff-top paths and also the North York Moors National Park.

MORNING Make an early visit (by 7:00 AM) to the **fish market**, and then stroll along the harbor for a view of town from the long, curving pier. Cross the river by the swing bridge to explore the **old town** on the east side – including the **Captain Cook Memorial Museum** – before climbing the 199 steps to the dramatic ruins of **Whitby Abbey**.

AFTERNOON Even if the beach beckons, don't miss **Whitby Museum** and its amazing collection of Jurassic period fossils. Fang-fans can also follow the **Dracula trail** around town – Bram Stoker set his famous novel here.

EVENING Walk up to the **Captain Cook Monument** to join an early evening guided "ghost walk" around the town's hidden alleys and lanes, before choosing a fish and seafood restaurant for dinner.

Essentials

GETTING THERE
Whitby is on England's northeastern coast, an hour's **drive** (or **bus ride**) from York. York lies on the East Coast **train** line between London and Edinburgh; there are also direct **trains** to York from **Manchester International Airport**.
A **steam railroad** runs to nearby Pickering.

WHERE TO STAY
Dillons (inexpensive) has classy, contemporary B&B rooms. www.dillonsofwhitby.co.uk
White Horse & Griffin (moderate) is a stylishly updated coaching inn and restaurant. www.whitehorseandgriffin.co.uk
La Rosa (expensive) offers quirky, vintage Victorian surroundings. www.larosa.co.uk

TOURIST INFORMATION
Whitby Tourist Information Centre, Langborne Road; www.discoveryorkshirecoast.com

WHITBY ENGLAND

The Great British Seaside Dish

It's hard to think of a more atmospheric UK coastal resort than Whitby in North Yorkshire, its red-roofed houses hugging the Esk River below the striking ruins of an ancient abbey. Generations of vacationers have wiggled their toes in Whitby's golden sands and strolled along the bustling harbor, building up an appetite for that greatest of seaside pleasures: deep-fried fish and chips.

The sea is embedded in Whitby's history – from humble medieval herring port to booming 18th-century whaling town – while its shipyards built the vessels that took England's greatest explorer, Captain James Cook, on his remarkable voyages of discovery. Even today, there's a real air of romance and excitement on any visit, from the steam trains that chug into the harborside station to the higgledy-piggledy cottages of the Georgian old town.

While Whitby and its glorious sandy beach remains at heart a traditional pail-and-shovel resort, there are boutique stirrings among the town's hotels and B&Bs, and a new wave of café-bars and restaurants doing great things with shellfish, sea bass, oysters, and lobster, along with other locally sourced produce. But there's still only one must-have dish on a day trip to Whitby – good old-fashioned fish and chips.

For such a well-known dish, its origins are obscure. The fried-fish dishes of immigrant Portuguese and Spanish Jews were already popular in London during Victorian times, while contemporary northern mill workers were enthusiastic consumers of fried "chips" made from potatoes dug from the rich Lancashire soil. When the two came together, a cheap, nutritious working-class delicacy was born. It quickly took hold across the nation – nowhere in England is more than 70 miles (110 km) from the coast – but for the quintessential fish-and-chips experience, there's still no beating the beguiling marriage of sand, sun, and sea air.

In Whitby, chunky cod and haddock fillets are the mainstays of carry-outs and upmarket restaurants alike, deep-fried in golden batter, sprinkled with salt and malt vinegar, and served with a mountain of chips. Batter recipes are zealously guarded, and the best places are proud to say they fry their fish and potatoes in traditional beef dripping or lard. For purists, the only accompaniment is mushy peas (marrowfat peas, cooked down to a purée), and if the whole lot is eaten out of paper on the beach, so much the better. The harborside cafés and restaurants of Whitby are selling more than just a dish – those heady salt-and-vinegar tones evoke nothing less than a collective national memory of seaside jaunts and happy holidays.

What Else to Eat

Fortune's *(www.fortuneskippers.co.uk)* is Whitby's only traditional smokehouse, tucked up a cobbled lane in the old town, just beyond the bottom of the 199 Steps. It's been a Fortune family concern since 1872, producing what many argue are England's best oak- and beech-smoked kippers – locals, visitors, and TV chefs alike all make the pilgrimage to the unassuming smokehouse and shop that lies sheltered under the east-side cliffs. Kippers are smoked Atlantic herring, still prepared by hand at Fortune's, alongside a delicious kipper pâté and smoked salmon, haddock, and bacon. A pair of Fortune's kippers is a true taste of Whitby, and many local hotels and restaurants serve Fortune's kippers to their guests.

Left Whitby viewed from the end of West Pier

The Best Places to Eat Fish and Chips

Magpie Café moderate

The venerable Magpie Café – run by three generations of the same family over several decades – is synonymous with fish and chips, both in Whitby and far beyond. It's a traditional-looking black-and-white building on the harborside, right by the fish market, unremarkable from the outside save for the line snaking down the steps and along the street, in any weather, at any time of the year (reservations aren't usually accepted). The lure is simply spectacular fish and chips – and not just cod and haddock, but plaice, skate, monkfish, lemon sole, or halibut, sourced wherever possible directly from Whitby fishing boats or fish merchants and perfectly fried in their own-recipe batter. The same fish also comes grilled or poached, while a very long menu also offers time-honored Magpie favorites from Whitby crab and kippers to seafood chowder and lobster thermidor. Portions are "Yorkshire-sized" (i.e., big), and the long-serving staff are helpful and motherly.

14 Pier Road, Whitby; open 11:30 AM–9 PM daily; www.magpiecafe.co.uk

Also in Whitby

The lines aren't so long, but the fish and chips are still excellent at **Trenchers** *(www.trenchersrestaurant.co.uk; moderate)*, where you can also watch the fryers at work. For posh fish and chips, and a more upmarket fish and seafood experience all around, **Green's** *(www.greensofwhitby.com; expensive)* sets the local standard – the boat skippers who land their fish are name-checked on the menu.

Also in England

Every town and city in England has a favorite local "chippy" (fish-and-chips restaurant or carry-out), and annual competitions and awards anoint the best, often in otherwise unsung places. **Colmans** in South Shields, also in the northeast *(www.colmansfishandchips.com; inexpensive)* is a classic of its kind, in business since 1926, and while **Harry Ramsdens** *(www.harryramsdens.co.uk)* is now a well-known national chain, the original restaurant in Guiseley, outside Leeds, still draws pilgrims.

Around the World

The dish has followed the English around the world, from New York to New Zealand. In Hong Kong, there's classic cod and chips at **Dot Cod** *(www.dotcod.com; expensive)*, an upmarket seafood restaurant and oyster bar, while Sydney, Australia, is renowned for quality beachside fish and chips, like those from **Mongers** *(www.mongers.com.au; inexpensive)*, found at Manly and Bondi beaches.

Three Days in Gruyères

Gruyères – a château-crowned, hilltop medieval town surrounded by snow-capped peaks – is in La Gruyère: rolling, cow-studded countryside in western Switzerland's French-speaking canton of Fribourg. It is the home of Gruyère, the most popular fondue cheese.

DAY ONE Head to **La Maison du Gruyère** (opposite the train station) to see Gruyère being made, then visit the 13th-century castle. On your way back down, see some exceptional Himalayan art at the **Musée Tibétain**, and then call in at the **H. R. Giger Museum**, which displays work by an Oscar-winning, Surrealist artist and designer.

DAY TWO Drive to **Bulle**, where folk art at the **Musée Gruérien** charmingly demonstrates the traditional life of dairy farmers. Take a tour of **Maison Cailler** chocolate factory in Broc. Wind down with a soak in the warm baths at **Les Bains de la Gruyère** in Charmey.

DAY THREE From May to September, high up in **Moléson-Village**, you can see cheese-making the old-fashioned way. After lunch, walk the two-hour **Cheese Trail** down to Gruyères–Gare.

Essentials

GETTING THERE
Fly to Geneva or Zurich **airports** and then either take a **train** to Gruyères via Palézieux (one change); or take a **train** to Bulle and then catch a **bus** to "Gruyères-Ville."

WHERE TO STAY
La Ferme du Bourgoz (inexpensive), outside the town walls, has three cozy guest rooms. Breakfast includes the farm's own cheese. *www.lafermedubourgoz.ch*
Hostellerie St-Georges (moderate) is a charming hotel in the town with a good restaurant. *www.st-georges-gruyeres.ch*
Romantik Hôtel Broc'aulit (expensive) in nearby Broc-en-Gruyère offers stylish rooms in a renovated 1830s building. *www.brocaulit.ch*

TOURIST INFORMATION
1 rue du Bourg; +41 848 424 424

Right A cheesemaker carries a wheel of Gruyère cheese to a cool cellar, where it will mature over 6–10 months
Below Diners enjoy spectacular views while eating alfresco on Gruyères' cobbled main street

GRUYERES SWITZERLAND

Cheese Fondue in Switzerland

Ensconced in fleecy falls of snow, or lit up by the clear spring sunshine, the walled and castle-topped town of Gruyères has a fairy-tale aura. It sits on a hill amid Alpine peaks, gently tinkling with the sound of cowbells as the animals graze on surrounding slopes. This is dairy paradise and the cradle of Gruyère cheese – one of the staples of a luscious, bubbling pot of fondue.

The tiny town of Gruyères sits high on a hill in the Fribourg pre-Alps, dominated by its medieval castle. Its name is said to come from the French word for crane, *grue*, because the bird adorned the heraldry of the counts of Gruyères, who lived here from the 11th to the 16th centuries. The town consists of little more than one pedestrianized, cobblestoned street, lined with beautifully maintained, centuries-old shopfronts, many bearing ornate wrought-iron signs. This is fairy-tale country, where geraniums tumble from every window box in summer, and twinkling lights shine on the cobbles at Christmas. Visitors come for two reasons: to see the chocolate-box town and to sample its more famous ware – Gruyère cheese – especially in the form of fondue, a pot of hot, melted cheese made for communal dipping.

Cheese has been made in the Gruyère region for centuries, and the apocryphal tale of fondue is that it was created by cowherds who had nothing to eat but stale bread and cheese, and discovered that the combination was better if the cheese was melted. Sadly, Swiss food historians dispute this, pointing out that cheese was too expensive for cowherds. They claim that fondue was a bourgeois dish invented just a few hundred years ago in Neuchâtel – once ruled by the French Dukes of Burgundy, but now part of Switzerland – and its fame later spread into Vaud, Fribourg, and beyond.

Fondue is simple to make: the cook rubs a heavy casserole dish (a *caquelon*) with garlic, adds and heats either white wine or water, then stirs in lots of cheese, sometimes with a little cornstarch, nutmeg, and Kirsch. The fondue is carried to the table and eaten communally from its pot, by diners who dip in small cubes of crusty bread held on long forks. The most popular fondue cheeses are Gruyère and the slightly softer Vacherin Fribourgeois. Sometimes Vacherin is used alone (as in *fondue Fribourgeoise*), but the most common form in Gruyères is the Swiss favorite, *moitié-moitié*: half-and-half Gruyère and Vacherin. Fondue is traditionally a winter dish, but in Gruyères its sheer popularity is such that it is served year-round.

Swiss Food Festivals

In late September the cowherds of Charmey don traditional jackets embroidered with edelweiss for **Désalpe**, a traditional festival when cows are led through the streets wearing headdresses of flowers. There are lots of food and craft stands too (*www.desalpe.ch*). Every village in the region holds a kind of Thanksgiving festival in September or October known as **Bénichon**, a feast that includes saffron-flavored *cuchaule* bread and *moutarde de Bénichon*, a jellylike sweet-and-sour spread (*www.fribourgregion.ch*). Also in October, the town of Bulle holds a huge event known as the **Salon Suisse des Goûts et Terroirs** – a veritable tumble of sausages, cheeses, baked goods, pickles, honeys, sweets, wines, and spirits, together with demonstrations by top-notch chefs – and you get to taste the results (*www.gouts-et-terroirs.ch*).

Above Cheese fondue is kept hot on the table so diners can dip their bread chunks

The Best Places to Eat Cheese Fondue

Café-Restaurant des Remparts
inexpensive–moderate

Locals and tourists blend at the no-frills Remparts as cozily as a good pot of fondue. Two types of fondue are served here: *moitié-moitié* ("half-and-half"), combining Gruyère and Vacherin Fribourgeois, garlic, and white wine; and *fondue au Vacherin* – a fondue of Vacherin Fribourgeois with garlic and water. Spear a piece of crusty bread or potato on your fondue fork and dip it into the cheese. As the pot begins to empty, ask the waitress to explain how best to get a good crust of cheese at the bottom that you can chip off and eat – it's delicious. The perfect accompaniments to fondue are *viande séchée* (air-dried beef, cut sliver-thin), pickles, and a cool glass of white Chasselas wine.

Berries are ideal for dessert, but you'll probably feel overwhelmingly tempted to have them with Gruyère double cream, so you might as well add in some good meringues too.

19 rue du Bourg, Gruyères; open 9 AM–9:30 PM daily; www.remparts-resto.com

Also in Gruyères

Try *moitié-moitié* at **Auberge de la Halle** (*www.la-halle.ch*) or **Hôtel de Ville** (*www.hoteldeville.ch*). **Le Chalet** (*www.chalet-gruyeres.ch*) has both good *moitié-moitié* and *fondue au Vacherin*, as does **La Fleur de Lys** (*www.hotelfleurdelys.ch*), which also serves fondue with boletus mushrooms (*aux bolets*). Prices at these restaurants are inexpensive to moderate, varying only marginally.

Also in Switzerland

Many eateries around Switzerland offer their own takes on cheese fondue. In Geneva, try *fondue au Crémant* (made with sparkling wine), a winter-only, dinner specialty at the **Buvette des Bains** (*www.buvettedesbains.ch; inexpensive*). Zurich's **Le Dézaley** (*www.le-dezaley.ch; moderate*) makes fondue using a good but secret "grandma's recipe." In the Swiss capital of Bern, **Restaurant Harmonie** (*www.harmonie.ch; expensive*) is renowned far and wide for its cheese fondue, which is served with morels, or truffles and Champagne.

Around the World

The **St. Moritz** (*www.stmoritz-restaurant.co.uk; moderate*) in London offers several kinds of fondue besides that perennial favorite, *moitié-moitié*. They also serve cheese fondue Valais-style (with tomatoes); Neuchâtel-style (Gruyère and Emmenthal); and *forestière* (with wild mushrooms). In New York, **Trestle on Tenth** (*www.trestleontenth.com; moderate*) has Fondue Sundays, when a trio of Gruyère, Emmenthal, and Vacherin go into the pot.

PORTO PORTUGAL

Bacalhau in the Port Capital

In Portugal's second city, Porto – famous for its port-wine lodges – the revitalized riverside Ribeira district is now a UNESCO World Heritage site and provides a magnificent backdrop for sampling that most Portuguese of foodstuffs: *bacalhau*, or dried, salted codfish. In skilled hands, this defies its unpromising beginnings to become no less than the country's national dish.

Arriving in Porto by rail or road, there's a first, dramatic view of the broad Douro River, which – more than any monument or museum, more than its stunning Baroque architecture – gives the downtown its distinct character. From the elevated medieval cathedral, an intricate jumble of stepped alleys tumbles down to the river's north bank and to the sparkling waterfront known as the Ribeira. Fish restaurants line the arcaded quayside, some tucked into former warehouses, while above looms the iconic Ponte Dom Luís I, the 19th-century double-decker bridge whose graceful profile frames both river and city. A meal here on the quayside, looking across the river to the port-wine lodges with their names emblazoned across their roofs, is an absolute must on a trip to Porto.

For all the Ribeira's alfresco restaurants and riverside promenades, Porto remains at heart a straightforward working city, something that is reflected in its down-to-earth cuisine. The locals, for example, are known as *tripeiros* – tripe-eaters – due to their penchant for tripe dishes, but there's another classic dish on the menu in every Porto establishment that's more palatable to most visitors.

In the 15th and early 16th centuries, the Portuguese were the world's greatest maritime explorers, opening up trading routes to Africa and India. Long sea journeys were made possible in part by the preservation of food, notably dried, salted codfish (*bacalhau*), which became one of the first truly global dishes – eaten from Portugal to Scandinavia, and in far-flung Portuguese colonies from Brazil to Macau.

After centuries of experimentation, the number of Portuguese *bacalhau* recipes is famously large – some say 365, one for every day of the year, others say a thousand. Every region has its own specialty, and so does every chef. In Porto, the favored preparation is named after the 19th-century cod merchant who invented it, *bacalhau à Gomes de Sá* – baked with potato and onion, and garnished with olives and hard-boiled eggs – but it also comes boiled, roasted, or fried, poached in olive oil, and cooked with everything from cream to chili peppers. It's a popular festive meal, with Portuguese families sitting down on Christmas Eve to *bacalhau com todos* ("with everything"), served with boiled potatoes, chickpeas, cabbage, and carrots. It may seem strange to anyone brought up on the idea of a Christmas turkey or ham, but the *bacalhau*-loving Portuguese wouldn't have it any other way.

A Day in Porto

Porto regards itself as the capital of northern Portugal, and it's a vibrant, cultural university city with a strong Baroque heritage and a fascinating riverside district.

MORNING Start with coffee and fresh bread in the **Mercado do Bolhão** market, then walk to the **Torre dos Clérigos** (Clérigos Tower) for an eagle-eye city view. Visit the medieval **Sé** (cathedral), after which you can descend the stepped alleys to the **Ribeira district**, where former merchant wealth is evident in buildings like the stunning Baroque **São Francisco church** and the **Palácio da Bolsa** (Stock Exchange).

AFTERNOON The Douro River has been at the heart of Porto's life and trade for centuries, and taking a **river cruise** under the city's famous bridges brings much of the history to life. Afterward, take the bus out to the **Fundação Serralves**, Porto's stunning contemporary art museum and sculpture park.

EVENING Drink an apéritif in the **Solar do Vinho do Porto**, the bar of the Port Wine Institute, before returning to the quayside restaurants of the **Ribeira**.

Essentials

GETTING THERE
Porto Airport is the main airport for northern Portugal. Fast, reliable **intercity trains** connect Porto and Lisbon (around three hours).

WHERE TO STAY
Grande Hotel de Paris (inexpensive) is a charming downtown mansion. *www.ghparis.pt*
Guest House Douro (moderate) has stylish B&B riverside rooms. *www.guesthousedouro.com*
Pestana Porto (expensive) is a classy boutique hotel on the quayside. *www.pestana.com*

TOURIST INFORMATION
Posto de Turismo Centro, Rua Clube dos Fenianos 25; *www.portoturismo.pt*

Above Port barrels on traditional *barcos rabelos* (flat-bottomed barges) by the Dom Luís I bridge

Left Stiff as a board and almost as weatherproof, the split and dried salt cod can be seen hanging from shopfronts all over Portugal

Above *Bacalhau a espanhola* – "in the Spanish way" – cooked with peppers, potatoes, fresh tomatoes, white wine, garlic, and green olives

On the Port Wine Trail

Since the 18th century, port wine has been shipped downriver from the Douro vineyards to large quayside warehouses – lodges – in Porto, with historic company names that resonate through the ages. All offer fascinating tours (often free) of their premises, and at lodges like Sandeman *(www.sandeman.eu)*, Cálem *(www.calem. pt)*, and Ramos Pinto *(www.ramospinto.pt)*, you can get to grips with the difference between a ruby, tawny, or vintage port before a tasting or two of their wines. There's more information on the Port Wine Institute website *(www.ivdp.pt)*, while the Rota do Vinho do Porto *(www.rvp.pt)* guides visitors on the Douro River "Port Wine Route."

The Best Places to Eat Bacalhau

Dom Tonho expensive

Dom Tonho occupies a favored position on the Ribeira quayside, its dining room windows and outdoor terrace looking directly onto the Douro River and Dom Luís I bridge. It has a sleek look that marries stylish design with the building's ancient, slabbed granite walls and arches, and visiting celebrities are very much on its radar, but for all its undoubted star attraction, it's what comes out of the Dom Tonho kitchen that seals the deal. The exciting menu puts a contemporary twist on traditional Portuguese dishes, not least its own take on salt cod, *bacalhau à Dom Tonho*, in which the fish is fried with potatoes and eggs and served with garlic-sautéed onion, bacon, and cabbage. This or another *bacalhau* dish is always on the menu, while for an appetizer try the tantalizingly named *peixinhos da horta* (little garden fish), which are actually deep-fried green beans – nothing less than Portuguese-style tempura.

Cais da Ribeira 13–15, Porto; open 12:30–3 PM & 7:30–11:30 PM daily; www.dtonho.com

Also in Porto

Filha da Mãe Preta *(+351 222 055 515; inexpensive)* is one of the best-known traditional Portuguese restaurants on the Porto quayside, its tiled arches and river views forming a charming backdrop for local dishes, including a daily *bacalhau* choice. **Café Majestic** *(www.cafemajestic.com; moderate)*, a gloriously decorated Art Nouveau café, also has *bacalhau* on its lunch menu, while a 30-minute metro ride from downtown takes you to the in-the-know suburb of Matosinhos for the city's finest fish and seafood restaurants.

Also in Portugal

Virtually every restaurant in Portugal serves a *bacalhau* dish – favorites to look for include *bacalhau à brás* (fried, with egg, onion, and potatoes), *com natas* (baked with cream), and *com piri-piri* (cooked in chili pepper sauce). At Lisbon's fashionable dockside **Bica do Sapato** *(www.bicadosapato.com; expensive)* they serve an unusual *bacalhau* risotto accompanied by deep-fried *bacalhau* fillets.

Around the World

Portuguese salt-cod preparations are rare outside the Portuguese-speaking countries, though *bacalhau* itself has traveled the world (as it was intended to) and turns up on menus as *bacalao* (Spain), *baccalà* (Italy), *klippfisk* (Norway), saltfish (Jamaica), and *morue* (France). In the Spanish capital, Madrid, one of the signature tapas dishes at the famous bullfighting tavern, **La Taberna de Antonio Sánchez** *(+34 915 397 826; inexpensive)*, is *tortilla de San Isidro*, a classic *madrileño* salt-cod omelet.

Right The *bouchons* of Lyon promise an old-fashioned warmth along with unpretentious, hearty regional food

Below *Saucisson chaud à la lyonnaise* is a simple dish of poached pork sausage and warm, dressed potato salad

A Day in Lyon

Old Lyon is a UNESCO World Heritage site, full of medieval churches and Renaissance buildings, and its narrow streets are full of surprises.

MORNING Explore the city's *traboules* (hidden passageways linking ancient streets). Map in hand, set out from **Place St Paul** in Old Lyon to explore the cobbled lanes. Visit **Cathédrale St-Jean** to admire the stained glass and the astronomical clock.

AFTERNOON Look for the giant modern murals that are splashed across Lyon, sometimes covering whole buildings. The architecture-rich **Presqu'île** area has some of the best, including **Fresque des Lyonnais**, picturing Lyonnais celebrities, and the nearby **Bibliothèque de la Cité**, where huge books decorate the building.

EVENING Take the funicular up to the gilt-rich basilica of **Nôtre Dame de Fourvière**, built in the 1870s on the site of a Roman temple. Alongside are two 12th-century chapels, and there's a sweeping view of the whole city from the terrace.

Essentials

GETTING THERE
There are **flights** (Lyon-Saint Exupéry Airport) and **high-speed trains** to Lyon from many European cities. The city has an efficient **tram, train,** and **bus** network, and free **bicycle** rental.

WHERE TO STAY
Collège Hotel (inexpensive) is a quirky school-themed hotel with all-white decor. *www.college-hotel.com*
Artelit Chambres d'Hôtes (moderate) has romantic rooms in a 16th-century building with a pink tower in Old Lyon. *www.dormiralyon.com*
Villa Florentine (expensive) is a restored 17th-century convent with a city panorama that's hard to top. *www.villaflorentine.com*

TOURIST INFORMATION
Place Bellecour; *www.lyon-france.com*

LYON FRANCE

The Lyonnais Bouchon

Travelers have passed through Lyon for thousands of years, en route from Italy to Flanders, or more recently from gray northern skies to southern sunshine. These days, it is a destination in its own right, luring visitors with its architecture, history, and homey *bouchons* – cozy traditional inns that specialize in the city's very own style of hearty cuisine.

"In the kingdom of good taste, Lyon's cuisine reigns above all others," or so says a popular adage in Lyon. There's certainly no shortage of wonderful ingredients – Lyon is surrounded by fine food, from Bresse chickens, Charolais beef, and Jura pork to the fish of the alpine Savoie lakes and the gleaming fruit of the Rhône Valley. Sitting at the crossroads between north and south, the city has cemented its gastronomic supremacy.

Once the capital of the Gauls, and still sometimes referred to in this way, Lyon has been a magnet for trade through the ages. During the Renaissance, its four annual fairs drew traders from all over Europe, and wealthy families soon began to ensconce themselves in the old town around St Jean, taking care to be close to both church and state (the governor's house, the cathedral,

and the archbishop's house). The regal former home of the Gadange family, influential Italian bankers, is now the Lyon history museum.

But the bourgeoisie did not make up the clientele at the local *bouchons*, which were the haunt of the workers, such as coachmen, who knew they could always count on a fresh, hearty meal and a pot of Beaujolais at a price to suit their meager wages. Pork was a menu constant, from *andouillette* (tripe sausage) and *petit salé* (pork belly) to fried crackling. It was not until the early 1900s that the *Mères Lyonnaises* (the mothers of Lyon) made Lyon a cuisine capital with their simple, subtle cooking. Mère Guy, Mère Fillioux, Mère Brazier, and Mère Bourgeois turned *bouchon* cooking into an art, and brought a new type of clientele to the table. Mère Brazier went on to become the first woman to win three Michelin stars, but it is often the modest Lyonnais cooking that draws the contented sighs: the pork and salty lentils, boiled pink sausages studded with pistachios, black pudding with melting apples, chicken softly braised in vinegar, salads of frizzy endive, egg, and chunks of smoky bacon, cheesy potato gratin, and butter-soaked apple tarts. Look out for an authentic *bouchon* by spotting the *Authentiques Bouchons Lyonnais* label, a guarantee of traditional warmth and astonishingly good food.

Cooking Classes

Veteran super-chef Paul Bocuse is a local treasure, known for his Michelin three-star restaurant and more pocket-friendly bistros, but he also runs the **Institut Paul Bocuse** (www. institutpaulbocuse.com), just outside Lyon in the Château du Vivier, which has been teaching cooking skills – from one- to three-day courses for amateurs to degree courses – for more than 20 years. Aurélie Chauvin is another passionate cook, who worked beside Michelin-starred chef Mathieu Vianney at Les Oliviers before deciding to open her own cooking school in Lyon, **Délicieusement Votre** (www.delicieusementvotre.com). You can learn to make an entrée, main course, and dessert in three hours or take a themed class – for example, in patisserie.

Left The Cathédrale St-Jean and Notre Dame de Fourvière on the banks of the Saône river, which joins the Rhône at Lyon

The Best Places to Eat Lyonnais Cooking

La Meunière moderate

Bouchon purists agree that they don't come much more atmospheric and traditionally French than La Meunière. The patron, Jean-Louis, has the spherical belly, handlebar mustache, and cheeky, welcoming smile of those long-disappeared bistro owners you might have glimpsed in sepia photos, but he's no phantom. And like Jean-Louis, the food is hearty, so prepare by running a triathlon, swimming the Channel, or walking up and down Lyon's Fourvière Hill at least twice. Start the meal with an apéritif known as a "communard" – a heady mix of red wine and red fruit syrup handed out with slices of cured sausage. Then launch into a range of robust salads (brains, tripe, lentils, herring, sheep's feet, or the ever-popular *salade lyonnaise* of bacon, croutons, *frisée* lettuce, and a poached egg). One of the city's oldest *bouchons*, La Meunière dishes up the classics with gusto: black pudding with apples, gratin of tripe sausage, chicken braised in vinegar, pistachio sausage and veal kidneys with mustard. For dessert, pears cooked in red wine or a plum tart are irresistible.

11 rue Neuve, Lyon; open noon–1:45 PM and 8:15–9:30 PM Tue–Sat; closed mid-Jul–mid-Aug and last week Dec; http://la.meuniere.free.fr

Also in Lyon

With its turned-wood and tiled street façade, **Chez Hugon** (+33 4 7828 1094; inexpensive) looks just like the convivial *bouchon* it is. Expect authentic Lyonnais food served up in plentiful quantities – potato and herring salad, pike quenelles in a creamy crayfish sauce, black pudding and apples, and for insatiable carnivores, *tête de veau* (calf's head).

Also in France

In Paris, **Aux Lyonnais** (www.auxlyonnais. com; moderate) is a delicious-looking place, from its extravagant mirrors and moldings down to its flowery *belle époque* tiles and period apéritif posters. As part of super-chef Alain Ducasse's L'Esprit Bistro group, Aux Lyonnais is more refined than rustic *bouchon*, but the cooking is definitely *bouchon*-inspired: calf's liver with parsley and garlic, farm-raised chicken in cream, pig's head sausage, and black pudding with potato purée arrive on the table in cast-iron pots and frying pans. All the cured meats and sausages are shipped up from Lyon.

Around the World

If you're in Los Angeles searching for French food with a hint of Lyon, slip into Thomas Keller's **Bouchon** (www.bouchonbistro.com; moderate). It has the casual, chattery vibe of a *bouchon* with the panache of a Paris bistro, and serves chunky country pâté, foie gras terrine, and blood sausage with caramelized apples.

BURSA TURKEY

Choice Kebabs in Anatolia

Despite its prestigious past and proximity to Istanbul, the ancient city of Bursa is often overlooked by visitors. It thrived under the Romans and was the birthplace of the Ottoman empire, which enriched the city as it experimented with new forms of architecture. Bursa today has much to offer visitors in its historic buildings and its cuisine, including the original form of the doner kebab.

The intriguing city of Bursa boasts a distinguished history dating back to 200 BC, when King Prusia of Bithynia established a kingdom on the remains of an ancient civilization here. The fertile plains, brisk trade, and healing thermal springs later made it a favorite of the Romans, but it was not until the Ottomans conquered the city in 1326 that the economic prosperity of the region was translated into art and architecture. Bursa was the Ottoman empire's first capital, and it became a kind of architectural laboratory – the city's 14th- and 15th-century buildings are uniquely important early examples of the developing Ottoman style.

Today's cosmopolitan city is littered with the majestic ghosts of its august past, with vast and magnificent mosques, exquisitely carved royal tombs, ornate medieval *medresesi* (seminaries), and elegant *hammams* (baths) seemingly haunting every corner. Bursa's spectacular setting beneath Mount Uludağ on the edge of a national park, its green spaces, café culture, and lack of hawkers pressing for business also add to the town's attractions. As does the Iskender kebab, invented here by Iskender Usta in 1867 when he first experimented with roasting lamb on a vertical spit.

Although the word "kebab" (or *kebap*) is thought to be Persian in origin, the dish probably developed from the nomadic lifestyle of the early Turkic tribes as they swept in from Central Asia in the 6th century. The world's first shish kebabs are said to have been hunks of meat skewered on the swords of marauding warriors as they sat around their camp fires. Today, the kebab is one of the most recognized and popular prepared foods in the world, but often serves as a cheap, easy stomach-filler after a night out. In fact, kebabs are a far more sophisticated and varied food form than the ubiquitous doner or shish commonly suggest.

In Turkey, where lamb and chicken most commonly fill kebabs, the meat is either compressed to form a giant cone for spit-roasting (*döner* means "rotating" in Turkish) and slicing, or cut into cubes and grilled on skewers (*şiş*), ground into meatballs (*köfte*), or steamed (*buğu*) and prepared as a casserole. The İskender *kebap* is quite an experience. In restaurants, waiters serve diamond-shaped slivers of spit-roasted lamb on warm *pide* (pita) bread, topped with fresh, fragrant tomato sauce and accompanied by grilled chili peppers and tangy yogurt, before drizzling the entire dish in lightly browned butter. Washed down with fresh grape juice, it's a veritable feast in the first city of the Sultans.

A Day in Bursa

Bursa is now a sizable and frenetic modern city, but its long and prodigious history is evident in its impressive mosques, tombs, houses, and pretty tea gardens.

MORNING Start the day admiring the 20 domes of Bursa's largest mosque, the 14th-century **Ulu Cami** (Grand Mosque). Just east of the square known locally as "Heykel" lies the exquisite 15th-century **Yeşil Cami** (Green Mosque) and the tiled **Yeşil Türbe** (Green Tomb). Then head for the covered market behind the mosque, where you can eat the town's famous candied chestnuts and drink Turkish coffee.

AFTERNOON West of the mosques are the 14th-century **tombs of Osman and Orhan**, the first sultans of the Ottoman empire, and just beyond them, the beautiful **Muradiye Complex**. Picnic in the adjacent **Kültür Parkı**, then take a cable-car ride up **Uludağ** for views over the national park and Turkey's largest ski center.

EVENING Head for the spa suburb of **Çekirge** or a city **hammam** for a revitalizing hot mineral bath, then enjoy a juicy Iskender kebab in one of the city's fine restaurants.

Essentials

GETTING THERE
Bursa's small international **Yenişehir Airport** is 33 miles (53 km) from downtown. Istanbul is within easy reach by fast **ferries** and **buses**.

WHERE TO STAY
Hotel Güneş (inexpensive) is a family-run, centrally located hotel. *+90 224 222 1404*
Safran Otel (moderate) is a restored Ottoman house near the Osman tomb. *+90 224 224 7216*
Hotel Gönlüferah (expensive) offers historic charm with modern comforts, including a spa. *www.gonluferah.com*

TOURIST INFORMATION
Just off Atatürk Caddesi; *+90 224 220 1848*

Above The Bursa İskender restaurant is the original home of the İskender *kebap*, the original form of the now-ubiquitous doner kebab

Left The serene interior of the 14th-century Ulu Cami mosque with its three-tiered ablution fountain and walls adorned with Koranic calligraphy

Below The delicately flavored *kebaps* of Bursa are served with various savory pastries, often topped with yogurt and chili peppers

Kebabs Around the World

Some sources claim that a shortage of cooking fuel led to the development and rapid spread of the quick-cooking kebab. Today, kebabs are found across the eastern Mediterranean and the Middle East, stretching as far as Central and South Asia.

TURKEY

Meşhur Köfteci Ali Usta inexpensive

Yali Caddesi, Tekirdağ; +90 282 261 1621

This popular kebab house has been serving up the regional specialty, *bugu kebabı*, along with the town's celebrated *Tekirdağ köftesi* spicy meatballs, in its promenade-facing restaurant since 1966. The food is authentic and competitively priced.

Dibek moderate

Hakkı Paşa Meydanı 1, Göreme; www.dibektraditionalcook.com

The Cappadocian town of Göreme is famous for its *köfte* and *testi kebap*, and Dibek serves both along with other enticing Cappadocian dishes in a cozy, atmospheric 16th-century building.

Kebapçi İskender expensive

Ünlü Caddesi 7, Bursa; +90 224 221 4615

Founded in 1867, and something of an institution, this kebab house takes its name from the inventor of the İskender kebab, from whom the current owners claim descent. It serves the İskender along with Bursa's other famous dish, the *inegöl köftesi*.

IRAN

Akin to a kind of national dish, kebabs dominate most Iranian menus. They are served principally in the form of shish kebabs, on bread or with steamed rice, or as *kubide* (like *köfte*). Grilled tomatoes, sliced raw onion, and sumac spice are typical accompaniments.

Ferdosi Sonnati inexpensive

Ferdosi St., Tehran; +98 21 6671 4503

With a firm local following, the Ferdosi prepares fresh, seasonal, and carefully cooked classic Persian dishes (including kebabs) at excellent prices. Try the homemade *dugh*, a refreshing sour yogurt drink that's the traditional kebab accompaniment.

The Khayyam Traditional Restaurant moderate

Khayyam St., Tehran; +98 21 5580 0760

After a trip around the Tehran bazaar, there's no better escape than to the Khayyam, lying on the bazaar's western periphery. Set in an early 18th-century building, this East-Asian-style oasis is atmospheric, cool, and relaxed and offers classic Iranian food and drink from a menu that's more eclectic than most in Tehran *(see also pp178–9)*.

Sofre Khane Sonnati Sangalag moderate

Park-e Shahr, Tehran; +98 21 6673 1075

Conveniently situated close to Tehran's Golestan Palace and city museums, the Sangalag makes a perfect pit stop while sightseeing. Set in the Park-e Shahr, it's tranquil and verdant and serves good home-prepared traditional fare, including kebabs and salads, at decent prices.

INDIA

Despite the significant rate of vegetarianism in India, meat kebabs (mainly chicken, lamb, and sometimes goat) have long featured in Indian cuisine, particularly in tandoori cooking and the meat-dominated Mughlai cuisine of northern India. The famous Arab traveler Ibn Battuta recorded a description of kebabs when he visited India in the 14th century.

Karim's inexpensive

168/2 Jha House Basti, Nizamuddin West, Delhi

Karim's may seem simple and unremarkable, but it's been serving first-rate Mughlai cuisine for nearly a century and is much loved locally for its succulent and subtly spiced kebabs. It's located down a side street opposite the south gate of the Jama Masjid (Great Mosque). Try the *burrah* (marinated lamb kebab) and finish with a creamy *firni* – a sweet rice pudding with cardamom, almonds, and pistachios.

Tunday Kababi moderate

Aminabad Rd., Lucknow; +91 522 552 4046

Although Lucknow is famous for its sophisticated Mughlai cuisine and its variety and quality of kebabs, the Tunday has established a near-iconic status both at home and abroad. Its mutton kebab, made of ground or minced lamb, is legendary. The *kathi kebab*, cooked on skewers in a tandoor oven, is also great.

Left (top to bottom) Carving a spit-roasted *döner kebap* in Istanbul; Greek lamb koftas served with mint yogurt; restaurant-sized souvlaki cooked outdoors in Greece

Below (top to bottom) India's *kakori* kebabs are spicy minced lamb or goat rolls, grilled on skewers; the classic shish kebabs take their name from the Turkish word for "skewer"

Khyber expensive

**145 Mahatma Gandhi Road, Fort, Mumbai;
www.khyberrestaurant.com**

Counted among Mumbai's top tables, the Khyber specializes in the meat-dominated Punjabi cuisine, including expertly flavored and cooked kebabs and *köfte*. With its reputation for fine dining, impeccable service, and hip decor, the Khyber boasts a fervent following among local celebrities, diplomats, and the business community.

PAKISTAN

In contrast to India, Pakistan's cuisine is firmly rooted in the carnivore camp, and kebabs feature frequently on menus, including *seekh* or *tikka* kebabs (shish kebabs), *shawarma* (doner kebab), and a few Pakistani variations such as *chapli* kebabs – spicy, minced mutton or beef patties shaped like a slipper *(chapli)* served with yogurt, rice, salad, and naan bread.

Gowal Mandi inexpensive

Off Railway Road, Lahore

The network of lanes just south of Railway Road in Lahore is known locally as "Food Street" for its rows of stands selling simple, fresh, and skillfully cooked Pakistani fare. At sunset, the roads close and all the locals congregate. It's a great place to try Pakistani dishes at rock-bottom prices in a great atmosphere.

Village Garden Restaurant moderate

Palace Cinema Bldg., Karachi; +92 21 521 2880

Karachi's oldest surviving restaurant also boasts one of the capital's best locations: an attractive and breezy garden filled with birdsong and shade where you can watch your *seekh* kebabs spit, sizzle, and emit tantalizing smells on the large outdoor grills.

GREECE

Some claim that the kebab originated in Greece in ancient times, alleging that writers such as Homer, Aristophanes, and Aristotle made reference to it in their works. The Greek *gyros* is akin to the Turkish *döner kebap*, although pork is often used, and *souvlaki* is akin to shish kebabs. They are as universally popular as their Turkish counterparts.

To Etsi inexpensive

Nikoforos Fokas 2, near the White Tower, Thessaloniki; +30 2310 222 469

Simple, basic, and garishly decorated, the To Etsi in Thessaloniki has won a cult following locally for its succulent *souvlaki* stuffed into freshly baked pita bread, served with crunchy salad and generous dollops of homemade hot, spicy, or garlicky sauces.

Varoulko expensive

Pireos 80, Gazi, Athens; www.varoulko.gr

As famous for its startling views of the Acropolis as for the startling modern-Greek creations of the country's only Michelin-star-rated chef, Lefteris Lazarou, the Varoulko is a must for the foodie. Seafood is the specialty, but the meat dishes don't disappoint. Book a rooftop table.

On the Menu in Turkey

There are dozens of varieties of kebab in Turkey. Many are local adaptations named after the place of origin or their founder.

Adana kebap Minced lamb spiced with chili peppers, garlic, parsley, paprika, pepper, and sumac, molded into a sausage and grilled over coals on a special long, flat skewer. The meat is served on top of warm strips of pita bread with a salad of tomatoes, peppers, and sliced onions tossed in sumac.

Buğu kebap Meat is steamed in a sealed terra-cotta pot along with pearl onions, garlic, thyme, sumac, and cumin.

Çiğ kebap Raw, ground lamb pounded with bulgur wheat and onions, spiced with cinnamon, cloves, paprika, and pepper.

Döner kebap Compressed meat (chicken or lamb) grilled on an upright and rotating skewer and sliced onto pita bread.

Erciyes kebap Lamb served on a bed of thinly sliced sautéed potatoes with garlic and yogurt.

Fıstıklı kebap Suckling lamb minced and mixed with herbs and pistachios.

İskender (Bursa) kebap Lamb *döner* layered on a bed of pita bread, topped with tomato sauce and tangy yogurt, then drizzled with lightly browned butter.

Patlıcan kebap Minced or cubed lamb grilled on skewers with eggplant.

Şiş kebap Cubed lamb or chicken marinated in oil, garlic, onion, and black pepper grilled on a skewer with onions and peppers.

Tavuk şiş kebap Chicken cubes marinated in olive oil, thyme, or rosemary, crushed garlic, black pepper, grated onion, and yogurt, grilled on a skewer over coals.

Testı kebap Lamb or chicken with vegetables (often onion and mushroom), slow-cooked in a sealed terra-cotta pot that is broken open at the dining table.

Tokat kebap Cubed lamb grilled on a skewer along with potato, eggplant, tomato, and garlic.

Urfa kebap Minced lamb, mildly spiced with chili pepper, garlic, paprika, pepper, and sumac, shaped like a sausage and grilled over coals; served with onion salad.

Yoğurtlu şiş kebap Grilled skewers of cubed lamb marinated in oil, garlic, and onion, along with grilled, skewered ground lamb *köfte*, served on a bed of butter-fried pita bread, sprinkled with sumac, salt, and thyme, and topped with fresh tomato sauce, yogurt, and fried strips of eggplant.

ROME ITALY

Jewish Artichokes in Rome

With such a richness of classical sights to savor, it is too easy to miss out on Rome's other fascinating histories. Peoples from all corners of the empire made their home here, and the city's Jewish population traces its presence back two millennia. Their chefs can take credit for one of Rome's culinary highlights – *carciofi alla giudia*, delicious fried artichokes.

Against the backdrop of its imperial Roman past and the Italian Renaissance, the Italian capital is very much alive and moving with the times, ever more international in flavor. It has a vibrant Film Festival, a modern auditorium by Renzo Piano, and MAXXI, a spectacular new contemporary art museum designed by Zaha Hadid.

However, the Eternal City's bottom line has changed not one iota. The stereotypes still run true, with scooters zooming along impossibly busy streets, flocks of robed nuns and priests everywhere, noisy neighborhood markets, and the *dolce vita* very much in evidence. The city's host of neighborhood trattorias could have been plucked straight from Italian films of the 1960s, when a *mezza porzione* (half a helping, and therefore cheaper) was commonplace. Down-to-earth and run by no-nonsense waiters, these trattorias serve exclusively traditional fare, rich, delicious, and tomatoey, like *coda alla vaccinara* (braised oxtail) and *spaghetti all'amatriciana,* with tomato, onion, chili pepper, and tangy cured bacon.

One item offered nonstop from October through to June is the typical plump, round Roman (or globe) artichoke. These are usually cooked in one of two ways, each radically different but both avoiding the tiresome ritual of scraping the flesh off the leaves. *Carciofi alla romana* entails slow-braising artichokes in garlic and parsley with a dash of broth. Soft as butter, they are a divine eating experience, as the whole artichoke can be simply sliced and eaten. A different and unusual technique is used for *carciofi alla giudia* ("in the Jewish way"); the artichokes are squashed "face down" to flatten and tenderize them, then fried in olive oil. The magic happens as the outer leaves turn deliciously crisp and golden. These crunchy delights are best eaten sizzling straight out of the pan.

The handsome artichoke is related to the wild thistle and hails from the Middle East. It made its appearance in Italy as an edible vegetable in the 1500s, but its origins can be traced farther back to another classical civilization – ancient Greece. Myths hold that mighty Zeus was infatuated with the exquisite nymph Cynara, but her capricious behavior made him insane with jealousy, so he turned her into a tough, spiky green plant. However, he did give her a sweet heart, and the "heart" of the artichoke, marinated in oil and herbs and served as antipasto or on pizza, is in fact probably better known throughout the world than the leaves lovingly embraced by the recipes of Rome.

Above Rome's Jewish Ghetto on the banks of the Tiber is now one of the city's most eclectic neighborhoods

Right The imposing dome of St. Peter's Basilica covers a huge and impressive interior – the space can hold 60,000 worshippers

Below *Carciofi alla giudia*, Jewish-style fried artichokes, are a specialty of the ancient Ghetto district of Rome

A Day in Rome

Central Rome, which holds the city's classic sights, is surprisingly compact and walkable, but you need to plan your time carefully to make the best of your day.

MORNING Go to the **Colosseum** and explore the stone tiers where spectators witnessed the ghastly blood sports of ancient Rome. Alongside is the **Forum**, with temples and public buildings, headquarters of the far-reaching Roman empire. Then walk through to **Campo de' Fiori** for its lively morning market and cafés.

AFTERNOON Head over to the forbidding **Castel Sant'Angelo** on the banks of the Tiber River. Designed for Emperor Hadrian as his mausoleum, over time it became a prison and even Papal apartments. Follow the broad **Via della Conciliazione** to the vast paved square in front of **St. Peter's Basilica**; the **Vatican museums** and the **Sistine Chapel** make a superb conclusion.

EVENING Pick a spot on **Piazza Navona**, resplendent with its gushing Baroque fountains by Bernini, for a magical alfresco dinner.

Essentials

GETTING THERE
Rome has two **airports**: Fiumicino has an express **train** to Termini central train station; while smaller Ciampino has a direct **bus**.

WHERE TO STAY
Hotel Panda (inexpensive) is a family-run hotel near the Spanish Steps. *www.hotelpanda.it*
Daphne Trevi (moderate) has two locations downtown. *www.daphne-rome.com*
Buonanotte Garibaldi (expensive) is a hidden oasis within the Trastevere district. *www.buonanottegaribaldi.com*

TOURIST INFORMATION
Via Parigi 11; +39 06 488 991

Artichokes Around Italy

The artichoke is highly prized in regional cuisines around Italy. Varieties of the vegetable are used in Cynar liqueur and even in tantalizing ice cream. Sardinia boasts the yellowish *spinoso sardo*, eaten raw with oil in springtime when fresh and tender. This is also peak time for prized tiny purple *castraure*, a variety jealously cultivated on Sant'Erasmo island in the Venice lagoon. These artichokes have a distinctive bitter tang due to the salt content of the soil. At the end of the artichoke season when the head becomes bristly, market stands across northeast Italy pare off the top and sell thick *fondi* disks, kept in water and lemon juice to prevent them from turning brown.

The Best Places to Eat Carciofi alla Giudia

Da Giggetto moderate

You'd be hard put to find a more pleasant place to have dinner on a balmy summer's evening in Rome than this venerated trattoria in the city's ancient Ghetto district, not far from the banks of the Tiber River. "Giggetto" was the nickname of Luigi Ceccarelli, a returned WWI serviceman who began this well-reputed trattoria back in 1923, and the current manager is his grandson. Dining is alfresco from spring through fall, a memorable experience as the tables are set up between shiny stone columns belonging to the Porticus of Octavia, steeped in history. Inside, old brick vaults and arches dangle with braids of garlic and dried herbs over spacious rooms. A bowl of plump globe artichokes in the entrance informs diners that the traditional Jewish-Roman dish – golden, crisp *carciofi alla giudia* – is available. Another typical offering here is *filetto di baccalà*, fillet of salt cod, battered, fried, and served hot with lemon.

Via Portico d'Ottavia 21/22, Rome; open 12:30–2:30 PM & 7:30–11 PM Tue–Sun; www.giggetto.it

Also in Rome

With long lines outside its otherwise inconspicuous entrance, **Sora Margherita** *(+39 06 687 4216; inexpensive)* is a tiny trattoria in the Ghetto. Once inside, you'll be elbow-to-elbow with other guests. However, it is well worth the wait – nobody ever complains about the food, especially the antipasto, which includes *carciofi alla giudia*, given rave reviews by guests new and old.

Also in Italy

The island of Sant'Erasmo in the Venetian lagoon is a giant vegetable garden, which has supplied Venice with flavorsome fresh produce since ancient Roman times. The menu at **Ristorante Cà Vignotto** *(+39 41 24 44 000; moderate)* on the island is dictated by the seasons, with winter to spring bringing the best *castraure* artichokes. With a bit of luck, their divine gnocchi with crab will be on the day's menu as well.

Around the World

Roman-style crisp-fried artichokes are one of the signature dishes of flamboyant master-chef Sandro Fioriti at his newest restaurant, **Sandro's** *(www.sandrosnyc.com; expensive)*, which attracts a cultlike following among New Yorkers. Another house specialty is *spaghettini al limone*, which can be varied with a melon or tomato sauce.

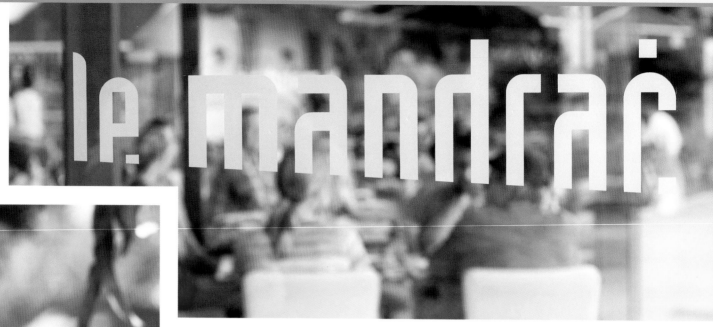

Right Modern seafood restaurants hug the water's edge on Volosko's picturesque harbor

Below Bread or polenta plus a glass of crisp *Vrbnička Žlahtina* are the perfect accompaniments to Kvarner scampi

Three Days on the Kvarner Gulf

The oldest resort on the Gulf, genteel Opatija offers plenty in the way of accommodations, culinary culture, and café life. Islands such as Cres and Lošinj, with their stone-built fishing villages and maquis-covered hills, offer more in the way of offbeat relaxed atmosphere.

DAY ONE Stroll **Opatija**'s palm-fringed seaside path, the **Lungomare**, which winds its way around a series of rocky bays and gravel beaches. Strike out to the former fishing village of **Volosko**, and southward toward **Lovran**, a town filled with picturesque Art Nouveau villas.

DAY TWO Explore **Rijeka**, the Gulf's one real metropolis, enjoying an espresso at one of the cafés lining the central **Korzo**, or browsing the stands at the bustling market. Take a trip to the hilltop suburb of **Trsat**, site of a ridge-top fortress, for spectacular maritime views.

DAY THREE Take the ferry to the conjoined islands of **Cres** and **Lošinj** (often called "the island of flowers"), where ridges of sheep pasture or Mediterranean maquis loom above sleepy fishing ports.

Essentials

GETTING THERE
International flights arrive at **Zagreb Airport**, a 112-mile (180-km) drive to the Kvarner's main city, Rijeka. **Buses** run from Zagreb's bus station to all of the Gulf's main settlements.

WHERE TO STAY
Pjacal (inexpensive) is a restful family-run B&B in Veli Lošinj. *www.pjacal.eu*
Palace-Bellevue (moderate) is a *belle-époque* hotel with fine high-ceilinged rooms in the center of Opatija. *www.liburnia.hr*
Draga di Lovrana (moderate) offers creature comforts and superb views in a hillside mansion high above Opatija and Lovran. *www.dragadilovrana.hr*

TOURIST INFORMATION
Nikole Tesle 2, Opatija; *www.kvarner.hr*

KVARNER GULF CROATIA

Scampi on the Adriatic Sea

Framed by gray-green mountains and dotted with arid ocher-colored islands, the Kvarner Gulf is one of the most starkly beautiful stretches of the Croatian Adriatic coastline. Its gin-clear seas yield an astounding variety of fish and crustaceans, although it is the famously succulent Kvarner scampi that occupy center stage in the local cuisine.

The Kvarner Gulf has been an essential stop-off for well-heeled visitors since the late 19th century, when Austrian dukes and duchesses descended on the region's coastal towns to enjoy the mild winters.

A sense of the *belle époque* still lives on in resorts like Opatija, where palm-fringed promenades are set against a backdrop of Art Nouveau hotels and vacation villas. A rather different atmosphere, however, prevails on islands such as Cres and Lošinj, where stone-built fishing villages huddle beside rocky coves, the neighboring scrubby maquis shrubland singing with cicadas. The vibrant city of Rijeka is the fulcrum around which the life of the Gulf revolves: a busy ferry and fishing port whose central market fills daily with the beckoning glisten of fresh fish, octopus, and squid. Indeed, it is this diverse array

of seafood that most characterizes the local diet. One culinary treasure particularly associated with the Gulf is the Kvarner scampi, a succulent crustacean that is highly valued on restaurant tables throughout Croatia.

The local scampi are Mediterranean cousins of the large prawn known as the Norway lobster. Blessed with a silty seabed perfect for burrowing, the Kvarner is one of the few parts of the Mediterranean where the scampi flourish in large numbers. In northern European countries, the fleshy tails of the scampi are frequently removed and fried in bread crumbs, although here in Croatia the creature is served whole and unpeeled and is eaten with the fingers – prying open the shells and scooping out the white meat is all part of the ritual. Indeed, locals who have grown up eating scampi will suck the shells dry and then bite open the animal's pincers in the hope of finding a final sliver of succulent flesh.

One recipe on almost every local restaurant menu, a culinary classic here and indeed all down Croatia's Dalmatian coast, is *skampi na buzari* – a simple but sensuous combination of scampi, garlic, tomato, and white wine. Eating the sauce-covered scampi is a fantastically messy process – so don't refuse your waiter's offer of a bib, unless you want a Dalmatian-style polka-dot pattern all over your favorite shirt.

Croatian Wines

Although not widely known as a wine-producing area, the Kvarner Gulf is home to one of Croatia's most highly regarded dry whites, Vrbnička Žlahtina, from the island of Krk. An indigenous Adriatic grape, Žlahtina (from the Slavic word meaning "noble") is cultivated almost exclusively in a green vale near the port of Vrbnik, one of the few fertile areas on what is otherwise an arid and unforgiving collection of islands. Vrbnik itself is a picturesque town built on a high cliff and is the perfect place to sample the crisp, dry Vrbnička Žlahtina wine; it has a fresh, young bouquet and is the perfect accompaniment to local specialties, such as homemade pasta, lamb, sheep cheese, and prosciutto, as well as the delicious Gulf seafood.

Left Boats in harbor on Lošinj Island, Croatia

The Best Places to Eat Scampi

Plavi Podrum expensive

Located on the northern fringes of Opatija, the fishing village of Volosko is something of a Croatian gastronomic Shangri-La, featuring several restaurants that regularly make the best-of lists of local food critics. Plavi Podrum, nestling on the curve of Volosko's boat-packed inner harbor, occupies a particular niche, marrying the best of local seafood with a modern European sense of culinary invention. Kvarner-caught fish and crustaceans form the backbone of the menu: seafood risottos, grilled squid, and scampi in all its varieties keep the locals coming back in droves. Other main courses are more experimental, mixing fish and meat flavors or making subtle use of Asian spices. Local ingredients, however, reign supreme, with wild asparagus and pungent Istrian truffles featuring heavily in season and a variety of Croatian olive oils arranged on the tables. The owner is one of Croatia's leading sommeliers, so if advice on the country's most intriguing wines is what you're after, this is emphatically the right place. The classy, starched-napkin interior is ideal for a formal meal, while the outdoor terrace, with its views of stone houses and fishing boats, has an altogether more romantic appeal.
Ulica Frana Supila 12, Volosko; open noon–midnight daily; www.plavipodrum.com

Also in the Kvarner Gulf

The road southwest from Opatija passes through the quaint seaside town of Lovran, where the **Najade Restaurant** (*+385 51 291 866; expensive*) serves up fresh scampi, squid, and fish dishes on a large sea-facing terrace. It's well worth venturing across the water to Lošinj, too, where the **Bora Bar** (*www.borabar.com; expensive*), overlooking Rovenska harbor, offers local scampi either *na buzari* or in a Grand Marnier sauce, alongside a range of homemade pastas.

Also in Croatia

Of the many seafood restaurants in the capital, Zagreb, **Gašpar** (*www.restoran-baltazar.hr; expensive*) offers an across-the-board selection of Adriatic treats, including a particularly good *buzari*. Gašpar's sister-restaurant **Baltazar**, in the same courtyard, is the place to sample the central Croatian repertoire of hearty grilled meats.

Around the World

Skampi na buzari is known all over the Adriatic, but is more difficult to find farther afield. In Slovenia's capital, Ljubljana, there is seafood aplenty: **Most** (*www.restavracija-most.si; expensive*) serves up scampi and other fresh crustaceans in a riverside setting right opposite the city's colonnaded fish market.

Above The iconic Eiffel Tower, built in 1889, towers over the pretty Parisian buildings in the 7th arrondissement

Above *Macarons* on display at Ladurée on rue Royale in Paris, where the family has been selling luxury cakes and pastries since 1871

A Day in Paris

Paris, the ultimate walking city, is teeming with sights. Skip your hotel breakfast and instead wander the neighborhood, taking in the scene, and grab your coffee and croissants at a café packed with locals.

MORNING Make your way to the chic **Marais** district and **Les Enfants Rouges**, Paris's oldest covered market, dating back to 1615. The evocative name recalls the children of a nearby orphanage, which closed in 1534, who uniformly wore red. Follow up with a *coup sur le zinc* (a pick-me-up – coffee or something stronger) at a local café.

AFTERNOON Ramble the *quais* of the Seine to the **Ile de la Cité**, stopping at the **Square du Vert Galant** to take in the grandeur of the **Louvre**. At the other end of the island, enjoy the view of **Notre Dame's** flying buttresses. Scour the art galleries of **St Germain**.

EVENING Head for **Place de la Concorde** to parade up the **Champs Elysées**. Look out over the city from the top of the **Arc de Triomphe**, tracing the 12 radiating avenues to arches and obelisks in the east and the contemporary **La Grande Arche de la Défense** to the west.

Essentials

GETTING THERE
Paris has **two airports**: Paris-Charles de Gaulle and Paris-Orly. The former has its own RER **metro** station; at Orly a **shuttle bus** links to the metro line.

WHERE TO STAY
Hôtel Jeanne d'Arc (inexpensive) is a cozy, family-run hotel in the history-soaked Marais district. *www.hoteljeannedarc.com*
Hôtels Paris Rive Gauche (moderate) boasts five bijou properties on the Left Bank. *www.hotels-paris-rive-gauche.com*
Paris institution **Le Meurice** (expensive) has public spaces by Philippe Starck (those chairs sporting ladies' shoes), while rooms channel luxurious Louis XVI. *www.lemeurice.com*

TOURIST INFORMATION
www.parisinfo.com

PARIS FRANCE

Marvelous Macarons in Paris

There's a lot to love about the French capital: temples of high art, sophisticated music haunts, cool *quartiers*, and lofty landmarks that span the centuries. But beyond the Louvre's masterpieces, Notre Dame's gargoyles, and the towering lights of the Eiffel Tower lies another tiny gem that never fails to draw crowds of Parisians and tourists: the perfect *macaron*.

An artistic city *par excellence*, Paris proffers an astonishing array of tempting pastimes. Culture vultures can swoop on highbrow opera and orchestral performances, or more bohemian attractions such as art-house cinema and circuses. Myriad museums satisfy cravings for any and all types of painting, photography, installations, and sculpture, while city parks and gardens – such as the 17th-century Jardin du Luxembourg – provide the tranquillity in which to reflect on it.

Visitors can soak up the ambience of centuries past through the city's astonishing architecture, from the 12th-century Gothic masterpiece of Notre Dame to the Renaissance buildings of the Marais or the high-tech Pompidou Center. The shopping is just as extraordinary; Paris is arguably the fashion capital of the world, and an afternoon's shopping can easily encompass both the *haute couture* of rue du Faubourg Saint-Honoré and the flea-market finds of Saint-Ouen. And then there's the food – reason enough for a visit on its own. Not simply fuel, food is more fine art here,

and nowhere is that better illustrated than in Paris patisseries. The most French of fancies – the *macaron* – is a byword for pastry perfection.

Henri II's Italian wife, Catherine de Medici, is credited with bringing the meringue to France in 1533, but it was a Frenchman, Pierre Desfontaines – cousin of Paris tea-salon owner Louis Ernest Ladurée (*see right*) – who first hit upon the idea, in the early 20th century, of joining two *macarons* together with a blob of chocolate ganache. Like all things painfully delicious, this ensemble requires real finesse. The ingredients are simple: egg whites, ground almonds, sugar, and flavoring. But it's the sifting, folding in, piping, letting them sit (or not), and baking at just the right temperature that determines whether they achieve that perfect crust and glossy dome. And it's the combination of chewy meringue and velvety center that causes people to sigh as they bite into ivory buttons oozing salted caramel, baby-pink disks encasing rose petals, or snowy puffs cloaking hazelnut and white truffle. Some connoisseurs insist they taste better the day after they're made, but who has the steely nerve to wait that long?

Above An alfresco café in the formal gardens of the Jardin du Luxembourg

Cooking Classes

There's no better place to learn the art of patisserie than in Paris. There are half-day, full-day, and multi-day courses, usually for 3–6 people. All the courses here need to be booked ahead. At **Promenades Gourmandes** (*www.promenadesgourmandes.com*), pastry and *macaron* master Joël Morgeat imparts an infallible technique for turning out perfect little meringue domes of chocolate, raspberry, or grapefruit, under the watchful eye of Parisian gourmet Paule Caillat. **Ecole Ritz Escoffier**, in the Ritz Hotel (*www.ritzparis.com*), runs classes showing how to whip up *macarons* in many flavors; expect to learn one flavor in 2 hours, or several in a 4-hour class. **La Cuisine Paris** (*www.lacuisineparis.com*) runs afternoon *macaron*-making classes in both French and English in the center of Paris.

The Best Places to Eat Macarons

Pierre Hermé expensive

Fourth-generation pastry-maker Pierre Hermé is the resident *macaron* magician, conjuring up creations that people cross town for. Hermé claims he only makes "what feels right" when it comes to these jewel-box disks, and there's no denying his surefire instincts. That crunchy shell and those creamy flavors: vanilla and olive oil, crème brûlée, wasabi and strawberry, and quince and rose are all life-enhancing combinations. Hermé started his career at the age of 14, when he was apprenticed to the famed *pâtissier* Gaston Lenôtre, and was head of the pastry kitchen at esteemed patisserie Fauchon by the time he was 24. Hermé now has his own sweet empire with four boutiques in Paris: those in rue Bonaparte and rue de Vaugiraud showcase his complete range of pastry pleasures, while those in rue Cambon and Avenue Paul Doumer concentrate solely on *macarons* and chocolates. It's worth making a pilgrimage to one of his two pastry shops in summer, when raspberries are in season, just to try "Ispahan" – two large rose-flavored *macarons* sandwiching rose petal cream, whole raspberries, and lychees. Ladurée may have invented the *macaron* but Pierre Hermé, dubbed "the Picasso of Pastry," perfected it.

4 rue Cambon and 58 Avenue Paul Doumer, Paris; open 10 AM–7 PM daily; www.pierreherme.com

Also in Paris

Ladurée, on rue Royale (*www.laduree.fr; expensive*), draws a constant stream of customers, lured by the unchanged, old-world interior and the delicious, ever-changing window displays: *croquembouche* made of rainbow *macarons*, *macaron* stacks anointed with papery butterflies, and tiers of pastel-colored *macaron* boxes lashed with ribbons. While Pierre Hermé (*see above*) opts for daring pairings, Ladurée turns out timeless classics: chocolate, vanilla, pistachio, orange blossom, lemon, and seasonal specials. There are other Paris branches, but this one is precious.

Also in France

Gastronomic Lyon has its own *macaron* masters. **Sève** (*www.chocolatseve.com; expensive*) dishes up to-die-for apple *tatin macarons* and savory domes filled with sesame and Gorgonzola, while **Sébastian Bouillet** (*www.chocolatier-bouillet.com; moderate*) dreams up fairy-floss *macarons* and salted caramel in a chocolate shell flaked with gold leaf.

Around the World

Pierre Hermé's **Aoyama** boutique (*+81 3 5485 7766; expensive*) in Tokyo was his first shop. The first floor is devoted to display, while upstairs in the Bar Chocolat, you can nibble on chocolates, pastries, and *macarons*.

A Day in San Sebastián

In July and September the beautiful people flock to San Sebastián for, respectively, the annual jazz and film festivals, but the decorous city and beachside promenade are just as delightful when the paparazzi and their targets have left town. Be sure to arrive hungry.

MORNING Explore the narrow streets of the **Parte Vieja**, or old quarter, which was rebuilt on the medieval street plan after Napoleon burned the city. At the harbor, explore the fishermen's docks and visit the **Palacio del Mar**, San Sebastián's intriguing aquarium, focused on the marine life of the Bay of Biscay.

AFTERNOON Walk up the circular road around **Monte Urgull** to see the 12th-century ruins of the **Castillo de Santa Cruz de la Mota**. Then catch some sun on **Playa de la Concha**.

EVENING Ride the funicular to the summit of **Monte Igueldo** to survey the city from this western headland. Then return to town for an evening of bar-hopping to sample the city's inventive *pintxos* (Basque tapas) before winding up at a fine restaurant for dinner.

Essentials

GETTING THERE
San Sebastián Airport has domestic flights; the **international airports** of Bilbao and Biarritz are relatively close. The city can also be reached by **train** on the **TGV Paris–Madrid** route, and by **bus** from many European cities.

WHERE TO STAY
Hotel Niza (inexpensive) offers airy rooms with Playa de la Concha views. *www.hotelniza.com*
Hotel de Londres y de Inglaterra (moderate) is a restored *belle époque* resort hotel with traditional furnishings. *www.hlondres.com*
Hotel María Cristina (expensive) is San Sebastián's most palatial hotel, with luxurious appointments in even the simplest rooms. *www.luxurycollection.com/MariaCristina*

TOURIST INFORMATION
Boulevard 8; *www.sansebastianturismo.com*

Right Monkfish and minted beans with Iberian tomato ravioli and Jerez vinegar by Basque chef Juan Mari Arzak

Below The uninhabited island of Santa Clara lies just off the scallop-shaped coastline of San Sebastián

SAN SEBASTIAN SPAIN

Basque Coast Innovation

Napoleon sacked and burned San Sebastián in 1813, but the resort that rose from the ashes is the epitome of refined hedonism. Royalty and movie stars bask in the sizzle of the Spanish sun, while San Sebastián's Basque chefs demonstrate the innovative Modern Spanish cuisine that has raised the bar for European gastronomy, much as Picasso rewrote the rules for modern art.

Playa de la Concha, San Sebastián's main beach, nestles between the twin headlands of Monte Urgull and Monte Igueldo. Its 4-mile (6-km) swath of white sand makes the city the pearl of the Basque coast. Once the sun goes down, beach-goers wash off their tanning lotion, dress for dinner, and prepare for an evening at the tables of San Sebastián's world-class restaurants. The city has more Michelin three-star establishments per capita than Paris or Tokyo, and a host of wonderful cafés, taverns, and bars where the quality of the food belies the humble surroundings.

San Sebastián is an intriguing mix of the old and the new. The broad avenues of the sophisticated modern town, lined with upmarket shops and restaurants, give way to the atmospheric streets of the old town beneath the base of Monte Urgull. Centered around the ancient Plaza de la Constitución, these narrow lanes hide treats such as the church of Santa Maria del Coro, a masterly example of Basque Baroque. The old town's sheltered harbor curls around a series of stone embankments, where a small fishing fleet unloads its rich daily catch of bream, sardines, anchovies, shrimp, spider crab, mullet, monkfish, and hake. The Basques are legendary fishermen and inventive cooks – Basque cuisine was a culinary revolution waiting to happen. With its emphasis on perfect ingredients artfully presented, Basque cooking proved the perfect foil to French nouvelle cuisine.

When San Sebastián's chefs began bringing theater to the plate in the 1970s, they championed local produce, fish, and meat, and jettisoned the elaborate, time-intensive preparations of traditional *haute cuisine*. They had fired the opening salvo of Modern Spanish cuisine – and have wowed diners ever since. They experiment with flavors like an artist expanding his palette, endowing each plate with an element of surprise. But the emphasis here is on flavor rather than culinary pyrotechnics: parsley foam brings out the sweetness of spider crab steeped in spicy tomato sauce; a sprinkling of crispy garlic wafers provides a crunchy counterpoint to pan-fried codfish with clams. Every dish is a sublime medley of texture and tastes.

Basque Wines

There are two distinctive wine regions in the Basque lands of Spain: the **Rioja Alavesa**, where the famous bodega of Marqués de Riscal is based; and the **Basque coast**, where the Txakolí wines are produced. The red Tempranillo and Cabernet Sauvignon blends of **Rioja** are justly famous as bold accompaniments to roasted meats and hearty stews. The mostly white, often slightly fizzy **Txakolí** wines are characterized by a bracing acidity that makes them the perfect foil for Basque seafood. Although Txakolí has been cultivated for at least 1,200 years, it has been the Basques' carefully guarded secret, and did not enter the export market until the 21st century. Three Txakolí districts are recognized, but the pale yellow to green wines from **Getaria** and **Zarautz** on the coast between Bilbao and San Sebastián are considered the best.

Above Basque Michelin three-star chef Juan Mari Arzak and his daughter Elena

The Best Places to Eat Modern Spanish Cuisine

Restaurante Arzak expensive

One could say that Juan Mari Arzak got his revenge on Napoleon by launching Modern Spanish cuisine – a revolution that toppled French *haute cuisine* from its gastronomic throne. This was Spain's first restaurant to be awarded three Michelin stars, and eating at Arzak remains as exciting today as it was in the 1970s, when the unknown provincial chef first applied the principles of French nouvelle cuisine to the traditions of Basque cookery. Arzak reduces dishes to their essential flavors, then plates them with unfussy but witty theater. Now working with his daughter Elena, Arzak continues to experiment with new twists on familiar foods – his "perfect egg" dishes are legendary among Spanish chefs – without sacrificing the integrity of the ingredients or the surprise of the presentation. Most diners opt for the astonishing tasting menu, which allows the broadest experience of Arzak's creative and experimental approach. It begins with a half-dozen or so small dishes, explodes into three to four "main" dishes built around meat or fish, and then segues into a series of sweet and delicious surprises.

Avenida Alcalde José Elosequi 273, San Sebastián; open for lunch Tue–Fri, dinner Tue–Sat; www.arzak.es

Also in San Sebastián

Pedro Subijana is the master magician of **Akelare** (*www.relaischateaux.com; expensive*), where mountainside views of the Bay of Biscay match his culinary sleight of hand. Martín Berasategui crafts a roller coaster of flavor surprises at his flagship **Berasategui** (*www.martinberasategui.com; expensive*) while offering an affordable sampling of his free-form imagination at **Restaurante Kursaal** (*+34 943 003 162; moderate*).

Also in Spain

In Madrid, diners greet dishes at **Villa Magna by Eneko Atxa** (*www.villamagna.es; moderate*) with either a hearty laugh or an exclamation of delight. At **Sergi Arola Gastro** (*www.sergiarola.es; expensive*), also in Madrid, Catalan star chef Sergi Arola composes just a few strong flavors per plate, cooking much like fellow Catalan Joan Miró painted. Innovator Ferran Adrià's greatest hits form the menu at **Hacienda Benazuza** (*www.elbullihotel.com; expensive*), in Sanlúcar la Mayor, near Seville.

Around the World

Spanish-born and trained, José Andrés launched a craze for Modern Spanish cuisine in the US. His most theatrical and magical restaurant, **The Bazaar** (*www.thebazaar.com; moderate*), in Beverly Hills, California, won *Esquire* magazine's Restaurant of the Year award in 2009.

SANTORINI GREECE

Golden Fava on Santorini

A magnet for honeymooners, Santorini has more five-star hotels and fancy restaurants than any other Greek island. Yet its signature dish, fava, is a humble staple food. This golden bean purée owes its rich, nutty flavor to Santorini's volcanic terrain. An eruption blew out the heart of the island 3,500 years ago, and this natural disaster proved an unexpected blessing for fava farmers.

Its red cliffs frosted with whitewashed hamlets and fringed with black sand beaches, Santorini has a savage beauty. The volcanic eruption that created the flooded caldera, or basin, in 1500 BC also buried the island's biggest settlement at Akrotiri. This Bronze Age city was discovered barely 30 years ago, buried beneath 33 ft (10 m) of ash. Recreations of the stunning frescoes unearthed at Akrotiri are on display in the island's capital, Fira, which can be reached by a thrilling cable-car ride from the port of Gialos.

The dramatic landscape makes for wondrous sunsets, but made it difficult for locals to eke out a living until the advent of tourism. Only a few crops can be coaxed from the island's arid soil – succulent grapes, sweet white eggplants, cherry tomatoes bursting with flavor, piquant capers, and the resilient fava bean. More prized (and much pricier) than fava grown elsewhere in Greece, this plain little bean has been cultivated on Santorini since the Bronze Age, its flat plants able to absorb moisture from the porous pumice stone. After harvesting, the beans are left to dry, then stripped of their brown husks to reveal yellow grains, bright as jewels.

Primarily a Lenten food in much of Greece, fava is eaten year-round on Santorini and always served warm. Simmered gently until it dissolves into a smooth paste, fava remains a popular foil for seafood – it forms a pillowy bed for octopus stewed in sweet wine, salty sardines, or crunchy calamari rings. Amazingly versatile, it might be topped with raw onions, doused in lemon, or flecked with dill. *Fava pandremeni* ("married fava") is a lyrical euphemism for leftover fava jazzed up with fried onions, capers, and a swirl of tomato paste. The less evocative *fava tis grias* ("crone's fava") is a winter variation with smoked pork. As it cools, a well is made in the fava and filled with olive oil; hence the Greek expression "there's a hole in the fava," which loosely translates as "there's something fishy going on."

Once a peasant food, fava is now an expensive gourmet product cultivated by fewer than 200 farmers. Most producers focus instead on the island's wines, following a tradition as old as Akrotiri. Vaulted wine cellars and humble cave dwellings have been converted into glamorous hotels teetering on the brink of the volcano, with infinity pools suspended between sky and sea. They make ideal vantage points from which to ponder whether the flooded crater does indeed conceal the lost city of Atlantis.

Three Days on Santorini

For all its black-sand beaches and wealth of antiquities, Santorini's main attraction is the spellbinding volcanic caldera. Boat trips to and around the islets are a must.

DAY ONE Sailing into the caldera is like floating into an open-air geological museum. Sizzling in the center is the crater of **Nea Kameni**, which you can climb if you dare. Wallow in the hot springs of **Palea Kameni**, then shin up the **Islet of Thirassia** to **Manolas**, a clifftop time-warp with astonishing views of the archipelago.

DAY TWO Hike the daredevil path running along the rim of the caldera from **Fira** to **Oia**, the quintessential Cycladic village. Zigzag down the red cliffs for just-caught fish and iced ouzo at **Ammoudi**, a fishing port with half a dozen good tavernas.

DAY THREE Admire reproductions of the frescoes unearthed at Akrotiri at the Petros Nomikos Foundation in **Fira**. Travel south from Fira to **Vothonos**, where you can buy top-quality fava beans to take home at the **Yiannis Nomikos Estate**. Continue onward to **Pyrgos**, a beautifully preserved village built around a medieval castle.

Essentials

GETTING THERE
There are direct flights to **Santorini Airport** from Europe, and regular domestic flights from Athens. The high-speed **ferry** from Athens takes about five hours.

WHERE TO STAY
Zannos Melathron (moderate) is a grand manor house in Pyrgos. *www.zannos.gr*
Kapari (moderate) has spectacular caldera views and snug rooms. *www.kaparisantorini.gr*
Perivolas (expensive) offers laid-back luxury on the outskirts of Oia. *www.perivolas.gr*

FURTHER INFORMATION
www.santorini.net

Above Selene restaurant in Pyrgos is world-renowned for its authentic Greek cuisine and imaginative use of local ingredients

Left The whitewashed church of Agios Gerasimos in Firostefani ("The Crown of Thira") is dramatically perched on the cliffs of the volcanic caldera

Above The much-prized fava beans of Santorini are simmered until they dissolve into a delicious paste, then eaten with fresh fish or octopus

Santorini Wines

Santorini's mineral-rich *terroir* yields some of the most delicate and distinctive wines in Greece. Around 40 indigenous grape varieties have been cultivated on the island for centuries. The bone-dry Assyrtiko and potent Vinsanto (unique to Santorini) are world-class. Wineries all over Santorini offer tours and tastings. Savor the sunset with oaky Oia Vareli and stuffed vine leaves straight from the surrounding vineyards at the peaceful **Sigalas Winery** (*www.sigalas-wine.com*) in Baxedes. Or drink in the 360° views with a glass of crisp Nyxteri from the **Santo Cooperative's Enotourism Center** (*www.santowines.gr*).

The Best Places to Eat Fava

Selene expensive

A mentor to many of Greece's finest chefs, Selene's Yiorgos Hatziyannakis was one of the first restaurateurs to put indigenous dishes such as fava on the menu. But there's nothing rustic about his refined reinterpretation of classic Greek dishes. Since opening Selene in 1986, he has created more than 20 variations of fava: mashed with the crystallized sap of the mastic tree and served with smoked mackerel and almond flakes; fava fritters stuffed with tomato and caper *confit*; fava risotto with grilled sea bass; and even fava ice cream garnished with caper leaves as an intriguing *amuse-bouche*. Other local ingredients are showcased to equally startling effect in dishes such as white eggplant salad with octopus carpaccio and *millefeuille* with cherry tomato marmalade. An informal wine bar below the restaurant serves less experimental but equally sophisticated Greek cuisine at half the price. The restaurant also holds cooking classes once a week.

Pyrgos Village, Santorini; open 7 PM–midnight daily, mid-Apr–mid-Oct; www.selene.gr

Also on Santorini

There are also many less expensive places to try fava in Santorini. At **To Psaraki** (The Little Fish) (*www.topsaraki.gr; moderate*), award-winning chef Thanasis Sfougaris has gone back to basics. His *fava pandremeni*, topped with caramelized onions, is divine, and a phenomenally good buy. **Ta Dichtia** (*www.tadichtia.gr; moderate*) sits on a pretty terrace on Perivolos beach, serving lemony fava, cuttlefish, and bulgur pilaf, and baked grouper. **Kyra Roza** (*+30 22860 24378; inexpensive*) is off the beaten track at Vourvoulos, but attracts off-duty chefs with its creamy fava, crispy red mullet, and mint-flecked *domatokeftedes* (tomato fritters).

Also in Greece

Santorini locals mourned when Chrysanthos Karamolegos, one of Greece's most inventive chefs, moved from the island to Halkidiki. His restaurant **Tomata** (*www.sani-resort.com; expensive*) features fava in unusual ways, such as paired with sea bass in ouzo vinaigrette, or with feta croquettes and watermelon coulis.

Around the World

Greek-American chef Michael Psilakis has single-handedly elevated Greek cuisine several notches. He has moved on from the Michelin-starred Anthos in New York, but you can sample his innovative fava with sea urchin sashimi as part of the post-modern meze at **Eos** at the Viceroy Hotel, Miami, FL (*www.viceroymiami.com; expensive*).

A Day in Munich

Munich's focal Marienplatz square, bustling with street musicians and artists, is the perfect place to start a day's tour.

MORNING Catch the Rathaus carillon (chiming bells) in **Marienplatz** at 11:00 AM; pop into the **toy museum** in the Altes Rathaus, then climb the **Peterskirche tower** for fantastic views. Stop at the **Viktualienmarkt** (food market) to eat a *Weisswurst*, Munich's famous white sausage, en route to the Renaissance **Residenz palace**.

AFTERNOON Walk to the **Pinakothek** museums, Munich's clutch of excellent art museums, and view either old masters or modern and contemporary art. Or take a bus to Munich's grandest museum: the **Deutsches Museum**, with its science and technology collection.

EVENING Choose between high culture – perhaps one of Munich's three first-rate **symphony orchestras** – or head to **Hofbräuhaus**, to while away the evening in the classic Bavarian way.

Essentials

GETTING THERE
Trains link Munich's **airport**, 18 miles (30 km) from the city, to its main **train** station, west of Marienplatz. Central Munich is easily walkable, but **public transportation** is excellent.

WHERE TO STAY
Pension Seibel (inexpensive) is simple, central, and very Bavarian. *www.seibel-hotels-munich.de*
Torbräu (moderate) is a dependable, family-run four-star choice close to the Viktualienmarkt. *www.torbraeu.de*
Charles Hotel (expensive) is a top-class hotel with huge rooms. *www.thecharleshotel.com*

TOURIST INFORMATION
Neuen Rathaus, Marienplatz; *+49 89 23 39 65 00*

Right Bacon and herb dumplings in a rich broth of mushrooms and cream is Bavarian comfort food at its finest

Below Munich's Hofbräuhaus, once the royal brewery, is one of the oldest beer halls in Germany

The Best Places to Eat Dumplings

Wirtshaus in der Au moderate

This lovely old Bavarian inn lies just far enough from downtown Munich to put it off the beaten track, yet it's still an easy walk from the Deutsches Museum. It has been serving beer and dumplings since 1901, and its simple, airy interiors with high vaulted ceilings, tiled floor, and rustic wooden furniture still speak of that time. But this is not a restaurant hamstrung by tradition; it likes to innovate by offering dishes such as spinach or beet dumplings and organic cheeses. All are executed with great success, as you might expect from a restaurant that has published its own dumpling cookbook (in English, too) and runs dumpling cooking courses. Dedicated to serving nothing but dumplings, and with waitresses who bustle in their traditional dirndl dresses, this is a cultural and gastronomic experience not to be missed.

Lilienstrasse 51, Munich; open 5 PM–1 AM Mon–Fri, 10 AM–1 AM Sat & Sun (kitchen closes at 11 PM); www.wirtshausinderau.de

Also in Munich

Dumplings combine with a jolly beer hall experience amid the long benches at the **Augustiner Bräustuben** *(www.braeustuben. de; moderate)* on Landsberger Strasse, perhaps less the complete tourist experience than the Hofbräuhaus, but just as good. The dumplings are served with duck or pork knuckle, smothered in mushroom sauce, or as liver dumpling soup.

Also in Germany

Knödel are thinner on the ground in northern Germany, but you can find potato dumplings. In Frankfurt, **Klabunt** *(www.klabunt-frankfurt. de; moderate)*, a simple pub, is fussy about using the finest ingredients; the specialty is half-and-half dumplings, made from equal measures of cooked and raw potatoes.

Farther north in Berlin, only southern German restaurants serve dumplings, such as **Spätzle & Knödel** on Wühlischstrasse *(+49 30 2757 1151; moderate)*. They even offer *Marillenknödel*, delicious apricot dessert dumplings.

Around the World

Austrians, particularly Tyroleans, are every bit as fond of dumplings as Bavarians, so excellent Austrian versions, such as those served in Innsbruck at **Lewisch** *(+43 51 258 6043; moderate)*, are fairly easy to find. Their menu includes *Serviettenknödel*, a large dumpling that is sliced like bread before serving.

It's an Austrian, too, who has opened one of the best dumpling restaurants in the New World: **Kinski** *(www.kinski-nyc.com; inexpensive)*, a modern eatery in New York City's diverse and hip Lower East Side. Its savory goulash-smothered dumpling and the many different sweet *Knödel*, served with nougat, raspberry, or apricot, are as good as they are far from home.

MUNICH GERMANY

Dumplings in Munich

As jolly and hearty as Bavaria itself, dumplings, or *Knödel*, have been a cornerstone of this region's cuisine since records began. Local legends even talk of dumplings being thrown at an enemy to end a 13th-century siege of the town of Deggendorf. With dumplings on the menu of most of its inns and beer halls, Bavaria's largest city, Munich, is the perfect place to sample them.

At least as old as their first mentions on 11th-century parchments, *Knödel* (or *Klöse* to north Germans) are one of Germany's most enduring and adaptable dishes. In the Middle Ages, meat dumplings, or *Fleischknödel*, were popular among the wealthy, who commonly used bread to bind them; the peasant version, reversing the proportions, was the *Semmelknödel* – a bread dumpling incorporating scraps of meat. The potato, arriving from Latin America in 1565, hardly challenged the *Knödel* at all, simply inspiring the potato dumpling. By the 19th century, Bavarians considered and declared the *Knödel* a national dish.

Like the *Knödel*, Munich is a Bavarian icon and has been its capital since 1503. Its remarkably compact medieval core boasts a glorious Renaissance palace, atmospheric squares, venerable churches, and museums that can keep art-lovers occupied for days. Yet much of Munich's charm today lies in its vibrancy, as the energetic, modern capital of Germany's high-tech industry. This energy shines in the summer when beer gardens, street cafés, and bars are in full swing, or during the world-famous Oktoberfest beer festival, when the city loses its head. Fortunately, if you need to escape the madness, these are also great times to visit the Alpine lakes and mountains that are only an hour's drive or train ride from the city.

Such a journey will take you through traditional Bavarian countryside, from which the ingredients of Munich's *Knödel* still come. Of the three main types of dumpling – meat, bread, and potato – the most popular is the *Semmelknödel*, based on stale rolls soaked in milk and broken down into doughy crumbs, mixed with onion, parsley, and lemon peel, though countless variations exist: *Speckknödel* have bacon bits in the mix, and *Leberknödel* are made with liver.

Dumplings can be served in soups or as a side order, but come into their own in classic main dishes, smothered with tangy beef or venison goulash or a rich and creamy mushroom sauce – one of Germany's few traditional vegetarian meals. But it doesn't stop there – only by ordering dessert *Knödel*, either served cold or sliced and fried and accompanied by stewed fruit, will you prove yourself a dedicated dumpling diner.

German Beer

Bavaria's extensive high plateaus are particularly well suited to growing the wheat and barley required by Germany's 1,300 or so breweries to make the country's favorite drink. Only the Czechs drink more per capita than the Germans, whose variety of beers is astonishing – all the way from summery golden lagers and cloudy wheat beers to dark brown Bock, traditionally brewed in winter and drunk in spring. Beers also vary tremendously in strength, up to a staggering 28 percent alcohol. Bavaria's classic beer is its Märzenbier, the mid-brown brew of its most famous annual celebration, the Oktoberfest. But even when it's not on, drinking in a jovial summer beer garden or hunkering down in a high-arched beer cellar, to lock arms with neighbors, sing, and stomp, remains a quintessential part of enjoying German beer.

Above An Oktoberfest waitress in traditional Bavarian costume

Above Astonishing Baroque stonework supports the balconies of the Palazzo Nicolaci di Villadorata in Noto

Above Glorious Sicilian lemons are used to make sorbet, a palate-cleansing contrast to the wealth of creamy, rich *gelati* flavors

Three Days in the Val di Noto

The old cities of the Val di Noto boast an exceptional artistic and cultural heritage. But this small corner of the island is also known for its dramatic, fertile interior landscape and stunning coastal scenery.

DAY ONE Visit the Baroque cathedral of **San Nicolò** in Noto and explore the nearby **palazzi** (palaces). After lunch, head inland to **Noto Antico** (old Noto) and wander around this atmospheric "ghost town."

DAY TWO Jump in a car or taxi and head south out of town, through the agricultural and wine-producing center of **Pachino** and onward toward **Capo Passero** – Sicily's southernmost headland. Here you can spend time in the charming seaside town of **Portopalo**, and enjoy the view of the lighthouse from **Capo delle Correnti**.

DAY THREE To the north of Noto in the **Monti Iblei**, deep river valleys have shaped the plateau housing the wonderful ancient site of **Pantalica**, where a scattering of tombs are smothered by wild flowers in spring. Below, the shady **Anapo River** can be followed on foot along the track of the former railroad.

Essentials

GETTING THERE
Sicily's main **airport** is Catania Fontanarossa. There are **buses** to Noto from the airport and there is a single-track **railway** from Noto to Ragusa, Modica, and Scicli. A **rental car** is useful for exploring the area and the island.

WHERE TO STAY
Agriturismo Calamosche (inexpensive) is a simple place with rooms and a campsite, 6 miles (10 km) outside Noto. *+39 347 858 7319*
La Fontanella (moderate) is Noto's only central hotel, located in a 19th-century palazzo. *www.albergolafontanella.it*
Terre di Vendicari (expensive), a stylish country house, lies in a nature preserve south of Noto. *www.terredivendicari.it*

TOURIST INFORMATION
Piazza XXVI Maggio; *+39 931 573 779*

NOTO ITALY

Gorgeous Gelati in Baroque Sicily

Built on a hill a few miles from the sea, Noto is the apogee of Sicilian Baroque. Much of its charm lies in its limestone buildings, their colors changing from gold to apricot depending on the light. Sicily has been defined as a place where "doing nothing is not seen as a waste of time, where people still eat jasmine ice cream" – and Noto, on a summer evening, is a fine place to do both.

In the wake of the terrible earthquake of 1693 that devastated Sicily, the ruined hill town of Noto was completely reconstructed, building by building, on a flatter location closer to the sea. Through the 18th century this became an enormous construction site run by the prominent architects of the day. Today, the town's Baroque architecture is unique in Sicily and, after substantial restoration, its long-decaying buildings are being revealed in all their glory. The steps that lead up to the cathedral from Largo Landolina are a good place to start a tour of the town's voluptuous *palazzi* and grandiose churches, replete with ornamental detail.

Designed specifically to include vistas of the surrounding countryside, Noto's urban plan was people-friendly and still works well today. Steps lead to the upper part of town and breathtaking views. One of the most popular tourist activities in Noto is just to wander the picturesque streets, taking in golden stone buildings with their handsome facades and elegant balconies, and enjoying spectacular vistas. The other

favorite pastime for visitors – and locals – is to savor the delicious *gelato* (ice cream) and almond sweetmeats for which the town has become famous.

Noto's reputation for ice-cream making originated 1,000 years ago, when Sicily was under the rule of the Arabs. They planted citrus and almond groves across the island, and brought with them the technique of making sherbet, or *sharbat*, from fruit syrups, flower essences, and snow from the slopes of Mount Etna. It seems probable that it was a resourceful Sicilian who first had the idea of making a good thing even better, freezing a mixture of milk, sugar or honey, and fruit, and giving the world one of its favorite foods.

By the 18th century, ices were so popular in Italy that almost the entire revenue of Sicily's Bishop of Catania came from selling the snow from Mount Etna. Not far from Noto you can still see *neviere*, limestone pits roofed with domes of stone, where snow was buried in winter, remaining frozen for months. Warm winters provoked national crises: in 1777 a boat thought to be carrying snow was attacked and its precious cargo seized – by Syracusans, desperate for ice cream.

The Best Places to Eat Gelati

Corrado Costanzo inexpensive

Tucked into a narrow lane below Noto's luscious central piazza, Largo Landolina, is a café that looks like any other in Sicily. But the ice cream created in *gelateria* Corrado Costanzo is judged by connoisseurs from all over the world to be the best on the planet. Eating a Costanzo ice cream is one of the world's most voluptuous gastronomic experiences, melting neither too slowly nor too fast on the tongue, suffusing the mouth with the unadulterated essence of mandarin, almond, rose, pistachio, mulberry, jasmine, or whichever locally grown fruit, nut, or flower is in season.

The death of Costanzo himself in 2003 has changed nothing – his daughter and son continue to produce ice creams and granitas like no one else. In spring, opt for rose, jasmine, or wild strawberry, and in summer pistachio, ricotta with cinnamon, or dark chocolate with orange. Unlike most, Costanzo's *gelati* contain no gums, using only egg white as a thickener.

Via Spaventa 7 (behind the Palazzo Ducezio), Noto; closed Mon; +39 931 835 243

Also in Noto

Noto is blessed with another great dessert-creating family, the Assenza brothers, Carlo and Corrado, who own the popular and authentic **Caffè Sicilia** *(+39 931 835 013; inexpensive)*, which has been operating since 1892. The cakes, pastries, and homemade jellies here are as superb as the innovative *gelati* – people come from far and wide to sample the flavors, which include almond blended with cinnamon, lemon, saffron, mulberry, wild strawberry, and a radical basil-scented ice.

Also in Italy

When in Rome, eat *gelato*. The Italian capital's favorite place to do so is **San Crispino** *(www.ilgelatodisancrispino.it; moderate)*, a short walk from Rome's own Baroque masterpiece, the Trevi fountain. It is famous for subtle flavors, including cream with honey or figs. Venice boasts **Alaska** *(+39 41 715 211; inexpensive)*, beloved of *gelato* gourmets who appreciate Carlo Pistacchi's fresh ingredients and experimental flavors such as celery and peach, and licorice and artichoke.

Around the World

Americans eat more ice cream than any other nation in the world, and one of their most famous ice-cream producers, **Ben & Jerry's** *(www.benjerry.com; moderate)*, offers tours of its factory in Vermont – on snowshoes in winter. Arguably even tastier ice cream can be found in Buenos Aires, Argentina, at family-owned **Persicco** *(+54 11 3339 7377; expensive)*, which has several branches.

Above Farmers harvesting almonds with poles and nets in southern Sicily

What Else to Eat

Sicily and sweet things go together. The superb offerings from local *pasticcerias* feature locally grown **almonds**, and the pastries have a divine melt-in-the-mouth quality. Try Pasticceria Mandolfiore *(www.pasticceriamandolfiore.com)* or Caffè Sicilia *(see right)*, whose nougat and homemade jellies make perfect gifts. Look for **biancomangiare** – blancmange as you've never tasted it, not unlike the *panna cotta* of northern Italy. The **chocolate** of nearby Modica is still made using the Aztec technique, with pure cocoa and sugar, so that it has a crunchy texture. You may be able to peep at the Iacono family making it in the kitchen behind the bar at Caffè dell' Arte, on Modica's Corso Umberto *(+39 932 943 257)* – or cross the road to the more famous Bonajuto *(+39 932 941 225)*, founded in 1880, for free chocolate tastings.

MADRID SPAIN

Sweet Surrender in Madrid

Spain's traditional capital reveals its playful side in the early hours, when office-bound bankers cross paths with hungry clubbers in the *churrerías*. These small shops work around the clock crafting *churros* – deep-fried strips of dough that are Madrid's classic breakfast or afternoon snack and a powerful late-night restorative, especially when dipped in thick hot chocolate.

From its formal old-world plazas and medieval lanes to its modernist offices and galleries, Madrid comes alive each day to the smell of *churros*. This essential breakfast fuels office workers and laborers alike, and it also provides a morning jump-start for museum-goers making their pilgrimages to the treasure houses on the city's Golden Triangle of art: the eclectic Museo Thyssen-Bornamisza, the legendary Museo del Prado with its works by Goya and Velázquez *(see also pp136–7)*, and the thought-provoking, sometimes controversial Museo Nacional Centro de Arte Reina Sofía, Spain's national museum of 20th- and 21st-century art.

By mid-afternoon, there are shopping bags at every table in the *churrerías*, as intrepid boutique warriors pause for the *merienda*, or afternoon snack, whether in the cluster of designer shops and custom cobblers of the Salamanca neighborhood or along the bustling streets in the vibrant barrio of Chueca. *Churros* are often hard to find after dark in other Spanish cities,

but not in Madrid, where the tasty fritters imbue *Madrileños* with the stamina to keep going until they drop. When the flamenco show ends at 1:00 AM or the sky shows dawn's early streaks as the dance clubs close, the *churrerías* beckon.

Thought to have been created as an easy breakfast for mountain shepherds (*churra* is an ancient breed of Iberian sheep), *churros* are among the simplest of sweets – a basic batter of flour, salt, and water piped into bubbling vats of oil. Fried into finger-sized sticks that are soft on the inside but brown and crisp on the outside, they must be eaten before they cool – ideally dusted with sugar and dipped into coffee or a cup of mud-thick Spanish hot chocolate – for an explosion of warmth that radiates from mouth to fingertips.

So central is the shepherd's breakfast to *Madrileños* that no festival in the city is complete without *churro* carts. As the street music rises to a proper Spanish din, vendors fire up their gas heaters to bring their oil to a bubbling sizzle, squirt in the dough, and transform a simple batter into a sweet celebratory treat.

A Day in Madrid

Madrid remains as vibrant at night as during the day. The monumental fountains of Neptuno and Cibeles along the Paseo del Prado are most dramatic when illuminated. The complex rhythms and mournful song of flamenco only begin after dinner (that is, midnight), and the trance beat of the dance clubs starts throbbing in the *madrugada*, or early morning.

MORNING Picasso's masterpiece, *Guernica*, is reason enough to visit the **Museo Nacional Centro de Arte Reina Sofía**, but don't miss the extensive collection of paintings and sculptures by Madrid-born Juan Gris and the ever-cryptic and mercurial Joan Miró.

AFTERNOON Seek out fashions by many of Spain's young, avant-garde designers in the trendy **Chueca** neighborhood, also known for its gay-friendly nightlife. For the best in Spanish footwear at bargain prices, peruse the shops on **Calle Augusto Figueroa**.

EVENING Begin with drinks in the upmarket culinary center of **Mercado San Miguel**. Eat dinner and watch Madrid's best flamenco at **Casa Patas**. After the show, dance until dawn at **Disco-Teatro Joy Eslava** and end the evening's revelries with *churros* and chocolate.

Essentials

GETTING THERE
Madrid lies near the geographical center of Spain. Most international airlines fly into **Madrid-Barajas Airport**, 7 miles (12 km) from downtown Madrid. The best way to get around the city is by **metro**.

WHERE TO STAY
Hotel Plaza Mayor (inexpensive) is a welcoming option in a 200-year-old church building. *www.h-plazamayor.com*
Room Mate Oscar Hotel (moderate) is a playful designer hotel in hip Chueca. *www.room-matehotels.com*
Catalonia Las Cortes (moderate) offers rooms in a converted 18th-century palace. *www.hoteles-catalonia.com*

TOURIST INFORMATION
Plaza Mayor 27; *www.esmadrid.com*

Left The chocolate for *chocolate con churros* should be rich, dark, and thick, perfect for dipping

Above The long, curled form of the Madrid *churro* is cut into small pieces for serving

Below A modern addition to the Museo Reina Sofía has enhanced the display space for 20th-century art

Doughnuts Around the World

Madrileños eat *churros* around the clock, but many cultures have their own love affairs with sizzling deep-fried dough. Whether they are called doughnuts, fritters, *beignets*, or *sopapillas*, they are often eaten as breakfast food or sweet treats at street fairs and markets.

MADRID

Chocolatería San Ginés inexpensive
Pasadizo de San Ginés 5; +34 913 656 546
Neat rows of cups and saucers on a marble bar greet customers at this institution beloved by generations of *Madrileños*. At midnight, dawn, and noon, San Ginés serves the thick chocolate and lightly crisp *churros* against which all others are judged.

Chocolatería Valor inexpensive
Calle Postigo de San Martín 7; www.valor.es
Founded in 1881, Valor is one of Spain's most famous makers of premium chocolate, used for baking, cooking, and confectionery. The company's signature *bonbonería* (sweets and bakery store), just a few steps from Puerta del Sol, serves rich hot chocolate with unusually large, unfluted *churros*.

Maestro Churrero inexpensive
Calle Atocha 19; www.maestrochurrero.com
This popular *churrería* traces its roots to a rolling cart from 1902 that allowed a *Madrileño* named Don Florencio to cater to theater-goers. Five generations down the line, his successors continue to warm hungry breakfast patrons and revelers needing a sweet bite after hours of tapas and drinks.

VALENCIA, SPAIN

Deep-fried pastries are as integral to Valencian cuisine as paella. Street vendors even sell hot chocolate and pumpkin *buñuelos* (a small bun similar to a *churro*) during the March carnival of Las Fallas (the Fires).

Estación del Norte inexpensive
Calle Xàtiva 24
Whether travelers are arriving or departing, they can always count on a quick pick-me-up of toasty *churros* and hot chocolate from the gleaming

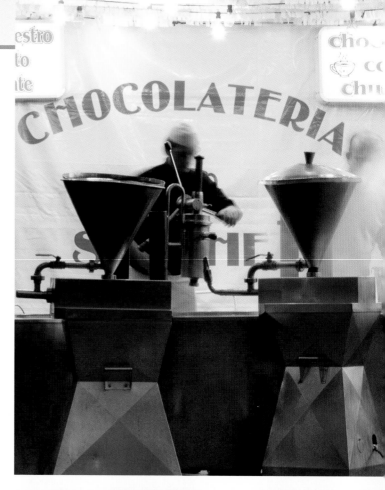

stainless steel outdoor kiosks that operate from dawn to midnight in front of Valencia's Art Nouveau train station in the heart of the city.

Horchatería El Siglo inexpensive
Plaza Santa Catalina 11, +34 963 918 466
Founded in 1836, this venerable café is celebrated for its milky *horchata* drink made from *chufa*, or tiger nuts. Cool and refreshing, it is usually served with *churros* or *buñuelos* (cheese doughnuts) – which staff often cook outdoors to attract customers, as the aromas are virtually irresistible.

Horchatería Santa Catalina inexpensive
Plaza Santa Catalina 6;
www.horchateriasantacatalina.com

Decorated in classic Valencian painted tiles, this rival to El Siglo is acclaimed for its hot chocolate, often ordered with *churros*. A larger sweet bread called a *farton*, which lacks the fluting of a *churro* and is sometimes glazed, usually accompanies *horchata*.

UNITED STATES

The United States spawned the sweetened fried dough known as the doughnut – a spherical or ring-shaped variation on the *churro*. But the country's many immigrant groups have not forgotten their own ethnic variations on deep-fried sweet fritters.

Doughnut Plant inexpensive
379 Grand Street, New York, New York;
www.doughnutplant.com

This artisanal doughnut shop in the Lower East Side of Manhattan has become a confectionery cult, in part because it incorporates fresh seasonal fruits such as strawberries and blueberries into the glazes. Weekend lines stretch out the door.

Dunkin' Donuts inexpensive
543 Southern Artery, Quincy, Massachusetts;
www.dunkindonuts.com

Dunkin' Donuts opened its first shop in Quincy, Massachusetts, in 1950, featuring fresh coffee and a doughnut with a small handle, allowing it to be dunked. The chain has since spread the American doughnut – in 52 varieties, including the perennially favorite plain, glazed, and jelly-filled types – to 31 countries around the world.

Left (top to bottom) A *chocolatería* stall serving hot chocolate at the carnival of Las Fallas in Valencia, Spain; coffee and doughnuts provide on-the-go urban fuel on Times Square, New York

Below (top to bottom) Sugar-coated ring doughnuts; a mariachi band performing near Churrería El Moro in Mexico City; *churros* dipped in chocolate in Oaxaca, Mexico

Morro Castle inexpensive
2500 Northwest Seventh Street, Miami, Florida; (305) 642 4747

This classic 1950s drive-in is known for its Cuban sandwiches and *fritas* (burgers) made with a mixture of ground beef and chorizo sausage. But many locals also believe that Morro Castle serves the best traditional Spanish-style *churros* and hot chocolate in Miami.

Spudnut Shop inexpensive
228 Williams Boulevard, Richland, Washington; www.richland.tri-cityshopping.com/spudnuts

A family-run bakery in the same location for more than 60 years, Spudnut uses a combination of potato flour and wheat flour to produce unusually airy yeast-raised and cake doughnuts. The family also bakes a line of spudnut muffins and cakes.

Café du Monde moderate
1039 Decatur Street, New Orleans, Louisiana; www.cafedumonde.com

A stalwart of the city's French Quarter, this marketplace café creates legendary *beignets* – high and puffy squares of fried dough covered in powdered sugar. They are served in orders of three to accompany coffee given a nutty, slightly acrid taste by roasted chicory.

Maria's New Mexican Kitchen moderate
555 West Cordova Road, Santa Fe, New Mexico; www.marias-santafe.com

This restaurant is justly famed for its authentic northern New Mexican cooking, based on fresh and dried chili peppers. The perfect conclusion to the hot and spicy courses comes in the form of soothing, honey-drizzled *sopapillas* – small, hollow, triangular "pillows" of sweet, fried dough.

Sra. Martinez moderate
4000 Northeast Second Avenue, Miami, Florida; www.sramartinez.com

Diners at this stylish bistro in a former post office in the Design District understand that *churros* are no longer just street food. For dessert, chef Michelle Bernstein serves *churros* with a chocolate dipping sauce that she spikes with cayenne pepper.

MEXICO

It is said that when the Spanish explorer Hernán Cortés arrived in Mexico in 1519, the Aztecs mistook him for an incarnation of their god Quetzalcoatl, and served him up a feast including *xocoatl*, a cocoa-bean drink. The Spanish kept the popular drink's ingredients a secret for 100 years, and eventually returned the favor by introducing Mexicans to the pleasures of *churros* dipped in thickened hot chocolate.

Cafe San Agustín inexpensive
Calle San Francisco 21, San Miguel de Allende; +52 5154 9102

Both *churros* and chocolate at this popular café come in three degrees of sweetness: Spanish, French, and Mexican. The sweetest is Mexican, and it is spiced with the brassy, bright flavor of the papery Mexican *canela*, or cinnamon.

Churrería El Moro inexpensive
Calle Lázaro Cárdenas 42, Mexico City; +52 5512 0896

Even the bespangled mariachi musicians from nearby Plaza Garibaldi patronize this 1935 landmark *churrería* for bags of *churros* doused with grainy sugar and the specialty hot chocolate, which is frothed with carved wooden *molinillos* (whisks) and served up in earthenware jugs.

ARGENTINA

Café culture is central to the Argentine capital, and *Porteños* (the inhabitants of Buenos Aires) often treat their favorite cafés as second living rooms – places to entertain friends and even conduct business over plates of *churros* and cups of hot chocolate.

La Giralda inexpensive
1453 Avenida Corrientes, Buenos Aires; +54 11 4371 3846

This erstwhile hangout for Argentine intellectuals and theater-goers is the most famous of the cluster on Avenida Corrientes. It caters to the *Porteño* sweet tooth by filling its *churros* with chocolate cream or with *dulce de leche*, the city's signature milk caramel. Early risers and clubbers on the way home compete for morning tables.

Café Tortoni moderate
825 Avenida de Mayo, Buenos Aires; www.cafetortoni.com.ar

Possibly the oldest café in Argentina, the historic and atmospheric Tortoni has been an integral part of *Porteño* life since 1858. A long-time favorite of politicians, intellectuals, and artists, its cigar-shaped, thick, and somewhat crunchy *churros* are best enjoyed with a *submarino* – a cup of hot milk served with a bar of dark chocolate (the "submarine") which melts when dipped.

A Day in Colmar

Colmar is one of the most captivating towns in Alsace, with intriguing medieval and Renaissance buildings, winding canals, and pretty gardens.

MORNING Head for the huddle of pedestrianized streets of the old town. Wander past the **Maison des Têtes** (House of Heads), with its facade of 111 faces, to the wooden **Pfister House**, which has glorious Renaissance balconies. Then visit the **Bartholdi Museum**, the former home of Frédéric Auguste Bartholdi, creator of the Statue of Liberty.

AFTERNOON Start with the **Unterlinden Museum**, a former Dominican convent full of Alsatian treasures, including the striking Isenheim Altarpiece, created in around 1515 – a riot of grisly monsters and demons. There's a fine batch of gargoyles, too, at the Gothic marvel on Place de la Cathédrale: **St. Martin's Collegiate Church**.

EVENING Walk down to the **Quai de la Poissonnerie** in Petite Venise. Cross the flower-draped bridges, and look down the canals along the rows of houses teetering drunkenly on the water's edge. Stop in a waterside café to sample some *tarte flambée*.

Essentials

GETTING THERE
Fly to either **Basel-Mulhouse** or **Strasbourg airports**; Colmar lies between the two, with good rail links. There are also fast **trains** three times a day from Paris.

WHERE TO STAY
L'Hôtel Beausejour (inexpensive) is a charming hotel in a restored early-20th-century building with family rooms. *www.beausejour.fr*
La Maison des Têtes (moderate), built in 1609, is chock-full of history and Alsatian appeal. *www.maisondestetes.com*
L'Hôtel Quatorze (expensive) is an ancient pharmacy turned into a designer hotel with hip paintings by Spanish artist Alfonso Vallès. *www.hotelquatorze.com*

TOURIST INFORMATION
www.ot-colmar.fr

Right *Tarte flambée* with the classic white cheese, bacon, and onion topping
Below Half-timbered houses sit alongside the canal in Petite Venise, Colmar

COLMAR

COLMAR FRANCE

Fiery Tarte Flambée in Alsace

Colmar's old town reflects a time when half-timbered houses were all the rage and you could never have enough gables, balconies, or spires. Delightfully Alsatian in look and attitude, the town is a little more German than French, and so is the food: pretzels, sausage, cabbage, and *tarte flambée*, a satisfyingly crispy crust anointed with a rich cream and bacon topping.

Colmar has both French and Germanic traits in its cooking, its architecture, and its festivals.

Full of Alsatian atmosphere, from its half-timbered houses to its medieval alleyways, the town is a vivid reminder not just of the proximity of the German border, but of the many disputes over its allegiance; it has been alternately part of France and Germany many times in its history. In the Middle Ages, Colmar was the region's port, and farmers were still using the canals to deliver their produce to the central covered market right up until the 1950s. The farmers are long gone, and the area – now known as Petite Venise – features tourist boats, a tootling train, and quayside cafés, but still something of the old-world charm remains, as the canals gently weave among the tall, ornately carved 16th-century buildings.

It was not until the 19th century that the Alsatians invented their famous tart – *tarte flambée* – and it was more by accident than intention. The canny farm women of the Kochersberg region used to roll out their left-over bread dough and pop it in among the wood-stoked flames to check the readiness of their oven for bread-baking. Its place in the oven flames explains its name, although some like to think it's also because the edges are always singed black, or flamed.

Pantry staples began to grace the rectangular, ultra-thin crust: a slather of homemade cream, some thinly sliced onions picked from the field, and chunks of home-cured bacon. In the fierce oven heat, it took a matter of minutes to cook – the ultimate fast food. At first the lunch of choice for just a small clutch of farmers in the Lower Rhine, it soon became emblematic of all Alsace. Towns both high and low on the Rhine now serve up "flame tart," or *flammekueche*. There's even a *Confrérie de la Veritable Tarte Flambée d'Alsace* (Brotherhood of the Real Alsatian Flamed Tart) to ensure the quality of the crust dished up in Alsatian restaurants. They insist on a certain recipe, cooked in a wood-fired oven, but they are open to variations on ingredient ratios, and even sanction a sweet version with sliced apple. In keeping with all things Alsatian, a happy blend is finally what counts.

The Alsatian Wine Route

Colmar is the "capital of Alsatian wine" and part of the 106-mile (170-km) *Route des Vins* (Wine Route). Threading through vast vineyards dotted with cobblestone villages and castles, it's easy to follow and a great way to explore the region. The route runs from Marlenheim to Thann, along the eastern foothills of the Vosges mountains, and there are more than 40 vineyards with wines to try along the way. Around 90 percent of Alsatian wine is white – Riesling, Sylvaner, Gewürztraminer, and Pinot Gris. If you'd like to do some wine tasting but don't want to drive the wine trail, try cellars in Colmar that are open for tastings, such as **Domaine Viticole de la Ville de Colmar** *(www.domaineviticolecolmar.fr)*, **Domaine Robert Karcher et Fils** *(www.vins-karcher.com)*, or organic wine grower **Martin Jund** *(www.vin-bio-jund.com)*, who also offers accommodations.

Above Dining alfresco in the Place de l'Ancienne Douane, Colmar

The Best Places to Eat Tarte Flambée

La Maison Rouge inexpensive

A Colmar gem known for its warm welcome and well-priced food, La Maison Rouge has been serving up Alsatian favorites for more than 30 years. In keeping with its name, there's a lot of red splashed around, from lamps and red-trimmed tablecloths to the blazing *rouge* walls of the cellar dining room. It's whispered, however, that the name dates back to a less cheery time, when the executioners from the guillotine stayed here and the red was a reference to the blood on their hands. There's nothing to fear these days, though, and the delicious food runs from *bibalakas* – a rib-sticking mix of *fromage blanc* (soft white cheese), chives, and garlic served with sautéed potatoes, cheese, and ham – to the house favorite of ham spit-roasted on the bone *(jambon à l'os braisé à la broche)*. But locals flock here for the four kinds of *tarte flambée*, including one garnished with goat cheese and basil, and a deluxe Upper Rhine version made with Munster, a high-fat, full-cream-milk cheese.

9 rue des Ecoles, Colmar; open noon–2 PM and 6:30–10 PM Tue–Sat; www.maison-rouge.net

Also in Colmar

Aux Clefs de Colmar *(+33 3 8923 9215; inexpensive)* serves up traditional regional food, from pork knuckle baked with a Munster-cheese crust to a host of *flammekueche*, or as they're known here, "flams." There's a basic flam of bacon, onion, and *fromage blanc*, several cheese versions (with Emmental, Munster, and goat cheese), plus one with smoked salmon and another with mushrooms.

Also in France

La Strasbourgeoise *(+33 1 4205 2002; moderate)* in Paris sits appropriately opposite the Gare de l'Est, the station for trains to and from Alsace. In place since 1950, this is a little corner of Alsace in the French capital, from the choucroute piled high with pork to the traditional *tarte flambée*, a crispy thin crust painted with cream and specked with bacon and finely sliced onion. Wash it down with a mug of Alsatian beer or a pitcher of Riesling.

Around the World

Alsatian specialties litter the menu at Boston's **Brasserie Jo** *(www.brasseriejo.com; inexpensive)*, including *tarte flambée*. They serve the classic — with fresh white cheese, bacon, and onions — plus two new versions that might earn the disdain of traditionalists but please the locals, with spinach, Gruyère cheese, and garlic chips, or blue cheese and walnut.

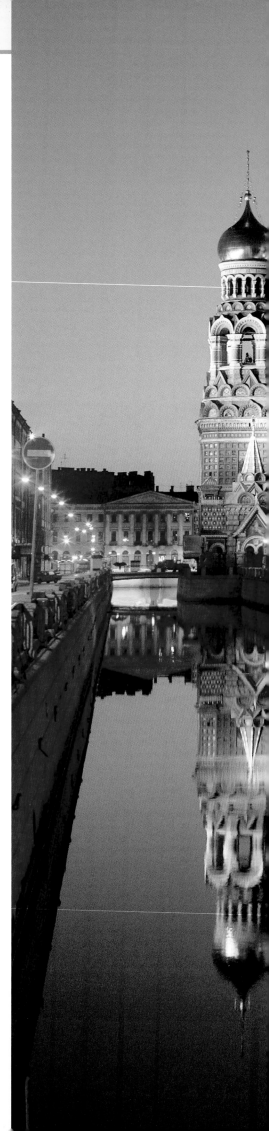

ST. PETERSBURG RUSSIA

Blinis and Caviar on the Baltic

Russia's hauntingly beautiful former imperial capital has been justly described as the Venice of the North. Since Czarist times, its cuisine has combined the simplicity of peasant cooking with the epicurean delights of this vast nation's rivers. Blinis with caviar are cherished by every Russian as their culinary birthright, whether eaten in a humble café or a fancy restaurant.

Founded by Czar Peter the Great to be a "window on the West" that exposed backward Holy Russia to the European Enlightenment, St. Petersburg is said to have been "built on bones" by forced labor, on a desolate swamp where the Neva River flows into the Baltic Sea. It supplanted Moscow as Russia's capital and remained so until Lenin returned the seat of power to the Kremlin. As the second city of the Soviet Union – renamed Leningrad – it withstood the epic 900 Days of Nazi siege, when 670,000 citizens perished from starvation, cold, or shelling.

Although the last czar, Nicholas II, once remarked that "St. Petersburg is Russian – but it is not Russia," the city is associated with a host of renowned figures. Here, Tchaikovsky, Stravinsky, and Shostakovich composed; Pushkin, Gogol, and Dostoevsky wrote; Rasputin, Lenin, and Trotsky made political history; and Catherine the Great defined decadent living. The city's historical associations abound, from unbridled autocrats to suicidal poets and ruthless revolutionaries.

The city's layout was determined by Peter the Great, who regulated the size of dwellings for each social class and plotted the great avenues that converge on the golden-spired Admiralty. Nevsky Prospekt, the city's main street, has examples of every style of architecture, from Baroque and Neo-Classical to Art Nouveau and Constructivism. The facades of this harmonious ensemble are painted in cool grays and blues or warm tawny hues, producing luminous reflections in the dark waters of the Neva River, its tributaries, and the numerous canals.

Ever since pagan times – before Russians adopted Christianity – the winter festival of Maslenitsa has been celebrated by gorging on blinis oozing melted butter, symbolizing the sun and hopes of fertile crops for the year ahead. The pancakes are traditionally prepared from buckwheat or wheat flour, mixed with butter, eggs, milk, and yeast; they can be topped with anything, but the classic accompaniment is caviar.

Red caviar *(krasnaya ikra)* is the plump orange eggs of salmon roe; it is far cheaper than black caviar *(chornaya ikra)*, harvested from four varieties of Caspian sturgeon. The most treasured is the pea-sized, black-to-silvery-grey Beluga, followed by the smaller, golden Sterlet, the brownish Osetra, and lastly the gray Sevruga. Canapé-sized blinis are the perfect foil to their oily saltiness, garnished with lemon slices, a dollop of sour cream, and a sprig of dill. Each one is a delicious testament to the decadence of the czars.

A Day in St. Petersburg

The Neva River defines the city; its majestic bridges link the downtown (on the mainland) to Petrograd Side and Vasilevsky Island. During the mid-summer White Nights, crowds gather to watch the bridges being raised; in winter the Neva freezes over, with spectacular ice floes during the spring thaw.

MORNING Tour the **State Hermitage Museum**, an architectural ensemble that includes the magnificent **Winter Palace** and houses a collection of artworks that rivals the Louvre's. Then stroll along the **Moyka** canal to the **Church of the Savior on the Spilled Blood**, marking the spot where Alexander II was assassinated.

AFTERNOON Visit the **Peter and Paul Fortress**, where the Romanovs (now buried in the Peter and Paul Cathedral) imprisoned generations of revolutionaries. Walk on the cruiser **Aurora**, whose guns heralded the October Revolution in 1917.

EVENING Explore the **Haymarket** district (the setting of Dostoevsky's *Crime and Punishment*), before attending a performance at the **Mariinsky Theater**.

Essentials

GETTING THERE
St. Petersburg's international **airport**, Pulkovo, has **buses** and **taxis** to downtown, 11 miles (17 km) away. It's easy to get around by **metro**, **bus**, *marshrutka* (**minibus**), or on foot.

WHERE TO STAY
Randhouse (inexpensive) is a hip B&B chain with good locations. *www.randhouse.ru*
Casa Leto (moderate) is an elegant mini-hotel near the Hermitage. *www.casaleto.com*
Grand Hotel Europe (expensive) is true old-style decadence. *www.grandhoteleurope.com*

TOURIST INFORMATION
www.visitrussia.org.uk

Above Mounds of caviar with sour cream and a sprig of dill constitutes the classic blini topping

Left The Church of the Resurrection of Christ, also known as the "Church of the Savior on the Spilled Blood," was built in 1883 in the style of 16th- and 17th-century Russian churches

Above Once the food of poor villagers living by the Caspian Sea, caviar became the choice of the elite before becoming widely available across Russia

Zakuski

On restaurant menus, blinis with caviar (or mushrooms or puréed herring) come under the heading of *zakuski*, or hors d'oeuvres. Salted sprat or herring, gherkins, pickled garlic, spiced feta, cold meats, gelatins, and salads are also popular, together with the oddly named *selyodka pod-shuby* – herring "in a fur coat" of beet, carrot, egg, and mayonnaise. *Zakuski* form the basis of the *Russky stol*, or "Russian table," which among the Czarist upper classes was merely the prelude to the main meal of the day. The *Russky stol* can be enjoyed at restaurants or private parties celebrating New Year, Orthodox Christmas (January 6–7), or "Old New Year" (January 13–14).

The Best Places to Eat Blinis

Caviar Bar & Restaurant
expensive

If money's no object, reserve a table at the Caviar Bar & Restaurant in the Grand Hotel Europe, where Tchaikovsky spent his honeymoon. Founded in the 1870s, the Yevropeyskaya (as locals call the hotel) became an orphanage after the 1920s Civil War and was only restored to its previous splendor six decades later. Though there's no formal dress code, you'll feel underdressed in casual wear amid the Caviar Bar's Art Nouveau marble decor, damask upholstery, and tinkling fountain.

Its menu offers such delights as Kamchatka crab, Siberian *pelmeni* (ravioli) in Champagne sauce, sturgeon and salmon mousse – and blinis with caviar. Their blinis are cooked to perfection – thin and crispy – and the caviar is mouthwatering, from the finest Beluga and Sterlet to unsalted *(malossol)* red caviar (which elsewhere tends to be over-salted). Served with panache, they are best washed down with shots of ice-cold vodka, of which there's a vast range of different flavored brands available.

Mikhailovskaya ul. 1–7, St. Petersburg; open 5 PM–midnight daily; www.grandhoteleurope.com

Also in St. Petersburg

You needn't spend a fortune to enjoy blinis with caviar. Provided they're freshly made, they can be delicious in cafés or as carry-outs from street kiosks serving Russian-style fast food. Some chains serve deep-frozen blinis, defrosted in a microwave, which are truly revolting. If in doubt ask, "*Oni svyezhi*?" ("Are they fresh?"). One sure-fire option – that also offers an all-you-can-eat *zakuski* buffet – is **Yolki Palki** *(inexpensive)*, a rustic-style chain of Russian tavernas with 24-hour branches at Malaya Konyushennaya 9 and Nevsky Prospekt 88. Besides a selection of vodkas, they also serve *kvas*, a delicious beverage made from fermented rye bread. Neither branch takes reservations.

Also in Russia

Yolki Palki *(see above)* is ubiquitous in Moscow, but **Teremok** *(www.teremok.ru; inexpensive)*, a chain with kiosks near metro stations, is a good alternative for a carry-out. For a sit-down meal in Moscow, try the funky **Café Margarita** *(www.cafe-margarita.ru; inexpensive)*, named after the heroine of Mikhail Bulgakov's classic novel, *The Master and Margarita*.

Around the World

Blinis are also a feature of Polish, Yiddish, Lithuanian, and Ukrainian cuisine, and feature on the menu in restaurants from Vilnius to Berlin and beyond. In the US, there are many Russian restaurants in Brooklyn; the **Baku Palace** *(www.bakupalace.com; moderate)* also has Azerbaijani dishes on its menu.

A Day in Ulm

Central Ulm is easily explored on foot: most places of interest lie between the Danube and Ulm Minster, which are just minutes apart.

MORNING Climb the 768 tight stairs of the **minster spire** while you are fresh, then admire the church's 15th-century choir stalls and its fine stained glass. Head downhill to the **Fishermen's Quarter** on the banks of the Danube and the 1443 **Schiefes Haus**, or crooked house, which leans alarmingly over a stream.

AFTERNOON Walk along the medieval riverside **city wall** to the equally crooked **Metzgerturm**, a 14th-century defensive tower uphill of which lies the **Rathaus**. It contains a replica of the world's first hang-glider and is decorated with frescoes of Ulm's medieval heyday. Cross the square to enter the striking modern **Kunsthalle Weishaupt** and enjoy its contemporary and modern art, then visit the adjoining **Ulmer Museum** for an overview of city history.

EVENING When there's no festival in town, travel ½ mile (1 km) south of downtown to the **Roxy**, a huge, happening cultural venue.

Essentials

GETTING THERE
Stuttgart International Airport lies an hour's **train** journey from Ulm. The rail station is within **walking** distance of all central attractions.

WHERE TO STAY
Pension Rösch (inexpensive) offers basic but clean and quiet rooms in the riverside Fishermen's Quarter. *+49 7316 5718*
Hotel Bäumle (moderate) is a welcoming hotel with good-value standard rooms in a 500-year-old building by the minster.
www.hotel-baeumle.de
Hotel Schiefes Haus (expensive) is an eccentric Ulm landmark – a half-timbered 1443 house that is "the most crooked hotel in the world."
www.hotelschiefeshausulm.de

TOURIST INFORMATION
www.tourismus.ulm.de

Left The roughly shaped pieces of handmade *Spätzle* are often mixed with cheese and herbs for a simple meal
Below The soaring spire of Ulm Minster rises above the city to an astonishing height of 530 ft (161 m)

ULM GERMANY

Swabian Noodles in Ulm

Most visitors to the pretty city of Ulm are drawn there to see the world's tallest church spire, a staggering piece of Gothic architecture that demonstrates the city's prosperity in medieval times. But this city – the birthplace of Albert Einstein – is full of surprises, not least the fine cuisine of the Swabian Alp region and its Italianate little egg noodles known as *Spätzle*.

On the banks of the Danube River sits Ulm, a sleepy old city that was first mentioned as a royal domain in 854 and became rich in the Middle Ages through the linen trade. Its magnificent church dates back to 1377, though its ambitious spire wasn't completed for another 500 years. On clear days even the Alps are visible from the top, making it well worth the long climb. The streets leading downhill from the minster to the Danube are scattered with fascinating buildings, from the attractive jumble of half-timbered 15th-century houses in the Fishermen's Quarter to the Rathaus (town hall) with its historic frescoes. The Eagle's Bastion, a nondescript 17th-century building by the river, is worthy of a visit in memory of the "tailor of Ulm," who attempted the first recorded (unsuccessful) flight from here in 1811.

The city's symbol is the sparrow. The legendary tale relates that while building the church, workmen were unable to get one of the huge wooden beams through the city gates, until they were inspired by the sight of a sparrow carrying a twig vertically in its beak.

The legend of the *Ulmer Spätze* (sparrow of Ulm) was born. Interestingly, the city's best-loved dish, *Spätzle*, means "little sparrow," although no one is quite sure why; it may refer to the legend or to the *Spätzle*'s original hand-pressed shapes, evident in medieval drawings.

Spätzle are served at most of Ulm's restaurants and at all of its many, boisterous festivals. Shaped like tiny dumplings or thin ragged fingers of pasta, *Spätzle* are made from white wheat flour, egg, and milk dough, to which minced pork liver is sometimes added to make *Leberspätzle*. This dough is then either finely chopped, forced though holes in a strainer, or grated into boiling salted water where it is cooked until it surfaces.

As a standalone dish, *Spätzle* most commonly appear as *Käsespätzle* (in a cheese sauce) or as *Krautspätzle*, which includes sauerkraut, onion, butter, marjoram, and caraway. *Spätzle* also make an important appearance in the regional beef stew *Gaisburger Marsch*, along with chopped potatoes and butter-fried onions, but most often they simply take the place of potatoes or dumplings in traditional German meat dishes such as sauerbraten (*see pp92–3*).

Ulm Bread Museum

Bread had religious importance in Germany for many centuries as an offering in pagan rites. This explains the many shapes still available today: round flat loaves once represented the sun, while braided loaves symbolized shorn hair. A tradition also developed of shaping bread into nature's creations, such as horses, birds, deer, fish, or sheaves of wheat for special occasions. Ulm's **Museum der Brotkultur** (bread museum) confirms bread's historical importance with its staggering 25,000 related objects and books. Most Ulm bakeries offer a wonderful range of breads to admire and buy, spanning from coarse, dark, and slightly sweet rye pumpernickel to multigrain loaves sprinkled with poppy or sunflower seeds. Many end up in a simple evening meal; the German word for dinner, *Abendbrot*, literally means "evening bread."

Above The elaborately painted walls of the 14th-century Rathaus

The Best Places to Eat Spätzle

Zunfthaus der Schiffleute
moderate

Once the local guild headquarters for fishermen, this 15th-century half-timbered house is home to one of Ulm's oldest restaurants. Inside, stone floors with timeless, heavy wooden furniture set the perfect scene for traditional Swabian foods, many of which involve outstanding homemade *Spätzle*. Virtually the whole range of possibilities are here; among them the standard *Käsespätzle*, in its rich cheese sauce, and the fairly common *Linsen* (lentils) *mit Spätzle* and *Krautspätzle*. More unusual meal options include the *Zunfthaustöpfle*, with its creamy herb-heavy mushroom sauce; and the robust *Ulmer Pfännle*, in which pork kebabs are smothered in fiery pepper sauce. Often the most interesting choices are on the restaurant's seasonal menu, where delicious ingredients such as asparagus, chanterelle mushrooms, and venison are served with *Spätzle*. A good selection of local beers is on hand to provide the perfect accompaniment to this rustic fare. But be sure not to overindulge on the main courses, as the vanilla ice cream with hot figs is well worth leaving space for.

Fischergasse 31, Ulm; open 11 AM–midnight Mon–Sat; www.zunfthaus-ulm.de

Also in Ulm

If you'd rather have your *Spätzle* served with a gourmet twist, try charming **Zur Forelle** *(www.zurforelle.com; expensive)*, which is also based in a 15th-century Fishermen's Quarter house. Its *Gaisburger Marsch* (Swabian beef stew) is particularly wonderful.

Also in Germany

Elsewhere in Swabia, in the venerable university town of Thübingen, the **Hotel am Schloss** *(www.hotelamschloss.de; moderate)* is largely famous for its *Maultaschen* (Swabian ravioli) and fine views of the city, but it always serves great *Spätzle* too and isn't afraid to experiment with dishes such as venison pot roast with hazelnut *Spätzle*. While it's easy to find good *Spätzle* in Swabia, it's much harder elsewhere in Germany, particularly in the north, which makes Berlin's **s'Brätle** *(+49 30 8862 7138; moderate)* all the more valuable. Its range of southern German specialties include superb *Spätzle*.

Around the World

With many Swabians emigrating to North America, it's also possible to find good *Spätzle* there too. In Alameda, California, the **Speisekammer** *(www.speisekammer.com; moderate)* provides San Francisco's Bay Area with a *Käsespätzle* to be proud of. On the east coast, **Cafe Steinhof** *(www.cafesteinhof. com; inexpensive)* does a first-rate job of the same dish, even though it classifies itself as an Austrian restaurant.

Above The main square in Brussels – the Grand Place – dates back to the Middle Ages

Above Steamed *moules marinière* cooked with garlic, white wine, parsley, and shallots are eaten using empty shells as pincers

Three Days in Brussels

Brussels is full of wonderful sights, food, and drink, and its attractions can easily be sampled by walking or taking the hop-on, hop-off buses.

DAY ONE Begin at the magnificent **Grand Place**, and take a short detour to the city mascot, the little bronze figure of the **Manneken-Pis** ("Peeing Boy"). Walk back through the elegant **Galéries St-Hubert** arcade to the Gothic **Cathédrale des Saints Michel et Gudule**. End the day at the **Musée des Instruments de Musique**.

DAY TWO Start the day at the **flea market** in the **Place du Jeu de Balle**. Then walk through the **Place du Grand Sablon**, with its upmarket antique and chocolate shops, to reach the **Musées Royaux des Beaux-Arts**, a monument to Belgian art.

DAY THREE Visit the **Horta Museum**, a shrine to Art Nouveau set in the home of its pioneer, Victor Horta. Then head for the wonderfully quirky **Musée Wiertz**, a 19th-century art studio. Continue to the **Parc du Cinquantenaire**, with its three museums: military, historic automobiles, and world-class antique treasures.

Essentials

GETTING THERE

Brussels has an international **airport** at **Zaventem**, three major **train stations**, and an extensive city network of **trams** and **buses**.

WHERE TO STAY

Sleep Well Youth Hostel (inexpensive) is more of a budget hotel than a hostel, with a good choice of accommodations close to downtown. *www.sleepwell.be*

Noga (moderate) is a neat, elegant, well-run hotel in a tranquil location, close to the Place Sainte-Catherine. *www.nogahotel.com*

Le Dixseptième (expensive) is a stylish boutique hotel in the 17th-century residence of the Spanish ambassador, close to the Grand Place. *www.ledixseptieme.be*

TOURIST INFORMATION

Grand Place; *www.visitbrussels.be*

BRUSSELS BELGIUM

Mussels in Brussels

Brussels is an hour's drive from the Belgian coast but, as a great medieval trading city, it has a historic connection with the sea. It's no surprise, therefore, that the classic Belgian dish of mussels and fries is the mainstay of many of the capital's restaurants. It's a simple, hearty, and nutritious dish that depends crucially on fresh, quality ingredients being cooked to perfection.

In 1561, an ambitious new waterway – the Willebroek Canal – was completed, leading to the heart of Brussels and giving the city a direct link to the sea. The canal terminated at Place Sainte-Catherine, a stone's throw from the city's splendid centerpiece, the Grand Place. In the late 19th century, when the canal's course was diverted and the basins at the city's center filled in, the area became the site of a huge fish market, the Marché aux Poissons. The fish market has since disappeared, but the connection with the sea remains in the wonderful fish restaurants of Place Sainte-Catherine.

Belgium has acquired a dizzying reputation for good food in recent decades, and its capital is also the effective capital of the European Union, attracting a cosmopolitan crowd that demands high standards. In the Belgians themselves, a culture of good food is instilled from an early age: they like to eat well, but have little tolerance of pretension. *Moules-frites* (mussels and fries) falls into this tradition. The high-end restaurants here are too grand to serve such a simple dish, and you're more likely to find it in bistros and family restaurants, but *moules-frites* is not to be sniffed at. It's a simple enough dish: the mussels are usually cooked *marinière* (steamed with chopped shallots, celery, parsley, thyme, bay leaves, and a glass of white wine), then served in large casseroles accompanied by copious *frites* (fries). But its creation en masse in lively restaurants creates glorious scenes reminiscent of the festive village celebrations painted by Pieter Brueghel the Elder, a resident of Brussels in the mid-16th century.

There is plenty for the visitor to see and admire in Brussels, including a fine cathedral and excellent art museums. But the real joy of visiting the city lies in glimpsing something of its individual character, which nurtured the Surrealist vision of René Magritte, and gave birth to Art Nouveau architecture and Tintin, the famous cartoon reporter. In the same spirit, the Belgian artist Marcel Broodthaers produced his most famous sculptural work in 1964–6 in several versions. His *Grande Casserole de Moules* is just what it says – real mussel shells filling a blackened casserole.

Above The old district of Les Marolles is renowned for its comic-strip murals

Les Frites Belges

Belgian *frites* (French fries) set the gold standard: when properly prepared, there are simply no better fries in the world. There are several factors involved. First, the choice of potato: only certain varieties (such as Bintje) are sufficiently sweet and floury to produce the optimum flavor and crispness. Second, the chips must be cut into just the right shape – about the size of a woman's little finger. Third, the oil (traditionally beef dripping) must be clean and piping hot. Lastly – and crucially – the *frites* are cooked twice: once to a pale softness; then, after cooling and resting, to a crispy, golden finish. The traditional Belgian accompaniment is mayonnaise. In Brussels, perfection is achieved not just in restaurants, but also in humble roadside stands (called *friteries* or *frietkoten*). A cornet of hot *frites* and a dollop of mayonnaise can be a meal in itself.

The Best Places to Eat Moules-Frites

La Marée moderate

Portuguese-born Mario and Teresa Alves have been building a solid reputation for delicious fish for over 30 years. Their restaurant's name means "The Tide," and the pretty 17th-century red-brick building is full of seafaring memorabilia, alongside old photos of the Marché aux Poissons. But essentially an easy simplicity prevails, so clients can concentrate on the food concocted by Teresa and her team in a kitchen open to view. It is a perfect setting for *moules-frites*: hospitable, unpretentious, yet with careful attention to detail. Prepared in four different ways (*marinière, au vin blanc, à la provençale*, and *maison*), the mussels come to the table in large, cast-iron casseroles. You can dig them out of their shells with a fork or by using an empty pair of shells as pincers; then drink the cooking juices with a spoon. Simple, beautifully done, and classically Belgian.

Rue de Flandre 99, Brussels; open 12–2 PM and 6:30–10 PM Tue–Sat; www.lamaree-sa.com

Also in Brussels

In't Spinnekopke (*www.spinnekopke.be; moderate*) is a delightfully atmospheric *estaminet* (traditional tavern) dating back to 1762 that specializes in Belgian beers and dishes, including *moules-frites*. **Chez Patrick** (*www.chezpatrick.be; moderate*) is another splendidly traditional eatery close to the Grand Place that has been serving *Bruxellois* favorites including *moules-frites* for over 70 years.

Also in Belgium

Go to the coast to sample some really delicious mussels and other seafoods. **Oesterput** (*www. oesterput.com; moderate*) stands right by the harbor at Blankenberge, and this workmanlike warehouse with a cafeteria-style restaurant serves first-class seafood of all kinds. **A l'Improviste** (*www.a-l-improviste.be; moderate*) is a stylish, modern seafood restaurant with a terrace overlooking the sea at Knokke-Heist that serves classic dishes such as *moules-frites* with great flair.

Around the World

The high international reputation of Belgian cooking has spawned outposts abroad in numerous formats. London has the **Belgo** chain (*www.belgo-restaurants.co.uk; moderate*) – brasserie-style restaurants specializing in Belgian dishes and beer. There are two **Belgian Beer Cafés** (*www.belgianbeercafemelbourne. com; moderate*) with a similar mission in Melbourne, Australia. Elsewhere, look for restaurants specializing in authentic Belgian cuisine. **Jeannine's Bistro** (*www. jeanninesbistro.com; moderate*) in Houston, Texas, is a fine example.

UMBRIA ITALY

Buried Treasure in Umbria

The dramatic, mountainous landscapes of Umbria in central Italy have inspired some of the world's greatest artists, including Michelangelo, Giotto, and Fra Angelico. Medieval and Renaissance towns tumble down its mountainsides like living history, many hiding exquisite art. In the fertile soil, hunters look for another Italian treasure: the knobby fungi known as truffles.

Beautiful enough to make painters of us all, Umbria seems to hide a masterpiece in every little church and chapel. It produced more saints than any other part of Italy, including St. Francis of Assisi, whose kind friendliness seems to live on in the spirit of Umbrians today. This landlocked region of Italy has witnessed the passage of marching armies, pilgrims, and traders over the centuries, but remains supremely hospitable to those wishing to admire its landscape, art, and rare, regional produce.

The culture and economy here are based on farming and hunting. In southeastern Umbria, the splendid towns of Spoleto and Norcia are surrounded by countryside, some carefully cultivated, some still wild and wooded as of old. From December to March, when dawn mists cloak the hills and valleys, a curious but well-rehearsed pas de deux performance takes place in this wondrous landscape. A solitary hunter sets out with his dog across a field of stubble lined with pale, pencil-thin birch trees. The animal sniffs the clay earth, its olfactory senses trained to pick up the scent from the prized *Tuber melanosporum*: the black truffle. Unearthed and cleaned, these deeply aromatic rhizomes become a transformational ingredient.

The sophisticated Romans and ancient Greeks revered truffles for their therapeutic and aphrodisiacal properties, and believed they were created as a result of the sacred thunderbolts that Jupiter periodically hurled to Earth. In reality, the Umbrian *tartufo nero* (black truffle) is a rather dull, woody fungus that needs a light brushing to remove the dirt clinging to it. Its otherworldly qualities are not evident until it is cut and tasted – at which point the all-pervading aroma of the freshly cut tuber translates into a fleeting moment of gustatory heaven that is rarely matched.

Less prized than the white truffles of Piedmont, which have sold in the past for prices exceeding €100,000 per kilo, the aromatic black truffle is still a rarity with the capacity to amaze. Though never cooked, the raw truffle is occasionally warmed, and in Umbria it is popularly grated sparingly over simple, hot pasta, such as *stringozzi*, an Umbrian form of pasta that's akin to spaghetti. The only other ingredient is a drizzle of olive oil, and Umbria boasts the best in Italy – all of its olive oils have DOP ("*denominazione origine protetta*") status. Black truffle is also used sparingly in the region's almost indefinably good meat and fish dishes, and in risotto – whose simplicity belies the glorious taste that awaits, courtesy of Umbria's "black diamonds."

Three Days in Umbria

Umbria is an Italian Renaissance painting come to life. Its medieval hilltop towns and stunning countryside provide many opportunities for great sightseeing and dining.

DAY ONE Spend the morning in the lovely walled town of **Norcia**, birthplace of St. Benedict. Try the delis – the butchers here are so renowned they gave Italy its word for butcher: "*norcino*." Take an afternoon bus to **Preci**, where pastel houses dot the steep hillside, and walk on to the splendid nearby abbey of **Sant'Eutizio**.

DAY TWO Magnificent **Spoleto** is dense with captivating buildings where the Roman, medieval, and Renaissance periods are pieced together. Unmissable sights are the open-air **Teatro Romano** and the **Ponte delle Torri**, a spectacular stone bridge.

DAY THREE Drive up to the breathtaking spread of the **Piano Grande**, the basin of an ancient subsided lake. It is crowned by the rugged peaks of the **Sibillini mountain range** in one of Italy's newest National Parks, and pans out below the iconic village of **Castelluccio di Norcia**, the perfect starting point for a walk in the park.

Essentials

GETTING THERE
There are **trains** and **buses** to the area from Perugia, the closest international **airport**.

WHERE TO STAY
Fonte Antica (inexpensive) offers B&B within a 700-year-old farmhouse in the National Park of Monti Sibillini. *www.fonteantica.com*
Hotel agli Scacchi (moderate) in Preci has home comforts and a swimming pool. *www.hotelagliscacchi.com*
Hotel Gattapone (expensive) is a boutique hotel in Spoleto. *www.hotelgattapone.it*

TOURIST INFORMATION
www.english.regioneumbria.eu

Above Freshly made ribbon pasta with shavings of black truffle and slices of ceps, or *funghi porcini*, which also grow in the Umbrian valleys

Left The enchanting village of Castelluccio di Norcia is famous for its lentils, traditionally cooked in Italy as part of New Year's Eve celebrations

Above Truffle hunting in the valleys here is a painstaking business, using specially trained dogs to sniff out the precious truffles

What Else to Eat

Norcineria roughly translates as "pork sausages." These are a serious business in Norcia, as testified by the abundance of shops crammed with rows of weird and wonderfully shaped dried and cured **salamis** tied up in string bundles. The *cremoso* variety is soft and perfect for spreading on bread for your picnic lunch, while the richer *cinghiale*, made with wild boar, is more often used in cooked dishes. The tiny, sweet, nutty **lentils** from the vast grassed plain that surrounds Castelluccio di Norcia are famous throughout Italy. At other times of year, sheep graze there, and their milk is lovingly transformed into the tangy and instantly recognizable **pecorino cheese**.

The Best Places to Eat Truffles

La Locanda di Cacio Re
moderate

The delights begin even before you reach the doors of this well-reputed restaurant, as the Locanda is set in the beautiful medieval village of Vallo di Nera, still ringed by old stone walls. The restaurant itself is a refurbished 16th-century farmhouse; in summertime, guests can relax over their meal on a spacious terrace overlooking the wild wooded valleys, and there's a light-filled dining room for cooler weather. Three wonderful varieties of truffle are served – the black summer truffle, the winter "special black," and the white. Chef Paolo Brunelli has put together a choice of four-course menus, one entirely devoted to the truffle. As well as being shaved over fresh *tagliolini* pasta, it accompanies smoked beef carpaccio, stars in truffled lamb, and flavors local cheeses such as *caciotta*. The signature dish is *stringozzi* pasta with sage, *guanciale* cured pork, and flakes of pecorino sheep cheese. Cooking courses, local products, and guest rooms are also offered.

I Casali di Vallo di Nera, Vallo di Nera; open for lunch and dinner Tue–Sun; www.caciore.com/locanda

Also in Umbria

The **Taverna Castelluccio** in Castelluccio di Norcia *(www.tavernacastelluccio.it; moderate)* is a wonderful institution, run by a welcoming host who is an expert on all matters local. As well as classics such as *tagliolini al tartufo nero di Norcia* (tagliatelle with Norcia black truffles), he serves *violatri* – wild spinach and hearty sausage stewed with organic lentils grown on the plain below the taverna.

Also in Italy

In a lovingly renovated Piedmont farmhouse in Madonna di Como, Alba, **Locanda del Pilone** *(www.locandadelpilone.com; expensive)* is a superb place to savor the white Alba truffles, as well as other Piedmont specialties. Desserts such as *millefoglie* with cocoa, chestnuts, and vanilla sauce are superb.

Around the World

In California's Bay Area, **Poggio** in Sausalito *(www.poggiotrattoria.com moderate)* regularly gets rave reviews. The menu changes on a daily basis, but throughout the fall, diners are guaranteed delicate white truffles imported from Alba, which on request are shaved over pasta dishes such as gnocchi fashioned from Yukon Gold potatoes smothered with ultra-creamy Valle d'Aosta fondue. Organic vegetables are grown on site and the mozzarella is made in-house.

VALENCIA SPAIN

The Original Paella in Valencia

The pearl of eastern Iberia, Valencia was contested between Christians and Moors in medieval times, and the old town echoes with these ancient cultures. In stark contrast, the City of Arts and Sciences may be the world's most futuristic complex. Old or new, every quarter of the city cherishes paella, a dish that perfectly captures the salty, earthy essence of Valencia.

Valencia's medieval center, its exceptional white-sand beaches, and its gleaming modern yacht harbor should be enough to satisfy anyone. But after the Turia River flooded catastrophically in 1957, Valencia remade itself by rerouting the river and creating a parkland in the dry riverbed. The capstone of civic reinvention was the astonishing City of Arts and Sciences, a "city within a city" designed by native son and avant-garde architectural superstar Santiago Calatrava. So marvelous is this paean to artistic and scientific discovery that visitors are torn between just wandering among the buildings, which function as giant-scale outdoor sculpture, and going inside to wander among first-class exhibitions and performances.

No such transformation has ever been necessary to Valencian cuisine, where paella is king. When the Moors introduced rice to Europe through Valencia in the 8th century, the dish became all but inevitable. The original *paella valenciana* uses the bounty of the garden plot to create a dish that is simultaneously light and earthy, as crisp green beans combine with sweet tomatoes and peppers and the chewy, meaty morsels of land snails and hare. The more famous *paella de mariscos* bristles with the sweet, crunchy shrimp and other shellfish of the Valencian coast. But in every form of paella, the rice is key.

Valencian rice can absorb up to four times its volume in liquid while still remaining firm, swelling prodigiously as it soaks up wine, fish broth, chicken stock, squid ink, or vegetable juices. Cooked in a *paellera* – the shallow, wide iron pan that gives paella its name – the dish forms a definitive nutty, caramelized golden crust, or *socarrat*, at the base of the pan. The best paellas also absorb a smoky flavor from cooking over a wood fire.

Some of the city's leading paella restaurants are found on Playa Malvarossa, the broad beach where locals and visitors swim and bask in the Mediterranean sun. Diners patiently await tables, knowing that the rituals of paella cannot be rushed. First comes the difficult choice over the type of paella, then the wait, as the dish is prepared to order, before – finally – the waiter presents a *paellera* big enough to serve the entire table. It is a celebration of centuries of gastronomic fusion in a single dish.

Above The futuristic buildings of the City of Arts and Sciences include a science museum (pictured), opera house, planetarium, and the largest aquarium in Europe

The Mercado Central

More than 400 vendors fill Valencia's central food market, and many more spill out on to the adjoining sidewalks and streets. The 1928 Modernista building is often cited as one of the largest covered markets in Europe. With its soaring ceilings and ornate central dome, it is a modern cathedral of gastronomy. Yet the fanciful architecture is upstaged by the bounty and beauty of the food stalls – pyramids of sweet oranges, glistening clear-eyed fish splayed out on crushed ice, thick green pods of fresh fava beans. The rich choices perhaps explain why Valencia's cooks have invented so many variations of paella. Stall-hopping yields the essentials – large cloth bags of heirloom Bomba rice, heaping mounds of bright paprika, small tins of precious saffron, and an iron *paellera*.

A Day in Valencia

The ages of Valencia's long history are evident everywhere. The Cathedral alone incorporates Roman relics and a Moorish minaret as its bell tower. As the city radiates outward, it becomes ever more modern, culminating in the futuristic fantasies of the architecture at the City of Arts and Sciences.

MORNING Marvel at the restored Renaissance-era frescoes in the stately **Cathedral**, then climb the minaret-turned-bell tower for a panorama of the old city. Across **Plaza de la Reina** in an extravagant Baroque palace, the **Museo Nacional de Cerámica** features a charming tiled Valencian kitchen.

AFTERNOON After photographing the interplay of forms in the **City of Arts and Sciences**, visit the planetarium at **L'Hemisfèric** or catch the graceful play of beluga whales and bottlenose dolphins at **L'Oceanogràfic**.

EVENING Stroll the narrow streets of the old fishermen's quarter, **El Cabanyal**, until you reach the broad strand of **Playa Malvarossa**. Catch the last rays of the sun at this urban beach or join the Valencians as they promenade along the shore before an evening of socializing and dining.

Essentials

GETTING THERE
Many European and Spanish airlines fly into **Valencia Airport**, and the city is well-served by **train** services from points all over Spain.

WHERE TO STAY
Hostal Venecia (inexpensive) has modest but cheerful rooms in a landmark building downtown. *www.hotelvenecia.com*
Hotel Meliá Valencia (moderate) offers stylish, modern rooms near the City of Arts and Sciences. *www.melia-hotels.com*
Hotel Neptuno (expensive) makes the most of its beachfront location on Playa Malvarossa with a rooftop solarium. *www.hotelneptunovalencia.com*

TOURIST INFORMATION
Calle Paz; *www.comunitatvalenciana.com*

The Best Places to Eat Paella

La Pepica moderate

Ernest Hemingway, Orson Welles, and their matador friends all heaped praises on La Pepica, where the menu features a modest eight rice dishes. These encompass all that is great about Valencian rice cookery, from the classic *paella valenciana* and the shellfish-topped *paella marinera* to the squid-and-its-ink *arroz negro*. The formality of the wait staff, smartly clad in white shirts and black waistcoats, heightens the sense of ceremony, especially when the paella is presented with a slight bow. The restaurant was established in 1898 on Playa Malvarossa and remains the principal temple of paella in the city that invented the dish. The front door is on the beach, but entering through the back from Paseo Neptuno gives customers a look behind the scenes at the voluminous kitchen of blue-and-white tiles and stainless-steel appliances where *paelleras* of every size dangle overhead.

2, 6, 8 Paseo Neptuno, Playa de la Malvarossa, Valencia; open for lunch Mon–Sun, dinner Mon–Sat; www.lapepica.com

Also in Valencia

At the edge of the old city, **Restaurante de Ana** *(www.restaurantedeana.com; moderate)* is a stickler about using exquisite fresh snails in its *paella valenciana*. Its *arroz estilo Albufera* is a paella with succulent duck. Traditional paella at the chic eatery of superchef Vicente Chust, **Restaurante Chust Godoy** *(www. chustgodoy.com; expensive)*, is well worth the one-hour wait for its preparation.

Also in the Valencia Region

Literally across the road from rice fields in the Albufera, **La Matandeta** in Alfafar *(www.lamatandeta.com; moderate; open Easter–Sep only)* often prepares its sublime paellas in the outdoor courtyard during the summer months. The casual **El Pescador** *(+34 965 842 571; inexpensive)* in Altea creates excellent seafood paellas as well as grilled local fish. In Elche, **Els Capellans** *(+34 966 610 011; moderate)* is famed for its Alicante-style paella studded with meatballs and topped with fluffy egg.

Around the World

Many restaurants in the great Mexican fishing port of **Veracruz** (try **La Choca**) make a delicious New World seafood paella called *arroz a la tumbada*, seasoned with hot peppers and usually topped with clams, shrimp, conch, squid, and red snapper. In New York City, **Socarrat Paella Bar** *(www. socarratpaellabar.com; moderate)* serves five different kinds of paella, including the traditional *paella valenciana* and a vegetarian version, and waiters offer to help you scrape up the crunchy *socarrat* at the bottom of the *paellera*.

Above Many cooks today add smoked paprika to give their paella the earthy, smoky taste traditionally imparted by cooking over a wood fire

Left The secret to a great paella lies in the *sofrito*, a slow browning of meat and vegetables, before the rice is added to the *paellera*

YORK ENGLAND

Afternoon Tea in Historic York

To the English, tea is more than a drink – it is the universal pick-me-up, the "cup that cheers." Combined with scones, sandwiches, and cakes, the English afternoon tea – served with near-ceremonial reverence – approaches an art form. There's nowhere better to indulge in this tradition than in heritage-drenched York, one of northern England's most alluring cities.

York has a central place in English history that makes it one of the country's most popular visitor destinations. It's a picturesque riverside city of pale stone buildings, with a central old-town area that's entirely concealed within a great fortified wall. Unsurpassed as a touring base for northern England, it's within easy reach of genteel Harrogate, stately Castle Howard, and the bluff North Yorkshire coast.

A day in historic York will find you walking around the stunning medieval walls or exploring York Minster, Britain's biggest and most impressive Gothic building. Getting lost in the tangle of cobbled streets is half the fun, happening upon fascinating timber-framed houses and grand Georgian buildings, while a score of innovative museums, hands-on history centers, and restored churches reveal the city's Roman, Viking, industrial, and religious heritage. Worn-out visitors need no persuasion to fall gratefully into a welcoming café for a restorative "cuppa" and something to eat.

The English have had a taste for tea since the 17th century. King Charles II's Portuguese queen, Catherine of Braganza, is usually credited with popularizing the drink, first brought back from India and China by Portuguese traders. By the 19th century, taking afternoon tea – a light meal between lunch and dinner – had become a social occasion in upper-class circles, and it's a tradition that survives today in the grand salons of fancy hotels, where pristine-jacketed waiters serve tiered platters of wafer-thin sandwiches and dainty cakes.

Away from the starred hotels, there's a more rustic tradition of cheery, old-fashioned tearooms serving generous slabs of homemade cake or, most typically of all, warm scones with clotted cream and strawberry jam – the so-called "cream tea." Whether this originated in Devon or Cornwall, both in England's rural southwest, is a hotly contested point – wars have been started over less – as is the correct method for eating the scones. A true Devonshire cream tea, for example, requires that the cream should be spread first, followed by the jam second, and there's even a campaign to seek for the cream tea the same European protected status afforded to Champagne or Gorgonzola cheese. That an afternoon snack could arouse such passions might appear strange, but as with the perennial question about the beverage itself – milk or tea in the cup first? – the vexed social habits of the English are a window to their very soul.

A Day in York

Exploring York on foot is easy, as most of its attractions lie within the city walls. This compact area is a treasure trove of architecture and heritage.

MORNING Start at **York Minster** to see England's finest stained-glass windows, and then walk down the former main road in Roman times, now called **Stonegate**, lined with shops, boutiques, and historic buildings. The nearby **Shambles** – the site of York's medieval butchers' shops – is equally photogenic.

AFTERNOON Simply choose a historical period and pursue your interest, either at **Jorvik** (the Viking-era attraction), **Fairfax House** (Georgian period), the **Castle Museum** (Victorian and Edwardian times), or the fantastic **National Railway Museum** (railroad history and working steam engines).

EVENING Evening **ghost walks** are a York specialty, following guides around the walls and alleys and hearing tales of royal villains, treasonous nobles, Civil War battles, and dastardly highwaymen (Dick Turpin was hanged in York).

Essentials

GETTING THERE
There are direct trains to York from **Manchester International Airport**. York is just under two hours from London by **train**.

WHERE TO STAY
Bar Convent (inexpensive) has simple but comfortable guest rooms in a working Georgian-era convent. www.bar-convent.org.uk
The Blue Rooms (moderate) are contemporary studio-style apartments. www.thebluebicycle.com
Hotel du Vin (expensive) is in boutique style, with a classy bistro. www.hotelduvin.com

TOURIST INFORMATION
1 Museum Street; www.visityork.org

Above Afternoon tea is served all afternoon and may include dainty sandwiches with their crusts cut off, as well as cakes

Left A church has occupied the site of York Minster since the 7th century; the present building was completed in 1472

Below Little Bettys is a smaller, cozier branch of York's famous Bettys Tearoom; it sells provisions downstairs and delicious teas upstairs

Below (top to bottom) Cakes await service at Bettys, purveyor of exquisite afternoon teas since 1919; the Piccadilly frontage of Fortnum & Mason in London, grocer to the English gentry

Right (top to bottom) A staunchly colonial tea in Hong Kong, with scones, clotted cream, and strawberry jam; afternoon tea at Raffles, Singapore; taking tea English-style in Jaipur, India

Afternoon Tea Around the World

The gentle tinkling of china teacups announces the civilized interlude between 3 and 5 PM when the world stops for tea in both cozy English tearooms and fancy East Asian hotels. This is the time to sit back and savor a long-standing and treasured ritual.

YORKSHIRE

Bettys moderate

6–8 St. Helen's Square, York; www.bettys.co.uk

Established in 1919, Bettys has six tearooms scattered around Yorkshire. The York establishment must be the most glamorous tearoom in England, an Art Deco gem whose elegant interior was inspired by the famous ocean liner *Queen Mary*. From the craft bakery emerge extraordinary breads, cakes, and confections, including the specialty cherry-and-almond "Fat Rascals," while Bettys' house-blend Yorkshire Tea is an English classic.

The Black Swan Tearoom moderate

Market Place, Helmsley; www.blackswan-helmsley.co.uk

Yorkshire's market towns are full of traditional, honest-to-goodness cafés, but there's far more style in evidence in this boutique tearoom and patisserie (a Tea Guild award-winner) attached to a classy country hotel. A rare and exotic tea menu ranges far and wide, or order afternoon tea with Champagne for a real indulgence.

Swinton Park moderate

Masham, Ripon; www.swintonpark.com

For a taste of the noble life, take tea in Swinton Park castle hotel, which is set in 200 acres of private parkland on the eastern fringes of the Yorkshire Dales. The local choice here is a "Wensleydale Tea," served with the crumbly, eponymous cheese from the Dales and Yorkshire fruitcake.

ALSO IN ENGLAND

London offers a stylish introduction to afternoon tea in a score or more famous hotels and glitzy stores, while in every region of England there's a seductive café or tearoom devoted to serving the perfect cream tea.

Otterton Mill inexpensive

Otterton, Budleigh Salterton, Devon; www.ottertonmill.com

Of the many contenders for the best Devonshire cream tea, they go the extra mile at Otterton Mill, which is set in a glorious riverside location in the wildlife-rich Otter Valley. The scones are made daily using their own milled flour, both clotted cream and jellies are supplied by nearby artisan producers, and the tea is organic and fair trade.

Cavendish Rooms moderate

Chatsworth House, Bakewell, Derbyshire; www.chatsworth.org

Enjoy a gracious afternoon tea that's entirely in keeping with the surroundings at Chatsworth House, Britain's finest Baroque stately home, the ancestral digs of the Dukes of Devonshire. Dainty cakes and pastries made by Chatsworth's own bakers are served in what is surely the most elegant stable block in the land, a glorious 18th-century space given a contemporary makeover.

De Grey's Tea Rooms moderate

Broad Street, Ludlow, Shropshire; www.degreys.co.uk

In central England's foodie capital, Ludlow, afternoon tea is at its traditional best at De Grey's, a half-timbered Tudor town house with an atmospheric oak-beamed interior and black-and-white-clad staff. An in-house bakery produces wonderful cakes and pastries, and if you eat more than is wise, you may be grateful to learn that there are also very cozy guest accommodations.

The Secret Garden moderate

Mersham-le-Hatch, Hythe Road, Ashford, Kent; www.secretgardenkent.co.uk

In the county of Kent – the so-called "garden of England" – afternoon tea and handsome locations go hand in hand, as in this restored coach house and impressive Victorian walled garden. The strawberry cream tea served here incorporates locally sourced jellies and clotted cream, while seasonal variations add a glass of Kentish sparkling wine or even mince pies and mulled wine at Christmas.

The Tea Cosy moderate

3 George Street, Kemptown, Brighton, East Sussex; www.theteacosy.co.uk

In the south coast's most flamboyant resort, this charming tearoom is dedicated, with its tongue

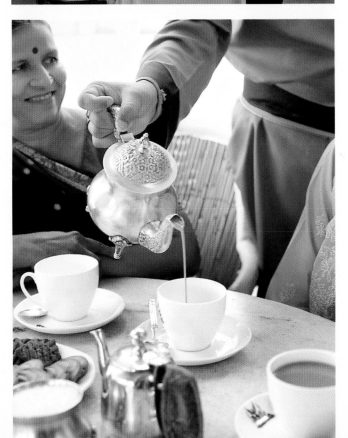

firmly in its cheek, to the gracious art of taking tea. Etiquette and manners are explained for beginners and visitors alike, from the use of the sugar tongs to the allowable volume of conversation at the tea table, while on Sunday afternoons everyone rises for a rendition of "God Save the Queen."

Fortnum & Mason expensive
181 Piccadilly, London W1;
www.fortnumandmason.com

Few places can offer as wide a range of teas as Fortnum's, the fashionable London grocery store *par excellence* founded in 1707. Their tea department offers over 70 blends and single-estate teas, available as part of afternoon tea or a grander High Tea in the store's elegant St. James's restaurant.

The Ritz expensive
150 Piccadilly, London W1;
www.theritzhotel.co.uk

For many, there is simply no better place to experience the quintessential afternoon tea in all its pomp and glory than the Ritz Hotel's magnificent, gilded Palm Court. This is tradition poured straight from the pot and, as befits the surroundings, you are expected to dress up; no jeans or athletic shoes, and gentlemen require a jacket and tie.

NORTH AMERICA

Coffee has long been the more popular drink in North America, but across the US and in Canada there are Anglophiles and tea fanatics who keep alive the genteel traditions of a bygone age.

Crown & Crumpet Tea Salon
moderate
207 Ghirardelli Square, 900 North Point, San Francisco, CA; www.crownandcrumpet.com

The Crown & Crumpet presents a mix of English wit and San Francisco style in a bright and breezy tearoom that offers a playful take on traditional afternoon tea. All the right ingredients are in place — well-sourced teas, homemade scones and cakes, toasted crumpets — but this creative California café is never in danger of taking itself too seriously.

Tea & Sympathy moderate
108 Greenwich Avenue, New York City, NY;
www.teaandsympathynewyork.com

Greenwich Village, original heart of New York's counterculture, is a melting pot of ideas and influences, including this self-styled "corner of England," known for its home-away-from-home food. Scones and jam are always on the menu, alongside other teatime favorites like rarebit or sardines on toast, and the teas include both English-style house blends and specialty brews.

Fairmont Empress Hotel
expensive
721 Government Street, Victoria, British Columbia, Canada; www.fairmont.com

For over a century, Victoria's dashing *grande dame* hotel has been serving afternoon tea with a harbor view in its glorious imperial lobby. There's every attention to detail, from tea tasting notes to the signature raisin scones that form the centerpiece of this most elegant of experiences.

ASIA

As the British Empire touched every corner of the world, so did the taste for a reviving mid-afternoon break. The English took tea back to its Eastern roots, and in Singapore, Hong Kong, and India, the ceremony lingers on in upmarket hotels.

Mandarin Oriental expensive
5 Connaught Road, Central, Hong Kong;
www.mandarinoriental.com

Even on the most hot and humid of days there's an air of calm in the Mandarin Oriental's legendary Clipper Lounge, where the great and good of Hong Kong come to see and be seen. Here, in one of the world's most renowned luxury hotels, afternoon tea is a truly magnificent repast, including artistic creations from the hotel's own patisserie.

Raffles Hotel expensive
1 Beach Road, Singapore; www.raffles.com

White-jacketed waiters glide effortlessly around the period-piece "Tiffin Room" in one of Southeast Asia's most emblematic hotels. Much like having a Singapore Sling (the iconic cocktail invented in the hotel), taking High Tea at Raffles is part of the whole colonial-revival experience and not to be missed.

Rambagh Palace expensive
Bhawani Singh Road, Jaipur, Rajasthan, India;
www.tajhotels.com

This former royal guest house and hunting lodge, later a Maharajah's palace and now a sumptuous hotel, makes for a wonderfully extravagant backdrop for afternoon tea. Pots of tea and dainty bites, impeccably presented, are served overlooking the stunning palace gardens.

NICE FRANCE

Flavors of the Southern Sun

In Nice's Bay of Angels, the limpid blue water laps the shore, but when the summer sun is pulsing like a furnace, it's the old town that beckons. Shade is offered by the pedestrian-friendly alleys with their pale facades and myriad galleries, while bars and bistros provide refreshment. A freshly made salade niçoise, a taste of sea and land, perfectly captures the essence of the city.

Nice has long lured artists and the idly affluent escaping a wintry north, attracted by the pastel-colored old town, the glitzy marina lifestyle, the palm-trimmed seafront, and the gloriously fresh food dished up in bistros, seaside cafés, and deluxe hotels. The city is a delicious culinary and cultural combination, proudly flaunting the influence of successive waves of outsiders. The Greeks were here, the Romans, too, and the northern Italians via the powerful Counts of Savoy. Nice finally passed into French hands in 1860 but the strong Italian influence, especially tableside, remains. This is, after all, the birthplace of ravioli and of Garibaldi.

The British, who have been visiting since the 1730s, also left their mark. Nice became the sundrenched sandbox of choice for aristocrats in the 19th century, even entertaining Queen Victoria. Luxury hotels sprang up to accommodate them while they built villas and raised a subscription to erect a walkway by the sea, the aptly named Promenade des Anglais.

When it comes to living and cooking, the Niçois keep it simple. You won't find rich sauces blanketing food; instead, it's subtle seasoning with an emphasis on newly picked, freshly caught, just made, and preferably enjoyed alfresco. There's no mistaking, then, that salade niçoise is a dish born of Nice. Each ingredient evokes the sun-soaked Mediterranean city, from the fragrant summer tomatoes to the salty, sea-kissed anchovies.

Some argue that a true niçoise contains only tomatoes, artichoke hearts, bell peppers, tiny, black niçoise olives, and anchovy fillets, dressed with rich local olive oil and fresh herbs: no vinegar – and certainly no tuna or lettuce. Others insist on tuna – canned, not fresh – but counsel against hard-boiled eggs. An infamous ex-city mayor turned cookbook author was adamant that potatoes, or any kind of cooked vegetables (those pesky green beans, for example), had no place in his niçoise salad bowl; and it's either tuna or anchovies, never the two together.

Today's innovative chefs insist, however, that the humble niçoise is at its best when it takes its lead from the seasons. Thus arugula, radishes, ruby-ringed onions, fava beans, and even thinly sliced cucumber may stake their claim among the flavor-infused tomatoes, olives, tuna, anchovies, and just-cooked eggs. And therein lies the key. The supremely generous Côte d'Azur climate enriches both the cuisine and the city so that, whatever its makeup, the signature dish of this southern city tastes like summer on a plate.

A Day in Nice

This historic seaside resort, nicknamed *Nice la Belle* (Nice the Beautiful), has buzz and beauty in spades, and there's plenty to see when the beach doesn't beckon.

MORNING Opt for a lazy café breakfast in **cours Saleya** and watch market vendors spin their spiel. Take to the cobbled alleyways, stopping at **Palais Lascaris** to glimpse how the very well-heeled once lived. Catch the elevator to **Castle Hill** for a Nice panorama, via **Tour Bellanda**, where Berlioz composed his *King Lear* overture.

AFTERNOON Hike up to **Cimiez** to pore over Henri Matisse's paintings, drawings, and sculptures in the **Musée Matisse**, the 17th-century villa in which the artist spent his last 34 years. Wander the nearby **Franciscan monastery** and its gardens, and on to the cemetery where Matisse and his fellow artist Raoul Dufy are buried.

EVENING Come sunset, walk or cycle the **Promenade des Anglais** along the cherubic **Bay of Angels**, past the swaying palms, pausing for a sundowner in the Relais bar of the flamboyant **Hotel Negresco**.

Essentials

GETTING THERE
Buses run from **Nice airport** to the central train station, with trains to Monaco, Cannes, Marseille, and Paris. Get around the city on **foot**, by **bus**, **taxi**, or free *vélo bleu* **bicycles**.

WHERE TO STAY
Villa la Tour (inexpensive) is a family-run gem in the heart of the old town. *www.villa-la-tour.com*
The Hotel Windsor (moderate) is full of contemporary art. *www.hotelwindsornice.com*
La Perouse (expensive) is a chic oasis looking over the Bay. *www.hotel-la-perouse.com*

TOURIST INFORMATION
5 Prom des Anglais; *www.nicetourisme.com*

Above In the old town, traditionally color-washed walls glow in the southern sunshine

Left The crescent-shaped city hugs the curve of the Baie des Anges – the Bay of Angels – backed by the soft contours of the Alpes-Maritimes

Above Today's chefs embellish the core niçoise ingredients with fresh herbs and blanched young vegetables such as green beans and baby leeks

Cooking Schools

Food writer and Cordon Bleu-trained cook Rosa Jackson runs **Les Petits Farcis** *(www.petitsfarcis.com)* from her restored 17th-century apartment in Nice's old town. Passionate about locally grown, organic food, Rosa dishes out cooking hints, recipes, and city tips during a class. Join her for a market tour, then learn to cook, then enjoy, a four-course niçoise lunch. Alternatively, stay in a farmhouse looking over the Côte d'Azur and learn to make tarts, tapenades, fragrant roast lamb, and other authentic Provençal goodies, or take a Nice food tour, with Tricia Robinson from **A Taste of Provence** *(www.tasteofprovence.com)*. Programs run Apr–Jun, Sep, and Oct.

The Best Places to Eat Salade Niçoise

Bistro d'Antoine moderate

The outside terrace sheltering beneath a cheery red awning and the snug upstairs dining room of Bistro d'Antoine are unfailingly loaded with patrons, so chef Armand Crespo is definitely doing something right. Since he and his wife took over the bistro a few years ago, it has rapidly gained a loyal following, with locals and Nice blow-ins seduced by its breezy ambience and uncompromisingly seasonal, and suave, menu. It's the kind of place you wish was in every French town. Scallop carpaccio with slivers of turnip, lightly fried calamari with mixed wild leaves, lentils with plump sausages, and gravadlax with shaved fennel fresh from the morning market showcase the chef's technique and imagination. The salade niçoise is another winner. Naturally, there are the tiny black niçoise olives, tuna, anchovies, and, at the height of summer, tomatoes that taste of the Mediterranean sun. Depending on the market, fine slices of sweet red onion or tiny violet artichoke might make a guest appearance on the plate. The wine list also draws applause.

27 rue de la Prefecture, Nice; open noon–2 PM & 7:15–10 PM Mon–Sat; +33 4 93 85 29 57

Also in Nice

Acchiardo *(+33 44 93 85 51 16; moderate)* on rue Droite is one of those homey family-run concerns that seem so perfectly in tune with old-town surrounds. From its elbow-to-elbow tables to the blackboard menu touting *"cuisine nissarde"* (that's "niçoise" in the local dialect), it's honest and unassuming. The Acchiardo salade niçoise has the obligatory tuna, tiny black olives, eggs, tomatoes, and anchovies, often with a surprise from the morning's market – maybe small red radishes or artichoke hearts.

Also in France

From April to October, **Plage 45** in the impeccably slick Grand Hotel at Cannes *(www.grand-hotel-cannes.com; expensive)* serves up salade niçoise with the works, all raw – not counting the hard-boiled eggs, tuna, and anchovies. That means cucumber, tomatoes, celery, red peppers, radishes, fava beans, black niçoise olives, and *cébette* (similar to leek but eaten raw), tossed with fresh basil.

Around the World

While French pastry great François Payard parades his favorite sweet treats at **François Payard Bakery** in New York's Soho *(www.fpbnyc.com; inexpensive)*, he also finds room for savories, including a snap-fresh salade niçoise. It's tweaked according to the season and dressed with a mustard vinaigrette, not olive oil, but tuna, hard-boiled eggs, plum tomatoes, and anchovies feature.

TREVISO ITALY

Luscious Tiramisu in the Veneto

The deliciously creamy coffee and chocolate taste of tiramisu puts it high on any list of sweet indulgences. Yet this rich and regal dessert had its origins not in a Renaissance court, but in a family-run restaurant in Italy's Veneto region, an often overlooked part of the country that delivers exquisite food, wine, and cultural experience in equal measures.

While many hurry through the Veneto on their way to Venice, few stop to sample the delights of this historic region. The relative lack of visitors only adds to the appeal of its small towns and cities, such as Verona, the setting for *Romeo and Juliet*, Vicenza, a UNESCO World Heritage site for its outstanding Palladian buildings, and Treviso, which makes a charming base for exploration.

Pretty and prosperous, Treviso has authentic Italian charm within its impressive city walls and gateways. Its porticoed main square, Piazza dei Signori, comes to life every evening when locals meet to exchange news and indulge in the ritual of apéritif-taking in the shade of an elegant medieval *palazzo* with a majestic external flight of stairs.

The peaceful heart of the old town is a maze of narrow alleyways crammed with tiny wine bars serving sparkling local Prosecco. As in Venice, albeit on a smaller scale, water is a big theme. Pretty shaded canals, lined with willow trees and parks, thread through the town – artificial offshoots of the Sile River that rises at a spring on the outskirts before flowing southeast through to the Venice lagoon. Despite its apparent charms, Treviso is no chocolate-box town; it has moved with the times, becoming one of Italy's leading fashion centers – labels such as Benetton and Sisley are based here – making it a great place to refresh your wardrobe.

Treviso's famous tiramisu is also a recent innovation. It was developed in the kitchens of the town's Ristorante Beccherie *(see facing page)* in 1962 from *sbatudin* – a pick-me-up for nursing mothers that comprised egg beaten with sugar accompanied by coffee and *savoiardi* – light-as-air sponge finger biscuits. With the addition of creamy mascarpone and powdered cocoa, the dish gradually evolved into the tiramisu we all know and love today, complementing the bountiful cuisine of the Trevigiano countryside.

The area's trademark *radicchio rosso* (red chicory) is also a constant on most restaurant menus, as a delicious wine-red salad, as pâté, or braised and canned. Fresh salad leaves are also served with the traditional *pasta e fagioli* (bean and pasta) soup, an effective twinning of bitter flavor and soft texture that makes for a classic lunch in the Veneto.

Above Grapes are grown for the Veneto's celebratory drink, Prosecco, in vineyards north of Treviso, where the gentle hills provide a perfect microclimate

Prosecco Wine

Grown in the Veneto, in the gentle sun-blessed hills around Treviso, Prosecco grapes are used to make the eponymous light white wine. The wine continues to ferment when bottled, producing tiny bubbles that give Prosecco its characteristic sparkle, giggling their way to the surface when the wine is poured. Unlike *spumante* dessert wines, Prosecco is invariably dry and has been dubbed "Italian champagne." It can be enjoyed on its own, to accompany a dessert, or mixed with fresh peach purée to make a refreshing Bellini cocktail. It is also widely found in the hugely popular Spritz apéritif consumed of an evening in every piazza of the Veneto. Here it is combined with a bright orange or red mixer – either Campari, Select, or Aperol – and soda, lemon, and a juicy fat green olive.

Three Days in the Veneto

Treviso itself is well worth exploring and is a fine base for trips to Venice and other towns of the Veneto, and for touring the gentle surrounding countryside.

DAY ONE Stroll through the heart of **Treviso** starting at the cobbled **Piazza dei Signori**, passing inviting delicatessens on Via Trevisi, to the **Pescheria**, the town's fish market in the middle of a canal. Adjacent is the atmospheric porticoed walkway, the **Buranelli**. Walk over to the other side of town for the **Cattedrale di San Nicolò** to admire its frescoes, which date back to 1352.

DAY TWO Drive northwest through cultivated countryside to the **Montello hills**, famous for their porcini mushrooms and vineyards around **Venegazzu**. Trattorias scattered through the woods and clearings serve the local specialties.

DAY THREE Take the train to **Venice** to wander the car-less streets, and treat yourself to a cappuccino at a canalside café. Don't miss the mornings-only fresh produce market at **Rialto**, close to the vast stone arch of the eponymous bridge. Afterward take a relaxing ride on a vaporetto along the **Grand Canal** to admire the magnificent line-up of *palazzos*.

Essentials

GETTING THERE

Treviso's **Canova Airport**, with flights to and from many European cities, is 3 miles (5 km) from the town; Venice's international **Marco Polo Airport** is 18 miles (30 km) away, and is well connected to Treviso by train and bus.

WHERE TO STAY

B&B Dolce Vita (inexpensive) provides cheery lodgings a short hop from downtown Treviso. *www.dolcevitatreviso.com*
Albergo Il Focolare (moderate) is good value in the heart of the town. *www.albergoilfocolare.net*
Relais Monaco (expensive) is a laid-back country villa with swimming pool and extensive parkland, a short drive out of town. *www.relaismonaco.it*

TOURIST INFORMATION

Via Sant'Andrea 3; +39 04 2254 7632

The Best Places to Eat Tiramisu

Ristorante Beccherie moderate

A gastronomic institution, this historic restaurant opened its elegant doors to diners in 1939 and the founder's grandson and his wife are continuing the tradition as ideal hosts. Unless you have some knowledge of the local dialect, you'd never guess that these lovely premises were a butcher shop back in the 1700s. Alfresco dining is delightful in summer when the tables spill out into the traffic-free square, whereas in winter they're moved back inside under dark timber beams. The service is both impeccable and friendly, with attention to details like warm plates and tasting portions of extra dishes. Tiramisu is just one dish that has made this restaurant so well known. Flat slices of the delicate dessert, its thin layers of mascarpone cream and sponge imbued with coffee and cocoa, are served year-round. The rest of the menu respects seasonal produce. Fall brings *faraona al forno* in *salsa péarada* – baked guinea fowl in a delicious sauce of liver and herbs. Flavorsome red radicchio stars in winter in delights such as a warming soup or crepes, then at warmer times of year there's *risi e bisi* – risotto with fresh peas.

Piazza Ancilotto, Treviso; open for lunch and dinner Tue–Sat, lunch only Sun; www.anticoristorantebeccherie.it

Also in Treviso

Run by a celebrated pastry chef, **Pasticceria Andrea Zanin** *(+39 04 2254 0437; moderate)* is a cake shop and café tucked down a narrow street near the main square. It is an ultra-modern haven for professionals and residents who pop in for a quick espresso and something sweet. Heavenly tiramisu is but one of the irresistible mini-portions lined up on the glass counter, a feast for the eyes as well as for the waistline.

Also in Italy

One of the oldest and most venerable cake shops in Venice, **Pasticceria Rizzardini** *(+39 04 1522 3835; moderate)* is a tiny standing-room-only establishment. It offers a tough choice: should you opt for an individual slice of luscious tiramisu, a freshly baked fruit tart, or a mini *beignet* with *zabaglione* with your cappuccino? The crunchy *croccantini* (peanut toffee) makes a perfect take-home gift.

Around the World

Run by a non-Italian brother and sister team, Sydney's **Alio** *(www.alio.com.au; expensive)* serves Italian-inspired food made with the freshest produce and immaculate attention to detail. The almost classic tiramisu is enhanced by the addition of Marsala wine to the fluffy mascarpone mixture, giving a more pungent flavor, while scrumptious albeit bitterish grated chocolate is the finishing touch.

Above Tiramisu – literally "pick-me-up" – is certainly an uplifting dish, with a kick of coffee and sometimes liqueur

Left Central Treviso is a maze of streets lined with arcaded walkways and dotted with tiny *osterias*

Right Aachen cathedral was built in AD 800 to symbolize the unification and political revival of the West; it is a UNESCO World Heritage site

Below The marinated beef of sauerbraten is served in a rich gravy, sometimes thickened with gingerbread

A Day in Aachen

Aachen's medieval Old Town is easily navigable on foot, but to explore its best museums and spa, you'll need to take a bus.

MORNING Head straight to Aachen's highlight, the **Dom**, which contains Charlemagne's remains in a gilded shrine and a treasury of extraordinary relics. Afterward, amble around the relaxed **Old Town**, visiting the **Rathaus**, whose facade is lined by the figures of 50 Holy Roman Emperors and whose top floor – the **Kaisersaal** (emperor hall) – has 19th-century frescoes and reproduction crown jewels.

AFTERNOON Take a 10-minute bus ride to the **Suermondt-Ludwig-Museum**, an art museum renowned for its stained glass collection and Old Masters such as Albrecht Dürer and Rembrandt. Or head around the corner to the **Ludwig Forum für Internationale Kunst**, a contemporary art museum in an elegant old Bauhaus-style factory.

EVENING Soak in the healing waters Charlemagne once enjoyed at the luxurious **Carolus Thermen** spa.

Essentials

GETTING THERE
Cologne/Bonn **airport** lies 45 miles (73 km) and 50 minutes by train from Aachen. High-speed **trains** connect Aachen to Brussels and Paris. There's a good **bus** service around the town.

WHERE TO STAY
Da Salvatore (inexpensive) has simple rooms above an Italian restaurant by the train station. *www.zimmer-in-aachen.de*
Drei Könige (moderate) is a boutique hotel with brightly colored rooms and apartments in a great central location. *www.h3k-aachen.de*
Pullman Aachen Quellenhof (expensive) is a grand old hotel with top facilities that backs onto the Carolus spa. *www.pullmanhotels.com*

TOURIST INFORMATION
www.aachen.de

AACHEN GERMANY

Gingery Sauerbraten in Aachen

Emperor Charlemagne's Frankish empire once covered most of modern-day Germany, France, and northern Italy. His capital was Aachen, on the border of Belgium and the Netherlands, which still has many impressive reminders of his rule, not least of which is an unusual dish he invented: sauerbraten. This slow-cooked, sour-sweet stew is commonly regarded as Germany's national dish.

Historical accounts suggest that the Emperor Charlemagne was a foodie. He loved Roquefort cheese, introduced peacocks as a dish at court, and made efforts to improve people's diets throughout his lands. He obviously liked the good life, because his main reason for choosing Aachen as his capital was its natural hot springs; relaxing in them was a favorite imperial pastime and they remain a major draw for visitors today.

Charlemagne was also a devout Christian, and his wonderful palace chapel, now incorporated into Aachen's Dom (cathedral), has been a destination for pilgrims for hundreds of years. The structure remains a highlight of any visit to the town today, thanks to the sense of history and devotion that seems fused into its brickwork and magnificent stained-glass windows.

Aachen's attractive Old Town is lovely to explore on foot. At its heart lies an expansive market square, encircled by some of the city's finest medieval houses and the 14th-century Rathaus (town hall), where around 30 of the Holy Roman Emperors that followed Charlemagne feasted after their coronations.

Much of this feasting almost certainly involved sauerbraten, the local delicacy. The dish is said to have been Charlemagne's clever idea for leftovers, and although it takes a long time to prepare, its practical and versatile nature has made it an enduring German favorite. The name means "sour roast" and much of its flavor comes from its marinade; the meat is marinated in strong vinegar for three days prior to its hours of roasting. This helps tenderize the meat – traditionally horsemeat, but today most often beef. The marinade also contains other ingredients, and it is these that bestow a uniquely delicious flavor on the dish. Marinades vary from region to region, and even between restaurants, but the key ingredients – wine, cloves, bay leaves, and juniper berries – are always part of the mix. The meat is then browned and put back into the marinade to cook for several hours before the sauce is thickened, often with ground gingerbread to give it a real zing. Eaten with noodles or potato dumplings, it's a food fit for emperors.

The Best Places to Eat Sauerbraten

Sauerbraten-Palast inexpensive

The priorities of this restaurant are obvious from its name, which translates as the "palace of sauerbraten." Certainly the quality of its sauerbraten would be fit for Charlemagne, though he might not appreciate rubbing shoulders with the complete cross-section of society that has made this restaurant a local institution for more than 20 years. The rather workaday, wood-clad pub interior is hardly a palace, although antiques and old prints of pre-war Aachen provide an atmospheric early 20th-century feel and time-honored authenticity. The unpretentious atmosphere rightly keeps the sauerbraten at center stage, and it is served here in giant portions, its meat so tender that it feels almost buttery in the mouth. Yet the real secret of the dish's success here is the sweet-and-sour gravy that uses the excellent local *Printen* form of gingerbread as an ingredient. The accompaniments – sweet-sour red cabbage and thick-cut Benelux-style fries – are also delicious. The only drawback is that improbably low prices ensure a popularity that frequently translates into a wait at the bar, as reservations are not accepted.

Vaalser Strasse 316, Aachen; open noon–3 PM & 5–11 PM Thu–Tue (closing at 10 PM Sat and Sun); +49 241 837 73

Also in Germany

Most traditional pubs and restaurants in Germany have sauerbraten on the menu, so there's often somewhere good for the dish, yet in Aachen nowhere comes close to the Sauerbraten-Palast. So if you're in Aachen and want to try it elsewhere, hop on a train for the short journey to Cologne, where the **Brauhaus Ohne Namen** *(+49 221 81 26 80; moderate)* on Mathildenstrasse has a region-wide reputation for the dish. Here it's served with dumplings, apple compote, and the fine local beer, Kölsch. It's rare to find sauerbraten on the menus of finer restaurants, so it's a welcome specialty of **Lutter & Wegner** *(www.l-w-berlin.de; expensive)* in Berlin, which has won national gastronomic awards for a dish that it has served in elegant surroundings since 1881.

Around the World

Outside Germany it's common to find good sauerbraten wherever Germans have settled. This particularly includes the American Midwest, where **Karl Ratzsch** *(www. karlratzsch.com; expensive)* does a superb rendition of Aachen-style sauerbraten in Milwaukee using a ginger-snap gravy. In South Africa, in the former German colony of Namibia, one of several places with good sauerbraten is the **Swakopmund Brauhaus** *(www. swakopmund brauhaus.com; moderate)*, a jolly German beer hall in an unusual setting.

Aachen's Christmas Market

As a city with an impressive history and a love of tradition, it's not surprising that Aachen has one of Germany's most atmospheric and popular Christmas markets, which attracts some 1.8 million visitors every year. Aachen's large medieval square provides the perfect backdrop for carousels, Nativity scenes, and a myriad stands selling traditional handicrafts. But the serious temptation lies in the seductive foods on sale. Roasted chestnuts and sausages sizzle on charcoal grills, their aromas mingling deliciously with the scent of waffles, potato cakes, and warming *Glühwein* (mulled wine). The Christmas cakes and cookies, including the favorite, *Printen* – a crunchy spiced gingerbread-style cookie – make ideal Christmas gifts.

Left Aachen was the principal coronation site of the Holy Roman Emperors

MOSCOW RUSSIA

Russia's Superpowered Soup

Moscow is a city where fusion isn't just a style of cuisine, but the leitmotif of local gastronomy. Even fast-food chains sell a range of sushi, Thai, Chinese, and Italian dishes to tempt Muscovites. This "mix and match" approach might seem new, but it goes back centuries – as does the Russian love of soup – and the two combine in *solyanka*, a soup that can feature almost anything.

Conspicuous consumption is the credo of this city, which revolves around power and money, and sees excess as a virtue. The global recession may have halted the construction of the world's tallest skyscraper, but menus still feature dubious exotica such as endangered species smuggled out of African war zones. From historic Red Square to the fashionable malls of the Garden Ring road, this febrile city has re-created and reimagined itself to become "the new New York." Radiating in concentric circles from its medieval hilltop citadel, or Kremlin, Moscow exemplifies the best and worst of Russia. Its beauty and ugliness are inseparable, its sentimentality the obverse of a brutality rooted in centuries of despotism and fear of anarchy. Private and cultural life is as passionate as business and politics are cynical.

Eating well has always been not only an affirmation of success but also a way of fortifying oneself for the hardships that may befall even the richest. As illustrated by the fate of Bolshevik leaders in Stalin's day, even the greatest can end up in Siberia – so it's important to enjoy life while you can. Traditionally, the main meal of the day has been *obyed* (lunch), with supper limited to leftover *zakuski* – Russian hors d'oeuvres *(see p75)*. Even today, when slimmed-down business lunches are widely available, many Muscovites expect to eat a hearty four-course lunch of *zakuski*, soup, a main dish, and a dessert, washed down with beer or vodka.

Soup has always been the mainstay of Russian cuisine; spoons appeared on Russian tables 400 years before forks did. Peasants subsisted on cabbage soup and buckwheat porridge, with flavorings limited to sour cream, garlic, honey, vinegar, dill, and a few other fresh herbs. These tastes – salty, sweet, sour, and pickled – remained the norm even among the nobility until Peter the Great introduced French chefs to his court. *Solyanka* is a rich jumble of a soup that combines indigenous with foreign ingredients. Its name derives from the Russian word for salt *(sol)*, but it also means "mixed" due to the wide variety of possible ingredients. The soup is prepared by cooking salted cucumbers, before adding the main ingredient: meat, mushrooms, or fish. The core ingredient dictates what else goes in, from allspice and dill to cabbage and breadcrumbs. Like a Dostoevskian fictional hero, cast aside any doubts and throw yourself wholeheartedly into the dish and into Moscow itself – you're sure to leave poorer but wiser.

A Day in Moscow

Be sure to travel between sights on Moscow's metro, deservedly famous for the lavish decor of its stations. Ploshchad Revolyutsii, Komsomolskaya, Park Kultury, and Mayakovskaya are among the best examples of the grandiose, High Stalinist style.

MORNING Visit **Red Square**, whose iconic **St. Basil's Cathedral** and **Lenin Mausoleum** symbolize Russia's tumultuous past, as does the **Kremlin**. See the crown jewels in the **Armory Museum**, the colossal **Czar Cannon**, and the world's largest bell before lunch at the nearby Shield and Sword restaurant *(see facing page)*.

AFTERNOON Take a cruise on the **Moskva River**, past the fairy-tale **Cathedral of Christ the Savior** and the 300-ft- (91-m-) high **Monument to Peter the Great**, bestriding a galleon. Disembark at the **Novodevichy Convent** to visit the cemetery where Gogol, Shostakovich, and other luminaries are buried beneath quirky effigies.

EVENING See what's happening on the scene at **Garage**, a wonderful Constructivist bus depot turned art space, like the Tate Modern's Turbine Hall in London.

Essentials

GETTING THERE
Domodedovo International **airport** is 22 miles (34 km) from the center of the city; there are regular Aeroexpress **trains** to the downtown.

WHERE TO STAY
Alfa (inexpensive) is a 3-star giant 20 minutes from downtown. *www.hotelizmailovo-alfa.ru/eng*
Akvarel (moderate) is very central, located off chic Tverskaya Ulitsa. *www.hotelakvarel.ru*
Savoy (expensive) is a historic 4-star hotel with an Art Nouveau restaurant and a sauna, extensively restored in 2005. *www.savoy.ru*

FURTHER INFORMATION
www.visitrussia.com; www.moscowcity.com

Above *Solyanka* is a rich mix of vegetables and meat or fish, enriched with a dash of sour cream

Left Legend has it that St. Basil's Cathedral, completed in 1561, was so beautiful that Ivan the Terrible ordered the architect to be killed, so he could not build its equal elsewhere

Above *Worker and Collective Farmer* (1937) is an iconic Soviet-era sculpture that is now located at an entrance to the All-Russian Exhibition Center

Russian Vodka

"Drinking is the joy of the Russians. We cannot live without it." So said the 10th-century Prince Vladimir, rejecting Islam as the state religion in favor of Christianity, which allowed the drinking of vodka. Over a millennium later, vodka remains central to Russian life – as much a curse as a joy, being the prime cause of falling life expectancy in Russian men. Russians seldom go for mixers, but never drink vodka without eating (if only bread). Vodka may be infused with lemon (*limonnaya*), hot peppers (*pertsovka*), bison-grass (*zubrovka*), juniper berries, cloves (*okhotnitchaya*), or other flavorings. Russians adore elaborate toasts, but you can get by with "*Za zdrovyie!*" ("To health!").

The Best Places to Eat Solyanka

Café Pushkin expensive

Named after the Romantic poet, whose ill-starred wedding occurred in the vicinity, this establishment would have delighted him. People gape as they enter the building, a former pharmacy with huge windows and rich, Biedermeier-style fittings; its upper floors formed part of an aristocrat's home in the 1820s. The apothecary prepared drugs in the cellar, which is now furnished like a mad scientist's laboratory, with Bunsen burners, a Morse telegraph, and other retro gadgetry. The first floor is grander, with a sumptuously paneled library of rare editions and a ballroom built for an ancestor of the composer Rimsky-Korsakov, which now serves as the VIP dining room. During the summer, there's also a rooftop terrace café. Each floor has a different menu – though all feature a rich meat *solyanka* that leaves just enough room for a main course. You can choose between medieval specialties such as baked sterlet (a small sturgeon) in caviar sauce or pike head stuffed with fish and apple *confit*, or Frenchified dishes such as crab salad with quail eggs and basil-and-raspberry mayonnaise. As befits the clientele of oligarchs, movie stars, and politicians, the wine list is princely.

Tverskoy bulvar 26A, Moscow; open 24 hours daily; www.cafe-pushkin.ru/en

Also in Moscow

Solyanka can be found in the humblest cafés, but visitors to Moscow usually prefer somewhere with a touch of style or sheer oddity. **Shield and Sword** (*+7 495 222 4446; inexpensive)* is a KGB-themed place whose dining room contains a replica of the statue of "Iron Felix" Dzerzhinsky that once stood outside the Lubyanka headquarters of the secret police, which he founded. Its Soviet-style menu includes *solyanka*, *pelmeni* (Russian ravioli), and chicken Kiev. Many dishes come with a shot of vodka. Alternatively, check out **Solyanka** (*http://s-11.ru/english; moderate)*, a hip restaurant, bar, club, and boutique, named after the street on which it stands (which once led to the Royal Salt Yard) rather than the dish (which only features on its lunchtime menu on Wednesdays). Solyanka offers plenty of alternatives to Russian food, from *tom yam* soup and chicken curry to Mediterranean salads and pasta dishes. There are lines outside on weekends, when DJs play hip-hop until 6:00 AM.

Also in Russia

In St. Petersburg, you can enjoy *solyanka* at the **Café Sunduk** (*www.cafesunduk.ru; inexpensive)*, a funky art-café that has live Spanish, blues, or jazz music.

Right The "old town" quarter of Patershol offers some of the best options for eating and drinking in Ghent

Below Creamy-white *waterzooi* fish stew includes delicate spices traded in Ghent since the Middle Ages

A Day in Ghent

All the main sights are within easy walking distance of the historic downtown, but the main art museums are in the Citadelpark in the south of the city, a tram-ride away.

MORNING Start with **St-Baafskathedraal** and a pilgrimage to Jan van Eyck's glorious painting, *The Adoration of the Mystic Lamb*. A short walk past the **Belfort** (belfry) and Gothic **St-Niklaaskerk** will lead you to the **Graslei** and **Korenlei**, where medieval and Renaissance guildhouses line the old river port. The **Groot Vleeshuis**, a medieval butcher's hall, showcases regional food specialties.

AFTERNOON Head for the cutting-edge museum of contemporary art, **SMAK**, or the nearby **Museum voor Schone Kunsten**, which has an impressive collection of pre-20th-century art.

EVENING For tickets at the **Vlaamse Opera** in the evening, you have to book well in advance; if this is impossible, head back to the old downtown for a stroll in **Patershol** district and a supper of *waterzooi*.

Essentials

GETTING THERE
The nearest **international airport** is Brussels (Zaventem), 37 miles (60 km) away. Ghent's main **train** station, Sint-Pieters, is near the Citadelpark, a tram-ride from downtown. The city has an excellent **tram** and **bus** network.

WHERE TO STAY
Flandria (inexpensive) is a small, family-oriented central hotel. *www.hotelflandria-gent.be*
Erasmus (moderate) is a delightful small hotel in a 16th-century house filled with antiques. *www.erasmushotel.be*
NH Gent Belfort (expensive) offers elegant, international-style comfort downtown. *www.nh-hotels.com*

TOURIST INFORMATION
www.visitgent.be

Waterzooi in Ghent

On a clear winter day, the tips of the medieval spires and gables of Ghent glint under the sun's low rays and the gilded skyline is freeze-framed in the mirror-still waters of the canals and rivers. Shoppers bustle among the busy streets and market squares, pausing at lunchtime for a warming dish of *waterzooi*, a creamy white stew that's Belgium's comfort food *par excellence*.

The Leie River forms a picturesque mini-port at the heart of medieval Ghent, surrounded by grand buildings that demonstrate the city's historic importance as a center of crafts and manufacturing. The soaring town belfry, muscular Gravensteen Castle, and grave Gothic churches give way at the riverside to the imposing guildhouses, magnificent examples of Renaissance architecture. Tucked away in the 14th-century St-Baafskathedraal lies one of the great masterpieces of northern European art – *The Adoration of the Mystic Lamb*, a huge, multi-paneled altarpiece painted in around 1432 by Jan van Eyck and his brother Hubrecht.

But Ghent also has a newer face. It was the first Belgian city to industrialize, initially around the textile trade. The beguiling Patershol district was the old weavers' quarter, but once industrialization got under way, Ghent began to acquire the grander adornments of a successful European city, with theaters, a fine opera house, and a respected university.

River links to the North Sea made Ghent into a prosperous trading city during the Middle Ages and the Renaissance, and the ingredients of its signature dish, *waterzooi*, reflect this history. This creamy stew uses the produce of the surrounding rural landscape, but its spices and wine were classic trading goods of the Middle Ages. Pieces of fish or chicken are poached gently in a cream-laden broth flavored with julienned leeks, shallots, carrots, celery, and white wine, and scented with parsley, saffron, pepper, and bay leaves. *Waterzooi* was originally cooked with river fish, but today it is usually made with fish from the North Sea, such as cod, turbot, monkfish, halibut, scallops, or shrimp.

Waterzooi is essentially simple and unpretentious; the name itself brings together the word "water" and a derivative of *kooksel*, "something cooked." But quality ingredients and the deft skills of the cook can also bring to it a smooth elegance. Said to have been the favorite dish of Charles V, the Holy Roman Emperor born here in 1500, it is – like the city itself – both down-to-earth and sophisticated; a heartwarming dish that has long been a favorite of peasants and kings.

What to Drink

Belgium is famous for the quality of its beer, with dozens of small, traditional breweries, numerous brands and labels, and a huge range of flavors and alcoholic strengths. The most celebrated beers are made by five Trappist monasteries, including Chimay and Westmalle. One good place to sample the range is the pub called **Dulle Griet** *(www.dullegriet.be)*, which is packed with character and beer memorabilia, and serves over 250 kinds of Belgian beer. Less well-known is Belgian *jenever*, a traditional and well-crafted form of gin, drunk straight or in its many flavored versions – lemon, apple, vanilla, hazelnut, and more. Try this at **'t Dreupelkot** *(www.dreupelkot. be)*, a cherished institution that offers 200 different flavors.

The Best Places to Eat Waterzooi

Bij den Wijzen en den Zot
moderate

Waterzooi is treasured as a home-cooked dish, often made to grandmother's cherished recipe, so it is not easy to find in restaurants, even in Ghent. You have to seek out the kind of welcoming, unpretentious restaurants that take pride in specializing in traditional Flemish dishes, such as Bij den Wijzen en den Zot. As suggested by its curious name – "At the House of the Wise Man and the Fool" – this is a restaurant full of character. It is set in the folksy Patershol area and occupies a beautiful 16th-century, step-gabled building that was formerly the guildhouse of the leatherworkers. The food is traditional Flemish cuisine, with dishes such as *gentse stoverij* (Ghent beef stew) made with Westmalle beer. They serve an award-winning *waterzooi* here, embellished with other seafood such as mussels and Dublin Bay prawns.

Hertogstraat 42, Ghent; open noon–1:30 PM and 6:30–9:30 PM Tue–Sat; www.bijdenwijzenendenzot.be

Also in Ghent

Two other restaurants in Ghent regularly have *waterzooi* on the menu. **'t Klokhuys** *(www. klokhuys.com; inexpensive)*, also in the Patershol district, is a charming, brasserie-style restaurant with wooden tables set out beneath exposed beams. **Brasserie 't Stropke** *(www. brasserietstropke.be; inexpensive)*, lying close to the Gravensteen Castle, is in a similar mold.

Also in Belgium

To find *waterzooi* elsewhere in Belgium, you need to look for restaurants that are not ashamed of presenting "home-cooked" dishes. In Brussels, **Aux Armes de Bruxelles** *(www.auxarmesdebruxelles.be; expensive)* is unusual for being a first-class, traditional Belgian restaurant in the Rue des Bouchers, where most restaurants are touristy and to be avoided. In Bruges, try the **Gran Kaffee de Passage** *(www.passagebruges.com; inexpensive)*, a wonderfully atmospheric, candlelit restaurant that serves well-priced traditional Belgian dishes.

Around the World

The **Belga Café** *(www.belgacafe.com; moderate)* in Washington, DC, prides itself on its authentic Belgian flavors and atmosphere. In New York, **Waterzooi Belgian Bistro** *(www. waterzooi.com; moderate)* enriches its signature dish with lobster, mussels, and clams. It's a similar seafood bonanza at the **Leuven Belgian Beer Café** *(www.leuven.co.nz; moderate)* in Wellington, New Zealand.

SAVOIE

SAVOIE FRANCE

Say Cheese in the French Alps

The French Alps are renowned for valleys sprinkled with story-book chalets, chic ski resorts, and impossibly pretty scenery. They are also famous for their food: sturdy stews and soups, *diots* (little sausages), mushrooms and game from the forests, and dairy produce from the rich alpine pasture: the Haute Savoie alone has more than 30 different varieties of cheese.

The snowy summits and ice-dipped peaks of the French Alps have long lured skiers chasing powder thrills and downhill speed, nourished in their conquest of the slopes by honest, robust French mountain food.

The Savoie, vestige of a kingdom that ruled this corner of Europe for eight centuries, sits at the heart of the French Alps. Divided into Savoie and Haute Savoie, it is home to many of France's most stylish ski resorts – Chamonix, Courchevel, and Val d'Isère – and some of its finest cheeses. These came long before the folks in chunky boots and salopettes. The first skis – simple wooden planks – made their debut in 1878, while local farmers were making cheese in the Middle Ages.

Thus, cheese has always been a mountain staple. Reblochon de Savoie, Abondance, and Beaufort are acclaimed local cheese celebs, while the region's most legendary dish is the dippy *fondue Savoyarde* (Beaufort cheese melted with local dry white wine and Kirsch).

Cheese is intrinsically linked to the gloriously scenic landscape. Beaufort, named after the pretty Beaufontain region, trumpets the flavors of the Savoie. In summer, the Tarentaise cows graze on alpine grasses high up on the mountains around the town of Beaufort, infusing the cheese with flowery-herb flavors. In winter, they remain in the barns on a diet of hay. Thus, the color and aroma of the poetically named Beaufort d'Alpage (literally "Beaufort from the high mountain pasture") is completely different from the ghostly winter Beaufort.

The region's next most famous *fromage* is the delicate-tasting Reblochon, from the eastern slopes of the Haute-Savoie; almost two-thirds is produced in the magical Aravis Massif, a stone's throw from Lake Geneva. In winter, the snow-covered slopes around the villages of La Clusaz and Le Grand-Bornand are the domain of skiers, but come spring, the dairy godmothers trot out to reclaim the grassy slopes. Again, the local diet bestows a unique taste to the cheese.

Lake Annecy, with its lofty backdrop and blue, blue water – dubbed "the purest in all of Europe" – is proof that lakes and mountains are inspiring cohorts. At its northern tip, the town of Annecy itself, former seat of the Comtes de Genève, makes a good base for exploring the country roads and *fromageries* of the Haute-Savoie. A trip to Chamonix will give skiers and mountain-climbers the wide open slopes they crave: this was, after all, the birthplace of mountaineering, as well as the site of the first Winter Olympics, in 1924.

Three Days in the French Alps

Annecy makes an excellent base: its public transportation links around the region are good, but taxis are also plentiful and car rental is available.

DAY ONE Explore Annecy's **medieval quarter** with its atmospheric canals and arcades. Visit the turreted **Château d'Annecy** to see traditional arts and crafts. In fine weather, opt for a three-hour guided bicycle tour of the town. Bird-fanciers can explore the **Sentier de découvertes des Roselières** around the lake to spy water fowl.

DAY TWO Visit a traditional **fromagerie** *(see overleaf)* to see how cheese is made. Farms around the village of **Grand-Bornand** make Reblochon, and **Beaufort** is charming. In summer, listen out for the clang of cowbells on the mountains.

DAY THREE Head for **Chamonix** and take a cable car up to **Aguille du Midi**, 12,300 ft (3,842 m) high, for sweeping views. Take a train up to France's longest glacier, the 4.3-mile (7-km) **Mer de Glace** (Sea of Ice). Spoon down *tartiflette* – potato, bacon, onion, and cream topped with melted cheese – at **La Bergerie** to ward off the chills.

Essentials

GETTING THERE
Trains run frequently from Lyon and Paris to Annecy. **Buses** serve the closest major airport, Geneva, with daily flights also from Paris to Annecy's **Meythet airport**.

WHERE TO STAY
Hôtel Les Cimes (inexpensive) in Annecy has a warm, chalet feel. www.hotel-les-cimes.com
Hameau Albert 1er (moderate) offers old-style comfort in Annecy. www.hameaualbert.fr
Auberge du Père Bise (expensive) has views over glorious Lake Annecy. www.perebise.com

FURTHER INFORMATION
www.lac-annecy.com; www.chamonix.com

Above Reblochon is a key ingredient in fondues and in the local dish *tartiflette*, a comforting baked potato and cheese concoction

Left The unmistakable peak of Mont Blanc, highest mountain in western Europe, rises up behind the train station in Chamonix

Below Moving at an imperceptible pace, the mighty Mer de Glace ("Sea of Ice") glacier travels down the valley it has carved in the rock

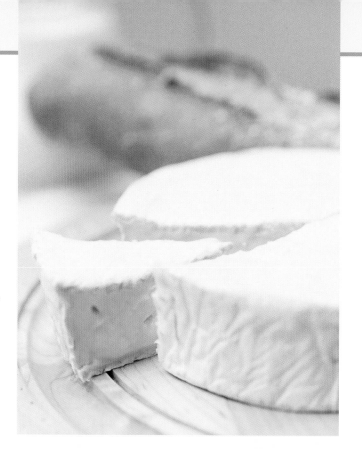

Cheese Around the World

While milk might taste the same throughout the world, cheese is the consummate individual. Climate, history, tradition, landscape, the eating habits and the breed of the animal, and the dexterity of the cheesemaker all help ensure that the slice is right, from the lofty French Alps to the flatlands of Holland and the heart-shaped island of Tasmania.

THE FRENCH ALPS

Coopérative Laitière de Haut Tarentaise

www.fromagebeaufort.com

The Dairy Cooperative of the High Tarentaise has shops in Bourg St-Maurice, Val d'Isère, Les Arcs, La Rosière, and Tignes selling Beaufort cheese, dubbed "the prince of Gruyères." A hard, cooked cheese, it is pressed into beechwood molds to shape it, then drained, turned, and rubbed with salt daily, and aged for six months.

La Laiterie des Halles

2 place de Genève, Chambéry; www.fromager-denis-provent.com

Denis Provent, who runs La Laiterie des Halles, is a master of Savoie cheeses; his family has been in the *fromage* business for three generations. His shop in Chambéry brims with Savoie cheeses, including Reblochon Fermier, Abondance, Beaufort, Tome de Bauges (semi-soft cow cheese), Tomette de Brebis de Savoie (sheep cheese), and Tarentais (farmhouse goat cheese). Provent ages many of the cheeses in his own cellars. He has a second cheese "boutique," Les Délices Savoyardes, on rue de Genève in Aix-les-Bains.

Le Grand-Bornand

www.legrandbornand.com

Farms in and around this pretty winter-sports village near Annecy welcome visitors during the summer months to see Reblochon Fermier (farmhouse Reblochon) cheese being made, from the milking of the cows to a tasting of the final creamy product. Le Grand-Bornand, with some 55 farms in operation, boasts as many cows (2,000) as people! Le Grand-Bornand Tourist Office organizes tours.

NORMANDY, FRANCE

The land of cows, apple trees, and thatched roofs produces one of France's most famous cheeses – the fruity Camembert – as well as Pont l'Evêque, Livarot, and Brillat-Savarin.

La Foire aux Fromages de Livarot

A festival featuring all the finest local cheeses is held in Livarot, in the heart of Camembert country, every August. Brave souls can attempt to win the title of fastest Livarot cheese-eater; the current record is 26 oz (750 g) in 1 minute 51 seconds.

La Fromagerie François Olivier

40 rue de l'Hôpital, Rouen; http://fromagerieolivier.free.fr

Possibly the best cheese shop in France, with a huge choice of French and Normandy cheeses, including exquisite artisan-made Camembert.

La Route du Fromage

Livarot; www.paysdelivarot.fr

A selection of farms in the picturesque Pays d'Auge region – which includes big-cheese villages such as Livarot, Pont l'Evêque, and Camembert – offer tastings as well as cheese for sale. Pick up a map of the touring route at a local tourist office.

FRANCHE-COMTE, FRANCE

This unspoiled region on the eastern edge of France produces tangy, traditionally made Comté, the country's biggest-selling hard cheese. Other popular local picks for the cheese board include Mont d'Or and Morbier.

Fromagerie Marcel Petite

22 rue Bernard Palissy, Granges Narboz; www.comte-petite.com

Here you can see how impressive 65,000 wheels of Comté look stored in a converted fort, and follow up the adventure with a tasting in these atmospheric surroundings.

La Fromagerie du Mont d'Or

2 rue du Moulin, Métabief; +33 3 81 490 236

A cheese shop specializing in the rich, runny Mont d'Or cheese, a French Christmas favorite that is only available from September to March. Morbier cheese is also offered. The fromagerie uses the milk from 13 regional producers.

Left (top to bottom) Silky Camembert, one of the world's most-copied cheeses; dairy cows in Normandy, France; turning Comté in Fort Saint Antoine cellars, home of Fromagerie Marcel Petite

Below (top to bottom) Traditionally dressed cheese porters load up at the Alkmaar cheese market in the Netherlands; artisanal cheeses on display on an Italian market stand

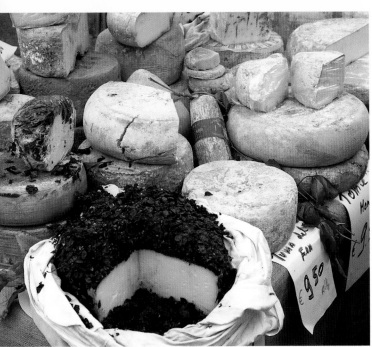

Les Routes du Comté
www.lesroutesducomte.com

Follow suggested itineraries or tailor your own driving tour along this route, and let local farmers demonstrate the care with which Comté is made and how good it is. Dairyman Jean François Marmier runs a herd of Montbeliarde cows, the ones most closely aligned with Comté, which visitors can help milk or feed for a more hands-on Alpine experience.

LOMBARDY, ITALY

Plump with natural beauty – rivers, lakes, mountains – as well as cities brimming with art and history, the kingdom of Lombardy is also rich in *formaggio*, with big hitters such as Gorgonzola, Grana Padano, and Taleggio.

Formaggi Galli
Piazza Wagner, Milan

Marco Galli's stand in Milan's huge Piazza Wagner food market specializes in Lombardy cheeses. Slow Food supporter Galli is known for sourcing exceptional Gorgonzola, some aged to mind-blowing maturity.

La Baita del Formaggio
Via Italia 42, Milan; www.labaitadelformaggio.it

This traditional cheese shop offers up a host of artisanal Italian cheeses. The Lariano Speziato, a soft cheese from the mountains surrounding Lake Como, is exclusive to the shop.

Rossi y Grassi
Via Ponte Vetero 4, Milan; www.rg.mi.it

In the classy Brera district, this top-quality gourmet food shop displays a tempting selection of Italian cheeses, including fruity Grana Padano and soft Taleggio, plus wines from Italy's greatest producers. There is another branch close by on Via Solferino.

THE NETHERLANDS

The Dutch have been making cheese since at least the 4th century, with Gouda and Edam now global favorites. Both towns are within easy striking distance of Amsterdam. Don't miss the legendary cheese carriers at the weekly summer markets.

Abraham Kef
Marnixstraat 192, Amsterdam; www.abrahamkef.nl

A little piece of France in central Amsterdam, this shop specializes in French as well as Dutch cheeses. Their philosophy is that good cheese is inseparable from good wine, and you can enjoy both in the shop's small dining area.

De Kaaskamer
Runstraat 7, Amsterdam; http://kaaskamer.nl

In the newly fashionable "Nine Streets" shopping area, this shop, with its floor-to-ceiling selection of cheeses – including organic Dutch offerings – is sure to keep cheese fans both happy and busy.

Kaashuis Tromp
Utrechtsestraat 90, Amsterdam; www.kaashuistromp.nl

Henk van Kol's "House of Cheese" has expanded into a small universe, with another three branches in Amsterdam and 10 more throughout the Netherlands. The flagship store, noted for its friendly service, is packed with Dutch cheeses of all kinds, including many from small-scale producers, along with 250 foreign cheeses.

TASMANIA, AUSTRALIA

With its pristine environment, clean, clear waters, lush green pastures, and fertile soil, Tasmania is home to many boutique dairy farms and artisan cheesemakers turning out creamy brie styles, full-bodied cheddar, and artisanal cow and goat cheeses.

Bruny Island Cheese Company
1807 Main Road, Great Bay, Bruny Island; www.brunyislandcheese.com.au

On this small island off Tasmania, famed for its fairy penguins and other wildlife, Nick Haddow churns out handmade cow, sheep, and goat cheeses, ranging from "Barney," a blue cheese, and the mild, Gruyère-like "C2" to specialties such as prosciutto-wrapped and olive oil-marinated cheeses. See and taste the cheeses being made, and don't miss their home-baked bread and homemade ice cream too.

King Island Diary
Currie, King Island; www.kidairy.com.au

Situated on another tranquil little island, Australia's best-known specialty cheese and dairy producer makes a range of creamy bries, pungent blues, and sharp aged cheddars, and has a tasting room in which they can be discovered.

Pyengana Cheese Factory
St. Columba Falls Road, Pyengana; +61 3 6373 6157

Australia's oldest cheddar is made following a method developed in the local cooperative in the 1890s by cheesemaker Jon Healey's grandfather. There are dairy and cheese factory tours by appointment, plus cheese sales in The Factory Shop.

Right Gaudí worked on the still-unfinished La Sagrada Familia for more than 40 years, famously declaring that "my client is not in a hurry"

BARCELONA SPAIN

Zarzuela in Stylish Barcelona

The cuisine of Barcelona can be as phantasmagorical as its architecture by Gaudí and his fellow Modernistas. Just as La Sagrada Familia makes the viewer wonder how the architect could possibly pile on so many ornamental encrustations, Barcelona's signature fish stew, zarzuela, makes the diner wonder if there is no end to the seafood delicacies hidden in a single bowl.

It seems perfectly natural that Barcelona, a city graced with free-flowing, fanciful architecture and a lively street life, would have developed a fish stew as studded with textures, shapes, colors, and flavors as the *zarzuela de mariscos a la catalana*. How this Catalonian cousin of Marseille's bouillabaisse (*see pp128–9*) and Provençal *soupe aux poissons* got its name is something of a mystery, but "zarzuela" is also a form of Spanish light opera that includes rustic dances, spoken dialogue, and songs. It is perhaps the similarly surprising and delightful mixture that has earned this fish stew – a veritable seafood operetta – the same name.

Spruced up for the 1992 Olympics, Barcelona nonetheless retains its character as a colorful beachfront town first settled by fishermen in 1754. The formerly disreputable shoreline district of working wharves and sailors' enticements is now an area of flourishing seafood restaurants, where Barcelonans and visitors alike go to promenade alongside a sandy beach that flows from the Olympic sports harbor to the Old Port. Here, the statue of the explorer Columbus marks the foot of the city's most famous pedestrian boulevard, La Rambla.

Barcelona springs to life along the broad, car-free expanse of La Rambla, with flower vendors, living statues, bird-sellers, newspaper kiosks, and cafés as still points in the flowing human river. Side streets branch off into the Barri Gòtic (Gothic quarter), where folk-dancers step through the *sardana* every Sunday in front of the cathedral. At the head of La Rambla, the 19th-century district of L'Eixample contains much of the city's famous Modernista architecture, including two buildings by Gaudí that are now World Heritage sites: the undulating, organic Casa Mila ("La Pedrera") and his most famous building, the uncompleted cathedral of the Holy Family – La Sagrada Familia.

No place looks like Barcelona, and likewise Barcelona's zarzuela stands apart from other fish stews. The easy-going Catalans improvise endlessly, and cooks can add any firm fish to the garlicky broth tinged sunset-golden with saffron, as long as they also include bright shrimp, earthy small clams, pink mussels in their blue shells, a king prawn, and half a lobster. This rich dish is served in wide, shallow bowls so diners can admire the jumble of colors, inhale the rising aromas, and sop up the ocean-salty broth with garlic-rubbed toast. Like Barcelona itself, zarzuela is a feast for all the senses.

Above The Plaça Reial, a large square in the Barri Gòtic, provides an atmospheric setting for its many renowned restaurants, cafés, and bars

Below The distinctive, saffron-rich fish stew called zarzuela is a riot of warm color, as red pepper curls among the gently poached pink and white seafood

A Day in Barcelona

As the capital of Catalan culture – neither precisely Spanish nor French – Barcelona is a city of rich artistic ferment. Joan Miró was born here, Pablo Picasso spent his formative years here, and Antoní Gaudí became the city's most famous architect, bequeathing it the iconic Sagrada Familia and a range of other Modernista masterpieces.

MORNING See a masterpiece nearing completion as the morning light strikes the spires of **La Sagrada Familia**. Then visit **Casa Mila**, Gaudí's finished crowning glory.

AFTERNOON Stroll through the circus-like scene of **La Rambla**, veering into the quieter **Barri Gòtic** to visit the **Museu Picasso**, repository of the artist's earliest works. Take the cable car up to **Montjuïc**, where the organic building designed by architect Josep Lluís Sert showcases the surrealism of Miró's paintings and sculptures.

EVENING As evening falls, stroll the **waterfront promenade** and enjoy tapas, then dinner, at the bars and restaurants of Barceloneta, the 18th-century waterfront district.

Essentials

GETTING THERE
Barcelona's **international airport**, El Prat de Llobregat, lies 8 miles (13 km) from the downtown, and has connecting **trains** and **buses**.

WHERE TO STAY
El Jardí Hotel (inexpensive) has bright rooms in the old town. *www.hoteljardi-barcelona.com*
Hotel Casa Fuster (moderate) is a historic Modernista building. *www.hotelcasafuster.com*
Hotel Arts Barcelona (expensive) provides luxurious comfort on Barcelona's revitalized waterfront. *www.ritzcarlton.com*

TOURIST INFORMATION
Plaza de Catalunya; *www.barcelonaturisme.com*

La Boqueria Food Market

There has been a fresh food market on La Rambla since 1701, although the current incarnation of the Mercat de la Boqueria – which resembles a Modernista train shed with its soaring steel roof – dates from 1914. If La Sagrada Familia expresses Barcelona's faith, La Boqueria expresses the city's obsession with good food. More than 300 stalls and dozens of mini-restaurants, cafés, and bars make up the market, which is among the largest in Europe. The fishmongers, their catch heaped on ice, fill the center, and butchers, fruit and vegetable sellers, and preserved-food dealers radiate outward. From wild mushrooms to baby squid, if Catalans eat it, someone in La Boqueria sells it.

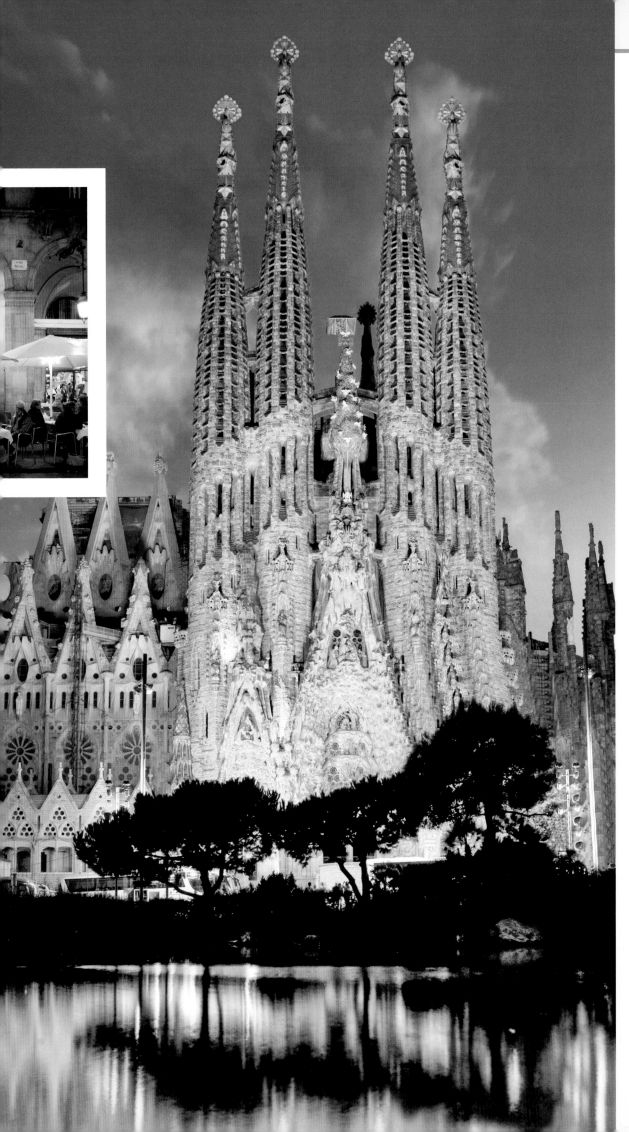

The Best Places to Eat Zarzuela

Restaurante Set Portes expensive

Everyone from Che Guevara to Errol Flynn, and from the King of Spain to Yoko Ono, has dined at Set Portes, and commemorative plaques even mark their favored seats. Founded in 1836, the restaurant famously has seven entrances, and shares the building where Picasso and his parents first lived when they came to Barcelona in 1895. After the Spanish Civil War, Set Portes emerged as the most elegant restaurant in Barcelona, and it has tenaciously clung to its crown by serving only brilliant preparations of the best ingredients. The restaurant's version of zarzuela always features a generous half (the one with the large claw) of an Atlantic lobster, as well as cuts of fish that other restaurants would reserve for grilling. The wine list is optimally paired with the menu and is particularly robust, with Priorat reds and Penedés whites from Catalonia.

Passeig Isabel II 14, Barcelona; open 1 PM–1 AM daily; www.7portes.com

Also in Barcelona

As the son of a fisherman, the proprietor of the Barcelona tavern **Can Majó** (*www.canmajo.es; moderate*) knows how to make a brilliant zarzuela. Book ahead for an outdoor table overlooking the harbor. **Can Culleretes** (*www.culleretes.com; inexpensive*) is a marvelously old-fashioned restaurant (founded in 1786) that often caters to large groups, and serves a good zarzuela among its many Catalan specialties.

Also in Catalonia

Few zarzuelas are so loaded with amazing crustaceans as the version served at **Restaurant Sa Gambina** (*www.restaurantsagambina.com; moderate*) in Cadaqués. Their "Gala-Dalí zarzuela" was named for painter Salvador Dalí and his wife Gaia, who ordered it frequently when living in Cadaqués. Considered by many to be perhaps Spain's greatest seafood restaurant, **Joan Gatell Restaurant** (*www.joangatell.com; expensive*) in Cambrils makes a transporting zarzuela as well as *suquet*, a humbler but similar soup without the crustaceans.

Around the World

Any seafood stew with crustaceans, clams, and mussels could technically be called a zarzuela, but in the resorts of coastal Colombia and Venezuela, cooks prepare a *mariscada* that traces its roots to the Spanish zarzuela. An excellent version is available daily at **Restaurante de Albahaca** (*+58 295 263 7552; inexpensive*) on Venezuela's Isla de Margarita. A *mariscada* made with dark beer and seasoned with cilantro is the house special of **Juan del Mar Restaurante** (*+57 5 664 5862; moderate*) in Cartagena, Colombia.

ALGARVE PORTUGAL

Cataplana in the Algarve

The Moors' conquest of the Iberian peninsula in the 8th century still resonates in Portugal. In the southern coastal province that they named "al-Gharb" – today's Algarve – the new settlers built walled towns and castles, planted rice and citrus trees, and influenced the native cuisine in the shape of the *cataplana*, a cooking utensil still used today to prepare Portugal's finest seafood dishes.

Like the brimming paella pan or clay tagine pot, the sight of a waiter bearing the burnished, domed copper *cataplana* immediately signals the arrival of a dish that's firmly rooted in place – in this case the long, alluring coastline of the Portuguese Algarve. The iconic shape of the *cataplana* – like a hinged, lidded wok – is as recognizable as the golden sands and rocky coves of the region itself, and, as the clasps are released, the steam within rises like wisps of cloud into the azure Algarve skies. It's a fanciful image, but there's a real majesty in both the dish and its presentation that goes far beyond a simple seafood meal.

The word "cataplana" refers to both the cooking vessel and the dish, and to add to the confusion, there is no single dish represented by the name. The most typical – and some would say most authentic – preparation is an *amêijoas na cataplana* (cataplana of clams), where clams are steamed in their shells along with chopped onion, tomato, garlic, paprika, a little piri-piri seasoning, and strips of *presunto* (smoked ham) and garlicky *chouriço* sausage. It's a wonderful combination, with the melded flavors and juices retained during cooking within the sealed *cataplana*. But it's by no means the only *cataplana* dish available, as many restaurants offer versions using other shellfish and fish, particularly *lagosta* (lobster), *gambas* (shrimp), *pescada* (hake), and *tamboril* (monkfish).

Common to all good *cataplanas* are the quality and freshness of the prime ingredients, and that's where the sunny, sea-facing Algarve comes into its own. It's one of Europe's finest resort regions, more relaxed than the heavily developed Spanish costas and featuring an undulating 125-mile (200-km) coastline that's synonymous with both fantastic beaches and terrific seafood. Away from the well-known resorts, on the wilder, far western stretches beyond Lagos or the idyllic eastern sandbank islands between Faro and Tavira, you'll find hidden grottoes, isolated beaches, and charming whitewashed villages that still retain echoes of their Moorish past, and small fishing ports with lively local fish markets that are centuries old but still play a central part in daily life. Rather like the *cataplana* itself, you only need to lift the lid to discover all that's best about the Algarve.

Above The Algarve is dotted with small coves and beaches, such as Praia do Carvalho in Lagoa, which offers sheltered sands and crystal-clear water

What Else to Eat

The classic sight – and smell – of the Portuguese coast is smoke rising off rows of salt-flecked sardines being cooked on an outdoor charcoal grill. Fresh fish, notably **robalo** (sea bass) and **dourada** (bream), get the same treatment, while **atum** (tuna) – a significant Algarve catch – is often baked in an earthenware dish with a caramelized onion sauce *(atum de cebolada)*. It's also well worth trying the delicious fish stew called **caldeirada**, but for a thoroughly Portuguese experience, there's no beating **arroz de marisco** served with an Algarve seaside view. This is a spicy, souplike combination of rice and shellfish (clams, certainly, and perhaps also mussels, crab, and shrimp), garnished with cilantro and served with a simple salad.

Three Days on the Algarve

Don't spend all your time on the beach, however tempting. It pays to explore the less-visited inland areas too, particularly the pretty Serra de Monchique (Monchique mountains) in the west and the shores of the Rio Guadiana, the river that forms the border with Spain, in the east.

DAY ONE From Faro airport, head east to the lovely riverside town of **Tavira**, which has a fish market, some fine boutique accommodations, and a line of simple riverside restaurants. Then catch the ferry across to the sandy beaches of the **Ilha de Tavira** (Tavira island).

DAY TWO Make attractive **Albufeira** your next base. Its magnificent cove beaches are within easy reach of town. Take a side trip by car up to the old hillside village of **Alte** for lunch, and return via the medieval walled town of **Silves**.

DAY THREE Visit the western headland of **Sagres**, with its historic fort and dramatic beaches. North of here along the western, Atlantic coast, as far as **Odeceixe**, lies a series of remote beaches and youth-oriented surf resorts, backed by the mountains of the **Serra de Monchique**.

Essentials

GETTING THERE
Faro **international airport** is used by many holiday operators and budget airlines. A **car** is the best way to get around, though there is a useful **train** service between Lagos in the west and Vila Real de Santo António in the east.

WHERE TO STAY
Hotel Lagosmar (inexpensive) is a traditional, family-run guesthouse in the centre of the busy resort of Lagos. www.lagosmar.com
Pousada de Sagres (moderate) is a quiet retreat in the far western Algarve. www.pousadas.pt
Casa Três Palmeiras (expensive) is a wonderfully sited cliff-top villa above the beach near Praia da Rocha. www.casatrespalmeiras.com

TOURIST INFORMATION
www.visitalgarve.pt

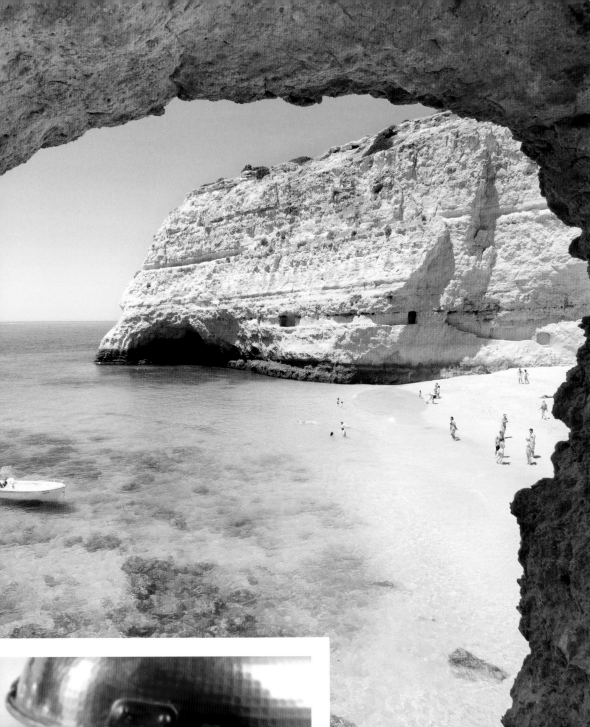

The Best Places to Eat Cataplana

Don Sebastião expensive

Don Sebastião is a welcoming restaurant on a central cobbled street in the western resort of Lagos, whose owner believes that for *cataplana*, simple is best. His enduringly popular *amêijoas na cataplana* (clam *cataplana*) is presented in the traditional copper vessel and sticks firmly to the basics: small local clams cooked with tomato, onion, garlic, peppers, and a splash of white wine, with *presunto* (smoked ham) and *chouriço* (garlic sausage) added for body and flavor. The *chouriço*, incidentally, makes an early appearance in any meal at Don Sebastião, served as a hot, sliced, and flaming appetizer, doused in *medronho*, a local firewater made from the fruits of the strawberry tree (which taste rather like lychees). You can eat outside on the cobbles, which is the best way to get a flavor of lively Lagos, though there's a warm, rustic interior too, as well as a rather fine underground *adega* (wine cellar), which the waiters can usually be persuaded to show off at the end of a meal.

Rua 25 de Abril 20–22, Lagos; open noon–10 PM daily; www.restaurantedonsebastiao.com

Also on the Algarve

In Lagos, dine on the rooftop terrace of the **Estrêla do Mar** *(+351 282 769 250; moderate)*. The restaurant couldn't be better placed for the ingredients for a *cataplana* – it's right on top of the fish market. In Tavira, the stunning **Pousada de Tavira** *(www.pousadas.pt; expensive)*, a boutique hotel fashioned from a 16th-century convent, has an excellent restaurant that puts a contemporary twist on regional dishes like the *cataplana*.

Also in Portugal

Many of Lisbon's inhabitants escape to the nearby coast at the small fishing port and resort of Ericeira, where the unpretentious **Mar à Vista** *(+351 261 862 928; moderate)* is the best place for *cataplana*. Farther north, the Atlantic-facing resorts of Nazaré and Figueira da Foz are both traditional summer boltholes for Portuguese families, with lots of great seafood restaurants. Try Figueira's renowned shellfish specialist, **Caçarola II** *(www.cacaroladois.com; expensive)*, which serves a fish, shrimp, and clam *cataplana*.

Around the World

Outside Portugal it's rare to find a genuine *cataplana*, cooked in the traditional copper utensil, but London's oldest Portuguese restaurant, **O Fado** *(www.ofado.co.uk; expensive)*, prepares a monkfish-and-mussels version in the correct manner.

Above Charcoal-grilled seafood, from sardines to lobsters, is a feature of life in the Algarve, and its tempting smell wafts along the coast

Left The two-handled copper *cataplana* has a hinged lid and seals completely, retaining all the flavorsome juices of the ingredients

Right Pedestrians rule in Højbro Plads, a lively square in the central, car-free Strøget shopping district

Below Careful attention to the aesthetics of presentation turns a simple sandwich into an elegant dish

A Day in Copenhagen

Central Copenhagen lends itself to easy strolling, and many parts are pedestrianized. Royal parks and gardens further add to the charm.

MORNING Take a stroll around the **harbor** area, starting at the **Kastellet** fortification for good views of the city. Nearby is the world-famous statue of Hans Christian Andersen's **Little Mermaid**, sitting on a rock in the harbor. From here it's only a short walk to the so-called **Marble Church**, with the largest dome in Scandinavia, and, almost opposite, the somewhat unassuming royal palace, **Amalienborg**.

AFTERNOON AND EVENING Continue your walking tour to **Nyhavn**; this colorfully painted waterfront quarter, dating from the 17th century, is full of restaurants, bars, and cafés popular with locals and visitors alike. Squeeze in a visit to **Rosenborg Castle** with its splendid gardens before hitting the shops. **Strøget** is the longest car-free shopping area in Europe, with all the big names, quirky designer shops, and eateries; many are open late in summer and for Christmas.

Essentials

GETTING THERE
Copenhagen is located on Zealand and Amager in eastern Denmark. Flights arrive into **Kastrup International Airport**, 5 miles (8 km) from downtown. There are **metro**, local **buses**, and **bike rental** options to get around the city.

WHERE TO STAY
Cabinn City (inexpensive) is a centrally located, comfortable budget hotel. *www.cabinn.com*
Hotel Alexandra (moderate) is a retro hotel with modern Danish art, not far from the shopping district. *www.hotelalexandra.dk*
First Hotel Skt Petri (expensive) is the city's latest über-cool hotel, and the birthplace of the Copenhagen cocktail. *www.sktpetri.dk*

TOURIST INFORMATION
Vesterbrogade 4A; +45 7022 2442

COPENHAGEN DENMARK

Denmark's Deluxe Sandwiches

Danes know how to turn a humble snack into a lavish feast, for the eye as well as the palate, with their traditional *smørrebrød* open sandwiches. In Copenhagen, entire restaurants are dedicated to this wonderfully versatile dish, and there are many other delights to sample, from shopping paradise Strøget to royal palaces and the colorful Nyhavn harbor area.

The Danish capital – "Wonderful, wonderful Copenhagen" as the old movie tune goes – has a long history as a center for trade and commerce, growing into one of Scandinavia's most diverse and cosmopolitan cities. Southern Sweden and all of Norway were ruled from here for several none-too-peaceful centuries, making Copenhagen the main hub of Scandinavia, a role it still lays claim to today. Warmongering among neighbors is now thankfully past; old enemies Denmark and Sweden are connected via Europe's longest bridge and the bartering in the harbor has been replaced by shopping in the fabulous pedestrianized district of Strøget.

Despite its size, Copenhagen has a nicely compact center, where most of the main sights can be visited on foot. A busy day's sightseeing can take in several royal palaces, the Little Mermaid of children's story fame, the old harbor area of Nyhavn, and much more – all fueled by *smørrebrød*, the most Danish of snacks.

Originally called *smør og brød*, literally meaning "butter and bread," the Danish open sandwich today has developed from a simple worker's packed lunch – perhaps a couple of slices of rye bread with cheese – into quite possibly the most varied dish in Denmark. While Swedes make their smorgasbord a feast of small dishes, Danes simply heap goodies onto slices of bread, piled high and beautifully arranged. Making these open sandwiches has become an art form, with the stylishly arranged toppings a perfect match of flavors, textures, and colors, all splendidly coordinated.

Traditionally, dark rye bread is used, setting off the other colorful ingredients, although it's not at all uncommon for *smørrebrød* toppings to be so heavily piled that you are left guessing as to whether there is actually a slice of bread hiding underneath. Popular toppings include pink slices of roast beef with pickles and golden roasted onions, roast pork with red cabbage and orange, smoked salmon with dill, cucumber, and lemon, or indeed whatever the chef has on hand. Find a cozy restaurant, pick your favorite(s), and dig in. *Smørrebrød* makes the "wonderful" in Copenhagen even more well-deserved.

Left Brightly painted canalside buildings in Nyhavn

What Else to Eat

Danes eat more **pork** than any other nationality, and not a single part of their most beloved of meats goes to waste. Roasted, salted, smoked, cured, even pickled pork is popular, and fabulous-tasting sausages, hams, and salamis abound. **Frikadelle**, pork meatballs or rissoles, is one of the best-known and loved national dishes, often accompanied by boiled potatoes, bright red beets, deep green pickles, and a warming, thick brown sauce. **Beef** is almost as popular, and a dish managing to fit in both meats is **biksemad**, a hash of cubed beef and pork, along with potatoes, carrots, and onions, all topped off with a fried egg, sunny side up: hearty food to keep the cold at bay in winter and energize you in summer.

The Best Places to Eat Smørrebrød

Ida Davidsen moderate

Five generations of Davidsens can't be wrong. Boasting the proudest *smørrebrød* tradition in Copenhagen, this family has been making open sandwiches since 1888. Today Ida Davidsen is queen of the kitchen, with her son Oscar running the cozy cellar establishment right in the heart of central Copenhagen. The original Oskar, the current proprietor's great-great-grandfather, was a wine merchant, aiming to quench thirsts, not fill bellies, when he first set up business. But customers weren't used to simply sipping without nibbling, and so the bar began selling *smørrebrød* to go with the wines. Today the restaurant has a selection of 250 different *smørrebrød* to choose from – the largest in Denmark. The humble sandwich has never looked so good, and the only problem is actually choosing what to have. Whatever your heart's desire, you can probably find it as a sandwich topping here, from the traditional to the more adventurous. Leg of lamb on a *smørrebrød*? Not a problem! Bacon, pâté, herring, meatballs, smoked cheese – anything goes, and usually very nicely too.

Store Kongensgade 70, Copenhagen (with another outlet at Ketchup in Tivoli Gardens); open 10:30 AM–4 PM Mon–Fri; www.idadavidsen.dk

Also in Copenhagen

Slotskælderen hos Gitte Kik on Fortunstræde **(+45 33 11 15 37; moderate)** is another long-runner in the *smørrebrød* stakes, celebrating over a century in business. Housed in what's known as the Castle Cellar, the restaurant lies directly opposite the Danish Parliament building, making this a busy spot at lunch time. Traditional recipes are used, and they even pickle their own herring and make their own schnapps.

Also in Denmark

Brøndums Hotel (+45 98 44 15 55; inexpensive) is beautifully located in Skagen, on the tip of Jutland – former home to Scandinavia's most famous colony of painters. It's perfect for old-fashioned *smørrebrød* in a scenic setting. The building oozes old-world charm and has picturesque terrace seating in summer overlooking the sea.

Around the World

At **Madsen Scandinavian Restaurant** *(www.madsenrestaurant.com; moderate)* in London's fashionable South Kensington district you can sample traditional *smørrebrød* in a trendy setting. They've even made up their own, slightly smaller lunch-snack version, called "Smushi," on either dark rye or sourdough bread. Toppings include well-known favorites such as roast beef with remoulade, roast pork with crackling and red cabbage, and several tasty vegetarian options.

BUDAPEST HUNGARY

On Budapest's Paprika Trail

One of Europe's great capitals, Budapest combines the drama of its Danube-spanning location with the mystique of a city that has witnessed great events in history. Ottoman conquerors, Habsburg monarchs, and Communist planners have all left their mark, but it is in Budapest's markets, coffeehouses, and restaurants that you will find the ebb and flow of Hungarian life.

The name Budapest literally links a city of two halves: tranquil, hilly Buda on the west bank of the Danube, and bustling Pest, with its shops, cafés, and museums, on the eastern bank. The castle district on Buda Hill recalls the glory days of Hungary's medieval monarchs and their Habsburg successors, while over the river in Pest, boulevards heavy with 19th-century buildings convey a palpable sense of national pride. Elsewhere, downtown facades are studded with decorative motifs, constituting a three-dimensional pattern book of early Hungarian (Magyar) folk art. Modern buildings such as the wonderful Ludwig Museum of Modern Art on the banks of the Danube River reveal that Budapest is a restlessly contemporary city too.

Hungarians take their food very seriously. Bakery counters groan under the weight of speckled loaves and rolls, café windows contain displays of delicate pastries and cakes, and chalkboards outside restaurants deliver the rich promise of roast breast of duck or fried liver of goose. However, no dish sums up Hungarian culinary culture more than goulash, the ubiquitous paprika-flavored stew whose origins are as old as the Hungarian nation.

For many, the word "goulash" is a catch-all term, but in Hungary itself the word *gulyás* usually refers to a rather thin stew that is served as a soup; the full-blooded stew that most non-Hungarians would consider to be goulash goes by the name of *pörkölt*. This is most often made with chunks of veal (*borjúpörkölt*), although there are many variations – *pörkölt* featuring huge, scaly chunks of freshwater fish is a favorite in the south. There is also a silkier version of goulash known as *paprikás*, thickened with lots of cream. All of these dishes originated in the simple stews prepared by Hungarian cattle-drovers over campfires, and you'll still see them served in traditional metal dishes, or *bogrács*, with a huge ladle protruding from the rim.

In Budapest you'll find goulash on menus everywhere, from bus station buffets to high-class restaurants. The one essential ingredient is paprika, the frequently fiery spice grown on a huge scale throughout southern Hungary. Strings of dried paprikas are a colorful feature of Budapest's markets, where they are labeled according to their heat and flavor – there are eight grades, ranging from the sweet and mild *különleges* to the maroon-colored, tongue-blisteringly hot *erős*.

A Day in Budapest

Bisected by the mighty Danube, Budapest has been destroyed and rebuilt over the centuries, giving it an eclectic appearance and elegant feel. The banks of the river have UNESCO World Heritage status, justifying the city's name, the "Pearl of the Danube."

MORNING Start off by visiting **Buda**, a historical quarter of 18th-century mansions and cobbled squares. The parapets of the **Fishermen's Bastion** provide sumptuous views across the Danube River.

AFTERNOON Cross the river to **Pest** and its animated main shopping street, **Váci utca**, pausing for coffee and cake in one of the many fine café-patisseries. Afterward, take a trip on the 100-year-old M1 metro line to leafy **Városliget Park**, where both a zoo and a reconstructed Transylvanian castle await. If you have time for a gallery, the **Museum of Applied Arts** is the ideal introduction to Hungarian visual style.

EVENING Promenade along Pest's Danube shore and admire the illuminated bridges before heading for **Ráday utca**, an up-and-coming area of cafés and restaurants.

Essentials

GETTING THERE
Flights arrive at **Ferihegy Airport**; buses travel the 10 miles (16 km) to the downtown.

WHERE TO STAY
Anna (inexpensive) is a small, homey B&B in a central Pest location. *www.annahotel.hu*
Ibis Centrum (moderate) is in a lively part of Pest. *www.ibis-centrum.hu*
Danubius Hotel Gellért (expensive) combines Art Nouveau elegance with proximity to the world-famous Gellért thermal baths complex. *www.danubiushotels.com/gellert*

TOURIST INFORMATION
Sütő u. 2, Deák tér; *www.budapestinfo.hu*

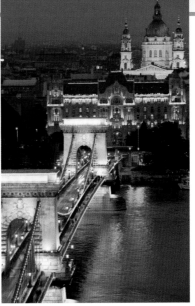

Above The 19th-century basilica of St. Stephen overlooks the Chain Bridge, which spans the Danube connecting Buda and Pest

Left Wrought-iron work and vaulting give the Great Market its spacious character

Above Paprika-hued *gulyás* (goulash) served in a metal *bogrács* cooking pot is considered an important part of Hungary's national heritage

The Great Market

Dating from the 1890s, Budapest's Great Market Hall or *Nagycsarnok* is one of the landmarks of the city, with steep-roofed corner towers giving it the air of a Transylvanian castle. Inside, cast-iron pillars preside over row upon row of stands, selling everything from fruit and veggies to embroidered blouses. Rows of salamis hang curtainlike above tins of goose-liver pâté arranged in pyramids. Many stands feature dried paprikas strung together into chains – ideal decorations for a rustic kitchen. If you're a fan of paprika in your cooking, a couple of chains will be enough to keep you going for a year or more.

The Best Places to Eat Goulash

Bock Bisztró expensive

With a bright creamy interior lined with cookbooks and wine magazines, Bock Bisztró doesn't at first sight look like the average Hungarian tavern. However, once you receive your "pre-appetizer" (a pot of spicy pork lard with plenty of crusty bread to smear it on), you quickly realize that there is more in the way of Magyar tradition here than at first meets the eye. By putting traditional national recipes and modern Mediterranean dishes on the same menu, Bock has done a great deal to make old-school Hungarian cooking fashionable again. Head chef Lajos Bíró is something of a national culinary celebrity, with several TV shows and coffee-table books to his name. Entrées like veal paprikash *(borjúpaprikás)* delight with their velvety texture and delicate paprika tones – extra spice is provided on the side if you feel the need to increase the temperature. Bock is also a wine shop, so you can get good advice on which Hungarian red to drink with your meal and the chance to buy a bottle as you leave.

Erzsebet korut 43–49, Budapest; open noon–midnight Mon–Sat; www.bockbisztro.hu

Also in Budapest

Ostentatiously decorated with Transylvanian folk motifs, 19th-century relic **Kárpátia** *(www.karpatia.hu; expensive)* is a long-established favorite with both locals and tourists, and its goulashes remain of unimpeachably high quality. Away from the tourist trail, **Régi Sipos** *(www.regisipos.hu; moderate)* serves up homey southern Hungarian delights such as carp goulash *(pontypörkölt)* or the much-prized catfish stew *(harcsapaprikás)*, accompanied by lasagna-like sheets of delicious cheesy noodles.

Also in Hungary

Gulyás and *pörkölt* can be found throughout the country, but are at their best in the rural south and east. Located in Kecskemét, close to the paprika-growing plains of the south, **Kecskeméti Csárda és Borház** *(+36 76 417 640; moderate)* excels in spicy traditional cooking. The southern town of Baja is famous for its paprika-meets-fish cuisine, with riverside restaurants like **Vendio** *(www.vendio.hu; moderate)* drawing in customers with catfish stew with cheesy noodles.

Around the World

One Hungarian restaurant that is the absolute equal of any establishment in Budapest is the **Gay Hussar** *(www.gayhussar.co.uk; expensive)* in London's Soho, famous not just for its fine goulashes and duck roasts but also for a clientele that has included media types and many a leading politician over the years.

ISTANBUL TURKEY

Meze by the Bosphorus

East meets West quite literally in Istanbul, the only city in the world that bestrides two continents. Set on the shores of the Bosphorus and Golden Horn, its majestic domes, elegant minarets, and towers float above the hubbub of 13 million people in motion. At meal times, a momentary lull sees locals and visitors settle into spreads of meze, one of the great joys of travel in Turkey.

Istanbul, the meeting point of two worlds, is one of the most vibrant, colorful, and heritage-rich cities on Earth. Capital of the Byzantine and Ottoman empires, it boasts the evocative remains of its Genoese, Roman, and Greek overlords. Its people live among some of the world's finest Byzantine and Ottoman architecture, including the Blue Mosque, Topkapı Palace, and the Roman emperor Justinian's famous church, Hagia Sophia. There's plenty to keep Orientalists happy too: medieval-era bazaars, markets selling pyramids of exotic produce, 14th-century hammams that still steam, and stands where master craftsmen still ply their ancient trades.

There's an almost overwhelming amount of choice, but there's one way in which Istanbul can be digested on even a short break – in its cuisine, and the platters of little bite-sized dishes known as meze. There are dozens of types of meze to try, all dressed with fresh herbs and spices and rich with intriguing flavors such as sesame, pomegranate, and walnuts. Plump olives and yogurty, garlicky dips; white beans and cheeses, salted fresh tuna, stuffed mussels, crisp little savory pastries and rissoles, stuffed zucchini flowers, and, everywhere, Turkey's glorious eggplants, braised with tomatoes,

roasted, grilled, or mashed into dips: this is a terrific way to sample the sophisticated and eclectic cuisine and flavors of Turkey's different regions.

The word "meze" is believed to derive from the Persian, meaning "pleasurable taste." According to Turkish tradition, meze have their roots in the opulent era of the great 16th-century sultan, Süleyman the Magnificent. Fond of throwing extravagant feasts, the Sultan nonetheless needed to ensure against intrigue and poisoning by keeping food-taster slaves in his court. Ordering the palace kitchen to prepare taster portions before he sat down to table, he inadvertently started a trend among Istanbul's courtiers and aristocracy.

Today meze are served both as appetizers and as a complete meal in themselves. Sample them in Istanbul's atmospheric *meyhanes* (traditional Turkish taverns) found in the Beyoğlu, Nevizade, and Sofyalı areas, where crammed tables of chattering locals pick from the large trays of meze wheeled around by waiters. Raki is the traditional accompaniment, an aniseed-flavored firewater with the kick of a Seljuk pony. To follow, relax with a thick, fragrant Turkish coffee, accompanied perhaps by the soothing bubble of a *nargileh* (water pipe), and feel blissfully satiated in the capital once justly dubbed "The City of the World's Desire."

Three Days in Istanbul

Istanbul contains enough to keep the visitor occupied for a month. Three days will give you a chance to take in the main sights, and plenty of opportunities to feast on meze.

DAY ONE Start in the historic **Sultanahmet** district with the iconic **Blue Mosque** and its famous, ethereal neighbor, **Hagia Sophia**, then visit the **Basilica Cistern**. Spend the afternoon shopping at the **Grand Bazaar**, and later the **Spice Bazaar** in Tahtakale.

DAY TWO Spend the morning taking in the magnificent **Topkapı Palace**, and after lunch, the collection of the **Istanbul Archaeological Museums**. Take a refreshing tea and a bath at an old Ottoman **hammam** (Turkish bath) before dinner.

DAY THREE Board a **ferry at Eminönü** and sail along the **Bosphorus** and **Golden Horn**. After a reviving coffee and baklava, head for the **western districts** of old Istanbul to admire the beautiful Byzantine mosaics and frescoes of the **Chora Church**. After lunch, head for Sultanahmet and the **Museum of Turkish & Islamic Arts**, before ambling via the Arasta Bazaar to the **Great Palace Mosaic Museum**.

Essentials

GETTING THERE
The **LRT** (Light Rail Transport) and **taxis** connect the **international airport** to central Istanbul.

WHERE TO STAY
Hotel Empress Zoe (inexpensive–moderate) is charming, in boutique style, with a garden and rooftop terrace. *www.emzoe.com*
Sirkeci Konak (moderate): central, comfortable, with a pool and hammam. *www.sirkecikonak.com*
Four Seasons Hotel Istanbul (expensive) is famous for its central location, sumptuous service and comfort. *www.fourseasons.com*

TOURIST INFORMATION
Divan Yolu, Sultanahmet; *+90 212 518 8754*

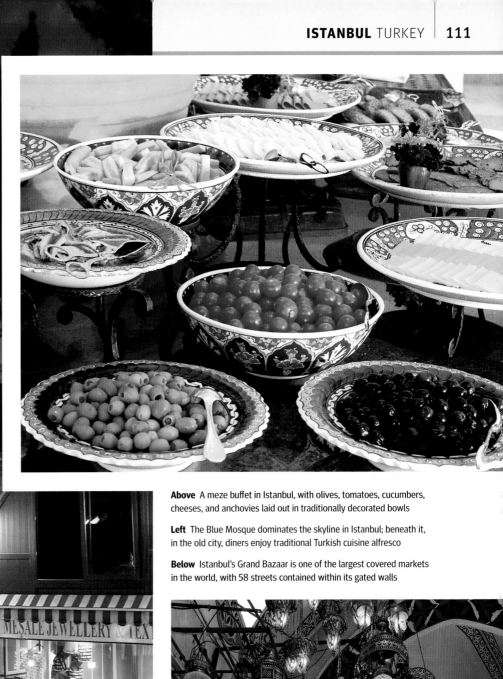

Above A meze buffet in Istanbul, with olives, tomatoes, cucumbers, cheeses, and anchovies laid out in traditionally decorated bowls

Left The Blue Mosque dominates the skyline in Istanbul; beneath it, in the old city, diners enjoy traditional Turkish cuisine alfresco

Below Istanbul's Grand Bazaar is one of the largest covered markets in the world, with 58 streets contained within its gated walls

Meze Around the World

Meze are found throughout the Middle East and Mediterranean, albeit under different names or forms. The fashion is believed to have spread from the Sultan's court in Istanbul at the height of the Ottoman empire.

ISTANBUL

Sofyalı 9 inexpensive
Sofyalı Sokak 9, Tünel; +90 212 245 0362

In an area famous for its *meyhanes* (taverns), this is one of Istanbul's best, serving superb meze and traditional Anatolian cooking in attractive surroundings and a warm, vibrant, and buzzing atmosphere. Try the specialty, *arnavut ciğeri* (fried lamb liver).

Asitane expensive
Kariye Camii Sokak 6, Edirnekapı; www.asitanerestaurant.com

Just south of the Chora Church, upmarket Asitane has established a specialty in and a reputation for fine Ottoman cuisine. Its dedicated chefs source original recipes from the kitchens of the old Ottoman palaces and employ original methods of preparation and cooking for all their dishes, including their sumptuous meze.

Mikla expensive
Marmara Pera Hotel, Meşrutiyet Caddesi 15, Tepebaşı; www.miklarestaurant.com

Considered the city's top table, Mikla is overseen by local "celebrity chef" Mehmet Gürs, who creates stunning modern Mediterranean dishes with Turkish ingredients, cooking methods, and flavors. Spectacular views, impeccable service, and sumptuous decor complement the food.

SYRIA

Syrian cuisine is one of the oldest, richest, and most sophisticated in the world, and the range of meze found in its restaurants reflects this, combining a wide range of raw ingredients with centuries-old culinary know-how.

Bab Al-Hara inexpensive
Sharia Al-Qaimariyya, Damascus; +963 11 541 8644

Set deep in the old city close to the Umayyad Mosque, Al-Hara boasts a fervent local following for its fresh, flavorsome, and authentic cooking, at excellent prices, served in an old courtyard house. The meze and grills are a particular specialty.

Bazaar Al-Charq moderate
Between Sharia Al-Mutanabi and Sharia Hammam Al-Tat, Aleppo; +963 21 224 9120

The cellar-like Charq is cozy, atmospheric, and welcoming. The kitchen offers an impressive variety of Damascene and Aleppine specialties, including a wide range of meze; the heavenly, smoky baba ghanoush (eggplant purée) is a must-try. There's usually live traditional music in the evening.

Al-Khawali expensive
Maazanet al-Shahim, Damascus; +963 11 222 5808

Considered one of Syria's best restaurants and counting its president among its customers, Al-Khawali is a great choice for sampling meze Syrian-style. Set in a restored Damascene courtyard house dating to 1368, it combines beautiful surroundings with first-class cooking and service.

Sissi House expensive
Just off Saahat Al-Hattab, Jdeideh, Aleppo; www.sissihouse.com

Considered a cut above in decor, ambience, and cooking, Sissi House attracts a well-heeled and glamorous local following. It specializes in Aleppine cuisine, beautifully prepared, cooked, and served, including a selection of over 50 meze. Classical Arabic music is often played live.

LEBANON

For many people, Lebanese cuisine forms their main experience of meze, aided undoubtedly by the large Lebanese communities and their eateries found in many Western cities. In Lebanon itself, eating out is an important part of social interaction.

Abdel Wahab moderate
Rue Abdel Wahab El-Inglizi, Achrafiye, Beirut; +961 1 200 552

With tables spread around the pretty garden and high-ceilinged rooms of an old Ottoman villa, the Abdel Wahab is an atmospheric and romantic place for dinner *à deux*. The lavish buffets are famous and include a wide range of meze, among them several varieties of heavenly hummus.

Left (top to bottom) The beautiful courtyard setting of the Al-Khawali restaurant in Damascus, Syria; alfresco dining in Istanbul, overlooking the Bosphorus; meze in Egypt

Below (top to bottom) Greek meze, with olives, fava beans (foreground), octopus, and (center left) char-grilled halloumi cheese; arranging cold meze dishes at a Lebanese restaurant

La Tabkha moderate
Rue Gouraud, Gemmayzeh, Beirut; +961 1 579 000
Modern, minimalist, and contemporary, La Tabkha serves a terrific array of modern Lebanese dishes with a touch of French influence, including an excellent lunch-time meze buffet that changes daily.

Shahrazad moderate
6th Floor, Centre Commercial de Yaghi & Simbole, off Rue Abdel Halim Hajjar, Baalbek; +961 8 371 851

The location may lack style or atmosphere, but it's the spectacular views over Baalbek's Roman ruins that draw a loyal following, along with the simple but hearty and well-prepared home cooking, including a good selection of delicious, freshly prepared meze.

EGYPT
At one time part and parcel of the Ottoman empire and today part of the Middle East, Egypt has long been influenced by both regions' cooking. It has also developed its own distinct versions of meze, using local ingredients and cooking traditions.

Samakmak moderate
42 Qar Ras At Tin, Alexandria; +20 3 481 1560
Established by a former belly dancer, the Samakmak is a cozy, intimate, and atmospheric restaurant. It is best known for its excellent, imaginatively prepared fish and seafood dishes, which include an unusual and very good meze selection.

Abou El Sid expensive
157 Sharia 26 July, Zamalek, Cairo; +20 2 2735 9640
Styled like an Orientalist boudoir-restaurant-bar, the Abou El Sid is one of Cairo's eating hot spots. Diners recline on cushions pasha-style around low brass tables while tucking into well-prepared traditional Egyptian cooking, including mouthwatering meze. Reservations are essential.

CYPRUS
Though unquestionably influenced by Turkey and Greece as well as the Middle East, Cyprus nonetheless proudly possesses its own culinary traditions. The Cypriots love and value their food and keep up a vigorous tradition of meze.

Fetta's inexpensive
Ioanni Agroti 33, Pafos; +357 2693 7822
One of Cyprus's top traditional restaurants, Fetta's bases its reputation on enduring culinary values: quality ingredients, locally sourced, and simple but sound home cooking passed down the generations. The meze platter of grilled meats is a specialty.

Zanettos Taverna inexpensive
Trikoupi 65, Lefkosia; +357 2276 5501
One of the oldest surviving tavernas in the Old City, Zanettos is a bit of an institution and retains a loyal local following. Though located in a rather lugubrious part of town, it's worth the journey: the meze are superb and the atmosphere convivial and fun.

On the Menu in Turkey

Acı domates ezmesi Spicy tomato dip.
Ançüz Pickled anchovies.
Arnavut ciğeri Diced, fried lamb liver with raw onion, sumac, chili pepper, and chopped parsley.
Barbunya pilaki Salad of red beans.
Beyaz peynir White sheep or goat cheese.
Cacık Yogurt with grated cucumber and mint, served either as a kind of soup or as a dip.
Çerkez tavuğu Literally, "Circassian chicken" – chicken, walnuts, and bread flavored with garlic.
Deniz börülcesi Samphire dressed with olive oil, garlic, and lemon and traditionally served with fish and seafood meze.
Enginar Boiled artichoke.
Ezme salatası Tomato and pepper dip.
Fasulye piyazı Salad of navy beans.
Fava or **fava salatası** A puréed fava bean dip.
Haydari Yogurt dip made with garlic and mint.

Kabak çiçeği dolması Stuffed zucchini flowers.
Kısır Salad made of spiced bulgur wheat.
Lakerda Tuna fish, sliced and salted.
Mercimek köftesi Spicy balls made of red lentils and bulgur wheat traditionally served at weddings and family feasts.
Midye dolması Stuffed mussels.
Patates köftesi Cheese and potato croquettes.
Patlıcan biber tava Fried eggplant and sweet green peppers with tomato sauce and chili pepper.
Patlıcan ezmesi Roast eggplant with yogurt.
Patlıcan kızartması or **salatası** Fried eggplant and tomato, served warm or as a salad.
Sarımsaklı havuç Grated carrot in a garlicky yogurt.
Semizotu salatası Salad of purslane in a yogurt and garlic dressing.
Sigara böreği Cigar-shaped pastries deep-fried and stuffed with cheese.
Yaprak dolması Vine leaves stuffed with pine nuts, rice, and herbs.

LOIRE VALLEY FRANCE

Tarte Tatin in The Regal Loire

The upside-down apple tart is quintessentially French – but one village in particular lays claim to its invention, saying that it was born in the tiny village of Lamotte-Beuvron when the Tatin sisters pulled it from their oven. Their name still clings to the dish, but every bakery and bistro throughout the château-strewn Loire Valley has a version of the apple and sugar-soaked *tarte Tatin*.

The year 1889 was a significant one for France: the Eiffel Tower was completed, and an apple tart blazed its way into the culinary chronicles. Stéphanie and Caroline Tatin, two sisters who ran a hotel in the little village of Lamotte-Beuvron, created their tart *tour de force* purely by accident, or so the story goes. While racing to get through a busy lunch service, Stéphanie threw a pan of apples, sugar, and butter into the oven, thinking there was pastry on the bottom. The apples caramelized, turning a luminous bronze, and she then attempted to "save" the dessert by adding a pastry lid and putting it back into the oven. Rather than admit a mistake, the sisters flipped over their "tart nouveau," carved it up immediately, and served it. That's the official story, at least, recounted by *La Confrérie des Lichonneux de Tarte Tatin* (The Brotherhood of the *Tarte Tatin)*, its vigilant protectors and promoters.

Sticklers for tradition, the Brotherhood insists the butter goes in first, followed by the sugar, with the apple quarters layered on top – then it's into the oven to bake, just as in the sisters' day. Not everyone follows this code; some cooks prefer to caramelize the butter and sugar separately before adding the apples to bake.

The tart has a formidable fan base, which grew from that first bunch of hunters at the sisters' hotel, who lined up again the following week for a taste of the new apple dessert. More than 120 years later, hunters still flock to the Sologne region in fall, hot on the trail of wild boar, deer, duck, pheasants, and mushrooms.

Tourists, however, stalk different prey: the châteaux of the Loire, which materialize at every curve and corner. In the 16th century, the French court moved between these pleasure palaces for days of hunting and nights of feasting. The vast Château de Chambord was the brainchild of François I, who at 25 vowed to show the world just how passionate he was about architecture and hunting; his extravagant white stone Renaissance palace is in the midst of a forest teeming with game. In October it rings with the sound of stags rutting, as they clash antlers and bellow to establish their superiority and claim to the best of the hinds.

Toward the north lies Orléans, once the capital of France and now the capital of the Loire Valley. It was here that Joan of Arc famously liberated the city of Orléans from the English in 1429, at only 17 years old. From castles and grand gardens, to deeds of great bravery and accidental culinary creation, the Loire is full of astonishing sights, tales, and tastes.

Three Days in the Loire Valley

Loved by kings and blessed by nature, the Loire Valley is an all-around crowd-pleaser.

DAY ONE Lamotte-Beuvron sits deep in the Sologne, a region rich in nature and known for hiking, hunting, and riding. Wander the tree-flanked **Canal de la Sauldre** just outside the town, or take to one of the many hiking tracks on foot or horseback – they're the ideal antidote to *tarte Tatin* overindulgence.

DAY TWO Visit **Orléans** and immerse yourself in history, specifically that of the Maid of Orléans, Joan of Arc. Her former home is now a museum – **Centre Jeanne d'Arc** – devoted to telling her story. The stained-glass windows of **Sainte Croix Cathedral** also pay tribute. There's even a Joan of Arc festival in May, complete with medieval fair.

DAY THREE Head for **Chambord**, to explore **Château de Chambord**, Renaissance status symbol *par excellence*. There's a magnificent interlocking double staircase, false windows, turrets galore, and an expansive roof terrace to which the king used to ascend in order to watch the start of the hunt, tournaments, and festivals.

Essentials

GETTING THERE
Fly to **Tours airport**, or take a **high-speed train** from Paris to the Loire Valley region.

WHERE TO STAY
Auberge du Cheval Blanc (inexpensive) in Yvoy le Marron has comfortable rooms in an old coaching inn. www.aubergeduchevalblanc.com
Château de Beauharnais (moderate) is grand, and just 7 miles (12 km) from Lamotte-Beuvron. www.châteaudebeauharnais.com
Grand Hôtel du Lion d'Or (expensive) *(see facing page)*. www.hotel-liondor.fr

TOURIST INFORMATION
www.loirevalleytourism.com

Above *Tarte Tatin* is an "upside-down" apple pie, where the golden-brown caramelized apples sit atop a layer of flaky, buttery pastry

Left The extravagant Château de Chambord, a hunting lodge for François I, is the largest of the Loire châteaux, boasting 440 rooms

Above Lamotte-Beuvron's Hôtel Tatin, where the Tatin sisters cooked up their famous tart, is still going strong today as a hotel and restaurant

Tarte Tatin Festival

The annual *Foire au Pays des la Tarte Tatin* (*tarte Tatin* festival) takes place in mid-September in Lamotte-Beuvron. There are tart-making demonstrations, often by a renowned, Loire-based chef employing only the ingredients used by the revered Tatin sisters. Baking aficionados can enter the *tarte Tatin* contest, and the winner walks away with a handsome trophy. This is, after all, a festival designed for people "wishing to taste, evaluate, and defend the *tarte Tatin*." It's a serious, if delicious, business. But individualists beware – any attempts to improve on the original recipe will be treated with the appropriate disdain.

The Best Places to Eat Tarte Tatin

Grand Hôtel du Lion d'Or
expensive

Didier Clément, chef at the Michelin-starred Lion d'Or in Romorantin-Lanthenay, is inspired by the produce of the Sologne and driven by the seasons. He's also a fan of long-forgotten varieties of herbs, spices, and heirloom vegetables and fruits, such as *reine de reinettes* ("king of the pippins") apples, and he works with gardeners and farmers in the region to grow them for his table. In fall and winter, he showcases his version of "*la tarte des demoiselles Tatin*," cooking up perfectly caramelized apples on a puff-pastry base that would have the sisters beaming. He admits, however, that he actually prefers to serve his "lighter version" of the apple classic: a millefeuille of *reinette* apples crowned with quince ice cream (an old-fashioned favorite that Clément champions) and frothy caramel. In summer, diners can eat in the flower-filled courtyard of the 16th-century hotel, and in winter they're ensconced in high-end country comfort in the formal dining room, with its chandeliers and starched white cloths.

69 rue Georges Clemenceau, Romorantin-Lanthenay; open for lunch and dinner Wed–Mon, closed 1–13 Aug, 19–29 Dec and 16 Feb–10 Mar; www.hotel-liondor.fr

Also in the Loire

A visit to sleepy little Lamotte-Beuvron wouldn't be complete without a pit stop at the **Hôtel Tatin** *(www.hotel-Tatin.fr; moderate)*, the alleged birthplace of the tart. It still has the same coal- and wood-burning tiled stove in which the famed sisters baked their tarts. *Reine de reinettes* remains the apple of choice, cut into slices, quarters, or chunks, layered in a special pan, cooked to golden perfection, and served comfortingly warm.

Also in France

Philippe Conticini is an artist when it comes to cakes, tarts, and all the finer, sweeter things in life. His Paris bakery, **La Pâtisserie des Rêves** *(www.lapatisseriedesreves.com; inexpensive)*, is chock-full of his creations, including an irresistible *tarte Tatin*. His rendition has slivers of apple piled high on a square of crispy puff pastry; the pale, almost translucent apple sheets on the bottom rise up the color scale to the caramel-colored beauties on top. The *tarte* is served with a pot of lime-flavored mascarpone.

Around the World

London's much-lauded **Le Gavroche** *(www.le-gavroche.co.uk; expensive)*, founded in 1967 by the Roux brothers, dishes up a delicious *tarte Tatin* that perfectly finishes a top-end French meal. Individual-sized tarts brimming with caramelized apples come with a dollop of Madagascan-vanilla-flavored ice cream.

Above Klädesholmen is one of 3,000 islands off Sweden's west coast, connected by bridge to the island of Bockholmen

Above Smorgasbord in Bohuslän's restaurants includes deliciously large helpings of fish and shellfish, such as lobster, crayfish, and shrimp

Three Days in Bohuslän

Bohuslän's coastline, featuring islands, skerries, Sweden's only fjord, and its only marine national park, can be explored in just a few days.

DAY ONE Drive north from **Gothenburg** following the archipelago, passing the two largest islands, **Orust** and **Tjörn**. After an hour's drive you reach the charming settlement of **Lysekil**, on Sweden's only fjord, **Gullmaren**. In the afternoon, continue to nearby **Smögen**, one of the most scenic fishing villages on the coast, now a popular vacation spot.

DAY TWO Follow the main coastal road north toward the unusual Bronze Age rock carvings at **Tanum**, a UNESCO World Heritage site. Reach the hub of **Strömstad**, near Norway, in the evening and treat yourself to some pampering at its renowned spa, before dinner at **Rökeriet**, a traditional smokehouse in the harbor.

DAY THREE Take the morning ferry to the **Koster Islands** and explore the car-free north island, hiking among the purple heather, yellow gorse, and pink-tinged cliffs before cycling or canoeing around the south island. Return to **Strömstad** by ferry in the evening.

Essentials

GETTING THERE
The coastal region of Bohuslän lies between Gothenburg and the Norwegian border. Flights arrive at **Gothenburg-Landvetter international airport,** 13 miles (20 km) from downtown. There are good local **buses** and **car** rental.

WHERE TO STAY
Strandflickorna (inexpensive) is an old-fashioned, peaceful hotel near the sea in the coastal town of Lysekil. *www.strandflickorna.se*
Salt & Sill (moderate), Sweden's first floating hotel, has 23 stylish rooms in two buildings off the island of Klädesholmen. *www.saltosill.se*
Quality Spa & Resort Strömstad (expensive) is a world-class hotel and traditional health spa. *www.stromstadspa.se.*

TOURIST INFORMATION
www.westsweden.com; www.vastsverige.com

BOHUSLAN SWEDEN

Smorgasbord in Sweden

The coastline between Gothenburg and the Norwegian border on the west coast of Sweden is teeming with islands, islets, and skerries, where small fishing communities still make a living from the sea. In the province of Bohuslän, they've given a twist to the traditional smorgasbord – a feast of buffet-style dishes – by adding the bounty of the sea to the luxurious spread.

The province of Bohuslän has a distinctive fishing culture, full of tall tales of hardy fishermen and howling storms. The area can have fierce winters, but is blessed with sizzling summers. Running the length of the west coast north of Gothenburg, right up to the Norwegian border, the province is replete with quietly picturesque fishing villages. Some 3,000 islands and 5,000 islets follow the line of the Bohuslän archipelago, and in summer many of the cozy settlements turn into lively seaside resorts. Pleasure boats line the harbors, and the cafés and restaurants open up their terraces along the seafront, serving the freshest of west coast cuisine. Many of the tiny islands just off the coast have old-fashioned fishermen's huts, some of which are now summer houses, perching on the gently sloping, pink-tinted granite cliffs. The air tingles with the smell of seaweed, smoked fish, and pickled herring.

The humble herring has been fished along the coastline of Bohuslän for centuries and no local smorgasbord would be complete without this little fish.

The smorgasbord – a buffet-style spread of mostly cold dishes – is said to date back to the mid-14th century, when the upper classes began offering guests a small side table of hors d'oeuvres to accompany the alcoholic schnapps, or *brännvin*, for which they had a penchant. Over the centuries, these little appetizers, initially just bread, butter, some cheese, and of course the occasional herring, went from plain and simple to increasingly lavish and elegant, moving from side table to main table, with all manner of dishes.

Today these colorful, abundant lunch buffets tend to have seasonal and regional twists, such as the emphasis on fresh fish and seafood in Bohuslän, where they often include "the Big Five" – lobster, oysters, shrimp, crayfish, and mussels. Most spreads include a variety of breads, from dark rye and crispbreads to flatbreads and seeded rolls, and plenty of pickled herring in various sauces, from strong mustard to a subtle onion. Add a mix of salads, cold cuts, eggs, pies, potatoes, and cheese, and the smorgasbord becomes a feast for the eye as well as the stomach, a rainbow of colors like the pretty painted houses of the wharves.

The Good Food Trail

Making all the difference to the culinary scene in the region, Taste of West Sweden has been highlighting the best of West Swedish food and produce for just over a decade. Member restaurants, food producers, and farm shops all focus on locally sourced produce and fresh ingredients, from seafood and fish to game and dairy products, including many of the ingredients of a good smorgasbord. The 25 restaurants, traditional inns, and old manor houses featured in the program *(www.vastsverige.com)* offer the finest in dining experiences, and many include a smorgasbord with Bohuslän's "Big Five." You can visit cheese-makers, dairies, and even a brewery as part of the scheme. Kosters Trädgård *(www. kosterstradgardar.se)* on Sydkoster Island is a particular highlight in summer, when their herb garden and café are open.

Above The quayside restaurants of Fjallbacka, on the Bohuslän coast

The Best Places to Eat Smorgasbord

Salt & Sill moderate

Hotel and restaurant Salt & Sill sits prettily on the tiny island of Klädesholmen, one of the west coast's most scenic locations and famed for its herring trade – they even celebrate a "Day of the Herring." The chef serves up one of the best classic smorgasbords in the region and as the name – "Salt & Herring" – might suggest, there are a few delights of the sea included in the spread. On Sunday lunchtimes, guests can pick and choose from the many nibbles lined up, with a particularly fine selection of herring – there are 40 different types of preparation. In December, the smorgasbord turns into a *julbord*, a Christmas version that features traditional festive dishes such as Christmas ham and salt-cod *lutefisk*, as well as the year-round favorites – different types of bread, cold cuts, cheeses, pickled gherkins, beet salad, sausages, roe, mackerel, and so much more. It's all traditionally washed down with strong spirits, such as aquavit, schnapps, or *brännvin* (literally "firewine"), which certainly lives up to its name.

471 51 Klädesholmen, Tjörn; open from 5 PM Fri, from 1 PM Sat, & 1–5 PM Sun for classical smorgasbord; www.saltosill.se

Also in Bohuslän

Lökeberga *(www.lokeberga.se; moderate)* is a family-run hotel and restaurant right by the sea, half an hour north of Gothenburg. It is renowned for its smorgasbord, which uses typical ingredients from Bohuslän, including seafood and goat cheese. There is even a cake and dessert smorgasbord to sample if the main dishes don't fill you up.

Also in Sweden

Operakällaren's smorgasbord was legendary in its day, and after a 15-year break, it's back *(www.operakallaren.se; expensive)*. Served in what is perhaps the best restaurant in Sweden, under cut-glass chandeliers in a historic Stockholm building, the lavish spread rivals the finest of culinary experiences. Expect plump soused herring, gravadlax, smoked reindeer, meatballs, and delicious side dishes from cheeses to pâtés. A true feast.

Around the World

Miss Maud *(www.missmaud.com.au; inexpensive)* opened as a Swedish hotel and restaurant in Perth, Australia, in 1971, offering a sumptuous smorgasbord at breakfast, lunch, and dinner. Open 365 days a year, Miss Maud boasts Australia's only authentic Swedish smorgasbord, with a few Aussie favorites snuck in for good measure, such as Princess Cake and the eternal favorite: "pavlova downunder."

A Day in Seville

Capital of Andalusia for more than 800 years, Seville is southern Spain's seat of power and glory, and boasts magnificent palaces and churches. The city's grace and joy are expressed in sweet gardens, tiled patios, and the catharsis of its signature flamenco, the *Sevillana*.

MORNING Begin with the wondrous **Real Alcázar** before touring the **Cathedral**, which holds the tomb of Columbus. Climb the ramps of **La Giralda** to survey the medieval maze of **Barrio Santa Cruz**, where whitewashed houses line narrow, cobbled streets and are interspersed with quaint tapas bars and centuries-old gardens.

AFTERNOON Visit the exquisite palace and gardens of **La Casa de Pilatos**. Don't miss the haunting paintings of saints by Zubarán in the **Museo de Bellas Artes**. Founded by a famous dancer, the **Museo del Baile Flamenco** charts the flowering of the art form.

EVENING Return to the **Museo del Baile Flamenco** if a dance performance is scheduled, or catch equally authentic flamenco music and dance at **Los Gallos**.

Essentials

GETTING THERE
Flights arrive into **Seville Airport**, 6 miles (10 km) from downtown Seville. **Buses** from the airport take 25 minutes and run every half-hour; **car rental** and **taxis** are available.

WHERE TO STAY
YH Giralda (inexpensive) squeezes intimate but cheerful rooms on three levels around a central courtyard in a former abbots' residence. *www.yh-hoteles.com*

La Hostería del Laurel (moderate) is a romantic and atmospheric old inn where *Don Juan* was written. *www.hosteriadellaurel.com*

Hotel EME Fusion (expensive) brings luxurious avant-garde designer sensibility to the plaza next to the cathedral. *www.emehotel.com*

TOURIST INFORMATION
Plaza de San Francisco; *www.turismo.sevilla.org*

Right Like a raw vegetable smoothie, gazpacho is often served chilled in glasses as a thirst-quenching appetizer

Below The Salon de los Embajadores (Hall of the Ambassadors) in the Real Alcázar

The Best Places to Eat Gazpacho

Restaurante Sabina moderate

Long before the Slow Food movement made "local" the mantra of modern gastronomy, Sabina championed Andalusian products and culinary traditions. Many restaurants in Seville serve Andalusian fare, but Sabina specializes in the dishes of the countryside.

A classic gazpacho, almost sweet from the inclusion of extremely ripe tomatoes, makes the perfect starter, especially when accompanied by a glass of one of the acidic Macabeo white wines from the mountains northwest of the city. The restaurant is set in a former shipyard building about halfway between the cathedral and the bullring, and impresses with its high vaulted ceilings. Hearty main dishes kissed by the heat of its ovens excel; try braised pig's trotters, roasted leg of lamb larded with rosemary, stewed partridge, or a fulsome rendition of the Spanish standard, *rabo de toro* (oxtail stew). The wine list abounds with sturdy Rioja and Ribera del Duero reds, which are able to stand up to such rich fare, but if you're feeling curious, try a more unusual Tempranillo from the Sierras de Málaga.

Calle Dos de Mayo 4, Seville; open 1:30–4 PM and 9 PM–midnight Mon–Sat; +34 954 562 547

Also in Seville

The elegant Triana restaurant **Rio Grande** (*www.riogrande-sevilla.com; expensive*) is known mainly for its simply grilled fish, but the kitchen also makes a quintet of gazpachos in season, each tinted a different color by their dominant vegetables. The venerable tavern of **El Rinconcillo** (*www.elrinconcillo.es; inexpensive*), with its decoration of Feria and bullfight posters, is one of the oldest bars in Seville; celebrated as a tapas bar, it also serves a purely authentic *gazpacho Sevillano*.

Also in Spain

In Marbella, superchef Dani García plays with seasonal fruits and vegetables to make gazpachos based on everything from spring vegetables to wine grapes at **Calima** (*www. restaurantecalima.com; expensive*). **Café de Paris** in Málaga (*www.rcafedeparis.com; inexpensive*) garnishes its *ajo blanco con uvas* with red wine granita. In Cácares, **El Figón de Eustaquio** (*+34 927 248 194; moderate*) showcases Extremaduran classics, including the white gazpacho.

Around the World

Centuries after Spain got tomatoes and peppers, gazpacho has returned to the Spanish-inflected American Southwest. **Inn at Loretto** in Santa Fe, New Mexico (*www.innatloretto.com; moderate*), serves its chilled gazpacho with unusual but delicious avocado sorbet and lump crabmeat.

SEVILLE SPAIN

Cool Gazpacho in Sultry Seville

Seville became the most ornate city in Europe in the 16th century, when New World gold and silver sailed up the Guadalquivir River. The ships also brought culinary riches – tomatoes and bell peppers – which *Sevillanos* added to the ancient Roman soup of bread, garlic, salt, vinegar, and olive oil to create gazpacho, the refreshing chilled soup often called "salad in a bowl."

Like its signature dish, the city of Seville melds layers of history and styles into a single unified masterpiece. The ceremonial tomb of the explorer Christopher Columbus, whose discoveries forever altered Seville, holds a place of honor inside the massive cathedral, where New World gold on the altars sends glints of light into the soaring darkness overhead. The cathedral was built on the site of the city's Arabic mosque; its glorious bell tower – the Giralda – was originally the minaret of Seville's great mosque, and the muezzin would ride on horseback up the ramped passage to its top to call the faithful to prayer.

Moorish and Christian pasts intermingle with ease in the city. The Muslim ruling family of the Almohads built the Torre de Oro on the Guadalquivir River in 1220, and three centuries later the Spaniards turned it into the custom house to count New World riches. Treasure barges no longer ply the river; these days, cruise boats motor from the Arenal shipyards to the artful, harp-shaped bridge of Puente del Alamillo.

Gazpacho is also history in a bowl. When the Moors conquered Andalusia, they took the basic stale-bread soup introduced by the Roman legions and dressed it up with ground almonds and fresh grapes to create a white gazpacho still favored in the coastal city of Málaga. But it was not until the conquistadors brought home the curious fruits of the Aztec and Inca empires – tomatoes and both sweet and piquant capsicum peppers – that something like modern gazpacho became the city's signature bowl of cold-soup refreshment. The sharp snap of green bell peppers, raw garlic, and onion brightens the unctuous blend of sweet tomatoes with faintly astringent but melonlike cucumbers and yeasty dried bread.

Contemporary chefs make gazpacho a blank canvas for painting with the flavors of fresh fruit, exotic nutmeats, and a world of spices. Yet cool, red gazpacho remains the pride of Seville, best showcased in clear glass bowls. Each diner can season to taste with garnishes of toasted croutons, slivers of green onion, diced tomatoes, peppers, and cucumber. Few dishes so quickly relieve a fevered brow.

Gazpacho Variants

Gazpacho has many traditional variants throughout Spain, most of which add either chopped ham or chopped hard-boiled egg as garnishes. But the Andalusian coastal region near Málaga clings to its Moorish dishes, including the white gazpacho that is a relic of an era before tomatoes and peppers entered the Spanish diet. **Ajo blanco con uvas** is based on ground almonds, garlic, bread, and peeled grapes, and is served with croutons and grapes. The white gazpacho of Extremadura, known as **gazpacho Extremeño**, is a complex dish of egg, bread, garlic, bell pepper, and cucumber that is then blended with a strained broth of simmered onion, parsnips, carrots, turnips, and celery and liberally laced with vinegar and a dash of hot paprika. This richer version of gazpacho, served very cold, really soothes and nourishes.

Above Sara Baras demonstrates the traditional Andalusian dance of flamenco

KRAKOW ↗

KRAKOW POLAND

Soft Dumplings in Kraków

Every hour, on the hour, a bugle call sounds from atop the northern tower of St. Mary's basilica, the russet-red church that dominates old Kraków's main square. Traditionally a warning to the people of Kraków to defend their city, the mournful tune is today just as much a reminder that lunch is approaching. For many, that means *pierogi* – versatile and delicious stuffed dumplings.

With a royal pedigree that stretches back over a thousand years, Kraków is a treasure trove of Gothic and Renaissance architecture. The Old Town was spared the bombing most other Polish cities suffered during World War II, and Kraków now contains more historic buildings, monuments, and artworks – some 2.3 million registered at the last count – than any other place in the country. Savor it slowly, preferably on foot, and you'll discover something pretty or old or curious or tasty around every corner.

You're not likely to wear yourself out, because all the major points of interest are contained within the thumb-shaped Old Town. Looming above it to the south is Wawel, a royal complex containing the mainly Renaissance castle, cathedral, royal tombs, and crown treasury. The views from what is the very symbol of the Polish nation are priceless, but get back on to the street and head north along ulica Grodzka to the Rynek Główny, the largest medieval square in Europe. Here you'll find not only Kraków's faithful bugler but some of the finest buildings in the city, such as the Sukiennice (Cloth Hall), once a focus for commerce in the city. At the main square you can also pick up one of the many colorful horse-drawn carriages and take a

leisurely tour of the city, or strike out to one of Kraków's cultural sights, such as the Czartoryski Museum, where you can see Leonardo da Vinci's famous painting *Lady with an Ermine*.

After a morning on your feet, you'll appreciate the prospect of a hearty Polish lunch, and nothing is more fitting or filling than a plate of *pierogi* – crescent-shaped flour-based dumplings eaten throughout the country. *Pierogi* are usually boiled but can be baked or fried; they come with a variety of savory fillings and are typically served smothered with lard, sour cream, butter, or onions. Unless, that is, they are of the sweet variety, filled with strawberries, blueberries, or plums.

The classic trio are those with cottage cheese, potato, and onion (or "Russian *pierogi*"); cabbage and mushrooms; and minced meat; but today you'll find new takes on this quintessential Polish dish. Venison and bacon, apples with rose petals, and smoked salmon are among the tasty modern fillings. Innovation is the *raison d'être* of the Pierogi Festival, held annually in Kraków in mid-August, as close as possible to the feast of the Assumption of Mary (a very big holiday here) on August 15. Hundreds of restaurants compete to produce the most inventive *pierogi*, and up to 200,000 of the crescent-shaped delights are consumed.

Above Outdoor dining in one of the many restaurants in the former Jewish Kazimierz quarter

Right Larger even than St. Peter's square in the Vatican, Kraków's busy main square is overlooked by the towers of St. Mary's basilica

Below *Pierogi* are for every day and for feast days; mushroom-filled variants are a Christmas Eve tradition

A Day in Kraków

Many of Kraków's notable sights lie within the pocket-sized Old Town. A strip of parkland called Planty, which was formerly a moat, marks its border.

MORNING Introduce yourself to Kraków by walking up to **Wawel** and exploring as much of the royal complex as the morning will allow. Don't miss the **Royal Crypts** in the cathedral (where Archbishop Karol Wojtyla – the future John Paul II – once preached) or the Flemish tapestries in the castle's **Hall of Senators**.

AFTERNOON Get lost in the **Old Town**, visiting **St. Mary's basilica** in the main square for its exquisitely carved altarpiece and the 15th-century **Cloth Hall**, which is still used as a market. Nearby is the **Collegium Maius**, where Copernicus studied. Check out the 15th-century college's awesome Renaissance hall and treasury.

EVENING After sundown, head south of Wawel for **Kazimierz**, the one-time Jewish quarter, which has been revitalized in recent years and contains a great choice of bars and restaurants, some featuring live bands playing *klezmer* (Jewish folk music).

Essentials

GETTING THERE
Flights arrive into **John Paul II International Airport**, 7 miles (11 km) west of the city.

WHERE TO STAY
Nathan's Villa (inexpensive) is a modern hostel at the foot of Wawel Hill. www.nathansvilla.com
Hotel Wit Stwosz (moderate) occupies a restored 16th-century town house in the heart of the Old Town. www.wit-stwosz.com.pl
Hotel Copernicus (expensive) has 29 rooms in two beautifully restored buildings in the Old Town. www.hotel.com.pl/copernicus

TOURIST INFORMATION
Ulica Szpitalna 25; www.krakow.pl/en

What Else to Eat

Another iconic Polish dish is a "hunter's stew" named **bigos**, which is made with sauerkraut, chopped cabbage, and meat (pork, beef, game, sausage, and/or bacon). Everything is mixed together and cooked over a low flame for several hours, then put aside to be reheated a few more times, enhancing the flavors. The best place to try it is in someone's home; every family has its own recipe. Very few meals in Poland start without soup: **żurek**, made with beef or chicken stock, bacon, onion, mushrooms, sour cream, and kwas, a mixture of rye flour and water that has been left to ferment for several days, is a classic. Just as Polish but less unique is **barszcz**, a red beet soup not unlike Russian borscht.

The Best Places to Eat Pierogi

Zapiecek Polskie Pierogarnia
inexpensive

Pierogi were a mainstay during Poland's years of Communist rule, and while a lot has changed in both Poland and *pierogi* fillings since then, cheap and cheerful *pierogarnie* (places serving *pierogi*) still seem to have the best dumplings. A quintessential example is Zapiecek in the Old Town and, to the eternal gratitude of party people and denizens of the dark, it's open around the clock. Nothing fancy here – Zapiecek is self-service with a half-dozen tables and garden seating in the warmer months. But the legions of locals frequenting the joint are here for the finest handmade *pierogi* in town, rolled and pinched before their very noses. It's a quintessential Kraków experience and one not to be missed.
Ulica Sławkowska 32, Kraków; open 24 hrs daily; www.zapiecek.eu

Also in Kraków

If you're looking for *pierogi* in more stylish surrounds, just cross the street to **U Babci Maliny** *(www.kuchniaubabcimaliny.pl; inexpensive)*, where the *pierogi* are fried, not boiled, and served on a real trencher – a piece of bread as a plate. The decor is faux-folksy, with rough-hewn wooden walls and sheepskins, but cozy and fun.

Also in Poland

One of Warsaw's finest restaurants, **Gessler Restauracja U Kucharzy** *(www.gessler.pl; expensive)* serves peerless *pierogi* along with more ambitious dishes in a delightful restaurant set inside the kitchen of a elegant old hotel.

Around the World

The Polish diaspora ensures that excellent *pierogi* can be sampled in many corners of the world, and notably in London. Gessler of Warsaw has taken over Daquise, the longest-established independent Polish restaurant in London and favorite of Polish emigrés. It now trades as **Gessler Restauracja at Daquise** *(www. gesslerlondon.com; moderate)* in spruced-up but still very homey surroundings, just around the corner from the South Kensington tube station. For something even more stylish, head north along Exhibition Road to **Ognisko** *(www. ognisko.com; expensive)*, a clubby place filled with oil paintings, chandeliers, and mirrors and overlooking a verdant square. It serves a variety of Polish specialties, including *pierogi z mie sem lub pierogi ruskie* (*pierogi* stuffed with meat or cheese and potatoes) and *watróbka ciele ca nieborów* (calf's liver with Polish smoked bacon, tomato, and mustard sauce).

Three Days in and around Capri

Stunningly beautiful views and spectacular sights are everywhere here, demanding to be admired from land, sea, and mountaintop.

DAY ONE Take a morning **boat trip** around the island to see the cliffs and fantastic rock formations such as the **Faraglioni rock stacks**. If the tide is right, boatmen will row you into the splendid recesses of the **Blue Grotto**. An easy afternoon walk from Capri town leads to **Villa Jovis**, former vacation home of the Roman emperor Tiberius.

DAY TWO From **Anacapri** take the dizzying chairlift up **Monte Solaro** to the brilliant belvedere and café. Afterward, take the bus to the landmark **Faro lighthouse** and enjoy a swim at the small beach.

DAY THREE Make a full-day boat trip to the mainland, to **Sorrento** and around the peninsula to the spectacular **Amalfi Coast**. Here the pastel-colored houses of **Positano** cascade down the mountainside to a beautiful bay. Surrounded by terraced lemon groves, **Amalfi** nestles at sea level, its majestic black-and-white-checkered *duomo* dominating narrow alleyways dating back to Norman and Arab times.

Essentials

GETTING THERE
Fast **hydrofoils** and **ferries** from Naples and Sorrento run many times a day all year round. Once there, a **funicular** climbs to the town itself, and orange **buses** make the trip to Anacapri and around the island.

WHERE TO STAY
Pensione La Tosca (moderate) is a peaceful, welcoming little hotel with a beautiful terrace. *www.latoscahotel.com*
Villa Eva (moderate), just out of Anacapri, has a pretty garden, swimming pool, and panoramic views from the terraces. *www.villaeva.com*
Hotel Tragara (expensive) is luxurious, with breathtaking views over the Faraglioni rock stacks. *www.hoteltragara.com*

TOURIST INFORMATION
Capri Harbor; *+39 81 837 0686*

Right The tempting *tricolore* of *insalata caprese*: ripe red tomatoes, pearly white mozzarella, and fresh green basil

Below The town of Anacapri is watched over by a statue of Caesar Augustus, first of the Roman emperors

CAPRI ITALY

The Colors of Italy on Capri

Capri, the divinely picturesque island getaway in the Gulf of Naples in southern Italy, sums up *la dolce vita*. Well known to the ancient Romans, who built sumptuous imperial villas on its spectacular headlands, Capri also spells meal after memorable meal. Its simple but delicious summertime signature dish, *insalata caprese*, is now prepared the world over.

A surprisingly rugged mountainous island with sheer limestone cliffs rearing out of the crystal-clear Mediterranean, Capri has a remarkably temperate climate. Its pleasant winters suit the cultivation of citrus fruits, both lemons and sweet oranges. Hot summers tempered by sea breezes encourage grapevines that produce superb red and white wines. In the island's villages, charming houses are surrounded by gorgeous gardens that overflow with all manner of exotic plants, from palm trees to vividly colored bougainvillea.

Picture-postcard Capri has attracted huge numbers of visitors for centuries, from fleets of day-trippers and cruise ship passengers to the international jet set and royalty. It was probably for the latter that the island's signature salad with its three colors – the red, white, and green of the Italian flag – was invented.

Insalata caprese is a simple spread of thick slices of fresh tomato alternated with mozzarella cheese. It is important that both the main ingredients be at room temperature, not chilled, so that their individual flavors are brought out. A little salt may be added to the tomato, but only just before serving to ensure that it stays firm. Aromatic fresh basil with its strong oily perfume is a crucial addition, either as whole leaves or torn or chopped, depending on the school of thought, and the whole is given a light drizzle of extra-virgin olive oil. Sometimes oregano and olives are added for extra fragrance and flavor.

The dish was eulogized by the Italian Futurist movement of the early 20th century for its lightness and flavor, in contrast to the ubiquitous starchy pasta they rejected as far too heavy for a modern diet in the industrial age. (Legend has it that Egypt's King Farouk, while vacationing on the island, managed to buck this healthy trend by having his *insalata caprese* served as the filling in his toasted sandwiches.) For a dish this light, fresh, and simple to succeed, the ingredients must be of superb quality – especially the cheese. The finest mozzarella, made from buffalo milk, has to travel from the mainland region of Campania, just across the water. But few would disagree that *insalata caprese* tastes best of all on the lovely island on which it was invented.

What Else to Eat

With a bounty of fresh seasonal produce from land and sea, Capri and the Amalfi Coast have plenty for gourmet visitors. Order **ravioli alla caprese**, luscious rounds of pasta filled with moist *caciotta* cheese blended with egg, and dressed with a light sauce of tomato and herbs. Otherwise go for **gnocchi alla sorrentina**, tiny potato dumplings smothered in a smooth cheesy sauce with a hint of tomato. **Totani** are tender squid, which are stewed slowly and deliciously with potatoes. This part of Italy is famed for its lemons, which grow to gargantuan size, and on the dessert front, one landmark is **delizia al limone**, a heavenly, frothy cream of lemon with egg white. A superb conclusion to any meal is a slender frosted glass of cold **Limoncello** liqueur, a delicious, tingly after-dinner drink made with lemon rind steeped in alcohol.

Above Water buffalo, whose milk is used to produce the finest mozzarella cheese

The Best Places to Eat Insalata Caprese

Ristorante Villa Verde expensive

Discreetly tucked out of the way down a quiet alleyway a short stroll from Capri's central Piazzetta, this smart restaurant has its fair share of suntanned VIP guests, whose photos adorn the walls of the entrance. A courtyard garden fringed by trees enables alfresco dining in candlelight. The *insalata caprese* comes on a vast white platter, with overlapping layers of luscious mozzarella, thickly cut, alongside piles of rich red tomato rounds. Giant dark green olives, whole basil leaves, a sprinkling of oregano, and a splash of olive oil are the finishing touches. Similar high-quality ingredients are used for the restaurant's pizzas, baked in a wood-fired oven to guarantee that authentic smoky tang. Seafood also ranks high on the menu, with daily specials depending on availability. The fried *moscardini*, tender baby octopus, melt in your mouth. The bulging wine cellar is well stocked with bottles from the key regions of Italy as well as Spain and Australia.

Vico Sella Orto 6, Capri town; open noon–4 PM & 7 PM–1 AM daily; www.villaverde-capri.com

Also on Capri

Down narrow Via Lo Palazzo in downtown Capri, down-to-earth **Verginiello** *(+39 81 8370944; inexpensive)* bustles nonstop as heavily laden waiters dash from the animated kitchen to the spacious, panoramic dining room. Excellent-value Neapolitan dishes include *linguine malafemmina*, with tomato, anchovies, capers, and black olives, while fresh ingredients are showcased in salads such as the *caprese*.

Also in Italy

In Alberobello in Puglia, snug beneath the ancient stone arches and vaults of a 1700s olive press, **Ristorante Casanova** *(www.casanovailristorante.it; inexpensive)* makes good use of fresh mozzarella and its twin *burrata*, a similar but richer cheese. Both are served alongside salamis as antipasti. The typical local dishes feature fava beans and broccoli.

Rest of the World

Buffalo mozzarella sourced from an organic farm in the UK goes into the *insalata caprese* served at the **Ristorante Carpaccio** in London *(www.carpacciorestaurant.co.uk; moderate)*. The mouthwatering menu also offers a unique range of carpaccio, with ultra-thin slices of ox tongue, smoked duck, and octopus, among others. The cuisine is basically Italian but with a creative twist, so the *frittura mista di pesce* (a platter of mixed, fried fish) comes with a sweet and sour condiment.

AMSTERDAM NETHERLANDS

Rijsttafel Feasts in Amsterdam

Vast riches have flowed between Asia and Holland for hundreds of years, from the 17th-century heyday of the Dutch East India Company to 20th-century plantation wealth. As well as funding the canal-threaded elegance of cities like Amsterdam, this historic link has left a delicious edible legacy, *rijsttafel* – an assemblage of classic dishes inspired by traditional Indonesian feasts.

Holland is home to over 170 nationalities, but the most intriguing food influence is Indonesian. The Dutch dominated this vast Asian archipelago – home to evocative locations like Java, Bali, and Sumatra – from the early 17th century, taking full political control of the "Dutch East Indies" from 1800 until its independence in 1945. Politics and palates were intimately linked, however, and Holland was forced to joust with rival nations for commercial control of spice treasures such as nutmeg and cloves.

Colonial leaders met – and ate – amid the ornate courtyards of opulent venues such as the long-gone Hotel des Indes in Batavia (now Jakarta). It was in places such as these that a new type of feast gained popularity in the early 20th century, bringing together favorite local dishes in a dazzling showcase of Indonesia's exotic flavors. Christened *rijsttafel* ("rice table"), it took inspiration from traditional Indonesian feasts such as *tumpeng*, where a mound of rice was flanked by dishes forming a taste symphony of spicy, sweet, sour, and salty. Classics included in the Dutch feast were *teri kacang* (tiny dried fish fried with peanuts), *telur pindang* (marbled boiled eggs), sweet dry-fried *tempeh* (a fermented soy product), and *sambal goreng ati* (liver in chili pepper sauce). The dishes were Indonesian but the combination was Dutch, and today's *rijsttafel* – consisting of 12 to 30 little dishes – is found mainly in Amsterdam and The Hague. Restaurants offering this delicious feast range from small, unadorned backstreet hangouts to upmarket foodie shrines that still nod to the ambitions of the old Indonesian chefs, who were renowned for trying to outdo one another with the quality and inventiveness of their dishes.

Amsterdam's Tropenmuseum is a fascinating place to visit for a colorful overview of Indonesia's influence on Holland over the past 350 years. Nearby, the Eastern Docklands showcase the city's contemporary style – old, run-down quays have been transformed with 21st-century modernism to provide a striking contrast to the cobbled lanes and historic facades of the more traditional old downtown. The old docks also offer another island called Java, though this one is home to modern design shops and cutting-edge architecture rather than exotic food and valuable spices.

Above Amsterdam is a wonderful place to walk or cycle around; its colorful streets hide a plenitude of laid-back cafés and multicultural restaurants

What Else to Eat

Cheese is Dutch gold. **Edam,** a low-fat delight, is named after a beautiful 12th-century town on the shores of the Ijsselmeer inland sea. Another charming medieval town gave its name to Holland's other famous cheese – **Gouda** – which is still sold in giant wheels on the cobbled main square; choose between sweeter *jong* ("young") or more pungent *oud* ("old"). Salty **raw herring** is a unique Dutch classic. Try it on its own (dangle by the tail and slip it into your mouth) or stuffed with onions in a roll. The perfect way to wash down the herring is with **genever,** a Dutch predecessor to gin. Also good on its own, you can enjoy a lip-smacking blast of this Netherlands gem in one of Amsterdam's cozy vintage genever bars, such as De Drie Fleschjes on Gravenstraat or Oloofspoort on Nieuwebrugsteeg.

Three Days in and around Amsterdam

Short distances and fast trains make it easy to discover how much more there is to Holland beyond Amsterdam's atmospheric canal-laced beauty.

DAY ONE In Amsterdam, reflect on artistic genius at the **Van Gogh Museum** and the **Rijksmuseum**, which houses works by Rembrandt. You can then visit his former home, the **Rembrandt House Museum**, or that of another much-loved Amsterdam inhabitant, **Anne Frank**. Then dive into the galleries, boutiques, and bars of the charming **Jordaan** area, or its neighbor, the multicultural **De Pijp**.

DAY TWO Combine culture and coast in Holland's capital, **The Hague**, where you can see Old Masters at the 17th-century **Mauritshuis**, discover Mondrian at the **Gemeentemuseum**, then sniff sea air amid the dunes at **Scheveningen** or hop on tram 1 for a 20-minute ride to lovely **Delft** for an afternoon on its historic tiles.

DAY THREE Visit **Utrecht** to climb **Domtoren**, Holland's tallest and oldest church tower, and see **De Haar**, a restored medieval castle. The city also has Europe's only **Aboriginal Art Museum** and is home to the iconic Rietveld–Schröder House, a modernist home designed by Gerhardt Rietveld and Truus Schröder in the 1920s.

ESSENTIALS

GETTING THERE
Amsterdam's large international **airport**, Schipol, is 15 minutes by **train** from central Amsterdam. There are also **shuttle buses** from the airport to around 100 of the city's hotels.

WHERE TO STAY
Citizen M (inexpensive) is an exciting modern hotel with great facilities at an affordable price. www.citizenmamsterdamcity.com
The Convent Hotel (moderate) is a central, 4-star hotel carved from two medieval monasteries. www.accorhotels.com
Hotel Pulitzer (expensive) offers canalside luxury in a row of 17th- and 18th-century houses in the Old Quarter. www.pulitzeramsterdam.com

TOURIST INFORMATION
www.iamsterdam.com/en

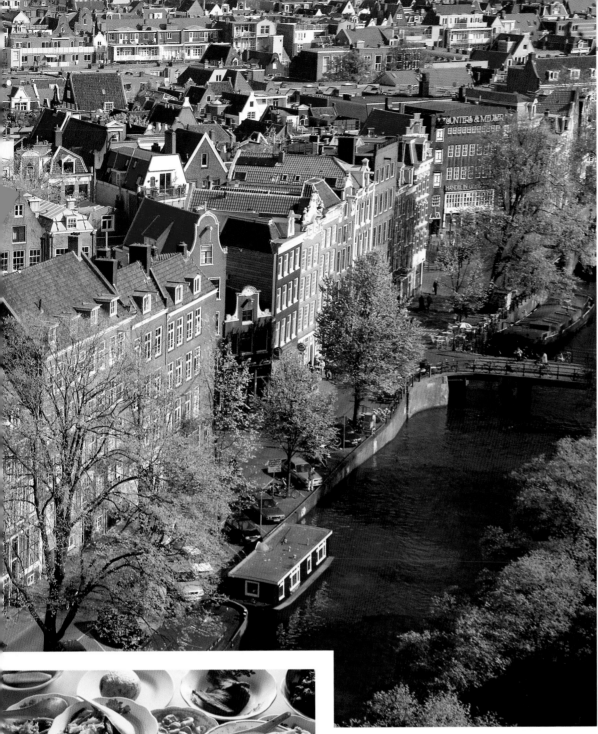

The Best Places to Eat Rijsttafel

Blue Pepper expensive

Amsterdam's Blue Pepper adds *haute* modern touches to the abundance of *rijsttafel*. Executive chef Sonja Pereira's interpretation of classic *rijsttafel* keeps the number of dishes down while adding flavors to maintain diversity of taste. Zesty additions to the traditional array include salads such as *salada asinan segar* (crab, mango, and pineapple with tamarind) and *salada bebek* (roasted duck with green turmeric leaves), while clever reinventions include grilled fish pâté in place of dried fish, or lime and soy replacing peanuts in a lamb satay sauce. Dutch shrimp adds a local presence to spicy green beans.

A more contemporary influence permeates the alternative Indonesian menu overseen by Pereira's colleague Tani Morabe. Shaped by modern Indonesia's vibrant culinary interactions with its Southeastern Asian neighbors, spicy chicken soup mingles with glass noodles and floating quail eggs, while grated coconut gives an East Indies tinge to wok-fried vegetables. "Indonesian cooking at its summit," raved one Dutch critic, and many would agree.

Nassaukade 366, Amsterdam; open 6–10 PM Wed–Mon; www.restaurantbluepepper.com

Also in Amsterdam

In the Eastern Canal district, restaurants line Utrechtsestraat, including the **Tempo Doeloe** *(www.tempodoeloerestaurant.nl; moderate)*, a well-regarded eatery that offers an air of restrained privacy along with attention to detail. It serves three different sizes of *rijsttafel*, from 15 to 25 dishes. Those on a budget should head for **Bojo** *(www.bojo.nl; inexpensive)* on Lange Leidsedwarsstraat, where huge portions don't mean compromising on quality, and the late hours make it a boon for night owls.

Also in the Netherlands

In The Hague, two places stand out: **Garoeda** *(www.garoeda.nl; moderate)*, which was opened by Indonesians resettling after independence in 1949; and **Raffles** *(www. restaurantraffles.com; expensive)*, which sits amid Archipel's beautiful streets and boasts an interior based on the Javan house of the owner's grandparents.

Around the World

The opulent **Oasis Restaurant** *(www.oasis-restaurant.co.id; expensive)* in Jakarta is one of the few places in Indonesia that now serves *rijsttafel*. This two-story mansion was built in 1928 as the private home of Dutch millionaire F. Brandenburg van Oltsende – who, in true colonial style, made his fortune from plantations of tea, rubber, and cinchona (a quinine-rich tree). Enjoy your "rice feast" here in grand style, served by up to 15 wait staff.

Above Modern Dutch restaurants, such as Amsterdam's Blue Pepper (pictured), offer innovative versions of classic Indonesian dishes

Left *Rijsttafel* today consists of 12–30 dishes; in the 1920s the Hotel des Indes in Batavia (now northern Jakarta) served 60 different dishes

A Day in Evora

Evora is the single most interesting destination in the Alentejo and it's also convenient for the nearby carpet-making town of Arraiolos and the elegant "marble towns" of Estremoz, Borba, and Vila Viçosa.

MORNING Visit the daily **Mercado Municipal** (municipal market) for Alentejan produce, but if possible, also go to the even more impressive open-air market held in Rossio square on the first Tuesday of the month. In the old town, don't miss the majestic **Sé** – the largest medieval cathedral in Portugal – or the Corinthian **Templo Romano** just a short walk away.

AFTERNOON Cafés line the central square, **Praça do Giraldo**, and after coffee and cakes, you can stroll to **São Francisco** church to see its macabre **Capela dos Ossos**, a chapel lined with the skulls and bones of former monks. The pretty public gardens lie beyond.

EVENING Watch the sun set from the outdoor café by the **Templo Romano** before investigating the traditional taverns and local restaurants hidden in the city's medieval alleys.

Essentials

GETTING THERE
From **Lisbon international airport** it's a 90-minute drive east to **Evora**. If you don't want to rent a car, there are direct **buses** and **trains** from downtown Lisbon.

WHERE TO STAY
Residencial Policarpo (inexpensive) is a charming if modest *pension* in a 16th-century manor house. www.pensaopolicarpo.com
Albergaria do Calvário (moderate) has boutique-style rooms in a former olive-oil mill. www.albergariadocalvario.com
Pousada de Evora – Lóios (expensive) is an elegant hotel in an ancient convent building, situated next to the Templo Romano in the center of town. www.pousadas.pt

TOURIST INFORMATION
Praça do Giraldo 73; +351 266 777 071

Right The black pigs of the Alentejo wander the region's oak forests, grazing freely on acorns

Below The view from Estremoz – the largest of the "marble towns" – over the plains of Upper Alentejo

Porco à Alentejana in Portugal

The Alentejo region, a vast area between Lisbon, the Tagus River, and the Algarve coast, is Portugal's agricultural heart – a giant patchwork of olive and wine estates, wheat and corn fields, rooting pigs, and grazing cattle. The regional cuisine is typically rustic, and boasts one of Portugal's best-loved dishes, the unusual meat-and-shellfish combination of *porco à alentejana*.

Any journey from Lisbon to the Algarve cuts right through the dramatic rural landscapes of the Alentejo, which has been the "bread-basket" of Portugal since Roman times. It's a land of burning summers and freezing winters, where a string of walled, medieval hill towns in the north gives way to endless, rolling plains that characterize much of the region.

In Baixo (Lower) Alentejo, quiet country roads run past shady stands of cork trees, isolated farmsteads, storks nesting on posts, and mile after sprawling mile of olive groves and vineyards. Among the few towns there's occasionally a magnificent surprise, like the so-called "marble towns" of Alto (Upper) Alentejo, whose buildings, roads, and monuments are all constructed from the same locally quarried pale stone. But there's only really one must-see historic destination in the region: the northern city of Evora, which boasts a stunning Roman and Moorish legacy, a fascinating tangle of late-medieval alleys, and a famous monthly open-air market showcasing local crafts and produce.

In such a rural area, it's hardly surprising that the local cuisine relies heavily on hearty peasant produce. Corn bread is used in many traditional recipes, crumbled into thick soups with fresh, aromatic cilantro (these dishes are known as *açordas*) or soaked, mashed, and fried with spicy sausage and paprika *(migas)*. Sheep cheese from the walled market town of Serpa is highly prized, while pork from the acorn-fed Alentejo *porco preto* (black pig) is fêted for its rich flavor.

It's loin of Alentejo pork that's at the heart of the one truly outstanding regional dish, *porco à alentejana*, which uses cubes of this fine meat marinated in a mix of white wine, garlic, paprika, and bay leaves. The twist in the recipe comes with the addition of clams, a surprising ingredient in a largely landlocked region, but explained by the ease with which (in pre-refrigeration times) shellfish could be transported from the coast and kept alive in buckets or trays until needed. Add cilantro, fried potatoes, and sometimes a helping of pickled vegetables, and you have a distinctive taste combination that has seduced the entire country.

The Best Places to Eat Porco à Alentejana

O Fialho (expensive)

O Fialho is the best place to sample Alentejan *cozinha típica* (regional cuisine) in Evora. Loved by locals for its easygoing charm, and considered a find by in-the-know visitors, the restaurant has been in the safe hands of the Fialho family since the late 1940s. It's a cozy and comfortable place to dine, with locally sourced ingredients and produce – cheese, olives, cured meats, seasonal vegetables, Alentejo pork, and game – at the heart of a typically rustic menu that demands a large appetite. While you might choose a hearty meal-in-itself soup, an unusual rice dish (with shredded hare, for example), or roast mountain lamb, this is undoubtedly the place to find out what *porco à alentejana* is all about. O Fialho serves a classy version of this classic dish, but even this more refined serving proves too large for many people – much to the disappointment of the restaurant staff, who offer an array of rich and creamy Portuguese desserts to follow.

Travessa das Mascarenhas 16, Evora; open 12:30–3:30 PM and 7:30 PM–midnight Tue–Sun; www.restaurantefialho.com

Also in the Alentejo Region

The road east from Evora to Spain passes through the attractive border town of Elvas, where **Restaurante O Lagar** *(www. restauranteolagar.com.sapo.pt; inexpensive)*, sited in a former olive-oil mill, is an excellent choice for *porco à alentejana* and other local dishes. In historic Beja, the capital of Baixo Alentejo, there's fine regional dining in the garden restaurant of the **Pousada de Beja** *(www. pousadas.pt; expensive)*, a splendid hotel fashioned from the former São Francisco convent.

Also in Portugal

The best place for Alentejan dishes in Lisbon, the Portuguese capital, is **Casa do Alentejo** *(www. casadoalentejo.pt; moderate)*, an Alentejan cultural center and restaurant with a palatial courtyard and impressive tiled dining room. *Borrego* (lamb) is also an Alentejan specialty, and the menu offers grilled *costeletas* (chops) served with rice as well as a typical lamb *ensopado*, a soupy, stewlike dish.

Around the World

It's rare to find the specific combination of pork and clams anywhere other than in a Portuguese restaurant, although the northeastern Catalonia region of neighboring Spain has a chicken-and-shrimp dish that mixes meat and shellfish in a similar fashion. To sample a true *porco à alentejana* in unexpected surroundings, visit the former Portuguese colony of Macau (now in China), where a score or more restaurants offer authentic Portuguese dishes. **Restaurante Litoral** *(www.restaurante-litoral.com; moderate)* has a loyal local following.

Alentejo Wines

The Alentejo is one of Portugal's best-regarded wine-producing regions, especially for reds. There is a long history of winemaking here, especially around the towns of **Borba, Reguengos, Redondo,** and **Evora,** but it's only since the 1980s that Alentejo wine has gained an international reputation – in particular since many Alentejo vineyards started producing gutsy modern wines in a "New World" style (some even have Australian winemakers on board). **Herdade do Esporão** *(www.esporao.com)* produces the Esporão Reserva, Monte Velho, and Alandra wines you'll find in restaurants and shops across the country, and offers tastings and wine courses. In Evora, there's a visitor center that provides information about all the winery tours along the Alentejo wine route (Rota dos Vinhos do Alentejo; *www.vinhosdoalentejo.pt*).

Above *Porco à alentejana* is a favorite in both cafés and high-end restaurants

MARSEILLE FRANCE

Fishy Feast in the South of France

Marseille may not be pretty in a traditional Provençal way, but France's oldest city is not short of appeal. Marseille's charm lies in its multicultural, Mediterranean vibe, charismatic scruffiness, and that most famous of all Marseille dishes, bouillabaisse – a rich, briny boil-up of the morning's catch fresh from the port, fragrant, silky, and golden-glistening in the luminous sunshine.

Bouillabaisse was originally a fishermen's stew – the unsold catch of, usually, the smallest and most unprepossessing fish, cooked up in a pot of bubbling water on the beach. Today it is a more sumptuous dish, enriched with butter and saffron, much more in keeping with the recipe's origins in legend – concocted by Venus to lull her husband Vulcan to sleep so she could have some fun with Mars. Lots of variations exist in Provence, but Marseille lays claim to the best: a jamboree of local fish and shellfish, olive oil, onions, garlic, fennel, tomatoes, potatoes, parsley, and the golden ingredient, saffron. The city even has an official Charter of Bouillabaisse listing the ingredients that "must" be used in the dish, including a minimum of four fish from a choice of red mullet, John Dory, *rascasse* (scorpion fish), monkfish, and conger eel.

Small, bony rockfish and *rascasse* provide the base for the broth, which is reduced and concentrated – the word bouillabaisse probably derives from *bouille abaisse*, or "boil and reduce" – until it's as pungent as Davy Jones' locker. The soup is served first, bobbing with, traditionally, a single large crouton daubed with garlicky *rouille* – a ruddy mayonnaise spiked with chili pepper – followed separately by a heaped platter of fish that have been simmered in the broth.

The fish is landed daily at the Vieux Port (old port), where fishermen have been selling their catch for 350 years. Marseille today may be a huge, modern city – multi-ethnic, soccer-crazy, and with one of the most hair-raising traffic systems in France – but it's rich in history, as vibrant and eclectic as its signature dish. Not for nothing was it voted European Capital of Culture 2013. Painted by Cézanne, Renoir, and Dufy, it is the home of the Château d'If, where Alexandre Dumas's *Count of Monte Cristo* was imprisoned, and of architect Le Corbusier's seminal Unité d'Habitation.

Rising up behind the Vieux Port, Le Panier is the oldest part of the city, a hub of narrow streets and steps with pale candy-colored houses and a cosmopolitan mood thanks to decades of immigration. Nearby is the souk-like Marché des Capucins, a North African-flavored market piled with exotic produce and pastries. On the other side of the harbor, surveying the designer hotels, lounge bars, galleries, and boutiques that have sprung up below, sits Marseille's "Good Mother" – the magnificent Byzantine church of Notre Dame de la Garde, keeping watch over a city that gave France one of its most classic recipes.

A Day in Marseille

A modern city whose 26 centuries of cultural heritage and, at its heart, a fishing village atmosphere, come together to make Marseille a compelling destination.

MORNING Set off from **Fort Saint-Jean** and meander the winding streets of **Le Panier**, stopping to check out local archaeological finds at **La Vielle Charité**. Once a poorhouse, it's now crammed with priceless ancient artifacts. Drop into Marseille's answer to Istanbul's Hagia Sophia, the huge **Cathédrale de la Major**.

AFTERNOON Contrast old and new at **La Joliette** docks, where the Euroméditerranée Project is making bold architectural statements, including the shimmering 485-ft (148-m) **CMA-CGM Tower** designed by Zaha Hadid. If fashion is more your passion, peruse the collection of 20th-century clothes and accessories in the **Musée de la Mode**.

EVENING Climb up to **Notre Dame de la Garde** to take in a sweeping, 360° city view. Meander back to the **Vieux Port**, grab a seat on the terrace of a quayside bar, order a tall pastis, and watch the sun fade before dinner.

Essentials

GETTING THERE
Shuttle buses and taxis run from Marseille's **international airport** to the city. **Trains** link to most of France and beyond, with **bus** services to Provençal towns, including Nice.

WHERE TO STAY
Hôtel Le Corbusier (inexpensive): perfect for 1950s design fans. www.hotellecorbusier.com
Casa Honoré (moderate): a tiny boutique hotel steps from the Old Port. www.casahonore.com
Le Petit-Nice Passédat (expensive): a fabulous family-run villa. www.petitnice-passedat.com

TOURIST INFORMATION
www.marseille-tourisme.com

Above A classic bouillabaisse in the Marseille style, with the broth and the fish, garnished with lemon and herbs, served separately

Left Seagulls wheel hopefully above a fisherman selling his catch on the Quai des Belges, Marseille's exuberant fish market

Above Boats moored in the Vieux Port, with the basilica of Notre Dame de la Garde reaching into the sky in the background

What Else to Eat

Pizza is big in Marseille, and even the pizza vans that dot the city dish up a mean crust. Best of all are the thin-crusted, wood-fired pizzas from Le Panier restaurant **Chez Etienne** *(43 rue de Lorette, no telephone)*. For North African delights, find delicious couscous, tagines, and pastries from boisterous Algerian canteen **Sur le Pouce** *(+33 4 9156 1328)*, near the Marché des Capucins. The weird and wonderful chocolates made by the Le Ray family at their shop, **La Chocolatière du Panier** *(+33 4 9155 7041)*, are also unmissable: try black cherry, ginger, lavender, basil, lime, and coriander, and even onion paired with chocolate.

The Best Places to Eat Bouillabaisse

Le Petit Nice expensive

Gérald Passédat's three-star Michelin eatery sits on an idyllic rocky point surveying the blue, blue Mediterranean. The chef is so attached to his surroundings and Marseille's culinary heritage that he's devoted an entire tasting menu to bouillabaisse. It's an extravagantly poetic, and expensive, version of the original, inspired by Passédat's childhood memories – he was born on this very spot. His dedication to achieving the most intense, authentic flavors begins with the fish stock, boiling down live rock crabs and an assembly of small rockfish (it takes some 6 lb of fresh fish to make a quart of stock) to fashion the fragrant base of the dish. The bouillabaisse menu is then served in three courses, kicking off with a mussel and clam carpaccio with fried strips of *girelle* (rainbow wrasse), followed by the catch of the day, perfectly cooked in a sea-spiked artichoke broth. Then comes the soup: red scorpion fish, sea bream, and potatoes in a saffron-rich broth, with *rouille*, of course.

Anse de Maldormé, Corniche JF Kennedy; open for lunch and dinner Tue–Sat (open Mon evening in July and August); www.petitnice-passedat.com

Also in Marseille

The lovely setting of **L'Epuisette** *(www. l-epuisette.com; expensive)* alone makes it worth a visit. Luckily, the bouillabaisse cooked up by Guillaume Sourrieu is just as impressive. Perched on the jetty in the tiny cove of Vallon des Auffes, this is an impossibly perfect spot for a plate of deluxe fish soup and a platter of squeaky fresh monkfish, red scorpion fish, John Dory, conger eel (all Bouillabaisse Charter-sanctioned), and waxy yellow potatoes, infused with the perkiest saffron broth around.

Also in France

Fittingly, it's a former fisherman's hut that's home to Saint-Tropez's top seafood soup. **Chez Camille** *(www.chezcamille.fr; moderate)*, perched at one end of the bay of Pampelonne, has been dishing up simple seafood since it was mistaken for a beach bistro back in the '50s by director Roger Vadim and his then-wife, Brigitte Bardot. Locals claim it serves up one of the best bouillabaisses on the Riviera.

Around the World

Whatever the weather in London, you can get a taste of sunshine at **Bistro Bruno Loubet** at the Zetter Hotel *(www.bistrotbrunoloubet. com; moderate)*. Ex-Michelin-star chef Bruno Loubet cooks up affordable French food, from rustic favorites like the bouillabaisse with *rouille* and croutons to classics with a modern bent, such as duck *confit* with honey and North African spice.

NUREMBERG

NUREMBERG GERMANY

Franconia's Mini-Bratwurst

Nuremberg is a small city with a big history. The unofficial capital of the Holy Roman Empire, it was a powerful trade center in the Middle Ages and the cultural heart of the German Renaissance in the 15th century. The modern city is no less energetic; it heads up the pretty Franconian region, where wine competes with beer and the sausages are delicious little bratwurst.

Probably invented by Chinese butchers in the 6th century BC, sausages began as an efficient way of using edible meat scraps. With the addition of herbs and spices, they quickly became popular enough for the idea to spread west, giving the ancient Greeks and Romans a chance to really popularize them. In medieval times, the Germans made them into a culinary art form, inventing around 1,200 different types, most of which were smoked, dried, or precooked. But in the early 15th century, cooks in the Nuremberg region invented the most popular German sausage, bratwurst – a fresh sausage that was designed to be cooked.

Central Nuremberg looks like a city frozen in time, from much the same era. It lost most of its medieval glories in the bombing of World War II, but some survive in the old town, where crooked half-timbered houses and surviving city walls hug twisting alleys and tight cobbled streets. A large part of enjoying the town is simply strolling around and soaking up the atmosphere. The Hauptmarkt, its bustling focal square, is often filled with colorful market stands and is overlooked by the Frauenkirch, a beautiful Gothic church. The next square to the north, the Rathausplatz, is equally attractive, thanks partly to the presence of the town hall and the 13th-century St. Sebald church, with its impressive bronze Gothic shrine. But the city's most magnificent single sight is its Kaiserburg (known locally as "The Burg"), the city's huge medieval castle, which took 400 years to complete and whose position above the old town provides impressive views over its red-roofed core.

Eating out in Nuremberg is a treat. Franconian fare is hearty and filling, and often served with the very good local wines. But beer goes best with wurst, and the wurst here is some of the finest in Germany. The *Nürnberger Rostbratwurst* was standardized by town council decree in 1497; each sausage must be 3 inches (7–9 cm) long and 0.8 oz (25 g) in weight. This was probably due to the high prices of meat at the time, but it turned out to be as important to the sausage as its ingredients. It makes for a large surface area around the marjoram-and-caraway-flavored pork, and the crispy outer skin readily absorbs the traditional beech-wood fire aromas. The tangy flavors beg for mouth-wateringly sharp German mustards, so the other natural accompaniment is something mild and forgiving, such as potato salad or sauerkraut. But the little sausages seem to taste best served three abreast on a warm bun, as comfort food on a cold day.

A Day in Nuremberg

Bombs obliterated Nuremberg's heart in World War II, but meticulous rebuilding since has reproduced the original, charming medieval core, ideal for enjoyable wandering.

MORNING Get a feel for the lively downtown at the **Hauptmarkt**, the focal market square, before taking in the attractive venerable buildings around the neighboring square of **Rathausplatz**. Then climb steadily on narrow cobbled streets north to the **Kaiserburg** to view its imperial living quarters and the old town from above.

AFTERNOON Cross Nuremberg's walled core to explore the city's two best museums on its southern side. Choose from stimulating your mind with the contemporary art of the **Neues Museum** or getting a better grip on German history in the **Germanisches Nationalmuseum**, which has many intriguing artifacts, including the world's first globe.

EVENING Head to a **beer hall** such as the Barfüsser Hausbrauerei (Hallplatz 2) to absorb the traditional atmosphere of a vast cellar where you can enjoy handcrafted blond and dark German beers and *Bierbrand*, a schnapps made of beer.

Essentials

GETTING THERE
Nuremberg's international **airport** is 4 miles (7 km) from the city and has a subway to the downtown. There are **buses** and direct **rail** connections to many European cities.

WHERE TO STAY
Elch (inexpensive) offers simple lodgings in a 14th-century house. *www.hotel-elch.de*
Dürer Haus (moderate) has bright and airy rooms near the castle. *www.duerer-hotel.de*
Le Méridien Grand (expensive) is a premier hotel with sleek styling. *www.lemeridien.com*

TOURIST INFORMATION
www.nuernberg.de

Above *Nürnberger Rostbratwürste* are a favorite from the market stands in the city, where they're sold *Drei im Weckla* ("three in a bun")

Left Most visitors choose to stay in the Altstadt ("Old Town"), close to the main square of the Hauptmarkt and the Frauenkirche.

Below The mini-bratwurst are often served with tangy sauerkraut and pretzel or rye bread and hot mustard

Sausages Around the World

The Nurembergers of Germany's Franconia region may lay claim to having invented the bratwurst, but a love of grilled sausage has long since spread throughout much of the Western world. Over time, many nations have developed unique and delicious twists that rival even the age-old recipes of Germany.

NUREMBERG

Bratwurst Herzle inexpensive
Brunnengasse 11; www.bratwurstherzle.de
This old-fashioned and down-to-earth little place, tucked away in a central old town alley, has served the perfect Nuremberg mini-sausages and sauerkraut since 1529. It's always so busy that most diners have to share a table.

Nassauer Keller inexpensive
Karolinenstrasse 2; +49 911 225 967
Worth visiting for the atmospheric medieval cellar dining experience alone, this restaurant is based in one of the only surviving medieval tower houses. It specializes in Franconian cuisine, such as *Schweineschäufele* (roast pork shoulder) and serves several types of sausages, including "original Nuremberg sausages."

Bratwurst-Häusle moderate
Rathausplatz 1, 90403; +49 911 227 695
This tiny historic restaurant in the shadows of St. Sebald church is so well known and touristy that it's often too packed for its own good. Yet it remains a great place to pick up bratwurst to go along with jars of cured or smoked sausages.

Bratwurstglöcklein expensive
Waffenhof 5; +49 911 227 625
This is the oldest bratwurst restaurant in Nuremberg, dating back to 1313, and its half-dozen set menus strive to create an interesting Franconian meal. They include dishes such as dumpling soup, pork knuckle, Nuremberg sausages that have been simmered with onions and vinegar before grilling, wine sauerkraut, homemade potato salad with a creamy horseradish sauce, and *O´batzder*, a rich local cheese dip made with Camembert and served with pretzels.

ERFURT, GERMANY

The German state of Thüringia also claims to have invented bratwurst. The city is certainly sausage-mad: every adult here consumes an average of two 6–7 inch (15–20 cm) bratwursts every day, and Thüringian sausage has become the German standard.

Faustfood inexpensive
Waagegasse 1; www.faustfood.de
A minimalist grilled meat and sausage eatery with modern interiors; you can sit at chunky wooden tables or perch at the busy counter to enjoy a quick barbecued *Thüringer Rostbratwurst.*

Wirtshaus Christoffel inexpensive
Michaelisstrasse 41; +49 361 2626 943
This medieval-themed restaurant has been serving its specialty sausage with bread and broth continuously since 1477.

Zum Wenigemarkt moderate
Wenigemarkt 13; www.wenigemarkt-13.de
Popular for alfresco eating in summer, this cozy restaurant excels at traditional Thüringian cuisine. It serves an especially crispy *Rostbratwurst* with fried potatoes and sauerkraut laced with bacon flakes.

BERLIN, GERMANY

A city that is always on the go is reliant on a good supply of snacks, and in Berlin this means sausages, especially "currywurst" – chopped sausage smothered in tomato sauce mixed with curry powder.

Curry 195 inexpensive
Kurfürstendamm 195, Berlin; +49 030 881 8942
A neon-lit sausage eatery known as much for its excellent, juicy currywurst sausages as its popularity with German celebrities – which explains the Champagne on the menu.

Konnopke's Imbiss inexpensive
Schönhauser Allee 44a; www.konnopke-imbiss.de
Berlin's most famous sausage kiosk sits beneath noisy elevated train tracks. It has survived the Nazis, World War II, and the privations of East Germany to continue to dole out some of the city's best currywurst: marvelously juicy, served with crispy fries and sprinkled with paprika.

Fleischerei moderate
Torstrasse 116–118; www.fleischerei-berlin.com

A place to actually sit and eat currywurst is a rarity in Berlin, which would give this central restaurant with its simple and functional decor an edge even if its wurst weren't so good.

THE LAKE DISTRICT, UK

Cumbria's contribution to sausage culture is peppery and made of chopped meat, rather than minced, giving it a real chunkiness. Its notable characteristic is its huge length, forming a great wheel on the plate.

Mason's Arms moderate
Cartmel Fell, Grange-over-Sands, Cumbria; www.masonsarmsstrawberrybank.co.uk

High-quality local food and a great selection of local ales make this fellside inn stand out. Its Cumberland sausage embarks on a successful European adventure on a toasted ciabatta, with caramelized onions, damson chutney, and thin fries.

The Yanwath Gate Inn moderate
Yanwath, Cumbria; www.yanwathgate.com

A quintessential northern English country pub, this old inn dates back to 1683. Its chunky and peppery Cumberland sausage comes with black pudding, mashed potatoes, broccoli, carrots, and gravy.

SOUTH AFRICA

The South African *boerewors*, or "farmer's sausage," is a spicy national signature dish. It's made largely from beef seasoned with coriander and is always barbecued on a braai.

Wandie's Place inexpensive
618 Makhalemele St., Dube, Soweto, Johannesburg; www.wandies.co.za

An unpretentious eatery with long tables, colorful tablecloths, bustle, and sociable chatter that started life as a *shebeen*, or illicit bar. It now specializes in a Soweto-style festive buffet including dishes such as mutton curry, beef *potjie* (a stew), *pap* (a porridge), *umqushu* (corn and bean stew), *ting* (soft porridge), and of course *boerewors*, served both fresh from the barbecue and dried as *wors*.

Karoo Cattle and Land moderate
Irene Village Mall, Irene, Pretoria; www.karoocattleandland.com

A great South African steakhouse that claims its *boerewors* would be the pride of any *karoo tannie* (local elderly aunt), which seems at odds with the

cosmopolitan black leather, chrome, and glass decor. But the mix is so successful that the restaurant has opened half a dozen branches.

Karibu expensive
Shop 156, The Wharf Centre, V&A Waterfront, Cape Town; www.kariburestaurant.co.za

Views of Table Mountain and the tranquil blue Atlantic prepare the palate perfectly for the restaurant's vibrant South African flavors. The chefs here are experts in barbecuing *boerewors* over open coals, then serving them with local breads such as *Kaapse broodjie*, or with *putu* and *chakalaka* (porridge and relish).

WISCONSIN, USA

Wisconsin's many German immigrants have developed old recipes to create their own signature "brats," by parboiling them in beer before grilling, part-filling them with cheddar, or lacing them with chili pepper, Cajun style.

Charcoal Inn South inexpensive
1313 South 8th Street, Sheboygan; (920) 458-6988

South Sheboygan's annual bratwurst festival is the big Wisconsin draw for sausage lovers, but when it's not on, the Charcoal Inn is the place to head to. The must-order meal here is a double brat with the works: two sausages in a bun with pickles, mustard, and raw onions, with butter oozing out on every side. As in Germany, the key to its great taste is the flavor of heavy spices unlocked by a smoky charcoal fire and superb traditional bread rolls with thin, crispy crusts and soft centers.

Milwaukee Brat House moderate
1013 3rd St., Milwaukee; www.milwaukeebrathouse.com

Though it only opened in 2008, this sausage specialist already has a cult following. Its late-19th-century brick town-house home, with stained glass, long dark-wood bar, and historic photos of Milwaukee, is the perfect backdrop for great brats from Fred Usinger's excellent butcher shop opposite the bar.

Water Street Brewery moderate
1101 N Water St., Milwaukee; www.waterstreetbrewery.com

Milwaukee has the only baseball stadium in the US where bratwurst outsell hot dogs; many of its pubs and bars feature it too. This microbrewery, with its brick warehouse interiors, adds its own signature by simmering its bratwurst in beer and mixed spices prior to grilling.

NORTH NORFOLK ENGLAND

Great Pub Grub in North Norfolk

The pubs along North Norfolk's windswept coast have long been cozy refuges, but these days they offer more than just a pint to warm your cockles. Old-fashioned drinking dens have been transformed into gastropubs, where you are now likely to be greeted by the delicious aroma of pan-fried scallops or duck with lavender sauce, served with real ale or a good choice of wines.

The famously flat North Norfolk landscape has a haunting atmosphere all its own, with sand dunes and saltmarshes stretching for miles along the shore. Tidal mudflats attract rare migratory birds, and colonies of seals inhabit the sandbars offshore. Popular in summer for seaside excursions and seal-spotting trips, the coastline's very bleakness draws visitors for birdwatching and bracing walks in winter. And once the fresh sea air has brought a rosy glow to your cheeks, there's nothing like ducking into a gastropub – one of the new breed of "dining pubs" dedicated to fine, locally sourced food – for a hearty meal.

All along the North Norfolk coast you'll find historic stone-walled pubs that are now gastropubs. In summer, vacationers breeze in from the beaches, while in winter, roaring wood fires and steaming damp dogs help build up a convivial fug in which locals gather in snug settles polished smooth by use – much as they have done for the last 500 years. At the Lord Nelson in Burnham Thorpe, you can draw your chair up to the hearth where the Admiral himself warmed his feet. And while you soak up the atmosphere, you can also sample the fruits of the sea and surrounding farmlands.

The fertile fields and grazing marshes support prime beef, lamb, and pork – and prime sausages in rich onion sauce are a gastropub staple. Game is a Norfolk specialty, too: pheasant, partridge, and pigeon abound in season. Pedigree incarnations of classic dishes, such as Sandringham Red Poll rib-eye steak – a rare breed that hit the headlines during a spate of cattle-rustling from the Queen's estate – or local game stew with thyme dumplings are enough to make the mouth of any carnivore water. But seafood is what the region is all about. The sea, the sands, and the winding saltmarsh creeks yield Stiffkey Blue cockles, Thornham mussels and oysters, Brancaster lobster, Cromer crabs, and fresh-caught North Sea fish. Samphire, a succulent marsh grass, is the perfect accompaniment, lightly steamed and salty.

Reinvigorated by a gastropub lunch, you might choose to visit 18th-century Holkham Hall, a Palladian masterpiece with impressive grounds; explore the picturesque villages of Blakeney and Cley next the Sea; enjoy British seaside fun in the brasher resorts of Wells next the Sea and Cromer; venture inland to the pretty towns of Burnham Market or Holt – or simply continue walking along the dreamy, timeless Norfolk coastal path, pausing to investigate the tide pools along the way.

Three Days in North Norfolk

It's less than 40 miles (65 km) from Hunstanton to Cromer, but between these two busy seaside resorts are plenty of delightful stopping-off points – and gastropubs.

DAY ONE Enjoy **Hunstanton**, with its fairground, promenade, and all the fun of the typical vacation resort. Visit the Queen's country home at **Sandringham House**, open to visitors most of the summer. In between the two is **Norfolk Lavender**, a lavender farm and visitor attraction where in summer the scent of these lovely plants fills the air.

DAY TWO Linger in the village of **Brancaster**, with its beach and nature preserve, before heading inland to **Burnham Market**, an attractive town with excellent shopping and dining, ideal for lunch. Nearby is **Holkham Hall**, a country house worth touring before taking the coast road to enjoy **Wells next the Sea** and **Blakeney**.

DAY THREE In Blakeney, book a boat trip to see the **seal colony**, before visiting nearby **Cley next the Sea**, a pretty village known for its pottery and fish smokery. Head east for an afternoon in the adjacent resorts of **Sheringham** or **Cromer**.

Essentials

GETTING THERE
King's Lynn and Cromer can be reached by **rail** from London and from Norwich, and **buses** run regularly up and down the coast.

WHERE TO STAY
The Gin Trap Inn (moderate) in Ringstead is a gastropub with lovely views from the bedrooms. *www.gintrapinn.co.uk*
The Neptune (moderate) has a Michelin-starred restaurant. *www.theneptune.co.uk*
Byfords (expensive), Holt's oldest building, is now a fun boutique hotel. *www.byfords.org.uk*

TOURIST INFORMATION
Staithe Street, Wells next the Sea.

Above The Rose and Crown pub in Snettisham is a traditional North Norfolk pub that offers locally sourced food, including samphire

Left At Blakeney Point, small boats take advantage of the incoming tide as it starts to fill the creeks winding through the saltmarsh

Above Tasty sausages and superb steaks from traditional, fourth-generation butcher Arthur Howell can be found on many Norfolk menus

Seasonal Produce

Cromer crabs are said to be at their finest from Good Friday onward, just in time to be eaten with buttery new potatoes and the glorious **asparagus** for which Norfolk is famed. Traditionally, the last asparagus is cut on Midsummer's Day, but before long **samphire** – a unique, salty edible plant known as "poor man's asparagus" – comes into season. **Lavender** reflects the intense blue of Norfolk's wide summer skies; introduced here by the Romans, its delicate flavor can be found in ice creams and sauces, and even perking up salads. Fall and winter bring a feast of **game**, including little-seen gamebirds such as teal and woodcock, and the plumpest **mussels**.

The Best Places to Eat Norfolk Pub Food

The Rose and Crown
inexpensive–moderate

The Rose and Crown in the village of Snettisham, 4 miles (6 km) north of Sandringham, is an unpretentious village pub that dates back to the 14th century, and it hasn't let its growing reputation as one of the area's best gastropubs spoil its historic feel or its place as a village local. It serves a good selection of Norfolk and Suffolk ales, and its warren of rooms provides cozy drinking corners as well as a choice of eating areas, in among the inglenook fireplaces and red-tiled floors. There are straightforward bar meals, such as fish and chips and Holkham Hall sausages with mash, or more elaborate dishes using local produce. Samphire is harvested on the coast nearby, herbs are grown in community gardens, and seafood is bought direct from the fishermen who bring it to the pub's kitchen early in the morning. Brancaster mussels and oysters sit on the menu alongside Norfolk pigeon breast and fresh grilled asparagus.

Old Church Road, Snettisham, Norfolk; open for lunch and dinner daily; www.roseandcrownsnettisham.co.uk

Also in North Norfolk

With a few exceptions, prices vary little across the area. Food in the 17th-century **Hoste Arms** *(www.hostearms.co.uk; moderate)* on Burnham Market's village green is exceptional. Meats come from the Great Ryburgh Farm, venison from Holkham Hall, and oysters from nearby Burnham Creek. With stunning coastal views, the **White Horse** in Brancaster *(www. whitehorsebrancaster.co.uk; moderate)* has exceptional shellfish, from the beds at the shore of their property. Another **White Horse**, in the iconic village of Blakeney *(www. blakeneywhitehorse.co.uk; moderate)*, is an old coaching inn that fields an impressive range of local suppliers on its menu: look for Morston mussels, Firs Farm lamb, Binham Blue cheese, and beer from microbrewery Yetmans.

Also in England

Heston Blumenthal is just one of several celebrity chefs now running gastropubs, and one of them, **The Hinds Head** in Bray, Berkshire *(www.hindsheadhotel.co.uk; expensive)*, was recently chosen as "Pub of the Year" by the inspectors for Michelin.

Also in the UK

A few miles outside Edinburgh in Lothianbridge, Dalkeith, is the Scottish Gastropub of the Year, the **Sun Inn** *(www.thesuninnedinburgh.co.uk; moderate)*. With its oak floors, wooden beams, and log fires, it's the epitome of the friendly old pub, but it uses superb produce obtained from top Scottish suppliers including Glen Lyon venison, Macsween haggis, Isle of Mull cheddar, and Strathdon blue cheese.

Above Plaza Mayor, Madrid's principal square, abounds in historic buildings and sidewalk restaurants

A Day in Madrid

When Madrid became the capital in 1561, Spain's monarchs went to work transforming the sleepy regional city into the gleaming seat of the crown. From monumental plazas to broad boulevards, and masterpieces of Spanish art to elegant garden parks, their legacies remain some of the most engaging sights of the city.

MORNING View wondrous renditions of the royal family by Diego Velázquez in the **Museo del Prado** – created when the crown transferred much of its collection to this public museum. Then stroll the gardens of the **Parque del Buen Retiro**, once a royal retreat.

AFTERNOON Ringed with cafés and restaurants, **Plaza Mayor** has been Madrid's central gathering spot since it was completed in 1619. Leave this bustling realm of the people to spend hours getting a glimpse of the royal lifestyle in the **Palacio Real**.

EVENING Dress for the red carpet to attend a concert, recital, opera, or ballet in the **Teatro Real**, the 19th-century jewel-box concert hall ordered by Queen Isabel II.

Essentials

GETTING THERE
Most international airlines fly into **Madrid-Barajas Airport,** 7 miles (12 km) from downtown. There are **buses, metro trains,** and shared and standard **taxis** to the central city. Use the fantastic metro to get around the city.

WHERE TO STAY
Hostal Macarena (inexpensive) has spacious but simple rooms near Plaza Mayor. *www.silserranos.com*
Hotel Moderno (moderate) is a gracious family-run property. *www.hotel-moderno.com*
Husa Hotel Paseo del Arte (expensive) is a sleek, stylish hotel near the Reina Sofía art museum. *www.hotelhusapaseodelarte.com*

TOURIST INFORMATION
Plaza Mayor 27; +34 915 881 636; *www.esmadrid.com*

Above *Cocido madrileño* traditionally includes a mixture of salt meat, fresh meat, and smoked sausages, made tender by slow cooking

MADRID SPAIN

Hearty Cocido in Old Madrid

Behind its gloss of 21st-century chic, Madrid reveals itself as an imperial capital of dazzling Baroque monuments and atmospheric warrens of narrow streets. No dish is more emblematic of this old Madrid than *cocido madrileño* – a comfort meal of delicate soup, earthy vegetables, chickpeas, smoky meats, and sausages, perfectly suited to the measured pace of a family lunch.

Few dishes stir such primal nostalgia in the hearts of *Madrileños* as *cocido*. This is the soul food of the Madrid de las Asturias – the old city that sprawled out from the Puerta del Sol under Habsburg rule between 1561 and 1665. The dish can be sampled at its traditional best in the ancient taverns below Plaza Mayor, so little changed that it is easy to imagine Velázquez tipping a lunchtime glass during a break from painting royal portraits.

Tradition and ritual not only define Spanish dining but infuse every interaction that Spaniards at leisure have with their capital city. To fully understand Madrid, follow suit, perhaps by capping a morning in the Velázquez and Goya galleries in the Museo del Prado with people-watching from a café table in Plaza Mayor. In a similar vein, no visit to the lavish rooms of the Palacio Real is complete without pausing to admire the statues and fountains in the Jardines de Sabatini surrounding the royal residence. On Sunday, Parque del Buen Retiro is full of families watching

puppet shows or rowing on the lake, and Madrid's restaurants come alive with diners enjoying the social and gastronomic pleasures of *cocido* – the dish that everyone's grandmother used to make. This hearty stew is a winter favorite, though it can be sampled in many of the city's restaurants throughout the year.

Some of Madrid's *cocido* restaurants are old-fashioned folksy establishments where the stew simmers in earthenware jugs. Others are fine-dining icons where this working-man's hotpot – itself derived from a stew devised by Spain's Sephardic Jews that could be cooked slowly and without human intervention on the Sabbath – achieves an elegance and formality that belies its origins.

Cocido is served in three courses of increasingly intense flavor: first the savory broth with slender noodles, then a plate of toothsome chickpeas and boiled vegetables, and a final plate of hearty meats – heaps of sausages, pork, roast beef, chicken, slabs of bacon, and chunks of ham. The result is a taste of old Madrid and one of the most bounteous and filling dishes in Iberian cuisine.

A Celebratory Dish

Spain was one of the first countries in Europe to grow sugar cane, and there is no denying the Spanish penchant for devouring a special sweet themed to each holiday. The biggest celebration in the city honors Madrid's patron saint **San Isidro** with a nine-day fiesta centered on his feast day, May 15. Pastry shops fill their windows with the special *buñuelos de San Isidro*, an intensely sweet pastry deep-fried until crisp and injected with a creamy custard that spurts out on first bite. Celebrations include parades, concerts, and traditional dance performances, as well as the *corridas* (bullfights) at Madrid's Moorish-influenced **Las Ventas** bullring – a huge red-brick edifice decorated with ceramic tiles. Impromptu bars spring up along the main streets at night to sell what the Spanish call "minis" – big plastic cups of beer, wine, and mixed drinks.

Above Older restaurants advertise *cocido madrileño* on their wall tiles

The Best Places to Eat Cocido Madrileño

La Bola Taberna moderate

Cocido has been a menu centerpiece since this beloved tavern opened in 1870. In the early days, the Verdasco family (who still operate La Bola) served three versions: a noon stew for laborers, a 1:00 PM version with stewed chicken popular with students, and the full-fledged *cocido* with mixed meats and pork fat at 2:00 PM – a favorite of politicians and journalists, according to newspaper reports of the era. The restaurant still prepares *cocido* by letting it bubble slowly in colorful ceramic casseroles over oak charcoal in ancient stoves. As a nod to modernity, service for small tables is in two courses – soup followed by vegetables and meat together. However, it is common for at least half of the *taberna* to be occupied by groups of a dozen or more, enjoying the complete three-course presentation on white tablecloths in the wood-paneled rooms. La Bola also serves a celebrated version of *callos*, Madrid's signature tripe dish.

Calle Bola 5, Madrid; open for lunch daily, dinner Mon–Sat; www.labola.es

Also in Madrid

For a refined *cocido* experience, try the glittering upstairs dining room at **Lhardy** *(www.lhardy. com; expensive)*, which first opened its doors to diners in 1839. A less daunting meal can be had at **Taberna de Antonio Sanchez** at Calle Méson de Paredes 13 *(+34 915 397 826; moderate)*, which offers miniature *cocido* servings as a tapa.

Also in Spain

A regional variety of *cocido* found throughout Andalusia, *cocido andaluz* uses Arabic spices (mostly cumin and saffron), fresh beans, soft squash, and spicy sausages. One of the best is served in the city of Jaén at the **Parador de Jaén** *(www.parador.es; moderate)*. In Galicia, *cocido gallego* pairs the region's famous pork and veal with turnips, potatoes, and white beans.

Around the World

In **Portugal**, a variant of the stew, *cozido à portuguesa*, can be found in most restaurants in the city of Coimbra, such as **Zé Manel Dos Ossos** *(+351 239 823 790; inexpensive)*. It differs from Spanish *cocido* by including Braganza cabbage and several varieties of smoked sausages, and using rice and beans instead of chickpeas. In **Brazil**, the national dish, *feijoada (see pp320–1)*, is a South American adaptation of Portuguese *cozido*, with black beans, pork ribs, and dried beef.

ZURICH SWITZERLAND

Striking Gold in Zurich

Big money is never far away in the small city of Zurich – it is in the gleaming facades of its financial institutions, historic guild halls and churches, abundant cultural offerings, and opulent shops. The city's classic dishes – liver with herbs, or veal in cream sauce – also have a soul-satisfying richness, especially when served with the delicious potato pancakes known as rösti.

Zurich is a city of commerce. The clink of coin has accompanied trade, manufacturing, and not least – from 1755, with the creation of Bank Leu & Cie – the banking sector, which has made this city of around 400,000 inhabitants one of the world's leading financial centers. Nestled on the shores of Lake Zurich and straddling both banks of the Limmat River, Zurich saw the passage of Celts and Romans before settling into its solidly Teutonic mold, which has shaped the diet of the city's burghers. *Zürcher Geschnetzeltes*, strips of tender veal cooked in a cream sauce, and *Leberli*, calf liver pan-fried with garden herbs, are two favorites, especially when accompanied by rösti. These buttery potato cakes are made by boiling unpeeled potatoes until semisoft; they are then peeled and grated, and shaped in the frying pan into a round pancake. The taste of butter and a little salt permeates the cake, which is soft within and a crusty golden brown without.

Rösti may be a local star, but Zurich has much more to offer the taste buds. From *Kaffee und Kuchen* (coffee and cake) in a bakery tearoom to bistro food,

ethnic restaurants, and temples of Michelin-starred refinement, there's much to savor. Very much part of the mix is the street market held twice weekly at Bürkliplatz near the lake – a riot of seasonal fruit, vegetables and flowers, and wild mushrooms in fall.

Despite its wealth, Zurich remains a small city – and its manageable size is what makes getting around downtown on foot, or via Zurich's clean and efficient tram system, the preferred option. Leading straight down toward the lake from the Hauptbahnhof, or main train station, is Bahnhofstrasse, Zurich's answer to Bond Street and Fifth Avenue. Some of the largest banks mingle along this stretch with a lush spread of retail havens. Off to the left is part of Zurich's Old Town, linked by several foot bridges to the rest of the Old Town on the other side of the river. Aside from its medieval guild halls, crowning Old Town glories include the Chagall-windowed Fraumünster church and the Grossmünster (cathedral), surrounded by art galleries, antique stores, chic boutiques, eateries, and food shops. Mixing art, café culture, and shopping is Cabaret Voltaire, a reminder that the Dada movement began in Zurich in 1916.

Above Surrounded by snow-clad peaks, Zurich's Old Town straddles the Limmat River, which flows out from the northern end of Lake Zurich

What Else to Eat

Savory Swiss cuisine can be rich, but be sure to leave room for Zurich's many sweet treats. **Confiserie Sprüngli** (*www.confiserie-spruengli.ch*) on Paradeplatz is not only a favorite meeting point but also the place to buy sinfully good macaroons called *Luxemburgerli*. **Café Schober** (*http://peclard-zurich.ch*) on Napfgasse in Zurich's Old Town is deservedly popular. Its decor is as Baroque-extravagant as its pastries, cakes, and cookies; the hot chocolate is not to be missed. **Teuscher** (*www.teuscher.com*) on Storchengasse is one of the world's finest chocolatiers; don't miss their superlative Champagne truffles, made with Dom Perignon. There's no café here, but visitors enjoy the extravagant decorations that change with each season. There's a smaller branch on Bahnhofstrasse.

A Day in Zurich

Switzerland's largest city is not just for shopping and eating, but also for culture, as a considerable amount of Zurich's wealth – private and public – goes into art and performance. The Old Town bears witness to a rich history, and the lake, particularly in summer, lends the waterfront an almost Riviera-like quality: walk along the promenade parallel to Utoquai to soak up that vibe.

MORNING Visit the **Kunsthaus**, a world-class fine art museum with an extraordinary collection of work by Swiss artist Alberto Giacometti, as well as significant works by Edvard Munch, Van Gogh, Picasso, and leading Expressionists. Leave some time for shopping in the **Old Town** and **Bahnhofstrasse**.

AFTERNOON Check whether the **E. G. Bührle Collection** is having a public viewing, or visit the **Museum Rietberg**, a Mecca of non-Western art housed in part in the villa where German composer Richard Wagner wrote the *Wesendonck Lieder*. Families may prefer the **Swiss National Museum** or **Zurich Zoo**.

EVENING Enjoy chic wine bars, trendy dining, and clubbing, or book a concert at the **Tonhalle** or a performance of opera or ballet at Zurich's **Opera House**.

Essentials

GETTING THERE
Flights from around the globe land at **Zurich Airport**. Trains leave every 10 minutes for the 10-minute ride to Zurich's main **train station**. Zurich's **tram** system covers the city.

WHERE TO STAY
Hotel Leoneck (inexpensive) uses Swiss icons such as dairy cows to create a fun, friendly space. *www.leoneck.ch*
Romantik Hotel Florhof (moderate) is a charmingly converted patrician home. *www.florhof.ch*
Hotel Widder (expensive), in imaginatively converted Old Town buildings, is pure luxury. *www.widder.ch*

TOURIST INFORMATION
Zurich main train station; +41 44 215 40 00

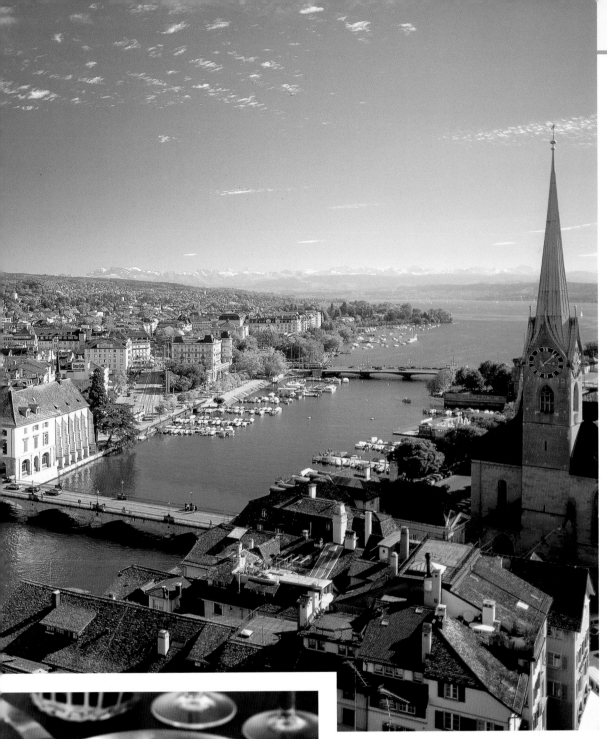

The Best Places to Eat Rösti

Kronenhalle expensive

In Switzerland, many fashionable city eateries either don't serve rösti or reinterpret them into dainty patties. However, at Kronenhalle there's no fooling around with the rösti; it's the real thing – a large, rich, buttery potato cake that's eaten with the restaurant's Châteaubriand steak, Wiener schnitzel, or veal bratwurst.

This establishment has been home to Zurich's *crème de la crème* for generations and has a collection of art by masters such as Miró and Chagall. Whether you're in the front room or one of the two dining rooms, the buzzy atmosphere is that of a chock-a-block brasserie rather than a hallowed hall of gastronomic distinction (although the food is very savvily done). With so much history – it opened its doors in 1862 – to go with the art and the beautiful people, the Kronenhalle is quintessential Zurich.

Rämistrasse 4, Zurich; open noon–midnight daily; www.kronenhalle.ch

Also in Zurich

Once the home of the city's mayor, the building housing **Restaurant Bierhalle Kropf** *(www.zumkropf.ch; moderate)* is a magnificent piece of heritage, dating back to the Middle Ages; try their house specialty of *Würstplatte* – a selection of sausages – *mit Rösti.* At the **Rössli** *(www.roessli-zollikon.ch; moderate)* in Zollikon, an upmarket area just outside the downtown, try your rösti with calf liver, garlic, onions, and herbs. **Zunfthaus zur Haue** *(www. zunfthaus-zur-haue.ch; moderate)* serves its *Geschnetzeltes mit Rösti* with added calf kidney for that extra zing.

Also in Switzerland

Lucerne's iconic **Wirtshaus Galliker** *(+41 41 240 10 02; moderate)* is a bastion of homely Swiss cooking, with rösti galore. **Café du Grütli** *(www.cafedugruetli.ch; inexpensive)* in Lausanne serves up Swiss classics with rösti including local *saucisse à rotir* (roast sausage). **Restaurant Schnabel** *(www.restaurant-schnabel.ch; moderate)* in Basel has a whole selection of rösti dishes as main courses as well as accompaniments to liver dishes such as the Basel specialty *Suuri Läberli* (sour beef liver).

Around the World

In Canada, order rösti as a side dish with the Swiss classic *eminçé de veau à la Zurichoise* (strips of veal cooked in a cream sauce) at Montreal's **La Raclette** *(www.laraclette.ca; moderate).* In Hong Kong, **Chesa** *(www. peninsula.com; moderate)*, at the Peninsula Hotel, serves rösti (which they pronounce "roastee") with both *Geschnetzeltes* (listed on the menu by its French name, *eminçé de veau*) and bratwurst *(see pp130–1).*

Above Zurich is a city of sober efficiency and clean streets, served by a smooth-running network of trams and trolley buses

Left Classic Swiss rösti may be served with a fried egg on top as a weekday meal, or as an accompaniment to veal or liver dishes

TINOS GREECE

An Easter Feast on Tinos

Easter is the biggest event of the year in Greece – and nowhere is it celebrated with greater aplomb than on the island of Tinos in the Cyclades. The solemnity of the midnight mass is finally broken by firecrackers; congregations embrace and depart in candlelit processions that shimmer through the villages, descending on the tavernas to break the 40-day Lenten fast with 24 hours of feasting.

Every year, thousands of Greeks in search of salvation flock to the miracle-working church of Panagia Evangelistria, on a hill above Tinos town (also known as Chora), the island's capital. But Tinos is also a Mecca for epicures and artists seeking solace in the whitewashed villages lodged in the folds of thyme-scented hills. Ancient footpaths crisscross the terraced valleys, and a hiker's sole companions are inquisitive goats and indifferent sheep.

Traditions run deep on Tinos, an island saved from overdevelopment by the all-powerful Greek Orthodox church. Apprentices still chip away at the marble sculpture school in Pyrgos. Old men thread baskets by hand in Volax, a hamlet built around a mysterious cluster of boulders like giant bowling balls. Kids play hopscotch among the flowerpots on the main street of Agapi – a village endearingly called "Love."

Easter is the main event on the island, and the centerpiece of the Orthodox Easter feast is spring lamb, naturally flavored with the wild herbs on which the animals graze. None of the sacrificial lamb goes to waste. Once mass is over, the midnight feast begins with a bowl of *magiritsa* soup, made from lamb's liver, lungs, head, and intestines, *avgolemono* (egg and lemon) sauce, and seasoned with green onions and dill. This pungent broth prepares the stomach for the meat spree to follow – a kind of digestive purgatory after 40 days of Lenten fasting. The ordeal is sweetened with slices of *tsoureki*, a braided brioche flavored with the resinous sap of the mastic tree, and *lychnarakia*, sweet cheese pies shaped like miniature toques.

Traditionally, the Easter lamb is marinated in olive oil, lemon, and oregano, then roasted whole on a spit. This laborious process is an essential part of the culinary ritual: a pit must be dug, a fire built, then everyone must take a turn at the spit (secretly tearing off bits of crispy skin). It takes several hours for the lamb to cook; meanwhile, hard-boiled eggs, dyed red to represent the blood of Christ, are cracked open, wine is drunk, songs are sung, and cigarettes are smoked. Squeamish cooks and lazy restaurateurs often slow-roast a leg of lamb in the oven instead – but the result is almost as good. Potato wedges drenched in lemon and garlic are tucked into the cooking dish, and a simple green salad with a zingy lemon dressing is all that's required on the side. It would be almost sacrilegious to serve anything else.

Three Days on Tinos

The travel writer Lawrence Durrell dubbed Tinos "the Lourdes of modern Greece." But with spectacular vernacular architecture, a thriving crafts industry, and scores of sandy beaches, there's much more than churches to explore.

DAY ONE There are around 50 villages on Tinos – each one lovelier than the last. Buy baskets in **Volax**, where cottages crouch beneath colossal boulders. Visit the Museum of Marble Crafts in **Pyrgos**, where every doorway bristles with sculpted marble birds, boats, and hearts; the village is also famous for *galaktoboureko*, sticky custard pie.

DAY TWO Admire some of the island's 800 carved, decorated dovecotes, found everywhere. Visit the Venetian fortress at craggy **Exobourgo**; return to Tinos town and light a candle at **Panagia Evangelistria** before visiting the neighboring bazaar.

DAY THREE Aeolos, god of the winds, allegedly resides on **Mount Tsiknias**, the island's highest peak. Make the most of winds at the surf school on **Kolimbithra beach**, or head for a sandy cove such as **Livada**, **Apigania**, or **Pachia Ammos**.

Essentials

GETTING THERE
There is no airport; **ferries** from Athens take 3–5 hours. You'll need to rent a **car** to explore.

WHERE TO STAY
Tinion (inexpensive) in Tinos town is a basic but charming *pension*. www.tinionhotel.gr
Vega Apartments (moderate) in Agios Markos offer vacation rentals in sleek Cycladic style. www.vegaapartments.gr
Anthia (expensive) is a family-friendly hotel with a pool and restaurant, close to Agios Fokas beach. www.anthia.gr

FURTHER INFORMATION
www.tinos.gr

Above On Easter Sunday, lamb marinated in lemon juice, olive oil, and oregano is spit-roasted over coals as the centerpiece of the Easter feast

Left The small, medieval village of Triantaros lies 4 miles (6 km) northeast of Tinos town, and is home to the picturesque Church of the Holy Apostles

Above A Greek Orthodox priest prays over the *epitaphios*, a sacred cloth carrying an image of Christ, taken into the sea at Tinos on Good Friday

What Else to Eat

Lamb is often stewed with **artichokes** here: it's one of the few crops that thrive on the wind-whipped island. Locals battle it out for the best recipe at the Artichoke Festival in the village of Komi in May. Buy marinated artichoke hearts *(aginares)* and other Tinian delicacies straight from the source at the daily farmers' market by Tinos port: **thyme honey** thick as treacle, slabs of **louza** (cured pork), **graviera** cheese, and necklaces of **sun-dried tomatoes**. Many of these find their way into **fourtalia**, the delicious frittata of the Cyclades. The ultimate comfort food is *fourtalia* with **fennel-seed sausage** at To Agnandi *(+30 22830 21095)*, a quaint *ouzeri*/grocery in Ktikados.

The Best Places to Eat Greek Lamb

Ta Isternia inexpensive

It's extremely hard to have a bad meal on Tinos, but some tavernas are quietly but consistently sensational. This unassuming local haunt is one of them. While two (admittedly excellent) rival restaurants – Thalassaki and Naftilos – battle it out on the waterfront at Isternia bay, those in the know escape the crowds and head up the treacherous, winding road to the village of Isternia proper. Tucked away on a back street near the parking lot, this is the only taverna in town. Despite the lack of competition, its owners Nikos and Anna maintain very high standards. They serve traditional Greek food with a Tinian twist: caper croquettes, garlic and potato dip, black-eyed beans with sun-dried tomatoes. The traditional Easter feast is cooked exactly as it should be: tender lamb that falls off the bone, lemony potatoes that fall apart in your mouth, and crisp lettuce salad. The small terrace has a handful of tables with ravishing views of the Aegean.

Isternia, Tinos; open 1 PM–midnight Easter–Sep; +30 22830 31005

Also on Tinos

Douar *(+30 22830 41231; inexpensive)* in the village of Steni is a *hasapotaverna* (a butcher and no-frills restaurant) that is strictly for carnivores. Gruff service and cramped tables don't deter the regulars, who come from miles away to gnaw on the addictive lamb chops.

Also in Greece

The tradition of roasting whole lambs on a spit comes from **Roumeli**, a region in central Greece. On Easter Sunday, residents in its towns of **Livadia**, **Amfiklia**, and **Amfissa** set up makeshift barbecues on the streets and offer hunks of roast lamb and *kokoretsi* (skewered innards encased in intestines) to all passers-by.

Around the World

George Calombaris is one of Australia's most influential chefs. **The Press Club** *(www.thepressclub.com.au; expensive)*, his flashy but accessible flagship restaurant in Melbourne, is an exemplary showcase for modern Greek food. Dramatically presented, deceptively simple dishes include roast loin of lamb with beet *horiatiki* (a salad with feta cheese) and almond *skordalia* (a thick, garlicky purée). Greeks eat leftover lamb sandwiches for days after Easter, and you can recreate the experience in Palo Alto, California, at **Evvia Estiatorio** *(www.evvia.net; moderate)*. This upmarket Greek restaurant in Silicon Valley serves roasted-lamb pita-bread sandwiches with tzatziki, tomato, and seasonal greens.

A Day in Toulouse

Toulouse is pretty, prosperous, and rich in culture. Known as *La Ville Rose* (the Pink City), the Place du Capitole lies at its heart; head here for a relaxing coffee and people-watching between visiting sights.

MORNING Visit the **Théâtre du Capitole** to marvel at its painted ceilings. From there walk the **rue du Taur** to Europe's largest Romanesque church, **St Sernin Basilica**.

AFTERNOON Explore the fortress-like **Jacobins Convent**, with its soaring "palm tree" pillars and vaults. Call into the **Musée des Augustins**, a 14th-century convent, for Gothic statuary. Contrast the old with the new at **Les Abbatoirs**, where more than 2,000 pieces of modern art are housed in what was a 19th-century slaughterhouse.

EVENING Come sunset, take up a seat on the terrace in **Place du Capitole** and watch the 18th-century red-brick buildings that cast a rosy tint by day begin to blush and glow lilac as dusk falls. Wander along the banks of the **Garonne River** to see the vaults of the old **New Bridge** lit up at night.

Essentials

GETTING THERE
Aéroport Toulouse Blagnac is a 7-mile (11-km) **drive** or **bus** ride from the city, and has flights to most major European cities. There are also **high-speed trains** from Paris and Lille.

WHERE TO STAY
Le Clos des Potiers (inexpensive) is a refined retreat with Empire style and plenty of atmosphere. *www.hotel-closdespotiers.com*
Hôtel Le Grand Balcon (moderate) is a 1930s hotel, much loved by French author Antoine de Saint-Exupéry, and now completely renovated. *www.grandbalconhotel.com*
Grand Hôtel de l'Opéra (expensive) is a former 17th-century convent-turned-plush hotel on the Place du Capitole. *www.grand-hotel-opera.com*

TOURIST INFORMATION
Donjon du Capitole; *www.toulouse-tourisme.com*

Right The Toulouse version of cassoulet always includes garlicky sausage and either goose or duck

Below Dining alfresco in the Place du Capitole, which hosts a market on Saturdays

TOULOUSE

TOULOUSE FRANCE

Full of Beans in Toulouse

Several towns in the southwest of France claim the earthy pork and bean cassoulet as their own, and Toulouse stands tall and proud among them. Cassoulet is as emblematic to the city as its rugby-loving locals, rowdy bistros, and dusky red bricks. Slow-cooked, smoky, thick with handmade sausage and goose, this classic French stew is a symbol of warmth and country comfort.

Toulouse's links with the past are omnipresent, from its medieval spires to its rich peasant food. The city's streets are lined with mansions built on the wealth of the *pastel* (woad plant) dyeing industry, and they open onto cascading fountains, quiet squares, and the banks of the Canal du Midi, a waterway to the Mediterranean constructed in the 17th century for the burgeoning grain trade. But this is a city that's also firmly anchored in the present; it's a flourishing student town with an enviable nightlife, and an enclave for sharp-minded scientists toiling for the airline and space industries. Ancient and modern rub shoulders comfortably in Toulouse.

Toulousains often claim to have more in common with Barcelona, a two-hour drive away, than Paris. There is a definite laid-back, Latin ambience here, and the view, like the stone of the city buildings, is generally rose-colored. But things were quite different during the Hundred Years War of the 14th and 15th centuries, during which the nearby town of Castelnaudary came under siege. It's said that

desperate citizens created a collective dish – the heart-warming cassoulet – so full-bodied that it perked up everyone sufficiently to fight the good fight. The Académie Universelle du Cassoulet, however, begs to differ, maintaining that cassoulet evolved around the family hearth as simple peasant fare, not combat cuisine. As time passed and rural folk left the farms to seek work as cooks or domestics in the city, their recipes went with them and on to bourgeois tables.

Whatever the truth of the matter, this hearty casserole of white beans and meat is steeped as much in history and legend as in flavor. Castelnaudary, Carcassonne, and Toulouse have been dubbed cassoulet's "holy trinity," with each boasting their own variation of it. In Toulouse, chefs add garlicky *Toulousain* sausage, pork rind, and goose or duck *confit* to enrich the bean mixture. Experts insist that the secret to a great cassoulet lies in the beans: they must be cooked just long enough and lie in a stock that's smooth and thickened by the pork rind. Then follows hours of patient slow-baking in a traditional earthenware pot – the *cassole* – that gives the dish its name.

Food Shopping in Toulouse

The covered market in **Place Victor Hugo** has 100 stands open for business from Tuesday to Sunday. Pick up *confit de canard* (preserved duck) and local *saucisse* (pork sausage) for your cassoulet, and a slab of foie gras for an appetizer. The **Saint Aubin** Sunday market offers the best of the season, such as wild mushrooms and oysters from Arcachon, and live pigeons and geese fresh from local farms, while **Place du Capitole**'s Saturday's market is organically themed. If you prefer not to jostle for your food, **Maison Busquets** on rue Rémusat has a vast array of regional goodies, including wine and prepared cassoulet. **Violettes et Pastelles** on rue St Pantaléon is the place to visit for everything violet, from bonbons to syrup. The violet, supposedly brought back from Italy by Napoleon's soldiers, is the city's symbol.

Above Toulouse lies on the banks of the Garonne River in southwest France

The Best Places to Eat Cassoulet

Le Cantou moderate

With its leafy garden, interspersed with flowery color bursts, Le Cantou feels more like a country house than an elegant city restaurant just 10 minutes from the center of Toulouse. That may be because it reflects the cooking style of chef Philippe Puel, who grew up watching his grandmother cooking cassoulet in her farmhouse kitchen – her passion for the dish and the region still infuses his doggedly seasonal cooking. While an ardent fan of her original dish, which took days to prepare, Puel believes old recipes can be made new. So, in as much as it's possible with a dish this hearty, Puel's version is light! There's the requisite Toulouse sausage, some thinly sliced pork rind, and the essential duck *confit*, which he trims of excess fat. (*Confit*, meaning "cooked in its own fat," developed as a way of preserving meat before refrigeration. It renders the meat tender.) Puel adds thin-skinned, sweet white beans from Tarbes, then puts everything into the oven for several hours to emerge bubbling, browned, and begging for a spoon.

98, rue de Velasquez, St-Martin-du-Touch; open for lunch and dinner Mon–Fri; www.cantou.fr

Also in Toulouse

Die-hard cassoulet fans can follow one of two cassoulet trails: the Route de Cassoulet or the Route Gourmand du Cassoulet. Chef Claude Taffarello's **Auberge du Poids Public** *(www.auberge-du-poids-public.fr; moderate)* in pretty Saint-Félix-Lauragais is on the latter. His cassoulet, served in a traditional *cassole*, is a rich mix of beans, duck and goose *confit*, and sausage, bobbing in a thick, plentiful sauce – good, sustaining stuff, all sourced locally, including the earthenware *cassole* in which the the dish is cooked. The restaurant also has a wonderful view across the surrounding countryside.

Also in France

If you can't make it to the south, upmarket **Au Trou Gascon** *(www.autrougascon.fr; expensive)* in Paris will transport you there with its cassoulet. The chef's favorite just happens to be this famous dish, and here it's a marvelous melding of lamb, pork, duck, and incomparable Tarbais beans.

Around the World

Toulouse-style cassoulet is always on the menu at Anthony Bourdain's New York temple to everyday French cooking, **Les Halles** *(www. leshalles.net/brasserie; inexpensive)*. Close your eyes, take a spoonful, and, just for a minute, you could almost be in the pink city itself.

BRUGES BELGIUM

Silky Chocolate in Bruges

Bruges was the leading commercial center of Europe in the 15th century, famed for its wealth and luxury products. Its later poverty ensured that its buildings remained miraculously untouched, while its extraordinary paintings bear witness to the elaborate craftsmanship of its jewelers, dressmakers, and cabinet-makers. The skills of its fine chocolatiers can still be sampled today.

Bruges still looks and feels like a medieval city. Trapped in time, its network of cobbled streets are lined with stepped-gabled facades and threaded with mirror-still canals that reflect the spires and towers of the skyline. In the early 1500s, vital trade transferred to Antwerp, and for centuries Bruges quietly decayed, remaining largely untouched by the industrialization that transformed other Flemish cities. So its glory days were already over when the Spaniard Hernán Cortés first brought cocoa beans to Emperor Charles V in 1528. Charles V ruled over many countries in Europe, including Belgium, and it was his governor, the Duke of Alba, who first introduced chocolate to the country. The Belgians at first consumed it as a drink, in much the same way as the Mayans and Aztecs had produced *xocolātl*. It was not until the 19th century, when British and Swiss chocolate-makers experimented with cocoa beans, that the modern form of hard chocolate was invented.

It was the Belgians, however, who invented filled chocolates. Jean Neuhaus of Brussels was the pioneer, creating his first pralines in 1912 and selling them in boxes still referred to as *ballotins*. Belgian chocolatiers have been working on techniques for filling chocolate ever since, conjuring up little gems using ingredients such as fruit and nut pastes, liqueurs, marzipan, and fresh cream. Meanwhile, the base ingredient – Belgian chocolate itself – has acquired a worldwide reputation for its outstanding quality. Carefully sourced from top-quality cocoa beans, it contains a high percentage of cocoa solids and valuable cocoa butter – a volatile oil that provides the remarkable cooling sensation as the chocolate melts in the mouth. Similar high standards have been brought to the subtle blend of cocoa butter, milk, and sugar that lies behind the famous Belgian white chocolate.

In the 19th century, Bruges was rediscovered by travelers and antiquarians, who recognized the unique survival of its historic fabric and set about preserving it, mixing in a fair dose of Neo-Gothic fancy to reinforce the mood. Bruges, restored and revived, is now one of the most popular tourist destinations of northern Europe, and this has brought a new era of prosperity back to its old streets, visible in the elegant shops, numerous boutique hotels, and excellent restaurants. The city's feel for consumer luxury today recalls its golden age, and the fabulous, gilded *ballotins* from its chocolate shops have become the treasure caskets of the modern age.

Three Days in Bruges

Bruges is a wonderfully walkable city that boasts extraordinary paintings and historic buildings; in three days you have ample time to see everything at leisure.

DAY ONE The **Markt** is the old central marketplace, dominated by the **Belfry**, which offers fine views over the city. Close by, in the **Burg**, is the beautiful Gothic **Stadhuis** (town hall). For a different perspective on the city, take a canal trip, and then go to the **Groeninge Museum** to admire its exceptional collection of early Flemish paintings.

DAY TWO The **Gruuthuse Museum** is a city mansion full of the domestic artifacts that wealthy Bruges families once craved, and the **Memling Museum** has wonderful 15th-century paintings. End with a relaxing stroll to the historic **Begijnhof** (a haven for religious women in the Middle Ages) and the lake called the **Minnewater**.

DAY THREE Go shopping in **Steenstraat** and **Zuidzandstraat**. Then visit the **Friet Museum**, dedicated to Belgian fries, or the **Museum voor Volkskunde** (folk museum). End with a walk to the old windmills by the **Kruispoort** medieval city gate.

Essentials

GETTING THERE
Frequent **trains** connect Bruges to Brussels, which has an international **airport** and **fast-train** connections to other European cities.

WHERE TO STAY
Charlie Rockets (inexpensive) is central and affordable. *www.charlierockets.com*
Alegria (moderate) offers charming family-run rooms near the Markt. *www.alegria-hotel.com*
Martin's Orangerie (expensive) is an exquisite boutique hotel in a historic town house. *www.hotelorangerie.com*

TOURIST INFORMATION
www.brugge.be

Above The chocolatiers of Bruges have taken chocolate-making from a conservative skill to a cutting-edge art, calling upon a long tradition

Left The enchanting city of Bruges is made up of perfectly preserved medieval and Gothic buildings towering above long, still waterways

Above Belgian chocolates are made from a vast array of natural ingredients, offering an exquisitely tempting choice at virtually every corner

The Best Places to Buy Belgian Chocolate

Chocolaterie Sukerbuyc expensive

Paule Helen Depreter founded Chocolaterie Sukerbuyc (the name means "sugar belly") in 1977, in the same premises it still occupies in Katelijnestraat, close to the museums. It is the oldest chocolate-making establishment in Bruges, and although it has remained a family business, it has come a long way in 35 years, increasing its production tenfold and establishing a reputation for superb handmade chocolates. You'll find a wide variety of pralines using dark, milk, and white chocolate based on 100 percent cocoa butter. Clients are encouraged to choose their own selection to fill the pretty boxes, and can see through the store into the workshop where the chocolates are made. The shop also produces fun pictures of Bruges by screen-printing dark chocolate onto a white chocolate background. Their café, De Proeverie ("the tasting place"), is opposite the shop, and is famed for both its exquisite patisserie and its hot chocolate drink, made by slowly melting a chocolate bar into hot milk.
Katelijnestraat 5, Bruges; open 8:30 AM–6:30 PM daily; www.sukerbuyc.be

Also in Bruges

Several of the major Belgian manufacturers of high-quality chocolates have high-street outlets in Bruges. These include **Neuhaus** *(www. neuhaus.be)* and **Leonidas** *(www.leonidas. com)*. Although their products are made on an industrial scale, they maintain very high standards and the volume of sales means that their prices are relatively low, given their quality.

Also in Belgium

The major manufacturers all have numerous outlets in Brussels, but there are also smaller makers of exceptional quality. This includes the rising star **Pierre Marcolini** *(www.marcolini.be)* and the splendid traditional *pâtissier-chocolatier* **Wittamer** *(www.wittamer.com)*, both on Place du Grand Sablon. Another noted producer is **Mary** *(www.mary.be)*, supplier to the Belgian royal family, whose delightfully decorated Rococo-style shop is worth a visit in itself.

Around the World

Manufacturers producing top-quality chocolate are rare. **Valrhona** *(www.valrhona.com/fr)* is a French company founded in 1922 and based in the small town of Tain-l'Hermitage near Lyon; it prides itself on its careful sourcing of cocoa beans and its ability to extract their distinctive flavors. The US company **Knipschildt** *(www.knipschildt.com)*, founded in 1999 by the Danish-born chef Fritz Knipschildt, has quickly built up a phenomenal reputation for the quality of its filled chocolates, truffles, and bars.

Museum of Chocolate

Choco-Story *(www.choco-story.be)* is a museum that tells the story of chocolate from its origins to today. It has thousands of artifacts on display, from cocoa beans, chocolate-making utensils, machinery, and molds to hundreds of examples of ingenious packaging and much more. Visitors can stop off to watch demonstrations of chocolate-making techniques by expert chocolatiers. The collection is designed to appeal to all levels, including those who are interested in the finer details, such as the distinctive qualities of the various cocoa "vintages." The museum building itself is a historic 15th-century wine tavern.

BOLOGNA

BOLOGNA ITALY

Tortellini in Italy's Gourmet Heart

The down-to-earth city of Bologna is renowned for the world's oldest university, a lively central district, and long, elegantly porticoed streets. But the majority of visitors from Italy and beyond flock here for food, either eaten in the excellent trattorias or bought to take home from the mouthwatering gourmet shops. The simple, fresh *tortellini in brodo* is a firm favorite.

Bologna hums with activity. A stroll through the compact downtown in the company of fleets of bicycles reveals innovative bookshops, cafés blending chocolate and spices packed to the rafters, and time-tested restaurants that are crowded with diners every day of the week. Resting on a foundation of ancient Roman buildings, the city has grown up in a compact layout, with delightful architectural gems such as Romanesque chapels slotted between butcher shops or apartment buildings. This is a city that can easily be explored on foot, and most tourists start in the oldest part of town, the Quadrilateral, which is dominated by Bologna's favorite church, the vast 14th-century San Petronio.

Bologna is nicknamed *La Grassa* (meaning "the fat one"), and it is widely regarded as the gastronomic capital of Italy. The city is located in Emilia-Romagna, a region synonymous with good food; it is home to the aromatic balsamic vinegar from Modena, *parmigiano* (Parmesan) cheese and prosciutto from Parma, Felino

salami, Bologna's own enormous, pistachio-studded mortadella sausage, and, last but not least, fresh egg pasta. A perfect combination of nearly all of these regional delights comes in the shape of tortellini, tiny knotted parcels of thinly rolled pasta filled with a finely minced, delicate blend of *prosciutto crudo*, mortadella, *parmigiano* cheese, and a hint of nutmeg. Tradition dictates that tortellini be both cooked and served in *brodo*, a delicate consommé made from beef and capon or chicken. They should be served sprinkled with more *parmigiano* and very much *al dente* – almost disconcertingly undercooked. This is because the pasta continues to cook in the hot liquid in the bowl.

There are two stories about the invention of tortellini. The first is practical yet poignant – it was a way for locals departing for the Crusades to take the tastes of home with them. The second seems somehow more Italian: during a convention of the gods that took place in mythical times, an innkeeper inadvertently glimpsed Venus naked, and was inspired by the beautiful sight to create these golden "belly buttons."

Three Days in and around Bologna

This fascinating region is packed with historic churches and monuments, and fantastic food markets that spell heaven for gourmet travelers.

DAY ONE Start in Bologna's **Piazza Maggiore**, the vast square edged by brick palaces and the imposing medieval church of **San Petronio**. Take narrow-flagged **Via Orefici** into the old district lined with mouthwatering gourmet delicatessens, pork butchers, and greengrocers.

DAY TWO Make the 20-minute train trip to **Modena** for its priceless Romanesque art and architecture, recognized on the World Heritage list by UNESCO. The **Duomo** and **Torre Ghirlandina** are outstanding. Then head for the town's **covered market** to sample the famous balsamic vinegar and sparkling Lambrusco wine.

DAY THREE One hour away by train is prosperous **Parma**, where the sights are all within walking distance. Visit the graceful 11th-century **cathedral** and baptistry with their art treasures, then move on to **Palazzo Pilotta** and its gallery of works by **Correggio**. Don't miss the magnificent opera house, **Teatro Regia**, or the birthplace of the great conductor Arturo Toscanini, but leave plenty of time for the specialty gourmet shops and restaurants.

Essentials

GETTING THERE
Bologna's **international airport** is a 20-minute **bus** ride from the city, which is well served by **trains**. Take an orange **city bus** to get around; the best way to explore the historic center is on **foot**.

WHERE TO STAY
B&B Centrale (inexpensive) offers good-value, light-filled accommodations handy for the station. *www.bbcentrale.com*
Hotel Metropolitan (moderate) is a smart, modern, Eastern-inspired hotel. *www.hotelmetropolitan.com*
Casa Sant'Angelo (expensive) is a small, beautifully renovated 15th-century palace with a roof terrace and spa. *www.casasantangelo.com*

TOURIST INFORMATION
http://iat.comune.bologna.it

Left *Tortellini in brodo* are dished up with nothing but their cooking broth for a classic, simple Italian dish

Above Bologna is the capital city of Emilia-Romagna, and conforms to a medieval street plan

Below Bologna has one of Italy's largest food markets, which sells a huge variety of fresh pasta

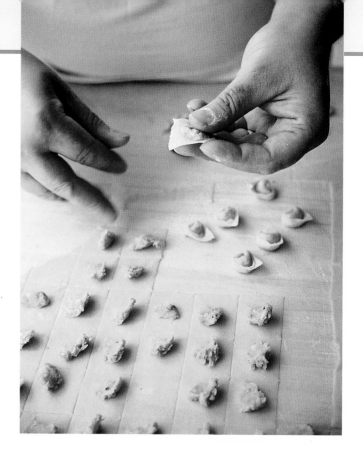

Pasta Around the World

Pasta was brought to Italy from the Middle East in the 13th century and became the simple staple that still reigns supreme there today. Luckily, the rest of the world caught on in the 20th century, and you can now eat delicious pasta – simply dressed or enveloped in rich sauces – all around the world.

ITALY

Antica Focacceria San Francesco
inexpensive

Via Paternostro 58, Palermo, Sicily; www.afsf.it

Five generations of the Conticello family have cooked in this lovely old building, which has a spacious courtyard restaurant. It's renowned for typical Sicilian dishes such as *pasta con le sarde:* spaghetti with sardines, wild fennel, pine nuts, and currants. At lunch times it operates almost as a fast-food place, with dishes served on plastic plates to eat or carry out.

Trattoria Meloncello inexpensive
Via Saragozza 240, Bologna; +39 51 613 947

The decor is down-to-earth 1950s Italian, but the food is timeless; this is simple food at its best. The affable owner always explains the day's menu, rather than offering a printed version, which usually includes a very good homemade tortellini as well as tagliatelle with a rich *ragù*. The house wine is very good too.

Da Nello moderate
Via Monte Grappa 2, Bologna; www.ristorantedanello.it

This venerable institution is always packed. Diners are ushered downstairs amidst mouthwatering fragrances and uniformed waiters hurrying with steaming plates of *tortellini in brodo, pappardelle alla caccia* (game sauce), and *cotoletta alla bolognese* (escalope with *parmigiano* and Parma ham).

Ristorante Pappone moderate
Marina del Cantone 23, Massa Lubrense, Naples; www.hotelcertosa.com

The restaurant inside the Hotel la Certosa on the Amalfi Coast serves large platters of huge, pale *maccheroni* tubes cooked perfectly *al dente* and accompanied by the day's fish catch stewed in delicate tomato. The restaurant sits on a beachfront terrace overlooking a secluded cove.

PARIS, FRANCE

Italian cuisine in the French capital steps many rungs up the gastronomic ladder, from the basic trattoria to stylish restaurants in which both Italian and French chefs bring a creative intelligence to even the more traditional dishes.

L'Enoteca moderate
25 rue Charles V; www.enoteca.fr

Wine takes center stage in this cozy 17th-century locale in the Marais; the restaurant has won awards for its selection. Creative mouthwatering pasta options are *linguine ai frutti di mare* refreshed with citrus zest, and squid-ink black cannelloni filled with sea bass and ricotta.

La Locanda moderate
8 rue de Dragon; www.lalocanda.fr

This sun-filled restaurant in St-Germain-des-Prés is located in an 18th-century town house and offers a wonderful "Trio of Pasta": three of the day's specials as a surprise. Fresh hand-fished seafood arrives daily and also ranks high as a favorite – try the spaghetti with lobster or *vongole* (clams) from Brittany.

LONDON, UK

The "Italian Eating Place" was the first Italian restaurant set up in London. Joseph Moretti opened it in 1803 to cater mostly to Italians, but the cuisine later became fashionable thanks to the trend for traveling Europe on "Grand Tours." These days there are hundreds of Italian restaurants in London, which import genuine ingredients from Italy.

Carluccio's inexpensive
Garrick St., Covent Garden, WC2; www.carluccios.com

Brainchild of jovial TV chef Antonio Carluccio, his elegant flagship serves pasta dishes from all over Italy. The *penne giardiniera* is a tasty mix of zucchini, fried spinach balls, chili pepper, and garlic.

Locanda Locatelli expensive
8 Seymour St., W1; www.locandalocatelli.com

This Michelin-starred restaurant is reputed to serve the best Italian food in the city. The divine house pasta comes stuffed with pheasant and rosemary, or smothered with gently stewed octopus.

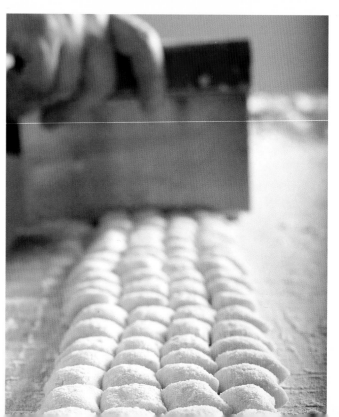

Left (top to bottom) Filling and shaping individual tortellini by hand; *penne alla puttanesca*, with tomatoes, capers, olives, and chili peppers; using a dough scraper to cut gnocchi dusted with cornmeal

Below (top to bottom) Every pasta shape, plain or ridged, is designed to suit the texture of individual sauces; Vincenzo Conticello of the Antica Focacceria San Francesco in Sicily

SYDNEY, AUSTRALIA

Port of call since the 1800s for settlers from both southern and northern Italy, this vibrant cosmopolitan city has many modern trattorias offering a unique Australian fusion slant.

Café Sopra moderate

7 Danks St., Waterloo; www.fratellifresh.com.au
Expect to wait at this trendy restaurant on the light-filled floor above their market shop. An enticing blackboard menu offers simple heaven such as linguine with seafood, lemon, chili pepper, and garlic.

Dolcissimo moderate

96–8 Ramsay St, Haberfield; www.dolcissimo.com.au
Housed in a renovated shop in an old Italian neighborhood, Dolcissimo offers a wide choice of simple favorites, such as gnocchi with Gorgonzola and an outstanding *penne carbonara*.

ST. LOUIS, MO

This city's Italian community began to settle on "The Hill" in the early 1900s. A curious Italian-American dish developed here: toasted ravioli, deep-fried and served with a sauce.

Adriana's on the Hill inexpensive

5101 Shaw Ave.; www.adrianasonthehill.com
This friendly café is run by Adriana Fazio and her daughters, who produce Italian specials for lunch. The pasta is usually penne with a choice of tomato and basil, spicy *salsiccia* (pork sausage), or meatballs.

Da Marcella moderate

3600 Watson Rd.; www.trattoriamarcella.com
This well-established restaurant has a vast menu that embraces elegant *agnolotti del plin* (stuffed pasta with truffle butter), as well as the local favorite: toasted ravioli covered in tomato sauce.

NEW YORK, NY

New York has the most – and the most varied – Italian restaurants in the US, and they can call upon fresh Italian-sourced ingredients, flown in daily to the Big Apple.

Osteria del Circo moderate

120 W. 55th St.; www.osteriadelcirco.com
Sirio Maccioni's restaurant produces fabulous Tuscan food under the watchful eyes of his talented chef wife, Egidiana. This busy eatery serves traditional dishes such as *fritto misto di mare* (mixed, deep-fried fish) and modern Italian favorites like roasted scallops wrapped in pancetta. Don't miss "Mamma Egi's ravioli," stuffed with spinach and ricotta.

Patsy's moderate

236 W. 56th St.; www.patsys.com
Based in New York's theater district, Patsy's is a classic Italian eatery that attracts big-name actors and actresses as clientele. It's only had three chefs in its 65 years of existence, who faithfully reproduce its much-loved favorites – from *linguine puttanesca* and *tortellini bolognese* to striped bass *marechiare* (poached in white wine, garlic, and tomato).

On the Menu

Aglio, olio, peperoncino Pasta simply dressed with garlic, olive oil, and chili pepper.

Ai frutti di mare, alla scogliera With mixed seafood and garlic.

Al nero di seppia With a black sauce of squid ink.

Alla norma With a rich Sicilian sauce of stewed eggplant, tomato, basil, and salted ricotta cheese.

Alle vongole With fresh clams.

Amatriciana A rich tomato sauce with bacon and sometimes chili peppers.

Bucatini Long, tubular pasta.

Cacio e pepe Melted Caciocavallo cheese and ground pepper.

Cannelloni Large pasta tubes filled with meat sauce or spinach and ricotta.

Capelli d'angelo Ultra-thin spaghetti.

Carbonara A creamy sauce of eggs, bacon, and Parmesan.

Fusilli Short, curly twists of pasta.

Gnocchi Small, soft dumplings of potato bound with a little flour.

Maccheroni General name for a wide range of short, tubular pasta.

Orechiette Dimpled buttons of pasta – also known as "small ears."

Pappardelle Wide ribbons of pasta.

Parmigiano Parmesan cheese.

Penne Short, quill-shaped tubes of pasta.

Puttanesca A type of sauce made with tomatoes, olives, and capers.

Ragù A rich meat and vegetable sauce.

Ravioli Flat pillows of pasta filled with meat, fish, vegetables, or cheese.

Spaghetti Long, round pasta.

Stringozzi Handmade Umbrian tagliatelle.

Tagliatelle Ribbons of pasta.

Trenette Like spaghetti but flatter and thicker, a Ligurian favorite with pesto.

LONDON ENGLAND

Roast Beef and Beefeaters

So associated are the British with traditional roast beef that the French call them "les rosbifs," but, far from being insulted, the nation still takes pride in its favorite Sunday lunch. Top London restaurants and down-to-earth pubs alike serve up oven-roasted beef with Yorkshire pudding, horseradish, and gravy – perfect fodder for visiting the old England symbolized by the dish.

"When Mighty Roast Beef was the Englishman's food, It ennobled our brains and enriched our blood," wrote Henry Fielding in his jingoistic ballad, *The Roast Beef of Old England*, evoking a nostalgic view of English national identity way back in 1731. The song was taken up as an unofficial anthem, sung in theaters and at naval dinners, and William Hogarth named a satirical painting after it in 1748: subtitled *The Gate of Calais*, it depicts starving French soldiers drooling as a side of beef is borne into an English tavern.

The origins of the dish itself are more prosaic. In the days before domestic ovens, households used to roast their beef in the baker's oven on Sundays, the day of rest. Yorkshire pudding, a batter cooked in the juices from the roasting meat, had been added by 1747, when English cooking writer Hannah Glasse included a recipe in *The Art of Cookery Made Plain and Easy*.

Old-fashioned London restaurants such as Rules and Simpson's in the Strand continue to serve old English roast beef with all the trimmings in historic surroundings, and Londoners vie to nominate the best pub roast. Alongside the Yorkshire pudding, which should be light and fluffy, classic accompaniments are crunchy roast potatoes and seasonal vegetables, piquant horseradish sauce and thick gravy. Prime cuts of rib and sirloin from prized Aberdeen Angus and Hereford herds yield the most tender, juicy meat, best served rare and thinly sliced.

Fuel up at one of these before a foray into old England. Start at the Tower of London, guarded by its Beefeaters, so called because these royal bodyguards were allowed to eat as much beef as they wanted from the king's table. Decide for yourself if "our soldiers were brave and our courtiers were good," as Fielding sentimentally suggested in his ballad: the 11th-century White Tower is where two little princes were imprisoned by King Richard III, while at Tower Green, countless Englishmen and women, among them Henry VIII's wife Anne Boleyn, lost their heads.

For a glimpse into Hogarthian England, visit Sir John Soane's Museum, a perfectly preserved 18th-century house where you can see the artist's *A Rake's Progress* and *The Election*, satirizing the world in which Fielding's rousing ode to roast beef took such hold. From here one can explore the Inns of Court, up Fleet Street and past the Old Bailey and into the back streets of St. James's and Mayfair, all redolent of a past when Englishmen "had stomachs to eat and to fight."

Three Days in London

London has so much to offer that visitors need to plan ahead, especially if time is short. But it's possible to pack in a few modern marvels among the traditional sights.

DAY ONE Start at the **Tower of London**, with its Crown Jewels and Beefeaters, then take a look at Tower Bridge. Walk through the City of London to **St. Paul's Cathedral**, then cross the Thames to visit the **Tate Modern** gallery in the afternoon.

DAY TWO Take an early stroll in Green Park to see **Buckingham Palace**. Ride the **London Eye** for a bird's-eye view of the city, then go to **Covent Garden** for lunch – perhaps at Rules. Spend the afternoon with the antiquities at the **British Museum**, or walk through Holborn to **Sir John Soane's Museum**.

DAY THREE In the morning see **Big Ben**, the **Houses of Parliament**, and **Westminster Abbey**, and then in the afternoon choose from one of the city's other exceptional museums, clustered together in South Kensington: the **Science Museum**, **Natural History Museum**, or **Victoria and Albert Museum**.

Essentials

GETTING THERE
London has three **international airports**, with public transportation to the center. Get around on **foot** or by **bus** or **subway train** ("tube").

WHERE TO STAY
The Hoxton (inexpensive) is chic and fun, but slightly out of the center. *www.hoxtonhotels.com*
The Hallam (moderate) is a bargain, moderately priced but central. *www.hallamhotel.com*
The Savoy (expensive), one of London's *grande dame* hotels, has been recently overhauled. *www.fairmont.com/savoy*

TOURIST INFORMATION
1 Lower Regent Street; *www.visitlondon.com*

The Best Places to Eat Roast Beef

Rules expensive

To step into Rules in Covent Garden is to step back in time: it was founded in 1798 and is the oldest restaurant in the city. In all that time it has been owned by only three families, and its history is told on the walls and in the various atmospheric dining rooms that fill the old building. Many famous people have dined at Rules, including Charles Dickens, Charlie Chaplin, and Laurence Olivier, and memorabilia from many of the illustrious diners is displayed for the entertainment of present-day diners. The menu remains resolutely traditional British, and they serve Aberdeenshire sirloin of beef with roast potatoes and Yorkshire pudding as a grand dish for two people. Game features heavily on the menu, changing with the seasons, and their British "nursery-style" desserts – golden syrup sponge, lemon meringue pie, and rice pudding – are renowned. Dining at Rules is more than just a meal, it's a British institution.

35 Maiden Lane, Covent Garden, WC2; open noon–11.45 PM Mon–Sat, noon–10.45 PM Sun; www.rules.co.uk

Also in London

Simpson's in the Strand (www.simpsonsinthestrand.co.uk; expensive) typifies traditional London formality with its wood paneling, chandeliers, silver-domed serving trays, and immaculate staff. Roast beef is one of its signature dishes, carved at the table and served with roast potatoes, Savoy cabbage, Yorkshire pudding, and horseradish. Or have your Sunday lunch with all the trimmings in the **National Dining Rooms** (www.thenationaldiningrooms.co.uk; moderate), the excellent restaurant that is part of the National Gallery on Trafalgar Square.

Also in England

The Hardwick Inn (www.hardwickinn.co.uk; inexpensive) in Derbyshire is a unique 15th-century sandstone inn owned by the National Trust, Britain's guardian of heritage properties, and a rare place that serves roast beef, locally sourced, from its Carvery restaurant almost every day of the week.

Around the World

The original **Lawry's The Prime Rib** in Beverly Hills (www.lawrysonline.com; expensive) specializes in ribs and roasts and serves its roast beef accompanied with Yorkshire pudding and creamed horseradish. Expect London gentleman's club decor, with dark wood and thick carpets; plenty of theatrics such as tableside carving and flambéeing; and impeccable service.

Above Rare roast beef, roast potatoes, roast parsnips, and Yorkshire pudding await the gravy

Left Old meets new on the Thames, where passengers on the London Eye look straight across the river at Big Ben

Above Interior of Rules restaurant, a London institution specializing in British cookery – roast meats and game, oysters, pies, and puddings

Borough Market

As colorful as London itself, Borough Market is one of the oldest, biggest, and most popular food markets in London. There has been a market here in the Southwark area near a crossing point on the Thames River since at least the 11th century. Here you'll find an amazing array of produce to buy and try, not just from in and around London and the UK but from all over the world. There are artisan bakers, butchers, and fishmongers selling everything from Lincolnshire sausages and Melton Mowbray pork pies to oysters and trout, along with stands selling nothing but olives or jellies, honey or pâtés. Open Thu–Sat; www.boroughmarket.org.uk

A Day in Bergen

You can easily explore Bergen in a day; walk around the center and use the funicular for the surrounding peaks.

MORNING Start the morning with a stroll around the harbor area and the **Bryggen UNESCO site** – a walk among these old wooden buildings is a step back in time. The Quarter has existed since the mid-14th century, but most of the wooden houses still standing date from 1704, after the great fire of 1702. Visit the **Hanseatic Museum and Schøtstuene**, the old Assembly Rooms.

AFTERNOON Walk to the **fish market** and wander around it to admire the stands of fish and seafood. Choose one of the great places serving lunch. Then take the **Fløibanen Funicular Railway** for a swift ride up to **Mount Fløyen** with gorgeous views over the city.

EVENING In summer the funicular is open until midnight so you can stay late in the mountains enjoying the extraordinary light. Beware that Bergen is "blessed" with abundant rainfall, and if the day starts off sunny, reverse the itinerary, starting with the funicular railway.

Essentials

GETTING THERE
Bergen lies on the coast of western Norway. Flights arrive at **Flesland International Airport** and there are **shuttle buses** and **taxis** to the downtown, 12 miles (20 km) away.

WHERE TO STAY
Hanseatic Hotel Bergen (inexpensive) has 16 unique rooms within the Bryggen UNESCO site. *www.dethanseatiskehotell.no*
Augustin Hotel (moderate) is the oldest family-run hotel in Bergen, with a cozy restaurant and bar. *www.augustin.no*
Clarion Collection Hotel Havnekontoret (expensive) is Bergen's most luxurious hotel. *www.clarionhotel.com*

TOURIST INFORMATION
Fresco Hall, Vågsallmenning Square (opposite the fish market); *+47 55 552 000*

Left The beautiful Lofoten Islands can be reached by plane or coastal liner from Bergen
Below Colorful merchant buildings line the wharf at the World Heritage site of Bryggen

BERGEN NORWAY

"Buried" Salmon in Bergen

When the rays are glittering across Bergen harbor on a sunny summer day, the fish market, or *fisketorget*, seems literally to sparkle as visitors and locals gather to shop, browse, and eat. The hub of this bustling port city for several hundred years, this famous market is full of stands heaped high with delights of the sea and that Scandinavian favorite, deep-hued gravadlax.

Bergen's history stretches back as far as the 11th century, and in its heyday it was a headquarters for the Hanseatic League – northern Europe's dominating trade alliance in the late Middle Ages. The league was made up of German and Scandinavian seafaring merchants, and the legacy of the German merchants can still be experienced in the oldest, most charming of the city's neighborhoods, known as Bryggen. A UNESCO World Heritage site since 1979, the 62 gently leaning wooden merchants' houses here have been lovingly restored to their former glory, and wandering among these rickety antique houses is like entering a wooden maze. Several have been opened up as museums, while others sell typical Norwegian handicrafts, from fluffy knitwear to ornate Sami reindeer-bone knives.

Fish has always played a vital role in Bergen – it was responsible for drawing the Hanseatic League to the town's shores in the 13th century, at around the same time that one of Norway's national dishes *par excellence*, gravadlax, appeared on the culinary scene.

This signature dish, today most often served as an appetizer, was invented by fishermen, who would salt and then bury their freshly caught salmon, leaving it to ferment in the sand at high tide. "*Grav*" literally means "grave," and "burying" the salmon gave it a very distinctive flavor. These days you won't see any Norwegians digging up their dish of the day from the beaches, but gravadlax remains just as tasty, having been "buried" and cured in a marinade of salt, sugar, dill, and often a dash of aquavit or gin.

Much has changed in Bergen since the fish-trading of the Middle Ages, but the scene at the fish market is every bit as lively, as gregarious sellers vie for customers against the backdrop of the Hanseatic houses. Stands are piled high with bright orange or pink gravadlax, smoked salmon, rosy shrimp, purple lobsters, red crayfish, and apricot-colored mussels. Open sandwiches stacked with fish and seafood call out to be eaten from improvised cafés with rustic wooden benches. It's not hard to imagine a merchant in the Middle Ages tucking into the same dishes on the same spot some 600 years ago.

Food with a View

Bergen is surrounded by *de syv fjell* ("the seven peaks"), mountains with stunning views of Bergen and the nearby islands and fjords. Several offer foodie experiences with a view. **Fløien Folkerestaurang** *(www.bellevue-restauranter.no)*, one of the Historic Restaurants of Norway, is reached by the Fløibanen Funicular Railway, one of Bergen's main sights. Its old, atmospheric building is open daily in summer for traditional Norwegian cooking. Mount Ulriken, reached by bus and gondola from central Bergen, has the city's highest restaurant, **Sky:skraperen** *(www.ulriken643.no)*. It serves gravadlax and other traditional dishes. **Jacob Aall Bar & Brasserie** *(www.jacobaall.no)* offers good views without the need to climb a peak first. Located on top of a tall downtown building, you can admire the views from the bar on the premises.

Above Gravadlax with fresh dill and black peppercorns

The Best Places to Eat Gravadlax

Enhjørningen Fish Restaurant
expensive

Enhjørningen Fish Restaurant, Bergen's oldest fish restaurant, is steeped in the city's history, housed as it is in an old Hanseatic wharf house in the Bryggen quarter near the harbor. Parts of the building date from the 14th century and the enchanting decor gives you the feeling of having stepped into the living room of an old merchant's house, complete with antique furniture and paintings.

The menu ranges from the traditional to the more adventurous, with an emphasis on fresh local fish and seafood. Top choice must be their gravadlax, which is cured in aquavit – a caraway-flavored schnapps – and served with mustard sauce. For those with a hearty appetite, there are plenty of other unusual dishes to sample, including *rakørret* (cured trout – another traditional Norwegian dish) and vendace roe, a specialty. The three-course tasting menus, one of which includes the gravadlax dish, are particularly good buys.

Enhjørningsgården 29, Bergen; open 4–11 PM daily, closed Sun Sep–mid-May; www.enhjorningen.no

Also in Bergen

To taste some exquisite homemade gravadlax, try newly opened **Cornelia Seafood Restaurant** *(+47 55 011 885; moderate)*, somewhat ironically located in the old meat market area. Alf Roald Sætre and Odd Einar Tufteland, the men behind the establishment, really know their seafood. In 2004 they opened one of the city's most popular seafood and fish restaurants, **Cornelius Restaurant** *(www.cornelius-restauranter.no; moderate)*, reached only by boat from central Bergen. Both restaurants are worth a visit for the sheer variety of fresh fish and seafood they offer; they also have no less than five different recipes for home-cured gravadlax, which is available to buy in the fishmonger's next door to the Cornelia Restaurant.

Also in Norway

In Stavanger, **Sjøhuset Skagen** *(www.sjohusetskagen.no; expensive)*, housed in an old, bright-red-painted timbered building, serves home-cured gravadlax with the traditional accompaniments of salad, mustard dressing, and dark rye bread.

Around the World

The Smörgås Chef *(www.smorgas.com; inexpensive)* has no less than three prime locations across New York, offering the very best of Scandinavian cuisine, including their own home-cured gravadlax. A special treat is their aquavit-cured salmon with traditional cucumber-dill salad and mustard sauce.

STRASBOURG FRANCE

Choucroute Garnie in Strasbourg

Strasbourg's outstanding historic architecture is now protected as a UNESCO World Heritage site; its medieval churches, grand public buildings, and tangle of narrow streets offer a unique insight into a bygone age. Long contested by both Germany and France, its shifting borders have also given it a distinctive cuisine, exemplified by a deliciously heaped platter of *choucroute garnie.*

The capital of Alsace, Strasbourg lies on the French/German border, and has habitually scuttled back and forth between France and Germany. In fact, from 1870 to 1945, it was alternately French and German no fewer than four times. Its checkered nationality is evident everywhere, from the medieval neighborhood of La Petite France to the grand Neo-Gothic German Quarter, both of which carry street signs written in French and the Germanic Alsatian dialect.

La Petite France is impossibly charming, with a web of waterways, half-timbered houses, and wooden bridges, but its hospital and noisy canal-boat workshops led the Germans to skirt the area when they annexed the city in 1870. They struck out instead past the old town, throwing up grandiose public buildings, private homes, and graceful gardens, spawning the German or Imperial Quarter. The buildings still sparkle today, and the German influence on local culinary habits remains as palpable. It's sometimes striking, in fact, just how "un-French" an Alsatian menu can seem. Thanks to Jewish immigration in the 1100s, foie gras is a firm

favorite, but German influence on local culinary habits is everywhere in evidence – sauerkraut *(choucroute)*, wursts, pretzels, braised meats, gingerbread, and *kougelhopf* still loom large on an Alsatian plate.

Choucroute garnie is the Alsatian dish *par excellence*: salt-pickled cabbage braised with salted and smoked pork, and seasoned with juniper berries. The dish seems encoded in Alsatian genes, and everyone has a favorite way of making sure the *choucroute* is silky, the sausages perfectly simmered, and the pork addictive. Most recipes also include bay leaves, garlic, onions, potatoes, white Alsatian Riesling wine, and a dollop of duck or goose fat to get it started. Above all, the flavor should be delicate, not tart, so the pickled cabbage is rinsed twice before it is added to the pot. Some like to go whole hog and add a titanic ham hock, smoked pork chops, or even liver quenelles (dumplings). When it is brought to the table, a glistening hillock of *choucroute* crested with slices of smoked and salted pork, fat sausages, and steamed potatoes should provoke a gasp of delight.

A Day in Strasbourg

With its picture-postcard houses and lapping canals, Strasbourg is full of charm. A good way to get your bearings in this city is to take a canal cruise.

MORNING Visit **Notre Dame Cathedral** with its pink-hued sandstone facade and soaring spire (at 465 ft/142 m, it was the tallest monument in the world from 1647 to 1874). Its elaborate astronomical clock parades the 12 apostles at 12:30 PM. Sidle into a *winstub* (wine room) such as the one in the marvelously medieval **Maison Kammerzell** for a glass of Sylvaner wine.

AFTERNOON Spend the afternoon at the **Musée d'Art Moderne et Contemporain (MAMCO)** appreciating the works of Kandinsky, Arp, and the German Symbolists, and admiring the museum's impressive collection of *belle époque* posters. Take tea (and cake) in the light-filled **Art Café**.

EVENING Wander the cobbled, illuminated streets of **La Petite France**, with their geranium-festooned Hansel-and-Gretel-like houses. Follow the canals to the **Ponts Couverts** and survey old Strasbourg from the **Barrage de Vauban**, a dam designed to protect the city. If you have time, walk through the grandiose **German Quarter** and ponder the historical to-ing and fro-ing of this fine city.

Essentials

GETTING THERE
Aéroport Strasbourg International is 6 miles (10 km) from the city; there's a **shuttle train**. Strasbourg has **high-speed train** connections across France and Europe, and a good network of **trams** and **buses** around the city.

WHERE TO STAY
Hotel 21 Siècle (inexpensive) is a minimalist, modern hotel that also offers apartments with kitchenette. *www.hotel-cyber-21.com*
The **Cour du Corbeau** (moderate) is housed in a 16th-century building. *www.cour-corbeau.com*
The **Régent Petite France** (expensive) is a contemporary riverside hotel in a former ice factory. *www.regent-petite-france.com*

TOURIST INFORMATION
17 place de la Cathédrale; *www.otstrasbourg.fr*

Above The canal-side restaurants of La Petite France allow diners to sample authentic Alsatian food in a time-honored setting

Left The Gothic towers of Strasbourg Cathedral form a stunning backdrop to the Christmas market, held here since 1570

Above *Choucroute garnie* is nostalgia on a plate for many Alsatians, evoking precious memories of childhood and home

The Best Places to Eat Choucroute Garnie

Chez Yvonne inexpensive

Chez Yvonne is something of an institution in Strasbourg. Sandwiched between 16th-century timber-fronted houses in a street just a step or two from the mighty cathedral, this woody *winstub* oozes old Strasbourg. Rustic and down-to-earth, it has a menu that includes all of Alsace's tried and tested, true and timeless dishes: goose foie gras, *presskopt*, *coq au Riesling*, *jambonneau*, and, of course, *choucroute garnie*. *Winstub* cooking is, above all, familial, and Alsatian families tend to have a favorite one that they like to call their own. Chez Yvonne is that kind of place. *Winstub* translates as "wine room," and the room *(stub)* refers to a cozy one in someone's house where everyone relaxes. Yvonne herself may have retired long ago, but the *kelsch* (gingham) curtains, warm wood paneling, and pottery live on, along with the generous plate of *choucroute garnie*, a happy confluence of pork liver quenelles, pork knuckle, blood sausage, Strasbourg and Monbéliard sausages, salted pork loin, smoked pork belly, and fermented cabbage. It's perfect with the restaurant's dry white Sylvaner wine.

10 rue du Sanglier, Strasbourg; noon–2:15 PM & 6 PM–midnight daily; www.chez-yvonne.net

Also in Strasbourg

Captivating **Le Clou** *(www.le-clou.com; inexpensive)* is everything you could wish for in a *winstub*: welcoming, warm, woody, and full of delicious smells. Tables are shared, so you'll be rubbing shoulders with strangers, but somehow that doesn't seem inappropriate when you're eating this kind of food. People dream of the consommé with bone-marrow quenelles and the *choucroute royale avec wädele*, a regal version of *choucroute garnie* that substitutes champagne for wine and adds a hefty pork knuckle to the meat contingent.

Also in France

Drouant *(www.drouant.com; expensive)* in Paris started out as a humble tobacco-bar in 1880, but today it's a first-class restaurant owned by three-star Michelin chef and Alsatian Antoine Westermann. Its founder Charles Drouant also hailed from Alsace, and his former customers included the artists Renoir, Rodin, and Pissarro. Westermann champions French products and traditions and has a particular penchant for his childhood home of Alsace. Come winter, *choucroute* pops up on the menu.

Around the World

The *choucroute Alsacienne* at **Brasserie Jo** *(www.brasseriejo.com; moderate)* in Boston, MA, is the real thing; founder and owner Jean Joho hails from Alsace and cooked for many years in Strasbourg and the award-winning Auberge d'Ill before decamping to Boston.

What Else to Eat

Centuries of shifting borders between Germany and France have imbued the city and its cuisine with a unique style. Try **baeckeoffe**, a hearty stew of potatoes, pork, beef, lamb, and white wine, which is always on the menu at **Le Baeckeoffe d'Alsace** *(www.baeckeoffe.com)*. **Fleischschnecke**, minced beef rolled in noodle dough, then sliced and cooked in a meaty broth, is good at **Le Clou** *(see right)*. For a quick snack, grab a **bretzel** (pretzel) from any bakery – they've been cooking them here since the 14th century. If you prefer something sweeter, try a **kougelhopf**, a brioche studded with raisins.

Above Manarola, one of the five picturesque Cinque Terre villages on the Ligurian coast

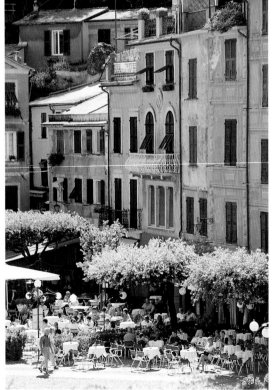

Above The elegant town of Portofino is part of the Riviera di Levante

Three Days in Liguria

The Italian Riviera is an easy place to spend time, whether you want to sightsee, hike, or relax in a spectacularly beautiful setting.

DAY ONE Genoa's spectacular **aquarium**, designed by architect Renzo Piano, is an excellent start to any visit. Then take a short stroll downtown to explore the medieval streets and visit the **Duomo**.

DAY TWO Pack your swimsuit and set out along the spectacular 7-mile (12-km) **Sentiero Azzurro** path that links the picture-postcard villages of the **Cinque Terre**. Begin at **Monterosso al Mare** and go southeast along the cliffs dotted with medieval watchtowers and through the fishing settlements, all the way to **Riomaggiore**. If you get tired, jump on a train or a ferry.

DAY THREE A rocky wooded peninsula east of Genoa is the stunning setting for "impossibly beautiful" **Portofino**, with its pastel houses and luxury yachts. From there, catch a ferry to the exquisite abbey of **San Fruttuoso**, which sits on the beachfront in a secluded bay. Continue on to hospitable **Camogli** either on foot or by ferry.

Essentials

GETTING THERE
Genoa's Cristoforo Colombo **airport** has flights from most European cities. There are **buses** every half-hour to the downtown, 4 miles (6 km) away. Extensive **bus** and **train** networks link the towns of the Italian Riviera.

WHERE TO STAY
Hotel Agnello D'Oro (inexpensive) is a quiet converted monastery close to the train station in Genoa. *www.hotelagnellodoro.it*
Hotel Cenobio dei Dogi (moderate) in Camogli is a beautiful seafront hotel in a refurbished 17th-century villa. *www.cenobio.it*
Hotel Splendido Mare (expensive) provides unabashed luxury in the heart of fabulous Portofino. *www.hotelsplendido.com*

TOURIST INFORMATION
www.turismoinliguria.it

LIGURIA ITALY

Pesto on the Italian Riviera

Renowned for its mild Mediterranean winters, the Italian Riviera runs all along the rocky Ligurian coastline. It represents old-fashioned glamour, and its romantic resorts – such as Portofino and San Remo – have long attracted the world's elite. But from the palaces of Genoa to the tumbling fishermen's houses of Cinque Terre, one simple sauce reigns supreme: *pesto alla genovese*.

The marvelous region of Liguria, in northwest Italy, is remarkably varied. It boasts landscapes stretching from the snowbound Alps to the dramatic coastline of the Mediterranean, where soaring cliffs rise from secluded bays and long beaches of yellow sand. At its heart stands the sprawling capital city of Genoa, a strategic port for more than 2,000 years and a supreme example of old-world capitalism from its heyday in the 16th century. The region retains much of its old appeal, easily enchanting visitors who wander the charming fishing settlements or medieval city streets. Elegant resorts dot the coast in both directions from Genoa: to the west, the Riviera di Ponente runs quickly to the star of the 1900s, San Remo; while to the east, the Riviera di Levante glories in upmarket Portofino and the pretty clifftop villages of Cinque Terre.

Genoa has produced many extraordinary people, from the 15th-century explorer Christopher Columbus to the 20th century's wondrous architect Renzo Piano, and the countryside around it produces equally famous food. Olives – such as the tiny, flavorsome Taggiasco variety – grow everywhere, flourishing on the sun-soaked terraced hillsides. They are pressed to make a superb, delicate extra-virgin oil, which then forms the basis of the area's best-known pasta sauce, *pesto alla genovese*. "Pesto" simply means "crushed," referring to the way that the basic raw ingredient, fresh basil, is traditionally pounded by hand using a mortar and pestle, along with pine nuts and (sometimes) garlic. Many cooks today crush the ingredients in an electric blender, before adding the finishing touches – olive oil and grated Parmesan cheese. A little water may be added if the paste is too thick, and then it is carried triumphantly to the table, where it silkily coats pasta or gnocchi with rich Ligurian flavors.

Pesto has spawned a huge number of variations, from the common Ligurian version with runner beans and potatoes to an exotic Sicilian one enriched with tomatoes and almonds. Chefs in other countries play with it freely, even trying other herbs and vegetables in place of basil. It seems that the basic mix – of leaf, oil, and nuts – is so fine that nothing is able to spoil it.

Ligurian Food Festivals

The pretty Cinque Terre village of **Monterosso al Mare** is the place to go if you love lemons; every spring it holds the Sagra del Limone, a fair celebrating lemons and everything made from them. The whole village is adorned in yellow, and a myriad products – from marmalade and lemon cakes to the alcoholic Limoncello – can be tasted and bought. Every May the village of **Camogli** hosts a unique Sagra del Pesce, a fish fair first held by local fishermen in 1952. A truly gigantic frying pan, rated as the world's biggest, is set up in the seafront square and plates of fried fish are handed out to all and sundry during festivities for the patron saint San Fortunato. Also in May, neighboring **Recco** celebrates another Ligurian specialty, the delicious *focaccia con formaggio*, a thin, fragrant bread spread with soft fresh cheese and baked quickly in a very hot oven.

Above Fragrant *pesto alla genovese* may be utterly smooth or deliciously grainy

The Best Places to Eat Pesto

Ristorante Da Genio moderate

Having reliably served up delicious traditional Ligurian cuisine for over 50 years, this restaurant has a devoted following of diners from both Genoa and farther afield. It is well worth the baffling walk through a warren of old streets to find the place. The decor is 1950s Italian, and the walls are lined with paintings by local artists. The signature dish is a classic pesto, freshly made in-house using a special variety of small-leaved Genoa basil blended with pine nuts and Parmesan. The resulting bright green, oily cream is tossed with hot *troffiette* – squiggles of pale, tender pasta – and sprinkled with grated Parmesan. They also serve pesto on *trenette*, a type of flat spaghetti, and as *corzetti con sugo di pinoli*, an ancient dish and a rarity these days in Liguria – flat pasta medallions in a pine nut dressing. Second courses focus on fish, notably a stew of *stoccafisso* (cod) with black olives and pine nuts. There's a great selection of Ligurian wines, too.

Salita San Leonardo 61r, Genoa; open 12:30–3 PM & 7:30–10 PM Mon–Sat, Sept–July; www.mangiareinliguria.it/dagenio

Also in Liguria

The tiny, friendly eatery of **Il Portico Spaghetteria** *(www.ilporticodicamogli.it; inexpensive)* in Camogli is tucked under the archways facing the beachfront. Aromatic pesto is served with ricotta on a *crostino* for antipasto, then with *trenette* as a first course. Try the good *intingolo di mare* dip of mussels and bread too.

Also in Italy

Trattoria Cantina Siciliana *(www.cantinasiciliana.it; moderate)* is a friendly Slow Food restaurant in Trapani, Sicily, that serves some memorable Sicilian food. One of the stand-out dishes is *busiate*, strips of fresh pasta curled into spirals around a knitting needle. They are dished up with delicious *pesto trapanese*, which is a superlative blend of finely chopped tomato, basil, garlic, and almonds with pecorino cheese.

Around the World

In New York, the "food temple" that is **Eataly** *(www.eatalyny.com; inexpensive)* consists of several restaurants and small food stores; it resembles a giant food exhibition. This is the first member of the chain outside northern Italy, and they make a great *pasta al forno al pesto*, Ligurian-style pesto spread on top of lasagna pasta sheets that have been layered with a cheesy béchamel sauce. The final touch is a sprinkling of toasted pine nuts and cracked black peppercorns.

Above Perfect cones of ground spices fill the air with aromas in the Mellah, the old Jewish quarter of Marrakech, Morocco

The Middle East and Africa

The Flavors of
The Middle East and Africa

Mention the Middle East in a culinary context and most people think of kebabs and kofte. In fact, the region's cuisine is as rich, colorful, and ancient as its history. The region is also renowned for its hospitality, where "a guest is a gift from God"; travelers often find themselves invited to sample dishes where they taste best: in the home. In contrast to the Middle East's homogenous approach, Africa's 61 territories have enormously varied cuisines, offering surprising delights.

Mesopotamia, as it was known in ancient times, is called the "Cradle of Civilization," and it was here, around 7,000 years ago, that man first turned from nomadic hunter-gatherer into settled farmer. Part of a wider region known as the "Fertile Crescent," which stretched sicklelike from North Africa's Nile along the Mediterranean coast all the way to the Persian Gulf, this was the home of the Biblical Garden of Eden, and it was long known as the "land of milk and honey."

It was the region's abundance of food and, in particular, wheat that first caught the covetous eye of the Romans, who occupied the area in the 2nd century AD. Hot on the heels of the Romans came other powers who introduced their own culinary traditions but also adopted the local ones. Later, they carried this culinary combination with them as they swept east or west, bequeathing the whole region an unusual culinary homogeneity. Like the magnificent ancient monuments of the Middle East, its foods are a legacy of the powers that passed through it. With the Arabs in the 7th century came dates and nuts as well as exotic spices from seafaring merchants, bringing turmeric, cardamom, cumin, peppercorns, cloves, and allspice from India and Southeast Asia. With the Mongols came dumplings

> *This was the home of the Biblical Garden of Eden, and was long known as the "land of milk and honey."*

and the roasting of meat on fires – the world's first kebabs. The Persians brought rice and poultry, sometimes combining both into such sumptuous dishes as *khoresh-e fesejan* and *polo*. The Ottomans introduced the fine art of sweet and savory pastry, conspiring to make such delectable delicacies as baklava, as well as the tradition of meze – dining on little dishes such as falafel and *kibbeh nayyeh* – and the fashion for drinking coffee.

The Phenomenon of the Souk

Nowhere are the region's riches more evident than in the souks, each one a labyrinthine warren of stands selling the finest local goods and produce. There's rice and waxy saffron from the Caspian Sea, honey-sweet soft fruits including translucent apricots from Lebanon, plump cherries, quinces, and melons from Iran, fragrant figs from Turkey, and beautiful artichokes, peppers, okra, zucchini,

Right Pomegranate on sale in Iran, where it has long played a key role in the cuisine
Below Women selling the daily catch of sardines on a beach in Maputo, Mozambique

and eggplants from all over. The souk is a unique phenomenon of the Middle East, found in almost every town of the region; some are virtually unchanged since medieval times.

Africa's Ever-Evolving Cuisine

The second largest landmass on Earth, Africa comprises over a billion people inhabiting environments that range from hot deserts and snow-capped mountains to tropical forests and coastal wetlands. The continent's diversity of both peoples and geography is reflected in the contrast of its cuisines.

In East Africa, cattle are kept as a form of currency and wealth, so beef is generally reserved for special occasions; lamb, goat, poultry, and game are all eaten too. Arabs who settled the coastal areas of East Africa over a millennium ago introduced rice and spices such as cinnamon and cloves, together with golden saffron from Persia. Later, Indian settlers introduced their own cuisines, including spices and curry dishes as well as legumes such as lentils, pickled vegetables, and breads such as chapatis. European colonization saw the introduction of citrus fruit and yet more spices from their Asian colonies; chili peppers, peanuts, peppers, corn, and tomatoes from the New World; and tropical fruits from Brazil. Almost the only country in Africa to escape colonization – bar a brief, fiercely resisted seven-year period – was Ethiopia, which to this day retains much of its indigenous culture and cuisine, including its distinctive sourdough bread, *injera*.

North Africa, culturally part of the Middle East, shares that region's culinary traditions and influences, as well as boasting its own, particularly in regions close to the Atlantic and Mediterranean. South Africa's cooking is sometimes described as a "rainbow cuisine" because of the many influences that have shaped it. The indigenous Bantu-speaking people lived on wind-dried meat and wild game roasted over fires – traditions still seen today in the form of biltong and the South African love of braai, or barbecues. Other influences included the Dutch and British colonizers and Asian immigrants, who introduced legumes, soups, and curries. The resulting culinary synthesis of Asian and Dutch influence can be seen in dishes such as *bobotie*.

West African cuisine is best known for its starchy staples made from the locally grown yams, cassava, cocoyams, corn, and plantain that accompany spicy stews and soups. Outside Muslim Africa, alcoholic drinks are widely brewed, from the wines of Tunisia and South Africa and the honey wine – *tej* – of Ethiopia to the widely consumed palm wine and millet beer. The Middle East and Africa are brimming with exciting tastes and sights.

> *The continent's diversity of both peoples and geography is reflected in the contrast of its cuisines.*

Left Seafood vendor in Forodhani Gardens, by the beach in Zanzibar, Tanzania
Below Spices for sale at the crowded Bzouriyah market in Old Damascus, Syria

A Day in Cairo

After a traditional breakfast of *fuul* (cooked, mashed fava beans), head first for the monumental 10th-century gateway, Bab Zowaylah.

MORNING Just outside the gate, take a look at the **Mosque of Salih Talay** and the **Souk Al Khayyameyyah**, which once furnished the Fatimid armies with tents and saddles. Climb the ramparts for spectacular views over the old city. After a visit to the **Mosque-Madrasah of Sultan Mu'ayyad Shaykh**, continue along Shari' Al Mu'ez Li Dinillah until you reach the 16th-century **Al Ghuri** complex.

AFTERNOON Visit the famous 10th-century mosque of **Al Azhar**, one of the oldest educational institutions in the world. Have Arabic coffee at Suliman Café and then shop for perfume, spice, and gold in the famous **Khan al-Khalili bazaar**. If you have time, visit the **Fatimid** and **Mamluk** complexes, containing the world's densest collection of mosques, madrasahs, mausoleums, and *khanqahs* (Sufi "monasteries").

EVENING See Sufi whirling dervishes at the **Wikala Al Ghuri**, then retire to a restaurant for falafel meze and delicious fresh seafood.

Essentials

GETTING THERE
Buses, minibuses, and **taxis** connect Cairo's international **airport** with the downtown, 12 miles (20 km) away. The **metro** and **taxis** are the simplest ways of getting around town.

WHERE TO STAY
Carlton Hotel (inexpensive) is centrally located in a 1930s building with simple but spotless rooms. www.carltonhotelcairo.com
Grand Hotel (moderate) is less grand than it once was, but the former five-story palace still offers large and comfortable rooms at good prices. www.grandhotelcairo.com
Mena House Oberoi (expensive) is a stunning 19th-century hunting lodge with breathtaking pyramid views. www.menahouseoberoi.com

TOURIST INFORMATION
www.egypt.travel

Left Fast food Egyptian-style: crunchy falafel in pita bread with cucumber, lettuce, mint leaves, and yogurt
Below One of the many glorious food and spice stands in the legendary Khan al-Khalili bazaar, Cairo

CAIRO EGYPT

Fast Falafel in Old Cairo

A world away from the tourist-thronged pyramids and the commotion of central Cairo lies the quarter known as "Medieval Cairo." This small area has 850 listed monuments, making it one of the most heritage-rich enclaves on Earth. Evocative, atmospheric, and little changed, the fascinating quarter is also believed to be the home of Egypt's version of fast food: the falafel.

For many, Egypt's capital Cairo is synonymous with pharaohs, pyramids, and sphinxes. But Cairo was never in fact a Pharaonic city, despite being situated close to the ancient capital of Memphis, and was only formally founded in the 10th century under the Fatimids, who marched in from modern-day Tunisia. Al Qahira ("the victorious"), as Cairo is still known in Arabic today, soon grew into a great and prosperous city ruled by a series of wealthy, tyrannical, and sometimes capricious sultans.

The magnificent monuments erected during this time made the city a legend in its own day, and many still survive. Extending from the old Fatimid gate of Bab Zowaylah in the south to Bab Al Futuh in the north, Al Qahira is as well preserved architecturally as it is atmospherically; it is quite simply one of the finest, most evocative medieval cities in the world.

Market-goers for centuries have had to dodge the donkey carts that still clatter down the alleyways. In the souks, the piles of pungent spices and the earthy aromas emanating from the food stands are a heady mix; and the competing cries of the *gallabiyya*-clad market vendors echo around the city walls.

From the 4th to the 6th centuries, the Copts, a very early Christian community, were the largest religious group in Egypt. They were eager to create a vegetarian alternative to meat for days of fasting and are credited with the invention of falafel (or *ta'amiya* as it's better known in Cairo) for this purpose. The popular fritter caught on throughout Egypt, then across the Middle East and beyond. It is usually made from uncooked, ground fava beans in Egypt (or from chickpeas or a combination of both elsewhere), which are mixed with garlic, parsley, sesame seeds, onions, pepper, cumin, and coriander, then deep-fried until golden brown.

Falafel is served as meze *(see also pp110–13)*, and sometimes as part of *iftar*, the meal that breaks the daily fast after sunset during Ramadan. But it's usually eaten as a kind of fast food, in pita bread or *lafa* (another flatbread), with salad, pickled vegetables, hot pepper sauce, and tahini (a sesame seed paste). Hot, crisp, and freshly made falafel is the perfect thing to eat while drifting among the beautiful buildings of old Cairo.

Egyptian Eating Etiquette

In the Arab world, the right hand only is used for eating. The left, reserved for toilet ablutions, is kept firmly tucked away. If eating from a communal plate, it's considered bad manners to dig in with too much relish – including reaching for dishes not placed near you, overfilling your mouth, or eating too fast. The refusal of at least some second helpings is equally frowned upon. Once full, locals sometimes place their right hand over their stomach or heart to show repletion and gratitude. During the Muslim month of Ramadan, it shows sensitivity and respect to avoid eating, drinking, or smoking in public. If invited to an Egyptian household, it's considered good manners to bring a small gift such as flowers, chocolates, or pastries. Shoes are left at the door, hands are washed, and guests are seated next to a person of the same sex.

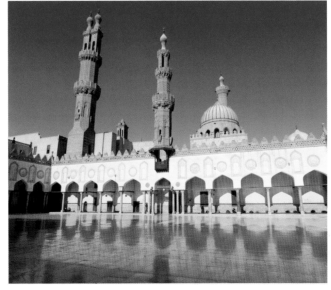

Above The Al Azhar mosque was completed in 972 for the new city of Al Qahira

The Best Places to Eat Falafel

Naguib Mahfouz Café expensive

Naguib Mahfouz is like an oasis amid the swirling motion and commotion of the Khan al-Khalili bazaar. Named after Egypt's 1988 winner of the Nobel Prize for Literature, who regularly came here, the café-restaurant provides a cool, serene, and civilized escape from Cairo's chaos. The elegant, marbled café is a great place for a fresh falafel snack, reviving cup of Arabic coffee or *sheesha* pipe – or better still, all three. Deeper inside, the lavish decor *à l'Oriental* of the formal restaurant provides an atmospheric and moody setting for a quiet lunch or dinner, particularly inside the private niches off the corridor. Specializing in classic Egyptian dishes that are well prepared, cooked, and served, the Naguib is an excellent choice for a first foray into Egyptian cooking or for a last-night splurge. The Naguib's *ta'amiya* (falafel) are prepared with finely diced green onion and garlic, subtly spiced with coriander and cumin, and topped with sesame seeds.

5 Sikket Al Baddistan, Khan al-Khalili, Cairo; open 10 AM–11 PM daily; +20 2 2590 3788

Also in Cairo

Run by the same family for 50 years, the **Felfella Restaurant** *(+20 2 2392 2833; moderate)* on Shari' Hoda Shaarawi has carved a niche and reputation for itself by offering fresh, wholesome, and good-quality Egyptian cooking at competitive prices in clean, convivial surroundings. *Ta'amiya* is the specialty: the crisp and carefully fried exterior hides a bright green fava interior that shouts of freshness and attentive cooking. For a good, inexpensive pit-stop when you're sightseeing, try **Al Halwagy** *(inexpensive)*, located 165 yards (150 m) east of Shari' Al Mu'ez Li Dinillah. Over a century old, this tiny, modest little place has survived through force of reputation: its *ta'amiya* and *fuul* are legendary.

Also in Egypt

Mohammed Ahmed *(+20 3 487 3576; inexpensive)* in Alexandria is an unassuming restaurant with a fanatical local following. Two staples have made it famous: *ta'amiya* and *fuul*. The menu (available in English) offers a good choice of salads, sauces, and condiments to accompany the little golden beauties, which can be eaten in or taken away.

Around the World

In central London, the **Ali Baba** *(+44 20 7723 7474; inexpensive)* near Regent's Park has developed something of a cult following for both nostalgic Egyptians and Londoners seeking fresh, decent Middle Eastern food at attractive prices, including the crunchy and flavorsome *ta'amiya*.

ISFAHAN IRAN

Khoresh-e Fesenjan in Isfahan

As the call to prayer rises from its minarets, Isfahan's famous mosque, Masjid-e Emam, glitters in the late afternoon sun. In the nearby bazaar, the air is filled with the scent of spices, and toward the city's edge an ancient fire temple is silhouetted against low, jagged hills. There is no more atmospheric place to sample *khoresh-e fesenjan*, one of the most opulent dishes in Persian cuisine.

Isfahan is an unforgettable place. Imagine a square – originally a polo ground – surrounded by some of the most exquisitely beautiful architecture to be found anywhere in the Islamic world. The Persian capital during the 16th and 17th centuries, Isfahan is for many synonymous with the art and architecture of Iran – refined palaces, elegant gardens, and mosques lavishly decorated with dazzling blue and turquoise tiles.

Iran (Persia) has an exceptionally long history. It was already a formidable empire some 2,500 years ago, against which first the Greeks and then the Romans measured themselves. Though there are plenty of signs of this long history in Isfahan, the city is most closely associated with the Safavid period, when the great ruler Shah Abbas turned it into his capital in the late 16th century. He laid out the Meydan-e Emam (a huge square) together with the Masjid-e Emam (the famous royal mosque on the south side of the square) and the smaller Masjid-e Lotfallah mosque. These buildings still constitute one of the greatest architectural ensembles on the planet, and along with the Meydan-e Emam are inscribed on the UNESCO World Heritage list.

The cuisine of the Persian empire also developed over the course of many centuries, and is equally refined. *Khoresh* is the Persian word for a stew or sauce, and it comes in many guises, of which *fesenjan* is one of the best known and certainly one of the richest. This dish – also called the king of stews – is often prepared at home for special occasions. Chicken, or more traditionally duck, is simmered with onion, ground toasted walnuts, and pomegranate syrup until literally falling off the bone. The resulting sauce is a rich, dark brown, with an exquisite sweet-bitter flavor from the walnuts, pomegranate, lemon, and cinnamon. Some say the dish originates in northern Iran, though it can be found across the country – at least, in restaurants serving a range of dishes rather than just kebabs, the nation's favorite fast food.

Khoresh-e fesenjan is served with rice, cooked slowly to perfection and topped with melting butter, a serving of tasty yogurt, and a wedge of the golden crust (called *tah-dig* in Persian) that forms at the bottom of the rice pan. This is the best part of the dish, as far as many Iranians are concerned. Of course, this being Iran, you won't be drinking wine with your meal – think more in terms of a glass of cool mineral water.

A Day in Isfahan

Most of Isfahan's main sights, including the Meydan-e Emam and the bazaar, are north of the Zayandeh River, while the Armenian quarter and a few other places lie south.

MORNING Start with the **Masjid-e Jame**, a 12th-century masterpiece that has an amazing carved stucco prayer niche from the Mongol period. Then walk through the streets of the **bazaar** to the **Meydan-e Emam**, the vast square laid out at the close of the 16th century, and visit the magnificent **Masjid-e Emam**.

AFTERNOON Visit other buildings on the Meydan-e Emam, including the breathtaking **Masjid-e Lotfallah** and **Ali Qapu Palace**, then take a short walk to the **Hasht Behesht Palace** in the gardens nearby. Share a taxi to the old Armenian quarter of **New Julfa**, with its fascinating churches.

EVENING Return to the river, ducking under one end of the **Si-o Se** bridge to stop at the atmospheric teahouse beneath the arches. Walk to **Restoran-e Shahrzad** in the centre of the city for *khoresh-e fesenjan*.

Essentials

GETTING THERE
Iranian Air and other Gulf states airlines fly into Isfahan's **airport**. There are **shared taxis** to the city 15 miles (25 km) away. **Trains** run from Tehran.

WHERE TO STAY
Amir Kabir Hostel (inexpensive) is the most popular low budget option. *+98 311 222 7273*
Hotel Julfa (moderate) in the Armenian quarter is another good choice. *+98 311 624 4441*
Hasht Behesht Apartment Hotel (moderate) is modern and just five minutes from the Meydan-e Emam. *www.ehbhotel.webs.com*

FURTHER INFORMATION
www.isfahan.ir

Above The Bazaar-e Bozorg is a 400-year-old market selling an astonishing array of goods, including a vast range of spices

Left It is said that nearly half a million tiles make up the exquisite mosaic patterning and calligraphy decorating the Masjid-e Emam, or Imam Mosque

Above The thick, dark sauce of *khoresh-e fesenjan* surprises the taste buds with its unique sweet-bitter flavor from pomegranates and walnuts

What Else to Eat

Khoresh-e fesenjan is a great example of a *khoresh* or sauce-based dish, but there are many others, such as **khoresh-e bademjan** (eggplant with chicken, lamb, or duck), **khoresh-e ghormeh sabzi** (lamb cooked in a sauce of fresh green herbs), and **khoresh torsh** (lamb with dried fruit). Along with plenty of fresh herbs and spices such as cinnamon and nutmeg, another popular ingredient you may encounter in these dishes is whole dried lime, which imparts a wonderful flavor. The accompaniment to *khoresh* is a mountain of perfectly cooked rice. Iranians generally eat their main meal in the middle of the day, so look for *khoresh* then, rather than in the evening.

The Best Places to Eat Khoresh-e Fesenjan

Restoran-e Shahrzad moderate

In the center of Isfahan and only a short walk from the Meydan-e Emam, Restoran-e Shahrzad serves some of the finest Persian cuisine in Isfahan – including a delicious *khoresh-e fesenjan*. There is a good range of dishes on the menu, from golden *tachin (see p179)* and other rice dishes to fish and sizzling kebabs. Portions are generous, the staff polite and efficient, and the interior decor suitably lavish, complete with wood paneling, colorful stained glass windows, and paintings in the style of Persian miniatures. Prices are slightly higher than average for Isfahan, but still very reasonable. As with most restaurants, the *fesenjan* here is made with chicken rather than duck – but it is nevertheless incredibly rich and fragrant, deep-colored and bursting with sweet and sour flavors. The buttery rice is, as always, a perfect partner to this heady stew. The long-established Shahrzad is understandably popular with locals as well as foreign visitors, and is both a great place to eat out in Isfahan and a wonderful introduction to the delicious Persian *fesenjan*.
Abbas Abad Street, Isfahan; open 11:30 AM– 10:30 PM daily; +98 311 220 4490

Also in Isfahan

The **Khan Gostar** restaurant *(+98 311 627 8989; moderate)* in the Hotel Julfa is one of the best places to eat in town – perhaps as good as Shahrzad – and a good place to try a range of Persian dishes. Popular with Isfahanis, this restaurant is farther from downtown, but an obvious choice if you're spending time in Isfahan's historic Armenian quarter. By far the most atmospheric place to sip tea in town is in the **teahouse** *(inexpensive)* under the Si-o Se bridge – you may even find *abgusht*, a thick meat and potato stew that's a specialty of Tabriz in northwest Iran, rather than *khoresh*.

Also in Iran

Ferdosi Sonnati *(+98 21 6671 4503; inexpensive)* is a busy place at the southern end of Ferdosi Street in Tehran, which serves plenty of traditional Persian dishes including several types of *khoresh*.

Around the World

One of the best Persian restaurants in London is **Shandi's** *(www.shandispersianrestaurant. co.uk; moderate)*. Smaller and less well-known than some others, this gem of a restaurant has excellent food, reasonable prices, and offers a genuinely warm welcome. The *khoresh-e fesenjan* is delicious.

CAPE TOWN SOUTH AFRICA

Bobotie Beneath Table Mountain

Situated near Africa's southern tip, cosmopolitan Cape Town is a city of singular natural beauty. Rising from a gorgeous natural harbor to the footslopes of iconic Table Mountain, it is also the home of *bobotie*, the definitive dish of the Cape Malay community, whose fusion of Indonesian, Dutch, and indigenous elements has created a unique cuisine emblematic of the city itself.

Above Cape Town sits at the foot of the spectacular Table Mountain, which dominates the city skyline; the summit can be reached in minutes by cable car

Boasting world-class restaurants that represent every conceivable global cuisine, Cape Town is Africa's culinary answer to London or New York – but with the added advantages of a warm climate, a tourist-friendly exchange rate, and one of the world's top winelands on the doorstep. It's ironic, then, that you could spend quite some time in Cape Town without realizing that it boasts its own distinctive cuisine; but possible, because Cape Malay cuisine, like the community, stands slightly outside the South African mainstream.

The Cape Malay are an anomaly. In a land whose history is dominated by the clash between indigenous Africans and European settlers, this tightly knit community is descended from Indonesian slaves and religious dissidents brought here by the earliest Dutch settlers. The community retains a strong Islamic identity, despite South Africa being predominantly Christian, yet its mother tongue is the Dutch derivative called Afrikaans, while the famously sentimental songs performed by its choirs are called *Nederlandsliede* (Dutch Songs).

Unsurprisingly, Cape Malay cuisine is a curious mixture. The curries are sweeter and milder than their Indonesian forerunners due to the use of fruit preserves. *Sosaties* – kebabs soaked in a sweet, spicy marinade – are a linguistic fusion of the Dutch *saus* (sauce) and Indonesian satay (skewered meat). And the inclusion of Cape pondweed in a lamb dish called *waterblommetjiebredie* (water-flower stew) is borrowed from the indigenous Khoikhoi. The national dish of South Africa, *bobotie*, was probably introduced to the Cape by early Dutch settlers before being re-adopted by their Indonesian slaves. Rather like a spicy moussaka, it comprises a fruity, curried ground meat base, topped with an eggy sauce that forms a crust when baked.

Cape Malay culture still thrives in the Bo-Kaap (Upper Cape), a residential district of brightly painted houses that offers superb views across the city bowl to the unmistakable flat top of Table Mountain – accessed from downtown by a thrilling revolving cable car. Farther afield, Cape Town offers limitless opportunities for memorable expeditions, including whale-watching in False Bay, a hike to the clifftop Cape Point Lighthouse, or a boat trip to Robben Island.

Cape Wines

Viniculture in the Cape dates back to 1659, when the colony's founder Jan van Riebeeck produced a small amount of doubtless rather rough wine. The subsequent arrival of French Huguenots prompted the fledgling industry to spread inland to **Stellenbosch, Franschhoek,** and **Paarl,** the site of historic vineyards such as Blaauwklippen, Boschendal, and Vergelegen. Today, South Africa is the world's seventh-largest wine producer, with about a dozen different grape varieties. **Cabernet Sauvignon,** the most widely planted red, produces heavy wines that complement red meats. **Pinotage,** a uniquely South African cultivar, makes a fruity, purple wine that often represents the best value among the reds. Of the whites, **Sauvignon Blanc** provides a crisp, zesty complement to Cape Malay dishes and seafood.

Three Days in and around Cape Town

Cape Town and its immediate environs could easily keep you busy for two weeks. It boasts iconic mountains, rustic wine estates, colorful botanical gardens, modern shopping malls, windswept oceanic cliffs, and superb swimming beaches, all set against the craggy spine of Table Mountain National Park (TMNP).

DAY ONE Head to the summit of **Table Mountain**, which is most easily reached by cable car. It has interesting wildlife and offers breathtaking views in all directions. After lunching at **Noon Gun**, head to the **Company's Gardens**, founded by van Riebeeck and encircled by historic landmarks such as the **Old Slave Lodge**, **National Museum**, **St. George's Cathedral**, and **House of Parliament**.

DAY TWO Take off for the **Western Cape Peninsula** and the **Constantia Winelands**, taking in the spectacular Cape of Good Hope sector of **TMNP** and the penguin colony at **Boulders**. Lunch at Groot Constantia's **Jonkershuis Restaurant**, then enjoy an afternoon stroll around **Kirstenbosch Botanical Garden**.

DAY THREE Visit sedate old **Stellenbosch**, famed for its wealth of Cape Dutch architecture, then go wine-tasting in the surrounding **Cape Winelands**.

Essentials

GETTING THERE
Most international flights land at **Johannesburg**, two hours by air from Cape Town; **trains** and **buses** connect the cities. There are also direct flights from Europe to **Cape Town International Airport**, 30 minutes from downtown.

WHERE TO STAY
For a cozy bargain, the **Lord Nelson Inn** (inexpensive) in historic Simonstown is hard to beat. *www.lordnelsoninn.co.za*
Cape Town Hollow (moderate) is a conveniently central hotel situated opposite the Company's Gardens. *www.capetownhollow.co.za*
The Cape Grace (expensive) is the epitome of contemporary five-star chic. *www.capegrace.com*

TOURIST INFORMATION
www.tourismcapetown.co.za

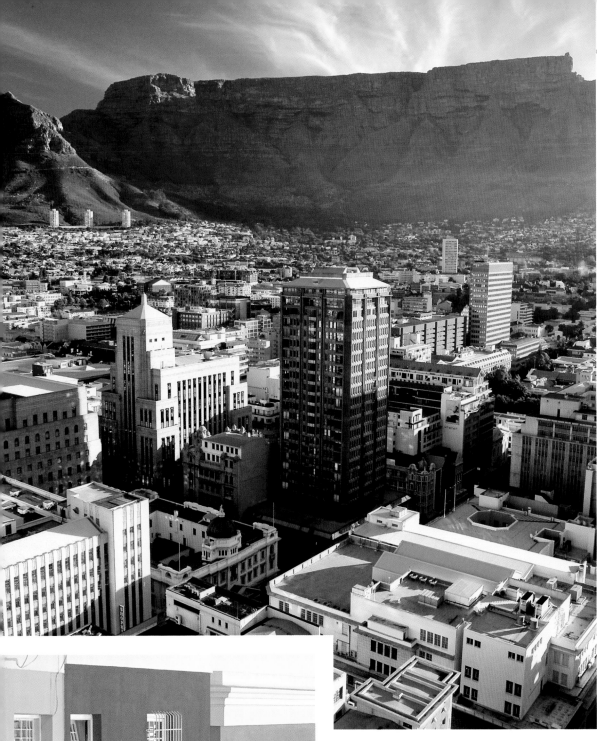

The Best Places to Eat Bobotie

Jonkershuis Restaurant moderate

A historic setting in suburban Groot Constantia, South Africa's oldest wine estate, is just one of many reasons why a relaxed lunch at the Jonkershuis ranks among the Cape Peninsula's most iconic dining experiences. The setting here really is lovely, with long leafy rows of vines sloping up to the base of the ragged peaks of the Constantia Mountain, and the option of dining alfresco in the oak-shaded gardens. If this doesn't appeal, you can eat inside the period-furnished main building, a thatched and whitewashed Cape Dutch edifice dating to the 18th century. Owned and managed by a team of the Cape's most experienced restaurateurs, Jonkershuis prides itself on its Cape Malay menu, which includes *bobotie* – here served with an accompaniment of *sambals* (chili pepper sauces) and almond-flavored yellow rice. For those seeking a one-stop introduction to the local cuisine, the restaurant produces a sumptuous Cape Malay "tasting plate," a kind of mini-buffet featuring *bobotie* alongside a rich lamb curry, a lighter chicken curry, and cinnamon-flavored roast butternut. There's a great choice of Cape whites, including the estate's own oaked Chardonnay and Sauvignon Blanc, and the dessert menu includes Cape specialties such as *melktert* (milk tart) and *malva* pudding, a spongy, apricot-flavored dish of Dutch origin.

Off Constantia Main Road, Cape Town; open 9 AM–10 PM Mon–Sat; 9 AM–5 PM Sun; www.jonkershuisconstantia.co.za

Also in Cape Town

The **Noon Gun Tea Room & Restaurant** *(www.noonguntearoom.co.za; inexpensive)* dishes up excellent *bobotie* along with the likes of *deningvleis* (a hearty sweet-sour lamb stew), chicken *breyeni* (a spicy rice-based risotto-like dish), and a good selection of characteristically sweet desserts to finish. Set in the world-famous Kirstenbosch Botanical Garden on the eastern slopes of Table Mountain, the **Silver Tree Restaurant** *(www. kirstenboschrestaurant.com; moderate)* is famous for its picnic hampers, but it also serves a good *bobotie* – made with super-lean ostrich meat in a traditional *potjie* (black pot) – and tasty Cape Malay curry.

Also in South Africa

Gramadoelas *(www.gramadoelas.co.za; expensive)* in Johannesburg has played host to luminaries as diverse as Queen Elizabeth II and the actor Danny Glover. *Bobotie* is a firm favorite on the menu, alongside other Cape dishes such as *waterblommetjiebredie* (water-flower stew) and piping hot, grilled *sosaties*.

Above In 1954, the curried *bobotie* was declared the national dish of South Africa by the United Nations Women's Organization

Left The lines of colorful houses in the Bo Kaap Malay quarter are occasionally broken by *kramats* (Muslim saint shrines) and mosques

MARRAKECH

MARRAKECH MOROCCO

Spicy Tagine in the City of Souks

The sunset tinges the distant Atlas Mountains a deep rose-red, and the call to prayer echoes from the turret of the Koutoubia Mosque. This is the time for the snake-charmers and henna artists of Jemaa el-Fna square to make way for the food-laden stands of Marrakech's night food market. Take a stroll around the spectacle before tucking into a traditional Moroccan tagine.

An oasis in every sense of the word, Marrakech was once a beacon for trading caravans that had traveled north through the desert and navigated over the often snow-capped Atlas Mountains. The fabulous palaces and lush palms of the city have always been where sub-Saharan Africa meets Arab North Africa, and even today this market town on the edge of nowhere remains a compellingly exotic port of call.

Life in the medina – the old walled city – revolves around the towering medieval minaret of the Koutoubia Mosque. For many visitors, though, this is eclipsed by the atmospheric Jemaa el-Fna, the nerve center of Marrakech, with its weird and wonderful cast of artists and performers – from water-sellers to fortune-tellers – and spectacular, frenetic food market.

Next head for the ancient souk – a vast area of higgledy-piggledy, cupboard-sized shops and stands filling dozens of narrow alleyways. Delicious smells draw you farther into the endless maze of lanes, where stands are laden with bundles of fresh mint, jars of plump olives infused with lemon and garlic, and bright pyramids of spice. Intricately made leather goods, metalwork, inlaid boxes, brass lanterns, carpets, and

jewelry overflow the tables and floor. Slightly less overwhelming are the food and spice markets of the Mellah, the old Jewish quarter; the Place des Ferblantiers, where tinsmiths make and sell their wares, is a relative haven from the hustle and bustle. Find a rooftop café terrace for a refreshing mint tea – and look for white storks, soaring to their nests on top of the old royal tombs and palaces.

After a day's sightseeing, shopping, or wandering the souk, there is nothing better than sitting down to enjoy a rich, fragrant tagine – the signature dish of Morocco. This aromatic dish combines meat – usually lamb, sometimes chicken – with fruit (often dried), vegetables, and a heady mix of herbs and spices, including saffron, cumin, coriander, and nutmeg.

The concoction is then braised slowly over a bed of charcoal in its distinctive and eponymous clay pot. The traditional conical-lidded dish synonymous with tagine – effectively a robust, portable cooking pot and serving dish all in one – originated with the Berber and Tuareg tribes of the Sahara. The use of dried fruits and the emphasis on aromatic spices also stem from this nomadic culture. Marrakech may have smartened itself up a little in recent years for the tourist trade, but its ancient desert heart still beats strong.

A Day in Marrakech

The rich history of Marrakech is reflected in its various quarters. The medina corresponds to the old town, with Jemaa el-Fna, the hub of all activity, at its heart. Within the ramparts are the souks, the kasbah, and the Mellah.

MORNING Start at **Jemaa el-Fna**, the vast square at the heart of the medina, which is as old as Marrakech itself. Just off the square, and dominating Marrakech's skyline, is the tower of the **Koutoubia Mosque**. Like most mosques in Morocco, it is closed to non-Muslims, but is an impressive sight nonetheless.

AFTERNOON Laid out in the narrow streets north of Jemaa el-Fna are a spectacular array of **souks**, or bazaars, selling everything from carpets and slippers to magic spells, in which you can while away whole mornings or afternoons. Continue to the **city walls** that enclose the medina, studded with 20 ornamental gates.

EVENING Return to **Jemaa el-Fna**, which transforms itself at night into a circus, theater, and restaurant, with itinerant musicians and entertainers drawing crowds.

Essentials

GETTING THERE
Menara International Airport is 2 miles (4 km) from the downtown. **Taxis** are readily available.

WHERE TO STAY
Hôtel Sherazade (inexpensive) has simple rooms within a *riad* (traditional Moorish town house). www.hotelsherazade.com
Tchaikana (moderate) is a beautiful *riad* within the medina. www.tchaikana.com
La Maison Arabe (expensive) was the first boutique hotel in Marrakech, and offers luxury and comfort. www.lamaisonarabe.com

TOURIST INFORMATION
Place Abdelmoumen Ben Ali (Av Mohammed V).

Above Richly colored and scented mounds of saffron, paprika, and cumin for sale in the souk

Left The Jemaa el-Fna at night becomes a noisy mass of food stands, suffused with the aromas of kebabs grilling on charcoal braziers

Above The rich meat stew of tagine is cooked in a distinctive earthenware vessel with a conical lid that releases fragrant aromas when lifted

Cooking Schools

Take more than just a tagine dish home from your trip to Marrakech – there are several great cooking schools in and around the city offering workshops and courses in Moroccan cuisine, and tagine is always on the syllabus. **Kasbah Agafy** *(www.kasbahagafay.com)* offers outdoor cooking courses in the organic herb and vegetable garden of a beautifully renovated 150-year-old fort, 20 minutes from Marrakech. **La Maison Arabe** *(see Where to Stay)* holds half-day cooking workshops for residents and guests. **Rhodes School of Cuisine** *(www. rhodeschoolofcuisine.com)* runs week-long courses with luxury *riad* accommodations.

The Best Places to Eat Tagine

Restaurant Al Fassia moderate

Restaurant Al Fassia faces onto a tiny but leafy courtyard and is decorated in warm, earthy colors in a modern Moroccan style. Here, chef Halima Chab and her all-woman team prepare and serve a repertoire of tagines, with up to 13 on the menu at any one time – and all of them supreme examples of the art. They might include tender lamb with caramelized onions and pumpkin, or dates and roasted almonds; chicken with olives and preserved lemons; or *kefta* (spicy meatballs) with eggs.

Begin your meal with a selection from Al Fassia's stunning range of meze, which includes a delicious honey- and cinnamon-scented squash purée, and finish with Halima Chab's signature dessert of *b'stilla* (a filo pastry) with almonds and milk.

Founded over 20 years ago, Al Fassia was once legendary – and loved – for its no-nonsense service. Since its move to a more upmarket venue in the residential Guéliz district, the atmosphere has become more refined – but the standard of cooking undoubtedly remains one of the high points of any visit to Marrakech.

55 Boulevard Zerktouni, Guéliz, Marrakech; open noon–2:30 PM and 7:30–11 PM daily, except Tue; www.alfassia.com

Also in Marrakech

To sample a tagine as part of a fine-dining experience, try the elegant and atmospheric **La Maison Arabe** *(www.lamaisonarabe.com; expensive)* or the historic **La Mamounia** hotel *(www.mamounia.com; moderate)*, with its magnificent terrace on the ground floor and bar and tearoom on the top floor. And for a simple but authentic tagine, as well as a jaw-dropping view over the city, opt for the rooftop tables of popular **Chez Chegrouni** at 4–6 Jemaa el-Fna *(no telephone; inexpensive)*.

Also in Morocco

Interesting regional variations on the tagine are offered around Morocco. In Fès, try **Al Firdaouss** *(+212 535 634 343; moderate)*. This is one of Fès's most enchanting restaurants and serves a delicious tagine. A short walk away is the traditional **Palais Tariana** *(+212 535 636 604; expensive)*.

Around the World

London's Moroccan community first started to arrive in the 1960s. Since then, Moroccan food has become increasingly available and fashionable. **Momo**, just off Regent Street *(www.momoresto.com; expensive)*, is London's most famous and glam Moroccan restaurant, serving high-quality food. Also in central London, **Original Tagines** *(www.original-tagines.com; inexpensive)* serves excellent tagines in contemporary Moroccan surrounds.

Three Days on Zanzibar

Though Stone Town boasts several striking architectural landmarks to head for, it is also conducive to whimsical exploration, routinely throwing up fantastic sights, sounds, and smells – and it's not so large that you could truly get lost.

DAY ONE Dedicate the day to Stone Town. Start at the **Palace Museum**, then follow the waterfront south to the **House of Wonders**, **Forodhani Gardens**, and the **Old Arab Fort**, a great spot for lunch. In the afternoon, browse the shops on **Kenyatta**, **Gizenga**, and **Hurumzi Streets**, or venture north into the tangle of alleys at the heart of Stone Town. Have a drink at the historic **Africa House Hotel**.

DAY TWO An organized **Spice Tour** will combine a visit to a local *shamba* (subsistence farm) with stops at several ruined 19th-century palaces and baths north of town.

DAY THREE Drive south to **Kizimkani** for a dhow trip and swimming with dolphins. Return via **Jozani Forest** to seek out the Zanzibar red colobus, a spectacularly coiffed monkey unique to this island.

Essentials

GETTING THERE
Zanzibar International Airport has flights from Ethiopia and Kenya; there's a larger airport at Dar es Salaam, a short trip away by **plane** or **ferry**. The town is easily explored on **foot**.

WHERE TO STAY
Hotel Kiponda (inexpensive) is a long-serving budget favorite that's centrally located with some period character. *www.kiponda.com*
236 Hurumzi (moderate–expensive) has an unbeatable atmosphere; it's a three-story, 19th-century mansion lavishly furnished in period style. *www.236hurumzi.com*
Zanzibar Serena Inn (expensive) is a more conventional and overtly luxurious hotel on the waterfront. *www.serenahotels.com*

TOURIST INFORMATION
www.zanzibartourism.net

Right *Mnazi wa kamba* (shrimp curry), bathed in the golden-brown sauce made from masala and coconut milk

Below The legendary food stands of Forodhani Gardens fire up their grills at sunset

ZANZIBAR TANZANIA

Swahili Curry on Zanzibar

For over 1,000 years, Zanzibar has been a cultural melting pot. Its historic center, Stone Town, has a captivating blend of African, Arabic, Asian, and European architecture, and there's a rich mix of languages and cultures among its inhabitants. Zanzibari dishes are equally cosmopolitan, such as *mnazi*, a tangy, coconut-milk curry that seamlessly blends Indian, Arabic, and homegrown elements.

The very name "Zanzibar" drips with exoticism; most visitors agree that the Spice Island, which lies in the Indian Ocean off Tanzania's Swahili coast, is one of those travel destinations that truly matches expectations. Around the coast, mysterious ruins recall a millennium of maritime trade with Arabia. The pristine swaths of palm-lined white sand give way to a sea that offers magical diving and snorkeling, and the opportunity to swim with dolphins.

Zanzibar's cultural heart is historic Stone Town: a labyrinthine knot of narrow alleys, ostentatious Omani palaces, and multistory Swahili homesteads emanating from a medieval harbor with an imposing 17th-century Omani fort. The town's prosperity peaked in the mid-19th century, when it served as a capital for the Sultan of Oman and formed the main trade conduit for slaves captured on the African mainland. One of the most symbolically resonant landmarks on the island is the Anglican Cathedral, built on the site of the town's notorious slave market.

Today, the giddying smell of spiced Swahili *kahawa* (coffee) permeates Stone Town, punctuated by tantalizing wafts of home cooking. There are stands piled with aromatic foodstuffs; fresh and dried spices vie with the heady scents of juicy fresh fruits.

Zanzibari cuisine has been influenced by centuries of trade with Arabia and Asia, and its most popular dish is Swahili coconut curry. Made with chicken, fish, or seafood – and sometimes even beef – it incorporates the golden-brown Zanzibari masala, a superb mix of ground cinnamon, roasted coriander, cumin and fennel seeds, chili pepper, and cilantro. This imparts a spicy tang that blends with fresh coconut milk to produce a curry with a deep, creamy texture and rich aftertaste. Accompanied by *wali na nazi* (rice boiled in coconut milk), chapatis, and spinach-like *sukuma wiki*, Swahili curry – *mnazi* –is the culinary embodiment of the glorious Spice Island and its cosmopolitan past. It's arguably best eaten from the overflowing dinner stands of the waterfront Forodhani Gardens, which emerge mysteriously by the shore as the sun sets over the Indian Ocean, offering a unique sensory treat.

The Best Places to Eat Swahili Curry

Monsoon Restaurant moderate

The ultimate Zanzibari night out is provided by this well-established traditional restaurant, especially if you time your visit to coincide with the live *taarab* (classical Swahili music) performances on Wednesday and Friday nights. The terrace is ideal for an early evening drink, allowing you to watch the sun set over Forodhani Gardens while sailing dhows billow romantically across the Indian Ocean. Inside, the restaurant is divided into two areas. The homey bar is the place to relax over a fresh cocktail or ginger-spiced coffee, accompanied perhaps by a sweet *kashata* (nutty cookie). The main culinary action takes place next door, in a large open area decorated in the Swahili way, with *mikeka* matting spread across the floor and ground-level seating on brightly colored cushions set around knee-high tables, their tops adorned with fragrant fresh jasmine. An imaginative à la carte menu combines traditional Zanzibari favorites – Swahili chicken curry, kingfish in coconut sauce, shrimp marinated in garlic, ginger, and lime – with fusion fare that incorporates influences from all corners of the Mediterranean. There's a four-course dinner for diners with adventurous palates.

Hurumzi St., Stone Town, Zanzibar; open 10 AM–midnight daily; www.monsoon-zanzibar.com

Also on Zanzibar

Situated on the ground floor of the historic "House of Tea" hotel on Kelele Square, **Beyt al Chai Restaurant** *(www.bluebayzanzibar.com; expensive)* might not look like anything special in daylight, but the food is arguably the finest on Zanzibar, and it's complemented by a lovely candlelit ambience at dinner. The cuisine can be categorized broadly as Swahili fusion, with keynote dishes including a Zanzibar casserole of seafood poached in coconut and lemongrass broth, and there is an excellent wine list.

Also in Africa

Traditional Swahili cuisine is poorly represented at restaurants in Dar es Salaam, the largest city in Tanzania and former capital, but **Sweet Eazy Restaurant & Lounge** *(www.sweeteazy.com; moderate–expensive)* is a notable exception, serving an imaginative menu of traditional and fusion dishes including a superb seafood coconut curry. The arched decor evokes traditional Swahili architecture and there's live music on weekends. On Shela Beach, on the outskirts of the time-warped Kenyan port of Lamu, the stylish "barefoot luxury" **Peponi Hotel** *(www.peponi-lamu.com; expensive)* is renowned for its fresh seafood, whether you like it sushi-style, grilled plain, or curried in the traditional Swahili manner.

What Else to Eat

Seafood features strongly on Zanzibari menus, with a particular favorite being marinated and grilled **shrimp**. These are served at a cluster of food stands on Forodhani Gardens, alongside other East African favorites such as **nyama choma** (grilled meat), **chapatis** (flatbreads), and **sugar cane juice**. Fresh fruit is also prominent, including oversized and super-tasty coconuts and pineapples, but the adventurous might want to try **embe keri** (unripe mango sprinkled with chili pepper flakes) or the delicious but foul-smelling, spiky-coated durian fruit. Other popular Swahili dishes on the island include **boko-boko**, an aromatic porridge-type dish made of shredded meat and bulgur wheat, and **urojo** (literally "mixed") soup, in which cubes of grilled beef are placed with potatoes, chickpea fritters, and whatever else is available in a fruity stock.

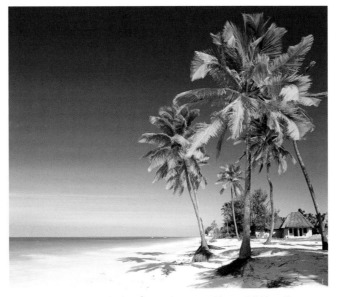

Above Zanzibar's uncrowded beaches are interspersed by small fishing villages

ALEPPO SYRIA

Cherry Kebabs in Ancient Aleppo

In the shadow of the looming Citadel, the souk of Aleppo teems and bustles with life. It is the beating heart of one of the world's oldest inhabited cities, and shimmers with vivid colors and smells as it has since the days of the Silk Road. It was here that merchants sold Eastern spices alongside fresh local produce, and that most Aleppian of recipes, *kabab bil karaz*, was born.

It is said that the covered souk in Aleppo stretches over 20 miles (32 km), making it the largest in the world. But size matters less than atmosphere in recreating the tumult and excitement of a medieval Arabian marketplace – and Syria's second city has atmosphere in abundance. This is not a touristy souk, although it is perfect for visitors who wish to wander beneath its impressive stone arches and browse without being harassed by traders. Aleppians pride themselves on their hospitality toward travelers, in traditional Bedouin fashion.

During Aleppo's 7,000 years of history, it has been overrun by Hittites, Assyrians, Persians, and Romans. Walk around the wonderful Old City, and you'll see architecture left by the Mamluks and Ottomans. Many civilizations helped shape Aleppo, but it was its position on the trade routes that provided its distinct character. As one of the main stops on the Silk Road between China and Europe, Aleppo became a commercial center that prospered from the flow of goods, wealth, people, and ideas. And it was this cultural exchange that helped to shape its proud culinary heritage.

Today Aleppo is heralded as the gastronomic capital of Syria, and a growing destination for food tourism. Surrounded by fertile land, it has always produced fine local ingredients, from fruit and vegetables to meat and poultry. But an influx of exotic spices from the East was to change the way those ingredients were prepared forever. The spice traders in the souks invented delicious recipes to entice customers and encourage trade. And their legacy became the bedrock of a sophisticated, globally recognized cuisine.

Exotic ingredients and local produce come together in *kabab bil karaz*, the cherry kebab. It is made with the sour *wishna* cherries grown in orchards on the outskirts of the city, and tender, locally reared lamb. The minced meat is rolled into small balls, broiled, laid upon thin flatbread, and drenched in a thick, dark cherry sauce. A *baharat* spice blend adds cardamom, cloves, cumin, and coriander to the mix, and a few spoonfuls of pomegranate molasses rounds it off with a sumptuously balanced sweet and sour quality. A fresh *fattoush* salad, splashed with lemon juice and a sprinkling of sumac, is all you need to complete a dish that's been thousands of years in the making.

Above The Citadel of Aleppo is one of the largest fortresses in the world; its walls sit above a moat that connects to underground passageways and caves

---

What Else to Eat

There's always a twist to Aleppine food, and **yabrak** is no exception. It's similar to **waraq enab** (cold vine leaves stuffed with rice and minced lamb), but served hot, which changes the flavor and texture of the dish. Aleppo has a large Armenian population, so you should certainly try its **soujouk**, slices of spiced sausage rolled in flatbread. **Basterma** is another Armenian delicacy of cured meat crusted in a peppery herb coating. Both dishes can be found at **Kasr Al-Wali** (www.kasralwali.com), but for one of the city's most traditional and heartwarming experiences, have a breakfast of **ful medames** at **Abu Abdo**'s tiny restaurant in Jdeideh. The old man has been serving the same dish of fava beans, tahini, lemon juice, and red pepper paste for around 50 years, and he's a legendary character in the city.

A Day in Aleppo

Few cities in the Middle East can match Aleppo for its mix of historical sites, calming mosques and churches, chaotic streets, and atmospheric souks. Wandering through the delightfully haphazard Old City, toward the yellow-taxi-thronged streets of the New City, is the best way to soak it all in.

MORNING Begin by ambling through the streets of the **Old Town** to the huge fortified mound of the **Citadel**. Tour the ruins, from the underground **hammam** to the old **amphitheater**, and then cool down at the café, with stunning views.

AFTERNOON Explore the famous and sprawling **souk**, for which a stern constitution and a good pair of shoes are essential. Enjoy the tumult of trade along mile after mile of stands, offering everything from silk and spices to Aleppine olive soap and the entrails of sheep.

EVENING Take refuge in the **Grand Mosque**, then grab a taxi for the **New City**. The shops in the quiet Christian neighborhood of **Jdeideh** begin to close their shutters by nightfall, which is when you should head to **Hatab Square** and a traditional Syrian courtyard restaurant for delightful Aleppine food and a cold beer.

Essentials

GETTING THERE

Aleppo International Airport is around 15 minutes from the city by **taxi**. There are **trains** from Istanbul to the north and Damascus in the south.

WHERE TO STAY

Baron Hotel (inexpensive) is the oldest hotel in Syria, and once played host to Lawrence of Arabia. A little faded, but full of history. *+963 21 210 880*
Yasmeen d'Alep (moderate) is a delightful hotel occupying a restored 17th-century mansion in the Jdeideh area. *www.yasmeenalep.com*
Sheraton Aleppo (expensive) is ideal for when comfort and cleanliness are more important than character. *www.starwoodhotels.com*

TOURIST INFORMATION

+963 21 21 228

The Best Places to Eat Cherry Kebabs

Zmorod expensive

There's a special ambience at this delightful restaurant, which sits in an elegant courtyard at the center of a beautifully restored 17th-century house. An ornate wrought-iron staircase climbs up a cool limestone wall, while overhead, intricate lanterns cast a lambent glow on the diners below. The atmosphere intensifies when the dining area is full of families and giggling couples, as fleet-footed waiters bring plate after plate of authentic Syrian delights to each table. The *kabab bil karaz* here is famous across Syria. The cherries and lamb are sourced locally, so both are wonderfully fresh. If you arrive early in the cherry season, the rich, spicy, dark sauce has a sourer edger to it, while later on it's sweeter, as the cherries ripen. Either way, the meat will be cooked to pink and tender perfection, and goes superbly with warm flatbread and fresh salad leaves. Like all Syrian spreads, a variety of dishes should be added, from a spicy *muhammara* red pepper paste with pomegranate molasses to a smoky *baba ghanoush* dip of mashed eggplant.

Raheb Bouhaira Street, Jdeideh, Aleppo; open noon–late daily; www.zmorod.com

Also in Aleppo

Club d'Alep *(+963 21 211 3500; expensive)* is quite possibly the best restaurant in the country, but unfortunately it's a private members club. In Syria, however, more than anywhere else on Earth, people are so friendly, warm, and welcoming that it shouldn't necessarily stop you from getting in. A friendly word with your hotel manager may be all that's needed. The reward is simply fantastic food, from the cherry kebabs to the desert truffles with lamb. **Bazar Al-Charq** *(www.bazaralcharq.com/aleppoe.htm; moderate)* is a cavernous restaurant in a stone cellar, offering all kinds of kebabs and even some rustic Bedouin dishes.

Also in Syria

Al Halabi *(www.fourseasons.com/damascus; expensive)* is one of the best restaurants in Damascus, but even this grand venue has a distinctly Aleppine bent. "Halab" is the ancient name for Aleppo, and Aleppine (Halabian) chef Mohammed Helal's food bears all the adventurous hallmarks of Aleppo's cuisine. Highlights are the cherry kebab and the *kebbeh saffarjaliyeh* (spiced lamb and bulgur wheat patties with quince, pomegranate, and rice).

Around the World

Elsewhere in the Middle East, Dubai has a number of good restaurants offering great, authentic Syrian food, including **Aroos Damascus** *(+971 221 9825; inexpensive)* and **Sarai** *(+971 438 0640; moderate)*.

Above The cherry kebabs in Aleppo have a unique flavor that comes from the small, sour cherries that grow just outside the city

Left Fresh, dried, whole, crushed, and powdered spices are sold in bins, bags, and pyramids in Aleppo's labyrinthine covered souk

TUNIS TUNISIA

A Tricky Treat in Tunis

Africa meets Europe in Tunisia's buzzing capital city, Tunis. Within the ancient medina, shoppers wander the labyrinthine paths of the souks, while in the modern city outside, businessmen sip coffee and read European newspapers. Come lunchtime, though, they're all likely to be tucking into the same dish: *brik à l'oeuf*, Tunisia's most delicious – and challenging – treat.

Tunis sits along Tunisia's northern coast, tucked into the innermost corner of the Gulf of Tunis. Its modern outlook and cosmopolitan air make it one of the most accessible North African destinations for visitors. But it exudes plenty of exotic atmosphere too, in the exquisitely tiled mosques and minarets towering above the rooftops, the arched courtyards and decorative doorways, the echoing cry of the muezzin calling the faithful to prayer, and the pungent smells of spice and perfume.

The city's impressive Roman history is another of its highlights, from the exquisite mosaics in the Bardo Museum to the outstanding ruins at Dougga, a day-trip away. The suburbs contain the remnants of an even more ancient empire, Carthage. From here the seafaring Phoenicians dominated the Mediterranean in the 6th century BC. Since then Arab, Ottoman, and French settlers have all influenced Tunisia's culture and cuisine.

Brik à l'oeuf is one such dish that Tunisians have made their own. This delicious triangular parcel of thin pastry, which may be filled with seafood, minced lamb, beef, or vegetables and herbs, but always includes an egg yolk, is fried in oil and eaten with the fingers.

It has its roots in the deep-fried *börek* of Turkish cuisine and in fact the unusual name, brik, is simply the local variation on the original Turkish word.

But with *brik à l'oeuf*, the Tunisians have made this humble snack food into a work of art. The most impressive briks are more than a hand-span wide, their paper-thin shells shaped like a fan and held daintily upright in a sliced lemon. The brik is often enlivened by fiery harissa, a spicy red mix of hot chili peppers and olive oil, mashed together into a paste. If you don't like hot sauces, don't even look at harissa – it might make your eyes water. However, it's so popular with the locals that many brik recipes include harissa in the filling, so if you can't stomach the heat, make sure to ask for one without. In Tunisia, harissa is almost always put on the table at the start of a meal, perhaps with some olives and bread as an hors d'oeuvre. Each chef or household will have their own recipe, and fancier versions might include cumin, coriander, and other herbs and spices.

The challenge in eating a *brik à l'oeuf* – especially the large, elaborate ones – is to control the runny egg yolk that explodes with the first bite. Once you can eat one without it running down your chin, then you've mastered the trick of the most Tunisian brik.

A Day in Tunis

The medina, Tunis's walled old town, is a UNESCO World Heritage site harboring a feast of Islamic architecture. From here, a short (and inexpensive) taxi ride will take you to sights in the surrounding new town and farther out along the coast.

MORNING Wander through the streets of the **medina** and soak up the atmosphere, admiring the beautifully carved and tiled decoration on the mosques and minarets. Dodge the carpet-sellers and go shopping in the mesmerizing bazaars of the souks.

AFTERNOON Visit the **Bardo Museum** to see the finest collection of Roman mosaics in the world. Then take a taxi to **Carthage** to see the **Antonine Baths**, the best of the scattered ruins of the once-great Phoenician civilization.

EVENING With its whitewashed, blue-shuttered houses and elaborate painted doors, the hilltop town of **Sidi Bou Saïd** is a favorite stop for visitors, just 12 miles (20 km) from Tunis. Its café terraces are grand spots from which to sip a mint tea and watch the sun set over the sea.

Essentials

GETTING THERE
Buses and **taxis** link Tunis-Carthage **international airport** with the downtown. Explore central Tunis on **foot**, or take **taxis** farther afield.

WHERE TO STAY
Hotel Majestic (inexpensive) is located on the edge of the medina. *+216 71 332 666*
Hotel Carlton (moderate) is a central, three-star Art Deco hotel. *www.hotelcarltontunis.com*
The **Oriental Palace** (expensive) is luxurious and sumptuously decorated. *+216 71 348 846*

TOURIST INFORMATION
Tunisia National Office of Tourism, 1 Avenue Mohamed V, Tunis; *+216 71 341 077*

Above Courtyard dining, North African *riadh*-style, at the Dar El Jeld restaurant in Tunis

Left Intricate tiling and stonework at the great mosque complex in Sidi Bou Saïd, a hilltop town a short metro train or taxi ride from the city

Above The crispy pastry of a *brik à l'oeuf* hides a secret: a golden egg yolk at its heart, waiting to burst at the first bite

What Else to Eat

Couscous, simply meaning "food," was originally a staple of the nomadic North African Berber tribes. These granules of semolina are typically layered on herbs and cooked in the top half of a *kiskas*, or double boiler, above a spicy meat, fish, or vegetable stew, absorbing the aromas and flavors as it steams. While any ingredients can form the base – camel and octopus are Tunisian specialties – couscous is always enriched by herbs, spices, and harissa. One delicious version, known as **burzqan**, is mixed with fresh butter, mutton, saffron, and chickpeas, sprinkled with hot milk, and garnished with raisins, almonds, pistachios, hazelnuts, and walnuts.

The Best Places to Eat Brik à l'Oeuf

Dar El Jeld expensive

This atmospheric old place in the heart of the medina is one of the finest restaurants in Tunis. It's in a beautiful 18th-century town house, and you might need some help to find it, but once through the flame-lit arched doorway and into the covered tiled courtyard that forms the dining area, you will experience everything that is magical and evocative about North Africa. By Tunisian standards this is an expensive place to eat, but it provides an unforgettable flavor of Tunis. The service is impeccably courteous, and reservations are essential. There is live music on most evenings. Several types of brik are available as appetizers, including a taster selection of mini-briks, and other specialties of the house include lamb couscous, an olive and beef stew, fish couscous, tajines, a North African-style paella, and an array of delicious pastry desserts. It is also the place to discover just how good Tunisian wines can be.

5–10 Rue Dar El Jeld, La Kasbah, Tunis; open for lunch and dinner Mon–Sat; closed for lunch in July and during Ramadan, and for all of August; www.dareljeld.tourism.tn

Also in Tunis

A venerable institution in the Souk El Trouk (the Turkish or tailors' souk) in the medina, **M'rabet Café Restaurant** *(+216 71 561 729; inexpensive)* is the perfect place to take a break from the hectic bustle of the souks and relax with a coffee or a mint tea, or something more substantial. It has a café downstairs; upstairs is an inexpensive restaurant that serves brik alongside many other Tunisian specialties, including lamb and chicken couscous. Live music is often featured.

Also in Tunisia

Restaurant Chargui *(+216 71 740 987; moderate)* is one of the best restaurants in Sidi Bou Saïd, the picturesque little hilltop town close to Tunis. Open daily, it has a lovely blue-and white-washed terrace with great views over the sea, and its menu includes a choice of briks, a range of couscous dishes, and locally caught fresh grilled fish.

Around the World

An authentic taste of both Tunisia and Morocco can be found on Sutter Street in the heart of San Francisco at **Cafe Zitouna** *(www.cafezitouna.com; moderate)*, an unpretentious café/carry-out specializing in the flavors of North Africa. Brik is naturally on the menu, along with a wide range of tajines, couscous dishes, hot and spicy *merguez* sausages, and sticky baklava desserts.

BEIRUT LEBANON

Raw Passion in Beirut

Invigorating and exasperating, vibrant and serene, beautiful and dilapidated – Beirut is all things to all people. Though plagued by strife, it refuses to be beaten. It has emerged from a troubled past as a cosmopolitan crucible of cultures, and from its street life to its nightlife, Beirut's impulses and passions are as raw as can be – just like the city's favorite meat dish, *kibbeh nayyeh*.

Built on a promontory jutting out into the Mediterranean, Beirut is ever the show-off. But as difficult as it might be to imagine today's vivacious capital playing second fiddle to a neighboring town, it was once deemed less important than the Phoenician trading ports of Sidon and Byblos. It wasn't until the Romans began using Beirut as a military base and commercial hub that it really began to blossom. The ruins of Roman bathhouses can still be seen in the central area, today a buoyant shopping and entertainment district, which itself sprang out of a more recent set of ruins left behind by the devastating 15-year civil war.

Bullet-peppered buildings and army checkpoints serve as a reminder of the city's struggles, but years of conflict and political instability have taught the people to seize life and live it with gusto. This natural energy and *joie de vivre* can be felt on any trip to Beirut, from the daily human tide that flows up and down its sweeping Corniche to the frenetic cafés and bars that line Gemmayze's vivid Rue Gourard. Amble along Hamra Street, and the street food of sizzling *shawarma* grilled meats and falafel will be hard to resist. But

leave room for lunch, which in Beirut is long, leisurely, and all about meze. Guaranteed to be among the array of dishes is *kibbeh nayyeh*, one of Lebanon's most famous delicacies. It's raw lamb, pulverized with cracked bulgur wheat and chopped onion until mousse-soft, often whipped into swirly shapes and served drizzled with olive oil and garnished with fresh mint. Its creamy texture and rich flavor goes perfectly with green olives, pickled chili peppers, and zesty tabbouleh (parsley and bulgur salad).

Like so many Levantine dishes, it may well have its roots in ancient Syria. Some villages, like Ehden in northern Lebanon – considered by some to be the capital of *kibbeh nayyeh* – have claimed it as their own. But for centuries, wherever there were sheep and goats in Lebanon, *kibbeh nayyeh* would be pounded in stone mortars called *jurns*, the sound resonating through the village. The beauty of finding *kibbeh nayyeh* in Beirut lies in discovering regional variations – one recipe might have coarse bulgur, while another might use more olive oil. But as any master of *kibbeh nayyeh* preparation will tell you, the secret ultimately lies in the freshness, quality, and leanness of the meat.

Above Much of Beirut's historic central district has required reconstruction, and is now a vibrant shopping, dining, and entertainment area

Beirut's Farmers' Market

Souk El Tayeb (*www.soukeltayeb.com*), which meets every Saturday on a site near the Exhibition Center, is Lebanon's first weekly farmers' market; it brings together over 100 producers and artisans. Founded by Kamal Mouzawak, the souk showcases the seasonal produce of farmers from all over Lebanon, but it's more than just a market. As well as aiming to preserve Lebanon's natural heritage, it also seeks to promote coexistence, social interaction, and an environmentally friendly lifestyle. **Tawlet** (*www.tawlet.com*) is the organization's cooperative kitchen, which offers the creations of a different regional cook each day. In addition, the team holds regular **Food & Feast festivals** across Lebanon, from the fruit-growing villages of Mount Lebanon to the herb-growers of the south.

Three Days in Beirut

Lebanon is small and geographically diverse, so it's possible to swim in the morning, ski in the afternoon, and go clubbing in the city at night. With a few days to explore, you can revel in Beirut's infectious energy, enjoy the resorts of Mount Lebanon, and recover at the beach clubs around the capital.

DAY ONE After a morning stroll along the **Corniche**, have an espresso in a **Hamra café** among the students from the American University. Head east to the beautiful **Mohammed al-Amin mosque** on the site of the Green Line that divided Beirut during the civil war. Then check out the cafés and bars in the Christian neighborhoods of **Achrefiyeh** and **Gemmayze**.

DAY TWO Drive or take a taxi to the **Jeita Grotto** to see the impressive stalactites and stalagmites in the subterranean caverns. Then head on to the slopes of **Faraya Mzaar**, where the après-ski culture is every bit as lively as the skiing.

DAY THREE If the weather's fine, kick back at one of Beirut's beach clubs. **AUB Beach** has a wonderful ambience, while the **St. George Yacht Motor Club** is where the beautiful people go to hang out.

Essentials

GETTING THERE
From **Rafic Hariri International Airport** it's just a 10-minute **taxi** ride downtown; if you dislike haggling, choose a marked, registered white cab.

WHERE TO STAY
Port View Hotel (inexpensive) in the Mar Mikhael area is within walking distance of the bars and restaurants of Gemmayze. *www.portviewhotel.blogspot.com*

Marble Tower (moderate) is a comfortable and recently renovated hotel in the lively Hamra district. *www.marbletowerhotel.com*

Le Gray (expensive) is a modern luxury hotel in the revamped Central district. *www.campbellgrayhotels.com*

TOURIST INFORMATION
I Rue Banque du Liban, Hamra; +961 1 343 073

Above With an almost diplike texture, creamy *kibbeh nayyeh* should be scooped up with Lebanese flatbread

Right The stunning new Mohammed al-Amin mosque is modeled on the Sultan Ahmed Mosque in Istanbul

The Best Places to Eat Kibbeh Nayyeh

Abdel Wahab moderate

A bastion of tradition in one of Beirut's most fashionable districts, Abdel Wahab is a sure bet for authentic *kibbeh nayyeh* in a charming setting. Occupying an attractive Ottoman house in a Monot side street, the dining area is an enclosed courtyard, which is suitably untainted by 21st-century trappings. The waiters are used to serving vast meze spreads, which they deliver with speed and efficiency.

From the olives and pickled vegetables to hummus and tabbouleh, the dishes begin arriving thick and fast. Abdel Wahab has a reputation for using only the best butchers, some of whom are from the famous meat markets of Sabra, so the *kibbeh nayyeh* here is one of the freshest in the city. Beautifully presented in pink swirls, it has a richness that will flood your palate with flavor, and a texture as smooth as paste. Those of a sterner constitution might enjoy *sauda nayyeh*, or raw lamb's liver and fat cubes, served with little mounds of pepper and ground spices for dipping. Meze is all about contrasts, so have a mix of hot and cold dishes, from barbecued chicken livers to stuffed vine leaves. When a long meze lunch in the mountains is just out of reach, Abdel Wahab is the next best thing.

El Inglizi Street, Monot, Achrefiyeh, Beirut; open noon–midnight daily; +961 1 200 550/1

Also in Beirut

You'll find a refreshingly contemporary take on Lebanese cuisine in **Babel** *(+961 70 425 777; moderate)*, a breathtaking new restaurant on the Dbayeh Highway on the outskirts of town. The cavernous dining room is high and wide, built of huge blocks of sandstone. It's like dining at a palace in ancient Baalbek, but the *kibbeh nayyeh* has a thoroughly modern twist – served in individual, bite-size portions, rolled and dotted with black sesame seeds like sushi.

Also in Lebanon

Twenty minutes' drive from Beirut is the mountain retreat of Brummana, where **Kasr Fakhreddine** *(www.fakhreddine.com; expensive)* has sweeping valley views of the Chouf Mountains and great *kibbeh nayyeh*. For a distinctly northern Lebanese version of the dish, **Le Mortier** *(+961 3 870 507; inexpensive)* in the town of Ehden near Tripoli has a beautiful setting and *kibbeh* in all of its wondrous forms, both raw and cooked.

Around the World

There are more people of Lebanese extraction living outside Lebanon than within. Brazil has one of the largest migrant communities, and São Paulo's **Almanara** *(www.almanara. com.br; inexpensive)* has been preparing and serving authentic meze, including *kibbeh nayyeh*, since the 1950s.

TEHRAN IRAN

Persian Polo in Tehran

Tehran is an almost frenetically busy city, with broad streets, roaring traffic, and a great, seething bazaar – not to mention some of the country's best restaurants – all lying in the shadow of the mighty, snow-capped Alborz Mountains. It's just the place to hunt down one of the many variations of *polo*, the most exquisite of Persian rice dishes.

The Iranian capital cannot really be called a beautiful city. A sprawling, exhaust-filled metropolis with some eight million inhabitants, it is a place more usually associated with concrete blocks and seemingly endless streams of traffic. But look a little beyond this and you will find green parks, opulent palaces, and some of the country's finest museums. To visit Iran without spending any time here is to miss something of what makes the country tick.

Though the history of Tehran stretches back several thousand years, it was not until the end of the 18th century that it became the Iranian capital under the Qajar dynasty. And if the modern city cannot itself be called beautiful, some of its surroundings certainly can. Tehran sits on a plain at the foot of the enormous Alborz Mountains. One of these, the volcanic Mount Damavend, is the highest mountain in Iran – an enormous, snow-streaked cone, almost perfectly symmetrical, that still belches sulfur from its summit. Rich in associations with Persian folklore, the Alborz are now best known for their ski slopes and resorts, in particular Dizin and Tochal, accessible by a cable-car route that stretches from the more affluent northern suburbs of Tehran.

Tehran also has some excellent restaurants, from simple kebab shops to traditional places serving luxuriant rice dishes, such as *polo*. The rice in *polo* dishes is prepared using an elaborate cooking method known as *chelo*, during which the rice is washed, soaked, boiled until almost cooked, spread on the bottom of a heavy-bottomed pan (already coated with butter or oil), and finally steamed, very slowly, with a cloth under the lid to absorb any drips. When cooked properly, a thick golden crust, called *tah-dig*, forms on the bottom of the pan; it is served separately and is always a much-sought-after item at the Persian table. *Chelo* rice is heaped high on plates and served in generous portions to accompany kebabs, *khoresh* (stews), and other dishes.

In *polo* recipes, half the cooked rice is added to the buttered pan, and then cooked chicken, meat, or other ingredients are added. A second layer of rice is spread on top, and finally the whole dish is steamed. There are numerous well-known *polo* recipes, from *zereshk polo-e morgh* (with saffron, chicken, and barberries) and *shirin polo* (with orange peel, saffron, almonds, and pistachios), to its most elaborate and decadent form, *tachin*. There's even a fresh herby version that is the perfect accompaniment to fish – *sabzi polo*.

A Day in Tehran

The majority of Tehran's sites are concentrated close to downtown, but a few – such as the Azadi Tower – are farther out; they can easily be reached by bus, metro, or taxi. The vast (and incomplete) Imam Khomeini Shrine is on the road to Ghom.

MORNING Start from Imam Khomeini metro station, and walk south to visit the 16th-century **Golestan Palace**, site of the Qajar court in the 18th century.

AFTERNOON Return to Imam Khomeini metro station, taking a slight detour to walk through part of Tehran's enormous **bazaar**, and stop at the **Khayyam Traditional Restaurant** for lunch. Visit the **National Museum**, which has a fascinating archaeological collection showcasing the country's long history, and the small **Ceramics and Glass Museum**, which has excellent modern displays.

EVENING Walk northwest, crossing the busy Enqelab Avenue to reach the **Carpet Museum**, the **Museum of Contemporary Art**, and **Park Laleh**, one of the most pleasant green spaces in the city.

Essentials

GETTING THERE
Imam Khomeini International Airport lies 22 miles (35 km) from Tehran; there are shared or private **taxis** into town. **Buses** and **trains** connect Tehran with most places in Iran.

WHERE TO STAY
Mashhad Hostel (inexpensive) is a hostel with rooms and dorms. www.mashhadhostel.com
Atlas (moderate) is a good mid-range hotel with a small garden. www.atlas-hotel.com
Ferdowsi Grand Hotel (expensive) is central and comfortable. www.ferdowsihotel.com

TOURIST INFORMATION
www.itto.org

Above The highly prized golden crust of *tachin polo* is achieved by slowly baking the cooked, layered rice and chicken in a buttered pan

Left The Golestan Palace was part of a group of royal buildings built within the mud-thatched walls of Tehran's historic *arg*, or citadel

Above Specialty rice dishes are always an important part of Iranian festivities, such as Yalda – the longest night of the year

A Celebratory Dish

Of the many delicious variations of *polo*, **tachin** is the best and most elaborate. Here the partly cooked rice is mixed with yogurt and saffron, and used to coat the inside of a heavy pan. The center is then filled with alternating layers of rice and chicken mixed with *zereshk* (barberries) before the whole dish is slowly baked until the outer surface forms a delicious golden crust. It is then turned out on to a plate. *Tachin* are sometimes seen stacked one on top of another, like the tiers of a wedding cake. It is not the sort of dish you find everywhere, and is typically made for festive occasions, but you have more chance of finding it in Tehran than anywhere else.

The Best Places to Eat Polo

The Khayyam Traditional Restaurant moderate

The Khayyam Traditional Restaurant, right in the heart of Tehran's frenetic bazaar near the Nasreddin mosque, is one of the most beautifully decorated traditional restaurants in the Iranian capital. The historic building (originally part of the Nasreddin mosque complex) was recently restored, and now has a main area with wooden tables and chairs as well as partly enclosed areas with cushions for seating. Its brick-vaulted interior is moodily lit, highlighting the decorative mosaic tiles. It can (and does) get extremely busy, particularly at lunch times, but the atmosphere always remains friendly and relaxed. The menu ranges from succulent kebabs served alongside a mountain of fragrant *chelo* rice to steaming plates of *khoresh* (see pp164–5), *abgusht*, or *dizi* (meat stews) and, of course, *polo* dishes, including *zereshk polo* served with the requisite wedge of butter. Portions are generous and the prices, while more than average for Iran, are still very reasonable.

Khayyam Street, Tehran; open 11 AM–11 PM daily; +98 21 5580 0760

Also in Tehran

The busy **Ferdosi Sonnati** *(+98 21 6671 4503; inexpensive)*, at the southern end of Ferdosi Street, serves plenty of traditional Persian dishes, including *zereshk polo* and *tachin*. Other good options are **Sofreh Khane Ayyaran** *(+98 21 6676 0376; moderate)*, which is sometimes inundated by tour groups but does serve a wider-than-average range of traditional Persian dishes, and the buzzing subterranean **Sofreh Khane Ali Ghapoo** *(+98 21 8877 7803; inexpensive)*.

Also in Iran

In Isfahan, *tachin* is served at **Nobahar** *(+98 311 221 0800; inexpensive)* and **Shahrzad** *(+98 311 220 4490; moderate)*. The **Khan Gostar Restaurant** *(+98 311 627 8989; moderate)* in the Hotel Julfa, Isfahan, is another excellent choice, and very popular with locals.

Around the World

There are many Persian restaurants in London, but the contemporary-styled **Lavash** *(www.lavash.co.uk; moderate)* at the top of Finchley Road is one of the few that serve *tachin*. **Little Persia** *(www.littlepersia.co.uk; moderate)* serves several *polo* dishes in its colorful interior, and **Alounak** *(www.alounak.co.uk; moderate)* is another longstanding favorite in the UK capital.

Above The Church of St. George, Lalibela, is carved in the form of a Greek cross, from an excavation 40 ft (12 m) deep

A Day in Lalibela

Lalibela's lovely churches can be split into three main groups: the first two, the Northern and Eastern Groups (conveniently containing some of the town's most impressive and important) lie with a short distance of downtown; the third group lies scattered outside town. For a tour of the churches, visit the tiny Tourist Office, where you can find a guide and the informative pamphlet *Lalibela: World Heritage*.

MORNING Visit the Northern and Eastern Groups of churches. The two most impressive are **Bet Giyorgis** (The Church of St. George), considered the most perfect of all the churches, and **Bet Medhane Alem**, which measures 110 ft x 77 ft (33.5 x 23.5 m), and is believed to be the largest rock-hewn church in the world. Other highlights of the Northern Group include **Bet Golgotha** and **Bet Mikael**. In the Eastern Group, don't miss **Bet Amanuel** and **Bet Abba Libanos**.

AFTERNOON Consider a trip to one of the churches outside the town. Particularly recommended are **Yemrehanna Kristos**, **Ashetan Maryam**, and **Na'akuto La'ab**.

Essentials

GETTING THERE
Lalibela has a domestic **airport** 14 miles (23 km) south of town and there are **minibus taxis** to the downtown. There is a daily **bus** from Addis-Ababa, which takes two days to reach Lalibela.

WHERE TO STAY
Seven Olives Hotel (inexpensive) has simple but peaceful rooms with views across lovely gardens. *+251 3 3336 0020*
Tukol Village (moderate) offers the option of staying overnight in a *tukul* (traditional Ethiopian hut). *+251 3 3336 0564*
Yemereha Hotel (moderate) has comfortable rooms furnished with traditional Ethiopian crafts. *www.greenlandethiopia.com*

TOURIST INFORMATION
Main Lalibela road (near St. Lalibela Secondary School); *+251 3 3336 0167*

Above *Injera* forms the base for *seg wat*, a spicy meat stew that traditionally uses *beri-beri*, a very hot Ethiopian chili pepper

LALIBELA ↗

LALIBELA ETHIOPIA

Injera in Holy Lalibela

Dubbed "Africa's Petra" for its astonishing rock-hewn churches, Lalibela has drawn Western visitors since the 16th century. It is hidden high in the Ethiopian highlands, and the journey is long and arduous for the thousands of pilgrims who travel there on foot. Many seek replenishment in its famous, pancake-like flatbread, *injera*, topped by a hot, steaming, and revitalizing stew.

Cradle of the Zagwe dynasty in the 12th and 13th centuries, Lalibela was once the country's capital and the home of kings. According to local tradition, the town's ruler and namesake, King Lalibela, was briefly forced into exile to Jerusalem by his evil, usurping brother. Amazed by the churches there, Lalibela vowed to build a holy city on African soil upon his return to his homeland.

Lalibela's churches are exceptional for three main reasons: their artistic refinement, their sophisticated construction (many are not just carved into the rock, but freed entirely from it), and their number – so many are found within such a small area. For the visitor, Lalibela's unique appeal also lies in its timeless continuity. Monks and deacons, traditionally robed, glide along the candlelit passageways and tunnels that connect the medieval churches, and the sound of chanting still rises from the hidden crypts and grottoes. The deep, cool recesses of the extraordinary church interiors are filled with the heady fragrance of incense and burning beeswax candles.

The taverns and restaurants of Lalibela have also been serving the pilgrims for centuries. They offer up an often quite sophisticated and eclectic cuisine that includes piquant meat *wats* (stews) and mild, smooth curries of vegetables and beans. Underpinning all – literally – is the country's staple, *injera*, a kind of large, round flatbread upon which the cooks heap one or more meat and vegetable dishes. Used as a base and also as a tool (small pieces are torn off with the right hand and used to pick at the dishes), *injera* famously serves as foodstuff, plate, and cutlery.

Injera is traditionally made from the flour of *teff*, a small-grained indigenous Ethiopian cereal that is found throughout the Ethiopian highlands. This distinguishes the higher-quality *injera*, which is lighter, smoother, thinner, and springier than non-*teff* varieties. After a day's exploration of Lalibela's wondrous churches, there's no better way to end the day than by tucking in to *injera* and a large, communal plate of steaming, slightly spicy stew with some new-found friends. Ethiopians believe that sharing a meal in this way cements a friendship forever.

What to Drink in Lalibela

Once the drink of Ethiopian emperors and kings, *tej* – a kind of mead – is now the popular local tipple. Made from locally produced honey and an Ethiopian shrub called *gesho*, it is found today in the *tej beats* (a kind of Ethiopian equivalent of pubs) in most Ethiopian towns, as well as in higher-end restaurants. Served in delightful little flasks known as *birille*, *tej* comes in varying degrees of sweetness. Ask for *derek* if you want it dry and strong (the drier it is, the more alcoholic the content), *mahakalenya* for medium-sweet, and *laslasa* or *bers* for a sweeter and less alcoholic version. Local men congregate at *tej beats* to gossip, cogitate, and commiserate. As in Western pubs, most men tend to gather during a weekend afternoon, while women traditionally drink *tej* from glasses during market days as they work and exchange news.

Above *Injera* dough is fermented overnight, then cooked like a pancake

The Best Places to Eat Injera

Blue Lal Hotel Restaurant
inexpensive

Although Lalibela and its extraordinary churches are becoming better known and visitor numbers are increasing, the range and quality of the town's restaurants (and hotels) remain rather limited. One of the better options for sampling Ethiopian food is the Blue Lal Hotel Restaurant. Designed like a *tukul* (traditional Ethiopian hut), complete with freshly cut grass strewn on the floor and multicolored *mesobs* (traditional, mushroom-shaped dining tables woven like baskets) dotting the dining floor, the Blue Lal Restaurant serves fresh, authentic, and good-quality Ethiopian dishes, including a well-prepared *injera*, at excellent prices. Try the unctuous *doro wat*: chicken drumsticks or wings accompanied by hard- boiled egg served in a hot sauce of butter, onion, and cardamom and a good sprinkling of *berbere* (a spice mixture of up to 16 ingredients, including the fiery *beri-beri*). If you don't fancy stew, try *kitfo*, minced beef or lamb traditionally served warm but not cooked – like a form of steak tartare – and flavored with the even hotter *mitmita* spice mixture.

Downtown Lalibela; +251 3 3336 0380

Also in Lalibela

The **Seven Olives Hotel** (*+251 3 3336 0020; inexpensive*) is furnished with Ethiopian arts and crafts and offers the classic range of *injera*-plus-*wats*, as well as *injera* and *ye som megeb* (vegetarian dishes traditionally served on Friday, the day of fasting). If you're eager to taste multiple Ethiopian dishes, request the *beyanatu* – you'll receive small portions of different meat and vegetable dishes.

Also in Ethiopia

Habesha Restaurant (*+251 3 3351 8358; moderate*) in Addis-Ababa is traditionally decorated and known for its good-quality, more eclectic menu, including *injera*-accompanied dishes such as *dulet* (minced tripe, liver, and beef fried in butter, onions, chili pepper, and cardamom) and *kwanta* (strips of beef rubbed in chili pepper, butter, salt, and *berbere*). In the evening, there's live Ethiopian music or dancing.

Around the World

London has a sizable Ethiopian community and **Wabe Shebele Restaurant** (*+44 20 7378 9009; moderate*) serves authentic Ethiopian food in a traditionally decorated dining room. Regulars include *gored gored* (warmed cubes of raw beef served with spiced Ethiopian butter) and *goden tibs* (lamb ribs sautéed with *berbere* and rosemary). On weekends, there is traditional Ethiopian dancing.

Right Fresh produce, seafood, and curios can be found in the covered Central Market

Below The chicken takes its color and heat from the small but feisty piri-piri pepper, also known as the bird's-eye chili or African red devil

A Day in Maputo

Easily and safely explored on foot, central Maputo is a compact grid of shady avenues filled with unexpected architectural curiosities.

MORNING Start at Praça dos Trabalhadores and **Maputo Railway Station**, the palatial 1910 creation of Gustave Eiffel. From here, the bar-lined **Rua de Bagamoio** (once known as the "Street of Trouble" by visiting sailors) leads through the old town to the 18th-century **Fortalezada Nossa Senhora da Conceição**, the city's oldest extant building and home to interesting artworks. Take a short ferry ride to rustic **Catembe** for fabulous views and an inexpensive seafood lunch at the redoubtable **Restaurant Diogo** on the beach.

AFTERNOON Take the ferry back and follow Av. Patrice Lumumba uphill to the prestigious **Polana District** and shady **Av. Friedrich Engels** for clifftop views over the harbor.

EVENING Dive into the fantastic **Barracas de Museu** for a drink or two before or after dinner.

Essentials

GETTING THERE
Maputo is Mozambique's main **port** of entry, and the **international airport** is only 10 minutes from downtown, traffic permitting.

WHERE TO STAY
Fatima's Place (inexpensive) is a popular owner-managed hostel with dorms and private rooms. www.mozambiquebackpackers.com
Hotel Villa das Mangas (moderate) is a small central boutique hotel set around a pretty garden with a pool. www.hipchichotels.net
The ocean-facing **Serena Polana** (expensive) has been Maputo's most prestigious address since it opened in 1922. www.serenahotels.com

FURTHER INFORMATION
Mike Slater's detailed www.mozguide.com is very useful.

MAPUTO MOZAMBIQUE

All Fired Up in Mozambique

Lapped by the balmy Indian Ocean, Maputo is probably the most characterful capital city in sub-equatorial Africa. A seaside port, its wide palm- and jacaranda-shaded *avenidas* are flanked by cozy street cafés and an oddly cohesive cocktail of architectural styles. The city possesses an engaging Afro-Mediterranean mood epitomized by the addictive, fiery zip of chicken piri-piri.

Five centuries ago, the desire to secure control of the spice trade inspired Portugal to establish outposts along the east coast of Africa, one of which grew to become the modern Mozambican capital of Maputo. Today, the most notoriously tongue-searing of these spices – the ferocious chili pepper known by the Swahili-derived name piri-piri – forms the cornerstone of Mozambique's best-known culinary export.

Mozambique's struggle for independence from Portugal ended as recently as 1974, and the legacy of colonial rule can still be seen in the fascinating architecture of its capital city. Antiquated colonial relics and handsome Art Deco and Bauhaus buildings stand out among bleak Soviet-style apartment blocks, relics of a period of Marxist-oriented government that

inspired a bitter civil war. And it is the juxtaposition of the city's contemporary African culture against this time-warped architectural exotica that makes Maputo so compelling. For example, one of Africa's most bizarrely misplaced buildings – a stately palace built in ornate Portuguese Gothic style that now houses the Natural History Museum – sits just around the corner from the utterly African Barracas de Museu. This unpretentious, vast warren of makeshift stands and bars is inhabited by a bustling cast of guitar-bearing rent-a-crooners, beer-swilling mamas, wild-eyed pool hustlers, and after-hours office workers. It is dedicated to the sale and consumption of alcohol and there is no better place to make new friends over a cold Mozambican beer and a sizzling plate of chicken piri-piri.

No other dish is quite so definitely Mozambican as this – spatchcocked chicken, grilled to perfection over hot coals in its mantle of piquant piri-piri sauce. Deep red and viscous, the sauce is dominated by the chili pepper for which it is named, which is finely chopped and soaked in vegetable oil, garlic, vinegar, lemon juice, and coarse salt – and whatever other secret ingredient it is that ensures that, whether you're ordering at a street stall, a hole-in-the-wall carry-out or an upmarket restaurant, no two versions of this unofficial national dish ever taste exactly the same.

What Else to Eat

Maputo, almost uniquely among sub-equatorial African capitals, has long been renowned for its dining-out scene. In the colonial era the city was noted, as it still is now, for its fine **seafood**. Particularly famous are the country's **shrimp** (often referred to in southern Africa as LM prawns, after Maputo's old colonial name, Lourenço Marques), which are usually served grilled, with garlic or piri-piri sauce on the side, or baked in a beer-based sauce. The **Costa do Sol** *(see right)* is renowned for its shrimp and seafood combos (try the grilled fish and calamari), and there's no finer exponent of sauce-baked shrimp than the **1908 Restaurant** *(+258 21 304 428)*, set in a beautiful colonial house on Av. Eduardo Mondlane.

Left High-rise buildings give way to beachside homes on the outskirts

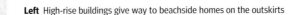

The Best Places to Eat Chicken Piri-Piri

Restaurante Costa do Sol
moderate–expensive

Boasting a prime seafront location 5 miles (8 km) north of downtown, the legendary Costa do Sol is the oldest eatery in Maputo, having operated continuously since the 1940s, and throughout the civil war that drove Mozambique to an economic standstill in the 1980s. Fittingly, this family-run institution has a somewhat time-warped Mediterranean ambience, with its Art Deco facade, wide terrace overlooking a palm-lined beach and gentle rolling breakers, reasonably priced daily specials chalked up on a board, white-starched tablecloths, and famously erratic (but invariably friendly) service. As with most restaurants in Maputo, seafood features heavily on the menu, but the Costa do Sol also arguably serves the city's finest grilled chicken: marinated in a spicy sauce, sealed and flame-grilled on an open fire and accompanied by a bowl of fiery red sauce whose searing chili pepper base is, like all the best piri-piri, offset by a delicious tang from the addition of preserved lemons. A chilled Sauvignon Blanc from neighboring South Africa provides the perfect accompaniment, though the locally brewed 2M lager might be a safer bet for dousing the fiery aftertaste.

Av. de Marginal; open 11 AM–10:30 PM Sun–Thu, 11 AM–midnight Fri & Sat; +258 21 450 115

Also in Maputo

As might be surmised from the restaurant's name, the chef at **Piri-piri** *(+258 21 492 379; moderate)*, an ever-popular eatery in the heart of the upmarket Polana district, isn't afraid of dousing his grilled chicken in antisocial quantities of delicious piri-piri sauce. Aside from the good food, the terrace here, where Av. 24 de Julho and Av. Julius Nyerere meet, has to be one of the city's top spots for people-watching.

Also in Mozambique

Tucked away on an anonymous dirt road in Vilankulo, one of Mozambique's top resort towns, is **Varanda** *(+258 29 382 412; moderate)*, a family-run restaurant famed for its seafood and superb chicken piri-piri. It overlooks a beach where fishing dhows come to land their catches in the evening.

Around the World

Unsurprisingly, Mozambique's most famous dish long ago made it across two oceans to its former colonizer, Portugal, where it has become a local specialty at the picturesque village of Guia, in the central Algarve. There are several restaurants to choose from here, but none finer than the veteran **Restaurant Ramires** *(+351 289 561 232; inexpensive)*, which has been firing up visitors' taste buds for over 25 years.

Above More than 4,500 years old, the pyramids of Giza are the sole survivors of the original Seven Wonders of the World

Above *Hamam mashi* – Egyptian stuffed pigeon with bulgur wheat

Three Days in Cairo

Cairo has enough to keep sightseers occupied for weeks. The following itinerary takes in all the iconic sites, as well some lesser-known but equally interesting areas, attractions, and activities.

DAY ONE Head first for the legendary **Egyptian Museum**. In the afternoon, take a tour of central Cairo, including the **Museum of Islamic Art**, interspersed with some coffee-and-cake stops. Later, browse the colorful **Khan al-Khalili bazaar**. End the day aboard a felucca (a traditional sailboat) for a sunset sail on the Nile.

DAY TWO Take an all-day tour of the **Pyramids** and **Sphinx** via **Memphis**, **Saqqara**, and **Giza**. Rest and replenish over meze and watch the sun set over the pyramids with a cocktail at Oberoi.

DAY THREE Spend the morning exploring **Coptic Cairo**. Start at the **Coptic Museum** and the **Hanging Church**. After coffee at nearby St. George's Café, continue the church tour and visit **St. Sergius** and **St. Barbara**. Spend the afternoon wandering the **Islamic Quarter**; be sure to visit the **Mosque of Ibn Tuloan**.

Essentials

GETTING THERE
Buses, minibuses, and **taxis** connect Cairo's international **airport** with the downtown, 12 miles (20 km) away. The **metro** and **taxis** are the simplest ways of getting around town.

WHERE TO STAY
Pension Roma (inexpensive) is a simple but well-run and homey B&B with evening meals available on request. *www.pensionroma.com*
Talisman Hotel (moderate) is a centrally located boutique hotel with attractive rooms decorated in oriental style. *+20 2 2393 9431*
Four Seasons at Nile (expensive) is sumptuous and furnished with original Egyptian art; it overlooks the Nile and is minutes from the Egyptian Museum. *www.fourseasons.com*

TOURIST INFORMATION
www.egypt.travel

CAIRO EGYPT

Stuffed Pigeon in Cairo

Long known locally as *Umm ad-Dunya* ("mother of the world"), Cairo still deserves deference: its museums house some of humanity's greatest historical and artistic treasures, and its old quarters contain some of the world's finest religious architecture. Cairo is also Egypt's culinary capital, and the perfect place to try its unofficial national dish, *hamam mashi*: stuffed pigeon.

Africa's largest city and one of the most densely populated metropolises on Earth, Cairo is also one of the world's most vibrant capitals. Though almost as famous for its overcrowding, congestion, and pollution as for its ancient treasures, the city's energy, entrepreneurship, and indomitable spirit are nonetheless enthralling. On the roads, camels and donkeys vie for position with the pickup trucks and dilapidated cars; above the roar of engines, the muezzin's age-old call to prayer rises above the cries of the street hawkers. The smog and exhaust fumes mingle with the aromas of street-sold roasted corn and freshly baked bread, along with the unmistakable waft of fruit-infused *sheesha* pipes.

Cairo's world-famous attractions include the astonishing Egyptian Museum and pyramids of Giza, but it has equally interesting, lesser-known sights, such as the Coptic Quarter and Islamic Cairo. Known as the "City of a Thousand Minarets," Cairo has some of the world's greatest Islamic architecture. Its beautiful churches – such as the 7th-century El Muallaqa (the "Hanging Church") – bear witness to the importance of its early Christian Coptic community.

Like many of its attractions, Cairo's unofficial national dish – *hamam mashi* or stuffed pigeon – is also said to date back to Pharaonic times. The birds were traditionally reared in conical, mud-built pigeon cotes, which can still be seen today lining the Nile Delta, although pigeons are also kept in the towns. For Cairo's millions of rural migrants, old habits die hard: birdcages are placed outside windows and doors and on rooftops and terraces. The dish is usually served during the winter months, when the birds are at their plumpest; only young, tender pigeons are selected.

Traditionally, the birds are served in pairs, stuffed with rice, onion, and chopped pigeon or chicken liver, then spiced with cinnamon, cumin, and pepper and sometimes nuts. Roasted or grilled on a spit, they are usually accompanied by tabbouleh (a salad of bulgur wheat, parsley, mint, tomatoes, and green onions) and tahini (sesame-seed paste). They are not everyday food, but mark special occasions, made "for those whom you love dearly," as the Cairenes say.

What Else to Eat

A great way to start the day (as Egyptians do) is with filling and sustaining **fuul** (cooked, mashed fava beans). For lunch or dinner, try the much-prized **Nile perch** from the Nile. Other culinary sightseeing might include **molokhiyya**, a popular mallow-based soup with a distinctly slimy texture and earthy flavor, or **koshari** (macaroni, rice, lentils, and chickpeas topped with fried onions and a spicy tomato sauce). Drinks worth searching out include the ubiquitous **shay bilnaana** (mint tea) and other herbal infusions such as **helba** (fenugreek), **yansoon** (anise), and **irfa** (cinnamon). **Sahlab**, a hot milky mixture of arrowroot or semolina, nuts, and cinnamon, is popular in winter, while **karkadeh** is a hibiscus infusion served as an antidote to the summer heat. **Zabaady**, a yogurt-based drink, accompanies meat dishes.

Above The busy alleyways of the ancient Khan al-Khalili bazaar in Cairo

The Best Places to Eat Stuffed Pigeon

Citadel View Restaurant
expensive

Aptly named, the Citadel View boasts the best appointment in town. Located in the lovely, landscaped gardens of the Al Azhar Park on a breeze-catching hillock, the Citadel commands panoramic views over the gardens, the Citadel, and all of Old Cairo. Housed in a neo-Fatimid palace, the complex comprises a good café and a couple of restaurants, of which the Studio Misr is the highlight. The Studio specializes in traditional Egyptian dishes (particularly grills), including stuffed pigeon, that are artfully prepared. At night, amid the niches, arches, and intimate spaces of the lantern-lit interior, the evening can seem like something out of one of Scheherazade's stories of the Arabian Nights. On weekends (Friday and Saturday), there's a fixed-price open buffet, which provides a welcome opportunity to taste a variety of traditional Egyptian and Middle Eastern dishes. The stuffed pigeon (ordered *à la carte* only) is cooked *à point* and is succulent and gamey, with a subtle hint of cinnamon.

Al Azhar Park, Shari' Salah Salem, Cairo; open noon–1 AM daily; +20 2 2510 9151

Also in Cairo

Old-world through and through, from the dark-paneled dining room to the besuited, taciturn waiters and deep, leather-clad seats, **El Mashrabiah** *(+20 2 3748 2801; moderate–expensive)* prides itself also on its traditional, old-school Egyptian cooking. Specializing in classic meat dishes including stuffed pigeon, grilled rabbit, quail, and duck, as well as offering ethereal kofta (spicy meatballs), *tagen* (a slow-cooked stew), and shish kebabs, it attracts a fervent local following among Cairo's well-heeled carnivores.

Also in Egypt

Sofra *(www.sofra.com; moderate)* has rapidly become known as one of Luxor's best eating options. Spread over a series of private dining rooms, a salon, and an attractive, atmospheric rooftop terrace, it is a great spot for a preprandial or dinner drink. Both decor and dining are traditional, and the menu is full of tried-and-tested classics, including a particularly flavorsome roasted stuffed pigeon.

Popular with Aswani families for its simple and traditional menu at excellent prices, the **Al Makka** *(+20 97 230 3232; inexpensive)* in Aswan additionally offers quality and consistency. Specialties include the stuffed pigeon, kofta, shish kebabs, and succulent grilled chicken, all served with tahini, salad, and flatbread. No alcohol is served.

Above Rattan panels shade vendors and their stands of produce at a busy street market in Bali, Indonesia

Asia and Australasia

The Flavors of
Asia and Australasia

Asia and Australasia contain virtually half the world's population and examples of most of the Earth's geography, so it's perhaps unsurprising that very few culinary opportunities are left unexplored among this melange of interconnected cultures and climates. Spices dominate the foods of Asia, but are used to flavor a huge range of cuisines with distinctive styles. Australasia has combined these with its European heritage to concoct a unique range of Pan-Asian dishes.

In the north of Asia, the arid Himalayan plateau descends to a vast swath of treeless steppes, where wheat is the staple and cooking is kept simple by the limited ingredients. Lower down, humid hills and river plains form the heartland of those two great Asian core crops – tea and rice – that pattern the upland slopes in terracing, color the landscape a rich green, and nourish half of humanity. Rice in particular holds the regional cuisines together, infinitely flexible in its uses: it's eaten steamed, fried, roasted, and boiled; made into noodles, cakes, and wine; ground into flour and used in desserts. The rice belt extends south into the tropics, where heat, rain, and rich soils create an extraordinary fertility in which all manner of spices, fruits, and vegetables flourish. Add to this the multitudes of farmed pigs and chickens and an abundance of marine life, and the menu becomes infinite.

Thailand, Malaysia, and Indonesia share a southern Indian love of spice pastes, coconut milk, and grilled foods.

A Rich Mixture of Cuisines

The story of Asian cuisine is one of cross-fertilization. In terms of variety and influence, India and China completely dominate the region. Migration, trade, and conquest spread the philosophies and cuisines of these two behemoths across Asia, though isolation and distance have preserved local variations: a cuisine might be identifiably "Asian," but there's a world of difference between a Cambodian *amok* fish curry and West Lake fish from China's Hangzhou. However, there are definite cooking "families": Thailand, Malaysia, and Indonesia share a southern Indian love of spice pastes, coconut milk, and grilled foods; the cooking of Laos, Cambodia, and Vietnam has clearer, cleaner flavors built around well-defined ingredients, perhaps closer to the studied simplicity and restrained palette of Japanese and Korean cuisine. India has no qualms about adapting foreign dishes – Mumbai's cosmopolitan *chaat* snacks, for example, embrace even Portuguese influences. Even that inward-looking cultural monolith, China, where alien ideas are absorbed so effectively that they eventually become Chinese, still shows evidence of contact with the outside world – in Peking duck, for instance, which probably owes a debt to Mongol cuisine.

Right Federation Square in Melbourne, Australia, is a major meeting and eating point
Below Chefs preparing sushi in Tokyo, Japan – as much an art form as a dish

Nothing demonstrates the extent of this trade in ideas more than the history of Asian spices, especially ginger, pepper, nutmeg, cloves, cinnamon, and cardamom, which are all used extensively in Southeast Asian cooking. Many reached Europe via India in Roman times, and by the Middle Ages had become so valuable (due partly to assumed medicinal properties) that they fired the 16th-century European voyages of global exploration to discover their source, Indonesia's fabled "Spice Islands." Spanish, Portuguese, Dutch, and British explorers (or invaders and colonists) dominated the regional economies of Asia for the next four centuries, and they made one massive contribution to their cuisine by importing chili peppers from South America. So ubiquitous is the chili today in Asian cooking – it's used in dishes as varied as Sichuanese *gong bao* chicken, Thai green curry, Vietnamese *pho* (noodle soup), and countless relishes and spice pastes – that it's impossible to imagine how local cooks once managed without it.

Food is such an expression of culture in Asia that people's lives seem to revolve around it for much of the time. Eating here is always more than simply topping off the body's calories; it is, rather, something to be indulged in or lavished upon others at every opportunity, with special dishes and feasting marking secular and religious festivals. Even the humblest meals can become social events; quiet, romantic restaurants are noticeably rare across much of Asia, where brightly lit, lively venues – the best of which are described in Chinese as being *renao*, or "hot and noisy" – are favored. That's not to say that there aren't rules; should someone inadvertently touch food with their left hand in Indonesia, onlookers would recoil in disgust at this breach of etiquette. But when wolfing down satay or nasi goreng at a street stand, or rubbing elbows with fellow diners in a south Indian thali house, the sheer enjoyment of eating seems to overwhelm the need to prescribe exactly how this should be done.

> *Food is such an expression of culture in Asia that people's lives seem to revolve around it for much of the time.*

Pan-Asian Cooking

The cuisine of Australia and New Zealand is very much that of the mostly European peoples who have colonized these islands in the last 200 years. Not that indigenous methods haven't had an impact: the famous Australian barbecue is only a step away from Aboriginal campfire cooking, illustrating a dominant "keep it simple" attitude to food. But the cuisine often self-consciously references European heritage or, in the case of Melbourne's Pan-Asian cuisine, fuses a whole region under one umbrella. Perhaps here, the setting is at least as important to the eating experience as the food; you can't really separate Balmain bugs from their coastal, Sydneyside spot.

Left Farm workers planting rice in a paddy field in Andhra Pradesh, India
Below Street food can be bought from stands and wandering vendors in Hoi An, Vietnam

HANGZHOU CHINA

The Lucky Fish of Hangzhou

In the Chinese town of Hangzhou in Zhejiang, the blue waters of West Lake slowly darken in the twilight, as couples take an evening stroll beneath the ornamental trees lining the shore. As diners marvel at the view from a waterside restaurant, a plate of fragrant West Lake fish arrives at the table, taking its place among a feast of other culinary delights.

A center of trade and business for over 1,000 years, Hangzhou sprang up during the Tang dynasty on fertile, newly reclaimed plains between eastern China's riverlands and the sea. The Grand Canal brought in merchants, whose money spawned a leisured class that grew fond of the gently poetic scenery of nearby West Lake. The city reached its zenith as China's capital during the 13th-century Southern Song dynasty, but the countryside – and West Lake in particular – has never lost its place in the Chinese mind as the epitome of cultural refinement and natural elegance. Poets, emperors, gastronomes, and even Marco Polo have all been drawn here, the latter writing that a cruise around West Lake was one of the most pleasurable experiences in the world.

Today the lakeshore shows off the subtlety of Chinese landscaping, taking nature as its starting point but skillfully tweaking it by adding strategically placed paths, arched bridges, temples, and historical monuments to the gently modeled parks and woodlands. A similar vein of artful conceit runs through the local food, which offers apparently simple dishes with clear flavors, often sweet and rich, whose appearance is refined to the point of pretension – all concealing a huge amount of exacting preparation.

West Lake and its surrounds have always provided a rich assortment of foods, and it has been a place for leisurely fun since its artificial formation from a natural bay in the 8th century. Its high point has long been the Mid-Autumn Festival, when families and friends gather to see the full moon over the water. Cruise boats on the lake traditionally served wine and food, and fish – considered auspicious – would naturally be on the menu.

The need to cook quickly in a confined space probably accounts for the simplicity of these dishes, many of which can still be enjoyed today. The West Lake fish itself is in fact a whole carp, which is poached with ginger and then coated with a sticky sweet-and-sour sauce made from its cooking liquid, sugar, and the local black vinegar. Served alongside crisply stir-fried shrimp, soy-braised pork, and a freshly opened parcel of "Beggar's Chicken," this famous fish completes a classic eastern Chinese meal.

Above The vast, tranquil expanse of West Lake (*Xi Hu*) is ringed by stunning tourist attractions, but its serenity is easily enjoyed from a simple walk along its shores

---

Longjing Tea

The gently undulating hills southwest of Hangzhou are terraced with plantations sprouting the renowned Longjing tea, one of China's most famous brews. Its name, meaning "Dragon Well," comes from the village and water source of Longjing, near West Lake, but the finest brew is said to be prepared using water from Hupaomeng Quan ("Running-Tiger Dream Spring"), a famous spring in Hangzhou. Longjing is a green tea, whose leaf-buds are picked and dried immediately without allowing them to ferment, creating a pale yellow, delicately aromatic tea. Hangzhou governor and man of letters Su Dongpo (1037–1101) recorded the wonders of this tea, and it was a favorite of the great emperor Qianlong (1711–99), who visited Hangzhou during the 18th century.

A Day around West Lake

There's no reason to linger in humdrum Hangzhou; the main attraction is West Lake itself and the sights scattered around its shore.

MORNING In the north lake area, visit the **tomb of General Yue Fei** (1103–42), a patriotic Song general who defended China against the invading Jurchen armies; the tomb features some extraordinary statuary, including a 15-ft (4.5-m) statue of the general himself. Then delve further into local history at the **Zhejiang Provincial Museum**. From here, cross south over the lake on foot via the **Su Di Causeway**, planted with willow and plum trees. Detour to tiny **Xiaoying Island**, covered in pagodas and reached over a bridge. On the south shore, enjoy a peaceful walk in attractive **Huagang Park**, which was laid out in Song times.

AFTERNOON Catch a cab to **Lingyin Temple**, a famous Zen Buddhist retreat some 2 miles (3 km) west of the lake at **Feilai Hill**. Then take a second cab ride to **Longjing** village to tour the family-run tea factories and plantations.

EVENING Return to **West Lake** and rent a wooden sampan for a short cruise, before finally tucking into local fare at one of the shoreside restaurants.

Essentials

GETTING THERE
Fly to **Hangzhou Xiaoshan International Airport** and take an **airport shuttle bus** or **taxi** to Hangzhou. You can also reach the town by **train** from many other Chinese cities. West Lake is immediately west of Hangzhou.

WHERE TO STAY
West Lake Youth Hostel (inexpensive) has friendly, basic dorms and doubles just south of the lake. www.westlakehostel.com
Crystal Orange Hotel (moderate) has boutique rooms near the shore. +86 571 2887 8988
Ramada Plaza (expensive) is an upmarket chain hotel with attentive service situated on the north shore of the lake. www.ramada.com

TOURIST INFORMATION
Hangzhou Tourist Center; www.hicenter.cn

The Best Places to Eat West Lake Fish

Lou Wai Lou expensive

If elegant food served in a lakeside setting is what Hangzhou is all about, then Lou Wai Lou – the "Tower Beyond Towers" – is the best restaurant in town. Right on the waterfront, this palatial institution has been in business since the 19th century. It is renowned for its West Lake fish, mooncakes (available during the Mid-Autumn Festival), and *dongpo rou* – fatty cubes of pork belly slow-braised to a buttery softness, attributed to the ubiquitous Su Dongpo. Other specialties include the banquet classic *bai niao chao feng*, a whole chicken braised in stock, and *xiang xia guoba*, shrimp soup poured over sizzling, crispy-fried rice crusts. The decor is a little heavy-handed – sparkling chandeliers, red carpets, gold wallpaper, and dark wooden screens and furniture – though you'd expect nothing less of a restaurant that has its own gilded pavilion moored in the lake. This is accessible only by private boat, and provides the ultimate location for a moonlit evening of gastronomic delight and contemplation.

30 Gu Shan Lu, Hangzhou; open 8:30 AM–8:30 PM daily; www.louwailou.com.cn (needs translation)

Also in Hangzhou

Tian Wai Tian *(+86 571 8796 5450; moderate)* is situated in the hills west of Hangzhou, outside the Lingyin Temple. This century-old restaurant features an extensive vegetarian menu alongside local dishes including West Lake fish, Beggar's Chicken (baked in a clay coating, cracked open at the table), and subtly scented freshwater prawns stir-fried with Longjing tea leaves. It is not as refined as some of the lakeside restaurants, but the food is reliably good.

Also in China

In Shanghai, **Xin Kai Yuan** *(+86 21 6439 7999; moderate)* is one of a stylish, city-wide chain of restaurants specializing in Hangzhou cuisine, with all the usual favorites, though you should concentrate on their immaculate *dongpo rou* and duck soup, both indulgently rich dishes without a trace of greasiness. After this, the inevitably oversized restaurant lobby, groaning under an ostentatious dressing of marble and auspicious decorations, is excusable in a city that cherishes conspicuous wealth.

In Hong Kong, **Tien Heung Lau** *(+86 852 2366 2414; moderate)* is a Hangzhou-style restaurant to which elegant furnishings and attentive service are completely alien. But don't be put off – the food is superb and fresh (many of their classic dishes have to be ordered in advance), including the outstandingly fragrant Beggar's Chicken, crispy eel, and succulent smoked yellow croaker. If you visit in the fall, try the steamed whole crab or fried shredded crab with noodles.

Above Hangzhou's signature dish is West Lake fish (*Xi Hu cu yu*), whose simple preparation is typical of Zhejiang cuisine

Left Tea has been harvested from the Longjing ("Dragon Well") plantations for more than 2,000 years

A Day in Mumbai

Mumbai's most interesting sights are quite widespread, but with some stamina and the help of an occasional taxi you can cover a remarkable amount of ground in a day.

MORNING The magnificent harborside **Gateway of India**, built for the visit of King George V in 1911, is the best place to start, though you'll need to keep the hawkers at bay. Then head inland to spend a couple of hours in the **Prince of Wales Museum** (now officially known as Chhatrapati Shivaji), which houses some of India's finest paintings and sculpture.

AFTERNOON Take a taxi up to **Malabar Hill** and stroll along its leafy ridge, passing by the eerie Parsi **Towers of Silence** and visiting the serene **Jain temple**, whose stunning interior is encrusted with mirrors. Farther down there is also the famous Hindu **Walukeshwar temple**.

EVENING As dusk falls, wind your way down the hill to the top end of **Chowpatty Beach** for some great people-watching while munching a plate of tasty *chaat* by the Arabian Sea.

Essentials

GETTING THERE
Mumbai lies on India's west coast and is a domestic hub for **rail** and **bus** networks. Chhatrapati Shivaji international **airport** lies 19 miles (30 km) north of Mumbai.

WHERE TO STAY
Sea Shore (inexpensive) is a good budget option in Colaba, with some sea-facing rooms, but only shared bathrooms. *+91 22 2287 4237*
City Palace (moderate) is a reliable and conveniently located hotel opposite VT station. *www.hotelcitypalace.net*
Taj Mahal Palace & Tower (expensive), colonial Bombay's oldest hotel, has views of the Arabian Sea and the Gateway of India; it now has a plush modern annex. *www.tajhotels.com*

TOURIST INFORMATION
www.maharashtratourism.gov.in

Left The puffed rice, noodles, and potatoes of *bhel puri* are tumbled with onions, cilantro, chili pepper, and tamarind sauce
Below A huge statue of Ganesh is transported through the water off Chowpatty Beach during the Ganesh Chaturthi Festival

MUMBAI

MUMBAI INDIA

Chaat on a Mumbai Beach

Mumbai is India's economic powerhouse and the cosmopolitan home of Bollywood, the world's most prolific film industry. The city also epitomizes the subcontinent's diversity: it has the worst slums in Asia as well as some of the world's priciest apartments. Frenetically fast-paced, many of its 17 million inhabitants eat on the go – and traditional *chaat* is the snack of choice.

The head-spinning modern city of Mumbai was originally seven islands populated exclusively by fishermen. The islands belonged to several different dynasties over the centuries, but fell under European control when the Portuguese invaded in 1508, renaming the islands *Bom Bahia* (the Good Bay). Some 150 years later, the Portuguese handed the islands to the British, who headquartered the East India Company in "Bombay." They reclaimed vast swaths of land to join the islands together and began a rapid expansion of the port. By the time India gained independence in 1947, Bombay was by far its most prosperous city, boasting a fine collection of Raj-era architecture, including the triumphal arch of the Gateway of India, the Taj Hotel, the VT train station, and the Prince of Wales Museum.

The city's reputation as a financial and trade center was augmented by the booming entertainment business, and Mumbai, as it was renamed in 1996, was soon displaying the brash confidence and wealth of the growing middle class. The constant stream of immigrants from other states and foreign lands added to the cosmopolitan atmosphere and to Mumbai's cuisine – so it is fitting that the most popular dish here is not a single item but a collection of snacks that fall under the blanket term *chaat*. They are available at thousands of stands and roadside *dhabas* (very basic restaurants) throughout the urban sprawl, but the most concentrated and famous string of *chaat* stands line the back of Chowpatty Beach at the end of Marine Drive.

If there is one common ingredient, it is crispy fried dough known as *puri*, which is mixed with a variety of ingredients to produce the different types of *chaat*. It is usually served on a tin plate or in a banana-leaf bowl and, of course, eaten with the right hand. Mumbai's favorite version is *bhel puri*, a mixture of *puri*, deep-fried vermicelli, puffed rice, potato, hot pepper paste, chopped onions, cilantro, and tamarind sauce. A popular variation, *pani puri*, includes a lentil and potato stuffing with sweet chutney. *Pav bhaji*, found virtually everywhere, is a Portuguese-style bun filled with a spicy vegetable stew. Hot, spicy, and nourishing, this is food for fueling enterprise.

Ganesh Chaturthi

Not actually a food festival in its own right, Mumbai's renowned Ganesh Chaturthi is an excellent occasion to sample the delights of *chaat* at Chowpatty Beach. It is a birthday party for the beloved elephant-headed deity Ganesh, and one of the most important and popular Hindu festivals. It falls some time between late August and late September and lasts for up to ten days, culminating in thousands of images of the chubby god being immersed in the soupy waters of the Arabian Sea. Given that the monsoon is often still in full swing during the event, visitors are just as likely to get completely soaked as participants, even if they do not assist in the deity-dunking. Ganesh is said to be fond of sweet desserts, so the *chaat-wallahs* come out in full force, making sure there are plenty of sweet and savory snacks available for his birthday.

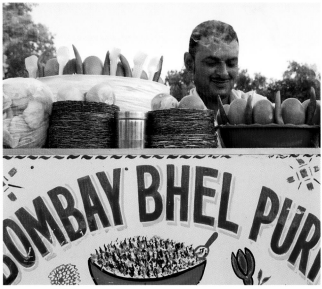

Above Mumbai's street stands are renowned for their great *chaat*, especially *bhel puri*

The Best Places to Eat Chaat

Chowpatty Beach Stands
inexpensive

The whole concept of Indian *chaat* is that it's sold by outlets that are as transient as their customers. Consequently, it is hard to pin down a specific stand amid the throng of *chaat-wallahs* who wheel their carts up and down the back of Chowpatty Beach, advertising their goods with piercing cries or clanging bells. What is indisputable is that locals in Mumbai will all tell you that this is the place to come.

So, let your senses lead you to the most appealing plate of *bhel puri* to suit your own palate. Rest assured that while the stand itself might be dented and grubby, the food will be freshly prepared and the high turnover ensures it remains so.

Chowpatty beach, Mumbai; open all day until late evening

Also in Mumbai

Chaat is available at every turn in Mumbai, but here are two well-known spots. Near the GPO (the main post office), in bustling Crawford Market's 3rd Lane, **Eden's Snacks** *(inexpensive)* is one of central Mumbai's most popular places for grabbing a quick plate of *bhel puri* or *sev puri* (with crispy *papri* wafers) while shopping. On Wodehouse Road in Colaba, where most foreigners stay, **Sunshine Snack Corner** *(+91 22 2215 0646; inexpensive)* is worth trying. If you would rather pass on such unadulterated street food, try **Chaat Lo** *(inexpensive)*, behind Chowpatty Beach opposite Bhavan's College, which makes many types of *chaat* as well as samosas and *chola bhature*, a Punjabi dish involving spicy chickpeas and fried *puri* bread.

Also in India

Different types of *chaat* are widespread throughout the country. In the capital, Delhi, **Chaat Corner** *(inexpensive)* on Arya Samaj Road offers a great range. In Chennai, in the south, you can find local versions of street foods at **Chit Chat** *(inexpensive)* on the city's main thoroughfare, Anna Salai.

Around the World

Apart from well-known snacks like samosas and pakora, Mumbai-style *chaat* can be hard to come by outside India, as most restaurants serve more conventional meals. However, London has quite a few options, such as **Santok Maa's Bhel Poori House** *(+44 20 8665 0626; inexpensive)* in Thornton Heath, which specializes in *bhel puri*, as the name suggests. In Canada, Toronto's **Bombay Bhel** *(www.bombaybhelrestaurant.com; moderate)* offers *pani, bhel, sev,* and chickpea-filled *dahi puri* among its appetizers.

Above The restaurant at Vasse Felix has beautiful views over its vineyards, which were the first to be established in Margaret River

Above The fine local venison and wines of Margaret River combine in dishes such as roasted venison with red wine and cranberry coulis

Three Days in Margaret River

The Margaret River region is characterized by its fantastic blend of natural beauty and phenomenal food and wine. Take it all in, but remember that distances are long and journeys can take time.

DAY ONE Hop on to the **food and wine trail**: join one of the many guided tours available in the area, or take a **Bushtucker Canoe Tour** along the Margaret River to experience native Australian bush foods.

DAY TWO Head south, exploring the rugged beaches and spectacular caves – the Lake, Mammoth, and Jewel show caves – that crop up along the scenic drive to **Augusta**. Have a picnic lunch in the **Boranup Karri Forest**, and finish the day with a visit to the **Cape Leeuwin** lighthouse and have fish and chips on the beach.

DAY THREE Go west to the coast at **Prevelly** for an ocean-view breakfast, then admire the surfing on nearby **Gnarabup Beach**. Head back to town for an afternoon viewing artisan workshops and galleries or get back to nature at the **Wildlife Center** featuring displays from Australia's largest collection of birds of prey.

Essentials

GETTING THERE
Fly to **Perth International Airport** then **rent a car** for the 3½-hour drive south to Margaret River, or take a **bus** with Southwest Coachlines.

WHERE TO STAY
Adamsons Riverside Apartment and Motel Accommodation (inexpensive) is on beautiful grounds by the river and forest, a short stroll from town. *www.adamsonsriverside.net.au*
Basildene Manor (moderate) offers stately accommodations close to town, surrounded by a huge and pretty garden. *www.basildene.com.au*
Merribrook Retreat (expensive) offers every conceivable luxury in a stunning rural setting. *www.merribrook.com.au*

TOURIST INFORMATION
100 Bussell Highway, Margaret River town; *www.margaretriver.com*

MARGARET RIVER AUSTRALIA

Venison Among the Vineyards

South of Perth, on Australia's wild western coastline, Margaret River is a region of natural abundance. Blessed with a maritime Mediterranean climate, its renowned vineyards thrive within the bush landscape, bordered by a river on one side and untamed coastline on the other. Local produce is king here, and the perfect match for the area's fine wines is venison, the meat of kings.

With its rich agricultural soils, life-giving river, dense bushland, and isolated setting on one of Australia's wildest stretches of untouched coastline, the commercial development of Margaret River was destined to evolve much more slowly than its natural industry. Alfred and Ellen Bussell built the first homestead here in 1875, but it was another 55 years before a scant collection of three houses allowed the area to declare itself a town.

Little has changed in the last 100 years. Though it now boasts a population of 11,000, the area is still dominated by farming and viticulture. Beef cattle, sheep, and deer graze in and around one of the nation's largest wine regions, farmed to feed the appetites of the questing gourmets who flock here each year to devour their favorites among the Margaret River delights.

It's the deer farming that inspires some of the area's greatest culinary experiences. Local couple Graham and Cynthia Morrison established their farm here in 1977, when few people were aware of the combined great taste and health benefits that venison

had to offer, but from its humble beginnings the venison farm has gone on to supply its lean and sweet meat to chefs in the local area and across Australia. Local cooks now serve up tender venison dishes that lend a new richness to old favorites, such as venison spare ribs, slow-cooked in a sticky-sweet barbecue-style sauce, or elegant venison carpaccio teamed with capers and Kalamata olives. Wintry venison osso bucco with chorizo and beans is ideal sustenance after a day spent relaxing on Margaret River's world-renowned surf beaches or trawling the cellars of its many internationally acclaimed wineries.

It is this diversity that propels the region from being a one-day stopover to a multidimensional vacation destination. This is a place to indulge every facet of your personality: the wine aficionado, the adventurer, the surfer, the artist, the naturalist, and the adventurous gourmand. Because as much as the region is a haven of natural splendor, it is the focus on food and wine that makes it stand out among the nation's coastal hot spots. Margaret River provides a heady change of pace – and tastes – from everyday life.

Above The shoreline of Prevelly Park, on the Margaret River Estuary

Margaret River Wines

Wine tasting is a feature of any trip to Margaret River, and most vineyards offer tastings alongside gourmet nibbles or elegant lunches. **Vasse Felix** *(www.vassefelix.com.au)* is the region's oldest vineyard and its wines are some of the most acclaimed. You can enjoy a tasting in its subterranean Cellar Door tasting shop, or try them with food in the winery's elegant restaurant, which has gorgeous views over the vines. **Leeuwin Estate** *(www.leeuwinestate.com. au)* lays claim to one of the region's best Chardonnays – which is no mean feat, given that the region is famed for its Chardonnay grape. Tasting is a must. **Bootleg Brewery** *(www. bootlegbrewery.com.au)* offers a change for those nearing vineyard saturation. Its award-winning ales and lagers can be enjoyed at tables outside in its large and pretty grounds.

The Best Places to Eat Venison

Voyager Estate expensive

Just as the glorious natural surroundings of the Margaret River region amaze visitors, so too does the Voyager Estate. The combination of atmospheric grandeur, striking rose gardens, and gastronomic excellence – all wrapped up in a pretty Cape Dutch architectural package – is almost too good to be true. And the food is as magnificent as the surroundings. Chef Nigel Harvey does his utmost with the astoundingly good fresh, local produce that comes under his fingertips, including, of course, Margaret River venison, farmed a mere cork pop away. Harvey's deft touch makes the meat shine, in dishes such as his delicately sweet venison carpaccio, matched innovatively with the fresh spiciness of radish and watercress and the bite of Manchego cheese. It is a dish complemented by the blackberry, dark-chocolate, and oaky aromatics of the estate's well-regarded Cabernet Sauvignon-Merlot blend. Dishes change with the season, so prepare to be surprised.

Lot 1, Stevens Road, Margaret River; open 10 AM–4:30 PM daily; www.voyagerestate.com.au

Also in Margaret River

Go to the source at **Margaret River Venison** *(www.mrvenison.com; inexpensive)* where you can pick up venison steaks, sausages, or marinated kebabs to cook on the barbecue. For something a little more formal there is **Must** *(www.must.com.au; expensive)*, a stellar wine bar and restaurant where venison takes on a more sophisticated tone.

Also in Australia

In the small South Australian town of Mount Compass, Judith Phillips is renowned for the venison meat pies she makes and sells at **Mount Compass Venison** *(+61 8 8556 8216; inexpensive)*. In Victoria, relish autumnal venison *pithivier* crammed with mushrooms and chestnuts at **Gigi's of Beechworth** *(www.gigisofbeechworth.com; expensive)* in this historic gold-mining town.

Around the World

The reindeer is native to Finland, and there are few better places to experience superbly cooked venison. The top spot in Helsinki is the two-Michelin-starred **Chez Dominique** *(www. chezdominique.fi; expensive)*, where venison and oyster tartare is a must. Also in the capital but lower on the price ladder is **Lappi** *(www. lappires.com; moderate)*, where traditional sautéed venison comes with mashed potatoes and lingonberries, served in a chic update of the traditional Scandinavian log cabin.

KYOTO JAPAN

Fine Dining in Kyoto

The imperial capital for half a millennium until 1869, Kyoto is the cradle of Japanese culture and its historical and spiritual heart. Geishas wander its cherry-tree-lined streets and lanterns are lit at night, when the appetizing smell of cooking fills the air. The pinnacle of Kyoto's culinary heritage – the highly refined, multi-course *kaiseki* – lives on in the city's historic *ryotei* restaurants.

Kyoto is such a perfect distillation of Japanese culture that at times it can feel like a theme park. Spared the destructive might of Allied bombing at the end of World War II, large parts of the city remain well preserved, affording evocative glimpses of life in feudal-era Japan. This is where you will find Japan's most seductive Zen gardens, its most impressive temples, and, of course, the fabled geishas, women who are formally trained to entertain men with music, dance, and conversation; they are easily distinguished by their formal white makeup, wigs, and elaborate kimonos. Costume geishas roam the main tourist district, Gion, for the benefit of the cameras, but you can sometimes spot the real thing on Pontocho, the restaurant and nightlife street.

Kyoto's famous tea ceremony represents the pinnacle of the city's ritual aesthetic, with its impressively controlled and precise choreography. Food-lovers owe it a debt of gratitude, as it led to the creation of a gastronomic treat. Needing some food to counteract all the bitter green tea, the imperial court came up with the similarly ritualized and prolonged multi-course *kaiseki*, Japan's answer to *haute cuisine*.

Perfection, subtlety, and above all seasonality are the watchwords of the *kaiseki* chef. *Kaiseki* meals are traditionally served to diners seated on *tatami* (rice-straw mats) in the minimally furnished private rooms of *ryotei* – traditional restaurants housed in old wooden buildings, usually overlooking immaculate gardens. The menu is fixed and can run to over 20 courses, each with a specific name; the finest *kaiseki* meals cost at least 50,000 yen ($600) – often much more. The *sakizuke* is the first dish, the all-important overture; ensuing courses draw attention to an aspect of Japan's seasonal bounty, such as spring mountain ferns in May or the fiercely expensive *matsutake* mushroom in fall. Even the tableware plays a role in reflecting the seasonal narrative of the meal.

For the *kaiseki* novice, there will almost certainly be alien and quite possibly alarming ingredients – sea cucumber roe, salted fish entrails, or snapping turtle, for instance – as well as unfamiliar mealy, soft, and crunchy textures. There will be little or no meat and some dishes might not even taste like very much, but everything will look exquisite. *Dashi*, a stock made from seaweed and *katsuobushi* (dried bonito flakes), forms the core of any *kaiseki*, but it will invariably end with rice, the foodstuff the Japanese hold most dear.

Above *Kaiseki* is a succession of courses that aim to balance texture, temperature, and flavor, while emphasizing the essential character of the season

Right The Golden Pavilion in the Rukuon-ji complex is one of many beautiful temple buildings in Kyoto

Below In Kyoto, geishas and *maiko* (apprentice geishas) dress their hair and bodies in 18th-century style

---

A Day in Kyoto

Kyoto has more than 2,000 temples, shrines, and gardens, many of them UNESCO World Heritage sites, so selectivity is the key for sightseeing Kyoto in one day.

MORNING Start at **Nanzen-ji**, which is a good example of the type of temple most common to Kyoto; it is also situated close to many other temples in **Higashiyama**, a wonderful area to wander. For lunch, make for the legendary **Nishiki Market**, a covered corridor filled with dried-fish vendors, grocers selling bewildering indigenous Kyoto vegetables, Japanese sweet shops, and ancient knifemakers who once fashioned samurai swords and still service the imperial kitchen equipment.

AFTERNOON Visit the **Kyoto International Manga Museum** for a modern take on Japan, or explore the **Imperial Palace** for a more historical one. Then stroll around the atmospheric residential area of **Kamigyo ku**; there is a surprise on every street.

EVENING End the day on the outdoor restaurant terraces of **Pontocho**, watching the bats swoop over the Kamo River.

Essentials

GETTING THERE
The **"bullet train"** from Tokyo takes around 2½ hours. The nearest **airport** is Kansai International, 75 minutes away by **train**.

WHERE TO STAY
Ryokan Ishihara (inexpensive) is a traditional Japanese inn that warmly welcomes foreigners. www.yado-web.com
APA Hotel (moderate) is a modern hotel close to the main station. www.apahotel.com
Tawaraya (expensive) is a superb, 300-year-old traditional Japanese *ryokan*. +81 75 211 5566

TOURIST INFORMATION
www.seejapan.co.uk

What Else to Eat

Kyoto is cradled on three sides by mountains that provide the clear, clean water so essential for its *sake* and tea. The soft, pure water is also important in the manufacture of Kyoto's renowned **tofu**, a key element of the city's cuisine. It used to be delivered fresh to homes every morning, like milk. Kyotoites enjoy tofu simmered in a hot pot, deep-fried (**agedashi tofu**), freeze-dried, or spread with miso and grilled as **dengaku**, among many preparations. They especially value dried tofu skin, or **yuba**. There are several excellent tofu restaurants in Kyoto, many of them located close to the main temples. One of the most famous is **Okutan**, close to the Nanzen-ji temple (*+81 75 771 8709*).

The Best Places to Eat Kaiseki

Kikunoi expensive

Kyoto's finest *kaiseki* restaurants can be rather daunting, impenetrable places – some shun diners they don't know – but there are a few that welcome *kaiseki* novices, offering proper seats instead of a *tatami* mat and explaining the courses to their guests. Of these, the most renowned is Kikunoi ("chrysanthemum well"), awarded three Michelin stars in 2011. It was founded in 1912 and is run by the third-generation chef Yoshihiro Murata in a historic *ryotei* surrounded by immaculate Zen gardens, home to the freshwater spring from which the restaurant gets its name. Courses during a *kaiseki* could include raw baby squid marinated in soy, exquisite sashimi, sumptuous monkfish liver, and, unusually for a *kaiseki*, duck and beef from Hyogo Prefecture's Wagyu cattle. Clients argue over the best time of year to visit – given the seasonal nature of the food – but fall is probably the most compelling season to dine at Kikunoi. Many of the world's greatest chefs have made a pilgrimage here.

459 Shimokawara-cho, Higashiyama-ku, Kyoto; open noon–2 PM and 5–8 PM (last entry) daily; www.kikunoi.jp

Also in Kyoto

Kaiseki comes in many forms. Its most perfectly realized expression is usually found in *ryotei*, but the term is just as often used to describe any vaguely traditional, multi-course Japanese meal served *omakase* (orchestrated by the chef). Kikunoi *(above)* has a less formal sister restaurant, **Roan Kikunoi** *(www.kikunoi.jp; moderate)*, but for a more contemporary yet still authentically Kyoto-style *kaiseki* in a restaurant, try **Aunbo** *(+81 525 2900; moderate)*, in the atmospheric Gion district. The meticulously crafted, super-fresh ingredients used by chef Tashima in his cuisine will include tofu, local *kyo-yasai* (Kyoto vegetables), and fish, which you can enjoy while gazing thoughtfully at the restaurant's equally immaculate Zen garden.

Also in Japan

One restaurant that has picked up a great deal of buzz – along with two Michelin stars – in recent years is **Ryugin** *(www.nihonryori-ryugin.com; expensive)* in Tokyo. In this tiny, ornate, windowless dining room in a back street of Roppongi, chef Seiji Yamamoto creates gorgeously elaborate, multi-course meals from super-fresh, seasonal Japanese ingredients.

Around the World

Kaiseki has been hugely influential on the multi-course, fixed menu style of *haute cuisine* dining that has spread throughout the top restaurants of Europe and America. You can see echoes of *kaiseki* in the elaborate cuisine of restaurants such as **The Fat Duck** *(www. thefatduck.co.uk; expensive)* in the UK and Copenhagen's **Noma** *(www.noma.dk)*.

Above Wide, tumbling rice terraces cut into the steep sides of ravines surround Ubud

Above Young Balinese dancers in traditional costume at the annual Bali Arts Festival, which features dance, theater, and shadow puppetry

Three Days in Bali

Bali is spectacularly beautiful, so wherever you go, you'll be blessed with glorious sights. The island's relaxed and rural artistic retreat – Ubud – is a good place to start.

DAY ONE Visit **Ubud** to shop for crafts or browse the **Neka Art Museum**. After lunch, follow narrow paths across the paddy fields, or head to **Tirta Empul**, a 1,000-year-old Hindu water temple with eerie stone carvings. After dark, catch a *barong* dance performance.

DAY TWO Rise very early to see dolphins at **Lovina**. Follow them into the water around **Menjangan Island**'s coral reefs, or hike easy trails through forested **Bali Barat National Park** to see monkeys, deer, and endangered Bali starlings. Returning to **Ubud**, stop at roadside viewpoints for views of the volcano **Gunung Agung**.

DAY THREE Spend the day on the beach enjoying **Kuta**'s lively bar scene, relax at the quieter resort of **Nusa Dua** or catch world-beating surf at **Uluwatu**. Enjoy the sunset from clifftop **Pura Luhur** temple, then head to beachside **Jimbaran** for a seafood barbecue.

Essentials

GETTING THERE
Bali's **international airport** (named the Ngurah Rai Airport, but commonly called Denpasar Airport) and its **sea port** are near the capital, Denpasar. The island is only 93 miles (150 km) wide; transport is by **bus**, **taxi**, or rental **car**.

WHERE TO STAY
Poppies Gang 2 (inexpensive) is a legendary street in Kuta with lots of clean, basic hostels. Ubud's **Desa Sanctuary** (moderate) features self-contained, traditional buildings with modern facilities in Bali's cultural center. *www.sanctuarythevillage.com*
Suluban Cliff Villa (expensive) pampers with superlative clifftop sea views from your bed. *www.sulubancliffbali.com*

TOURIST INFORMATION
www.balitourismboard.org

BALI INDONESIA

Satay on the Island of the Gods

As the gamelan orchestra's haunting chimes fade into the early evening dusk, it's clear that the shaggy-haired, good-natured *barong* has once again failed to defeat Rangda, a long-nailed witch who has been threatening the kingdom. The audience pours out of the temple theater and into the street, to be snared by the tempting scent of satay sticks charring over a roadside grill.

Bali is unique in Indonesia for its Hindu culture, as most of the islands are Muslim, though like everywhere else in the country, there's an unruly spirit world lurking under the surface of its organized religion. Out in the sunshine, terrific surf pounds the cliffs and brilliant beaches, villages celebrate life in seemingly daily festivities, and the highlands around Ubud – Bali's artistic retreat – are piled with vibrantly green rice terraces. But there's a darker side to Bali too: good and evil gods are kept in balance by offerings of flowers and food in doorway shrines, worship at intricately carved stone temples, the frankly spooky *barong* dance, and the paying of respects to Bali's religious pivot, the mighty and disturbingly active Gunung Agung volcano.

Balinese satay is different too. In popular opinion, these barbecued skewers of spiced meat have become Indonesia's national dish. Classically simple and infinitely variable, satay is as much at home on high-end restaurant menus as it is being served up at simple *warung* (home-based) cafés, street carts, or village festivals. But unlike their Muslim countrymen, the Balinese adore eating pork – one of the island's classic dishes is *babi guling*, roast suckling pig – and you'll find pork satay served everywhere here.

Aside from the meat used, however, pork satay is unremarkably familiar: a few little cubes of marinated meat threaded onto a bamboo skewer, grilled, and served with a peanut-based sauce. Where Balinese satay really excels is *satay lilit*, made from seafood. Shrimp and firm, white fish are mashed to a thick, moist paste with coconut milk and rich palm sugar; tangy tamarind pulp, chili peppers, minced turmeric, and ginger are blended in for flavor, with a touch of pungent *terasi* shrimp paste. The resulting doughy mixture is molded around the rib of a palm leaf (or, more prosaically, a thick wooden skewer), lightly oiled, and grilled over a glowing bed of charcoal made from coconut husks. Served with a dipping sauce of *sambal matah* – a chili pepper and lemongrass relish – all you need is some *ketupat* rice cakes and a vegetable dish such as *plecing kangkung* (water spinach dressed in a spicy lime juice sambal) to be in island heaven.

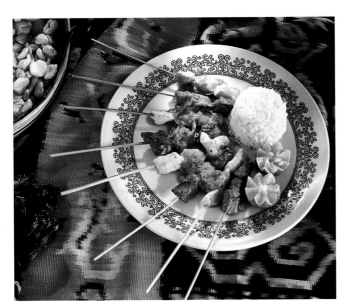

Above Satay is often served simply in Bali, with plain rice and a squeeze of lime

Indonesian Shrimp Paste

Fermented shrimp paste – *terasi* or *belacan* – forms the backbone of most soups, spice pastes, marinades, and *sambals* in Indonesian cooking. Made by pounding tiny shrimp into a paste and then leaving the resulting mixture to mature in the sun in wicker trays, it's sold in crumbly, reddish-brown blocks, usually in a tightly sealed tin, as its raw smell can only be described as "overpowering." Strangely, *terasi* loses its aggressive marine aroma when cooked, and fortunately it is roasted over a flame before being added – sparingly – to a dish. Indonesian food is so heavily spiced that you'd expect even *terasi*'s flavor to vanish under the onslaught of chili pepper and pungent gingers, but it's always there if you look for it, somehow mellowing, thickening, and binding together the overall flavor, making the dish unmistakably Indonesian.

The Best Places to Eat Satay

Bumbu Bali expensive

Bumbu Bali is a slightly touristy place to dine, but the modern courtyard setting is delightful and the menu uncompromisingly Balinese, thanks to the efforts of renowned chef and restaurateur Heinz von Holzen, who has been living in Bali since 1990. Start with *satay lilit* or perhaps *gedang mekuah*, a soup of pumpkin-like green papaya. For the main course, choose steamed fresh vegetables and festive yellow rice alongside *tum bebek* (minced duck meat seasoned with spices and steamed in a banana leaf parcel), or a simpler stewed beef and coconut milk curry, or the lighter *ikan bakar*, a simple whole grilled fish. Finish with fresh tropical fruit, such as the delicately scented mangosteen, or a selection of Balinese cakes made from sago, rice flour, and coconut.
Jalan Pratama, Tanjung Benoa; open 11 AM–11 PM daily; +62 361 774502

Also in Bali

Kafe Batan Waru *(+62 361 977 528; moderate)* specializes in regional Indonesian fare and so is a great place to sample half a dozen varieties of satay, including another Balinese version, *satay sapi*, made with succulent pieces of pork, and a great chicken satay from the island of Madura.

Also in Indonesia

Jalan Penghibur, the street above Losari Beach in the capital of Sulawesi, is famous for its long string of night-time mobile food carts known as *lima kaki* ("five legs" – three on the cart and two on the person who pushes it). You can get excellent, very inexpensive seafood satay here, though the local version, *satay makassar*, is for the curious only; it is made from grilled offal and served without sauces or *sambals*.

Around the World

Singapore's version of satay, served with the familiar sauce made from crushed peanuts, chili peppers, garlic, coconut milk, lime juice, and *kecap manis* (sweet soy sauce), was one of the first to be exported to the West via Chinese restaurants. **Lau Pa Sat** *(www.laupasat.biz; inexpensive)*, an airy 19th-century cast-iron building in Singapore that once served as a market, is now a food court with a score of counters offering all the old street-hawker favorites, including superb, freshly cooked satay sticks at very low prices. In London, **Satay House** *(www.satay-house.co.uk; moderate)* is a buzzy restaurant that serves authentic Malaysian foods, including meat and vegetarian satay, and a huge range of delicious curries.

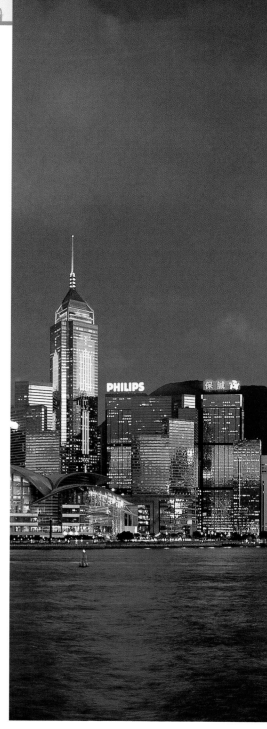

HONG KONG CHINA

Dim Sum by the South China Sea

"A dream of Manhattan, arising from the South China Sea" – modern travel writer Pico Iyer's description perfectly captures the East–West paradox that is Hong Kong. From imperial stronghold to opium port, Cold War enclave to today's global financial hub, this teeming city still delights in its traditional Cantonese cuisine, especially its bite-sized, delicious dim sum.

Prior to 1997 Hong Kong had been a British colony for 155 years, but this vibrant business center remains emphatically Chinese under its Western veneer. While you can shop for Armani suits or be serenaded by a string quartet over afternoon tea at an elegant colonial hotel, the dominant language is Cantonese and the city's ultra-modern harborside has been laid out according to the traditional aesthetic principles of feng shui.

As stores open and the engines of commerce fire up for the day, in the oasis of Kowloon Park, birds chirp and swoop between fig trees, and senior citizens greet each other after their morning tai chi exercises with "*Jousahn, yum cha, yum cha!*" – "Good morning, let's go for dim sum!" When it comes to eating, Hong Kong is the best place in the world to try Cantonese cooking, with its fresh flavors and contrasting textures, and there's no better way to sample its variety than with dim sum, or "little choices" – dainty portions of fried or steamed snacks. In Hong Kong, dim sum is better

known as *yum cha* – "with tea" – and a pot is an essential part of the meal. Favorite is *bo lei*, a dark, strong brew said to help the digestion.

The Hong Kong dim sum experience involves wading into a busy restaurant, finding a free table, then ordering from the carts laden with dishes and steamer baskets that constantly cruise by. *Har gau* dumplings, their shrimp fillings glowing pink through translucent wrappings; little steamed beef balls, smooth, springy-textured, and flavored with minced celery; fluffy steamed buns filled with scented *char siu* roast pork; aromatic sticky rice steamed in lotus leaves; *cheung fun*, meat wrapped in sheets of paper-thin rice noodles – the main problem is deciding what not to try, so it's no surprise that a dim sum brunch often stretches into the afternoon. It's the perfect way to fortify yourself for sightseeing and, above all in this city built on trade, for shopping, whether browsing in glitzy high-end Central, haggling in hectic Causeway Bay and Nathan Road, or diving into the heady Temple Street night bazaar.

Three Days in Hong Kong

Hong Kong has matchless shopping opportunities, but look beyond them and you'll discover an engaging mix of modern architecture, traditional temples, street markets, island life, and even fine beaches.

DAY ONE Explore Hong Kong Island by riding the Peak Tram to the **Peak** for views over the city, then catch a bus to explore traditional Chinese medicine shops and the smoky **Man Mo Temple** at Sheung Wan. After lunch, sunbathe or stroll on the south coast's **Shek O** beach, then mix with expats over a drink at one of **Lan Kwai Fong**'s many bars.

DAY TWO Catch the romantic Star Ferry across the harbor to **Kowloon** and Nathan Road's jewelers and clothing shops, then work north through the lively jade, goldfish, and ladies' markets. Ride the MTR to Diamond Hill's antique-style **Nan Lian Gardens**, before returning to the harbor for the classic nighttime view of Hong Kong Island's skyline.

DAY THREE Head to **Lantau Island** and ride the Ngong Ping 360° cable car to the serene, 110-foot- (34-m-) high **Big Buddha**, then visit the stilt fishing village of **Tai O** for a chance to see pink dolphins, before returning to Hong Kong Island by ferry.

Essentials

GETTING THERE
A major hub, **Hong Kong International Airport** connects directly to much of the globe. The **Airport Express** train has direct links to the downtown and Kowloon. **Buses**, the **MTR subway**, and **taxis** are comprehensive and efficient.

WHERE TO STAY
The **Eaton Hotel** (inexpensive) is friendly and functional. *www.eaton-hotel.com*
Hotel LKF (moderate) is classy and in boutique style. *www.hotel-lkf.com.hk*
The Peninsula Hotel (expensive) offers colonial-era luxury. *www.peninsula.com*

TOURIST INFORMATION
Find the helpful Hong Kong Tourism Board at Causeway Bay MTR station and Tsim Sha Tsui Star Ferry Pier (Kowloon); *www.discoverhongkong.com*

Left In the dim sum kitchens, tender dumplings are lifted gently from their traditional bamboo steamers

Above High-speed ferries dart across the harbor against Hong Kong's fabulous illuminated skyline

Below Chefs make their selection from lantern-lit market stalls piled high with artfully displayed produce

Dim Sum Around the World

Naturally, China is the best place to eat dim sum, but cities outside Asia with large Chinese communities come a close second. From London to Sydney and San Francisco, top-class dim sum is increasingly available in gastronomic hubs around the world.

HONG KONG

Tim Ho Wan Shop inexpensive

8 Tai Yuen Mansion, 2–20 Kwong Wa Street, Mong Kok, Kowloon; +86 852 2332 2896

The world's least expensive Michelin-starred restaurant, with lines stretching around the block – take a number and go shopping for an hour. Their flaky barbecued pork buns, richly flavored turnip cake, and perfect *har gau* are not to be missed.

Din Tai Fung moderate

3/F Silvercord Centre, 30 Canton Road, Tsim Sha Tsui, Kowloon; +86 852 2730 6928

Courteous service, bright, bustling, and everything above average. The specialties are various *xiaolong bao* (dumplings normally stuffed with pork, though one version here comes filled with taro paste), but save room for the crunchy jellyfish and radish salad.

Luk Yu Tea House expensive

24 Stanley Street, Central; +86 852 2523 1970

Perhaps a little overpriced, but it's the ambience that makes this not to be missed: pure 1930s teahouse, with ceiling fans, dark wooden booths, and ancient staff wearing crisply starched linen.

GUANGZHOU, CHINA

Sprawling, overcrowded Guangzhou, capital of Guangdong province, shares the same energy, language, and cuisine as Hong Kong. But at over 2,000 years old, it has rather more history.

Liwan Mingshijia inexpensive

99 Dishifu Lu; +86 20 8139 1405

This open-fronted cafeteria on Guangzhou's famous food street is always packed to bursting – sharing tables is inevitable and even Cantonese-speakers have trouble ordering above the din. It is best for exquisitely thin-skinned *cheung fun*, juicy won ton, and *shuang pi nai* (custardlike "double-skinned milk").

Chao Hao moderate

6/F World Trade Centre, 371 Huanshi Dong Lu; +86 20 8769 0888

Smart and sophisticated decor makes Chao Hao a favorite place for indulging in crispy-skinned pork, stewed chickens' feet, and Hong Kong-style mango pudding, though the specialty dish here is *fun gwor* – dumplings from northeastern Guangdong province.

Tao Tao Ju moderate

20 Dishifu Lu; +86 20 8139 9632

The roast goose – a Cantonese specialty – and the crumbly *char siu* rolls alone justify the reputation of this century-old restaurant, which claims to have more than 200 dim sum dishes on the menu. The greatest variety is available after 2:00 PM.

SINGAPORE

This tiny city-state sitting at the tip of the Malay Peninsula was, like Hong Kong, founded by the British. With its mix of colonial, Chinese, Malay, and Indian heritage, Singapore is one of Southeast Asia's trading hubs.

Yan Ting moderate

The St Regis Hotel, 29 Tangling Road; +65 6506 6866

Probably the finest dim sum in Singapore, served in suave surroundings by attentive staff. The *char siu* roast pork is meltingly soft, the *har gau* dumplings firm and smooth, and their soup stocks awash with complex but subtle flavors.

SYDNEY, AUSTRALIA

Chinese migrants came to Australia during the country's 19th-century gold rushes and stayed to run market gardens and stores. There are good-sized Chinatowns in all state capitals, but Sydney's is probably the liveliest.

East Ocean Seafood inexpensive

421–9 Sussex Street, Haymarket; www.eastocean.com.au

Come prepared to stand in line at this authentically busy, hot, and noisy dim sum legend, which delivers consistently fine scallop dumplings, steamed black-bean spare ribs, and fried vegetable rolls. Hong Kong expats get positively misty-eyed over their *dofu fa* (tofu custard).

Left (top to bottom) Four types of *gao*, or steamed dumplings; the main gateway into Sydney's Chinatown; dim sum dishes with, in the foreground, "phoenix talons" (chickens' feet)

Below (top to bottom) Paper lanterns strung across Gerrard Street, in the heart of London's Chinatown; rolled and skewered steamed pork with chili pepper and green onions

LONDON, UK

London's dim sum scene has exploded since the upmarket and innovative Hakkasan opened in the late 1990s, making Chinese food hip, upping the bar for dim sum cooking everywhere, and making London arguably the best city for Chinese food outside Asia.

Phoenix Palace moderate

5 Glentworth Street, NW1; www.phoenixpalace.co.uk

You know where you are with Phoenix Palace's enjoyably familiar dim sum selection – barbecued pork buns, sesame shrimp rolls, and crunchy fried yam dumplings – all cooked to perfection and served in a polite, bright setting.

Yi-Ban moderate

London Regatta Centre, Dockside Road, Royal Albert Dock, E16; www.yi-ban.com

A converted warehouse serving first-class dim sum with a stylish Docklands view. Their shrimp and chive dumplings, pork and preserved egg congee, and marinated pork with jellyfish are good enough to make you overlook the occasionally offhand service.

Hakkasan expensive

8 Hanway Place, W1; www.hakkasan.com

Hakkasan's success has brought it a Michelin star. The stylish wooden decor invokes a romanticized image of China, which suits the food – venison puffs and flying fish roe have never appeared on menus in dim sum's homeland. Don't miss the magnificent seafood dumpling consommé.

SAN FRANCISCO, CA

San Francisco's Chinatown is one of the largest outside Asia and the oldest in America. Beneath ornate 19th-century buildings, including a dragon-embossed Bank of America, lie dim sum restaurants that are fairly conservative, but with high-quality food.

Yong Kee inexpensive

732 Jackson Street; (415) 986 3759

A carry-out bakery that's a favorite with local Chinese, with many dim sum offerings – though it's pretty well mandatory to try their big chicken buns and handmade *char siu* rolls. There's no English sign outside, but it's not hard to find.

Ton Kiang moderate

5821 Geary Boulevard (between 22nd and 23rd Ave.); www.tonkiang.net

Though most of the excellent dim sum menu here is mainstream Cantonese, Ton Kiang is unusual in also serving Hakka dishes from northeastern Guangdong province, on the border with Fujian (Hokkien). Shrimp-stuffed eggplant is a Hakka classic.

Yank Sing moderate

One Rincon Center, 101 Spear Street; www.yanksing.com

This family-run institution has been feeding the community since 1958, building up an enviable reputation for fresh tastes and skillful presentation. Must-trys are the *xiaolong bao*, chicken *fan gwor* dumplings, and steamed rice packets.

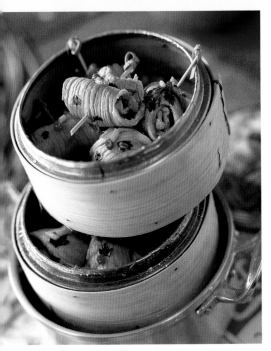

On the Menu

Char siu bao A steamed bun, light and fluffy around its savory stuffing of barbecued pork.

Cheung fun Thin, light rice noodle sheets folded around shrimp or roast meat fillings and flavored with a soy-oil dressing.

Chun goon "Spring roll," the best-known dim sum outside China, though not so popular at home. Usually stuffed with pork shreds and bean sprouts, and served with a sweet-and-sour sauce.

Dan ta Flaky pastry cup filled with egg custard. Macau's Portuguese-influenced version is grilled on top.

Fan gwor Clear-skinned dumplings from Chaozhou (Teochew) in China's eastern Guangdong province. Usually filled with seafood and light-flavored vegetables.

Foong jow Literally "phoenix talons," actually chickens' feet, prepared in various ways. The skin has a classic, gelatinous crunchiness, but they're fiddly things to eat, with dozens of tiny bones.

Har gau Steamed, clear-skinned shrimp dumplings; the shrimp should be slightly crisp and the wrapping light. A yardstick for a fine dim sum kitchen.

Jook Bland rice porridge, perked up with savory ingredients; an ideal complement to richer dim sum dishes. Sometimes known by its Indian name, "congee."

Law bak go Fried turnip-paste patty flavored with dried shrimp and *lap cheung* sausage.

Mong gwor pu deen A refreshing, un-Chinese dessert of Southeast Asian origins, comprising puréed mango pulp set with gelatin.

Nor mai gai Chicken pieces steamed inside a glutinous rice packet, wrapped in a scented lotus leaf. They tend to be rather heavy and filling.

San jook ngau yuk Steamed, springy-textured beef balls, served with a distinctive, aromatic soy sauce.

Siu mai Ubiquitous, open-topped steamed pork-and-shrimp dumplings. Inevitably ordered because of their good looks, they can be delightfully firm and juicy, but are often rather heavy.

Woo gok Crisp and curiously "hairy'" fried taro croquettes, filled with minced beef. Surprisingly filling.

Xiaolong bao Addictively tasty steamed pork and shredded cabbage dumplings from Shanghai. They fill with broth during cooking, making eating tricky – bite a hole in the side to drain them first.

PENANG MALAYSIA

Spicy Fish Soup in Penang

Georgetown, capital of the jungly Malaysian island of Penang, is steeped in a fusion of cultures, a legacy of Malay, Chinese, Indian, and Thai traders who settled here after the British set up shop during the 18th century. Colonial architecture aside, Penang's hallmark is its Nonya cooking – a blend of Chinese and Southeast Asian cuisines, typified by pungent, hot-and-sour *laksa*.

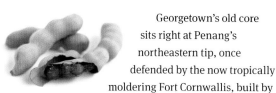

Georgetown's old core sits right at Penang's northeastern tip, once defended by the now tropically moldering Fort Cornwallis, built by the British at the spot where they first landed on the island in 1786. The streets nearby are a cultural mosaic of the peoples that followed them: the waterfront, where the magnificently colonial Eastern & Oriental Hotel stares out to sea; Little India, with its Hindu temples and tandoori chicken shops; the Chinese district, a maze of pastel-colored, colonnaded shophouses (a cross-cultural product of Chinese and Portuguese influences) and ornate southern Chinese guildhalls; the mosques of modern Malaysia; and a scattering of Thai restaurants. In fact, restaurants of all sorts are everywhere, filling the heavy, humid air with competing aromas, though it's around the markets and on the seafront – where people stroll in the evening, enjoying the cooling ocean breezes – that you'll find true Nonya cooking.

Laksa – spicy Malaysian seafood soup – is a classic Nonya dish, using a Chinese-style noodle soup as a vehicle for Malay flavors and ingredients. It takes several regional forms, but Penang's *asam laksa* stands out for being deliciously hot-and-sour. Scented galangal and lemongrass are used to flavor boiling fish stock, along with tart tamarind pulp – in Malay, tamarind is called "laksa," which also means "sour." The flavored stock is poured over rice noodles, topped with a healthy sprinkle of fresh and dried chili peppers, cucumber and pineapple shreds, mint leaves, sliced shallots, and pink, finely chopped ginger-flower buds, before pungent shrimp sauce is finally drizzled in to link all the flavors together. It's a powerful mix, enough to make any Westerner break a sweat.

Where to cool off? By day it gets pretty hot down on the coast, so heading inland to the heights of Penang Hill makes sense – especially as there's a funicular railway to the forested top, where the climate is a few degrees cooler and everything is shaded. Or, to give hot, tired feet a break, take a driving tour of the island – if you're interested in wildlife, don't miss the chance to see turtles nesting at Penang National Park. The lush Penang Botanic Gardens is another cooling sanctuary, with wonderful tropical trees, orchids, and ornamental ponds – and some bold rhesus monkeys. Much of the vegetation here has culinary uses, with helpful signage – from ginger to lychees, mangosteens to tamarind, it's a fascinating way to "meet the cast" of the local cuisine.

Above Penang-style *laksa* omits the coconut milk found in most Malaysian variants of the dish, for a much cleaner, more refreshing taste

Right Boisterous deities welcome you to the Sri Mariamman Temple, the oldest Hindu temple in Penang

Below The Asam Laksa stand at the Ayer Itam market is a legendary Penang food stop *(see facing page)*

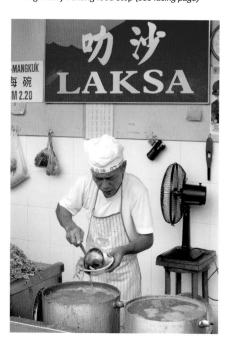

Three Days in Penang

Penang is a beautiful island, but for those unused to it, the climate can be punishing. Take it easy, and make plans for the day that are not too ambitious.

DAY ONE Kick off a walking tour of Georgetown at the site of **Fort Cornwallis**, before plunging southwest into **Chinatown** and its shaded, arcaded shophouses. Stop to admire the riotously decorated Hindu **Sri Mariamman Temple** on the edge of **Little India**, then continue south to a knot of ornate Chinese clan temples – **Khoo Kongsi** on Lebuh Pantai is the most splendid. If you've still got the energy, head west to **Cheong Fatt Tze mansion** for a guided tour of this magnificent Chinese pile.

DAY TWO Catch a bus or taxi to Georgetown's western outskirts and easy, well-marked walking trails at the **Botanic Gardens** and adjacent **Penang Hill**.

DAY THREE Save the third day for touring Penang's **north coast**: aside from slightly overdeveloped beaches around **Batu Ferringhi**, there's the delightful – if tiny – **Penang National Park** at Mukah Head, famed for its turtles and offering short jungle walks.

Essentials

GETTING THERE
Georgetown can be reached via **Penang International Airport**, and by **road** bridge, **train**, and **ferry** from the Malaysian mainland.

WHERE TO STAY
The **Old Penang Guesthouse** (inexpensive) is characterful, and nicely restored. *www.oldpenang.com*
The Cathay (moderate) is a faded but charming Chinese mansion. *+60 4262 6271*
Eastern & Oriental Hotel (expensive): grand, romantic, historic charm. *www.e-o-hotel.com*

TOURIST INFORMATION
10 Pesara King Edward; *+60 4261 6663*

Nonya Cooking

Nonya cooking (also called Straits Chinese cooking) is a blend of Malay and southern Chinese themes, with an occasional nod to Thai and Indian cuisines. The blend is not always even, and both sides adore fish and seafood. The Chinese bring rice dumplings and "cakes," noodle soups, and stir-fries to the party, but the Malay influence is clear in the use of chili-pepper *sambal* relishes, coconut milk, and cooking pastes made from complex blends of fresh and dried spices. The defining Nonya taste is a sharp, sour flavor rich in chili peppers, tamarind, lime juice, and noxious-smelling *belachan* shrimp paste (which mellows considerably when cooked) – of which *asam laksa* is the perfect example.

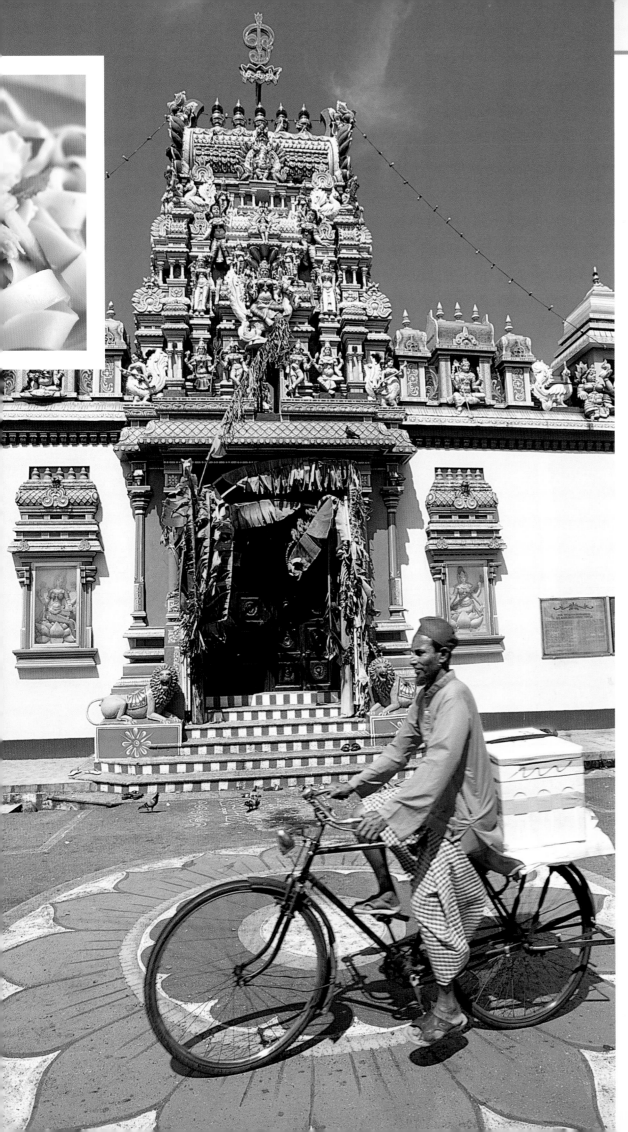

The Best Places to Eat Asam Laksa

Asam Laksa Stall inexpensive

Locals will tell you that this humble stand, west of downtown Georgetown near the foot of Penang Hill, serves the best *asam laksa* in Penang – in which case, it's probably the best *asam laksa* available anywhere. The local family running the show follows the classic recipe and, as everything is laid out at the front of the stand, you can follow the whole process, from chopping and slicing the ingredients through to spooning out the seasoned stock into the bowls of noodles and adding the garnishes. It's all ridiculously cheap but, as portions are generous, you won't need a second bowl. After your meal, be sure to visit the nearby Kek Lok Si, an absurd, pagoda-like temple on an octagonal base dating to 1893, full of brightly painted moldings and Buddhist statuary. On the hill behind the market is a spectacular, 100-foot- (30-m-) high bronze statue of Guanyin, the Chinese goddess of mercy, only completed in 2003.

Ayer Itam market, Jalan Ayer Itam; open noon–8 PM daily

Also in Penang

While the Asam Laksa Stall *(above)* might have a monopoly on the tastiest *asam laksa*, the **Pesiaran Gurney Night Hawker Centre**, around 1½ miles (3 km) west of central Georgetown – or rather the adjacent waterfront promenade – is definitely the most atmospheric place to eat it. Sit out here with sociable crowds and enjoy the dusk and fresh air, with excellent *laksa* served up fresh at dozens of street stands – just aim for the busiest one.

Also in Malaysia

In Malaysia's capital, Kuala Lumpur, **Mark's Asam Laksa** in the Weld shopping center *(+60 2487 0050; inexpensive)* is a central branch of a cheerful restaurant chain serving good-quality *asam laksa* in comfortable, if not exciting, surroundings; try their *hong dou sha* (sweet red bean soup) as an unusual dessert.

Around the World

For a different take on what *laksa* is all about, head to East Coast Road in Singapore, where **328 Katong Laksa** *(+65 9732 8163; inexpensive)* – along with hundreds of other restaurants across the city – serves the richer version with shrimp, coconut milk, and a heavier, more curry-oriented flavor. Katong's menu stretches to little but *laksa*, but their *otak-otak* (spiced, minced fish steamed in banana-leaf packets) makes a good side dish.

A Day in Chengdu

Though much of Chengdu is modern, there are many places in the city to soak up a more traditional atmosphere.

MORNING Greet the dawn among scores of martial artists in **Renmin Park**, then catch a cab out to Chengdu's **Panda Breeding Research Base** to watch these endangered creatures breakfasting on fresh bamboo shoots. Return to town for tea at the atmospheric **Green Goat Temple**, dedicated to Taoism's mythic founder, Lao Tzu.

AFTERNOON Ride the bus or walk to **Jin Li**, a lane full of antique-style shops and stands specializing in Sichuan's famous *xiaochi* snacks. Visit the adjacent **Wuhou Memorial Hall**, where emperor Liu Bei of the ancient Shu kingdom is buried, then take a bus to the extraordinary **Jinsha Museum**, packed with cultural relics from the Bronze Age.

EVENING After dark, have supper along **Kuan Xiangzi**, a maze of beautifully restored 19th-century stone lanes and buildings that house some great restaurants. Afterward, catch a short performance of Sichuan opera at the **Shufeng Yayun** theater.

Essentials

GETTING THERE
Chengdu has a **train** station and **international airport**. A **metro line** runs south through the city, and **buses** and **taxis** are everywhere.

WHERE TO STAY
Traffic Hotel Chengdu (inexpensive) is a backpacker favorite – clean, friendly, efficient, and in a good central location. *www.traffichotelchengdu.cn*
The BuddhaZen Hotel (moderate) is a boutique hotel with a traditional courtyard setting, located in the fascinating "old street" area of Wen Shu Fang. *+86 28 8678 1212*
The Sofitel Wanda (expensive) is Chengdu's best upmarket option. *www.sofitel.com*

FURTHER INFORMATION
194 Qintai Road, Chengdu; or check the listings magazine *GoChengdu*: *www.gochengdoo.com*

Right Drinking cups *(wan)* have lids *(gai)* to catch the leaves of the tea *(cha)*; together they form the *gaiwan cha* for drinking tea
Below The teahouses of Chengdu vary from grand old buildings to bamboo-pole stalls in temples and markets

CHENGDU CHINA

A Cultural Brew in Chengdu

It's a summer day in Chengdu, the humid capital of Sichuan province, and people are languishing at a riverside teahouse, paralyzed by the heat despite shade from overhanging ginkgo and willow trees. In front of each is a thermos of hot water and a steaming cup of tea – which, according to Chinese medicine, is in fact "cooling," making it the perfect thing to drink in this climate.

Chengdu, the capital of Sichuan province, is a modern, overcrowded metropolis – but patches of traditional culture survive among the expressways and offices, and especially in the people. The city dates back to prehistory, and became known as a base for rebel armies around AD 200, before blossoming as a trading nexus on the "tea-horse roads," which spread out from central China into distant Tibet by the 16th century. Tea has been drunk in China for millennia; there are hundreds of varieties of tea and as many ways of serving it. But teahouse culture – with teahouses serving as hubs of local communities, like a bar or pub in the West – really only survives nowadays in Sichuan, and most obviously in Chengdu.

Sichuanese teahouses take many forms, from a few chairs in the corner of a temple park to grand, antique-style buildings with heavy wooden furniture and a theater stage for watching Sichuanese opera. Take a seat in either and a waiter will materialize to offer you tea; sometimes there's not much choice – just jasmine or green tea – but other times you may be offered a three-page menu of regional specialties. Tea is normally served in a *gaiwan cha* – a squat, lidded cup and saucer, which is used as a teapot elsewhere in China for pouring the brew into thimble-sized cups, but here it's drunk from directly. Locals pick up the whole assemblage in one hand to take a sip, carefully holding the lid only slightly open to keep back floating leaves. Demanding far less skill, *zhuye qing*, a green tea from the forested foothills of holy Mount Emei, always arrives in a glass tumbler so that you can watch the tiny, spear-shaped buds rise and fall as the drink cools.

The waiter will leave behind a flask of hot water, or periodically return with a metal kettle. Some establishments serve Sichuanese snacks, or at least a plate of dried beans or melon seeds so you can munch on something as you watch your fellow drinkers chat idly in the Sichuanese dialect, or play cards or mah jong. If the teahouse is a theater, don't expect the audience to devote too much attention to the play; they'll know the story already, and catching up with friends or swapping stories is far more important.

Sichuanese Snacks

Sichuan is famous for the variety of its snacks, or **xiaochi**, which, unlike many Sichuanese main courses, are not always searingly spicy. Savory **"carrypole noodles"** (*dandan mian*) are named after the way street hawkers of this dish used to cart their wares around, while gruesome-sounding **"husband-wife lung slices"** (*fuqi feipian*) feature slivers of beef in a mild soy/vinegar/chili-pepper dressing. Both *chao shou* (**Sichuanese ravioli** in plain soup) and *tangyuan* (rice flour **dumplings** stuffed with sweet sesame paste) are pepper-free, though bland *douhua*, **soft tofu**, comes with hot relish on the side. Upping the heat considerably, *gege* (rice-coated **spare ribs** cooked in tiny steamers), *liang fen* (**cold bean noodles** in a chili pepper/vinegar sauce), and *ranmian* (the aptly-named **"incandescent noodles"**) are best avoided unless you have an asbestos mouth.

Above Tea-drinkers watch Sichuan opera at Wuhou Temple in Chengdu

The Best Teahouses in Sichuan Province

Heming Teahouse inexpensive

Everyone in Chengdu knows Heming Teahouse. Set underneath a wisteria vine just inside the city's most central park, this open-air teahouse looks out across a large ornamental pond. There's a large bronze kettle at the entrance (actually a water spout for you to wash your hands on the way in), the regulation bamboo chairs, and some solid, inconveniently shaped stone tables. Cruising hairdressers, shoulder masseurs, and even earwax removers move among the locals, some of whom seem to spend the entire day here. There's just the right blend of indifference and attention shown to you by the staff. Weekend crowds sprawl, chew sunflower seeds, and slurp their drinks cheerfully, as they gossip, browse their newspapers, or stare vacantly at youngsters bumping around in boats on the pond.

A cafeteria off to one side sells hot and cold snacks, and once a year there's a food fair in the park, where you can buy other local treats such as "three gunshots" – three sticky-rice balls that are bounced off a drum into a tray of toasted flour and served in dark caramel; more performance art than a meal.

North Gate, Renmin Park, Chengdu; open 6 AM–7 PM daily

Also in Eastern Sichuan

For a rural riverside setting, leave Chengdu and head to the village of **Huanglong Xi**, whose rickety antique streets and low-key temples have made it something of a tourist phenomenon. For a similar experience with less raucous crowds, try **Pingle**, about 55 miles (90 km) west of Chengdu. There are wonderfully atmospheric teahouses in **Zigong**, a former industrial town a day's journey from Chengdu; here you can relax over tea in the flagstoned courtyards of Wangye Miao and Huanhou Gong, two splendidly ornate merchants' guildhalls commemorating the town's salt-mining heyday.

Also in Western Sichuan

For a totally different take on what makes a good cup of tea in Sichuan, head to western Sichuan. The teahouses scattered through dusty backlanes in **Songpan** – a Qing dynasty garrison town encircled by stone walls and snowy mountains – make great perches for watching the Muslim, Tibetan, and Qiang population go about their business. In the remote monastery towns of **Litang** and **Langmusi**, pluck up the courage to try Tibetan butter tea: a rare mix of tea, yak butter, salt, and water churned into a soup.

FUKUOKA JAPAN

Hakata Ramen in Fukuoka

Ramen may be Chinese in origin, but the Japanese have made it their own. They are obsessed with ramen noodle soup, devouring media dedicated to following ramen trends and tracking down the finest versions. Among the different regional variations, one holds pride of place in the hearts of aficionados: Hakata ramen, made in the easy-going port city of Fukuoka.

Fukuoka is actually two cities that have grown together over the years. Hakata – from which the legendary ramen gets its name – is to the east, and in feudal days was the commercial center, while Fukuoka, to the west, was the home of the samurai. They sit on the north coast of the island of Kyushu, separated by the Naka River. Most importantly, what many "rameniacs" claim to be the best ramen in the world can be found for sale throughout this conjoined city, both at its celebrated ramen restaurants and from its unique *yatai*, the ramshackle food stands dotted throughout the downtown, notably beside the winding Nakasu River and in the Tenjin nightlife district.

The *yatai* are the soul and spirit of Fukuoka, contributing greatly to its reputation as one of Japan's more welcoming and habitable cities. Diners sit outside beneath the stars on cramped wooden benches, elbow to elbow, chinking their beer glasses, making cross-table conversation – all part of the city's relaxed vibe. This is a relatively compact city with some impressive mall and beach developments – prime among them

being Canal City – and a vibrant cultural life. Fukuoka Art Museum has one of the best collections of Western contemporary art in Japan, but the Hakata Machiya Folk Museum is the place to find out more about the culture and heritage of Hakata: its three buildings replicate life in past eras down to the tiniest detail.

As always in Japan, though, the main recreation for locals and visitors alike is eating – particularly ramen. Definitions of what ramen is and the ingredients used to make it vary wildly, but regardless of the recipe, this is the food that fuels Japan. Essentially, ramen is some form of broth with egg noodles and toppings that can include steamed pork belly, green onions, nori seaweed, hard-boiled egg... the list is endless. From this base, varieties and regional variations expand exponentially: Tokyo ramen (probably the type best known elsewhere in the world) has soy sauce added to the soup; in Sapporo ramen (the third main ramen type), the noodles are thick and crinkly. But in the famous Hakata ramen, the noodles are straight and thin, and the soup is made from mountains of pork bones *(tonkotsu)* cooked for endless hours over a low heat. It doesn't need soy sauce. It's perfect.

Above Hakata ramen is unusual in Japan for being served mainly at food stands, where conviviality is encouraged as an important part of the experience

A Dubious Delicacy

Apart from its much-prized ramen, Fukuoka is also famed for its fugu, the notorious puffer fish. Usually served either raw or deep-fried, every once in a while this dish kills a hapless diner with its deadly neurotoxin. The fish are landed at the nearby port of Shimonoseki and ideally kept alive during transit to Fukuoka – if possible, right up until the moment an order comes in. Then, working swiftly, the highly trained and licensed fugu chef beheads and skins the fish before scooping out its toxic guts: the liver is the worst offender, but all the innards are discarded. In terms of flavor, fugu rarely lives up to the hype – which is why the Japanese tend to slather it in spicy condiments. But it is certainly an experience and one of those dishes that have to be tried at least once.

A Day in Fukuoka

Fukuoka is the largest city in Kyushu, and it's thoroughly cosmopolitan. There's not a huge amount to see in the way of traditional culture, but it has some great modern architecture, vibrant nightlife, and wonderful food.

MORNING Head for **Canal City**, the city's top shopping mall and entertainment complex, which has hundreds of shops and restaurants and a multiplex cinema. Grab lunch at **Raumen Stadium**, which sells food from around Japan.

AFTERNOON The **Hakata Machiya Folk Museum** will fill you in on the social and cultural history of the region; alternatively, art lovers will find much to divert them at the **Fukuoka Art Museum**.

EVENING After dark, the only place to be is jostling for space on a bench outside one of Fukuoka's famous **yatai**. Afterward, if you aren't too full to move, head into the **Nakasu** district or head west to **Tenjin**; both are lively nightlife areas packed with restaurants and bars. Alternatively, check out what's on at the **Fukuoka "Yahoo" Dome**, one of Japan's best live music, sports, and concert venues; it's also home to the city's much-loved baseball team, the Daiei Hawks.

Essentials

GETTING THERE
Fukuoka Airport is a major international gateway. The city's train station (named "Hakata Train Station") is on the Shinkansen **"bullet train"** line from Tokyo (the journey takes around seven hours).

WHERE TO STAY
Arty Inn (inexpensive) is a well-priced and central business hotel. *www.arty-inn.com*
Canal City Fukuoka Washington Hotel (moderate) is part of a chain, but well located in the amazing Canal City mall. *www.fukuoka-wh.com*
Grand Hyatt Fukuoka (expensive) offers five-star luxury, including a spa, pool, gym, tea lounge, and martini bar, in the Canal City complex. *www.fukuoka.grand.hyatt.com*

FURTHER INFORMATION
www.fukuoka-tourism.net/e

Above Hakata ramen often includes *chashu* (simmered pork), *kikurage* (wood-ear mushrooms), and *karashi takana* (spicy pickled greens)

Left Cooks add ingredients for some made-to-order Hakata ramen at a night street stand, or *yatai*, beside the river in Fukuoka

The Best Places to Eat Ramen

Yatai by the river inexpensive

Festooned with lights and constantly buzzing with diners, the *yatai* stands beside the Nakasu River in the center of the city offer one of the world's greatest low-cost dining experiences. The lines to sample their hot, steaming bowls of gut-busting ramen can often be daunting, but people eat quickly here and you can always enjoy a beer while you wait. On the menu are not just magnificent examples of the ramen chef's art but also tempura, other noodle dishes, grilled fish, *yakitori*, and slow-cooked *oden*. *Oden* is a kind of Japanese *pot au feu* made with tofu, boiled eggs, *daikon* (a kind of white radish), *konnyaku* (a solid jelly made from a root vegetable), and *kamaboko* (colorful steamed fish-paste cakes), all bobbing in an everlasting savory brown liquid topped off every morning. Unthinkably, the *yatai* of Fukuoka are under threat from a local authority determined to "clean up" its streets, so visit while you still can.

Nakasu (by the river in front of Canal City); open sunset–midnight daily

Also in Fukuoka

If you are looking for a more civilized environment in which to sample Hakata ramen, **Ichiran Ramen** *(www.ichiran.co.jp/pc/hp/english; inexpensive)*, which opened in 1960, is a legend throughout Japan. Though it now has branches across the country, the original shop remains a place of pilgrimage for ramen fans. Each diner gets a questionnaire to fill in with which they can fine-tune their order, specifying the firmness of the noodles, the strength of the onion, the fattiness of the broth, and so on.

Also in Japan

In Tokyo, the **Ramen Jiro** *(inexpensive)* at 2-16-4 Mita, Minato-ku, is a legend: this grimy, rather forbidding place is famed for its mammoth bowls of "rustic" *tonkotsu* pork broth ramen, piled high with cabbage and the saltiest, fattiest pork. The chef at this Jiro – the original of a large chain – is one of a number of gruff, scarred ramen masters who have ascended to quasi-deity status, respected and feared like the feudal warriors of yore (albeit with their own pot-noodle ranges). Expect to line up around the block, whatever time of day, month, or season.

Around the World

Ramen has now conquered New York, with locals lapping up this quick, savory, filling dish in restaurants across Manhattan, but the most famous is **Ippudo** on Fourth Avenue *(www.ippudony.com; moderate)*. Having transferred from Japan – where there are Ippudos up and down the land – this branch has scored a notable hit with its uncharacteristically (for a ramen joint) slick venue in the East Village. Lines start every day up to an hour before it opens, and keep on going until closing time.

TAMIL NADU INDIA

Tasty Thali in Tamil Nadu

The southern Indian region of Tamil Nadu is a rich tapestry of soaring temple gateways, vivid green rice paddies, and towns abuzz with rickshaws, bullock carts, bicycles, and bustling humanity. As the majority of the devout population foregoes meat for religious reasons, the meal that keeps the Tamils going during a hard-working day is the unlimited vegetarian buffet known as the thali.

The practice of Hinduism has continued unbroken for millennia in Tamil Nadu, predating even the Vedas, the Hindu religion's oldest sacred texts. Some of the splendid temples with towering tapered gateways that dominate the towns of the region are over 1,000 years old. Tamil Nadu was one of the few places in India not to have been taken over by Mughal invaders during the 16th and 17th centuries, so the Tamils proudly claim to have preserved the purest form of Hinduism.

Consequently, Hindu beliefs pervade every part of everyday life. The dusty streets are full of shops nestled beneath temple towers selling brightly colored icons of deities, Shiva tridents, and the garlands of vibrant marigolds that are used to bring blessings to temples, homes, offices, and even cars and bicycles. In the country, trees guard shrines at their bases, while farmers in white dhotis plow fields using oxen – it all seems timeless, until a farmer whips out his cell phone. This is 21st-century India, and he'll probably be arranging where to meet his friends for a lunchtime thali, a small feast of a meal that has remained remarkably unchanged over the centuries; it is known in southern India simply as "meals."

Thali can be enjoyed by visitors in one of the ubiquitous hole-in-the-wall restaurants, inside one of the newer chains of eateries, and at some hotels. Each diner is served a pile of rice in the middle of a banana leaf, which is then surrounded by at least half a dozen small metal bowls containing various side dishes. Occasionally these are ladled straight onto the rice, but either way, waiters continually replenish your meal until you beg for mercy. The accompanying dishes can be almost anything. There are always various vegetable or potato curries and the ever-present trio of sauces – spicy lentil and tomato *sambar*; thick, chili-pepper-and-tamarind-based *vathal kozhambu*; and soupy *rasam*, a *dhal*-based thin sauce with a peppery tang. A *papad* (poppadom) and some lime pickle are usually thrown into the mix, along with palate-cooling curd and sometimes a sweet dish, such as rice pudding.

It can take outsiders a while to develop the knack of scooping up the messy food using just their right hand, but the trick is to copy the locals and press the mixture of rice and vegetables into a slightly firmer shape with your fingers before lifting it to your mouth. Eating off a neatly cut banana leaf is a novelty for most of us, but like so many other special things in Tamil Nadu, here it's just an everyday occurrence.

Three Days in Tamil Nadu

Tamil Nadu covers a vast area stretching from the Bay of Bengal coastline to the richly forested mountains of the Western Ghats. The northeastern part of the state, closest to the capital, Chennai, offers an excellent introduction to this cultural wonderland.

DAY ONE Leave the choking chaos of **Chennai** immediately by taking a prepaid taxi from the airport to the delightful seaside town of **Mamallapuram**. Take in the sea breeze beside the iconic shore temples, before strolling through the village past the **Arjuna's Penance** bas-relief and on to the "five shrines" **Pancha Rathas** monument.

DAY TWO Take a bus via Chengalpattu to **Tiruvannamalai**, famous for the atmospheric **Annamalaiyar** temple and the reddish-colored **Mount Arunachal**, where the revered guru Ramana Maharishi lived in a cave during the 20th century.

DAY THREE Connect by train to **Chidambaram**, which is centered on the enormous and imposing **Nataraja temple**, home to the special *dikshitar* caste of priests and the holy image of Shiva dancing in the eternal wheel of fire.

Essentials

GETTING THERE
Chennai has an **international airport** and a comprehensive **bus** and train **network**.

WHERE TO STAY
Mansoor Lodge (inexpensive) in Chidambaram is a very simple lodge conveniently located right opposite the temple. *+91 4144 221 072*
Greenwoods Resort (moderate) is a friendly family-run hotel in Mamallapuram near the beach. *+91 44 2744 2251*
Sparsa Resort (expensive) offers luxury in Tiruvannamalai. *www.sparsaresorts.com*

TOURIST INFORMATION
www.tamilnadutourism.org

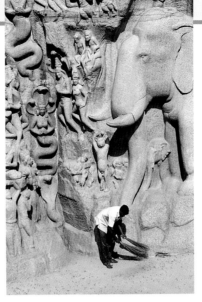

Above The 7th-century rock-hewn monuments of Pancha Rathas in Mamallapuram have been designated a UNESCO World Heritage site

Left The Nataraja temple in Chidambaram is one of the most ancient and celebrated shrines in India

What Else to Eat

Places that serve thalis tend also to offer a range of tasty south Indian snacks at certain times of day, generally from early morning until around 11 AM and then again from early evening until the restaurant closes. The most delicious snack option is **masala dosa**, a crispy rice-flour pancake stuffed with a lightly spiced potato and onion curry called **sabji**. *Masala dosa* is always accompanied by **sambar**, one of the sauces that comes with a thali, and coconut chutney. These two side dishes also accompany other popular snacks, such as **idli** (disk-shaped rice cakes) and **vada** (lentil and rice-flour savory doughnuts).

The Best Places to Eat Thali

Golden Palate moderate

The beautifully decorated and pleasantly air-conditioned vegetarian dining room of the Mamalla Heritage hotel in Mamallapuram continues the tradition started by the Mamalla Bhavan, the original village restaurant here, which still pulls in the crowds just up the road by the bus stand. At the Golden Palate, however, a little comfort and attentive service is added to the raw experience of thali-eating in most Tamil venues. Although eating with the hand is still the norm, you won't stick out if you opt for a spoon because many foreigners eat here.

The food itself has the reputation of being some of the best in northeast Tamil Nadu, and it is delicately prepared by a team of knowledgeable chefs. Some of the revolving selection of curry dishes that accompany the thali are not found elsewhere, such as okra with mustard seeds and beans cooked in a bright yellow turmeric sauce. The standard dishes — such as *sambar* and *rasam* — are as good as you'll find anywhere.

104 East Raja Street, Mamallapuram; open 7 AM– 10 PM daily; www.hotelmamallaheritage.com

Also in Tamil Nadu

Sri Ganesh Bhavan *(inexpensive)* on West Car Street, Chidambaram, backing on to the temple, is a quintessential thali haunt, with just a few creaky tables but superb fresh food. The food-only **Aakash Hotel** *(inexpensive)*, next to the bus stand in Tiruvannamalai, is another great spot to get a filling banana-leaf buffet. The **Saravana Bhavan** chain *(www. saravanabhavan.com; inexpensive)*, which has branches throughout Chennai and other parts of the state, is also highly recommended.

Also in India

Mysore's food-only **Hotel RRR** *(+91 821 244 2878; inexpensive)* does some of the best vegetarian thalis in Karnataka, while in Kerala's state capital, Trivandrum, top thalis can be had at **Hotel Arya Niwas** *(+91 471 233 0789; inexpensive)*. Delhi, the nation's capital, has a worthy northern outpost for south Indian fare in the very good **Anand** *(+91 11 2331 3554; inexpensive)* on Connaught Lane, a simple place that serves wonderful chicken delicacies.

Around the World

Although the great majority of curry houses outside India serve predominantly north Indian cuisine, there are still fine thalis to be found. Among over 10,000 Indian restaurants in the UK are six London branches of **Chennai Dosa** *(www.chennaidosa.com; inexpensive)*, where you can find authentic thalis, *dosas*, and other south Indian snacks.

Above The vegetarian meal of thali consists of many small dishes and aromatic sauces served alongside rice on a banana leaf

HOI AN VIETNAM

Street Food in Happy Hoi An

A powerful trading port for many centuries, Hoi An has a uniquely picturesque Old Quarter, its timeworn wooden buildings a testament to all the cultures that have traded and thrived here. Unscarred by war, the beautiful and easy-going town is also known for its multicultural street food, which blends the best fast-food elements from Vietnam, France, Japan, and China.

Hoi An sits roughly midway down Vietnam's coast; its position made it the country's largest and most successful trading port from the 15th to the 19th century. Evidence of the many foreign merchants that were drawn here – from China, Japan, India, and Europe in particular – can still be seen in the town's crumbling but beautiful architecture, miraculously untouched by the Vietnam War. It is an extraordinary record of the fusion of different cultures over time and as such has been declared a UNESCO World Heritage site.

The almost entirely wooden architecture of Hoi An, rich in tiling and lacquer, is a fascinating blend of Vietnamese and foreign designs and techniques. The Old Quarter's lanes and alleys are lined with small and grand homes, family cult houses (dedicated to the worship of ancestors), community houses, striking pagodas, and even a 17th-century Japanese wooden bridge. Despite the conversion of many interiors into shops, this old area has lost none of its charm.

Visitors able to drag their eyes away from the stunning buildings, with their craft shops, working artisans, and tailors, find that there is some fantastic street food available. Women in Chinese hats teeter through the cobbled streets, an entire restaurant hanging from a pole across their shoulders. When a suitable spot is found, the mobile restaurateur lays out a collection of plastic chairs, and before long customers are tucking into delicate seafood-topped rice pancakes or bowlfuls of sickly sweet desserts, fragrant with ginger and coconut. On the next corner a *banh mi* vendor can be found filling French-style baguettes with pâté and roast meat, before adding pickled daikon, chili pepper, and cilantro; it's another instance of East meets West.

The pedestrianized Old Quarter is undoubtedly Hoi An's main draw, but the new town offers an interesting, if noisy, glimpse into everyday Vietnamese life. An early-morning visit to the "wet market" is a must; it's here that the street sellers haggle over fish and all the exotic edibles that will go into making some of the freshest, tastiest street food in the world.

A Day in Hoi An

The Old Quarter of Hoi An is pedestrianized, and it's a joy simply to wander around its narrow streets, but watch out for motorbikes, which haven't yet been banned from the area. Aim for an early start, along with the locals.

MORNING Head down to the **wet market** before 7:00 AM as the locals descend to get their supplies for the day – this is an ideal place to sample some local dishes for breakfast too. While it is still early, take a walk through the **Old Quarter**, so you can appreciate the beautiful buildings and take photographs of the **Japanese Bridge** without interruption. As sites open, visit one of the preserved **old houses** or a **museum**. One special "tourist ticket" buys you entrance to five of the 18 historical sites.

AFTERNOON Leave the mainland behind and head across **Cam Nam Bridge** to **Cam Nam Island** and walk the streets to see glimpses of local life. Then indulge in some thrilling shopping, from artisan goods (such as ceramics and paintings) to custom tailoring at a fraction of the normal cost.

EVENING If you're in the town during a full moon, you'll be able to witness the monthly **lantern festival** in the Old Quarter: all street and house lights are turned off and the only light comes from glowing silk lanterns.

Essentials

GETTING THERE
Danang International Airport is around 22 miles (35 km) from Hoi An; there are **buses** and **taxis** to the town. All the sights in the town can be reached on foot.

WHERE TO STAY
Cua Dai (inexpensive) is a welcoming, pretty hotel with a large pool, 10 minutes' walk from town. *www.cuadai-hotel.com*
Long Life Riverside Hotel (moderate) is a modern boutique hotel on An Hoi Islet with views of the river and Old Quarter. *www.longlifehotels.com*
The Nam Hai (expensive) is located a short trip out of town and provides luxurious beachfront villas, some with their own pools. *www.thenamhai.com*

TOURIST INFORMATION
www.vietnamtourism.com

Left A blend of Japanese and Vietnamese food, *cao lau* is a pork noodle dish with greens and crispy fried pork skin

Above Impromptu seated "restaurants" spring up around the central market during trading hours

Below The Japanese Bridge, also known as the Pagoda Bridge, doubles as a temple with shrines to several deities

Street Food in Southeast Asia

Street food both scares and entices visitors to Southeast Asia, as worries about hygiene battle with the alluring sights and smells of the dishes on display. Put your fears aside and eat like the locals; you'll experience the best-value food Southeast Asia has to offer.

VIETNAM

Fresh and lighter than many cuisines in the region, Vietnamese cooking draws heavily on herbs, chili peppers, and lime. The street food of Vietnam is a frequent contender for favorite among travelers to the region, and rightly so.

Hoi An

Look beyond the Old Quarter's stunning buildings and you'll find excellent street food virtually everywhere. Keep an eye out for the moving vendors, such as the women who balance restaurants across their shoulders and the town's steamed bun *(banh bao)* merchant, who blasts pop music from his cart. Head north out of the Old Quarter for fantastic *banh mi*.

Old Quarter, Hanoi

From the moment the sun rises, the Old Quarter in Hanoi comes alive, with each corner seemingly bringing a new street-dining experience – pull up a plastic chair, order some *pho* or *banh cuon* (rice-flour pancakes stuffed with pork and wood-ear mushroom), and dig in.

Bac Ha

An overnight train plus a 2-hour minibus ride from Hanoi, Bac Ha's Sunday market is perhaps only for the dedicated traveler. But it's worth the effort when you sit down to eat pork noodle soup among the local Flower Hmong tribe, surrounded by a carnival of color that will stay with you for life.

THAILAND

Fiery from red hot chili peppers and pungent with shrimp paste and *nam pla* (fish sauce), Thailand's food is well known around the world, but its own streets still throw up lots of surprises, from fried cockroaches to sour orange curry and local sausages.

Chinatown, Bangkok

By day the main street of Bangkok's Chinatown is the city's busy gold-trading area, but by nightfall it is packed with street food vendors. Hungry visitors here snap up dishes such as *pla pao* (char-grilled fish), *tom yum koong* (the shrimp version of the sour and spicy soup), and *goong pao* (barbecued shrimp). For impressive displays of fresh seafood on ice, head to the T&K food stand on the corner of Thanon Phadung Dao and the Yaowarat Road.

Silom Road, Bangkok

This area is the business hub of the city and is home to many street stands at each end of the day. For a taste of real Bangkok – on many levels – get up early and go for the morning shift, when the road is filled to bursting point with hawkers plying their trade to the rat-race of workers. The delicious deep-fried pork and sticky rice is always a favorite.

Warorot Market, Chiang Mai

When the sun sets in Chiang Mai, the food vendors move into the roads around Tom Lamyai flower market near the river's pedestrian bridge. Try the northern Thai sausages and, if you're feeling adventurous, some of the deep-fried insects.

MALAYSIA

Malaysia is a wonderful meeting of cultures. Large groups of indigenous Malay, Chinese, and Indians have influenced each other's cuisines over the years, sharing techniques and ingredients to create unique dishes.

Gurney Drive Night Market, Penang
Persiaran Gurney (Gurney Drive), Georgetown

Penang is famed among Malaysians for its food, and this night market is the largest in the city. It opens until late and is busy until the end, packed with locals and tourists alike. The famous fried chicken skin and *asam laksa* noodles are must-tries.

Jalan Alor
Golden Triangle, Kuala Lumpur

In Kuala Lumpur's Golden Triangle, someone thrusts a menu at you approximately every five steps. The food here is a fantastic introduction to the Chinese dishes of Malaysia, such as *pan mee (see* On the Menu, *right)*. A roadside durian fruit makes a strong-smelling end to the meal that you'll either love or hate.

Left (top to bottom) Morning fish market, Hoi An, Vietnam; making roti by hand in Penang, Malaysia; neon-lit Chinatown in Bangkok, Thailand **Below (top to bottom)** Curries and toppings on sale at the evening market, Luang Prabang, Laos; *bak chor mee* (pork on egg noodles with chili peppers and vinegar) is served with a clear soup side-dish at Singapore's hawker stands

Little India Saturday Night Market
Masjid Jamek LRT, Kuala Lumpur

This bustling night market is the perfect place to try the Malay and Indian side of Malaysian street food. Don't miss satay and *apam balik*, thick pancakes with peanuts and corn.

SS2 Hawker Center
Petaling Jaya, Kuala Lumpur

The locals' favorite group of food stands is out of town but well worth the taxi ride. The Hawker Center has around 80 stands serving classics such as grilled stingray and *la la* (clams). The center's layout allows visitors to dine from as many stands as they wish and buy drinks from any of the many people that ply the aisles selling beverages.

LAOS

While Laos cannot compete with its larger neighbors for variety on the food front, there is still plenty to titillate the taste buds. The country's food takes influences from all its neighbors, and the setting can often be breathtaking.

Luang Prabang

The center of this city (a UNESCO World Heritage site) converts to a fabulous night market when evening falls. The air becomes thick with smoke, and banana leaves are piled high with delectable grilled meats. Try the *nem kao* (stuffed rice pancakes) or sticky rice with *sai gok* (local sausage).

SINGAPORE

Singapore is packed with street food, all of it inspected, regulated, and controlled for a degree of hygiene not seen elsewhere. Most of Singapore's 40,000 food stands are located inside "hawker centers."

Smith Street, Chinatown

Once a notorious red-light district, at night Smith Street is now home to many hawker stands. Look out for *char kway teow* (wok-fried noodles) and the sticky barbecued pork. Unusually for a food stand, China La Mian Steamed Buns makes a very delicious *xiao long bao* (juicy pork "small dragon" dumplings). For dessert, hunt out some *mochi*, little rice balls filled with crushed peanuts or sesame and served in pandan-leaf-flavored soup.

Little India, Rochor

Singapore's ethnic makeup is similar to Malaysia's trinity of cultures, and this area showcases the best of the Indian contingent's crafts and cuisine. The food stands here feature skillfully made *roti prata* (sweet flatbread), huge *dosai* (rice pancakes), and meals served on banana leaves.

Chinatown Complex Food Center
Trengganu Street

This is Singapore's largest hawker center, with more than 200 food stands. Favorites here include chicken rice, fried Hokkien prawn mee (fried noodles with shrimp), and claypot rice (chicken, Chinese sausage, and salted fish with crispy, lightly charred rice).

On the Menu

VIETNAM

Banh cuon Steamed and rolled-up rice-flour pancakes filled with pork and mushrooms, topped with fried shallots, and eaten with a spicy dipping sauce.
Banh mi French-style baguettes filled with meat and finished with pickled vegetables, herbs, and fiery pepper sauce.
Goi cuon A kind of Vietnamese spring roll: the rice paper roll holds pork, shrimp, rice noodles, herbs, and seafood.

THAILAND

Joke Rice porridge, which is common throughout this part of the world; in Thailand it is eaten for breakfast with minced pork and a soft egg.
Pad thai Tamarind and palm sugar combine into the sweet-and-sour sauce of this well-known fried rice-noodle dish.
Som tam A salad of crunchy green papaya topped with fermented freshwater crab or jumbo shrimp, served with a lime and fish-sauce dressing.

MALAYSIA

Laksa The most famous of Nonya (Chinese Malay) dishes bathes rice noodles, meat, seafood, and vegetables in either stock *(asam laksa; see pp204–5)* or spiced coconut milk (curry laksa).
Pan mee Freshly rolled noodles served dry or in soup, topped with crisp fried anchovies and minced pork, and finished with a spoonful of chili pepper sauce.
Satay Tender meat kebabs that are marinated before grilling and served with a spice-rich dipping sauce.

SINGAPORE

Char kway teow Wide, flat, rice noodles (*ho fun*) stir-fried with meat, seafood, and egg. The chefs deftly toss the ingredients near the stove's flame, imparting *wok hei* – the essence of the wok – to the dish.
Chili crab A delicious but messy, chili-pepper-sauce-covered crab.
Claypot rice A mix of marinated chicken, waxed Chinese sausages, and salted fish cooked in a clay pot with rice over charcoal, so the rice develops a crunchy base, similar to Persian *chelo (see p178)*, and a smoky flavor.
Roti prata These flatbreads arrived with southern Indian immigrants. Soft dough is deftly swung around the chef's head until it is paper-thin, then it is folded and fried into crisp layers. These are also sold all over Malaysia under the name *roti canai*.

Right Balmain bugs on sale in Sydney Fish Market – the second-largest in the world after Japan's Tsukiji market (*see p246*)

Below Juicy Balmain bugs, simply and quickly pan-fried with saffron

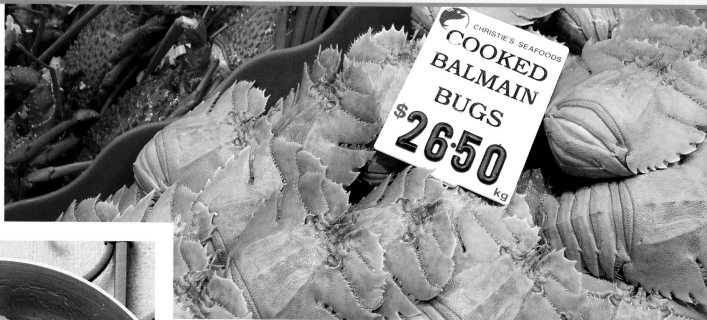

CHRISTIE'S SEAFOODS
COOKED BALMAIN BUGS
$2650 kg

A Day in Sydney

Sydney is dominated by its iconic harbor, and the foreshore abounds with culture and commerce, from the cobbled lanes of the historic Rocks to the celebrated Opera House and the ferry hub of Circular Quay.

MORNING Walk around the forecourt of architect Joern Utzen's **Sydney Opera House** and gaze upon its concrete sails. Saunter around **Circular Quay** and take a guided tour, complete with hard hat and harness, up that other city icon, the **Harbour Bridge**.

AFTERNOON Follow the shoreline through the **Botanic Gardens** to **Mrs. Macquarie's Chair** and survey the harbor, then on to the **Andrew (Boy) Charlton**, a glamorous public pool that begs a dip. Drop into the **NSW Art Gallery** and its 11,000 works.

EVENING Hop on a ferry to **Taronga Zoo**, **Balmain**, or **Manly Beach**, just to ride it back again to see the sparkling city lights. Head up to **Australia Square** for a cocktail in the **Orbit Lounge Bar** on the 47th floor. It has 360-degree views and revolves – very slowly.

Essentials

GETTING THERE
Sydney Airport, 5 miles (8 km) from downtown, is served by major international airlines. **Rail** and **bus** services link airport and city.

WHERE TO STAY
The Kirketon (moderate) is an oasis in the lively Darlinghurst area. *http://kirketon.com.au*
Ravesi's (moderate) has a relaxed Bondi beachside vibe with a shot of chic. *www.ravesis.com.au*
Establishment Hotel (expensive) is a sleek place to indulge your rock-star fantasies. *www.merivale.com/#/establishment/hotel*

TOURIST INFORMATION
City Host Kiosks are at the Town Hall, George Street, and Circular Quay (corner of Pitt and Alfred Streets); *www.visitnsw.com*

SYDNEY AUSTRALIA

Catching Bugs in Harbor City

Sydney and seafood go together like surf and sand. Few cities do it quite so deliciously: light-as-air fish and chips, oysters with a squirt of lemon, butter-poached scallops, and barbecued tiger shrimp. This harborfront city has a passion for all saltwater treasures, including the Balmain bug, a clawless crustacean with stacks of flavor, best eaten in a warm Sydney sea breeze.

Don't flinch when you see Balmain bug on the menu of one of Sydney's stylish seafood restaurants. This creature is in fact a type of lobster; its flat shell, five sets of legs, and armored body have earned it the "bug" moniker. Shy, retiring types during the day – tending to bury themselves in mud or sand – Balmain bugs emerge only after dark to scoot around. Despite their name, they don't hang around the bay with the other arty residents of Sydney's upmarket suburb of Balmain, but are mostly caught swimming off the coast of New South Wales. This means they're supremely fresh off the boat when they hit the briny Sydney Fish Market. Steamed, poached, pan-fried, or char-grilled, they're delicious drizzled with fennel vinaigrette, daubed with aïoli or pesto, or smeared in citrus butter.

If you've a yen to tour a lobster pen, set foot in a sashimi pavilion, or scrutinize shellfish shuckers, book an early morning tour of the fish market (6:55 AM), or alternatively, soak up the atmosphere in the harborside city. Explore the historic Rocks precinct, a cluster of sandstone alleys and courtyards dating back to convict times. It's an easy walk from here past the colonial architecture of Macquarie Street to Hyde Park Barracks, one of 11 Australian Convict Sites on UNESCO's World Heritage list.

Sydney is an outdoorsy city that begs to be explored on foot. Strike out along the cliffs from Bondi Beach via Tamarama (dubbed "Glamarama" for its fashionable vibe), Bronte, and Clovelly to Coogee Beach – the sea views are glorious. Or make the trek from Taronga Zoo to Balmoral Beach, through bushland, past historic buildings, former military bases, and spectacular harbor vistas. There's plenty of open-air summer entertainment too: catch a movie under the stars, soothed by a sea breeze, at St. George Open Air Cinema at Mrs. Macquarie's Point, or take in a free concert by the Sydney Symphony at Parramatta Park or the Domain. This huge site on the edge of the city's business district is next door to Sydney's Royal Botanic Gardens – one of the world's best – which itself hosts theatrical and artistic events.

Cooking Classes

With so much local expertise in seafood, Sydney is the perfect place to hone your cooking skills and cook up a fishy feast. **Sydney Seafood School** *(www.sydneyfishmarket.com.au)* at the Sydney Fish Market can show you how best to prepare anything with fins, shells, or tentacles. Its classes, which range from evening sessions to weekend workshops, are led by top chefs and take place in an auditorium featuring walls covered in Icelandic fish leather. Down-under food guru Simon Johnson's **Talk, Eat, Drink** classes *(www.simonjohnson.com)* in Alexandria's Providore's Market feature gifted chefs demonstrating their varied skills. You can sample the dishes, quiz the cooks, and even take part in the cooking.

Left Downtown Sydney and waterfront with the Opera House

The Best Places to Eat Balmain Bugs

Flying Fish expensive

Peter Kuruvita is a predawn regular at the Sydney Fish Market, and whenever he sees Balmain bugs, he swoops on them. They immediately sell out in his slick restaurant, Flying Fish. Head chef and co-owner Kuruvita grew up in a world permeated with fresh spices and flavors – he was born in Sri Lanka – and his menu perfectly reflects this. He serves the tender, sweet bug tail with a black pepper curry leaf sauce, a sauce of ginger, chili pepper, and shallot, or simply with salt and pepper. Sometimes, too, he boils them up to make a deeply flavorsome bisque. Sri Lankan curries made with kingfish or butternut squash and shellfish from the restaurant's live tank are popular alternatives. Flying Fish, with its old working wharf-meets-designer loft style, might be hard to find, but once settled in this harborside gem, it's hard to drag yourself away.

Jones Bay Wharf, 19–21 Pirrama Road, Pyrmont, Sydney; open noon–2:30 PM Tue–Fri, noon–3:30 PM Sun, 6–10:30 PM Mon–Sat; www.flyingfish.com.au

Also in Sydney

Diminutive and decidedly relaxed, **Fish Face** *(+61 2 9332 4803; moderate)* in Darlinghurst serves the best of Australian seafood, much flown in from around the country. Balmain bugs appear, sometimes in a salad with fennel and watercress, or whipped into an addictive mousse plumping out homemade ravioli in a bisque-like sauce made from the roasted shells, garnished with deep-fried shrimp and leek.

Also in New South Wales

Elegant **Zest** *(www.zestrestaurant.net.au; expensive)* on NSW's North Coast is delicious proof that great food isn't restricted to the big cities. Glenn Thompson, head chef and owner, is a master of flavor combinations. His crisp-fried zucchini flowers filled with Balmain bugs and sautéed bugs with goat cheese gnocchi are both to die for.

Other Seafood in Sydney

Slurp Sydney rock oysters and dig into fresh snapper pie with views of the city's skyline at **The Boathouse** *(www.boathouse.net.au; expensive)* as rowers skim the waters of Blackwattle Bay and fishing boats bob in the near distance. Catch a ferry to Watson's Bay to reach **Doyle's on the Wharf** *(www.doyles.com.au; inexpensive)*. This family-owned institution has been serving up seafood since 1885; try the carry-out beer-battered fish and chips and eat them on the beach or in the shady local park.

Three Days in Okinawa

Okinawa is made up of over 100 islands spread out over a considerable distance, so if you plan on seeing more than just the main island, you will need at least three or four days. However, many Japanese pop down to the main island simply for a long weekend by the beach.

DAY ONE Spend a day wandering the archipelago's capital, **Naha**. Go shopping (and eat) at the enormous **Makishi Market** and poke among the capital's shops for Ryukyuan lacquerware and glassware.

DAY TWO Head to the north of **Okinawa Honto** to enjoy the beaches or visit the **Ocean Expo Park**, which has a gigantic aquarium and is home to the **Native Okinawan Village**, featuring 20 houses from different eras. Then take a diving trip out to some of Japan's best **coral reefs**, or chill out at a beachside bar and try local delicacies like *goya chanpuru* and *umibudo* (caviar-like seaweed).

DAY THREE Take a short flight to the southernmost island of **Iriomote** and go hiking through the jungle in search of the super-rare Iriomote wild cat (fewer than 100 are thought to remain).

Essentials

GETTING THERE
There are regular flights from mainland Japan to Naha's **airport**, which also receives some international flights. There are decent **ferry** and **air** networks between the islands.

WHERE TO STAY
APA Hotel Naha (inexpensive) is a large, business-oriented hotel with reasonably priced rooms. *www.apahotel.com*

Okinawa Nahana Hotel (moderate) has large, modern rooms and a spa; it's also handily within walking distance of the market. *www.ishinhotels.com/okinawanahana/en*

Busena Terrace (expensive) is Okinawa's most lavish resort hotel, complete with underwater viewing tower. *www.terrace.co.jp*

TOURIST INFORMATION
www.pref.okinawa.jp/english/tourism

Right The vast Makishi Market in the center of Naha sells all kinds of foods, including some unique to Okinawa

Below Many of Okinawa's beautiful beaches have coral reefs and are great places for snorkeling

Goya Chanpuru in Okinawa

Mention of the Okinawan archipelago brings a misty-eyed look to many Japanese. These are their vacation islands, more relaxed than the mainland and with their own distinctive culture. The most famous dish of their indigenous cuisine is the stir-fry *goya chanpuru*, one of the super-healthy dishes credited with helping the Okinawans become some of the longest-lived people in the world.

The Okinawan archipelago lies 435 miles (700 km) south of mainland Japan and is made up of over 100 islands. Until the early 17th century, Okinawa was entirely independent from Japan. A few architectural traces of the Ryukyu kingdom from this pre-feudal era still remain, such as Shuri Castle on the main island of Okinawa Honto, and there are glimpses of its culture on the outlying islands of Taketomi and Iriomote.

Until the 17th century, Okinawa's culture and cuisine were more influenced by China, with which it had traded for centuries. The Ryukyus were a famously peaceable people – legend has it that they solved differences with guitars rather than swords – which makes it bitterly ironic that these islands were the scene of some of the bloodiest battles of World War II.

War veterans still make pilgrimages to Okinawa's main battle sites, but far greater numbers come for the diving, water sports, and wonderful beaches. Aside from its tourist industry, which is largely made up of Japanese along with Americans from the local US air base, Okinawa is a sleepy kind of place, particularly away from its capital, Naha. However, in recent years there has been a growing interest in the longevity of Okinawans born before 1939. The islands are said to have more centenarians per capita than any other part of the world, and the average life span for women is 85 years; it's 78 for men. Gerontologists have ascribed this to a variety of factors, but one of the main ones is thought to be their diet.

Chanpuru is the Okinawan for "stir fry" (it literally means "something mixed" and is also used to refer to the islanders' openness to foreign ideas, as in "*chanpuru* culture"). The most famous kind is *goya chanpuru*, made with *goya*, an indigenous knobby cucumber that has been proven to reduce blood pressure and has even been used to treat AIDs. Though unbearably bitter when eaten raw, *goya* is transformed when stir-fried with pork, tofu, vegetables, soy sauce, eggs, and sake. Word has caught on among the famously health-obsessed Japanese, and *goya*'s fast-spreading popularity means *goya chanpuru* is well on the way to becoming a Japanese culinary staple.

Longevity Food

Okinawa's typhoons make rice-growing tricky, but one crop that flourishes in this rain-washed, mineral-rich earth is the Okinawan purple sweet potato. These **beni imo**, as they are called, are high in flavonoids, which are antioxidants and act as hormone blockers, and they are also rich in carotenoids, vitamin E, fiber, and lycopene, which has been shown to help prevent prostate cancer. One of these sweet potatoes contains four times the daily vitamin A and half the vitamin C requirements of an adult. Recent research has also indicated that *beni imo* can help stabilize blood sugar levels and lower insulin resistance. Okinawans eat them in tempura and add them to cakes, but best of all is Okinawan sweet potato ice cream. Of course, this probably undermines a good deal of the health benefits, but the taste is ample compensation.

Above *Goya chanpuru* is a crunchy stir-fry with apparently wondrous health benefits

The Best Places to Eat Goya Chanpuru

Emi no Mise (Emi's Place)
moderate

The village of Ogimi in northern Okinawa Honto is famous for its large number of elderly residents, including several centenarians, most of whom have become quite used to the attention of interviewers from international TV channels. The only restaurant in this sleepy town is Emi's, the so-called "longevity restaurant," which is famous for its classic Okinawan cuisine. The eponymous Emi skillfully combines many of the ingredients that are thought to contribute to a long life: plenty of seafood, of course, including squid and octopus, plus lots of tofu – either plain and lightly poached, or the fiery red fermented type known as *tofuyo* (so assertively flavored that you are supposed to nibble at it using a toothpick). These are accompanied by simply steamed rice, crunchy-tart pickles and, of course, plenty of locally grown fresh vegetables and fruits, including dragon-fruit ice cream made from the fruit that grows outside the restaurant's front door. Some form of *chanpuru* is invariably on the menu, usually with the telltale smiling green slices of *goya* cucumber in the mix. Be warned, though – this is no ordinary diet food. Emi's dishes taste terrific and are beautifully presented, but one of the main reasons behind Okinawan longevity is thought to be calorific restriction – in other words, not eating too much. Here, this is tricky indeed.
61 Aza-Oganeku, Ogimi Village; open 10 AM–4 PM Wed–Mon; www.eminomise.com

Also in Okinawa

The largest collection of restaurants in Okinawa is found in its quiet, low-rise capital, Naha. Many serve *goya chanpuru*, but by far the best places to eat in town – for atmosphere at least – are the ramshackle restaurants on the first floor of the **Makishi Market**. As well as various *chanpurus*, you can make the most of the astounding selection of tropical seafood on sale in the market downstairs: point at what you fancy, and the vendors will send it upstairs to your restaurant to be cooked.

Also in Japan

Okinawan restaurants have begun to crop up in the larger cities of Japan. Tokyo has several, of which some are upmarket, but Okinawan food is somehow better eaten in the more rough-and-ready surroundings of an *izakaya*, or Japanese pub, such as **Okinawa** (*+81 3464 2576; moderate)* in the entertainment district of Shibuya. Be sure, too, to try the very special, potent Okinawan spirit *awamori*. It is distilled from rice and often sold with deadly (but dead) poisonous *habu* snakes coiled up in the bottle.

Right A gateway through the walls of the Forbidden City frames the Hall of Supreme Harmony, the ceremonial center of imperial power

Below Shredded meat from the roasted duck is wrapped in a wheat-flour pancake with green onion and cucumber

A Day in Beijing

Beijing's recent modernization hasn't quite managed to obliterate over 700 years of history – and the famous Great Wall is just an hour or so from the center of the city.

MORNING Catch a van to the **Great Wall** at Mutianyu and spend a couple of hours walking between watchtowers along this incredible structure, then head back to Beijing for a late lunch. Alternatively, start the day at the **Forbidden City**, the mighty imperial palace complex from which generations of emperors ruled China.

AFTERNOON Walk off lunch at the **Temple of Heaven Park**, admiring the splendid exterior of the temple itself, before heading to the *hutongs* for a stroll through the streets of old Beijing.

EVENING Grab a snack at **Dong'anmen Night Market** – you might want to avoid the scorpion kebabs – then decide whether to rub elbows with locals at one of the **Sanlitun** district's many bars, or settle in for a striking, if incomprehensible, performance of **Peking Opera**.

Essentials

GETTING THERE
Beijing is connected to China and the rest of the world by **air** and **rail**. Use a combination of **metro train**, **bus**, and **taxi** to negotiate the city's vast, gridlike street plan.

WHERE TO STAY
Beijing Downtown Backpackers (inexpensive) has clean, central rooms. *+86 10 8400 2429*
Bamboo Garden Hotel (moderate), down an old *hutong* alley, is full of character with a splendid landscaped garden. *www.bbgh.com.cn*
Haoyuan (moderate) is a traditionally furnished courtyard house. *www.haoyuanhotel.com*

FURTHER INFORMATION
Go to *www.cityweekend.com.cn/beijing* for English-language news and listings.

BEIJING↗

BEIJING CHINA

Peking Duck in Old Beijing

Beijing may be the capital of China, but it was founded by the Mongols under Kublai Khan. So it's hardly surprising that the city's signature dish is a marriage of foreign and native cuisine, in the same way that Beijing's palaces and maze of antique lanes reflect a Chinese refinement overlaying four centuries of alien rule, which ended with the last of the emperors in 1911.

On the surface, Beijing is a surprisingly modern metropolis, a somewhat soulless place in which individuals are dwarfed by a grid of enormously wide boulevards lined with glassy office blocks. But a far more traditional side lingers away from the main thoroughfares: the Forbidden City's mighty russet walls and endless puzzle of interlocking palaces, courtyards, and gardens, where the imperial families once lived among eunuchs and intrigue; the former homes of Manchu princes and officials, hidden among the intricate web of neighborhood alleys *(hutong)*; and the peerless symmetry of the Temple of Heaven's rotunda, where the emperors used to pray for good harvests. For their part, modern Beijingers are best observed still doing what they enjoy most, shopping in the stores or street markets and, especially, eating – in which case, you'll want to join them in sampling the one dish intimately linked to this city: Peking duck.

Preparation of this classic dish begins with the plucked, cleaned duck – a straw is inserted into the neck and the skin is gently blown away from the body. The ducks are then painted with malt extract and hung on a hook to wind-dry, then roasted in batches over a wood fire, the chefs shifting the birds constantly so that they color and cook evenly.

Eating Peking duck is a similarly staged process: a three-course study in taste and texture. First comes the skin, roasted to a translucent toffee color, crispy and succulent. The moist duck meat is then carved from the frame, to be seasoned with salty bean sauce and wrapped in elastic, paper-thin pancakes, with slivers of green onion and cucumber to add bite. Finally, a palate-cleansing bowl of velvety duck soup arrives, signaling the end of the meal.

Peking duck's origins are obscure, but as roasting only crops up in Chinese cooking where there's been outside influence, it's possibly a distant echo of Mongolian barbecues, where guests would be invited to carve their own portions off whole roasted animals. Only the Chinese taste for refinement could take such a crude cooking method and from it create a work of art.

Left Studded with towers, the mighty Great Wall winds across China

What Else to Eat

Another classic northern Chinese dish, now enjoyed country-wide, **jiaozi** are China's answer to ravioli. Nobody knows where they originated, but they've been around for a long time – a mummified bowlful was found at a Tang dynasty tomb on China's fabled Silk Road. Wheat dough wrappers stuffed with meat and cabbage and folded into a crescent shape, *jiaozi* are boiled, steamed, or fried before being tumbled into a bowl and served with a dipping sauce of your choice – try a mix of soy sauce, black vinegar, and crushed garlic. *Jiaozi* are not delicate: you order them by weight and northerners boast of how many they can put away at a single sitting. But as a hearty fuel, they are the ideal defense against Beijing's ferociously icy winters.

The Best Places to Eat Peking Duck

Quanjude moderate

Quanjude has been serving up some of the tastiest roast duck in Beijing since first opening its doors during the 1860s. It was one of the capital's first big restaurants to get back on its feet after China's stagnation during the Cultural Revolution, and by the 1980s getting a table here was a mix of luck and hand-to-hand combat, with the restaurant bursting beyond capacity every night and diners being hauled out of their chairs by waiting customers the moment it looked as though they'd finished eating. Nowadays things are far more relaxed, but make reservations or get here early if you don't want a long stint in the lobby. The decor is restaurant red-and-gold, service is flawless and efficient, and the duck – skillfully carved for you at the table – is certainly worth waiting for. Duck is what everyone orders, but the rest of the menu of northern Chinese specialties is extensive, and visiting dignitaries and tour groups are served a multi-course banquet.

14 Qianmen Xi Lu, Beijing; open 10:30 AM–8 PM daily; +86 10 6304 8987

Also in Beijing

Bianyifang *(+86 10 6711 6465; moderate)* can trace its history back to 1416, though the present business is contemporary with Quanjude. Unlike its rival, which cooks its birds over an open flame, Bianyifang slow-roasts its ducks in a closed oven which, according to partisans of this establishment, seals in a richer, juicier flavor. The restaurant lacks Quanjude's splendor, but it is comfortable enough.

Delivering a crisper, leaner duck than the average calorie-packed offering, **Da Dong** *(+86 10 8522 1234; expensive)* is emerging as one of Beijing's most talked-about contemporary restaurants. The menu is huge, the portions artistically small (except for the duck), and the cost somewhere in between.

Also in China

Hong Kong's **Dong Lai Shun** at the Royal Garden Hotel, Kowloon *(+852 2733 2020; expensive)* is the local representative of a famous Beijing restaurant chain specializing in Mongolian hotpot – a do-it-yourself meal featuring finely sliced raw lamb, a pot of boiling stock, and a host of vegetables and dipping sauces. Their Peking duck is excellent too, cooked to crisp-skinned perfection and served as the traditional three-course meal.

Around the World

Outside China, you'll want to head to Australia's finest Chinese restaurant, the **Flower Drum** in Melbourne *(+61 3 9662 3655; expensive)*. This bills itself as a Cantonese (southern Chinese) institution, but you wouldn't know it from their immaculate Peking duck – though don't expect to be able to fill up on the rather dainty portions.

YOGYAKARTA INDONESIA

Rice and Spice in Java

If the island of Java has dominated modern Indonesian history, the city of Yogyakarta has, thanks to its former sultan, spent the last 50 years at the heart of Javanese culture. To round off a day spent exploring Yogyakarta's palace area and shopping for arts and crafts, head to the night markets to indulge in a simple dish that is equally vital to Indonesian life: fried rice.

In a country where most food is fried and everyone eats rice three times a day, it's perhaps inevitable that nasi goreng – the classic Indonesian snack literally meaning "fried rice" – puts them both together. Precooked rice is stir-fried in smoking-hot oil with chili peppers, shallots, shredded chicken, and dried shrimp, and seasoned with *kecap manis* (sweet soy sauce). It's served in a neat dome on a plate, topped with strips of omelet or a fried egg, and garnished with slices of crisp cucumber and crunchy puffed shrimp wafers. Add an eye-wateringly spicy blob of chili-pepper *sambal* as a relish, and you have a meal.

Nobody knows where nasi goreng originated, but while it probably wasn't in Yogyakarta (usually shortened to "Yogya"), few other places provide a more historic setting for such an intrinsically Indonesian dish. The city – centered around the walled Kraton, the sultan's palace area at the heart of the old city – was founded in the 1750s by a disgruntled prince from the declining Mataram empire. His new kingdom endured a stormy few decades of family intrigue and colonial warfare before being pummeled into submission by the Dutch, and as Yogya's military power declined, the city became instead a cultural oasis, promoting the development of arts and crafts – especially batik work and the several forms of Javanese theater.

The Kraton is a cultural masterpiece in itself, though – oddly, given Java's ostensibly Muslim beliefs – its design reflects the region's earlier Hindu culture. The interior palace retains the most grandeur, with beautifully proportioned courtyards, pavilions, and main buildings still attended by traditionally dressed staff and sometimes hosting Javanese dance and *wayang kulit* shadow-puppet shows. The Taman Sari water palace nearby honors Loro Kidul, the seductive Goddess of the South Seas, with whom Yogya's sultans have always claimed a special relationship. For a return to earth, Jalan Malioboro – the street running north from the Kraton and originally intended as a triumphal route – now hosts Yogya's best-known tourist market, where you can buy endless quantities of local crafts. After dark, the businesses gradually close, to be replaced by food stands selling light meals and snacks – and nasi goreng assumes its rightful place, at the heart of life in the old city.

Above Though largely Muslim, Java is an island of many faiths. The serene Borobudur Temple, not far from Yogyakarta, is a relic of an earlier Buddhist kingdom

Rice – a Global Staple

Rice is a grass, first cultivated in prehistoric times along China's Yangtze valley – the Chinese still greet each other by asking, "Have you eaten rice yet?" Today rice is an essential, three-times-a-day fuel for a fifth of the world's population and is a staple throughout Asia, where brilliant green paddy fields and mountainsides terraced for rice cultivation are part of the scenery from India to China, Japan, and the Philippines, and south through Vietnam to Indonesia. Its uses are endless: after boiling, rice can be fried, roasted, stewed as a porridge, steamed inside lotus or bamboo-leaf packets, wrapped around seafood and rolled up in seaweed, fermented to produce wine, or puffed and served as breakfast cereal. Raw rice can also be pounded into flour and used for making noodles or cakes.

A Day in Yogyakarta

Yogya's Kraton and shopping alone can easily occupy a leisurely day, but you could alternatively set half the day aside for the 60-mile (100-km) round-trip to the incredible Buddhist complex at Borobudur, which predates the city by an entire millennium and was only fully restored during the 1980s.

MORNING Enter the **Kraton** area via the square where the sultan once settled public disputes and staged fights between buffaloes and tigers (the buffalo symbolized Java, while locals saw the tiger as representing the oppressive Dutch). Go on to browse artworks at the **Sono Budoyo Museum**, the **Taman Sari water palace** and the **Sultan's palace**, where Buddhist, Hindu, and Muslim motifs on the Bagsal Kencono pavilion illustrate Indonesia's complex religious relationships.

AFTERNOON After lunch, shop for Yogya's batik, silver, leatherwork, and crafts: **Jalan Malioboro** is the most obvious destination, but **Tirtodipuran Road** and **Beringharjo market** are less touristy – check quality and bargain hard.

EVENING Return to the **Kraton** for an evening stroll or take in a performance of Javanese puppetry, theater, or gamelan music.

Essentials

GETTING THERE
Yogya's **Adisucipto airport** has connections across Indonesia, plus Singapore and Malaysia. City transport includes **bus**, **taxi**, and **becak** (trishaw).

WHERE TO STAY
Rumah Boedi Pavilion (moderate) is central (near the train station), modern, and comfortable, with faux-ethnic chic furnishings. *www.rumahboedi-pavilionyogyakarta.com*
Dusun Jogja Village Inn (moderate) offers mid-range boutique comfort slightly farther from the center. *www.jvidusun.co.id*
The Phoenix (expensive) is a luxury modern revamp of a 1918 mansion. *www.mgallery.com*

FURTHER INFORMATION
Helpful information in English can be found at *www.yogyes.com*

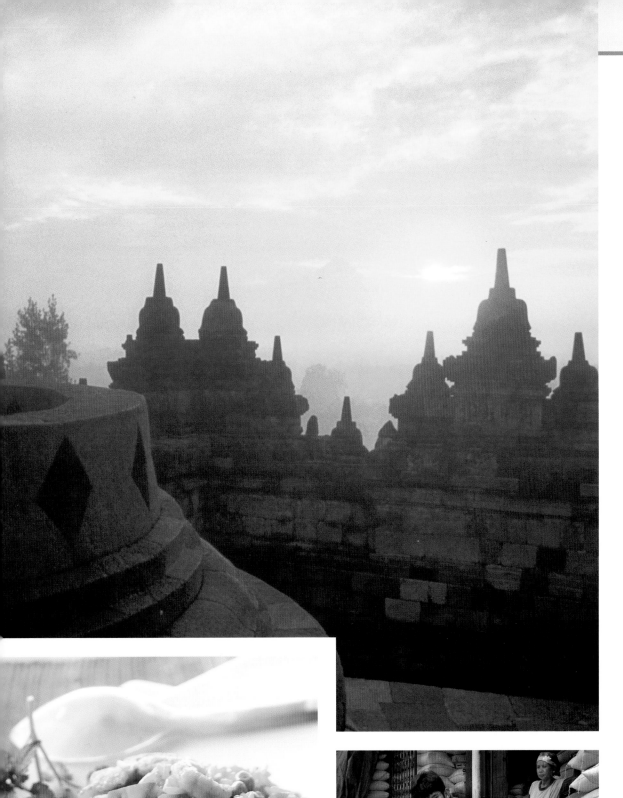

Above Turning rice at the market: the soil in this region, enriched by volcanic ash, is said to produce wonderfully aromatic grains

Left Nasi goreng knows no social barriers: Indonesians relish their national dish at street stands, in restaurants, and even at banquets

The Best Places to Eat Nasi Goreng

Jalan Malioboro Night Market
inexpensive

The best nasi goreng in Yogya is found in this wonderfully atmospheric market, where small restaurant stands give you the chance to try *lesehan* dining – sitting on bamboo mats at a low table, rubbing elbows with the locals while mouthwatering food is prepared in front of you. Aside from nasi goreng, try Yogya and Javanese specialties such as *nasi gudeg* (steamed rice with curry made from hefty, heavily scented jackfruit); tempeh (slightly sour, fermented soybean cake, usually sliced and fried); *nasi langgi* (steamed rice served on a banana leaf with a dozen spoonfuls of various curries and *sambals*); Kalasan chicken, stewed, fried, and flavored with copious garlic; and *bakpia pathok* (fried mung bean pastries, similar to Chinese mooncakes). For dessert, *cendol* is a drink of luridly colored jelly noodles in iced, sweetened coconut milk that – despite being served throughout Southeast Asia – locals insist originated in Java. Otherwise, *wedang ronde*, glutinous rice balls served in ginger syrup, is definitely a Yogya dish.

Jalan Malioboro, Kraton, Yogyakarta; open from dusk daily

Also in Yogyakarta

Also in the Kraton, **Bale Raos** *(+62 274 415 550; moderate)* serves excellent nasi goreng, though it specializes in recipes from the Yogyakartan Sultanate, some of them attributed to former rulers themselves. *Urip urip gulung* is fried catfish stewed in coconut milk flavored with ginger, *makrut* lime leaves, and lemongrass; while *sanggar* is, conversely, previously stewed beef cubes grilled on bamboo sticks like a satay.

Also in Java

In Jakarta, Java's hot, sprawling, chaotic, unwieldy capital, **Seribu Rasa** *(www. seriburasa.com; moderate)* sets the standard for mid-range restaurants serving regional Indonesian cooking, with stylish wooden decor. The menu includes several takes on nasi goreng: try *nasi sayur* (fried rice with vegetables) or fried-rice *sundah kelapa*, a seafood variation named after Jakarta's harbor area and fish market (where, incidentally, you can still see fleets of old-style wooden fishing boats pulled up at the wharf).

Around the World

BaliBali *(www.balibalirestaurant.com; moderate)* in London's West End is a relaxed, friendly place in which to try a host of Indonesian staples, including perfect nasi goreng, gado-gado (a salad with boiled eggs, tempeh, bean sprouts, and mild peanut sauce), plain Indonesian fried chicken, and spicy squid *sambal*.

Right Noise, color, and exotic smells characterize Phnom Penh's busy markets

Below Beautifully firm, translucent chunks of fish are suffused with subtle flavors in Cambodian *amok*

A Day in Phnom Penh

In addition to enjoying Khmer food, Phnom Penh is a great place to sample all things delicious and Gallic. Start the day with filtered coffee and fresh croissants or baguettes in one of the French-style eateries in and around Sisowath Quay on the Tonle Sap riverfront.

MORNING After breakfast, cross the road to the river bank and stroll down to the **Central Esplanade** in front of the glittering campus that is the **Royal Palace**. Then walk next door to the **National Museum**. This important storehouse holds artifacts and statuary from every region of Cambodia, including much from the glorious era of Angkor.

AFTERNOON Take a cyclo (bicycle rickshaw) ride to **Psar Thmei** (Central Market) – a magnificent, French Art Deco behemoth built in 1937. Head back to the **Tonle Sap** and enjoy a gentle river cruise as the sun sets behind the ocher of the city's buildings.

EVENING Finish the day with a display of classical Khmer Apsara dancing at the Bopha Penh Titanic Restaurant on **Sisowath Quay**.

Essentials

GETTING THERE
Phnom Penh International Airport is about half an hour from the center of town by **taxi**. One can navigate the city by **motorcycle taxi** (risky but fast) or by three-wheeled **"tuk-tuk."**

WHERE TO STAY
Goldiana (inexpensive) is a spotlessly clean and well-run Chinese hotel popular with visiting journalists and aid workers. *www.goldiana.com*
Villa Langka Hotel (moderate) is a stylish boutique hotel in a quiet and leafy setting. *www.villalangka.com*
Raffles Hotel Le Royal (expensive) is a glorious old French colonial hotel with real history and charm. *www.raffles.com*

TOURIST INFORMATION
www.tourismcambodia.com

PHNOM PENH CAMBODIA

Running Amok in Phnom Penh

Cambodia was once home to one of the most magnificent civilizations ever seen – the Khmer empire of Angkor, its story one of glorious conquest and savage defeat. The Cambodian dish *amok*, a coconutty fish curry cooked in banana leaves, is a reflection of the myriad influences that have swept over this small but charismatic nation: an echo of the ebb and flow of empire.

Until war and tragedy, in the shape of Pol Pot's genocidal Khmer Rouge, overtook the small kingdom of Cambodia, its modern capital, Phnom Penh, was known as the "Pearl of Asia" and was acknowledged to be one of the most elegant of all the colonial French-built cities in Indochina. Then, it was often called "sleepy" – but no longer. Phnom Penh today is frenetic with bustle. But while the beautiful but decaying French colonial architecture may be battling now with 21st-century sprawl, at the heart of the modern urban jungle still remain magnificent ocher-walled villas and wide, tree-lined boulevards, around which delicate Khmer temple and palace buildings and colorful food markets can be found.

One of the greatest pleasures of being in Phnom Penh is spending time on the riverfront. Lining the river is a series of small cafés and restaurants housed in pretty French colonial buildings. It is a great place to relax and watch people promenade – "*da leng*" as they say in Khmer – and to sample the local fare.

Cambodian cuisine shares much with its neighbor Thailand, but it's less spicy and has its own aromatic and distinctly lemony character. It is defined by two factors – rice in abundance from the fertile plains of the Tonle Sap Basin, and fish from the teeming lakes and rivers that bisect Cambodia and are its lifeblood. *Amok* – a creamy fish curry served with fragrant rice – is close to being the Cambodian national dish. Its base is coconut milk, to which are added galangal, kaffir lime, lemongrass, shallots, garlic, and chili peppers, with a touch of shrimp paste, palm sugar, and fish sauce. Egg yolk is also added, to set the sauce during steaming, and then the firm, white fish itself.

The mixture is steamed in a banana leaf "bowl," then served with a touch more coconut cream poured over the top and garnished with shredded lime leaves and a little red chili pepper. The resulting dish is both rich and sweet and also spicy, fragrant, and salty. It is not only a distillation of the subtle flavors that define Khmer cuisine; it is also, with its bright reds and greens, something of a visual feast, perfectly in tune with the lovely buildings that still grace this busy city.

What Else to Eat

Bok l'hong is a green papaya salad made with string beans, roasted peanuts, cherry tomatoes, tiny, savory crabs, and smoked fish, pounded in a mortar and pestle and flavored with chili pepper, lemon juice, and fermented fish paste. **Kralan** is a cake made from steamed rice, beans or peas, grated coconut, and coconut milk. **Loc lac** is a popular dish: cubed beef with red onions, served on a bed of salad with a dipping sauce of lemon juice and black pepper. **Pleah** is a grilled beef salad, flavored with fermented fish paste and tossed with onions and fresh herbs. Khmer meals usually feature at least one soup: **samlor machu** is a sour soup with a tamarind base and includes chicken or fish, tomatoes, lotus roots, water greens, and herbs.

Left The Silver Pagoda in the Royal Palace Garden

The Best Places to Eat Amok

Frizz Restaurant moderate

This unpretentious and airy little restaurant is in the heart of the city's boutique shopping district and not far from the Royal Palace. Many claim it serves the finest *amok* in Phnom Penh, with real care taken over both preparation and presentation. The atmosphere is cool and breezy with plenty of white soft furnishings, ocher floor tiles, and rattan furniture. In addition to *amok*, the Frizz offers a huge range of other Khmer dishes, including the hard-to-find *saik ko neung teuk kroch* – thinly sliced beef stir-fried with herbs and spices, served in an orange sauce on a bed of coleslaw. One can also order light Western food such as Mexican burritos, delicious baguette sandwiches, and healthy breakfasts. The Frizz runs a small cooking school that inspires respect from chefs both Khmer and foreign. The one-day classes come at a very reasonable price, and are fast becoming a "must-do" for foodies intrigued by the tangy mysteries of Khmer cuisine.

No. 67 Street 240, Phnom Penh; open 10 AM–10 PM daily; www.frizz-restaurant.com

Also in Phnom Penh

Khmer Kitchen *(+855 12 712 541; inexpensive)* is a traditional Cambodian restaurant offering indoor and outdoor seating beneath a grass-and-shingle roof in a wooden house set in leafy garden surroundings. If you prefer to be indoors, you can take an upstairs table and dine in comfort while reclining on silk cushions. In addition to the magnificent *amok*, the Khmer Kitchen serves numerous sour soups, including a variety with water spinach and a pleasing balance of sour tamarind with a hint of *prahok* (fermented fish paste).

Also in Cambodia

Any visit to Cambodia usually includes a visit to the spectacular ruins of Angkor Wat. When staying in the nearby town of Siem Reap, **Viroth's Restaurant**, behind La Résidence Hotel on Wat Bo Street *(www.viroth-hotel.com/restaurant.php; moderate)*, provides a perfect venue for sampling traditional Cambodian *amok* in a sleek boutique environment.

Around the World

Ties between Cambodia and France remain strong, and there is a noticeable Khmer presence in Paris. **La Mousson** *(www.lamousson.fr; moderate)* on Ave Emile Zola, in the 15th arrondissement of the city, specializes in traditional Khmer dishes, with *amok* in its original form or with scallops rather than white fish.

Above The changing of the guard at Gyeongbokgung Palace – the royal Palace of Shining Happiness – in the north of Seoul

Above Nighttime bustle in the Myeongdong shopping district

A Day in Seoul

Despite Seoul's size, the city's main sightseeing area is small enough to explore on foot. Here you'll find royal palaces, colossal markets, picturesque temples, and countless restaurants, cafés, and shops.

MORNING The majestic palace of **Gyeongbokgung** is at its best in the early morning, when its colorful wooden buildings slowly emerge from silhouette. The northern mountains provide the perfect backdrop, glowing pink and orange with the sun's first beams.

AFTERNOON Seoul is a shopper's dream. Hunt down calligraphic brushes, handmade paper, and artsy trinkets in the traditional stores of **Insadonggil Street**, or head just south to **Myeongdong** for more contemporary offerings. In between runs the gentle stream of Cheonggyecheon, whose quiet banks offer calming strolls.

EVENING It would be a shame to visit Seoul without hitting **Dongdaemun market**, parts of which are open all night. If you've not booked a banquet, you'll be able to pick up rice wine and mung-bean pancakes at the particularly photogenic Gwangjang stand area.

Essentials

GETTING THERE
Flights arrive at **Incheon International Airport**, around an hour away from the downtown by **express bus**. Seoul has an extensive **subway** network, though taxis are remarkably cheap.

WHERE TO STAY
Doulos (inexpensive) has spick-and-span rooms and is ideally located in the middle of the sightseeing area. *www.douloshotel.com*
Rakkojae (moderate) is a throwback to Joseon times, its wooden buildings set around a beautiful courtyard. *www.rkj.co.kr*
Westin Chosun (expensive) was Korea's first hotel and retains a gentle elegance, though a stylish overhaul has brought its rooms up to date. *www.westinchosun.co.kr*

FURTHER INFORMATION
http://english.visitkorea.or.kr

SEOUL SOUTH KOREA

A Royal Banquet in Seoul

In the sparkling Korean capital of Seoul, it really is possible to eat like a king – the banquets served here replicate those held for the kings of the Joseon dynasty, who ruled from the 14th to the early 20th century. These royal banquets have tables groaning under innumerable exquisite dishes, whose myriad tastes and colors nonetheless blend into a gentle Eastern harmony.

Bustling with commerce, drenched with neon, and pierced by innumerable skyscrapers, Seoul is one of the world's most absorbingly modern cities. However, it is also a place of substantial historical merit, having served as the seat of the Joseon dynasty from 1392 until its annexation by Japan in 1910. Joseon's first king, Taejo, was evidently hugely ambitious – the first few years of his rule saw the birth of two mighty palaces, a huge ancestral shrine, and a city wall studded with gargantuan gates. Amazingly, despite the passing of half a millennium, the Japanese occupation, and the devastating civil war of the 1950s, all of these sites remain, with superb restoration work bringing back their dynastic beauty.

Korea's wonderful cuisine has also emerged unscathed from troubled times, and the food of the Joseon royal court remains at the very top of the tree. Harmony is the key to these banquet-style feasts, with their near-perfect balance of color, flavor, aromas, texture, and shape. This is partly thanks to the Korean concept of *yeobaek*, which dictates that, for example,

fiery-red elements such as spicy *gimchi* or *kimchee* (preserved vegetables) are counterbalanced by bland soups and delicately seasoned roots.

Traditionally, banquets are made up of 12 main dishes, augmented by smaller side dishes known as *banchan*. Ingredients are always the finest the season can offer, culled from both land and sea. The variety is quite incredible, with offerings as diverse as buckwheat noodles, pumpkin congee, mung-bean pancakes, and pheasant-meat dumplings. Many of these dishes can be found in Korean home cooking, but two of the most visually arresting are unique to royal cuisine. The *sinsollo* is a bronze urn used at the table to make a richly aromatic meatball-and-vegetable stew, heated by charcoal embers. Most beautiful of all is the kaleidoscopically colorful *gujeolpan*, an octagonal tray of lacquered wood split into nine sections – the outer eight contain assorted roots, shoots, and marinaded leaves, to be wrapped up in paper-thin pancakes stacked in the central ninth segment. The only down-side, it seems, to feasting on royal Korean cuisine is that one must destroy what is effectively a work of art.

What Else to Eat

Royal court food represents the refined epitome of Korean cuisine, but at the other end of the scale – and much-beloved of local students – are homey restaurants, usually decked out with East Asian bric-a-brac, serving cheap but filling traditional dishes. Most popular are **jeon**, savory pancakes made from corn, mung beans, or even potatoes; the fillings are equally diverse, with sesame leaves and seafood being particularly common choices. One other item found on the menu at such places is **dubu-gimchi**, a delicious mix of hot *gimchi* and soft tofu. However, many are not here for the food, for these restaurants also serve milky rice wines known as **makkeolli** and **dongdongju**. Be warned – these taste deceptively weak and many a visitor has been known to "hit the wall" after a night on this uniquely Korean hooch.

Above The colorful *gujeolpan* often forms the centerpiece of a Korean royal banquet

The Best Places for Korean Royal Cuisine

Goongyeon expensive

This deceptively homey restaurant is Korea's only remaining link to the royal court cuisine of old. Its founder, Hwang Hye-seong, learned her trade from one of the last royal chefs of the Joseon dynasty, absorbing the ancient secrets over the course of several decades. These have now been passed on to her daughter Han Bong-nyeo; like her illustrious mother, Han has been designated an official national treasure. After taking your seat, you'll soon find the table blanketed with dishes, almost creaking under the weight of more than 30 individually prepared creations. You'll literally be eating like a king in almost every sense, since both the way in which the meal is laid out and the ingredients in the dishes are as close as possible to what Joseon royalty would have been presented with each evening. Celadon bowls, bronze chopsticks, and lacquered wooden trays heighten the air of authenticity, while floor-to-ceiling windows offer views of the pine-studded garden outside.

170–3 Gaheodong, Seoul; open noon–3 PM & 5:30–9 PM; www.goongyeon.com

Also in Seoul

Set within a clutch of traditional wooden buildings on Pildong Iga, **Korea House** (*www.koreahouse.or.kr; expensive*) serves up mammoth royal banquets – not quite scaling the heights of the cuisine in Goongyeon, but first-time visitors will scarcely be able to tell the difference. For a small extra fee you'll be able to watch colorful performances of traditional folk songs and dancing, which take place after the meal in an on-site theater. Attendants clad in silken *hanbok* – traditional Korean clothing – contribute further to the courtly air, while just north of the restaurant you'll find Namsangol, a small, re-created Joseon village.

Restaurants serving *yangbansik* – meals served to aristocrats during Joseon times – are cheaper and more numerous than those serving royal cuisine. One recommendation is **Doore** (*www.edoore.co.kr; moderate*), which serves what are essentially smaller versions of the royal feasts in a pleasantly rustic courtyard setting on Insadonggil, a street of tea shops, galleries, and craft workshops popular with visitors (*see* A Day in Seoul, *facing page*).

Yangbansik was essentially a derivation of royal court food, which was itself a take on Korea's traditional Buddhist temple food. Restaurants serving this meat-free cuisine can also be found around Seoul, the best being **Baru** (*www.baru.or.kr; expensive*), a pine-lined fifth-floor venue on Gyeonjidong in which to enjoy a delectable vegetable banquet overlooking Jogyesa, a major Buddhist temple.

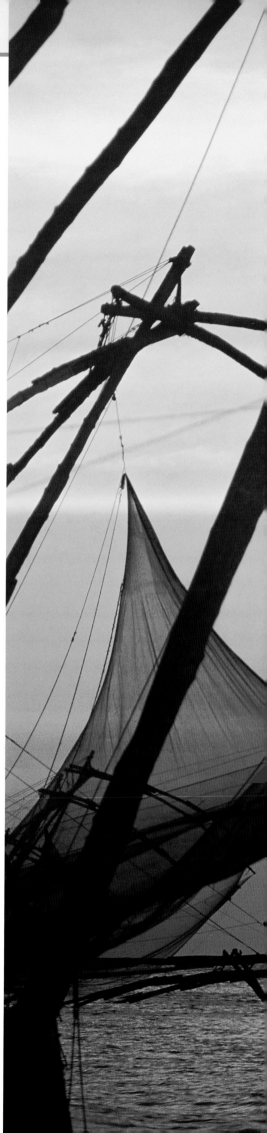

KERALA INDIA

Keralan Coconut Fish Curry

Hugging the tropical Malabar Coast in the southwest of the Indian peninsula, Kerala has a growing reputation as a destination for holistic vacations that include meditation courses or Ayurvedic treatments. Everyone relaxes under the swaying coconut palms, and the fruits of these ubiquitous trees deliver the creamy flesh and milk that are essential to *meen moilee*, a delicious fish curry.

Kerala has always relied on fishing, agriculture, and, above all, trade. There is evidence of the Sumerians and Phoenicians trading cotton, teak, sandalwood, and spices from the Malabar Coast as far back as 3000 BC, when trade ships fueled by the monsoon winds carried goods to Arabia, and overland caravans ferried those most highly prized westward toward the Mediterranean and Europe. Merchants continued to ply their trade through the 1st century, when St. Thomas arrived in Kerala and introduced Christianity to India, through centuries of Muslim and European domination, reaching new heights of freedom with Indian independence in 1947.

Trade has continued to flourish, but in Kerala it is now augmented by a booming tourist industry. The laid-back, ethnically Dravidian locals have a paradoxical reputation for maintaining a traditional lifestyle while espousing progressive political values – in 1957 they voted in the first democratically elected communist state government in the world. They prize education: this scenically alluring land of brilliant green rice paddies, shady palms, golden beaches, serene waterways, and the fertile Western Ghat mountains is home to a population with the highest literacy rate and most equitable division of wealth in the subcontinent. And it runs across religious divides: the bare-chested Brahmin priest you see entering one of the majestic Hindu temples is likely to be a card-carrying member of the same leftist party as a local Muslim fisherman or Christian farmer.

However, it is tradition, not modernity, that holds sway in Kerala's cuisine, and with fishing communities running the entire length of the coast, fish and seafood naturally play a huge role in local recipes. Combine this with the preponderance of coconuts and spices, and it's not surprising that a creamy coconut fish curry, *meen moilee*, is one of the state's signature dishes.

Any number of fish that inhabit the warm waters of the Arabian Sea can be used as the base, though the most common are kingfish, pomfret, and, best of all, full-flavored sear fish. The fish is added along with the coconut milk to a mixture of fried onions, garlic, chili peppers, ginger, turmeric, and cumin, then simmered until more coconut milk and chopped tomato is added, before a final garnish of tomato and fresh herbs. There is something wonderful about eating this exotic dish at a beachside restaurant looking out over the sea, where countless old wooden sailing ships once carried the spices you're tasting to other distant lands.

Three Days in Kerala

Even Kerala's state capital, Trivandrum, is laid-back by Indian standards, but it is the beaches, backwaters, rural retreats, and colonial splendor of Kochi (Cochin) that have far more appeal to most visitors.

DAY ONE After a filling breakfast of *dosas* (crispy pancakes) or *idlis* (steamed rice cakes), leave **Trivandrum** on an early morning bus or train for **Varkala**, where you can relax down on the golden sands or at one of the beachside cafés and restaurants.

DAY TWO Travel to **Kollam** in time to take a day-long backwater cruise, passing through peaceful lagoons where fishermen ply their trade. In the early evening you'll arrive in **Allapuzha**. You can stop en route at the fascinating ashram of the "living saint" **Mata Amritanandamayi**, or "Amma" ("Mother"), if you extend your tour by a day.

DAY THREE Take an early bus to **Ernakulam** and then a ferry across the harbor to atmospheric **Kochi**, where highlights include the much-photographed sail-like Chinese fishing nets, **Matancherry Palace**, and the **Pardesi Synagogue**.

Essentials

GETTING THERE
Beenapalli (in Trivandrum) and Kochi **airports** are international. Both towns are also hubs for **rail** and **road** connections.

WHERE TO STAY
Johnson's The Nest (inexpensive) in Alleppey is very friendly. *www.johnsonskerala.com*
Walton's Homestay (moderate) in Fort Cochin is a beautifully renovated Dutch mansion with a lovely garden. *www.waltonshomestay.com*
Villa Jacaranda (expensive) in Varkala is a boutique guesthouse. *www.villa-jacaranda.biz*

TOURIST INFORMATION
www.keralatourism.org

Above Awaiting a water-taxi in the Kerala backwaters, a series of connected lakes, rivers, and canals that runs half the length of the state

Left The graceful, counterweighted "Chinese" fishing nets of Kochi are raised and lowered into the water from the shore

Below Colorful *meen moilee* combines a taste of Kerala's renowned ocean fish with locally grown coconuts, tomatoes, and spices

Below left Chicken biryani **Below** The floating vegetable market on Dal Lake in Srinagar, Kashmir, is the only one of its kind in India **Right (top to bottom)** Sunset over a beachside restaurant in Goa; the fiery curry of vindaloo, developed in Goa, is a vinegar-and-chili-pepper-based meat dish; the Gariahat Fish Market in Kolkata is several decades old and the largest in the city

Curries Across the Subcontinent

From the majestic Himalayas in the north and the deserts and jungles of the center to the tropical southern coastline, each Indian region produces a range of delicious, distinctive dishes.

KERALA

Paragon inexpensive

Kannur Road, Kozhikode; www.paragonrestaurant.net

This is one of the oldest and most highly rated places to sample authentic Malabari cuisine, such as *meen moilee* (fish in coconut milk) or fish-and-mango curry.

Arca Nova moderate

Fort House Hotel, 2/6A Calvathy Road, Kochi; +91 484 221 7103

This hotel's peaceful candlelit jetty is a very romantic spot to enjoy *meen moilee* and other Keralan seafood specialties or more simple grilled fish steaks.

Costa Malabari moderate

Thottada, south of Kannur; +91 484 237 1761

This trio of homestay bungalows, just behind an idyllic strip of coast, can rustle up a mean *meen moilee*, as well as other home-style Keralan recipes.

KASHMIR

The idyllically situated Kashmir Valley, hemmed in by towering Himalayan ranges, has a predominantly Muslim population whose heavily meat-based cuisine, known as *wazwan*, includes the worldwide favorite *rogan josh* – meat in a richly spiced tomato sauce.

Juniper Hotel inexpensive

Lal Chowk, Srinagar; +91 194 247 1031

This popular restaurant is well known for its fine Kashmiri dishes, including *rogan josh* and *syun kaliya*, lamb curry with a yogurt and turmeric base.

Mughal Darbar moderate

Residency Road, Srinagar; www.mughal-darbar.com

This elegantly decorated restaurant within the hotel of the same name is a great place to sample authentic Kashmiri *wazwan* cuisine; it's a favorite with locals and visitors alike.

Pahalgam Hotel moderate

Main Bazaar, Pahalgam; www.pahalgamhotel.com

The restaurant at this smart alpine-style hotel is suitably lavish and serves up quality *wazwan* dishes such as *rogan josh*, as well as fresh trout from the adjacent Lidder River.

On the Menu

Bhel puri Popular form of *chaat (see pp192–3)*, made with *puri*, puffed rice, chopped onions and tomatoes, cilantro leaves, lime, and various spices.

Biryani Basmati rice cooked with meat, chicken, or vegetables and a seasoning of garlic, cardamom, cinnamon, turmeric, bay leaves, ginger, and sometimes cloves.

Chaat Street snacks, usually based on crispy fried *puri*.

Dosa Rice-flour and lentil pancake.

Garam masala Combination of spices such as ginger, turmeric, cloves, cumin, cardamom, and star anise; varies by region.

Gatta curry Gram-flour dumplings cooked in a yogurt and tomato gravy with garam masala, coriander, chili pepper, turmeric, and fennel.

Gram flour Chickpea flour.

Idli A circular steamed white patty made of ground rice and lentils.

Masala dosa The most popular south Indian pancake, stuffed with *sabji* and served with *sambar* and coconut chutney.

Pakora Vegetable fritters.

Paneer Unsalted white cheese.

Prawn malai curry A Bengali dish of shrimp cooked in a sauce of yogurt, cumin, chili peppers, coriander, turmeric, and ground coconut.

Puri Puffed flatbread, usually fried.

Rasam Very thin, yellow, lentil-based sauce, usually including tamarind.

Rogan josh Meat cooked in a rich tomato sauce with garlic, turmeric, coriander, cumin, chili pepper, and garam masala.

Sabji A dry vegetable curry, usually made with potato and onions and seasoned with garlic, turmeric, and chili pepper.

Sambar Spicy sauce with a tomato and lentil base that accompanies many south Indian dishes.

Samosa Triangular fried pastry snack; in India, usually filled with vegetables.

Tandoori Food cooked in a clay oven with a spicy yogurt marinade, tinted red by cayenne or chili pepper.

Thali South Indian rice plate with a set of accompanying vegetable curry dishes and sauces *(see pp210–11)*.

Tikka Lightly seasoned barbecued meat, often chicken.

Vada Small doughnut-shaped savory fritter, made from lentil and gram flours.

Vindaloo Meat cooked in a hot sauce of chili pepper, vinegar, cloves, cardamom, cinnamon, peppercorns, turmeric, coriander, and ginger. Potatoes are a Western addition.

KOLKATA

Formerly known as Calcutta, the humid capital of West Bengal is famed for its intellectual prowess. Bengali cuisine is spicy and aromatic, featuring many fish and seafood recipes, such as shrimp *malai* ("with coconut") curry.

Bhojohori Manna inexpensive
18/1A Hindustan Road; www.bhojohorimanna.com
The original branch of a small citywide chain churns out delicious Bengali fish and shrimp favorites as well as some tandoori dishes.

Kewpie's Kitchen moderate
2 Elgin Lane; +91 33 2475 9880
The best Bengali cuisine you can get aside from home-cooking, perhaps because the restaurant is the annex to a private home. As well as *malai* curry, you can get *malai chingri*, shrimp in cream.

6 Ballygunge Place expensive
6 Ballygunge Place; +91 33 2460 3922
Catering to the wealthier sector of Kolkata society, this classy restaurant places as much emphasis on its ambience and decor as on the freshly prepared seafood, including fish wrapped in banana leaf.

GOA

Goa is a former Portuguese colony, and the Christian culinary influence is evident in the presence of pork and wine, both rare in India. Fiery vindaloo, derived from the Portuguese *carne de vinha d'Alhos* (a wine-marinated pork dish) may contain both.

Cafe Xavier inexpensive
141 Municipal Market, Mapusa; +91 832 226 2229
This is an ideal place for a vindaloo, amid Goa's biggest market. You can also sample *xacuti*, meat or fish cooked in another fiery sauce of lemon juice, coconut milk, nuts, and red chili peppers.

George Restaurant & Bar inexpensive
Church Square, Panaji; +91 944 405 3656
A favorite local hangout that serves authentic Goan-Catholic cuisine, including vindaloo, kingfish curry, and shrimp-stuffed *papad* (poppadoms).

Ordo Sounsar moderate
North end of beach, Palolem; www.ordosounsar.com
This is a top beach-resort restaurant for sampling real Goan food, not dumbed-down for the Western palate. Try vindaloo-hot shrimp *balchao*, in chili pepper sauce, or shark *ambotik*, a hot-and-sour preparation.

HYDERABAD

Hyderabad is south India's most Islamic city but also the capital of overwhelmingly Hindu Andhra Pradesh. These two influences have combined to produce the biryani, a risotto-style dish of rice with vegetables or meat.

Paradise Persis inexpensive
Mahatma Gandhi Road, Secunderabad; www.paradisefoodcourt.com
This very popular spot in the thick of Hyderabad's twin city cooks delicious biryanis and other west Asian delights, such as mutton kebabs.

Hotel Shadab moderate
Madina Circle, Patthargatti; +91 40 2456 1648
A highly rated biryani joint situated between the river and the heart of the Muslim Old City, this has added fish and meat tandoori dishes to its menu and has an air-conditioned dining hall.

Firdaus expensive
Taj Krishna Hotel, Banjara Hills; +91 40 6666 2323
Biryanis are just one among many exquisite Indian dishes that you can feast upon in the chandelier-lit opulence of this luxury-class hotel restaurant.

RAJASTHAN

The colorful state of Rajasthan is a tapestry of desert, arable land, and imposing forts and palaces. The arid environment and roving lifestyle of the Rajputs (wealthy landowners) led to the development of a cuisine light on vegetables, such as *gatta* (dumpling) curry.

Monica inexpensive
First Fort Gate, Jaisalmer
Right by the entrance to the Arabian Nights-style fort, this modest but extremely popular restaurant serves a variety of Rajasthani dishes, including *gatta* curry and *thalis* (see pp208–9), as well as tandoori.

Chokhi Dhani moderate
Tonk Road, near Jaipur; www.chokhidhani.com
Dining in this theme-park-style restaurant complex is a unique experience; try the filling Rajasthani *thali* that includes *gatta* curry.

Marwar expensive
Taj Hari Mahal Hotel, Jodhpur; +91 291 243 9700
This is a fine place to treat yourself to luxurious surroundings and the traditional Marwari cuisine of Rajasthan, including *gatta di subzi*, a vegetable and dumpling combination, and *mas*, a spicy mutton dish.

Right Hosier Lane is one of Melbourne's many "laneways"; it is well known for its street art

Below Simple Pan-Asian fusion: trout steamed in banana leaf and lemongrass with wild and sticky rice

A Day in Melbourne

The flavor of Melbourne is best experienced by sampling a mixture of the city and some of its inner-city suburban neighborhoods: St. Kilda for beaches and glamorized grit; Fitzroy for eclectic urban cool; and the CBD (Central Business District) for its chic dining and bar scene.

MORNING Start in **St. Kilda** with breakfast on the deck of the **St. Kilda Sea Baths**. Walk the historic **pier** or drop into **Luna Park** before taking in the buzz of the **Acland Street Precinct**, famous for its continental cake shops and vintage clothing stores.

AFTERNOON Take a tram to **Gertrude Street, Fitzroy**, to experience Melbourne's hipster scene. There's kitsch housewares, intelligent fashion, alluring wine bars, and great contemporary art spaces.

EVENING Grab a tram or taxi back to the city bustle and **Federation Square** for a water-view apéritif at **Riverland Bar**. The rest of the night is for Pan-Asian drinks and nibbles: try hawker-style food at **Gingerboy** or a lychee martini at **Longrain**.

Essentials

GETTING THERE
Tullamarine Airport is 14 miles (23 km) from downtown Melbourne, which can be reached by **shuttle bus** (SkyBus) or **taxi**.

WHERE TO STAY
Bishopsgate B&B (inexpensive) offers good beachside accommodations in quaint St. Kilda. *www.bishopsgate.com.au*
Hotel Causeway (moderate) is a centrally located hotel in one of Melbourne's historic shopping arcades. *www.hotelcauseway.com.au*
The Olsen Hotel (expensive) is contemporary luxe with an artistic bent. It offers rooms, suites, and "residential suites" with kitchenettes. *www.artserieshotels.com.au/Olsen*

TOURIST INFORMATION
www.melbourneaustralia.org

MELBOURNE AUSTRALIA

Pan-Asian Delights in Melbourne

The fashion pack struts graffiti-adorned "laneways" to enter chic bolt-hole boutiques, while office workers clink glasses at riverside bars and sports fans cheer at Melbourne Cricket Ground. By nightfall, this city of many incarnations is united by a universal passion for food – and a love of Pan-Asian cuisine that owes directly to Melbourne's embrace of its vibrant immigrant culture.

Founded on the Yarra River in 1835, Melbourne's early development was defined by the gold rush: discovery of the precious nugget brought limitless riches and unprecedented development to the city's bluestone-paved streets. Before long, this resulted in an animated multicultural mix, as Chinese migrants joined wealth-seekers from as far away as Europe and North America, all packing their gastronomic heritage along with their dreams.

Today this legacy can be seen in vivid Pan-Asian cuisine, which blends Southeast Asian spice with modern cooking techniques to arrive at a culinary crossroads representative of the city itself. Part-artist, part-sports-fan, part-style-seeker, Melbourne is as layered as a Pan-Asian spice mix: the fire of chili pepper echoes in an electrifying night scene where unmarked doorways lead to dramatic rooftop cocktail bars; the piquancy of lemongrass bristles in the kitsch style of edgy Gertrude and Brunswick Streets; the sweet nuttiness of coconut hovers in the eclectic galleries.

But if the contemporary nerve center of the city lies in the challenging architectural style of Federation Square, the birth of Pan-Asian cuisine can be found a few blocks over in the historic stretch of Little Bourke Street's Chinatown. The second-longest continuous Chinese settlement in the Western world, it is from here that those once-challenging flavors were disseminated, scattering into Melbourne's modern culinary lexicon. Finding inspiration in the steaming dumplings, spicy soups, and textural curries of China and its Southeast Asian neighbors, today's chefs have respectfully turned tradition on its head to create a flavor canon as adventurous as those first émigrés. Within the industrial-chic space of South Melbourne's St. Ali, slow-roasted pork belly pairs with sweet fish sauce, *pat chun*, star anise, and jellyfish salad, while the greenhouse-style dining room of Verge serves barramundi with Chinese celery and smoked beets. But even among such bold, boundary-pushing flavors and the big-ticket cultural and sporting events, Melbourne and its exotic palate provide space for the subtleties – for laneways and lemongrass.

Food Shopping in Melbourne

The gastronomic tourist trail for gourmet junkies will lead you from one end of Melbourne to the other. **Victoria Street**, Richmond, is a short tram ride and a world away from the Central Business District (CBD). Home to an enormous array of Southeast Asian grocers and restaurants, it is a hub for exotic fruits, Peking duck, and cheap-but-good Thai and Vietnamese food. The **Queen Victoria** and **South Melbourne Markets** are the city's top open-air food markets, the latter being home to the best steamed dim sum in Melbourne. Not to be missed, the **Abbotsford Convent's Slow Food Farmer's Market** brings together stunning fresh produce and artisanal food producers in the beautifully scenic grounds of a former Catholic convent.

Left The many restaurants and bars of Federation Square, on the banks of the Yarra River, have made it a favorite meeting place

The Best Places to Eat Pan-Asian Food

Ezard expensive

Housed in the chic basement of Melbourne's *über*-hip Adelphi Hotel, Ezard has been setting the pace with its fabulously unobtrusive approach to experimental, Asian-inspired fine dining for more than a decade. The highly successful and well-regarded chef behind the plates, Teage Ezard, calls it "Australian freestyle" dining, but others simply call it unforgettable. Exhilarating dishes will test a diner's limits and still leave them wanting more: from the old Ezard favorites of Japanese-inspired oyster shooters and masterly stock-fried pork hock to seasonal treats such as Chinese-style roast duck with *shaosang* wine dressing, shiitake mushrooms, and steamed rice noodle roll. Ezard's success lies in combining the finest produce with an inherent talent for knowing when to shout and when to whisper. Dishes will stomp across your palate one moment (think five-spiced Bangalow sweet pork belly with yellow bean and peanut dressing) and tiptoe the next (perhaps steamed crab wonton dumplings with young coconut, mango, and crispy shallots). The bill may leave you gasping, but such sorcery will never come cheap.

187 Flinders Lane, Melbourne, Victoria; open noon–3 PM Mon–Fri, 6–10:30 PM Mon–Sat; www.ezard.com.au

Also in Melbourne

Experience Pan-Asian cuisine at its best with the winning trifecta of **Coda Bar and Restaurant** *(www.codarestaurant.com.au; moderate)*, the hawker-style cuisine of **Gingerboy** *(www.gingerboy.com.au; moderate)*, and the upmarket cocktail atmosphere of **Longrain** *(www.longrain.com.au; expensive)*. Or try a more traditional (and cheaper) option at the **Supper Inn** *(+61 3 9663 4759; inexpensive)* on Chinatown's Little Bourke Street.

Also in Australia

In Sydney, internationally lauded chef Tetsuya Wakuda marries the Japanese philosophy of natural and seasonal flavors with French technique at his restaurant, **Tetsuya's** *(www.tetsuyas.com; expensive)*, to riotous acclaim. For a beachside view try **Bistro C** *(www.bistroc.com.au; moderate)* in the vacation town of Noosa, Queensland.

Around the World

San Francisco is home to an enormous Asian community and is renowned for its stellar Pan-Asian cuisine. Enjoy Asian fusion (and amazing mojitos made with rice liquor) at **Lüx** *(415-567-2998; expensive)*, or – for a left-of-center dining experience – try the Chinese-style savory buns from the mobile **Chairman Bao Bun Truck** *(twitter: @chairmantruck; inexpensive)*.

OSAKA JAPAN

Okonomiyaki in Osaka

Osaka became a wealthy food-trading center in the 16th century, and has been famously serious about its food ever since. The third-largest city in Japan, it's also famously fast-paced, so it's not surprising that its inhabitants have become fast-food aficionados. Of all the city's superb snacklike creations, *okonomiyaki* is the favorite choice for food on the run.

Though it's not such an obvious choice for tourists as Tokyo, and not even the locals would ever claim it was pretty, Osaka is a dynamic, characterful city whose inhabitants are famed throughout the country for their sense of humor, their slightly contrary nature, and their gluttony (the local dialect even has a word for this: *kuidaore*, which means "eat till you bust").

Although Osaka doesn't tend to feature on tourist itineraries – it is rather overshadowed in this part of Japan by Kyoto and Nara – the city has put some effort into developing a few tourist attractions. It has Osaka-jo castle, a mostly re-created 16th-century residence, and a magnificent aquarium – which has one of the very few whale sharks in captivity in the world – as well as several excellent museums and the gigantic Universal Studios Japan fun park. The shopping is especially epic, with massive malls and the longest *shotengai* (covered shopping arcade) in Japan. More interestingly, in recent years travelers from around the world have slowly come to realize that thanks to the locals' famously insatiable appetites

and ceaseless curiosity about new things, Osakan cuisine is more open to innovation and foreign influence than other Japanese regional foods. As a result, this city has a great deal to offer foodies, particularly in the realm of fast food. This is the city that invented conveyor-belt sushi and instant noodles (both in 1958, curiously), but today Osaka's claim to fame lies in a triumvirate of unique fast foods: *tako yaki*, *kushikatsu (see box, below left)*, and, most famously of all, *okonomiyaki*.

Literally meaning "make it how you like," *okonomiyaki* usually features shredded cabbage, green onion, and pork (or shrimp or squid), all mixed together with a batter made from flour, *dashi* (stock), eggs, and, crucially for that chewy moistness, grated yam. This is then poured onto a hotplate where it is fried, flipped, fried some more, slathered with thick, dark, tangy-sweet sauce, and sprinkled with various toppings, including *kimchi* (Korean pickled vegetables), nori, Japanese mayonnaise, and *katsuobushi* (dried bonito flakes), before being cut into slices and devoured. It's a sociable dish, popular date food, and the definitive "must-have" in Osaka.

Above In 1583, the founder of Osaka, Toyotomi Hideyoshi, built the original Osaka-jo castle on the site of the Ishiyama Honganji Temple, to act as the center of a new, unified Japan

What Else to Eat

Along with *okonomiyaki* and instant noodles, Osaka has given the world other great fast foods. **Kushikatsu** are breaded, deep-fried skewers of vegetables, seafood, and meat dipped in yet another addictive, meaty-sugary, ebony-colored sauce. **Tako yaki** are chunks of octopus cooked in a doughnut-like batter, slathered with brown sauce and *katsuobushi* flakes – classic Osakan street food. But perhaps the perfect symbol of the famed impatience of Osakans is *kaiten* or **"conveyor-belt" sushi**, which was invented in the city in the 1950s. Though the quality at a *kaiten* place is no match for a "proper" sushi restaurant, it does meet the average Osakan's main criterion for a meal – speed of delivery. In fact, it is said that the conveyor belts are set to move faster in Osaka than they do in Tokyo.

A Day in Osaka

Osaka is the capital of Osaka Prefecture, and its busy beating heart. You're as likely to come across fascinating sights and food while wandering the city as you are when visiting tourist sites, so don't underestimate the value of a walking tour.

MORNING If you can make the 5 AM start, the **Osaka Municipal Wholesale Market** is legendary, and rivals Tokyo's Tsukiji for diversity and quality. Breakfast on a hearty bowl of *oden* (a kind of Japanese stew) upstairs in the cafeterias, then spend the rest of the morning at the **Osaka Aquarium**. Have lunch on the run, perhaps freshly cooked *tako yaki* from a stand on **Dotonbori**, the famous food street where (unusually for Japan) sidewalk snacking is positively encouraged.

AFTERNOON Hit the shops of **Minami** (Osaka is divided into two main neighborhoods: Kita in the north, with the main station; and Minami in the south). Walk Japan's longest covered shopping street, the 1½-mile- (2.5-km-) long **Tenjinbashi-suji** arcade, or opt for the more upmarket **Shinsaibashi**.

EVENING Return to **Dotonbori**, the life and soul of Osaka's 24/7 food party, which blazes with neon. Look for the giant crab – and eat *okonomiyaki*, of course.

Essentials

GETTING THERE
Osaka's **Kansai International Airport** is one of Japan's largest. The city has an extensive **subway** network as well as **trams** and **buses**.

WHERE TO STAY
The Dotonbori Hotel (inexpensive) offers large, modern rooms in the center of Dotonbori. *www.dotonbori-h.co.jp*
Dojima Hotel (moderate) is an uber-cool boutique hotel conveniently located between Kita and Minami. *www.dojima-hotel.com*
Imperial Hotel Osaka (expensive) is the sister hotel to the equally grand Imperial in Tokyo. Features include its own golf driving range. *www.imperialhotel.co.jp*

TOURIST INFORMATION
www.jnto.go.jp/eng

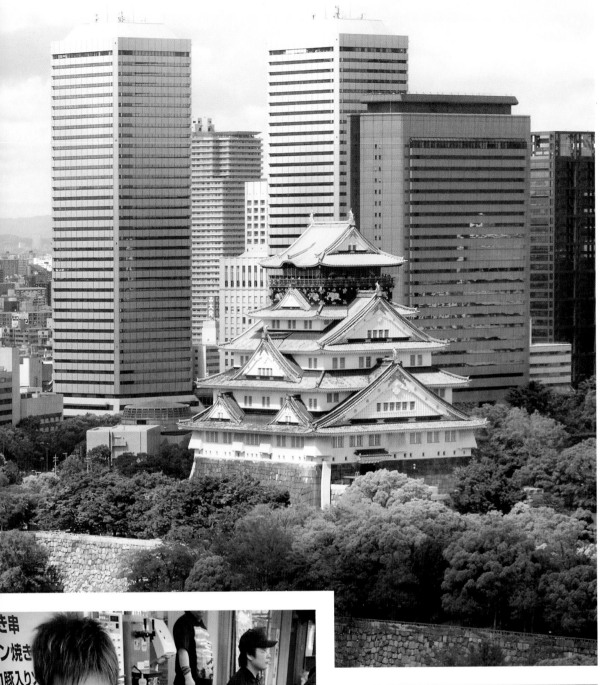

The Best Places to Eat Okonomiyaki

Dotonbori Street inexpensive

The search for fantastic *okonomiyaki* pulls everyone, inevitably, back to the Vegas-on-the-cheap glitz of Dotonbori – because this ceaselessly busy restaurant strip is its spiritual home. You'll find many of Osaka's 4,000 or so *okonomiyaki* restaurants here, most of them featuring a bewildering array of plastic models of *okonomiyaki* in their window to help you choose your variety of topping. In most places you'll be given a bowl of batter and some ingredients so you can make up your own mix. You then pour it on to a hotplate built into your table, flip the resulting thick disk with a metal spatula when one side is cooked, and finally divide it into pizza-style slices with the same spatula (the serving staff are usually happy to help *okonomiyaki* novices, of course). Brush with sauce, squirt with Japanese mayo, and sprinkle with nori, *katsuobushi*, *kimchi*, or whatever takes your fancy.

Dotonbori, Osaka; some restaurants open 24/7

Also in Osaka

For a more refined take on the meal-in-one miracle that is *okonomiyaki*, head for the rather more dressy **President Chibo** *(+81 6 6212 2211; moderate)*, also on Dotonbori. This five-floor temple to *okonomiyaki* opened in 1967 with the aim of taking the dish upmarket – hence the low lighting, marble counters, and chefs dressed in the French style. The *okonomiyaki* here are superlative, but purists might argue that having a chef cook them for you with tinkly music and attentive waiters is rather like having a *haute cuisine* hot dog.

Also in Japan

Both Tokyo and Hiroshima claim to have devised the ultimate incarnation of *okonomiyaki*. On **Monja Street** *(inexpensive)* in Tokyo's Tsukishima district you can try the local version, called *monjayaki*, which has the same basic ingredients as the Osakan version but is much runnier and doesn't shape up into quite such a pleasing patty. In Hiroshima, rather than mixing everything together, they prefer to layer their ingredients, sometimes adding *natto* (fermented soybean) or, more happily, a delicious, plump Hiroshima oyster. Try it in **Okonomi Village** *(inexpensive)*, a futuristic building with three floors of *Hiroshima-yaki* (rather than *okonomi-yaki*) eateries.

Above *Okonomiyaki* has been described as a Japanese pancake, omelet, or tortilla – it's a complete meal in a handy carry-out package

Left A cook at a food stand on Dotonbori demonstrates speed and skill, frying and flipping *okonomiyaki* to perfection

Above A reclining Buddha in the eccentric Buddha Park, constructed entirely from concrete by a Laotian mystic in the 1950s

A Day in Vientiane

One of the wonderful things about Vientiane is that the sights can be covered in one day: a pleasure best punctuated along the way with stops for a cup of fresh filtered Lao coffee or a glass of Lao beer.

MORNING Start with the **Ho Phra Kaew Art Museum**, a temple originally built to house the celebrated Emerald Buddha, later appropriated by Siam in 1779. Today it is a museum containing religious art. Then take in **Wat Phra That Luang**: this giant, golden Buddhist stupa is a defining symbol of Vientiane.

AFTERNOON The **National Museum**, in a rambling old colonial structure, is a fascinating collection of artifacts from various eras of Lao history. Then take a taxi 15 miles (24 km) along the river to the **Buddha Park**, a fanciful sculpture garden full of Hindu and Buddhist statuary.

EVENING Sunset over the Mekong is a show in itself. Back in town, if you're not heading for Nang Khambang for dinner, there are many traditional restaurants lining the river to the west of the main **riverfront promenade**. One of the best is Sala Khoun Ta.

Essentials

GETTING THERE
Wattay International Airport is a short **taxi** ride from the center of town. Alternatively, one can cross the **Mekong** from Thailand. Visa on arrival is available whichever route you choose.

WHERE TO STAY
Mali Namphu Guest House (inexpensive) is an atmospheric ocher-walled building constructed around a shaded courtyard. www.malinamphu.com
Hotel Khamvongsa (moderate) is brand-new and is situated in a converted French villa near the river. www.hotelkhamvongsa.com
Settha Palace Hotel (expensive) is a renovated French colonial masterpiece with great charm and excellent dining. www.setthapalace.com

TOURIST INFORMATION
www.tourismlaos.org

Above Dozens of small, unpretentious restaurants and food stands hung with lanterns line the banks of the Mekong at night

VIENTIANE LAOS

Laap in Leisurely Laos

Often dubbed the most laid-back nation in Asia, Laos is a country where people live by a very natural rhythm. Vientiane may be its capital city, but it remains as much a series of villages as a true metropolis. Lao cuisine shares much with that of Isan across the Mekong in northeastern Thailand, with a sharp and tangy palette of flavors typified by the dish known as *laap*.

While other Southeast Asian capitals have surged into the 21st century with swift economic development, mushrooming skyscrapers, jammed traffic, cluttered highways, and ever-spreading urban sprawl, Vientiane has set itself on a far more sedate path. Its leisurely spread along the northern shores of the Mekong River is still one mostly characterized by sparsely trafficked boulevards and quiet alleys.

The real name for the city is Wieng Chan – "City of Sandalwood." It has endured a torrid history over the last two centuries, being overrun by both Burmese and Chinese marauders. In 1828 it was comprehensively sacked by the Thais, leaving temples smashed and broken, streets empty, and Lao nationhood in tatters. The country rose again as a French protectorate toward the end of the 19th century, and it is their colonial-style buildings, together with magnificent Buddhist stupas and pagodas, that give the city its character, along with the slumberous movement of the mighty Mekong River that runs through it. The streets in the Chanthabuli district in the center of the city stretch back from the

Mekong, intersected by the main boulevards of Samsenthai Road and Setthathirat Road. This is the heart of the city and the place to wander, linger, and eat.

Lao cuisine, like that of neighboring Isan in Thailand – whose inhabitants are ethnically the same people – is defined by fragrant fresh herbs, citrus, and pungent fish sauce, and *laap*, the flagship Laotian salad, has them all in spades. It is most often made using beef, chicken, pork, or sometimes fish, thinly sliced, chopped, or minced, with flavorings that vary from region to region and, indeed, chef to chef.

Typically, the meat or fish is stir-fried quickly over high heat with chili peppers, lemongrass, and garlic, then mint, lime juice, lime rind, pepper sauce, peanuts, onion, and cilantro are stirred in. The whole mixture is then spooned onto lettuce leaves. Roughly ground, toasted rice *(khao khua)*, vital to the character of the dish, is added as a topping, garnished with mint leaves or heady Thai basil. Even when served with the meat still warm, and with the ubiquitous basket of sticky Lao rice on the side, the result is so delightfully refreshing that you'll soon be ready to stroll the streets once more.

What Else to Eat

Lao cuisine is derived using ingredients mainly from the wild or from the rice field. **Kop yat sai**, or stuffed frog, is something of a delicacy. **Naem khao** (rice-and-sausage ball) is a salad made with deep-fried rice balls, grated coconut, chopped peanuts, Lao fermented pork sausage, sliced shallots, mint, cilantro, lemon juice, and fish sauce. **Foe** (rice noodle soup) is very similar to Vietnamese *pho (see pp238–9)*, and is the ubiquitous breakfast dish in Laos. **Tam mak hoong** (green papaya salad), literally meaning "pounded papaya," is a sharp and spicy salad made from unripened papaya. Barbecued chicken, or **ping kai**, is a favorite in every street market in Laos. It is marinated in a delicious mixture of fish sauce, garlic, turmeric, coriander, and white pepper, then slowly grilled over low heat on a charcoal burner.

Above *Laap* combines all the sharp and tangy tastes so characteristic of the region

The Best Places to Eat Laap

Nang Khambang inexpensive

For a no-nonsense taste of *laap* at its finest in genuinely authentic, everyday Lao surroundings, Nang Khambang is the place. The name means "Mrs. Khambang," and it's a family-run eatery that has been in the same location for three generations. Everything here is of the highest quality, and the *laap* is no exception. The restaurant offers air-conditioned and non-air-conditioned seating and, in a country where service can be slow, the staff are very attentive and efficient. In addition to the *laap*, Nang Khambang offers excellent *paa neua on*, a kind of lightly grilled and seasoned freshwater fish. Also on the menu are Mekong River fish and a sour fish soup, not unlike Thai *tom yam*, called *kaeng som paa*. Their *tam mak hoong* (green papaya salad) is also excellent; here it comes with tiny freshwater shrimp and baby tomatoes. Although Nang Khambang is now well publicized among travelers and tourists, it is still also heavily patronized by a Lao clientele – always a sure sign of quality. Nor have the prices been raised beyond the reach of local people.

Khum Bulom, Vientiane; open noon–9 PM daily; +856 21 217 198

Also in Vientiane

Amphone *(+856 21 212 489; expensive)* is a gourmet affair where Lao cuisine is given an international "makeover." It is set in beautiful surroundings and the ambience is one defined by chic furnishings, subdued jazz, and a fine wine list. The *laap* here is one of many excellent renditions of Lao culinary standards, as is the steamed fish citronella in banana leaves.

Also in Laos

Luang Prabang is the ancient capital of Laos and is an exquisite little town in the mountains now protected as a UNESCO World Heritage site. In addition to the plethora of ancient temples and the beauty of the French-era colonnaded streets, it is home to some very fine restaurants. **Tamnak Lao** *(www.tamnaklao.net; expensive)*, housed in an old French colonial villa, offers an extensive menu of artfully prepared Lao dishes including *laap* with pork, chicken, or fish.

Around the World

Given the colonial history of Laos, it is no surprise that the best purely Lao restaurants outside the country itself are found in Paris (although Isan Thai restaurants are found all over the globe and the food is hugely similar). **Lao Lane Xang** *(+66 1 45 85 19 23; moderate)* is to be found in Paris's bustling Chinatown district. It is hugely popular for both lunch and dinner thanks to its low prices, excellent service, and the authenticity of the Lao fare served. It is a good idea to make a reservation.

A Day in Hanoi

You need to be up early to catch some of the best sights, but no day in Hanoi is complete without a breakfast of *pho*, so buy some on the run.

MORNING Take an early morning trip to **Hoan Kiem Lake** ("Lake of the Returned Sword"), in the heart of the **Old Quarter**, to admire the lake and watch locals exercising before work. Then take a taxi to **Ho Chi Minh's Mausoleum**, which is only open until 11:00 AM. The marble building is a place of pilgrimage for many Vietnamese, and its grounds contain the **Presidential Palace** and **Ho Chi Minh Museum**.

AFTERNOON Hop on a local bus (an experience in itself) or take a taxi to the **Vietnam Museum of Ethnology**. Vietnam is home to countless hill tribe minorities and this modern museum gives a fascinating insight into their history and way of life.

EVENING After a day of culture, some relaxation is overdue, so return to the **Old Quarter** and make your way to **Bia Hoi Corner** (Luong Ngoc Quyen/Ta Hien). Sink into one of the tiny plastic chairs on the sidewalk and drink the cheapest draft beer in town.

Essentials

GETTING THERE

Hanoi's **Noi An International Airport** lies 28 miles (45 km) outside the city. There are **taxis**, **minibuses**, and **public buses** to the downtown.

WHERE TO STAY

Make sure you have the address of your hotel, as unscrupulous operators can give their hotels the same names as successful ones.
The Hanoi Fortune Hotel (inexpensive) is close to Hoan Kiem Lake. *www.hanoifortunehotel.com*
Hotel Elegance Ruby (moderate) is a cool, classy retreat from the busy Old Quarter outside. *www.hanoielegancehotel.com*
The Sofitel Metropole (expensive) has long been the choice of diplomats and celebrities. *www.sofitel.com*

TOURIST INFORMATION

www.vietnamtourism.com

Right The many tastes and textures of *pho* come from its great mix of long-braised, freshly steamed, and raw ingredients

Below The busy district of Dong Xuan Market at the western end of the Old Quarter

HANOI VIETNAM

Steaming Hot Pho in Hanoi

Nestled in Vietnam's north, Hanoi harks back to a time before Southeast Asia's recent rapid growth. Its Old Quarter is a labyrinth of ancient, narrow streets, alive with people and a myriad motorcycles, their horns blaring. In the morning, everyone heads for a *pho* stand or restaurant for a bowl of this fresh noodle soup, brimming with crunchy vegetables and tender meat.

Over the centuries Hanoi has been the capital and political center of Vietnam for many different administrations, from conquering 11th-century Chinese dynasties and French colonialists to those of its own republic under Ho Chi Minh. In 2010 it celebrated its 1,000th anniversary and a long history that has included royalty and revolution along with Taoism, Confucianism, communism, and capitalism. Somehow it has managed to both preserve and integrate the past and present in its customs, architecture, and food, and visitors can enjoy the pace of modern Vietnam mingled with colonial Indochina.

The colonial period left its mark on the city, and beautiful examples of the architecture remain today, such as the stunning Grand Opera House and the many tree-lined boulevards. It is also responsible for the origins of the national dish – *pho* – which is said to have taken its name from the French *pot au feu*, a dish built upon the long, slow simmering of bones and aromatics. *Pho* uses the same initial process, but gains from the addition of noodles, spices, and herbs.

Breakfast is the ideal time to experience *pho*, giving you a glimpse into Hanoi life and setting you up for the day's exploring. Choose your restaurant, then stand elbow-to-elbow with locals, fighting to place your order at the busy counter. Vats of stock simmer and the air is fragrant with cinnamon, ginger, and star anise. Rice noodles and raw beef are given a quick hot bath before being placed in a bowl, then the diners follow their own routine, carefully squeezing lime juice and a squirt of hot sauce. A spoonful of sliced chili pepper makes the finished article unique. There is no talking, but this is a noisy affair, the clash of spoon with bowl and the slurping of noodles adding to the cacophony of service.

The bustle of the *pho* restaurant is a warm-up for the day ahead. Hanoi's Old Quarter is humid and busy and you take your life in your hands each time you dare to cross the road. But walking is still the best way to see this part of the city, as each corner brings a surprise, whether it's a street full of ironmongers or a hawker setting up for the day. Where exotic old Vietnam meets the new one head-on, Hanoi is the Asia of your dreams – you're bound to leave wanting more.

North and South

In the middle of the 20th century, during Hanoi's turn to communism, refugees fled from the north, taking their recipes with them, and *pho* appeared in the south. The dish is many-layered in both flavor and texture: the bite of rice noodles is a base for tender meat and the crunch of bean sprouts. But it is in the broth that the complexity of the dish really shows through. Formed from the slow simmering of beef bones, which gives the stock depth, it gains subtle nuances from charred onion, ginger, and the spices of the region – star anise, cinnamon, and cloves. No two recipes are the same. The *pho* of the north, *pho bac*, is a simple affair of rice, meat, and thinner noodles. In the south, *pho nam* is a more elaborate affair that might be filled with beef, chicken, offal, or seafood, and served with a plate of herbs and bean sprouts to add as you like.

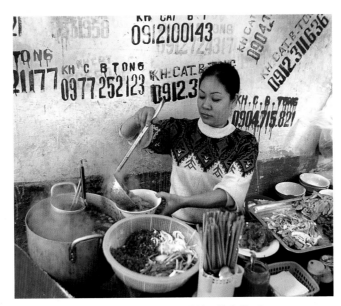

Above Fresh *pho* is on sale at most of the roadside cafés in Hanoi

The Best Places to Eat Pho

Pho Gia Truyen inexpensive

Nestled in Hanoi's Old Quarter, a short walk from Hoan Kiem Lake, Pho Gia Truyen (also known as "Pho 49 Bat Dan") is a *pho* restaurant of days gone by. You won't find fancy decor or attentive service, but you will find a version of *pho* that has few rivals. This is one for *pho bac* purists; there is nothing but beef available, although you can choose between *tai* (raw), *chin* (cooked), or *nam* (fatty brisket) by looking at the different cuts that sit tantalizingly behind glass at the service counter. Place your order and then enjoy watching the chef briefly cook the noodles and deftly slice your choice of beef from the display, filling the bowls with a fragrant, cloudy stock. It is then up to you to find a seat among the locals and drink in both the atmosphere and your very fine *pho*.

49 Bat Dan Street, Old Quarter, Hanoi; open 7 AM–11 PM

Also in Hanoi

Northern *pho* doesn't only come with beef: for a fine example of chicken *pho* (*pho ga*) head to **Pho Ga Mai Anh** *(+84 4 3943 8492; inexpensive)*. Like all the best *pho* restaurants this is a simple open-fronted affair, and its location on Le Van Huu, a short walk from beautiful Hoan Kiem Lake, is perfect for the Old Quarter-based tourist.

Also in Vietnam

In Ho Chi Minh City, **Pho Hua** *(+84 8 3829 7943; inexpensive)* is on Pasteur Street, just a short taxi ride from the main tourist area. It's been in business for over 40 years and caters to both locals and tourists. Spread over two floors, it's one of the best places for *pho* in the city.

Pho has not escaped the restaurant chain industry, and **Pho 24** *(www.pho24.com; moderate)* has many franchises that churn out dependable southern-style renditions of the dish and are popular with the younger Vietnamese. Their air-conditioned outlets are all over Vietnam and offer many different varieties of *pho* along with other dishes such as *com tam* (broken rice with pork) and spring rolls.

Around the World

After the fall of the south in the Vietnam War, many Vietnamese settled outside the country and a large community formed in London. Among the host of Vietnamese restaurants on Kingsland Road in the arty Hoxton district, **Song Que** *(+44 20 7613 3222; moderate)* easily stands out. It has the widest selection of *pho* in the city, with beef, beef offal, chicken, seafood, and vegetarian options, all bathed in a rich broth.

SOUTH ISLAND NEW ZEALAND

Bluff Oysters on South Island

New Zealand's South Island is wild and stunningly beautiful, with coves, fjords, and cliffs framing the cool, pristine waters of the Tasman Sea and Foveaux Strait. The cool-climate conditions at the island's southernmost point have produced some fascinating wildlife and delicious foodstuffs, and it's the world-renowned Bluff oysters that attract visitors from around the world.

The town of Bluff runs along the edge of New Zealand's most southerly peninsula, sheltered by the high range of hills that reach a peak in the old volcanic cone of "Old Man Bluff," or Bluff Hill. The South Island's State Highway No. 1 ends just outside town, where the waters of the Foveaux Strait lap around the Bluff Scenic Reserve – or Motupōhue – and its Glory Walking Track. From the summit of Bluff Hill there are panoramic views across the strait to Stewart Island, which offer a rare chance of glimpsing one of the rarest whales in the world, the southern right whale *(tohorā)*, or the charming little blue penguin *(titi)*.

For most of the year, Bluff is a sleepy addendum to the livelier nearby city of Invercargill, and it's inhabited by hardy folks who celebrate living at the extremity of a country. But from May to August each year, this laid-back town becomes the focus for the world's oyster lovers. *Tiostrea chilensis* oysters have been harvested commercially in New Zealand's deep south since the 1860s, originally off Stewart Island, but closer to Bluff from the 1880s, giving the oysters their name. Today, up to 10 million of the succulent bivalves are gathered annually, and they are considered to be the finest oysters in the world. The first catches of the year take place in early March, and the boats' return is eagerly awaited. In the restaurants of Auckland, a dozen of these delicious oysters cost more than NZ$50, but in Invercargill and Bluff, seafood suppliers sell the same number for less than half the price.

Tourists lucky enough to visit the area in May can attend the annual Bluff Oyster & Food Festival, which is proudly promoted with the tagline "Unsophisticated and proud of it!" The day's oyster-opening and -eating competitions are appetizers to heaped plates of local crayfish, *paua* (abalone), scallops, and blue cod, and of course more Bluff oysters. Around 20,000 are eaten at the festival, all washed down with the fine wines of the Central Otago vineyards or local beers such as the Pitch Black stout of the Invercargill Brewing Company.

Bluff's easy-going southern ambience infuses travel throughout the surrounding region. To the west lies the dreamlike scenery of the Fiordland National Park. In a country of astounding landscapes, Fiordland trumps everywhere else, with its jagged mountain peaks, fjords, lakes, vast alpine river valleys, and beautiful walking tracks. To the east, the isolated coves and clifftop lookouts of the Catlins coast provide the perfect places for impromptu seafood picnics.

Three Days on the Southern Scenic Route

This is a region of astonishing natural beauty – allow plenty of time to be captivated by the views and charmed by some of the southern hemisphere's most engaging wildlife.

DAY ONE From **Dunedin** head south along the rugged **Catlins** coastline. At **Roaring Bay**, *hoiho* (yellow-eyed penguins) waddle from the ocean at dusk. At **Papatowai**, visit Blair Sommerville's quirky **Lost Gypsy** gallery. Detour to the spectacular **Cathedral Caves**, then look for dolphins in the surf along the graceful sweep of **Porpoise Bay**.

DAY TWO Explore **Invercargill**. The **Southland Museum** has a great display of tuatara, New Zealand's reptiles, which haven't changed in 220 million years. Catch the ferry from nearby **Bluff** to **Stewart Island** for an opportunity to see kiwis in the wild.

DAY THREE Continue west to the **Fiordland National Park**. Head for **Doubtful Sound** to go kayaking in a beautifully isolated spot – just getting there takes a languid combination of two boats and a bus. Or visit **Milford Sound**, punctuated by the iconic profile of **Mitre Peak**, the spectacular end point for the Milford Track.

Essentials

GETTING THERE
Dunedin has regular **flights** from Auckland, New Zealand's main international airport. The airport has a **bus** shuttle and **car** rental.

WHERE TO STAY
Living Space (inexpensive) has sleek rooms in a restored 1907 warehouse. *www.livingspace.net*
Nugget Lodge (moderate) has two beachfront cabins in the Catlins. *www.nuggetlodge.co.nz*
Te Anau Lodge (expensive) is a luxurious and stately B&B that was originally built as a convent in the 1930s. *www.teanaulodge.com*

TOURIST INFORMATION
www.southernscenicroute.co.nz

Above Freshly shucked oysters, eaten raw with just a squeeze of lemon, are everyone's favorite in Bluff

Left The 40-mile (53-km) Milford Track takes walkers past Mitre Peak, in the breathtaking wilderness of Milford Sound

Below The shy kiwi bird is indigenous to New Zealand and is found nowhere else in the world – it is the country's national symbol

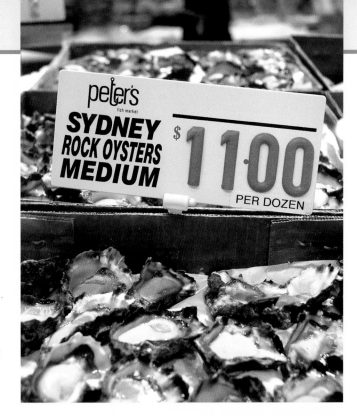

Oysters Around the World

Although most food now seems to be available virtually anywhere at any time of year, the only way to sample the finest oysters is to eat them close to their native waters. The exceptional oyster restaurants tend to be close to the best oyster beds.

NEW ZEALAND

Niagara Falls Café moderate

256 Niagara-Waikawa Rd., South Catlins; www.niagarafallscafe.co.nz

Part roadside restaurant and part funky art gallery, the Niagara Falls Café partners Bluff oysters with flinty Central Otago Riesling or zingy Marlborough Sauvignon Blanc. Seafood aficionados should definitely follow up with the blue cod in a herb and Chardonnay sauce.

Redcliff Restaurant & Bar
expensive

12 Mokonui St., Te Anau; +64 3 249 7431

A dozen Bluff oysters or house-smoked salmon at Te Anau's Redcliff Restaurant & Bar is the perfect celebration after completing Fiordland's iconic Milford Track. Redcliff's cozy bar is also the place to catch live music on summer weekends.

On The Menu

Oysters Bienville These are grilled oysters with béchamel sauce and garlic, shrimp, mushrooms, white wine, and Tabasco sauce. A New Orleans classic.

Oysters Kilpatrick An Australian and New Zealand dish that combines grilled oysters with Worcestershire sauce, diced bacon, and chopped parsley.

Oyster po' boy A traditional Louisiana "poor-boy" sandwich: a baguette filled with breaded, deep-fried oysters.

Oysters Rockefeller Created in 1899, and named after oil magnate John D. Rockefeller, these oysters are grilled with finely diced herbs, spinach, and butter.

Oyster shooter Fresh oyster served in a shot glass, often in a Bloody Mary cocktail.

TASMANIA, AUSTRALIA

Seafood from Australia's verdant island extension is venerated by mainland chefs in Sydney and Melbourne, especially oysters from Tasmania's pristine, cooler waters. Eating a freshly shucked half-dozen at the source is an essential Down Under experience.

Get Shucked inexpensive

1650 Bruny Island Main Rd., Bruny Island; www.getshucked.com.au

Keep it simple with a splash of Tabasco and a squeeze of lemon at Get Shucked's roadside stand on rugged and robust Bruny Island. An essential complement is a zingy chili pepper (nonalcoholic) brew from the Tasmanian Chilli Beer Company.

Freycinet Marine Farm moderate

1784 Coles Bay Rd., Coles Bay; www.freycinetmarinefarm.com

Simple wooden tables belie a sophisticated combo of oysters fresh from nearby Great Oyster Bay and the best of Tasmanian beer and wine. Improbably plump mussels and rock lobsters – from December to May only – are other tasty diversions.

Marque IV expensive

Elizabeth St. Pier, Hobart; www.marqueiv.com.au

Hobart's brilliant southern light shimmers on rows of fishing boats as Marque IV's elegant harborside dining room showcases the best Tasmanian produce. For oyster fans, the most delicious and innovative enhancements include limoncello and chili pepper or cucumber sorbet and Avruga roe.

SYDNEY, AUSTRALIA

One of the world's great harbor cities is also a brilliant destination for fresh seafood. The oyster experience here stretches from humble market stands to stylish waterfront bars. Fine Australian wine is usually close at hand.

Sydney Fish Market inexpensive

Bank St., Prymont; www.sydneyfishmarket.com.au

After the fish bazaars of Japan, Sydney Fish Market offers the world's widest variety of seafood. Curious foodie travelers can seek out and sample at least ten different types of oysters, together with only-in-Australia seafood such as leather jackets, yabbies, and Moreton Bay bugs.

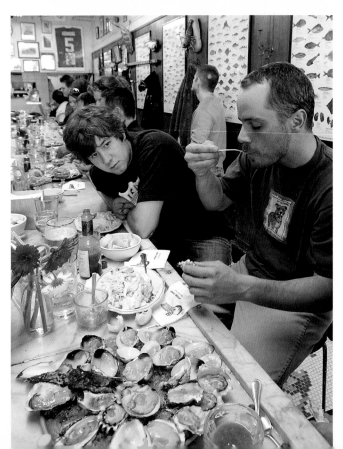

Left (top to bottom) Pacific oysters on sale in the Sydney Fish Market, Australia; fishing boats and Mures Seafood Restaurant, reflected in Victoria Dock, Hobart, Tasmania; eating fresh oysters at the Swan Oyster Depot, San Francisco **Below (top to bottom)** Preparing oysters at the Galway Oyster Festival, Ireland; oysters on sale in Cancale, France

Doyles on the Beach moderate

11 Marine Parade, Watson's Bay; www.doyles.com.au
With harbor views to downtown Sydney and a beachfront location, Doyles at Watson's Bay is one of Australia's iconic dining experiences. Highlights include creamy oysters Mornay and oysters Kilpatrick.

Sydney Cove Oyster Bar expensive

1 East Circular Quay; www.sydneycoveoysterbar.com
With unbeatable views of the cosmopolitan waterborne buzz of Circular Quay, this quintessential Sydney restaurant specializes in seafood – especially oysters – caught off New South Wales.

NEW ORLEANS, LA

From oysters Bienville and Rockefeller to po' boys, New Orleans has inspired more iconic oyster recipes than any other city.

Felix's Restaurant & Oyster Bar moderate

739 Iberville St., French Quarter; www.felixs.com
Felix's stays true to its 100-plus years of French Quarter history, and remains a favorite for New Orleans natives. After a night out on Bourbon Street, freshly shucked oysters and a Cajun-style Bloody Mary cocktail make for a reviving brunch.

Drago's Seafood Restaurant expensive

3232 North Arnoult Road, Metairie; www.dragosrestaurant.com

Grilled oysters dot the menus of many New Orleans restaurants, but reputedly Drago's served them first in 1993. Try the locally grown Louisiana bivalves with peanuts and red pepper aïoli, or with sun-dried tomatoes and pine nuts for a Mediterranean spin.

SAN FRANCISCO, CA

The oldest of this city's oyster bars opened in 1912, and San Francisco's love affair with briny bivalves shows no sign of slowing down. North America's best farmers' markets are here too, and keep the local culinary scene buzzing.

Swan Oyster Depot moderate

1517 Polk St. (between California St. & Sacramento St.); (415) 673 1101
Behind a century-old marble counter in this impossibly narrow restaurant, the wisecracking Sancimino brothers serve up oysters from around North America and the Pacific. Customers usually have to stand in line, but both the jokes and the oysters are worth waiting for.

Hog Island moderate

Ferry Building Marketplace, One Ferry Building #11; www.hogislandoysters.com

Pacific? Atlantic? West Coast? East Coast? There's a different selection of American oysters every day at this sleek, modern oyster bar in San Francisco's iconic Ferry Building. On Saturday mornings the action flows outside to the weekly farmers' market.

GALWAY, IRELAND

Caressed by brisk Atlantic gusts on Ireland's west coast, Galway's combination of salt water and fresh water produces exceptional oysters. This slice of natural good fortune is celebrated each September at the Galway International Oyster Festival (www.galwayoysterfest.com).

Conlon & Sons moderate

Eglinton St., Galway City; +353 91 562 268
Surrounded by Galway's best pubs, a big night in the city often kicks off at Conlon & Sons. From September to April, Galway oysters are served at the granite bar, and salmon, scallops, and mussels prove irresistible to seafood buffs.

Moran's Oyster Cottage moderate

The Weir, Kilcolgan; www.moransoystercottage.com
Moran's treats local Clarinbridge oysters simply and with respect; freshly shucked and served with a silky pint of Guinness and some Irish soda bread. A restaurant that's been run by the same family for seven generations really doesn't have a lot to prove.

CANCALE, FRANCE

The Romans, King Louis XIV, Marie Antoinette, and Napoleon Bonaparte were all fans of oysters from Cancale, in northwest France. Local *huîtres* include the delicate and nutty Plate Belon, and the robust and rare Pied de Cheval.

Quai Gambetta inexpensive

Just yards from Cancale's oyster beds, several enterprising locals on the quay offer a fresh dozen with a wedge of lemon for around €4. Ad hoc and alfresco dining is enhanced by salty Atlantic breezes.

A Contre Courant moderate

3 Place du Calvaire, 'Le Port', Cancale; www.acontrecourant.net

With modern decor and regular exhibitions from local artists, A Contre Courant resembles a breezy slice of the Med on France's Atlantic coast. Oysters are treated simply, and the wider menu includes scallops with *andouille* sausage and grilled shrimp skewers.

Above The Temple of the Emerald Buddha, in the compound of the Grand Palace in Bangkok

A Day in Bangkok

Take advantage of the cool of the morning for a walking tour of the cultural center, then use the river as an "expressway" to other sights.

MORNING Start the day in **Ko Ratanakosin**, which rests in a bend of the **Chao Phraya River** and contains some of the city's most historic architecture. **Wat Pho** is Bangkok's oldest temple and home to one of the largest reclining Buddha statues in the world. The nearby **Grand Palace** has been superseded by Chitlada Palace as the primary royal residence, but it is still used for ceremonial occasions. Adjacent **Wat Phra Kaew**, home to the "Emerald Buddha" (actually jade), is a gleaming example of Bangkok temple architecture at its most baroque.

AFTERNOON Catch a ferry across the river to **Supatra River House** to sample some great *tom yam*. From Chang pier, rent a long-tailed boat for a two-hour tour through **Thonburi**'s extensive canal network, admiring the old wooden houses and floating vendors.

EVENING Cool off by quaffing a cold beer and sampling more foodie treats at the **Soi 38 Night Market**, off Sukhumvit.

Essentials

GETTING THERE
Suvarnabhumi International Airport is 18 miles (30 km) from Bangkok; "Airport Express" **buses** and **taxis** go downtown.

WHERE TO STAY
Phra-Nakorn Norn-Len (inexpensive) is a trendy hotel with pretty, affordable accommodations in a quiet part of Bangkok near the river. *www.phranakorn-nornlen.com*

Conrad Bangkok (moderate) is conveniently located downtown near the BTS Sukhumvit line and shopping centers. *http://conradhotels1.hilton.com*

Chakrabongse Villas (expensive) are exquisite riverfront villas in the grounds of a century-old Thai palace. *www.thaivillas.com*

TOURIST INFORMATION
www.bangkoktourist.com

Above Bangkok has many night markets, full of chattering locals and tourists eating, drinking, and shopping until late

BANGKOK THAILAND

Tangy Tom Yam in Bangkok

Bangkok is the archetypal Southeast Asian metropolis. The humid air is thick with the heady scent of jasmine and the oceanic reverberation of distant traffic. Temple spires glitter alongside pounding discotheques, respectively temples to the ascetic and the hedonistic. The city's best-loved dish, *tom yam*, explodes with an energy that's perfectly in tune with this whirlwind of a city.

 Although intensely urbanized, Bangkok exhibits an uncompromised Thai identity beneath its modern veneer. Glass-and-steel buildings shaped like cartoon robots stand next to terra-cotta-tiled temples; wreaths of good-luck flowers dangle from the rear-view mirrors of buses and taxis; shaven-headed, orange-robed monks walk barefoot along the street beneath a bank of giant Sony screens carrying images of the latest global pop star.

Visitors can move across the city on water, via 18th-century canals; through the air, aboard the sleek Skytrain; or below ground, in the high-tech Metropolitan Rapid Transit Authority (MRTA) subway. Cultural highs are both high- and low-brow, from museums, galleries, and classical theater or dance performances to Thai boxing or club outings, to hear international DJs spin the latest house and hip-hop.

Just as the Bangkok Thai dialect has become standard Thai throughout the country, so Bangkok Thai cooking is today considered classic Thai cuisine. *Tom yam*, one of the most quintessential Bangkok Thai

dishes, has an ancient history, making use of the oldest ingredients and techniques known to Thai food historians. It is a spicy, tangy broth with lime and chili pepper overtones that's almost always made with seafood, though chicken is occasionally substituted.

Lemongrass, kaffir lime peel, and lime juice give *tom yam* its characteristic sour taste. Fueling the fire beneath the broth's often velvety surface are fresh whole bird chilis and sometimes half a teaspoonful of roast chili pepper paste. Improvisation comes into play with this dish more than most, as Thai cooks try to out-do one another in providing a savory soup with at least one or two "mystery" ingredients. Many cooks add galangal to give the mix an extra fragrance. For color and flavor, halved cherry tomatoes will sometimes work their way into the recipe. Aside from the lemongrass and galangal that will remain at the bottom of the serving bowl, solids in this soup are usually limited to shrimp and straw mushrooms, jostling beneath a sprinkle of leafy cilantro. Like Bangkok itself, the first taste often leaves the uninitiated delighted but gasping for breath.

Cooking Schools

You can amaze your friends back home with deft preparations of *tom yam* and other Thai delights by attending a cooking course in Bangkok. The oldest and best-known program in the city is the plush **Oriental Thai Cooking School** *(www. mandarinoriental.com)*, opposite the Mandarin Oriental Bangkok, which teaches four dishes a day, Monday to Saturday. At **The Thai House** (www.thaihouse.co.th), visitors choose from one- to three-day residential cooking courses held in a traditional Thai teak house about 40 minutes north of Bangkok by boat. The family kitchen lies next to a fruit orchard growing mangoes, bananas, papayas, and coconuts, and the perfect herb garden. **Baipai Thai Cooking School** *(www. baipai.com)* is one of the newer schools and its popular nonresidential programs are held in a two-story townhouse in Bangkok.

Above *Tom yam* is an everyday treat for many people in Thailand

The Best Places to Eat Tom Yam

Taling Pling moderate

One place that scores highly on all counts is Taling Pling, where the cooks make *tom yam* from scratch using ingredients purchased fresh every morning. The restaurant name comes from a venerable taling pling tree *(Averrhoa bilimbi)* that still stands alongside the old Thai house that houses the restaurant. Don't let the trendy mauve walls fool you; this is local food, with a central/southern Thai slant, and you'll get no mercy from the kitchen when it comes to spices. Every dish is prepared with the utmost attention, yet the prices are affordable for middle-class Thais, who make up most of the clientele. Other exemplary dishes that will go well with your *tom yam* include *phanaeng* curry with roast duck and *thawt man plaa* (fried fishcakes with a cucumber-peanut dipping sauce). If you want to try the restaurant's namesake fruit, order *yam plaa salit taling pling*, a fresh salad made with taling pling (a juicy, sour fruit) and small Gulf fish, fried whole. At lunchtime, Taling Pling is crowded with local office workers, so it's best to arrive after 1:00 PM or in the early evening to guarantee a table.

60 Pan Road, Bangkok; open 11 AM–10:30 PM; +66 2234 4872

Also in Bangkok

Most locals rate **Supatra River House** *(www. supatrariverhouse.net; moderate)* as the best restaurant on the river; it's an old teak house with wonderful views of the Grand Palace and Wat Arun. Enjoy great *tom yam* either alfresco or indoors with extremely efficient air-conditioning. **Raan Jay Fai** *(+66 2223 9384; inexpensive)* on the Maha Chai Road was once a local secret but is now quite well known among foodies. This open-air café serves a delicious *tom yam haeng*, a dry-fried (rather than soupy) version of the dish, and its *pad khee mao* (drunken noodles) are legendary.

Also in Thailand

If you find yourself on the resort island of Phuket, head to the historic town of the same name and look for **Nai Yao** *(+66 7621 2719; inexpensive)* on Phuket Road. It's one of the oldest seafood restaurants on the island, and uses fish straight from local fishing boats.

Around the World

The world's first Michelin-starred Thai restaurant, **Nahm** *(www.halkin.como.bz; expensive)* is found not in Thailand but in London, where Australian virtuoso chef David Thompson holds court. Try his version of *tom yam* with fresh mussels, or *geng jeut pla meuk yord sai*, another clear soup, made of squid, chicken, samphire, and shiitake mushrooms.

Three Days in Tokyo

Tokyo has no center; think of it instead as several cities that vaguely orbit the Imperial Palace and are connected by the Yamanoto Line railway. The main places visitors gravitate to are Ginza/Marunouchi, Roppongi, Shibuya/Omotesando/Harajuku, Shinjuku, Ikebukuro, Ueno, Akihabara, and Odaiba, but there are many more areas to explore.

DAY ONE Visit the **Tsukiji fish market** at the crack of dawn and breakfast at one of its famous sushi bars. From there head to **Ginza** for shopping, before moving on to the vast **Imperial Palace** complex and gardens. End the day amid the liquid crystal lights of **Shinjuku.**

DAY TWO **Shibuya**, **Harajuku**, and **Omotesando** are great for watching the best-dressed people in the world go about their business. If all the Gothic Lolita/Hello Kitty craziness gets too much, take a break amid the green spaces of **Yoyogi Park.**

DAY THREE If there is a tournament on, head to **Ryugoku** to see some sumo. For a final retail splurge, go to **Tokyo Midtown** in **Roppongi**, a vast and elegant mall with great restaurants, shops, and galleries.

Essentials

GETTING THERE

Two international **airports** serve Tokyo: Narita (an hour-and-a-half north of the city by **bus** or **Metro**) and Haneda (40 minutes south of the city by **monorail** or **bus**). Tokyo has a peerless network of **subways** and overground **trains**.

WHERE TO STAY

The Welcome Inn (inexpensive) has several traditional Japanese *ryokans* (inns) that are a good deal in an expensive city. *www.itcj.jp/eng*
Citadines Shinjuku (moderate) is reasonably central, modern, and spacious, at a fair price. *www.citadines.com*
The Mandarin Oriental (expensive) has stunning views, gorgeous rooms, and great restaurants. *www.mandarinoriental.com*

TOURIST INFORMATION

www.seejapan.co.uk

Right A sushi bar at breakfast time at Tsukiji fish market, where around almost 3 tons (2,700 kg) of fish is auctioned every day
Below The busy Shinjuku district boasts Tokyo's largest concentration of skyscrapers

TOKYO JAPAN

Fresh Sushi in Towering Tokyo

During the first decade of the 21st century, Tokyo finally edged aside New York, Paris, and London to claim the title of the undisputed culinary capital of the world, and its greatest food is sushi. Whether feasted upon at a lavish members-only restaurant or from a cheap and cheerful *kaiten,* where tempting portions roll by on a conveyor belt, the sushi here is invariably delicious.

Tokyo is one of the world's great cities, with cultural, historic, and culinary attractions to rival any capital. It is built on a daunting scale and its cityscape changes ceaselessly, but amid the liquid-crystal screens, nonstop rivers of people, and towering overpasses, there remain pockets of ancient Japan in the form of the city's temples and gardens, which are soothing oases of stillness.

No one takes food more seriously than the Japanese. Tokyo doesn't just offer every kind of global food and cuisine imaginable; it aims to better the originals. The city has also given the world several great dishes, not least sushi, which dates back to the 7th century, when the Japanese acquired the Chinese habit of preserving pieces of fish in rice. The rice was discarded when the fish was eaten, but by the 15th century the Japanese had started to speed up the process using rice wine vinegar, then eating both the fish and the rice. The seasoned rice became known as *sushi.* A further breakthrough occurred in the early 1800s, when a Tokyo inhabitant named Yohei Hanaya came up with the idea of squeezing rice into small blocks and adding toppings. This hand-shaped form of sushi became known as *nigiri* (meaning "to squeeze"); along with *maki* rolls (seaweed-bound rice rolls), it was to become the best known form of sushi around the world.

Now that sushi has become as ubiquitous as sandwiches in the supermarkets of the West, it can seem a little strange to discover that in Tokyo the Japanese don't really think of it as a cheap fast food. You can buy packs of prepared sushi in supermarkets (and it will be better than any supermarket sushi you've ever tasted), but the Japanese – and Tokyoites in particular – take their sushi much more seriously than that. Here, sushi is a treat, an extravagance. The rice is served at body temperature and very rarely topped with salmon; Tokyo favorites include chilled squid, bream, octopus, sea urchin, turbot, whitebait, shrimp, fish eggs, plaice, sea snails, and, of course, various cuts of tuna. Look for grilled eel and lightly pickled mackerel too. Eating sushi in Tokyo is a ritual to be savored, from the moment the freshly grated wasabi falls from a sharkskin board onto your colorful, sushi-laden plate.

Japanese Food Halls

For a jaw-dropping glimpse into the Tokyoites' glorious obsession with food, visit one of the city's great *depachika*, or department store food halls. Always to be found in the basement, they are a testament to the Japanese fixation with quality, variety, and innovation in food. They sell up to 30,000 different items, including a vast array of local and international ingredients and finished dishes. The *depachikas* of, for example, the **Seibu, Odakyu,** or **Takashimaya** department stores in the Tokyo neighborhoods of Shinjuku, Shibuya, Ginza, or Ikebukuro rank among the greatest food halls in the world. You'll find great carry-out tempura, sushi, tofu, noodles, Wagyu beef, fresh fish, *wagashi* (traditional Japanese sweets), and immaculate fruit and vegetables. In general, *depachikas* are great places to eat cheaply, or even for free – there are usually dozens of free samples offered.

Above Sushi is eaten as finger food, and each piece should be eaten in one bite

The Best Places to Eat Sushi

Tsukiji Fish Market inexpensive

There are sushi restaurants in every Tokyo neighborhood, ranging from six-seater bars to larger chains and conveyor-belt or *kaiten* sushi places. But the spiritual home of sushi are the restaurants in the heart of the world-famous Tsukiji fish market, the largest fish market in the world. The most famous of these restaurants is Daiwa, but its neighbors, particularly Sushi Dai, are just about as good, and they all serve what is perhaps the freshest sushi in the world. Annoyingly, they don't take reservations, so you need to arrive seriously early (around 5:00 AM) to avoid the lines. Set some time aside for a walk around the market itself, too, because it is one of the greatest food sights on Earth. Finally, if you want to be guaranteed a sushi meal to remember, there is one word with which you must greet the chef as you take your seat – *"Omakase,"* which means: "I'll leave it up to you."

Tsukiji, Tokyo; open 5 AM–2 PM Mon–Sat (closed on alternate Weds); www.tsukiji-market.or.jp

Also in Tokyo

The Ginza district in Tokyo is home to fiendishly expensive, exclusive, and often impossible-to-get-into sushi restaurants. The most famous of these is **Sukiyabashi Jiro** *(+81 03 3535 3600; expensive),* which was awarded three Michelin stars in 2009 and is run by the eponymous and legendary 84-year-old Jiro-san. He has been making sushi for over 60 years and is said to size up each customer's jaw and adjust the size of the *nigiri* to fit their mouth accordingly. Jiro-san's son runs a more accessible branch in the Roppongi Hills mall.

Also in Japan

Though the style of sushi we know best in the West originated in Tokyo, sushi has its historic roots in Kyoto and Osaka, where it was originally made in large portions that were pressed into boxes and typically topped with pickled mackerel. This *zaba-sushi* can still be eaten in Kyoto and Osaka. The most famous restaurant for this surprisingly hearty specialty – which is not served with wasabi or soy sauce – is **Izuu** *(+81 075 561 0751; expensive)* in Higashiyama-ku, Kyoto, which was established in 1781.

Around the World

Sushi's other great spiritual home is the US, where they have added their own quirks and ingredients to the mix to create wonders such as the inside-out-roll and the California roll. New York's **Sushi of Gari** *(www.sushiofgari.com; moderate)* and LA's **Asanebo** *(818-760-3348; expensive)* are highly recommended.

DUJIANGYAN

DUJIANGYAN CHINA

Peanut Chicken in Dujiangyan

Gong bao ji ding is one of the most instantly recognizable Chinese dishes, served up as "spicy chicken with peanuts" in restaurants around the world. History links it to Dujiangyan, a small Sichuanese town just north of the provincial capital, Chengdu, and also to an ancient engineering project that long ago turned this region into one of China's prime agricultural areas.

 Gong bao (sometimes *kung po*) chicken is named after Ding Baozhen, the Governor of Sichuan in the 1880s ("Gong Bao" was his official title), whose household is said by some to have invented this dish. Others claim that it is, in fact, an old recipe from neighboring Guizhou province, where Ding Baozhen was born, or that it was served up to him at a banquet by an obsequious subordinate looking for favors. It doesn't really matter which story is true: this stir-fried assemblage of juicy chicken cubes, crunchy peanuts, chopped dried chili peppers, and aromatic Sichuan peppercorns (called *huajiao*, or "flower pepper" in Chinese), all held together by a malty-sour sauce, is deliciously addictive.

The combination of peppers and *huajiao* is distinctly Sichuanese, though *gong bao* chicken isn't actually a hot dish by local standards. Some Sichuanese food is so fiery that even hardened locals glow crimson when eating it; to watch diners at a back-street night market tucking into innocuously named "boiled beef slices" or a communal, pepper-rich hotpot is to wince in sympathy. After a while, though,

this eye-watering diet becomes a necessity, and the Sichuanese justify their pepper cravings on health grounds, claiming that eating them warms you up in winter and helps you perspire during the summer, ultimately cooling you down.

Ding Baozhen is also famous for restoring Sichuan's agricultural self-sufficiency. Dujiangyan sits where the farmland plains of eastern Sichuan meet the abrupt "foothills" – in reality, steep-sided mountains – of the Tibetan Plateau. Watercourses tumble off these hillsides into the notoriously capricious Min River, which used to cause havoc by alternately drying out or flooding the plains. In 256 BC the Han dynasty governor Li Bing designed a simple-looking collection of dams, dikes, and spillways to channel the river into an irrigation system. Ding Baozhen restored his work, and today's vast waterways offer spectacular views over the channels and dams to the mountains and forests beyond. In taming the waters, Li Bing created an area of rich agricultural land, thereby granting the people a livelihood, and his efforts are commemorated in the temples of Erwang Miao and Fulong Guan – "Dragon-Taming Hall."

Above Erwang Miao, the Two Kings Temple, is a tribute to Li Bing and his son, who first irrigated the plains during China's Warring States period, 2,200 years ago

Sichuan Pepper

The characteristic Sichuanese taste is *mala*, literally "hot and numb," created by combining the spicy heat of chili peppers with the aromatic tingle of Sichuan pepper. Also known as prickly ash, these peppercorn-sized fruits grow on ferociously thorny bushes in western Sichuan – market vendors often hold up scratched hands to prove how fresh their wares are. They contain a volatile oil that creates a weird pins-and-needles sensation in the mouth when eaten. The dried peppercorns are either cooked whole in a dish, as in *gong bao* chicken (be warned, it's a bit of a shock when you bite into one) or ground to a powder and sprinkled over everything at the end. Sadly, the oil's numbing effect doesn't age well and peppercorns bought overseas rarely retain enough volatile oil to surprise an unwary diner.

A Day in Dujiangyan

Dujiangyan town itself is a functional transportation hub, so once you've arrived here from Chengdu, there's no reason to put off heading straight for the riverside parkland surrounding the ancient irrigation works.

MORNING Head for **Lidui Park** and admire the main channel from venerable **Fulong Hall**, then catch a cable car over the Min River or cross more adventurously via the narrow **Anlan** suspension bridge. Either way you'll reach **Erwang Miao**, the Two Kings Temple. Seek out the painted bust of Ding Baozhen in an alcove here, then walk through woodland back to town along the flagstoned **Songmao Path**, one of the ancient "tea roads" between Sichuan and Tibet.

AFTERNOON After lunch at one of the many riverside restaurants, head 15 miles (25 km) west to **Qingcheng Mountain**, a small but sacred Taoist peak. Climb the steep flights of steps through thick forest, pausing along the way to admire some small but beautiful temples and shrines.

EVENING Return to **Chengdu** for an evening stroll around the old streets surrounding Kuan Xiangzi, followed by a performance of traditional Sichuan opera.

Essentials

GETTING THERE
Dujiangyan is 20 miles (30 km) north of Shuangliu **international airport** in Chengdu. A **train** service also runs from Chengdu's north train station.

WHERE TO STAY
Dujianyan is short on foreigner-friendly hotels, so it's best to stay in Chengdu.
Sim's (inexpensive) is centrally located and offers very friendly, helpful service. www.gogosc.com
The Holiday Inn Express (moderate) is business-oriented and very used to dealing with foreigners. www.holidayinnexpress.com.cn
The Jinjiang Hotel (expensive) is a Chinese-style luxury hotel downtown. www.jjhotel.com

TOURIST INFORMATION
194 Qintai Road, Chengdu; or check the listings magazine *GoChengdu*: www.gochengdoo.com

Above Lanterns decorate one of the many small canals that are used to control the level of the Min River in Dujiangyan

Left *Gong bao* chicken combines chicken, peanuts, hot peppers, and Sichuan pepper with ginger and garlic in a light sweet-sour sauce

The Best Places to Eat Gong Bao Chicken

Alfresco restaurants in Dujiangyan inexpensive

For the best *gong bao* chicken experience in Dujiangyan, head to the host of waterside restaurants lining the overflow channel off Fuxing Road, just outside Lidui Park. Places here specialize in river food – including fresh frogs, snails, and little crayfish, all kept alive in buckets – but also include a broad range of Sichuanese favorites on the menu. The best way to choose a restaurant is to walk around and pick the busiest. The trick to finding a good plate of *gong bao* chicken (as it lends itself to endless variations, some better than others) is to look for one that includes chicken cubes, peanuts, Sichuan peppercorns, and chili peppers, and is not swamped in chili oil or sticky sauces. The best variations produce a relatively mild, dry dish with sharp, clear flavors. Whichever establishment you end up in, choose an outdoor table (most have awnings to protect you from the elements) and enjoy the setting, with the water racing roughly past along the broad, stone-lined channel. Make sure you check prices as you order, or you might get a shock when the bill arrives.

Around Lidui Park, Dujiangyan; open dawn–dusk daily

In Chengdu

The excellent **Manting Fan** *(+86 28 8517 7958; moderate)* serves up first-rate *gong bao* chicken, alongside other Sichuanese favorites such as *mapo tofu* (soft tofu cubes in a hot bean sauce), smoked duck, dry-fried green beans, "fish-flavored" pork shreds, sweet rabbit threads with steamed buns, and sautéed bamboo shoots. **Lao Fangzi** *(+86 28 8509 8822; moderate)* has a similar menu, and their "mouthwatering chicken" is well worth a try.

Also in China

Baguo Buyi *(+86 10 6400 8888; expensive)* is the Beijing branch of a Chengdu chain, featuring excellent *gong bao* chicken, twice-cooked pork, and performances of Sichuan opera to enjoy with your meal. **Chuanguo Yuanyi** *(+86 21 5836 8826; expensive)* does the same job in Shanghai, while in Chongqing, **Waipo Qiao** *(+86 23 6383 5988; moderate)* serves some of the best Sichuanese food in town.

Around the World

In London, both the cooking and decor at **Barshu** *(www.bar-shu.co.uk; moderate)* are extraordinarily close to an authentic Chengdu experience. New York's **Grand Sichuan** chain *(www.thegrandsichuan.com; moderate)* is well-regarded for staples including *gong bao* chicken. In Melbourne, aim for **Dainty Sichuan** *(+61 3 9663 8861: inexpensive)*, a crowded, unsophisticated place that likes its spices.

A Day in Old Delhi

Mesmerizing Old Delhi is just a mile or so (a couple of kilometers) north of Connaught Place, the modern hub of New Delhi. Unmistakably Islamic despite the nation's Hindu background, it is a thoroughly rewarding area in which to explore historic sites and markets.

MORNING From sturdy **Delhi Gate**, at the old city's southern edge, stroll up **Netaji Subhash Marg** until you see the massive ramparts of the **Red Fort** (Lal Qila) on your right. You can spend several hours visiting the exquisite halls, palaces, and museum within, including a relaxing stroll in the delightful gardens.

AFTERNOON Head west along crowded **Chandni Chowk**, perhaps dipping into the Hindu **Lal Mandir** temple, then bear south into the jumble of winding lanes that constitute one huge and vibrant market. Getting lost is part of the fun.

EVENING Find your way to **Jama Masjid** mosque, whose minarets tower above the old city. It is at its most magical around the time of evening prayers. Then it's tandoori time.

Essentials

GETTING THERE
Delhi's **Indira Gandhi International Airport**, due to be connected to the new **metro** system, is 9 miles (15 km) southwest of downtown. The metro provides a hassle-free and air-conditioned way of getting around the city.

WHERE TO STAY
Rak International (inexpensive) offers a bargain in the bustling backpacker area of Paharganj. *www.hotelrakinternational.com*
Godwin Deluxe (moderate) is a bright, modern hotel conveniently located in Ram Nagar, near the old city. *www.godwinhotels.com*
Maidens (expensive) gives you a taste of real Raj-style luxury in a converted colonial mansion in Old Delhi. *www.maidenshotel.com*

TOURIST INFORMATION
88 Janpath, New Delhi; *+91 11 2332 0008*

Right Spices, dried fruits, and nuts fill the alleys of Old Delhi's Khari Baoli market

Below Jama Masjid, the largest mosque in India, was commissioned by the Mughal emperor Shah Jahan

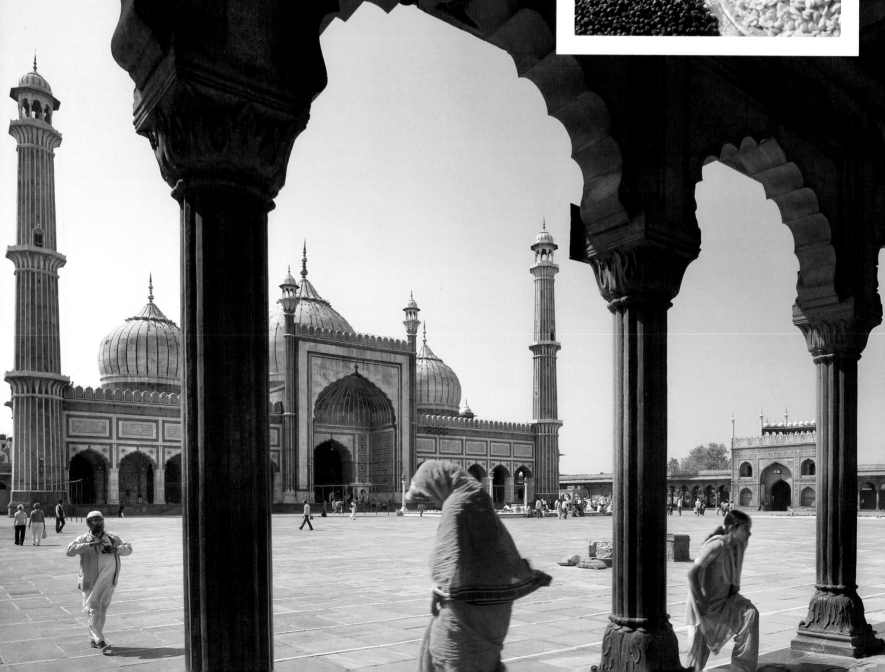

DELHI INDIA

Tandoori in the City of Mughals

The sprawling city of Delhi may boast the manicured avenues of the British Raj and be encircled by high-rise suburbs, but at its heart remain the atmospherically chaotic lanes of Old Delhi. This area grew up during the Islamic Mughal empire, and its heritage is reflected in its cuisine. It offers some of the best places in the world to eat tandoori dishes, cooked in a traditional clay oven.

Exploring India's capital is a journey of rich historical discovery, for this is not one but seven successive cities. Predating the New Delhi of the British Raj, settlement began with Rajput-era Lal Kot and culminated in the crowning glory of the Mughal empire: Shah Jahan's eponymous city, Shah-jahanabad, now known as Old Delhi. In between, a succession of Muslim conquerors left behind majestic monuments such as the towering Qutb Minar minaret and the elegant domed tomb of Emperor Humayun, but it is the remains of Shah Jahan's city, founded in 1638, that most captivate the imagination.

Within the space demarcated by the old city's four remaining stone gates and beside the expansive Red Fort and imposing Jama Masjid, India's largest mosque, life goes on in many ways as it did during the Mughal era. Wandering through the web of narrow lanes and bazaars, you will encounter rows of tiny shops selling by turns gleaming metal pots and other household items, sparkling jewelry, or colorful spices piled high in bulging sacks.

Old Delhi is a true melting pot of people from all over the Indian subcontinent and beyond. At every turn, restaurants vie for attention with street vendors selling snacks called *chaat (see pp192–3)*, but most distinctive among them – signaled by racks of ruddy-colored chickens fresh from the oven – are the tandoori restaurants. "Tandoor" is the word for the clay oven in which meat, fish, and some vegetables are cooked at temperatures as high as 750°F (480°C). This method of cooking, popular in the Punjab region, was said to be a favorite of the Mughal emperor Jahangir, father of Shah Jahan. However, tandoori cuisine as we know it today is widely credited to the restaurateur Kundan Lal Gujral and his Delhi base, Moti Mahal *(see right)*.

Tandoori dishes are fairly simple, with chicken as the most common ingredient. It is slit and marinaded in a mixture of yogurt, lime juice, garlic, and spices such as chili pepper, garam masala, coriander, cloves, and ginger before being baked in the oven. The marinade keeps the meat succulent and moist. It is served with an onion-based salad and usually eaten with naan flatbread, also fresh from the hot tandoor oven.

The Spice Market

Khari Baoli, named after its stepped well or *baoli*, once used for bathing and watering livestock, is the largest spice market in Asia. It is a fabulous place to stock up on Indian cooking ingredients and soak up the atmosphere of Old Delhi. Located just beyond the western end of Old Delhi's main street, Chandni Chowk, its crowded stands, separated by narrow lanes, are still often owned by the same families who began their businesses here ten generations ago. Every kind of spice, seasoning, and herb is on display amid a heady mixture of exotic aromas and a psychedelic palette of varying hues. The constant cries of porters carrying huge sacks and spice merchants advertising their wares adds sound to the sensual overload. You only need to take a pinch of garam masala and touch a little to your tongue to complete a sensory feast.

Above The precise mix of spices used determines the color of tandoori chicken

The Best Places to Eat Tandoori

Moti Mahal moderate

This restaurant – the epicenter of tandoori cuisine – was established in Delhi by Kundan Lal Gujral over 60 years ago and has since spawned a series of franchises, even beyond the boundaries of India. However, the prototype still has to be the place to sample tandoori cuisine at its best. There is plenty of seating within the relatively plain interior and a large leafy courtyard to dine in for most of the year. Some nights there is live *qawwali*, Islamic devotional music, to accompany your meal.

It is the food, however, that really does the talking. A wide range of tandoori dishes is available, including chicken or fish tikka, lamb kebabs, shrimp, and a variety of vegetables such as cauliflower, potato, and mushroom, as well as some *paneer* (cheese) dishes. Unsurprisingly, tandoori chicken is the most popular main dish on the menu, but the traditional butter chicken is another favorite. And, of course, there is a range of freshly baked naan breads to help you mop up any remaining juices.

3704 Netaji Subhash Marg, Daryaganj, Old Delhi; open 11 AM–11:30 PM daily; +91 11 2327 3661

Also in Delhi

The perfect example of how local cuisine has been taken upmarket to suit the lifestyle of Delhi's nouveaux riches, **Punjabi By Nature** *(www.punjabibynature.com; expensive)* has subtle lighting and decor, smart and attentive service, and delicious food that preserves its traditional roots. This is a fine spot for a special night out, sampling mouthwatering specialties such as tandoori shrimp, fish tikka, and *raan-e-punjab* (leg of lamb).

Also in India

Tandoori cuisine has spread to become a staple throughout India. In the city of Jaipur, **Niro's** *(+91 141 221 8520; moderate)* offers a succulent range of dishes from the tandoor as well as Rajasthani specialties. There's no problem finding good tandoori in the south, either: Chennai's **Bismillah Biryani Centre** *(+91 98 8464 8345; inexpensive)* is a typical street corner joint that turns tasty items out of its oven, as well as serving biryanis.

Around the World

In London, look no farther than the branch of **Moti Mahal** *(www.motimahal-uk.com; expensive)* in Covent Garden. This stylish restaurant offers top tandoori, expertly prepared by chef Anirudh Arora, as well as a variety of other traditional dishes. Over in San Francisco, the place to go is **India Clay Oven** *(www.indiaclayoven.com; inexpensive)*, which offers a wide range of tasty tandoori dishes.

PHUKET THAILAND

Green Curry in Phuket

Centuries before Phuket began attracting sand-and-sea hedonists, it was an important trade center for Arab, Indian, Malay, Chinese, and Portuguese traders. Indian and Arab merchants brought green curry to Ayutthaya, the ancient Thai capital north of Bangkok, in the 14th to 16th centuries, but southern Thailand – especially the island of Phuket – claims its cooks are the masters.

Dubbed "Pearl of the South" by the tourist industry, Phuket (pronounced "Poo-get") is Thailand's largest, wealthiest, most populous, and most visited island, and a province in itself. The jagged coastal terrain of this 310-sq-mile (810-sq-km) island encompasses broad sandy bays, rocky peninsulas, limestone cliffs, and tropical vegetation. Phuket's interior supports rice paddies and rubber, cashew-nut, cacao, pineapple, and coconut plantations, along with one last remnant of rainforest.

Formerly called Ko Thalang, and before that Junk Ceylon (an English corruption of the Malay "Tanjung Salang" or Cape Salang), Phuket has a culture all of its own. It combines Chinese and Portuguese influences with that of southern Thais and the *chao naam* (sea gypsies), an indigenous ocean-going people. About 35 percent of the island's population are Thai Muslims, and there are about as many mosques as Buddhist temples. There's lots for visitors to do (and spend money on), from sampling the delicious seafood to taking scuba-diving or snorkeling trips. And while most entertainment-seeking tourists flock to the flashy beach towns of Patong, Karon, and Kata, there are calmer spots, notably Nai Han and Kamala, and even relatively untouched coastal areas in the north, such as Nai Yang, Nai Thon, and Mai Khao.

Phuket cuisine combines Chinese, Malay, and Thai elements to create brightly colored, heavily spiced dishes. One favorite is *kaeng khiaw-waan* – literally "sweet green curry" – which is served with roti (a round wheat flatbread descended from Indian paratha), *khanom jeen* (thin rice noodles, served cold), or rice. The curry's green color derives from the plentiful presence of green chili peppers, cilantro root, kaffir lime peel, and green peppercorns, which are pounded with roasted coriander seed, fresh lemongrass, fresh galangal, fresh garlic, and salty shrimp paste to create the distinctive thick, green, pungent curry paste. This is cooked with coconut milk and eggplant, to make the curry slightly sweet and creamy, together with red chili peppers and the main ingredient – which might be chicken, beef, or seafood. Before serving, the dish is garnished with whole fresh sweet basil and chopped cilantro leaves, giving it a final fresh, tangy fragrance that's hard to resist.

Above The crews of traditional longtail boats such as these at Kata Beach – one of the most popular in Phuket – offer swimming and snorkeling trips

---

What Else to Eat

Favorite Phuket dishes tend to draw from two primary sources, Chinese and Malay. **Ba-mee moo op hong teh** (egg noodles with roast pork in a soy-mushroom sauce) is a Chinese-sourced dish, as is **khao man kai**, literally "chicken oily rice," but more commonly known as "Hainanese chicken rice." From the Malay side comes **roti kaeng**, a simple meal of griddle-cooked round flatbread with curry *(kaeng)*. One of the best-known southern Thai curries is **matsaman**, a fragrant Indian curry with peanuts and potatoes as well as chicken or beef. **Kaeng kayi** is a more local curry made with boiled cashew nuts. One dish that combines both Chinese and Thai elements, **khanom jeen**, is a delicious mix of thin rice noodles with a thick curry of fish, Chinese ginger, chili peppers, and coconut milk.

A Day in Phuket Town

Food is key to enjoying a great day out in Phuket town, so start the day with an eye-opening cup of *kopi* (strong Chinese-style black coffee) at Kopi de Phuket in the historic On On Hotel, accompanied by a plate of *roti kaeng kai* (flatbread with chicken curry) or some local candy from the large jars on the counter.

MORNING Meander through the historic **central district**, taking in the colorful Straits Settlement architecture, a 19th-century tradition. Walk up **Khao Rang**, sometimes called Phuket Hill, northwest of town, for views of the city, jungle, and sea. Take an outdoor table at Tungka Café for a lunch of egg noodles with smoked pork, a local specialty.

AFTERNOON Wander through the **Ranong Road Day Market** to shop for southern Thai fabrics and rattan crafts. Then visit the atmospheric **Shrine of the Serene Light**, off Phang-Nga Road, a Chinese temple that is nearly 200 years old.

EVENING Finish the day with a hand-crafted bowl of green curry at Krajok See *(see facing page)*. If you feel like an evening out, head to **Timber Hut** on the Yaowarat Road to enjoy music from local bands.

Essentials

GETTING THERE

Phuket **airport** has international flights. There are **planes** and **buses** from Bangkok. A **rental car** is worth considering to get around the island.

WHERE TO STAY

Thalang Guest House (inexpensive) offers simple, clean rooms in a Straits Settlement town house. *www.thalangguesthouse.com*

Sino House Phuket Hotel and Apartment (moderate) is a boutique hotel mixing vintage and modern decor. *www.sinohousephuket.com*

Royal Phuket City Hotel (expensive) in the capital of Phuket provides the town's most luxurious accommodations, with a gym and pool. *www.royalphuketcity.com*

TOURIST INFORMATION

www.tourismthailand.org

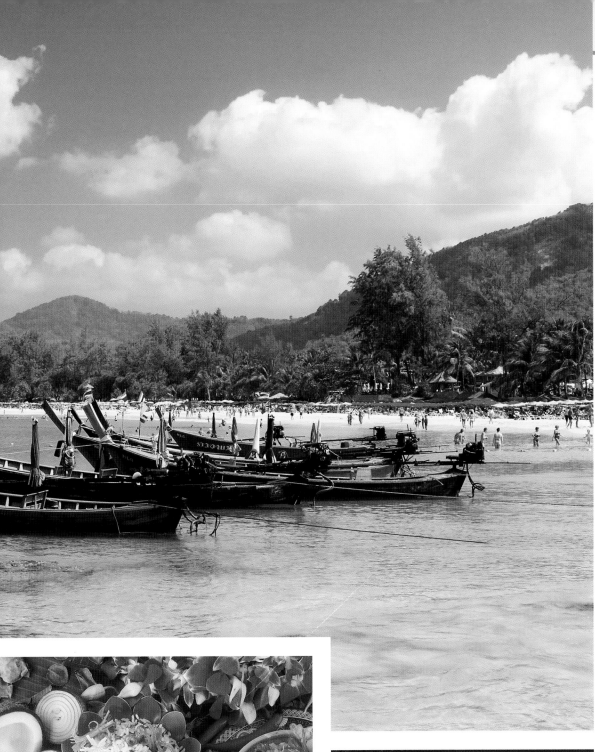

The Best Places to Eat Green Curry

Krajok See moderate

Krajok See used to be a closely guarded secret in Phuket town. It is named for the antique colored glass panes *(krajok see)* in its windows, and aside from the impressive cuisine, regular customers are drawn by the cozy and friendly atmosphere, enhanced by wooden ceilings and candlelight. Nowadays the restaurant is so well known that reservations are a must, as there are only about eight tables and one sitting per night (the restaurant is not open for lunch). Apart from green curry, another dish to look for here is *kung sarong*, shrimp wrapped in vermicelli, fried, and served with a tangy dip. Be sure to bring cash, as credit cards are not accepted. After 10 PM, the tables are pushed against the wall, a DJ spins tunes, and everyone dances.

26 Takua Pa Road, Phuket town; open evenings only, Tue–Sun; +66 7621 7903

Also in Phuket

A more down-to-earth, no-frills version of green curry can be found at legendary **Roti Chao Fa** *(+66 7622 1771; inexpensive)*, run by local Muslim Thais for over 30 years on the southwestern outskirts of Phuket town. As the name suggests, the large open-air restaurant specializes in roti, the unleavened flatbread derived from India's paratha. Customers dip roti into any of several curries, including green curry, served from large stainless-steel cooking pots. Rice is also available.

Also in Thailand

In Bangkok, **Roti Mataba** *(www.roti-mataba. net; moderate)* serves green curry very much in the southern Thai style, with roti or rice, in a charming two-story shophouse overlooking Santichaiprakarn Park. It's famous for its many variations of *mataba* (stuffed *rotis*), offering sweet and savory fillings from curried chicken, fish, or beef to banana or condensed milk. You can also sample other classic Thai-Muslim dishes here, such as *matsaman*, a tasty Indian-style curry with potatoes and peanuts.

Around the World

On the other side of the world, in San Francisco, California, **Manora's Thai Cuisine** *(www. manorathai.com; inexpensive)* offers one of the more authentic versions of Thai green curry found in the city, and at a reasonable price. Here it is served with a choice of chicken, beef, pork, or shrimp, and comes with both eggplant and green beans.

Above Many colorful rows of Sino-Portuguese "shophouses," which doubled as shops and homes, were built in Phuket in the 19th century

Left Thai green curry has a sweeter flavor and lighter texture than Indian curries; lime and lemongrass add refreshing citrus undertones

Above In midtown Manhattan, New York, a classic diner captures the streamlined, chrome-and-neon dream of 1950s America

North America

The Flavors of
North America

Ask most people around the globe to name the quintessential food of North America and the answer will most probably be "the hamburger." It is true that a good hamburger is available in almost every small town or big city across the US. But North American cuisine – including its fast food – is far more complex and varied, encompassing everything from homemade pies and perfect barbecue to succulent seafood, southern "soul food," and fiery Mexican dishes.

As Europeans discovered when they began colonizing the New World 500 years ago, the American continent is almost embarrassingly rich in natural food sources and fertile land. The icy waters of the northeast coast yield some of the world's finest shellfish, while much of the world's wheat springs from the black soil of North America's plains. Fruit trees groan with the weight of peaches in Georgia, apples in the Okanagan Valley, and oranges, lemons, and limes in Florida and California. Tomatoes and peppers grow as far as the eye can see in Mexico, and rippling corn stretches to the horizon through the American Midwest.

> *Nowhere is the taste of North America so celebrated as in northern California, where almost anything will grow.*

Nowhere is the taste of North America so celebrated as in northern California, where almost anything will grow. It was here that the farm-to-fork movement took root in the late 1960s, and so-called "California cuisine" – the concept of eating only fresh and local foods – has evolved into the driving force behind fine dining across virtually the whole of North America.

Yet North American cuisine has a distinctly casual streak. The slapdash grill menu – hamburgers included – met the American love affair with automobiles, especially in southern California, to give birth to the roadside diner. Even the streamlined architecture of this icon of American gastronomy reflects the worship of speed. While Americans hardly invented handheld food, few cities boast such a variety of street food as New York, where the diner on the move can chow down on German wurst in Midtown or Sri Lankan *dosas* in Washington Square Park.

Indigenous Ingredients

Transplanted ethnic cuisines are emblematic of North American gastronomy, yet certain dishes are rooted in their geography. Thanks to air freight, Maine lobster can be tasted all over the world, but never with such resonance as on the dock where it is landed. Clam chowder may trace its ancestry to Breton fish stews, but the clams that define it are limited to New England shores. And few dishes are so location-specific as New Orleans jambalaya, which

Right Cooking up a huge pot of chili at the Kansas State Fair Chili Cookoff
Below New York City's love of street food is indulged at its many street fairs

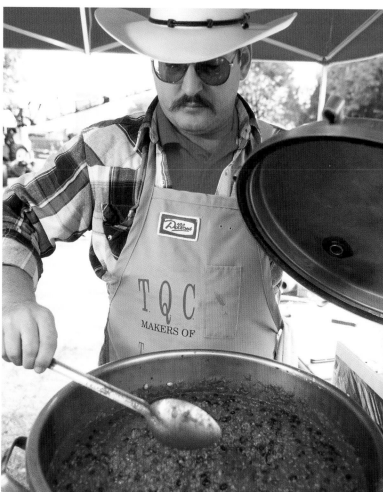

relies on the crayfish and rice of the bayous and the piquant tabasco strain of chili pepper. In fact, native North American peppers in their hundreds of varieties could be said to be the taste of the continent. The pork rib barbecue of Memphis carries just a hint of chili pepper heat, while in San Antonio, Texas, spicy stewed-beef chili contains nearly as much hot pepper as meat. But capsicum peppers have many more qualities than sheer heat: the sweetness of pimientoes, the smokiness of chipotle, and the spicy, fruity flavors of the habanero, for example. Farther up the Rio Grande, these are wonderfully exploited in the subtle cuisine of New Mexico, where Spanish colonists married Native American corn tortillas and chili-pepper-based sauces with an old-world taste for meat fillings.

Overseas Influences

A similar collusion between Native American and Spanish cookery took place in Mexico, where the people of Puebla combined their indigenous heritage ingredients of chocolate and chili pepper with spices introduced by the Spanish to create the rich brown sauce called *mole*. Indeed, it is a rare dish in Mexico that does not contain some form of chili pepper; it forms a part of even the *taco al pastor*, or rotisserie taco, so similar to the Middle Eastern doner kebab. The hottest of all the capsicums – the Scotch bonnet pepper found throughout the Caribbean basin – electrifies Jamaican jerk cooking, lending both heat and citrus notes to the smoky, spicy tang of Jamaican pimento wood, from the shrub that yields allspice. While jerk meat (usually chicken or fish) can be traced back to the original Arawak inhabitants of Jamaica, other Caribbean specialties reflect the islands' cultural overlays. So many East Asians were relocated to the Caribbean islands during colonial times that curries, *aloo* (spicy potato dishes), and the friendship bread of *dosti roti* are standards in the West Indies.

The African diaspora played a profound role in North American cooking as well. African slaves in the cotton and sugar cane regions of the American South cooked with African provender – okra, peanuts, and melons – along with leafy greens and cheap cuts of pork. In time, the hearty fare became known as "soul food," from collard greens cooked in bacon fat to the unctuous sweet potato pie.

Pennsylvania Dutch cooks are wont to encase every berry or tree fruit they grow in a flaky crust.

Americans have always had a sweet tooth, whether for thick cheesecakes made with the cream cheese of Philadelphia or for the sweet pastries of Pennsylvania Dutch country. A farming society with roots in central Europe (where pastry is king), Pennsylvania Dutch cooks are wont to encase every berry or tree fruit they grow in a flaky crust. It is, as the saying goes, as American as apple pie.

Left Local produce for sale at a market in Guadalajara, Mexico
Below A love of cars and fast food came together perfectly in the creation of the diner

Right Lobster-trap marker buoys decorate a shingled Maine lobster pound

Below The sweetest lobster is pulled from icy-cold Maine waters, steamed almost as soon as it is brought ashore, and simply served

Three Days along the Maine Coast

Picturesque fishing villages, lighthouses, and yachting harbors dot this meandering coastline, made famous by American painters from Winslow Homer (1836–1910) to Marsden Hartley (1877–1943).

DAY ONE Swim in the surf at **Reid State Park**, the longest sandy beach on this rocky coast, before peninsula-hopping to the yachting center of **Boothbay Harbor**. Fish for striped bass or tuna, or take a wildlife cruise to search for whales and puffins.

DAY TWO Clamber over the massive boulders of **Pemaquid Point** for a dramatic view of the lighthouse on the headland. Then drive to the fishing hamlet of Port Clyde and take a ferry to **Monhegan Island**, a summer art colony where painters open their studios to visitors.

DAY THREE After stopping at **Tenants Harbor** to visit the lobster-fishing museum, spend the day in the port of **Rockland**, with its world-class Farnsworth Art Museum and Wyeth Center, its child-friendly **Maine Lighthouse Museum**, and its excellent restaurants and cafés.

Essentials

GETTING THERE
Several domestic US carriers and Air Canada serve **Portland International Jetport**. Rent a **car** to drive north on Route 1.

WHERE TO STAY
Prices vary little across the region.
East Wind Inn (moderate) has lobster boats moored outside its windows in the picturesque fishing village of Tenants Harbor. *www.eastwindinn.com*
Grey Havens Inn (moderate) is a classic shingle-style 1904 hotel on a craggy bluff in Georgetown near Reid State Park. *www.greyhavens.com*
Limerock Inn (moderate) occupies a turreted Rockland manse in a Rockland neighborhood within walking distance of the Farnsworth Art Museum. *www.limerockinn.com*

MAINE USA

Sweet Lobster on the Maine Coast

From dawn to dusk, wooden boats motor across the tiny harbors of Maine's central coast. Men in rubber bib overalls toss lobster crates onto floating wooden docks, then abruptly cast off to haul more traps. Cooks hustle the crustaceans from dock to steamer to plate. The feast begins as diners crack shells, dig out the meat, and revel in the deep-sea flavor of the sweet-salty flesh.

Early European settlers of what would become the State of Maine wasted little time harvesting the virgin forests to build ships and turning to the sea to build a rich fishery. Maine's maritime heritage remains a way of life on the long, rocky peninsulas that trail off the coast between Casco and Penobscot bays, where briny villages are famous for the quantity and quality of their lobster catch. Drivers who detour down these peninsulas can spend days exploring a coast ruled by summer's long sunlight and the epic rise and fall of the tides. Twisting roads through spruce forest suddenly emerge into open vistas of the swelling green sea. Hidden coves are dotted with lobster boats, and craggy headlands are capped with stocky lighthouses that guide the boats to safe refuge through swirling currents and rocky straits.

Down every peninsula lies a harbor, and in every harbor is a "lobster pound" – originally a saltwater impound where lobsters were held for market. Most are still no-frills wooden facilities built right at the shore – some even hanging over the water.

Today most "pounds" also serve as casual seafood eateries. Few even have a dining room, serving meals through a carry-out window, but such shortcomings are of no consequence to connoisseurs of Maine's signature crustacean. A burly chaos rules the kitchens of these pounds, where cooks walk a narrow path next to monstrous steam vessels to load bags of lobsters, soft-shell clams, and potatoes tumbled with cobs of corn. Twelve to fifteen minutes later, the brownish-green lobsters have become bright red; the order is plated up and at the pickup window, the order number is yelled out loud enough for everyone on the wharf to hear.

The ensuing lobster feast is a messy experience, which is why most aficionados like to eat at picnic tables at the water's edge. Breaking the tail and claws sprays juices all around, and fingers quickly grow sticky picking the meat from the shell and dipping it into melted butter. Bibs, of course, are for sissies. But the sweet, succulent, and salty flesh makes all the mess and effort worthwhile.

The Maine Lobster Festival

More lobster comes ashore at the venerable fishing port of Rockland than anywhere else on the Maine coast, and for more than six decades the haul has been celebrated here with the annual Maine Lobster Festival. It takes place from Wednesday to Sunday on the first full weekend of August and draws thousands of visitors. A colorful parade, led by King Neptune and the newly crowned Sea Goddess, is among the highlights. One of the most popular events is the "Great International William Atwood Lobster Crate Race." Contestants vie to avoid falling into the sea as they run across 50 partially submerged lobster crates. Whoever touches the most crates before taking the plunge wins. Lobster, of course, is served daily.

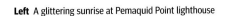

Left A glittering sunrise at Pemaquid Point lighthouse

The Best Places to Eat Lobster

Five Islands Lobster Co. moderate

This quintessential lobster pound offers the perfect synthesis of place and taste, serving classic lobster dinners and other seafood on one of Maine's prettiest harbors, ringed with five spruce-tufted islands. Dining is strictly alfresco, and diners must watch out for brazenly thieving gulls. Lobster is the mainstay. In addition to simply steamed crustaceans, the pound also prepares one of the tastiest lobster rolls on the coast. The kitchen picks the meat daily from steamed lobsters, blends it with just enough mayonnaise to hang together, and serves the lobster salad on a grilled soft bun. Since local lobstermen also haul up many Jonah crabs in their traps, the pound steams and picks their unusually sweet flesh to make crab rolls and crab cakes, which are usually served with a homemade tartar sauce full of chopped dill pickles and capers. Diners who prefer their seafood fried generally rate the restaurant's fried clams as among the best in Maine.

1447 Five Islands Rd., Georgetown, Maine; open 11:30 am–8 pm daily, mid-May–mid-Oct (may close at 7 pm late in the season); www.fiveislandslobster.com

Also in Maine

Coastal Maine is rife with excellent lobster pounds. **Shaw's Fish & Lobster Wharf** in New Harbor *(207 677 2200; moderate)* has the distinction of serving several local draft beers. In Rockland, chef Melissa Kelly often uses lobster in elegant preparations at **Primo** on Main Street *(www.primorestaurant.com; expensive)*.

Also in New England

Boston chef Jasper White literally wrote the book on ways to cook lobster. His pan-roasted lobster with bourbon and herbs is served at **Jasper White's Summer Shack** on Dalton Street *(www.summershackrestaurant.com; moderate)*. The hot lobster roll – lobster meat reheated in butter and served on a grilled bun – is a specialty of coastal Connecticut. Some of the best are found at **Lobster Landing** in Clinton *(860 669 2005; moderate)* and in Noank, at **Abbott's Lobster in the Rough** *(860 536 7719; moderate)*.

In Quebec

Maine lobsters also frequent the waters of Quebec's Magdalen Islands, where the short season, from May to July, yields superb lobster, much of it shipped to Montreal and Quebec City. To enjoy it at the source, visit **Restaurant La Marée Haute** in Havre-Albert *(418 937 2492; moderate)*, which serves a distinctively local cuisine that features marvelous lobster in season.

A Day in San Antonio

Many of San Antonio's sights are downtown, within walking distance of each other, including the Alamo, the fashionable River Walk, and the bustling Market Square. South of downtown, the atmospheric La Villita and King William historic districts are fun to stroll around.

MORNING Visit the **Alamo**, where frontier heroes including Jim Bowie and Davy Crockett were besieged for 13 days by the Mexican army in 1836 and gave their lives for Texan independence. Then make your way via the French-Gothic **San Fernando Cathedral** to Market Square and **El Mercado**, the vivid Mexican marketplace filled with colorful merchandise, crafts, jewelry, and lilting mariachi music.

AFTERNOON Drive to the South Side, where four lovely colonial churches lie within the **San Antonio Missions National Historical Park**. On the way back, catch the sunset from the observation deck of the landmark **Tower of the Americas** in Hemisphere Park.

EVENING Stroll along the **River Walk**, where the twinkling lights of the many bars and restaurants make a romantic end to the day.

Essentials

GETTING THERE
San Antonio International Airport is 7 miles (11 km) north of downtown; **shuttles**, a **bus** service, and **taxis** run into the city center. Once there, the downtown can be **walked**, though a **rental car** is useful for exploring farther afield.

WHERE TO STAY
Bonner Garden (inexpensive) is an award-winning B&B in the Monte Vista Historic District. *www.bonnergarden.com*
Crockett Hotel (moderate), a historic building, is just steps from the Alamo and has a friendly atmosphere. *www.crocketthotel.com*
Omni La Mansion del Rio (expensive) is an historic gem offering rustic-style luxury. *www.omnihotels.com*

TOURIST INFORMATION
317 Alamo Plaza; *www.visitsanantonio.com*

Right Chunks of prime beef, not ground beef, are used in an authentic chili, with soft beans tempering the fire of the spice
Below An evening river cruise is a perfect way to experience the music, color, and lights of the River Walk

SAN ANTONIO, TEXAS USA

On the Texas Chili Trail

Streetlights cast shadows over the dusky, silent buildings on San Antonio's Military Plaza. It's a far cry from the nights of yore, when this was one of the rowdiest places in Texas. Trail-hardened cowboys rode in from the range and headed straight for the Plaza, where the "Chili Queens" lit mesquite fires, hung bright lanterns, and dished out fiery ten-cent "bowls o' red" all night long.

Though San Antonio is now one of America's largest cities, its Mexican character and laid-back pace linger at its core. Colonial buildings such as the adobe Spanish Governors' Palace and San Fernando Cathedral resonate with history, and four of its beautiful 18th-century Spanish missions are still active places of worship. The fifth is better known as the Alamo, site of the heroic battle in 1836 for Texan independence. For modern contrast, San Antonio has the delightful downtown River Walk, lined with bustling restaurants, cafés, and entertainment, but with quiet stretches that let you enjoy the city's natural beauty. There are also fine art museums and lovely parks and gardens.

Chili is the official state dish of Texas, and San Antonio is the city where it was probably invented. Texas chili remains in a class of its own: the hottest you'll find anywhere, scorching the taste buds, stinging the sinuses, and sending chili-lovers into a state of bliss. In 1828, Houstonian diarist J. C. Clopper became the first person to describe it, writing of seeing poor families stewing a little meat into "a kind of hash with nearly as many peppers as pieces of meat." This blending of spicy peppers from Mexico with the pioneer love of beef made chili the earliest Tex-Mex dish. Chili became a trail food for Texas cowboys, who hammered dried beef, peppers, suet, and spices into bricks that could be boiled into stew. While preachers decried the "soup of the Devil, hot as Hell's brimstone," writers such as O. Henry immortalized the "Chili Queens," formidable Mexican women who served chili from their wagons on San Antonio's central Military Plaza. When the San Antonio Chili Stand opened at the Chicago World Fair in 1893, chili went national. By the 1930s, almost every town had a chili parlour.

When the ornate City Hall was built on Military Plaza, San Antonio's street life moved to nearby Market Square, today lined with the colorful shops and Mexican restaurants of El Mercado. During the many Hispanic festivals held in the square, the Chili Queens return, and the mouthwatering, piquant aroma of Texas chili wafts through the heart of San Antonio once more.

True "Texas Red" Chili

The term *chili con carne* (with meat) is superfluous here, for meat is the key ingredient – usually beef, but anything from bison to armadillo has been known to go into the pot. For real connoisseurs, beans are a travesty, and even tomatoes don't feature in the original dish. In Texas, the Chili Appreciation Society International (CASI) sets the rules for cooking true Texas red. Their biggest event is the World Chili Championship, held east of San Antonio in tiny Terlingua. On the first weekend of November, over 10,000 chili-hounds flock to this dusty ghost town. Country music plays, barbecues sizzle, and beer flows freely from coolers perched on groaning tailgates. Competition is intense, but the cooks and judges take the heat while a good time is had by all. Get yourself a pickup truck and come on down!

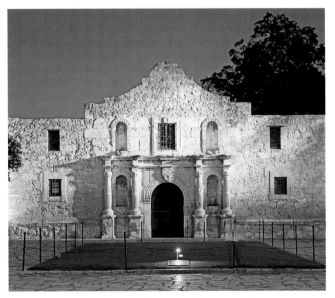

Above The Alamo, scene of past conflict but also fierce Texan pride

The Best Places to Eat Chili

Casa Rio moderate

Casa Rio has been serving food down by the river since 1946 and still sticks to its tried-and-tested recipes. It was the very first business down on the waterfront, and the boats and canoes that would arrive here, bringing hungry diners, helped build up the area to the River Walk that exists today. Colorful umbrellas shelter tables that are right by the water alongside one of the bridges, making it one of the prettiest dining spots around. Casa Rio serves the whole range of Mexican dishes, with starters including a tortilla soup, nachos, *flautas* (wheat-flour tortillas), and a *chili con queso* (with cheese). There's a range of chili options as main dishes, but if you only eat here once, you must have the Regular Plate of chili with Mexican rice and refried beans, which has been on the menu since opening day in 1946. If you get a second shot, then the slightly grander Deluxe Dinner is the local favorite.

430 E. Commerce Street; open 11 AM–11 PM daily; www.casa-rio.com

Also in San Antonio

Although San Antonio is regarded as the birthplace of chili, it can be surprisingly hard to find it on restaurant menus, perhaps because it's so strongly associated here with family recipes and festive gatherings. The best place to eat it is in just such an environment, so look for street fairs, festivals, and chili cook-offs going on around – and at weekends outside – the city, which are usually open to everyone.

Also in Texas

The **Texas Chili Parlor** *(www.txchiliparlor. com; inexpensive)* only opened in Austin in 1976 but it seems like it's been there forever. It's a popular student and sports bar that has a great chili section on its menu. You can choose from mild, spicy, or hot-hot-hot, have a chili taster of three different bowls of their best recipes, or try a white chili made with pork or even a vegetarian chili. In Grapevine, near Dallas, **Tolbert's** *(www.tolbertsrestaurant. com; moderate)* on Main Street has won all kinds of awards and accolades for its chilis. Founded in 1976 by Texan journalist Frank X. Tolbert Sr., it's a lively place with music several days a week and a menu that includes house Original Texas Red Chili, and a chili pie too.

Around the World

You can get your chili fix in London at **Automat**, a chic little American brasserie in the heart of Mayfair *(www.automat-london.com; expensive)*. Their *chili con carne*, served as an appetizer or a main course, is made only with premium Nebraska corn-fed beef.

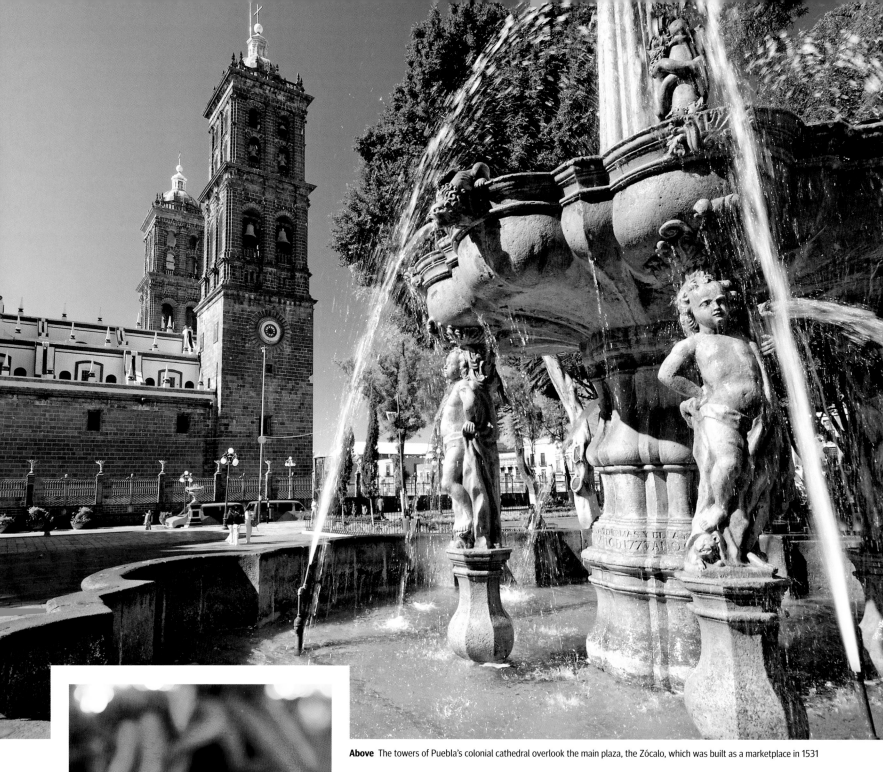

Above The towers of Puebla's colonial cathedral overlook the main plaza, the Zócalo, which was built as a marketplace in 1531

Above *Mole poblano de guajolote* (turkey) is a variation that often crops up during Puebla's Festival de Mole Poblano, held every July

A Day in Puebla

Puebla is rich in art, architectural, and archaeological interest. The best shopping opportunities arise on a Saturday or Sunday.

MORNING After a hearty breakfast of *huevos rancheros* (spicy eggs with tortillas), head for the antique and flea market in **Callejón de los Sapos** ("The Side Street of the Frogs") to browse for quirky bargains. Drop in to the nearby artists' district of **Barrio del Artista** to buy an original piece from one of the residents, or some of the city's famous blue-and-white pottery, known as *talavera*.

AFTERNOON Visit **Cholula**, 10 miles (16 km) east of Puebla. This is an ancient Indian town (Puebla was wholly built by the Spanish) dating back to the earliest civilizations of Mexico. Climb the huge **pyramid** and catch your breath at the **Iglesia de los Remedios** church atop it to enjoy sweeping views of neighboring volcanoes. Try a cup of *popo*, made of rice, cocoa, and chupipi fruit, on your way down, then explore the tunnels, crypts, and tombs beneath the pyramid.

EVENING After all that activity, you'll have earned a quiet supper.

Essentials

GETTING THERE

Puebla is 80 miles (125 km) from Mexico City, around two hours' drive from the capital along a good highway via **rental car** or **bus/coach**. Its small **airport** receives international flights from Houston, TX, and domestic arrivals from Cancún.

WHERE TO STAY

Hotel Colonial (inexpensive) is a friendly B&B near the main square. *www.colonial.com.mx*
Camino Real (moderate) is a beautifully restored convent in the city's historic center. *www.caminoreal.com/puebla*
La Purificadora (expensive), formerly a water purification factory, has been transformed by an architect into a contemporary design hotel – the pool is amazing. *www.lapurificadora.com*

TOURIST INFORMATION

www.visitmexico.com

PUEBLA MEXICO

Chocolate Chicken in Puebla

Just two hours from Mexico City, Puebla – the "City of Angels" – sits in a mountain valley surrounded by dramatic peaks and smoking, snow-capped volcanoes. Its gentle atmosphere owes much to its graceful colonial buildings, and visitors are kept busy photographing the magnificent architecture and eating *mole poblano* – this foodie city's namesake dish.

Puebla's immaculately preserved colonial architecture is arguably the best in Mexico, and has won the city UNESCO World Heritage status. Most of its 5,000 Spanish colonial buildings were built in the grand Baroque style of the 16th century, around graceful squares that found room for later additions in the 17th and 18th centuries. The magnificent cathedral dominates the main plaza, but the city also boasts the oldest library in the Americas, the Biblioteca Palafoxiana, and dozens of fascinating houses, convents, and churches. Domes crowd the skyline, pretty tiles line the walls and floors, and the gentle spray of fountains cools the many courtyards. Visitors browse for handicrafts in the markets or pottery workshops, or set off to wander the national parks, hike around the volcano, or visit the giant pyramid of Puebla's neighboring town, Cholula.

But Puebla is also an industrialized modern city with a large university, and it has a real buzz about it. There's a thriving café and restaurant culture, and the city is famous for its wonderful food, especially *mole poblano*: chicken in a chili-pepper-and-chocolate sauce. This is the best-known of several *mole* (pronounced "MO-lay") varieties and follows a complex recipe. The word *mole* comes from the indigenous ancient Aztec Náhuatl language, as do other more familiar words, such as avocado, tomato, and chocolate. *Mole* means something like "sauce", so guacamole is a sauce of avocado. *Poblano* simply means "of Puebla."

There are many interpretations of *mole poblano*, but the classic version comprises chicken breast covered in a voluptuous spicy sauce made of chili pepper and dark, unsweetened chocolate, subtly flavored with toasted seeds, dried fruits, corn, and spices, then left to bubble and reduce over many hours. Top of the menu at any special occasion, *mole poblano* is synonymous with celebration, starring at all weddings and on national holidays. Puebla's countless churches regularly host jubilant ceremonies and religious processions, which spill out onto the cobbled streets, making it impossible not to get caught up in this radiant city's colorful, joyous atmosphere.

The Best Places to Eat Mole Poblano

Sacristia de la Compañía
expensive

Undoubtedly one of the most upmarket dining options in Puebla, the eclectic Sacristia de la Compañía restaurant has two intimate rooms and a large patio, and offers a tasting menu alongside the à la carte list. Find it in the attractive Callejón de los Sapos – the same location as the weekend antique and flea market – in the historic center of the city. Part of a boutique hotel and antique shop (all the pieces on display are for sale, adding to the atmosphere) and housed in an 18th-century colonial mansion, the restaurant serves the best local and regional recipes and describes its *mole poblano* as the restaurant's "host." The Sacristia version of the classic dish is smokier and fierier thanks to charred chipotle (a smoked jalapeño pepper). You know you're in good hands when the chef behind a restaurant also offers cooking lessons, as this one does, lasting either one, three, or seven days. The week-long course is part of a package that includes hotel accommodations (wonderfully romantic) and meals.

6 Sur No. 304, Callejón de los Sapos; open 10 AM–10:30 PM Mon–Sat, 10 AM–5 PM Sun; www.mesones-sacristia.com

Also in Puebla

The most central of the three lively **Fonda de Santa Clara** restaurants *(www.fondadesantaclara.com; moderate)*, on 3 Poniente, specializes in local dishes and ingredients, with *mole poblano* as the centerpiece, and has traditional music and decor.

Also in Mexico

Three hours south of Puebla, the beautiful colonial city of Oaxaca cannot of course boast *mole poblano* but is home to the so-called "seven *moles* of Oaxaca," the most famous variety being *mole negro*. This should be jet-black in color due to the precise cooking (almost burning) of the ingredients. It uses six kinds of chili peppers and an array of nuts, dried fruit, seeds, and spices, as well as chocolate. The restaurant **Como Agua Pa Chocolate** *(www. comoaguapachocolate.com; moderate)*, named after the Mexican novel by the same name *(Like Water for Chocolate)*, has a balcony overlooking the Alameda Park, and while undoubtedly somewhat touristy, serves good chicken *mole* with a choice of five colorful Oaxacan sauces.

Around the World

Authentically prepared *mole poblano* is difficult to find outside Mexico and the southwestern United States; however, the four London branches of "market eating" restaurant chain **Wahaca** *(www.wahaca.co.uk; moderate)* do serve it enchilada-style with shredded chicken, using a recipe from Guanajuato, a picturesque town northwest of Mexico City.

Above A family produce stand at the weekly market in neighboring Cholula

What Else to Eat

Considered to be the gastronomic center of Mexico, Puebla has a varied cuisine that blends pre-Hispanic, Arabic, East Asian, French, and Spanish influences. Alongside *mole poblano*, other nationally and internationally renowned dishes include **chiles en nogada**, stuffed chili peppers with walnut sauce traditionally garnished with pomegranate seeds to provide the three colors of the Mexican flag – red, green, and white. Another classic is **pipián verde**, a fantastically tasty green *mole* sauce made from a base of toasted pumpkin seeds and usually served over chicken or pork. More casual street food comes from Puebla's covered food market, where **cemitas** – Mexican sandwiches – abound, with a dizzying array of possible fillings. Cheese-lovers should make straight for the oozing, stringy delights of the **quesadillas**.

NEW YORK, NY USA

Deli Delights in Manhattan

If imitation is a form of flattery, then New York's delis receive the highest praise. Even outside New York, many delis add "New York-style" to their name to evoke their rich history, classic ingredients, and gargantuan portions. New York's vibrant immigrant heritage, from Jewish to Italian to German, produced the USA's most popular deli cuisines, and today, it's hard to imagine one without the other.

New York's impressive immigrant history is best experienced in Lower Manhattan. Historically, the Lower East Side was the essence of the American "melting pot," with newcomers settling here from around the globe. In the late 1800s, this was one of the most densely populated neighborhoods in the world, with over half a million Jewish arrivals, followed by working-class Chinese and Puerto Ricans. Its story is told in the superb Ellis Island Immigration Museum, brought to life via historical photographs and voice recordings.

On the Lower East Side, you'll come across vestiges of "old New York" around every corner: the elegant, 1887 Eldridge Street synagogue; the well-known Tenement Museum depicting immigrant life; and perhaps most importantly, a still-lively Jewish food culture, from delicatessens to pickle purveyors. New York's deli history can also be traced back to the Italian immigrants who arrived in droves from 1850 to 1930. Little Italy in Lower Manhattan and, even better,

Arthur Avenue in the Bronx are studded with old-time Italian family delis filled with fat-streaked prosciutto, marinated artichokes, and tangy balsamic vinegar. German immigrants also made their mark on New York's deli history. For a taste of Bavaria, explore Yorkville on Manhattan's Upper East Side: the only area left in Manhattan that exhibits the city's German immigrant history, it is home to a couple of hearty delicatessens that peddle wursts of all kinds.

For all its colorful past, these days the Lower East Side seems to define gentrification, with trendy cocktail lounges and sleek boutiques. This is all the more reason to be impressed by the staying power of the deli tradition, which may have its roots in Lower Manhattan, but has since come to symbolize New York cuisine. Hot corned beef slathered with mustard; ruby-red slices of pastrami towering on rye; warm bagels smeared with cream cheese... peruse the menus of New York's quintessential delis, and you'll understand what inspired the classic image of a Jewish grandmother urging you to "eat, eat!"

Three Days in Manhattan

This is one of the top US destinations for visitors, with its world-class museums, iconic skyscrapers, great shopping, and lively nightlife.

DAY ONE Start the day with a waterfront walk around the southern tip of Manhattan, from the lively **South Street Seaport** to lush **Battery Park**, where you can catch a boat to visit the **Statue of Liberty** and **Ellis Island**. Afterward, explore the boutiques and cafés of the **West Village**, and then groove to a jazz show at the famous **Blue Note Jazz Club**.

DAY TWO Immerse yourself in the superb **Museum of Modern Art** (MoMA), which offers a double draw: the world's largest collection of modern art, and a building that's a work of art in itself. Keep an eye out for superstar paintings, from Picasso's *Les Demoiselles d'Avignon* to Vincent van Gogh's *The Starry Night*. A couple of blocks away is the legendary **Radio City Music Hall**; take the Stage Door tour, or check at the box office for evening show tickets.

DAY THREE Explore the lovely **High Line park** in the **Meatpacking District**, with views of the breezy Hudson River. In the afternoon, head north to the **American Museum of Natural History**, which is filled with fossils, skeletons, and life-size models of elephants and dinosaurs.

Essentials

GETTING THERE
New York City is served by three **airports**: JFK and LaGuardia (both in Queens), and Newark (in New Jersey), with **subway** and **shuttle** links to the city. The easiest way to get around Manhattan is by subway and on **foot**.

WHERE TO STAY
The Pod (inexpensive) has mod, thrifty rooms in Midtown. *www.thepodhotel.com*
The Mayfair (moderate) offers mid-range boutique comfort in the Theater District. *www.mayfairnewyork.com*
60 Thompson (expensive) in the SoHo district is elegant yet endearing. *www.60thompson.com*

TOURIST INFORMATION
Times Square Visitor Center, 1560 Broadway; *www.nycvisit.com*

DELICATESSEN STAGE RESTAURANT

Left The Statue of Liberty, first sight of the United States for generations of European immigrants

Above Classic pastrami sandwiches on the zinc countertop at world-famous Katz's (see overleaf)

Below Founded by Russian émigré Max Asnas in 1937, celebrity hangout The Stage is a Broadway landmark

Deli Food Around the World

Delicatessens flourish around the world from New York to Bologna, offering an authentic glimpse into the flavors and ingredients of a country's cuisine. The wonderfully varied choices include bagels heaped with cream cheese in New York; paper-thin slices of pastrami in Montreal; springy rounds of mozzarella in Italy; and pickled herring in Denmark.

NEW YORK CITY

2nd Avenue Deli inexpensive
162 East 33rd St.; www.2ndavedeli.com
Fill up on triple-decker sandwiches of peppery pastrami and grilled salami with plenty of Russian dressing; mushroom-and-barley soup; broiled chicken livers; and potato pancakes sweetened with warm apple sauce. This time-worn deli may have moved from Second Avenue, but it still offers the same quintessential deli fare, giant portions, and no-nonsense service.

Katz's Deli moderate
205 East Houston St.; www.katzdeli.com
There are sandwiches, and then there are sandwiches. For the latter, make for Katz's Deli, the renowned Jewish deli established in 1888 on the Lower East Side. Here, pastrami comes towering on rye, and giant, steaming *knoblewurst* (garlic beef sausage) dwarfs the bread it sits on. For dessert, try an egg cream, a uniquely New York concoction of milk, chocolate syrup, and carbonated water.

Russ & Daughters moderate
179 East Houston St.; www.russanddaughters.com
This shrine to smoked fish dates back to 1914, when Joel Russ began selling salt-cured herring and salmon. Since then, Russ & Daughters has continued to satiate the smoked-fish cravings of New Yorkers with curried herring, smoked Danish salmon, and one of the finest caviar selections in Manhattan, from Siberian Osetra to salmon roe.

Eataly expensive
200 Fifth Avenue; www.eatalyny.com
This temple to Italian cuisine, with marble-topped bars and high ceilings, showcases a superb array of Italian specialties: fat-streaked prosciutto from Parma; crumbly *reggiano* Parmesan from Emilia-Romagna; Rome-style pizzas bubbling with mozzarella and pepperoni; and Chianti and Brunello wines from Tuscany. In short: you can skip the trip to Italy – Eataly pretty much has it all.

LOS ANGELES, CA

Los Angeles, with its rich Jewish heritage, features a broad array of historic delis that serve all the traditional favorites, from matzo ball soup, brisket, and corned beef to smoked fish, chopped liver, and blueberry blintzes.

Factor's Famous Deli inexpensive
9420 West Pico Blvd.; www.factorsdeli.com
Slip into a roomy booth at this legendary deli, on Pico Boulevard since 1948, and fill up on rich deli specialties, including hot peppered beef, smoked liverwurst, and whitefish salad.

Nate and Al's inexpensive
414 North Beverly Dr.; www.natenal.com
Nate and Al's claims to be a "deli with heart" – and chances are you'll agree. It's lively and inviting, and serves homemade specials that might rival those of a Jewish grandmother. Try chicken noodle soup, corned beef and cabbage, and bursting frankfurters.

Canter's moderate
419 North Fairfax Ave.; www.cantersdeli.com
This historic Jewish deli, long a favorite with the show-business crowd, serves up hearty fare, including matzo ball soup, *challah* (braided bread), and brisket.

Langer's moderate
704 South Alvarado; www.langersdeli.com
Deli-lovers from all over LA make a pilgrimage to Langer's for its famous pastrami sandwich (No. 19 on the menu), piled high with thick-cut pastrami and Swiss cheese and served with creamy coleslaw.

MONTREAL, CANADA

Montreal's delicatessens are famous for their smoked meats, often served between huge chunks of rye bread with pickles on the side. The city is also known for its tasty bagels, which Montrealers say are even better than in New York City. You be the judge.

Left (top to bottom) Grab an espresso and panini at New York's Eataly, or sit down for a leisurely Italian feast; deli food Danish-style; Schwartz's in Montreal, famed for its portion sizes

Below (top to bottom) Air-dried hams hang from the ceiling in every Italian neighborhood grocery store; smoked meats and sausages take center stage in Bavarian *Delikatessens*

Fairmount Bagel Bakery
inexpensive

74 ave Fairmount ouest; www.fairmountbagel.com

Sink your teeth into one of Fairmount's warm bagels, made with unbleached flour, hand-rolled, and – here's the secret – baked in a wood-fired oven, and you'll understand why this is Montreal's best bagelry. There are more than 20 varieties to choose from.

Wilensky's Light Lunch
inexpensive

34 ave Fairmount ouest; (514) 271-0247

The frozen-in-time decor is as much a draw as the delicious bologna sausage and salami at this deli, which hasn't changed since 1932 – and that includes the grill and drinks machine. The prices, happily, also seem stuck in the past.

Reuben's Deli moderate
1116 rue Ste-Catherine ouest; www.reubensdeli.com

Taste your way through an array of smoked meats at this amiable deli. For variety, Reuben's also serves juicy steaks, Greek salads, and even cheesy lasagna. Enjoy a Canadian beer (or three) with your meal.

Schwartz's moderate
3895 boulevard St-Laurent; www.schwartzsdeli.com

This Montreal institution serves colossal smoked-meat sandwiches, with brusque service thrown in as part of the package. Be prepared to wait (and salivate) on weekends, when the line stretches out the door and down the sidewalk.

MUNICH, GERMANY

The word "delicatessen" is derived from the German, although in Germany, delis are more like specialty food halls – emporiums selling delicacies and fine food, from herb-scented sausages and caviar to exquisite tarts.

Feinkost Käfer moderate
Prinzregentenstrasse 73; www.feinkost-kaefer.de

Gourmands flock to this upmarket delicatessen, market, and restaurant, which is filled with local and international delicacies, including over 350 types of cheeses, roast ham, smoked meats, walnut-studded bread, and their justly famous raspberry tart.

Dallmayr expensive
Dienerstrasse 14–15; www.dallmayr.com

Enjoy everything from smoked sausages and caviar to rich coffees, fragrant teas, and flaky pastries at this luxury delicatessen and restaurant that dates back to the 17th century.

BOLOGNA, ITALY

The region of Emilia-Romagna and its capital, Bologna, are celebrated for their rich culinary traditions *(see also pp146–7)*. Bologna's nickname is La Grassa ("the fat one"), and the city's delicatessens feature a bounty of cheeses, olives, and especially cured pork meats, from prosciutto to salami to mortadella.

La Salumeria Bruno e Franco
inexpensive

Via Oberdan 16; www.la-salumeria.it

Widely considered one of Bologna's best delis, Bruno e Franco features traditional Italian fare, including superb olive oils, fresh and cured meats, Modena balsamic vinegar, the regional *reggiano* Parmesan cheese, jellies and preserves, and also excellent seafood salads, from octopus to shrimp.

A.F. Tamburini moderate
Via Caprarie 1; www.tamburini.com

Ham haunches and fat salami hang from the ceiling and pungent cheeses fill the counter at this venerable delicatessen. Sit in the warm café where you can also order fresh tortellini topped with rich Bolognese sauce, which got its name from the city.

COPENHAGEN, DENMARK

In Copenhagen, traditional delicatessen fare is served in a variety of forms, perhaps most famously as the country's beloved open-face sandwiches, *smørrebrød (see also pp106–7)*, which are heaped with everything from tangy herring and capers to roast pork.

Hansens Gamle Familiehave
moderate

Pile Allé 10; www.hansenshave.dk

Dig in to splendid *smørrebrød* at this historic outdoor eatery (which has a sliding roof so that patrons can stay toasty in winter). Take your pick from thinly sliced roast beef on dark rye, herring topped with a quivering egg, smoked eel, meatballs, and more. As for what to drink: Danish beer, of course.

Meyer's Deli moderate
Gammel Kongevej 107; www.meyersdeli.dk

This popular deli and restaurant is helmed by chef and gastronomic entrepreneur Claus Meyer, an enthusiastic proponent of locally sourced Nordic cuisine. Enjoy a wide range of deli fare, including organic bread from the on-site bakery, grilled sausage with homemade ketchup, and salami with fennel. If you're here on a weekend, don't miss the superb brunch.

SAN FRANCISCO, CALIFORNIA USA

Farm-to-Fork California Cuisine

San Francisco and the surrounding Bay Area are geographically blessed. The sparkling waters of the Pacific frame gorgeous vistas at every turn, from pastel-hued Victorian houses and vertiginous city streets to the famous Golden Gate Bridge. The region's cuisine rivals the setting, with innovative farm-fresh dishes to sample throughout the Bay Area.

A bird's-eye view of California reveals a wave-battered coastline, towering sequoia forests, lush vineyards, peach orchards, and orange groves. California may have given the world Hollywood, but the grand outdoors is its true celebrity. The influence of nature also pervades California's eponymous cuisine, which is rooted in the simple concept that ingredients should be healthy and homegrown.

It's easy to be part of the San Francisco feel-good spirit: join the locals on the bike trails that crisscross the city or test your balance rollerblading along the shaded paths in Golden Gate Park. Try a walk on the breezy waterfront, from lively Fisherman's Wharf (keep an eye out for its loudest residents – braying sea lions) to the sun-speckled Presidio parkland. North of the city lies Marin County – the birthplace of the mountain bike – where rugged Mount Tamalpais continues to offer the region's most exciting two-wheel adventures. The East Bay – and the progressive city of Berkeley – is also laced with green spaces, including Tilden Park. Take a dip in Lake Anza; stroll the aromatic Botanic Gardens; and hop on an antique carousel.

The "farm-to-fork" culinary movement – in which fresh, locally sourced ingredients rule – began in San Francisco and the Bay Area. One heady whiff in an outdoor market – and a juicy bite into a tender white peach – and you'll understand why. At San Francisco's popular Ferry Plaza Farmers Market on the Embarcadero, you can sniff and sample local produce while enjoying views of the Bay Bridge. Equally impressive is the Berkeley Bowl, which has the largest produce selection in northern California. Here, you'll see locals picking out organic pomegranates, hefting eggplants, and holding persimmons up to the light to choose the best of the best.

Many Bay Area chefs cultivate close relationships with regional growers, so what arrives at your table may have been pulled from the soil only hours before. Fusing fresh seasonal ingredients with cooking skills honed in the finest French kitchens gives delicious perfection – dishes like roasted scallops with Belgian endives and lemon gremolata, and parsnip and apple soup, populate the menus of California's gastronomic heroes, such as Alice Waters at her exceptional Chez Panisse (*see facing page*).

Above Unbeatable vistas of the San Francisco skyline and its surrounding hills can be had from the Golden Gate Bridge, the emblem of the city

California Wines

Viticulture began in California in the 18th century, when Spanish missionaries planted vines for their sacramental wines. Today, the Golden State produces more wine than the whole of Australia. California's most famous wine region is perhaps the **Napa Valley**, just north of the Bay Area, where the Mediterranean climate, favorable geology, and skilled modern winemaking techniques come together in some of the finest wines in the world. A visit to the Napa Valley, combining travel and frequent stops for tasting, is a must. You can explore independently by car, enjoying farm-fresh California cuisine along the way and spending the night at lovely B&Bs, or opt for the relaxed luxury of the **Napa Valley Wine Train** – a restaurant housed in vintage train cars (www.winetrain.com).

Three Days in the Bay Area

The Bay Area is anchored by the gorgeous city of San Francisco, with its world-class museums and impressive restaurants. To the east is the bohemian university town of Berkeley, and to the north, nature-filled Marin County.

DAY ONE Explore urban nature at **Golden Gate Park**, followed by a bike ride across Golden Gate Bridge into **Marin County**. Stop by the lovely harbor town of **Sausalito**, filled with art galleries and cafés. Ease into the evening in San Francisco's Italian **North Beach** neighborhood. Savor a grappa (or three) at **Tosca Café**, where you can enjoy the nostalgic atmosphere while listening to opera on the jukebox.

DAY TWO Visit the **Museum of Modern Art (SFMOMA)**, where the eye-catching building is as impressive as the art. Then shop till you drop at **Union Square**, which is ringed with boutiques and cafés where you can refuel over an ink-black espresso.

DAY THREE Head across the Oakland Bay Bridge to **Berkeley**, home to the famous University of California, and stroll colorful **Telegraph Avenue**, packed with street vendors and bookstores. For a dose of cultural history, stop in to the **Hearst Museum of Anthropology** on the University of California campus.

Essentials

GETTING THERE

San Francisco International Airport is 13 miles (21 km) from downtown. Get around on foot or by **BART** (Bay Area Rapid Transport) or **Muni** (San Francisco Municipal Railway).

WHERE TO STAY

The Greenwich Inn (inexpensive) is located in the Marina District. www.greenwichinn.com
Hotel Bijou (moderate) celebrates cinema history, with cozy rooms, red velvet curtains, and a small theater. www.hotelbijou.com
Claremont Resort (expensive) in the Berkeley Hills has leafy grounds, a splendid spa, and wonderful views. www.ksiresorts.com

TOURIST INFORMATION

San Francisco Convention and Visitors Bureau; www.onlyinsanfrancisco.com

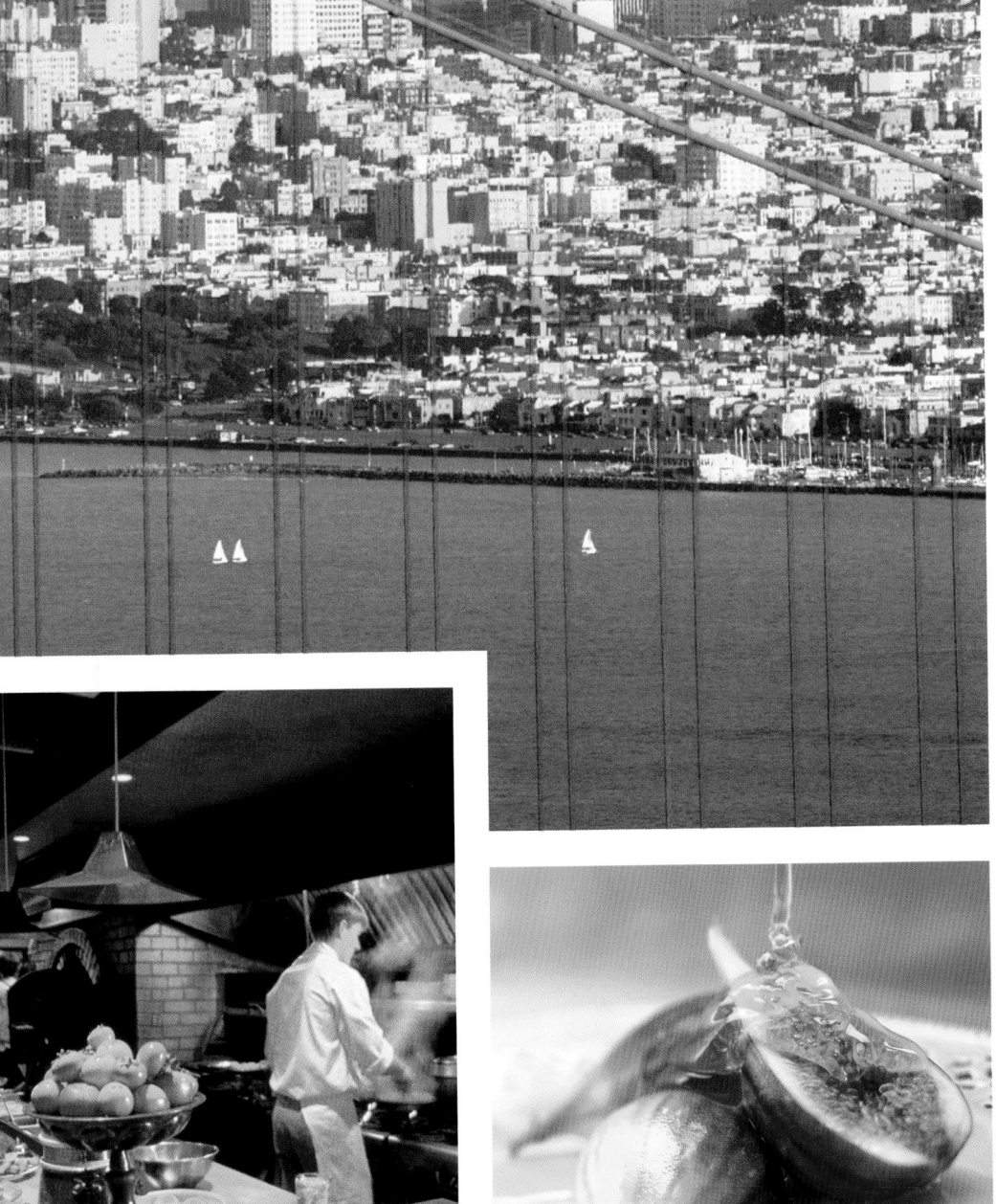

The Best Places to Eat California Cuisine

Chez Panisse expensive

With California cuisine, a dish is only as good as its ingredients. A juicy heirloom tomato picked off the vine or a sweet summer squash becomes the catalyst for the meal, the natural flavors enhanced by light dressings, such as a tart lemon vinaigrette. Chef Alice Waters founded Chez Panisse – and California cuisine itself – in 1971 on the belief that fresh, sustainable cuisine should be a right, not a privilege. At Chez Panisse the seasons reign supreme, and menus are developed around what's fresh at the market. Summer warmth brings forth glossy berries, while the autumnal cool reaps broccoli, artichokes, and acorn squash. Typical dishes include mesclun salad studded with creamy spoonfuls of avocado, poached salmon drizzled with citrus vinaigrette, and guinea fowl in a Provençal tomato sauce. After a multi-course dinner here, you will believe in transformative culinary experiences.

1517 Shattuck Avenue, Berkeley; open for dinner (two sittings) 6–6:30 PM and 8:30–9:15 PM Mon–Thu; 6–6:30 PM and 8:30–9:30 PM Fri–Sat; www.chezpanisse.com

Also in San Francisco

California's most famous vegetarian restaurant, **Greens** *(www.greensrestaurant.com; moderate)* has a setting that matches the cuisine. Built in a spacious warehouse constructed of reclaimed wood, the floor-to-ceiling windows offer views of the Golden Gate Bridge and the Marin headlands. Greens opened in 1979 under the auspices of the San Francisco Zen Center, and it continues to uphold Buddhist philosophies while paving the way for vegetarian restaurants around the country. The seasonal menu includes mesquite-grilled brochettes of mushrooms, tofu, small potatoes, and white corn; spinach salad with red dandelion, feta, and croutons; and a rich summer squash ragout. For a high-end night out, try **Michael Mina** *(www.michaelmina.net; expensive)* where the eponymous celebrity chef showcases a creative menu based on organic ingredients, from diver-caught scallops with lemon-accented caviar to pulled pork with apple ravioli.

Also in the US

One of New York City's first organic restaurants, **GustOrganics** *(www.gustorganics.com; inexpensive)* serves superb Latino-inspired farm-fresh cuisine, with plentiful vegan, vegetarian, and gluten-free options from breakfast through dinner.

Around the World

Fresh, seasonal Italian cuisine is a staple at **Il Bocconcino** *(www.ilbocconcino.com; inexpensive)* in Rome. The restaurant is popular with followers of the "Slow Food" movement, which, like California cuisine, places a premium on locally sourced, organic produce.

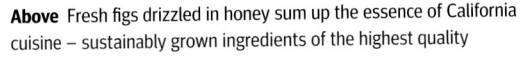

Above Fresh figs drizzled in honey sum up the essence of California cuisine – sustainably grown ingredients of the highest quality

Left French-inspired but thoroughly Californian, Chez Panisse has become a culinary institution

TRINIDAD CARIBBEAN

A Tropical Taste of Trinidad

In the Caribbean Sea's southernmost reaches, Trinidad forms a vibrant multicultural crossroads between South America and the West Indies. A sun-drenched, palm-scattered multilingual isle, Trinidad's richly diverse ethnicity mixes Indian, African, Amerindian, and European ancestry in a cultural mix that has resulted in fantastic multiethnic cooking styles and exotic food traditions.

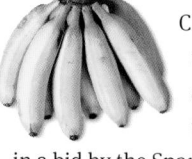

Claimed by Columbus for Spain in the 15th century, Trinidad soon acquired African slaves in addition to its native Amerindian population in a bid by the Spanish to create a flourishing plantation colony. In the early 18th century, French planters arrived to cultivate sugar and cocoa, followed shortly afterward by the British, who took control of the island in 1802. Spanish-speaking laborers from Venezuela and black laborers from the United States also settled in Trinidad in the 19th century, as did 150,000 workers from India's northern tip, Portuguese-speaking sailors from Madeira, and Cantonese farmhands from China. Today, the influences of Trinidad's colorful racial makeup have permeated every aspect of the island, including its cuisine.

The food of Trinidad is deliciously rich in exotic flavors, mixing the robust spices of India with the fresh local fruits, nuts, and vegetables of the Caribbean. From flavorsome Creole dishes of pot-stewed chicken with red beans and plantains to delicate Cantonese-style stir-fried vegetables, Trinidadian foods are well seasoned, and each one is a dish to savor. Yet it is the humble roti (or rosti) flatbreads that characterize "Trini" kitchens across the island, from the buttery paratha, yellow lentil *dhalpourie*, and potato *aloopourie* to the perennial favorite – *dosti*. *Dosti* is made using two disks of roti dough rolled out one on top of the other to form a "sandwiched" double layer; they are said to be like two friends – *dosti* – meeting, hence the name. The bread is cooked on a lightly greased hot *tawah* (baking stone) and served alongside dishes such as thick soups of curried chickpeas and potato dishes spiced with turmeric and fenugreek. It often accompanies a traditional curried duck recipe, where the birds are cooked in large iron cauldrons over an open flame on the banks of the Ortoire River.

Much has changed since Columbus first set foot on Trinidad, but this small island still epitomizes the Caribbean idyll. Almost 20 sandy stretches punctuate its coastline, and its natural attractions have been protected: there are wildlife sanctuaries, bird breeding centers, and eco-conservation areas. In the capital, Port of Spain, crowded street markets bustle among fine colonial mansions set around the capital's 260-acre (105-hectare) Queen's Park Savannah. All Trinidadians relish social gatherings and have made "the Savannah" and its surrounding zoo, botanical gardens, plazas, and cricket grounds central meeting points for the convivial consumption of feather-light, flaky *dosti*.

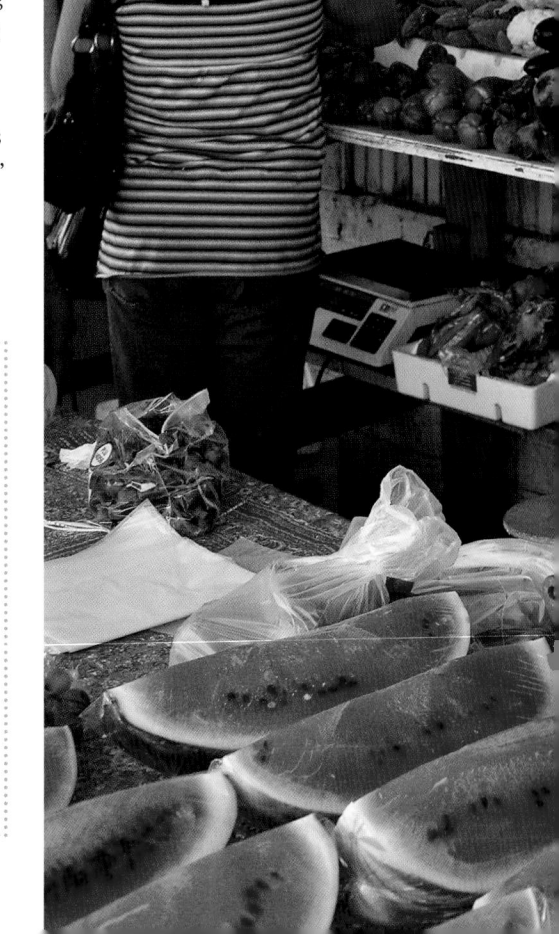

Three Days in Trinidad

Trinidad's 90-by-40 mile (145-by-65-km) landscape rolls out mountain peaks, beaches, streams, rivers, coconut palms, tropical flora, and rustling sugar cane crops.

DAY ONE Spot scarlet ibis at the 40-sq-mile (100-sq-km) **Caroni Bird Sanctuary**, Trinidad's most prized ecological site and a vast butterfly-rich swampland interlaced with waterways trimmed by blue, mauve, and white lilies.

DAY TWO Discover picturesque sands at **Maracas Bay**, Trinidad's most stunning soft white-sand beach. As the sun goes down, join local night owls to revel in calypso music. **Port of Spain**'s vibrant nightlife scene boasts numerous musical venues that offer a riot of color, dance, costume, and pulsating beats.

DAY THREE Spend the morning exploring **Pitch Lake**, a mysterious, otherworldly watery expanse dating back millions of years, discovered in 1595 by Sir Walter Raleigh. After lunch visit Port of Spain's **"Magnificent Seven"** – a collection of fine historical landmark buildings built on mudflats once tangled by knots of mangroves.

Essentials

GETTING THERE
Trinidad's **Piarco International Airport** lies 20 miles (32 km) southeast of the capital. Use **cars**, **taxis**, and **minibus taxis** to get around.

WHERE TO STAY
Orchard View Guest House (inexpensive) is a friendly family-run B&B located east of the airport in lush countryside. *(868) 313 0459*
Laguna Mar Resort (moderate) is an oceanfront retreat for nature-lovers. *www.lagunamar.com*
Hyatt Regency Trinidad (expensive) offers luxury in Port of Spain. *www.trinidad.hyatt.com*

TOURIST INFORMATION
www.gotrinidadandtobago.com

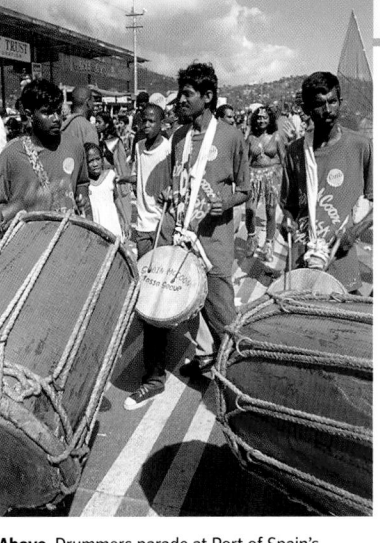

Above Drummers parade at Port of Spain's colorful five-day pre-Lenten Carnival

Left Trinidad has many produce markets selling fresh fruits, vegetables, and meat (including live chickens), visited by locals early each morning

Above Roti, especially in the form of *dosti*, is often eaten in the form of a wrap filled with seafood, chicken, or vegetable curry

Food Markets

Trinidad's multicultural ancestry is easily identified in Port of Spain's noisy Central Market, where you can rummage through piles of fresh-plucked dasheen leaves, succulent okra, water chestnuts, yucca, and bunches of blood-red chili peppers, and breathe in the intoxicating aroma of coconut milk sprinkled with crab meat, cilantro, or thyme. Nibble on richly seasoned, fried chunks of *geera* pork and tender pig's trotters, or glug down generous cups of corn soup topped off with a cloudlike dumpling, as hordes of food shoppers from all creeds jostle for paper-wrapped bargains around the seller's weighing scale.

The Best Places to Eat Roti

Siparia-Erin Road

To feast on a wide range of delectable roti, head to the Siparia-Erin Road in Debe, Port of Spain, where Trinidad's huge Indian community is centered. Dozens of vendors ply their mouthwatering wares at red-hot roadside *tawas* (griddles) that sizzle and spit with curried lentils, chickpeas, meat, shrimp, and strips of spicy vegetables. Choose from cold prewrapped rotis or freshly cooked warm breads on which to ladle generous dollops of filling, with a spoonful of piquant sauce on the side. With bare fingers, rip the flaky, buttery roti apart to delight in peppery beans, sweet tomatoes, sautéed *baigan* (eggplant), and lightly spiced spinach bhaji.

Also in Port of Spain

Other exquisite rotis can be found in the district of Penal, where Indian-owned curbside huts sell candied delicacies, hot spicy snacks, and sweets along Main Street. Imbibe the aromatic temptations of a host of scrumptious nibbles such as fried potato pies, *pholourie* (fried balls of ground split peas served with chutney), *barfi* (coconut fudge), *goolab jamoom* (milk balls in sweet syrup), and piles of roti stacked under towels to keep them perfectly moist and warm.

Also in Trinidad

D'Roti Hut *(868 681 8717; inexpensive)* on Eastern Main Road, Sangre Grande, in Trinidad's northeast, is a low-key, fast-food carry-out joint, but its menu offers about half a dozen mouthwatering variants to street stand food. Staff here use the local lingo when it comes to roti talk, and when you "buy roti" it means committing to a dish of curried vegetables, lentils, or meats wrapped up burrito-style in buttery griddle-cooked bread – unless you order a "buss-up-shot," in which the meat or vegetables are served on the side. D'Roti Hut is reliably good and everyone knows it.

Around the World

At **Roti Houpa** *(+44 20 7627 8637; inexpensive)* on Clapham High Street in South London, a highly skilled team of roti-makers hail from Debe and Penal's huge Indo-Trinidadian community. You can watch these roti masters at work as you peruse a carry-out menu of authentic Indo-Trinidadian cuisine. Also in London, the **Trinidad Roti Shop** *(+44 20 8838 4800; inexpensive)* on Nicoll Road, Harlesden, is unmissable, as it boasts a Trinidadian flag the size of a family car. Run by a friendly family from Port of Spain, this delightful red-and-white-painted hole-in-the-wall is a snug fit when it's busy. Join a line that often snakes out of the door to witness your order being fulfilled at a rhythmic pace. Choose from curried potato fillings and spicy sauces from a menu of sweet and savory rotis.

SOUTHERN CALIFORNIA USA

Road Food in Southern California

The surf's up and the convertible top's down on Highway 101, southern California's famous coast road. Along with its cross-country counterpart, Route 66, it helped make the road trip a classic American experience. The endless miles soon became dotted with neon beacons, beckoning hungry, weary travelers into a pit stop that became a fast-food icon – the American diner.

Diners have their roots in the horse-drawn lunch wagons that set up on street corners in the late 1880s to feed hungry shift workers, newspapermen, and theater-goers, looking for food after the restaurants closed. They evolved into rolling restaurants with a few seats inside, known as "dining cars" and then simply "diners." By the late 1920s, companies – most famously O'Mahony's of New Jersey – were manufacturing prefabricated diners built to look like railroad dining cars, in Art Deco designs, which were then shipped to their locations. By the 1930s they had acquired all their trademark characteristics: gleaming stainless-steel bodies, shiny chrome counters with swivel stools, tile floors, Formica tables in deep leather booths, and flashy jukeboxes full of dance records.

Today, as always, diners serve inexpensive homemade fare. Daily "blue-plate specials" might feature chicken and dumplings or Mom's meatloaf, with a hearty helping of potatoes and vegetables. All-day breakfasts range from sunny-side-up eggs and biscuits to whopper stacks of buttermilk pancakes with maple syrup. The soda fountain churns out thick, creamy chocolate malts and strawberry milk shakes to accompany juicy burgers, fries, and chili dogs hot off the grill. There's hot fudge sundae or a fat slice of banana cream pie topped with a tower of whipped cream to finish, and all the coffee you can drink.

By the 1950s there were over 6,000 diners across the country, and car culture came into its own. In the balmy nights of southern California, teenagers cruised "the strip" looking for fun (or trouble) and diners became drive-ins, where you placed your order over a speakerphone and ponytailed carhops brought it to your car, often on roller skates. Though the cars and hairstyles have changed, the fascination with the California lifestyle continues. Highway 101 has it all: the surfing hotspots of Oceanside and Huntingdon Beach, the swanky yachts of Newport Beach, and the bright lights of Hollywood – and along the way, flashes of neon and gleaming steel that promise bottomless cups of coffee and homemade pie.

Three Days in Southern California

Southern California offers a great range of sights, activities, and environments. You can go from big, bustling theme parks to quiet coves, or small, exotic cactus gardens to huge wetland bird preserves and even old mission churches to modern art galleries, all within a couple of hours' drive of each other. December to March is whale-watching season, with excursion boats leaving from several locations. Whether you're a surfer, a beachcomber, or a sunset-watcher, the coast is a highlight all year round.

DAY ONE Spend the day at **SeaWorld San Diego** for a close encounter with dolphins, sharks, sea lions, penguins, and other aquatic creatures. The impressive shows feature performances with dolphins and orcas.

DAY TWO Visit **Mission San Luis Rey**, the largest of California's 18th-century Spanish missions, at Oceanside. Then head for Oceanside's **Buccaneer Beach** to watch the surfers. In the afternoon, browse the art galleries at **Laguna Beach**, or admire the yachts at **Newport Beach**.

DAY THREE Take a morning stroll along the pier at **Huntington Beach**, another top surf city. Then head into **Los Angeles** and don a pair of roller skates to watch the wilder characters on the boardwalk at **Venice Beach**.

Essentials

GETTING THERE
Fly into an **international airport** at either San Diego or Los Angeles and **rent a car** – this is absolutely essential for exploring.

WHERE TO STAY
The Dana (inexpensive) in Mission Bay is a short walk from SeaWorld and the beach. *www.thedana.com*
Casa Laguna Inn (moderate) in Laguna Beach has charming rooms with ocean views in a mission-style inn. *www.casalaguna.com*
Oceanside Marina Suites (expensive) has spacious rooms with balconies looking over the ocean or harbor. *www.omihotel.com*

TOURIST INFORMATION
California Welcome Center, 928 North Coast Highway, Oceanside; *www.californiawelcomecenter.org*

Left Generous helpings of pancakes, syrup, and blueberries are a staple of California's diners

Above Large, comfortable cars and Art Deco–style diners are classic symbols of 1950s America

Below A road trip up the Pacific Coast leads through the magnificent scenery of Big Sur, California

Diners Around the World

Many American diners had closed by the 1970s, victims of the onslaught of fast-food chains. But nostalgia for the simpler postwar lifestyle and a love of '50s kitsch and Art Deco has sparked a new wave of retro-styled diners, in the US, Europe, and beyond.

SOUTHERN CALIFORNIA

101 Cafe inexpensive
631 South Coast Highway, Oceanside; www.101Cafe.net

Built in 1928, the 101 Cafe has gone from diner to drive-in and back again. Painted with bright murals and filled with Highway 101 memorabilia, it serves classic diner meals and sandwiches, from French toast or buttermilk pancakes with bacon to meatloaf or double cheeseburgers with fries. The peanut butter malt is to die for.

Mel's Diner moderate
8585 Sunset Blvd., West Hollywood; www.melsdrive-in.com

The original Mel's opened in 1947, and starred in the film *American Graffiti*, forming the backdrop for teenagers "cruising the strip" in California in 1962. Unfortunately, it was demolished shortly after shooting, but this second-generation diner – opened by the original owner's son – has recreated all the best parts, and has an outdoor patio where you can enjoy burgers and diner dinners under the neon lights.

The Nickel Diner moderate
524 South Main St., Los Angeles; www.nickeldiner.com

Located in an old vaudeville theater in the newly-gentrified area around Skid Row, the Nickel Diner plays with the classic diner repertoire to create some truly exceptional dishes: try the Big Time Cheddar, maple bacon doughnuts, and the red velvet cake.

Ruby's Diner moderate
1128 W Lincoln Ave., Anaheim; www.rubys.com

Nab one of the carhop spaces here and you'll get your chili fries served on roller skates. Vintage decor and a great menu make it a blast from the past. Also at Laguna Beach, Huntington Beach, and other locations around the US.

REST OF THE US

From homey neighborhood hangouts to slick retro-style restaurants, everyone in America has a favorite diner. Those listed below stand out for their history – some are original O'Mahony prewar models – and their decor, atmosphere, and authenticity, as well as their delicious diner fare.

66 Diner inexpensive
1405 Central Ave. NE, Albuquerque, New Mexico; www.66diner.com

Located right on historic Route 66, this fabulous diner has turquoise booths and golden oldies playing on the jukebox, and serves deluxe plates, blue-plate specials, and thick, creamy milk shakes from behind its shiny chrome and tiled counter.

Mickey's Dining Car inexpensive
36 West 7th St, St. Paul, Minnesota; www.mickeysdiningcar.com

Fresh farm eggs, hand-shredded hash browns, spindle-blended milk shakes, and tasty family recipes have been served in this authentic O'Mahony diner since 1939. It's now considered so precious that it's listed on the National Register of Historic Places.

Summit Diner inexpensive
1 Union Place, Summit, New Jersey; (908) 277 3256

Appropriately located opposite the train station, this 1938 Art Deco chrome beauty is another of the few remaining O'Mahony diners in the US. Enjoy Taylor ham (pork roll) and eggs with hash browns at the marble counter or in a red-leather booth.

Ed Debevic's moderate
640 N Wells St., Chicago, Illinois; www.eddebevics.com
Rude waitresses in beehive hairdos and horn-rimmed glasses who dance on the counter to '50s hits are all part of the experience at this fun, retro diner. Great shakes and burgers.

Rosie's Diner moderate
4500 14 Mile Rd. NE, Rockford, Michigan; www.rosiesdiner.com

A long menu of home-cooked favorites, from their signature slow-roasted beef and noodles to sloppy-joe sandwiches and blue-plate specials, are served in this authentic 1946 diner.

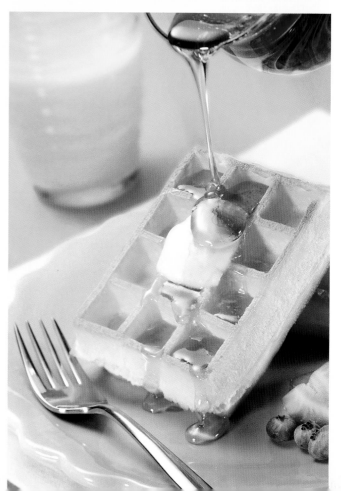

Left (top to bottom) A classic diner snack – French fries and a strawberry milk shake; a typical US diner in San Francisco; syrup and butter over waffles, with fresh fruit on the side

Below (top to bottom) Red Formica tables, checker-patterned plates, and jukeboxes help create the retro-diner look; Ed's Easy Diner, in Soho, London, is a haven for exhausted shoppers

ENGLAND

It's not surprising that London, with its fashionable restaurants and love of quirky style, embraced the retro diner craze, but now shiny silver American-style diners are springing up in the rest of the country too.

Ed's Easy Diner inexpensive
12 Moor St., London W1; www.edseasydiner.com
The all-day breakfast, juicy burgers, and creamy shakes are a hit at this colorful diner with a prime corner spot in Soho. Hot pepper addicts will love the "atomic" American fries and onion rings. Grab a red swivel chair at the shiny chrome counter.

Good Life Diner inexpensive
128–130 Curtain Rd., Shoreditch, London EC2; www.goodlifediner.com
Leather booths, lots of neon, and a '50s soundtrack form the backdrop to the burgers at this trendy American diner, which has four other London locations, in Camden, Islington, Soho, and Kensal Rise.

The 50s American Diner moderate
John St., Church Gresley, Derbyshire; www.the50samericandiner.bravehost.com
Burgers, steaks, and hot diggity dogs are served in this authentic, gleaming steel O'Mahony diner, shipped over from Boston to the National Forest in Derbyshire and filled with '50s memorabilia. Friendly waitresses wear vintage dresses to serve up food in four-seater booths and the jukebox plays rock 'n' roll.

IRELAND

With their long connections to America, it's no wonder that the fun-loving Irish have taken classic American burgers, shakes, and diner dishes along with 1950s nostalgia into their hearts, and opened some great diners.

Eddie Rocket's inexpensive
7 South Anne St., Dublin; www.eddierockets.ie
Fresh-ground burgers, foot-long hot dogs, red-basket specials, and hand-dipped Shake Shop malts come with a huge helping of '50s attitude. There are 20 Eddie Rocket's diners in greater Dublin and more around the country.

Springsteen's Diner moderate
633 Lisburn Rd., Belfast; www.springsteensdiner.com
With its flashy neon jukebox, all-day breakfasts, Whitehouse burgers (named after US presidents), and big menu of American favorites, this characterful diner could have been born in the USA.

REST OF EUROPE

Retro diners have crossed over to the Continent too. Paris may be the preserve of French culture and cuisine, but even here the stylish appeal of old-style American diners flourishes on the Left Bank.

Breakfast in America inexpensive
17 rue des Ecoles, Paris, France; www.breakfast-in-america.com
An ex-pat American filmmaker, longing for a stack of pancakes and a "bottomless mug o' Joe," opened this popular diner serving tasty all-day breakfasts, burgers, and blue *plat du jour*.

Happy Days Diner inexpensive
25 rue Francisque Gay, Paris, France; www.happydaysdiner.com
Enjoy mega-burgers, Long Island bagels, milk shakes, and more along with rockabilly music and a '50s ambience at this cheery diner sporting turquoise booths and pastel-pink countertops.

Flamme und Feuer moderate
Klein Breitenbach 2, Mörlenbach, near Mannheim, Germany; www.flammeundfeuer.de
Flamme und Feuer ("Flame and Fire") has a long American menu, but it's the all-you-can-eat burger and spare-rib nights and breakfast buffets that draw the Harley- and classic car-loving crowds.

AUSTRALIA

American diners seem completely at home in the land of road trains and beach barbies, especially in the cities, where the 1950s memorabilia, rock 'n' roll music, and diner fare add up to a really fun place to meet.

Big Rig Diner moderate
231 Oxford St., Darlinghurst, New South Wales; + 61 2 9332 3197
Tasty burgers, homemade chili, and other American favorites come with a big dollop of '50s style amid Elvis posters and great music on the jukebox. Check out the Houndstooth Bar at the back.

Misty's Diner moderate–expensive
103–105 High St., Prahran, Victoria; www.mistysdiner.com.au
Misty hails from Phoenix, Arizona, and her Aussie diner serves fare with a Southern flair, from deep-fried pickles and corn dogs to a bucket of pork ribs or "trailer-trash" fried steak. Misty's motto: "Bring your appetite, it's gonna get messy."

A Day in Macon

This moderately sized city is perfect for strolling, whether admiring the cherry blossoms, nibbling on peaches and pecans from the State Farmer's Market, or building up an appetite for the next meal.

MORNING Explore the ancient Indian mounds at the **Ocmulgee National Monument**, with structures and exhibits telling the story of 10,000 years of Southeastern Native American habitation and the distinctive Mississippian culture.

AFTERNOON Visit the **Tubman African American Museum** with its art, artifacts, cultural exhibits, and a huge mural depicting the journey from Africa to America. Cross the road to the exhibits of music and memorabilia in the **Georgia Music Hall of Fame**, then wander down to the river where a statue of Otis Redding gleams in the sun.

EVENING Take the self-guided Lights on Macon walking tour of the **Historic District** to see grand antebellum houses, such as magnificent Hay House ("Palace of the South"), and the pretty Lee Alumni House, with its archetypal southern verandas, lit up in all their glory.

Essentials

GETTING THERE
The closest **international airport** is Hartsfield-Jackson Atlanta, 80 miles (130 km) away. There are some commuter flights to **Middle Georgia Regional Airport**, 10 miles (16 km) from Macon. Renting a **car** is recommended.

WHERE TO STAY
Ramada Plaza (inexpensive) has a pool and is a short walk from the Georgia Music Hall of Fame. *www.ramada.com*

Marriott Macon City Center (moderate) is conveniently located for the downtown historic sites. *www.marriott.com/mcnfs*

1842 Inn (expensive) has romantic rooms in an antebellum mansion. *www.1842inn.com*

TOURIST INFORMATION
Downtown Visitors Center, 450 Martin Luther King, Jr. Blvd; *www.maconga.org*

Right Crispy southern-fried chicken uses crushed crackers or even cornflakes for the crunchy coating

Below The thousands of Yoshino cherry trees that line Macon's streets are a froth of white blossoms in March

MACON, GEORGIA USA

Soul Food in the Deep South

America's Deep South is known for soul music and soul food, and Macon, Georgia, is the place to get a taste of both. Famous in spring for the blossoms on the 300,000 cherry trees that line its streets, it's also a city rich in southern and, in particular, African-American heritage. It's a pretty town to explore, and full of places to enjoy old-fashioned home-cooking and hospitality.

While the term "soul food" denotes a heartwarming style of down-home African-American cooking, it has its roots in sadder days of slavery on southern plantations. African staples such as rice, sorghum, black-eyed peas, and okra were brought across the Atlantic on slave ships. Slaves supplemented their meager diet with greens disdained by their masters: collards, kale, and turnip tops. They adopted corn, an ancient staple crop of southern Native Americans, to make sweet cornbread and grits, a coarse porridge. Poor households made do with the cheapest cuts of meat, and nothing was wasted.

The term "soul food" came into use in the 1960s, by southerners both black and white who had migrated north and missed the regional cooking they grew up with. It has evolved into more nourishing, tastier menus of tender baked ham, fried chicken and pork chops, beef stew and barbecue ribs, side dishes of okra, collards, squash, or black-eyed peas, and desserts such as sweet bread pudding or potato pie. Greens are cooked with smoked or salted meats, diced onions, vinegar, and seasonings in tasty broths, and even lowly grits have made it on to fashionable menus today, often mixed with cheese in the manner of Italian polenta.

Deep in the heart of Georgia, Macon is a good place to discover both soul food and southern culture. Its roots go back thousands of years to the ancient Native Americans who built ceremonial mounds here. The city was founded in 1823 and prospered as a market hub for surrounding farms and cotton plantations. Handsome antebellum mansions and Victorian homes grace its historic neighborhoods. Sites like the Tubman Museum and Douglass Theatre pay tribute to Macon's strong African-American heritage.

Macon has a great music legacy as a cradle of soul and southern rock. The Georgia Music Hall of Fame pays tribute to local boys Little Richard and Otis Redding, and others who launched their careers here. Later, Mama Louise's soul food (*see panel, right*) kept the Allman Brothers Band going when they were still struggling musicians. In Macon, a little soul food and music is all the southern comfort you need.

Macon Festivals

Macon hosts several lively festivals throughout the year. Among the highlights are:

International Cherry Blossom Festival The town is painted pink for this 10-day festival, held in mid-March when the blossoms are at their peak. It features concerts, events, exhibitions, food fairs, parades, and hot-air balloons.

Tubman Pan Africa Festival African music and dancers, Caribbean steel bands, masquerades, and cultural demonstrations foster peace, love, hope, and unity at this April celebration.

Georgia State Fair Also in April, the oldest state fair in the Southeast offers amusement park rides, agricultural exhibits, and entertainment.

Ocmulgee Indian Celebration Indian nations of the Southeast gather at the Ocmulgee Monument in September to celebrate their heritage through storytelling, dancing, music, and art.

Above A thousand-year-old earth lodge of the Mississippian culture

The Best Places to Eat Soul Food

H & H Restaurant inexpensive

Soul food and music go hand in hand at H & H Restaurant in downtown Macon. It was founded in 1959 by the late Inez Hill and her goddaughter and cousin, Louise Hudson, and "Mama Louise" is still cooking up a storm and welcoming customers with her warm smile. The restaurant is situated in an unassuming red-brick building with a small sign. Inside are simple tables with red-checked tablecloths, and walls covered with autographed photos of the Allman Brothers. Mama Louise fed the penniless band in their early days in Macon, and when they became famous, they took her on tour with them. Otis Redding and other Macon musicians also feature on the jukebox.

The "meat-and-three" menu, which changes daily, offers main dishes such as fried chicken, roast beef, fried fish, or baked ham, accompanied by collard greens, okra, black-eyed peas, corn, and green beans. Leave room for the potato pie and other desserts. Breakfast is also served, with grits, of course, and homemade biscuits.

807 Forsyth St., Macon; open 6:30 AM–4 PM Mon–Sat; http://mamalouise.com

Also in Macon

Jeneane's at Pinebrook (www.jeneanes.com; *inexpensive*) is another Macon restaurant where you can choose from a daily menu of tasty meats, fish, and soul-food side dishes: greens and creamed corn, rutabagas, mashed potatoes and gravy, and cheese grits. The pecan and chocolate pies are highly rated.

Also in the South

Mama Dip's Kitchen in Chapel Hill, North Carolina (www.mamadips.com; *inexpensive*), features traditional country cooking in a pleasant, airy dining room with a wrap-around porch. House specialties include chicken-fried steak, pan-fried pork chops smothered in gravy, and chicken and dumplings. **Swett's** (*www. swettsrestaurant.com; inexpensive*) in Nashville, Tennessee, is for anyone who loves southern cooking. Family-owned since 1954, it may feature pig's feet or pork shoulder alongside such daily favorites as fried chicken, meatloaf, turnip greens, and fried cornbread.

In New York

Located in New York's Harlem, **Sylvia's** (www.sylviasrestaurant.com; *moderate*) is one of the most famous soul food restaurants in America, run by fabled southern matriarch Sylvia Woods and her family. Main dishes include Southern classics like smothered chicken and pork chops, oxtail, gumbo, chitterlings, fried catfish, and short beef ribs. The Sunday Gospel lunch with live music is legendary.

LANCASTER COUNTY

LANCASTER COUNTY, PENNSYLVANIA USA

Dutch Pie in Lancaster County

A visit to Pennsylvania's Lancaster County is a step back in time. Bearded men in wide-brimmed black hats drive horse-drawn buggies through the streets, while women in plain 19th-century dresses and bonnets sell quilts and jellies in the farmers' markets. And drifting from the bakeries and kitchen windowsills is the sweet, heavenly smell of home-baked Pennsylvania Dutch pie.

The quaint towns and neat family farms of Pennsylvania Dutch country are a world away from the urban buzz of Philadelphia. Head off the beaten tourist track onto the quiet rural roads here and you'll enter a landscape of rolling green hills and woodlands, dotted with large whitewashed farmhouses, covered "kissing bridges," windmills, and sturdy old barns built to last a century or two. In winter the farmers plow the fields using horses, not tractors, and in summer they bale hay with pitchforks onto wooden wagons.

The term Pennsylvania "Dutch" is a corruption of the word "Deutsch," the name for the German-speaking settlers who came here in the early 1700s. It includes the Amish communities, who live a simple life based on family and religious values, eschewing all things modern, such as cars and electricity. An otherwise closed community, the Amish open up to the outside world most readily through their crafts and food. They are known for hearty, home-cooked meals, served at communal tables in Amish restaurants, and their most famous dish is their pie – a pie so delicious

that local people often eat it for breakfast. The combination of traditional German recipes and a natural bounty of fruit and nut trees and lush berry patches makes these the finest fruit pies in the world. From juicy apple and ripe peach to sour cherry, tangy rhubarb, plump raisin, sticky pecan, or wild huckleberry, Pennsylvania Dutch pies have the perfect blend of tart and sweet flavors, oozing through a flaky lattice crust or hiding under a crunchy crumb topping.

There are special pies, too, that are rarely found elsewhere. Like the famous schnitz pie – normally made with dried apple slices, this uses green tomatoes in late fall when the apples run low. Or the syrupy, cakelike shoo-fly pie, made with molasses and brown sugar, which comes in thick, gooey "wet-bottom" or thin "dry-bottom" varieties. Its whimsical name came from the need to shoo the flies away as the pies cooled. The popular whoopie pies are not really pies at all, but more like huge cookies, consisting of a sandwich of two small, thin rounds of chocolate cake filled with icing. A Pennsylvania Dutch table is always laden with wonderful home-cooked dishes, but it's the scrumptious desserts that keep everyone coming back for more.

Above Horse-drawn travel is a sign of the Amish commitment to tradition and the virtue of living in a simple, unhurried, natural way

Amish Markets

One of the delights of visiting Lancaster County is visiting the food markets. Lancaster City's **Central Market** is the oldest farmers' market in the US, and a good place to buy cheeses and fresh-baked desserts. **Columbia Market** sells lots of local produce, and is housed in a historic structure with a dungeon beneath (there are guided tours). In Bird-in-Hand, the **Farmers' Market** has fresh produce and local crafts, while **Kauffman's Fruit Farm and Market** has delicious homemade sweet apple cider, apple dumplings, and deli items. In Ephrata, the **Green Dragon Farmers' Market & Auction** sells baked goods and Amish-made items, and the **Village Farm Market** has a wonderful selection of fresh-baked pies and specialty bakery items. Markets have different opening days and hours, so check locally.

Three Days in Lancaster County

There's lots to enjoy, apart from the food. You can explore the Amish way of life from old-fashioned horse-and-carriage rides to tours of Amish homesteads. There are historic mansions and museums, and dozens of art galleries. Shop for antiques, hand-stitched quilts, and other crafts, or expertly fashioned Amish furniture.

DAY ONE Immerse yourself in the Amish life with a visit to the **Amish Country Homestead** at **Bird-in-Hand**, or the **Landis Valley Village and Farm Museum** in **Lancaster**. Admire antique quilts at the **People's Place Quilt Museum** in **Intercourse**. Take an afternoon **horse-and-buggy ride** through the countryside.

DAY TWO Take a foodie tour of Lancaster County. Watch Pennsylvania Dutch cooks making pies and putting up canned jams, preserves, and more at the **Jam and Relish Kitchen** in **Intercourse**. Try your hand at twisting pretzels at the **Intercourse Pretzel Factory** or **Sturgis Pretzel Bakery** in **Lititz**. Nearby, watch candy-makers at the **Wilbur Chocolates Candy Americana Museum**.

DAY THREE Follow a scenic driving – or cycling – route and discover some of the region's **covered bridges**. The tourist office has several itineraries.

Essentials

GETTING THERE

There is an **international airport** in Philadelphia; Lancaster has a small airport that connects to BWI (Baltimore Washington International). **Trains** and **buses** run to Lancaster County from Philadelphia. A **rental car** is essential for touring.

WHERE TO STAY

Stone Haus Farm B&B (inexpensive) is a 200-year-old working farm. *www.stonehausfarmbnb.com*

After Eight Bed and Breakfast (moderate) is an antique-filllled 1818 colonial home in Paradise, Pennsylvania. *www.aftereightbnb.com*

The Inn at Twin Linden (expensive) is an elegant retreat in the heart of Amish country. *www.innattwinlinden.com*

TOURIST INFORMATION

501 Greenfield Rd.; *www.padutchcountry.com*

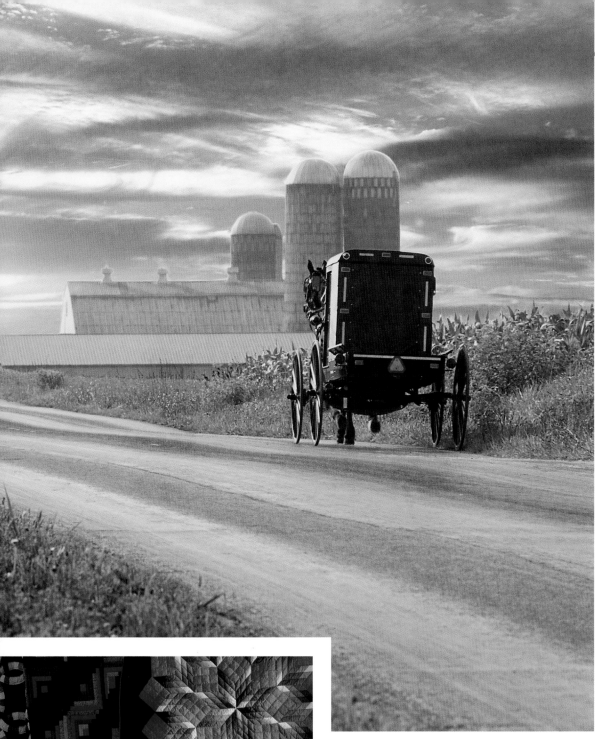

The Best Places to Eat Pennsylvania Dutch Pie

Good 'N Plenty Restaurant
moderate

Good 'N Plenty is housed in a two-story farmhouse built in 1871; the large "Dutch room" (main restaurant area) was added a century later to accommodate the customers lined up out the door for Christ and Dolly Lapp's delicious home-cooked Pennsylvania Dutch dinners. They still run the restaurant with their children and grandchildren. Dining is family-style, with tables seating 10 to 12 people. Once the tables are full, the platters start coming, laden with such favorites as crispy fried chicken, baked country ham, roast beef, mashed potatoes, baked country sausage, pork and sauerkraut, noodles, chow chow (a traditional relish), pepper cabbage, homemade bread, and more, followed by shoo-fly pie and other scrumptious desserts. No wonder it's been rated one of the best down-home dining spots in the country. And there's plenty more in the Bake Shop and Store, where you can buy freshly baked pies, cakes, and breads, and jars of apple butter or homemade chow chow to take home.

150 Eastbrook Road, Smoketown; open 11:30 AM–8 PM Mon–Sat; closed Christmas, Jan and early Feb; www.goodnplenty.com

Also in Lancaster County

You won't find a setting much more authentic than **Stoltzfus Farm Restaurant** *(www.stoltzfusfarmrestaurant.com; moderate)* in Gordonville for a Pennsylvania Dutch country meal. It's served in the Amish farmhouse where Amos Stoltzfus grew up. The family-style menu includes homemade hamloaf and homemade sausage, made in their own butcher's shop right on the farm, accompanied by candied sweet potatoes, brown buttered noodles, and many other country favorites, along with shoo-fly, cherry, and apple pies.

Also in the US

There are Amish communities scattered across 22 states of the US. Two of the largest are in northern Indiana and southeast Iowa. At **Das Dutchman Essenhaus Restaurant and Bakery** *(www.essenhaus.com; inexpensive)* in Middlebury, Indiana, large tables fill the rustic wood-paneled dining room, where family-style dining features old Amish recipes passed down through generations. The restaurant serves 30 kinds of pie; if you can't choose, take some home from the bakery next door. In Amana, Iowa, the family-run **Ox Yoke Inn** *(www.oxyokeinn.com; moderate)* has been a local favorite since 1940. It serves traditional old-world recipes, family-style or à la carte, using produce from neighboring farms and smokehouses. A tray of fresh-baked desserts is presented at the end of your meal.

Above The dark, sticky filling of shoo-fly, made from rich sorghum molasses and brown sugar, makes this pie a local favorite

Left Amish quilts are renowned worldwide for their quality and distinctive patterns, often contrasting bright colors with black

Above An adobe building decorated Southwestern style with a turquoise-mosaic steer skull and *ristras* – bunches of dried peppers

Above Fiery red salsa is often served with blue corn tortilla chips, made from a variety of corn that is unique to New Mexico

A Day in Santa Fe

Santa Fe is brimming with art and history, and its world-class galleries form the second-largest art market in the country (after New York). It has a feast of striking architecture and several fascinating museums.

MORNING Start at the Plaza to browse the **Indian Market** outside the Palace of the Governors, then step inside to visit the **New Mexico History Museum**. For more art, choose from the nearby **Fine Arts Museum** and the **Georgia O'Keeffe Museum**, then stroll along the **Old Santa Fe Trail** to see the miraculous staircase in **Loretto Chapel** and the 17th-century **San Miguel** mission chapel.

AFTERNOON Go gallery-hopping along **Canyon Road**, or head to **Museum Hill** to visit the outstanding **Museum of International Folk Art** and the **Museum of Indian Arts and Culture**.

EVENING Return to the Plaza for souvenir shopping and admire the facade of **St. Francis Cathedral** glowing in the setting sun. Take a patio table at one of the lively restaurant bars and relax with a margarita before dinner, soaking up the Southwestern atmosphere.

Essentials

GETTING THERE
There is limited commercial service to **Santa Fe Municipal Airport**, so most visitors fly to **Albuquerque International Sunport** and make the hour's drive to Santa Fe by **rental car** or **shuttle service**.

WHERE TO STAY
Santa Fe Sage Inn (inexpensive) has small but comfortable rooms in an adobe motel near downtown. *www.santafesageinn.com*
Hotel Santa Fe (moderate) is Native American–owned and features beautiful artworks. *www.hotelsantafe.com*
Inn on the Alameda (expensive) has stylish adobe buildings and *casitas* (little houses). *www.innonthealameda.com*

TOURIST INFORMATION
201 W. Marcy Street; *www.santafe.org*

SANTA FE, NEW MEXICO USA

Fiery Chili Peppers in Santa Fe

In the soft, clear light of a Santa Fe morning, Native American artisans spread their jewelry-laden blankets before the Palace of the Governors, built by Spanish settlers 400 years ago, while Anglo-American tourists stroll in the plaza below. This mix of cultures has given the city some wondrous arts and architecture, and a cuisine that calls on over 100 varieties of chili pepper.

Set high against the backdrop of the Sangre de Cristo mountains, Santa Fe is the capital of New Mexico, the oldest state capital in North America, established when Spanish conquistadors from Mexico founded a colony here in 1610. Its mix of cultural history and contemporary Southwestern style offers plenty for everyone to explore. At its heart lies the Plaza, lined on three sides by storefronts – a shopper's delight for Southwestern clothes, jewelry, arts, and crafts. The surrounding streets are as likely to lead to the earthy curves of old adobe houses as they are to hotels and public buildings sporting Spanish Colonial or Pueblo Revival styles, their soft pink and beige facades gleaming against a brilliant blue sky.

Old mission churches, sanctuaries, and a magnificent cathedral evoke the city's colonial roots. There are excellent museums highlighting Native American traditions, culture, and contemporary arts, and a wealth of fine art galleries and museums. Artists have long come to northern New Mexico for its clear light and spectacular hues. But in the restaurants of Santa Fe, only two colors matter: red and green, the colors of piquant chili peppers.

The local foods of the Native Americans have always used corn, beans, and above all, chili peppers, and these form the basis of the cuisine of New Mexico. It's the hot peppers that set these dishes apart from Mexican cuisine found elsewhere in the US. Instead of the standard tomato-based salsas, here you'll find fresh sauces of puréed green or ground dried red chili peppers, lightly seasoned with garlic, salt, or herbs to let the smoky, pungent flavors of the peppers shine through. Great with burritos or enchiladas; try both the red and green salsas by asking for "Christmas."

As well as forming the base for the zesty sauces of burritos, enchiladas, and meat entrées, peppers are used in mouthwatering dishes such as crispy deep-fried *chiles rellenos* (stuffed peppers) and *carne adovada* (marinated pork). Other exotic local ingredients, such as blue corn, *nopales* (prickly pear cactus), and *chayote* (vegetable pear), also tickle the taste buds; Southwestern cuisine offers plenty for everyone to explore.

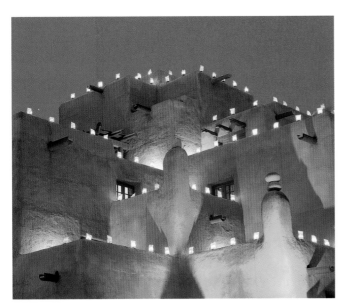

Above *Luminarias* light up the 300-year-old adobe buildings in Santa Fe

Cooking Classes

Whether you want to roast a chili pepper or stuff one for a *chile relleno*, the **Santa Fe School of Cooking** *(www.santafeschoolofcooking.com)* is the best place to learn the secrets of New Mexican cuisine. Courses at this internationally renowned culinary academy are taught by some of the city's best chefs, but are geared toward recreational cooks as well as budding professionals. Courses range from morning or afternoon classes on a single topic or dish to the three-day **Southwest Culinary Boot Camp**, which covers everything from the history of the region's foods to in-depth cooking techniques. Demonstration and hands-on classes are offered. There are also classes on New Mexican cheeses and wines, as well as restaurant walking tours. Participants can stock up on regional ingredients at the adjoining market.

The Best Places to Eat New Mexico Cuisine

The Shed moderate

Some of the best New Mexico cuisine in Santa Fe comes with loads of atmosphere at The Shed. Just east of the Plaza, a wooden gateway leads to a sunny, flower-filled patio and the old adobe hacienda, which dates from 1692. Its nine cozy, adjoining rooms are charmingly decorated with folk art, its niches and doorways are brightly painted, and there is alfresco dining on the patio in summer.

Family-owned for three generations, The Shed's menu features time-tested recipes such as the smoky-flavored green chili pepper chicken enchiladas, and red chili pepper enchiladas topped with a fried egg, a local favorite. All of The Shed's chili peppers are grown to order on local farms and ground daily in their own mill, making the food some of the freshest and tastiest around. It's also very spicy. Traditional entrées are served with blue corn tortillas, and may be accompanied by *posole* (a hominy stew), *calabacitas* (a squash dish), and pinto beans. Reservations are advised for dinner. The always-busy lunchtime operates on a first-come, first-served basis.

113½ East Palace Avenue, Santa Fe; open 11 AM–2:30 PM & 5:30–9 PM Mon–Sat; www.sfshed.com

Also in Santa Fe

Several Santa Fe restaurants deserve a place on the "must try" list. **La Choza** *(505 982 0909; inexpensive)*, The Shed's little sister, near Railyard Park, is less busy but serves the same great food. **Maria's New Mexican Kitchen** *(www.marias-santafe.com; moderate)* is famous for its margaritas, but the menu is fantastic too; *carne adovada* (marinated pork) is a specialty. **Tomasita's** *(505 983 5721; moderate)* is another local favorite, with delicious *chiles rellenos*.

Also in New Mexico

New Mexican food tends to be low to moderately priced, though dishes often feature in pricier Southwestern restaurants such as **Doc Martin's** in the historic **Taos Inn** *(www. taosinn.com; expensive)*, Taos. **Orlando's New Mexican Cafe** *(http://orlandostaos.com; inexpensive)*, also in Taos, serves superb dishes in hearty portions. In Albuquerque, head for the **Church Street Cafe** *(www.churchstreetcafe. com; moderate)* in the Old Town.

Around the World

It's hard to find authentic New Mexican cuisine outside the state of New Mexico, but **Little Anita's** *(www.littleanitas.com; moderate)* has several locations in Denver, CO. In Seattle, head for **Santa Fe Cafe** *(www.santafecafeseattle.com; moderate)* for blue corn tacos and chili peppers sourced from Hatch, New Mexico.

NEW ORLEANS, LOUISIANA USA

Jambalaya in the Big Easy

The mellow notes of a saxophone drift on the warm Gulf breeze through New Orleans' French Quarter, past elaborate wrought-iron balconies toward the jazz bars of Bourbon Street, mingling with the spicy scent of jambalaya wafting from restaurant windows. Welcome to the Big Easy – an extraordinary cultural and culinary melting pot where the good times roll.

New Orleans – nicknamed the Big Easy – is a sultry city that drawls its way through the daytime heat but snaps into life after dark, when the laughter, liquor, and music flow in the bars of the French Quarter. Set along the Mississippi River, it is also a vibrant port, known around the world for its music and its exuberant Mardi Gras festival.

New Orleans is a city of districts, each with its own character. Uptown – home to two universities – has a young vibe, while the Warehouse District offers art lovers the Contemporary Arts Center and Ogden Museum of Southern Art. The Garden District, with its grand antebellum houses, was created by Americans after the 1803 Louisiana Purchase. Its sobriety is a stark contrast to the frenetic French Quarter, where you can see the city's historic Creole townhouses decked with ornate wrought iron, visit antique shops, and enjoy plentiful entertainment.

At night, it's time to explore the city's musical heritage: New Orleans is the home of Dixieland jazz, but you'll also hear big band, jazz fusion, Delta blues, zydeco, funk, and rock music bursting through the doorways on Bourbon Street in the French Quarter.

Jambalaya is the dish that perfectly embodies the city's history. Founded by the French in 1718, New Orleans remained culturally French through subsequent years of Spanish rule, and long after it became an American territory in 1803. The descendants of the French and Spanish settlers – the Creoles – lived alongside African slaves and Haitian refugees, as well as Cajuns, French-speaking exiles from Acadia (present-day Nova Scotia).

Acquiring its name from the Provençal word for "mixture," jambalaya was born in the French Quarter when Spanish settlers tried to recreate their favorite rice dish, paella, using ripe tomatoes instead of saffron. Caribbean spices such as cayenne enhanced the trinity of peppers, onions, and celery cooked with chicken, peppery *andouille* sausage, and fresh seafood. The result was Creole, or red, jambalaya. Cajun-style brown jambalaya is an earthier version of the dish that gains its color from meat drippings browned in a cast-iron pot. It can contain such wild game foods as crawfish, alligator, duck, or venison. But whether juicy red or smoky brown, the best jambalaya is simmered slowly for an hour or more, allowing the rice to absorb the pungent blend of meat, seafood, and spices that makes it so delicious. The result is a dish both hearty and exotic, much like New Orleans itself.

A Day in New Orleans

With its many museums, plentiful live music, Audubon Zoo, and Aquarium, New Orleans has plenty to offer visiting families, but it is best known as a party city, with festivals throughout the year. The partying reaches frenetic levels during Mardi Gras, or "Fat Tuesday" – a season of carnivals, parades, and masked balls centered around the day before Ash Wednesday.

MORNING See the highlights of the **French Quarter**, including the **Presbytère** and **Cabildo**, **St. Louis Cathedral**, the **French Market**, and **Madame John's Legacy**. There are quirkier attractions, too, such as **Lafitte's Blacksmith Shop** and the **Historic Voodoo Museum**.

AFTERNOON Head to the riverfront in the **Warehouse District** for Blaire Kern's **Mardi Gras World** at Kern Studios. It's the next-best way to experience New Orleans' biggest street party if you can't be there in person.

EVENING Return to the French Quarter and party the night away on **Bourbon Street**.

Essentials

GETTING THERE
Major airlines operate from **Louis Armstrong New Orleans International Airport**, 15 miles (24 km) west of the city.

WHERE TO STAY
Bon Maison Guest House (inexpensive) is a good budget choice at the quiet end of Bourbon Street. www.bonmaison.com

Claiborne Mansion (moderate) has an air of elegance. www.clairbornemansion.com

Hotel Monteleone (expensive) is the pick of the French Quarter. www.hotelmonteleone.com

TOURIST INFORMATION
2020 St. Charles Avenue; *(800) 672 6124*

Above New Orleans hosts a renowned spring jazz festival, but live music energizes the city throughout the year

Left Tall, three-story Creole houses, with shallow wrought-iron balconies, are typical of the French Quarter of New Orleans

Above Like its name, which fuses French and African influences, jambalaya brings together ingredients as diverse as seafood and game

What Else to Eat

Gumbo is the Creole answer to bouillabaisse and may be seasoned with *file*, a Native American spice made from dried, ground sassafras leaves, and served over white rice. **Etouffée** is a thicker stew typically made of crawfish, though shrimp, crab, or chicken can also be used, cooked in a roux with vegetables and spices. **Red beans and rice** is a typical New Orleans dish that may be served with grilled fish "blackened" with a coating of spices. **Po'boy** sandwiches of fried seafood or meat on foot-long baguettes are classic New Orleans street food, as are **beignets**, square doughnuts covered in powdered sugar.

The Best Places to Eat Jambalaya

K-Paul's Louisiana Kitchen
expensive

Chef Paul Prudhomme is a Louisiana legend, the first chef to make New Orleans food respectable to the modern gourmet diner. His Louisiana Kitchen is now a city landmark, and though the atmosphere is casual café-style, the food is upmarket, the quality superb, and reservations essential. The restaurant building dates from 1834, with dining rooms on both floors, and alfresco tables in the atmospheric courtyard or on the balcony in season. Prudhomme uses only fresh ingredients, so the menu changes daily. Appetizers might include a cup of his chicken and *andouille* gumbo, made with his own *andouille* sausages; turtle soup; or his own inimitable version of Cajun jambalaya, simmered for hours in a rich stock with just the right amount of rice. The main-course temptations might feature another classic, crawfish *étouffée* – a stew simmered with the lid on, or "smothered" – or an eggplant pirogue (the name for a Cajun canoe) deep-fried and filled with Bay scallops, Louisiana shrimp, and crawfish.

416 Chartres Street, French Quarter, New Orleans; open 11 AM–2 PM Thu–Sat, 5:30 PM–10 PM Mon–Sat; www.kpauls.com

Also in New Orleans

You can sample the Creole version of jambalaya at **Mr. B's Bistro** *(www.mrbsbistro.com; expensive)*, where dishes like gumbo ya-ya, seafood gumbo, and Gulf shrimp with grits offer more tastes of the Creole south. Come for the Sunday Jazz Brunch, when a jazz trio lends a festive air. **The Gumbo Shop** *(www. gumboshop.com; inexpensive)* offers an atmospheric taste of old New Orleans, from its faded decor to the long menu of Creole and Cajun favorites.

Also in the US

For authentic New Orleans food and atmosphere in southern Florida, head to **Jambalaya Jeb's** *(http://jambalayajebs.com; inexpensive)* in Bonita Springs. This simple place in the Flamingo Island Flea Market is run by a family from Louisiana. They love the home cooking they grew up with and make their jambalaya, gumbo, and other dishes fresh each day and serve tasty New Orleans-style beignets.

Around the World

In the southern hemisphere, **South Restaurant** *(www.south-restaurant.com; moderate)* brings Creole cuisine to Sydney, Australia. Dishes include Creole jambalaya, gumbo, crawfish *étouffée*, and the traditional New Orleans muffaletta sandwich – a round loaf filled with salami, cheese, ham, and garlic, topped with an olive salad – which owes its origins to Sicilian immigrants to New Orleans.

Above Colorful *trajineras* (gondolas) offer a unique way to tour Xochimilco, an Aztec site just outside Mexico City

Above Soft tacos – tortillas stuffed with spicy meat, beans, fresh vegetables, and jalapeño peppers – make a great picnic on the run

A Day in Mexico City

One day is precious little time in a city as large and interesting as Mexico City, but with careful planning and taco-fueled stamina, it's surprising how much can be enjoyed and achieved.

MORNING Start the day in the cultural heart of the **Centro Historico**. In the huge main square (the **Zócalo**), take a guided tour of the ruined Aztec **Templo Mayor** and then drop into the **National Palace** to admire the Diego Rivera murals of revolutionary scenes.

AFTERNOON Take Line 2 of the metro as far south as it goes and change on to a Tren Ligero (light train) to explore the floating gardens of **Xochimilco**. It's best on a Sunday, when it's usually thronged with families and gaudily decorated barges. Join a punting trip and drift past lamb barbecues, mariachi musicians, and endless stalls.

EVENING Begin with alfresco drinks in **Plaza Garibaldi**. Then choose between a top-flight restaurant or a simple eatery, before hopping into a taxi to **Zona Rosa** for late-night clubbing; or head for home, stopping off for *churros* (see pp70–71) and chocolate on the way.

Essentials

GETTING THERE
Benito Juarez International Airport is 10 miles (16 km) east of the city, around 30 minutes by authorized **taxi** or the **metro** (Line 5). Get around the city on the excellent metro or use the iconic VW Beetle "bug" taxis.

WHERE TO STAY
Casa de la Condesa (inexpensive) is a modern, clean, and comfortable hotel in Roma Norte. All rooms have kitchens. www.casadelacondesa.net
Hotel Casa Vieja (moderate) is a boutique gem in Polanco that offers luxurious suites and roof-terrace dining. www.casavieja.com
Condesa DF (expensive): minimalist design hotel in upmarket Condesa with a noted Japanese-fusion restaurant. www.condesadf.com

TOURIST INFORMATION
www.visitmexico.com

MEXICO CITY MEXICO

Tackling the Taco in Mexico

Informal, exuberant, fast, yet satisfying, tacos are perfectly in tune with Mexico City. It was the powerhouse of pre-Hispanic America and still burns brightly today, mixing ancient traditions with high-tech, urban sophistication. Whether you're in arty Roma, the *centro histórico* or well-heeled Polanco, pick your *taquería* and enjoy a taco or two alongside the 25 million locals.

Without setting foot outside the massive metropolis of Mexico City, travelers can experience cultures nearly 700 years apart, all in the midst of teeming humanity, streaming traffic, and – more often than not – the unmistakable sound of an approaching mariachi band. Mexico's vast capital city is full of urban energy. Made up of a series of neighborhoods, each has a very distinct character, and many warrant exploration. It's almost impossible to miss the historic downtown, which includes the huge Zócalo (the central square) and the ruins of the Aztec Templo Mayor (the Great Temple). The best hotels are found in the elegant Polanco district, which sits alongside the vast green space of Chapultepec Park, near the renowned Anthropology Museum. Just outside the city, the Pyramids of the Sun and the Moon rise up in ancient Teotihuacán.

In such heady surroundings, the tasty, speedy taco could have been invented with the regular and robust refueling of Mexico City's overwhelmed visitors in mind. In fact, however, its origins may well date back as far as the Mayans and Aztecs. It makes use of that most traditional of Mexican foodstuffs – the corn tortilla – and the ubiquitous taco is a mainstay of the national diet. The name "taco" is a generic way to describe some kind of filling wrapped inside a tortilla, so it's essentially a Mexican-style sandwich. Many of the country's indigenous crops feature as fillings, such as chili peppers, tomatoes, avocados, and beans, usually accompanied by some type of meat or fish.

Most common at lunch time, tacos make ideal late-night snacks too, with recipes and ingredients varying according to family traditions and regional influences. The *taco al pastor*, or shepherd-style taco, is a favorite; this usually contains pork, sliced directly and showily from the rotisserie into the tortilla, although it can also be made with chicken or shredded steak. Fishy versions commonly consist of grilled or fried fish or shrimp along with lettuce or cabbage. The trick is to pile two or three of your choice onto a gaudy plastic plate, then retire to the condiments counter for lime, onion, cilantro, and guacamole, topped off with fiery salsa. Roll, fold, and devour – no cutlery required.

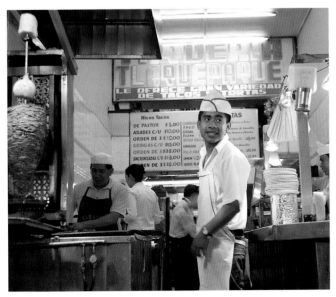

Above A *taquería* (taco restaurant) often has a *maestro taquero*, a master-taco maker

What Else to Eat

European and North American chain restaurants churning out "Mexican" dishes do no justice to a varied and imaginative national cuisine that makes full use of fresh indigenous produce. When you've had all the tacos you can take, be sure to try **tamales**, tasty and inexpensive snacks often sold from baskets by street sellers and once eaten by pre-Colombians. A *tamal* is a steamed parcel of corn dough with a sweet or savory filling, wrapped within a corn husk or banana leaf. Alternatively, seek out a **torta** (sandwich) or tortilla containing **nopal**: chopped, de-spined prickly pear cactus "paddles," or leaf pads, which look and taste a little like avocado. Although Mexico City is inland, the fish dishes are superb; tuck into shrimp in tangy sauces from Veracruz or whole fish fresh from the market, accompanied by hot, fresh salsa.

The Best Places to Eat Tacos

El Califa inexpensive

There are four El Califa *taquerías* in Mexico City, but the Condesa branch is the easiest to find, and it buzzes with a healthy mix of visitors and locals. This canteen-style restaurant is sufficiently stark and industrial to feel "authentic," but the quality of its food and hygiene make it a perfect entry to the world of the *taquería* – start here, and head for the street stalls when you and your palate are ready!

Vegetarians will struggle here, but carnivores can choose from various cuts of beef steak, rib, or chop, and chicken or pork. El Califa's specialty is to serve the meat griddle-roasted and in whole pieces, rather than minced. Tortillas come to you fresh from the oven, liberally laden with melted Oaxaca cheese, golden from the grill. Choose an *al pastor* (pork in guajillo chili salsa and grilled pineapple) and your marinated meat will be shaved off the spit in front of you. The *gaonera* (a slice of tender beef fillet with raw tomatillo sauce in a thick, handmade tortilla) is delicious. Take care when ordering from the salsa menu – they're all hot, despite what the menu might say.

Altata 22, Condesa; open from 1 PM "until the early hours"; www.elcalifa.com.mx/califa.html

Also in Mexico City

El Borrego Viudo ("the widowed sheep") *(Avenida Revolución Tacubaya; inexpensive)* is certainly authentic and well worth a late-night pilgrimage to this less-than-glamorous spot alongside the viaduct. Armies of servers clad in chef's whites bustle around the cavernous feeding house, taking tacos out to drive-through clients in the huge parking lot. Open 24 hours a day, it specializes in tacos *al pastor*.

Also in Mexico

Around six hours' drive southeast of Mexico City, Oaxaca is one of Mexico's most beautiful colonial cities. Follow the billowing smoke from **Mercado 20 de Noviembre**, an atmospheric and inexpensive food market, to find sizzling tacos. The stands are mostly frequented by local people, and best at lunch time; pick the stand with the longest line.

Around the World

Serving from a small gazebo with the menu propped up against it on a blackboard, **Buen Provecho** *(inexpensive)* is a one-man band consisting of Arturo Ortega Rodriguez, who serves up what must surely be London's most authentic Mexican food. He's in Waterloo (Lower Marsh) lunchtime market during the week and Elephant and Castle market on Sundays. Tacos come with a choice of marinated meat fillings, and the salsa is for sale, should you want to reproduce the experience at home.

Right Meaty Atlantic quahog clams are still harvested with wound-wire rakes and baskets

Below Clam chowder, which is thought to have developed from a 16th-century French fish stew, *la chaudrée*

A Day in Boston

Boston often seems more European than American, perhaps because it is a compact, walkable city where the streets meander pleasingly and buildings are mostly at human scale.

MORNING Begin a spin through Boston history at **Faneuil Hall**, the 18th-century meeting house where brewer and political agitator Samuel Adams demanded independence from Great Britain. Adjacent are the long granite buildings of **Quincy Market**, built in the 1820s and now a lively center of shops and restaurants. Head to the waterfront to visit the fish, penguins, and seals of the **New England Aquarium**.

AFTERNOON Book a **harbor cruise** at Long Wharf to admire Boston from its seaward side. Disembark in **Charlestown** to visit the world's oldest commissioned warship, the 1797 wooden frigate USS *Constitution*, known affectionately as "Old Ironsides."

EVENING Check listings for a drama or comedy in the restored early-20th-century playhouses of the lively **Theater District**.

Essentials

GETTING THERE
Domestic and international airlines fly into Boston's **Logan International Airport**. Boston is also served by Amtrak **train** from New York. The city has a combined **public transport system** of subway, trolleys, and buses known as the "T."

WHERE TO STAY
Constitution Inn (inexpensive) offers bargain accommodations near "Old Ironsides" at Charlestown. *www.constitutioninn.org*
Harborside Inn (moderate) occupies a former spice warehouse, just steps from Faneuil Hall marketplace. *www.harborsideinnboston.com*
Boston Harbor Hotel (expensive) is a showpiece of the revived waterfront. *www.bhh.com*

TOURIST INFORMATION
148 Tremont Street; *www.bostonusa.com*

BOSTON, MA USA

Creamy Chowder in Boston

Bankers, brokers, and tourists bustle down the Boston streets once walked by British soldiers and colonial revolutionaries. In this vibrant modern city, preservation is the watchword for historic buildings and gastronomy alike. No one has truly experienced Boston without tasting its dearest culinary legacy: the rich, creamy, buttery broth known as New England clam chowder.

For all its modernity, Boston revels in its early history. Founded in 1630 as "a city on a hill," Boston was the epicenter of American foment against British rule and the cradle of the American Revolution. On the Freedom Trail, the red-brick path that snakes 2½ miles (4 km) through the city linking its historic sites, 12 of the 16 buildings predate the Revolution and some stand cheek-by-jowl with glass skyscrapers. Visitors can enter the hall where patriots rallied for liberty and can even board the world's most venerable active warship, USS *Constitution*, which bobs at anchor near the shipyard where it was constructed. In Boston's theater district, new dramas unfold in the ornate interiors of some of America's oldest active playhouses.

Although the first English settlers of New England dismissed clams as "the meanest of God's blessings,"

by the 18th century clam chowder had become a mainstay of the region's cuisine and a gastronomic benchmark for authentic Yankee cooking. Probably an offshoot of New England fish chowders – so named because they were made in large iron cauldrons, or *chaudières*, as French-speaking Newfoundland fishermen called them – clam chowder is a felicitous marriage of clams, onions, butter, and milk. Devotees disagree over whether the onion should be sautéed with salt pork or butter, and whether the chowder should be thickened with potato or ship's crackers. Even with such minor variations and controversies, creamy clam chowder is ubiquitous in Boston establishments, from hip new bistros to some of the oldest restaurants in the United States.

Clam chowder remains New England's favorite comfort food – a savory, slightly salty, and perfectly silken antidote to a chill November day or a restorative pick-me-up after an afternoon cruising Boston Harbor. In the perfect chowder, each little clam explodes with flavor against the rich backdrop of the broth. Made from simple ingredients, it is one of the most democratic of luxuries. Historian Joseph C. Lincoln even deemed clam chowder "as American as the Stars and Stripes, as patriotic as the national anthem. It is 'Yankee Doodle' in a kettle."

Chowder Variants

In Boston, even the trendiest chef knows better than to mess with New England clam chowder, perhaps daring only to add a sprig of chervil or parsley to provide a spot of color in the milky sea of the bowl. But there are certain variants that appear in southern New England and elsewhere in the US. The rarest is the clear Rhode Island clam chowder – little more than clams and their steaming juices, butter, onion, and celery. The soup that most offends purists, however, is Manhattan clam chowder, a tomato-based vegetable soup to which clams are added, often served with cream to make a thick pink slurry. Scoffed one New England travel writer in 1940: "Tomatoes and clams have no more affinity than ice cream and horseradish."

Left Sailboats add old-world charm to Boston's modern waterfront

The Best Places to Eat Clam Chowder

Union Oyster House moderate

Opening in 1826 as Atwood and Bacon Oyster House, this venerable establishment is the oldest restaurant in Boston and the oldest eatery in continuous operation in the United States. Its semicircular oyster bar on the ground floor has been a favorite of Boston society since the days when famed orator and politician Daniel Webster (1782–1852) daily drank a brandy-and-water with every half-dozen raw oysters (he usually ate six plates). John F. Kennedy's favorite wooden booth on the upper level is marked with a commemorative plaque.

Although the Union Oyster House is most celebrated for its raw seafood bar of clams and oysters, the chefs make a meaty clam chowder dotted with small, juicy cherrystone clams – a young hard-shell clam indigenous to the Massachusetts coast – in a perfect broth, neither too thick nor too thin. A frequent winner of various chowder contests, it is served as both an appetizer and a main dish. Departing from tradition, the restaurant serves its chowder with corncakes instead of crackers.

41 Union Street, Boston; open 11 AM–9:30 PM Sun–Thu, 11 AM–10 PM Fri & Sat; www.unionoysterhouse.com

Also in Boston

Diners still eat at communal tables at **Durgin-Park** *(www.arkrestaurants.com; moderate)*, in the Faneuil Hall Marketplace, which opened to feed the hungry traders of the 19th-century Quincy Market. Its clam chowder is a bastion of Yankee taste. More modern but equal as a Boston gastronomic icon, **Legal Sea Foods** *(www.legalseafoods.com; moderate)* evolved from a fishmonger into a celebrated chain of restaurants. Its several Boston branches include one located near the Aquarium on State Street.

Also in New England

Captain Parker's Pub in West Yarmouth, Massachusetts *(www.captainparkers.com; moderate)* is famed for making Cape Cod's finest clam chowder. Set in Rhode Island's fishing port of Galilee, **Champlin's Seafood Restaurant** *(www.champlins.com; moderate)* makes both creamy New England chowder and the clear-broth Rhode Island variant. In South Norwalk, Connecticut, **Sono Seaport Seafood** *(www.sonoseaportseafood.com; moderate)* is, like Champlin's, both a fishmonger and a restaurant, and offers creamy New England and tomato-based Manhattan clam chowders.

Around the US

Bistro Boudin *(415 351 5561; moderate)*, a restaurant on Fisherman's Wharf in San Francisco, CA, merges two culinary icons by serving New England clam chowder in a loaf "bowl" of San Francisco sourdough bread.

MEMPHIS

MEMPHIS, TENNESSEE USA

Barbecue and Blues in Memphis

The old cotton capital of Memphis, Tennessee, rises on a bluff overlooking a wide, lazy stretch of the Mississippi River. During the long, sultry summer afternoons, its residents lie low to escape the humid heat. But after dark, in the back-alley rib shacks and the blues clubs of Beale Street, the River City comes alive with what made it world-famous – music and barbecue.

Memphis is the home of the blues. From the 1920s onward, black musicians from the Mississippi Delta made a beeline for Beale Street, where W. C. Handy, Howlin' Wolf, Muddy Waters, and B. B. King jammed in its legendary "juke joints." In 1954, Memphis became the birthplace of rock 'n' roll when, in the tiny Sun Studio, local boy Elvis Presley recorded a blues number, "That's All Right," but with a daring new sound that set the world on fire. Then, in the 1960s, the artists at Stax Records – including Otis Redding, Isaac Hayes, and Sam & Dave – turned Memphis into "Soulsville USA."

Memphis is also home to one of the oldest and most popular styles of Southern barbecue. This down-home food is a perfect complement to the raw, earthy music that sprang from the city's streets. In Memphis, home of the World Champion Barbecue Contest each May, barbecue means baby-back pork ribs. They come "wet" – cooked and served with a tangy sauce made from tomato, vinegar, and spices – or "dry" – seasoned with a rub of dried spices, primarily paprika, which gives the meat a lusty red color. Dry ribs are lightly mopped with just enough spiced vinegar during cooking to keep them juicy.

What makes Memphis barbecue so delicious is the cooking. The ribs are smoked "low and slow" over a hickory wood fire, giving them plenty of time to absorb the smoky scent and coating them with a dark crispy crust while remaining succulent and tender inside, with all the flavor of the meat shining through. The result is hot, melting, and sweet – just like Memphis music.

A passion for music still pulsates through Memphis today, whether you come to tour its music museums, pay homage to the King, buried at his Graceland mansion, or soak up some electric blues or R&B, moody jazz, or a boogie beat in the neon-lit nightclubs on Beale Street. But there's a more sober side to Memphis too: in 1968, Martin Luther King, Jr. was assassinated here, on the balcony of his room at the Lorraine Motel. The National Civil Rights Museum now located at this tragic spot is one of the most inspirational destinations in the US, and it surely has a fitting home in this city, where music brought all races and classes together.

A Day in Memphis

Most of the top sights in downtown Memphis are a short walk or taxi ride from Beale Street. Many can also be reached by bus or the vintage downtown trolley cars. Farther out are Soulsville: the Stax Museum of American Soul Music, and Graceland, Elvis Presley's former home. The city has many non-music attractions too, from botanic gardens and riverboat rides to film festivals and galleries, but on a one-day itinerary, it's almost inevitable that music-lovers are going to set the pace.

MORNING Get an early start at **Graceland** to see Elvis's sumptuous home and treasures, and pay your respects at his grave. Then head back downtown to the **Memphis Rock 'n' Soul Museum** for a fascinating look at the city's music history.

AFTERNOON Let your musical tastes decide whether to visit **Sun Studio** for an entertaining tour of the little studio that first recorded Elvis, Jerry Lee Lewis, and Johnny Cash, or head to the **Stax Museum** to hear the phenomenal story of the label that launched American soul music and ogle Isaac Hayes's gold-trimmed blue Cadillac.

EVENING After a monster meal of Memphis barbecue, lick your fingers and head for **Beale Street** and a night of Memphis blues.

Essentials

GETTING THERE
Memphis International Airport is only 15 minutes by taxi or shuttle from downtown. A **rental car** is useful for visiting Graceland.

WHERE TO STAY
Doubletree Hotel Memphis Downtown (inexpensive) has comfortable rooms just two blocks from Beale Street. *www.doubletree.com*
Memphis Marriott Downtown (moderate) is the city's largest hotel, right on the trolley line. *www.memphismarriottdowntown.com*
The Peabody Hotel (expensive): *the* place to stay in Memphis. *www.peabodymemphis.com*

TOURIST INFORMATION
Memphis Visitor Center, 3205 Elvis Presley Boulevard; *www.memphistravel.com*

Left Hail to the King: Elvis Presley's Graceland home welcomes more than half a million visitors each year

Above Sizzling "wet" pork ribs are brushed with a sauce made from tomatoes, vinegar, and spices

Top Follow the "Brass Note Walk of Fame" on legendary Beale Street, home of the blues

Barbecue Around the World

The first Southerners to barbecue were native Florida Indians, but as America developed, so did several regional styles of barbecue, using different cuts of meat, sauces, spices, and cooking methods. Other countries, such as South Africa, Kenya, and Brazil, have their own strong barbecue traditions.

MEMPHIS

Central BBQ inexpensive–moderate
2249 Central Ave.; www.cbqmemphis.com
Join the college students on the outdoor deck for award-winning pork plates, ribs, and hot wings, cooked up by two veterans of the Memphis in May World Championship Barbecue Contest.

Charlie Vergos' Rendezvous
moderate
52 South Second St.; www.hogsfly.com
Customers form a line down the alley to enter this basement rib joint, which has been serving up some of the city's best barbecue since 1948. Red-checked tables and Memphis memorabilia are arranged around the barbecue pit.

Corky's moderate
5259 Poplar Ave.; www.corkysmemphis.com
Old-fashioned, slow-cooked, hickory-smoked ribs and hand-pulled pork, the hits of the '50s and '60s, and the down-home decor of barn wood walls and cheery neon make this a Memphis favorite.

TEXAS

Barbecue means beef in Texas, where there are several regional styles. The East Texas (marinated in sweet tomato-based sauce) and Central Texas (dry-rubbed with spices and smoked over oak or pecan) barbecues are most popular.

Black's Barbecue inexpensive
215 N. Main St., Lockhart; www.blacksbbq.com
Black's is the oldest family-run barbecue restaurant in Texas (since 1932), and still the best, according to its many fans. Their tender beef brisket and homemade sausage are made to secret family recipes.

Railhead Smokehouse inexpensive
2900 Montgomery St., Fort Worth; www.railheadonline.com
This simple but lively Fort Worth barbecue joint is the place to go for the tenderest and tastiest beef brisket, ribs, pork tenderloin, and smoked sausage here in "Cow Town."

Artz Rib House moderate
2330 South Lamar, Austin; www.artzribhouse.com
Mesquite-smoked baby back ribs, country-style pork ribs, brisket, and sausage top the menu here, and you can order some of each. They're served up with a nightly helping of country and bluegrass music.

NORTH AND SOUTH CAROLINA

Pulled pork is king in North Carolina, where either a whole hog or a choice shoulder of pork is slow-cooked until it pulls gently off the bone. South Carolina tops it with Carolina Gold, a unique yellow sauce made from mustard, brown sugar, vinegar, and spices.

Speedy's Barbecue inexpensive
1317 Winston Rd., Lexington, North Carolina; www.speedysbbqinc.com
Set in a former drive-in, Speedy's still offers curbside service for those who can't wait for their barbecue sandwiches, plates, and trays – all served in extra-large portions with their delicious special sauce.

Sweatman's Bar-b-que inexpensive
1313 Gemini Drive, Holly Hill, South Carolina; (803) 492 7543
In an old wooden house under a pecan tree, this weekend barbecue joint serves some of the most delicious, pit-cooked pulled pork and ribs you'll find, served with authentic mustard sauce and "cracklins" (crispy pork crackling).

Wilber's Barbecue inexpensive
4172 Highway 70 E., Goldsboro, North Carolina; www.wilbersbarbecue.com
They cook the whole hog at Wilber's. Presidents Clinton and George Bush Sr. have tucked into their pit-cooked, oakwood-flavored pork, chopped and served with potato salad, hush puppies (cornbread fritters), and coleslaw.

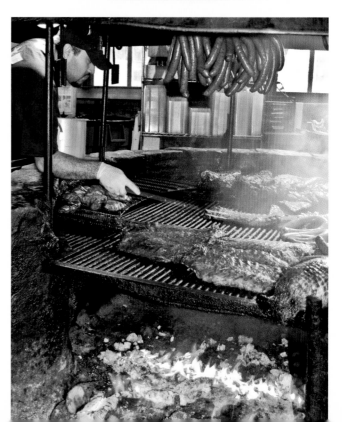

Left (top to bottom) "Dry" ribs, rubbed with a dry spice mix, are served with sauce on the side; "wet" ribs, cooked and served with sauce; a Texas barbecue pit with ribs and smoked sausage

Below (top to bottom) Grilled fish features on South African menus, where "linefish" simply means any fish caught by line from the sea; herding cattle in Brazil, where beef is king

MISSOURI

Kansas City's sweet, thick barbecue sauce, made from molasses and tomatoes, is in a class of its own. A variety of meats are rubbed with spices, smoked over hickory wood, and smothered with sauce at the table.

Arthur Bryant's Barbecue moderate

1727 Brooklyn Ave., Kansas City; www.arthurbryantsbbq.com

Rated the best barbecue in Kansas City (if not the world), Arthur Bryant's simple restaurant near the ballpark has been praised by baseball players and presidents for its delicious sauce.

B.B.'s Lawnside Bar-B-Q moderate

1205 E. 85th St., Kansas City; http://bbslawnsidebbq.com

The "B.B." stands for blues and beer, and here you'll have a big helping of the former, either from live bands or from the blues-loving owners' enormous collection of recordings, along with delicious slow-smoked ribs, pulled pork, beef, sausage, and chicken from the 60-year-old-barbecue pit.

Fiorella's Jack Stack Barbecue expensive

101 W. 22nd St., Kansas City; www.jackstackbbq.com

The high ceilings and see-through fireplace in a converted freight house in the Crossroads Arts District make a stunning setting for this top-rated barbecue, cooked in hickory-fired brick ovens.

BRAZIL

In Brazil's ranching region, the gauchos (cowboys) created their own style of barbecue, called *churrasco*. Try it in barbecue houses *(churrascaria rodízio)* around the country, where tender cuts of beef and other meats are grilled on long skewers over an open fire and served at your table, all-you-can-eat style.

Marius moderate

Av. Atlántica 290, Copacabana, Rio de Janeiro; www.marius.com.br

A mouthwatering choice of some 30 grilled meats is accompanied here by an amazing salad bar with fresh seafood and side dishes, amid artifacts from antique ships and farms.

Barbacoa expensive

Rua Dr. Renato Paes de Barros 65, Itaim, São Paulo; www.barbacoa.com.br

Serving over 20 scrumptious cuts of meats grilled without smoke over heated rocks, including wild boar

and the prized hump of the zebu, or Brahma steer, this popular barbecue house is great for vegetarians too, who can fill up on the extensive salad buffet.

Fogo de Chão expensive

Av. Moreira Guimarães 964, Moema, São Paulo; www.fogodechao.com

An extensive wine list complements the delicious grilled meats and superb salad bar here. Of the three locations in the city, this one has stylish, contemporary decor and a lively atmosphere.

KENYA

Barbecue is popular throughout Africa. In Kenya, *nyama choma* (Kiswahili for roasted meat) is usually beef, goat, or mutton; it's often ordered by weight. Be prepared, however, for even more unusual meats on some upmarket menus.

Summit Resort moderate

Lake Nakura National Park; +254 51 850 165

The open-air complex of lounge bars, dance floor, pool, and dining areas surrounding this friendly resort just outside the main entrance to the park includes a restaurant serving delicious *nyama choma*.

Carnivore expensive

Langata Road, Nairobi; www.tamarind.co.ke

Ostrich and crocodile are among the huge skewers of meats cooked on an enormous barbecue in the center of Kenya's most famous restaurant. It's served at your table by waiters in zebra-striped aprons.

SOUTH AFRICA

A South African braai, or pit barbecue, is a great social event where friends feast on steaks, lamb cutlets, and spicy sausage. The best restaurants serve up this relaxed, festive atmosphere along with good food.

Mama Africa moderate

178 Long Street, Cape Town; +27 21 424 8634

If you want to try roasted game meat, this is the place to find kudu, ostrich, springbok, and crocodile on the menu, with three African marimba bands providing a lively atmosphere.

Die Strandloper expensive

Langebaan, West Coast; www.strandloper.com

The delicious ten-course fish and seafood braai is cooked right on the beach at this informal restaurant. With the guitar music, the beach, and the endless stream of seafood, a meal lasts several hours.

Above New York street food is an intriguing mix of fast foods from around the world, often all for sale in one place

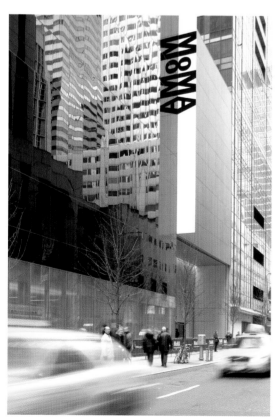

Above The Museum of Modern Art (MoMA) is a modernist building that houses one of the largest collections of contemporary art in the world

Three Days in New York City

New York has it all: iconic skyscrapers, lush parks, world-class museums, dazzling Times Square, and glitzy Broadway shows.

DAY ONE Go to the top of the **Empire State Building** for jaw-dropping 360° views, to get a better idea of the city you'll be exploring. Spend the afternoon being wowed by art at the **Museum of Modern Art**.

DAY TWO Head to **Central Park** in the morning, focusing your explorations on the area between 59th and 79th streets, where you can saunter along shaded paths from the wooded **Ramble** to the elegant **Bethesda Terrace**. Then up the cultural stakes by admiring the Picasso masterpieces and the Roman Temple of Dendur at the **Metropolitan Museum of Art**.

DAY THREE Start the day with a brisk walk across the **Brooklyn Bridge**, the largest suspension bridge in the world when it was built in 1883. Afterward, head to **SoHo** to shop in exquisite designer boutiques, and then cap off the day with a visit to neon-lit **Times Square** and a **Broadway** show in the nearby theater district.

Essentials

GETTING THERE

New York City is served by three airports: **JFK**, **LaGuardia**, and **Newark**. All share one website: *www.panynj.gov*. Travel into town by **subway**, **bus**, or **taxi**.

WHERE TO STAY

Off SoHo Suites Hotel (inexpensive) features simple but clean rooms. *www.offsoho.com*
Hotel Chelsea (moderate) has large, well-maintained rooms, and sits in the middle of hip Chelsea. *www.hotelchelsea.com*
Enjoy Midtown luxury at the well-known **Waldorf Astoria** (expensive), with its sumptuous lobby and spacious rooms. *www.waldorfnewyork.com*

TOURIST INFORMATION

Times Square Visitor Center is the most central tourist office, at 1560 Broadway; *(212) 768 1560; www.nyc.gov*

NEW YORK
NEW YORK

The Best Places to Eat Street Food

Super Tacos inexpensive

As the sun sets on weekdays, dinner rolls into town for the Upper West Side. Teetering stacks of corn tortillas are unwrapped, gas grills fired up, and the Super Tacos Sobre Ruedas ("On Wheels") truck at 96th and Broadway slides open its windows for business. The tacos are a study in simplicity: grilled meats are heaped onto corn tortillas and sprinkled with chopped onions and cilantro. Eating them is simple too: the warm, foldable tacos are wolfed down at the dented, stainless steel bar that's lit by a buzzing fluorescent light. The roast pork and *barbacoa* chicken tacos are the runaway winners, tender and juicy; and the supple slivers of boiled tongue are tenderly robust.

Southwest corner of 96th St. and Broadway, New York City; open 6 PM–2 AM Mon–Thu, 6 PM–3 AM Fri, noon–2 AM Sat–Sun; (917) 837 0866

Also in New York

NY Dosa *(212 431 1733; inexpensive)*, on the southern edge of Washington Square Park, serves spicy South Indian vegan food. For tasty burritos, tacos, and creamy guacamole on the run, try SoHo's **Calexico** *(www.calexicocart.com; inexpensive)*. The company won the hard-contested Vendy Award (also known as "the street food Oscars") in 2008. In 2010 the award was won by Middle Eastern food vendor **King of Falafel & Shawarma** *(www.thekingfalafel.com; inexpensive)*, normally found parked up at 30th Street and Broadway serving unbeatable falafel and chicken rice platters. **Jamaican Dutchy** *(www.thejamaicandutchy.net; inexpensive)* specializes in juicy jerk chicken. Satisfy your sweet tooth with warm waffles at **Wafels and Dinges** *(www.wafelsanddinges.com; inexpensive)*, a company with trucks at various locations around Manhattan, including a permanent one on Fulton and Front streets.

Also in the US

Los Angeles matches New York for superb food trucks. Abbot Kinney Boulevard in Venice features a range of street eats, including **Slammin' Sliders** *(www.slamminsliders.com; inexpensive)*, with juicy Kobe-Wagyu beef sliders (small burgers); and **Che Che's Argentinian Cuisine** *(twitter.com/chetruck; inexpensive)*, with tasty chicken *empanadas*.

Around the World

In the rest of the world, street carts offer one of the most memorable ways to sample local cuisine, from spicy soups in Southeast Asia to crepes in Paris. The pushcarts of Istanbul are outstanding, particularly those on the Galata Bridge waterfront on the European side of the Bosphorus. These are laden with treats including juicy kebabs, skewers of sausage, grilled corn on the cob, and silky pastries stuffed with feta.

NEW YORK, NEW YORK USA

New York's Urban Fuel

There's good reason for the famous phrase "in a New York minute." It's another way of saying fast, and it sums up the furious pace of New York life, which has given rise to the city's wildly popular "street food." This urban fuel for a city on the go reflects all of New York's diverse cultures, as food trucks offer everything from spicy Middle Eastern falafel or Jamaican jerk chicken to Belgian waffles.

Spend a day in New York, and you'll understand why it's one of the most popular destinations on Earth. The "city that never sleeps" features looming skyscrapers, elegant bridges, the vast Central Park, world-class museums, and intriguing bohemian neighborhoods lined with vintage boutiques. Equally diverse are New York's international cultures – and attendant cuisines – which you can sample at street carts across the city.

New York has a long history of street food, perhaps best exemplified by the basic hot dog. In 1936, Oscar Mayer rolled out the first portable hot dog cart – called the Wienermobile – and hot dogs have been sold on the streets of New York ever since. You'll spy vendors everywhere, from Battery Park to Times Square, and at a dollar and 50 cents for a hot dog heaped with condiments, it's one of the best deals in New York. For a taste of old New York, track down Nathan's Famous Hot Dogs, which began as a nickel counter in Coney Island in 1916, and is still the best place to sample a dog slathered in sauerkraut and relish.

If America is a melting pot, New York's culinary variety is one of its finest manifestations. You could find your way around New York on the scent from street carts alone, wafting the delicious smells of Italian pizza, Chinese crackling duck, Middle Eastern lamb kebabs, and freshly baked bagels smeared with cream cheese, first introduced by Jewish immigrants.

The street carts of Washington Square Park and nearby Bleecker Street specialize in spicy Asian fare, served up in a lively performance space jostling with buskers, chess players, and skateboarders. The historic neighborhood of SoHo offers the chance to see 19th-century architecture and quaintly cobblestoned streets, while eating from street carts selling everything from luscious chopped steak in corn tacos with salsa to brightly colored cupcakes. Midtown is the quintessential Manhattan neighborhood: skyscrapers glint in the noonday sun, spilling out office workers who continually appear to be in a mad dash. Not surprisingly, this area is a happy hunting ground for street carts, which cater to those on the hunt for a fast, hot lunch, whether they're workers or tourists.

Above The Empire State Building, Manhattan, has been a landmark since 1930

Classic New York Bars

Munching on street food builds up a thirst, which is easily assuaged by turning to New York's famous beer bars. Drink in history along with the beer at the oldest pub in New York City, **McSorley's Old Ale House** *(www.mcsorleysnewyork.com)*. This landmark bar opened in 1854, and its clientele has included both President Lincoln and ex-Beatle John Lennon. It serves only one drink: its own ale, available in light or dark. The bustling **P.J. Clarke's**, in Midtown *(www.pjclarkes.com)*, is one of the city's most famous alehouses, with a superb lineup of international and domestic beers. Wrap up the night at the **Ear Inn** *(www.earinn.com)*, a historic pub built in 1817 near the Hudson River that functioned as a speakeasy during Prohibition. It features a good mix of beers on tap and serves hearty American bar snacks.

JAMAICA CARIBBEAN

Fiery Jerk Chicken in Jamaica

Jamaica is renowned for its vivid colors, from the alabaster beaches and indigo-hued mountain peaks to rain forests filled with tropical blooms. Old traditions are upheld with pride in the fishing villages and colonial-era towns, from bygone culinary secrets to riotous folkloric festivals and rhythmic dance. But reggae and food – Bob Marley and jerk chicken – remain Jamaica's lifeblood.

From swanky coastal resorts and handsome colonial towns to neon-lit nightlife, Jamaica offers a variety of historic and cultural attractions. Lively Negril and Montego Bay, Jamaica's two main tourist areas, boast a mix of plush bars and rustic reggae-and-rum shacks together with long stretches of soft sands, popular restaurants, and world-class golf. Montego Bay, known colloquially as Mo' Bay, upholds its reputation as a party town with great gusto with after-dark haunts that run from funky lounge bars and pumping discos to steel-pan gigs on the beach. Sleepy villages hug the 620 miles (1,000 km) of coastline, offering the quieter natural attractions of scenic Treasure Beach, Port Antonio, and Oracabessa. Fertile farmlands and meadows form a colorful patchwork between mountainous ridges and forested ravines in a setting of palm-flanked azure seas, where fishing boats drag their nets ashore and sell their haul at tables on the sand.

In historic central Kingston, the hypnotic, pulsating rhythm of languid reggae is a laid-back beat in Jamaica's otherwise fast-paced metropolis. Snack vendors vie for attention over tooting horns, blaring car stereos, and the cries of street hawkers; housewives swap gossip over plates of ackee and saltfish as the aromas of slow-cooked seafood stews, seasoned chicken, and fire-roasted meats hang in the air. No local snack is more commonly sought out than the full-flavored "jerk," a uniquely Jamaican way of preserving and cooking meats and poultry.

Believed to have derived from the ancient hot-stone cooking practices of the indigenous Arawak people, jerk fuses smoky Jamaican pimento with the fiery-hot, blood-red chili peppers originally brought here from South American shores by 16th-century mariners. Salt is added as part of the marinade, and then the meat is roasted much as it was in times gone by, when escaped slaves, known as maroons, spent years living in the Blue Mountains battling attempts at recapture by the British troops. Today, the deep, intense and complex jerk flavor is synonymous with Jamaican kitchens and a true test of culinary prowess. Every home has its own "secret" recipe, handed down through generations. Pride runs high among jerk cooks in Jamaica – each of whom considers "their" jerk the best.

Above Rick's Café sits beside a favorite jumping-off point, and its position on the West End Cliffs of Negril makes it a great place to enjoy sunsets with a cold beer

Food Markets

Few experiences in Jamaica excite the senses quite like a stroll around the island's many colorful food markets. Flower stands stacked with a rainbow of scented blooms sit among food stands selling Blue Mountain coffee, freshly cut coconut, and sugary cakes still warm to the touch. Housewives haggle over breadfruit, pimentos, codfish, plantain, avocados, and callaloo, near red-hot grills that sizzle with skewers of seasoned pork, beef, and chicken wedged between juicy green peppers. Choose from rice and peas, jerk chicken, beef patties, or freshly cooked johnny cakes (fried dough biscuits) or banana fritters in Kingston's chaotic Coronation Market, Linstead Market in charming St. Catherine, Brownstown Market in St. Anne, or the Savanna-la-mar Market in Westmoreland.

Three Days in Jamaica

Jamaica's extraordinary natural beauty runs through its mountain, beach, and rain forest regions. Its villages and colonial settlements have enthralling histories, and central Kingston has an irrepressibly vibrant nightlife.

DAY ONE Stroll around the historic streets of Kingston's **Spanish Town** in the relative cool of the morning to marvel at the magnificent homes, plaza, and monuments. After lunch, visit the city's harbor museum, **Port Royal**, a memorial to the ancient capital city that was submerged following an earthquake in 1692. Then head to Hope Road to the **Bob Marley Museum** to revel in his writings.

DAY TWO Pack a picnic to hike through the bird-filled vegetation and coffee plantations around the **Blue Mountains**, perpetually cloaked in blue-tinged mists.

DAY THREE Spend a morning chilling out on ultra-hip **Doctor's Cave Beach** in **Montego Bay** to enjoy beautiful white sands and sparkling spring-fed waters. After lunch, explore a rainbow of underwater gardens in Mo' Bay's outlying shallow spurs from a glass-bottomed tour boat, a snorkel boat, or in a group dive; an old anchor from a Spanish galleon begs discovery on the marine park's western side.

Essentials

GETTING THERE
Montego Bay International Airport is 2 miles (3 km) north of Kingston and there are **shuttle buses** into town.

WHERE TO STAY
Klem's Homestay (inexpensive) is a charming place to experience typical Jamaican hospitality. *www.klemshomestay.hostel.com*
Rockhouse Hotel (moderate) is an affordable boutique hotel set on secluded cliffs in Negril with an infinity pool. *www.rockhousehotel.com*
Ritz Carlton Rose Hall (expensive) offers beach-fronted luxury with a golf course, spa, and five restaurants. *www.ritzcarlton.com*

TOURIST INFORMATION
www.visitjamaica.com

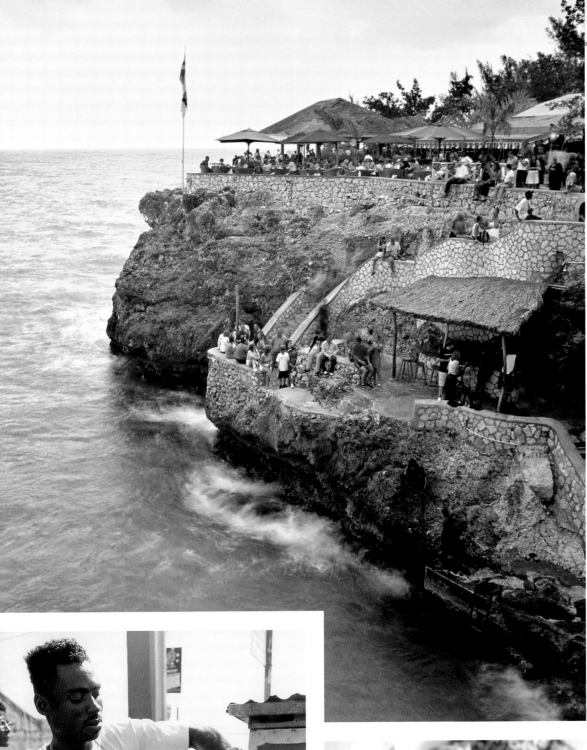

The Best Places to Eat Jerk Chicken

The Pork Pit inexpensive

You'll find plenty of food options among the character-packed beach restaurants, bars, and rum-and-seafood shacks of Montego Bay. But for those who seek the very best in jerk chicken, there is only one place to go – the Pork Pit, near Walter Fletcher Beach. A favorite haunt of beach-goers, who descend on its outdoor tables en masse at noon, the Pork Pit serves a large lunch of melt-in-the-mouth jerk meat (not just pork but poultry and seafood as well), corn cobs, and baked yams at shoestring prices. Delightfully informal with a seemingly unlimited supply of bottled Red Stripe beer, the Pork Pit favors plastic cutlery and throwaway plates over fancy tableware and simply lets the food speak for itself. Marvel at the guys in neon-yellow Pork Pit T-shirts as they carve up the jerk with gusto onto old iron griddles amid considerable smoke and sizzle.

27 Gloucester Avenue, Montego Bay; open 11 AM–11 PM daily; (876) 940 3008

In Kingston

Head to the **Chelsea Jerk Centre** *(876 926 6322; inexpensive)* on Kingston's Chelsea Avenue for an urban take on this Jamaican food favorite. Jerk chicken, pork, and seafood come with old-style corn fritters. True jerk aficionados also rave about **Our Place** *(876 927 7886; inexpensive)* on Hope Road, where locals trade tales over a sweet-smelling jerk pit with an after-work beer. Unmarked and tucked away among the billboards of the commercial district, this secret hideaway boasts blissful anonymity away from the jostle of the fast-paced city.

Also in Jamaica

The most relaxed place to try piquant jerk ribs is **Ocho Rios Jerk Centre** *(876 974 2549; inexpensive)* on Da Costa Drive, Ocho Rios. This delightfully rustic open-air jerk joint is one of Kingston's finest. Daily specials are posted on a chalkboard menu. Beers are frosted, the rum is strong, and the exotic array of fresh fruit juices are thirst-quenchingly good.

Around the World

In the UK, British-Jamaican reggae musician, chef, entrepreneur, and record producer Levi Roots brings plenty of spicy passion to his restaurant **Papine Jerk Centre** *(www.100acres.com/papinejerk; inexpensive)* in Wandsworth, South London. Using lip-smacking, zingy marinades to spice up chicken, fish, and simple cuts of meat, Roots – the man behind "Reggae Reggae Sauce" – creates authentic mouthwatering West Indian cuisine. You can't miss the restaurant – it's decked out in the bright Jamaican colors of yellow, red, and green. Drop in, swap gossip, and eat great-tasting jerk.

Above Jerk chicken is usually served with char-grilled corn or *tostones* (fried green plantains) and rice mixed with beans

Left Some of the best jerk chicken in Jamaica comes from street sellers at the roadside or in "jerk shacks" around the island

Above One of the largest museums in the US, the Philadelphia Museum of Art (foreground) sits beside the Schuylkill River

Above Cheesecake straddles the line between dessert and cheese, especially when topped with a heap of fruit in syrup

A Day in Philadelphia

Philadelphia is an easy city to navigate. To get your bearings, remember that the enormous City Hall sits on a square at the intersection of the two main thoroughfares, Market Street and Broad Street.

MORNING Explore the cobbled alleys of **Independence National Historical Park**. Don't miss the **Liberty Bell** on Market Street, or **Independence Hall** where the Declaration of Independence was signed. There are some fascinating exhibits in **Franklin Court**, a museum devoted to Benjamin Franklin. Nearby is elegant **Christ Church** and tiny **Elfreth's Alley** with its early colonial houses.

AFTERNOON Grab a snack at **Reading Terminal Market**. Then immerse yourself in the impressive collections at the **Philadelphia Museum of Art** or the **Rodin Museum**, which holds the largest collection of the sculptor's work outside France.

EVENING Catch a Broadway show or a performance by the Philadelphia Orchestra, Opera Company, or the Pennsylvania Ballet at the **Kimmel Center for the Performing Arts**.

Essentials

GETTING THERE
The **Airport Rail Line** is the quickest and cheapest way to get downtown from **Philadelphia International Airport**. There are **subways**, **trains**, and **buses** in the city.

WHERE TO STAY
The Gables (inexpensive) is an award-winning B&B in an 1889 mansion; it has comfortable rooms in Victorian decor. *www.gablesbb.com*
Penn's View Hotel (moderate) is a traditional hotel in the Old City, close to most main attractions. *www.pennsviewhotel.com*
Four Seasons Philadelphia (expensive) is an award-winning 5-star hotel whose Fountain Restaurant is one of the city's best. *www.fourseasons.com/philadelphia*

TOURIST INFORMATION
6th and Market Streets; *www.visitphilly.com*

PHILADELPHIA

PHILADELPHIA, PENNSYLVANIA USA

Cheesecake in Philadelphia

In the leafy grounds of Philadelphia's Independence National Historical Park, visitors admire some of the most venerable buildings in America. Shoppers fill the bustling Market Street shopping district, while culture-seekers browse the city's fine art museums. When they need to recharge their batteries, only one thing will do: a cup of coffee and a slice of creamy Philadelphia cheesecake.

Philadelphia is one of the oldest cities in the United States. Its Quaker founder William Penn named it after a Greek word meaning "brotherly love," and from 1682 it became a refuge for those seeking religious and political freedom. Less than a century later, Thomas Jefferson wrote the Declaration of Independence here.

From Chinatown to Little Italy, Philadelphia's neighborhood enclaves have given America some of its favorite foods, but creamy, dreamy Philadelphia cheesecake is the dish most likely to induce a feeling of brotherly love. Like the city's name, cheesecake has Greek origins, and it was baked for athletes at the first Olympic Games in 776 BC. Centuries later, Europeans brought their recipes to America, and it was here that cream cheese first became a key ingredient.

William Lawrence, a dairyman in New York's Hudson Valley, developed the process for making cream cheese by accident in 1872 while trying to make Neufchâtel, a soft French cheese. As his new cheese grew in popularity, he started selling it under the name of "Philadelphia," trading on the city's reputation for quality food. He later sold it to a larger company, and the cheese became a global phenomenon.

Philadelphia-style cheesecake has a rich, creamy texture but is lighter than other variations. More cheese than cake, its basic ingredients are simple – cream cheese, sugar, and eggs – but from there the sky's the limit. Chefs may add sweet almonds, tangy key lime, luscious chocolate, or syrupy liqueurs to the batter, which is poured over a crunchy crust made of vanilla wafers or gingersnaps, possibly mixed with nuts. A simple cheesecake is heavenly on its own, but a topping of fat juicy cherries, fresh blueberries, or other seasonal fruits turns it into a work of art.

Fortunately, Philadelphia is a perfect city to build up your appetite for cheesecake. Its historic neighborhoods are packed with attractions – from the Liberty Bell to the renowned Philadelphia Museum of Art – and refreshed by sweeping green spaces. There's much to admire in the home of the Declaration that so famously stated a person's inalienable right to life, liberty, and the pursuit of happiness.

Above The Liberty Bell, cast in 1751, is a traditional symbol of US freedom

New York Cheesecake

Thick, smooth New York cheesecake is one of the most popular styles of cheesecake in the United States. While it is also made with cream cheese, it is denser and richer due to the addition of egg yolks in the recipe, and sometimes lemon or cottage cheese is used to give it a sharper taste. New York cheesecake is baked in a pan standing 5–6 inches (13–15 cm) high, so its slices stand impressively tall. Although some chefs dribble a dash of strawberry or chocolate sauce into the batter, New York cheesecake is traditionally served plain without any toppings. Arnold Reuben, a German immigrant and creator of the Reuben sandwich (a delicious mix of cheese, beef, and sauerkraut on rye), is also credited with developing the first New York cheesecake in 1929. He served it at his Turf Restaurant on Broadway, where it became an instant hit.

The Best Places to Eat Cheesecake

Darling's Café and Famous Cheesecakes moderate

Darling's Café is the home of the original Philly cheesecake and makes the best cheesecakes in the city. It now has two branches, and both are unpretentious, charming little cafés with candles on the tables and some courtyard seating. They serve simple but hearty breakfasts such as bagels, oatmeal, or French toast, and lunches including a range of salads and Philadelphia sandwiches. But it's the cheesecakes, of course, that keep people coming back for more, and there's a range of tasty choices. There are usually about ten cheesecakes available at any one time, at a modest few dollars a slice. You might want to start with the Philly Classic before going on to indulgences like the Perfect Pumpkin, the Peanut Butter Silk, the Key Lime Pie, the wicked Belgium Chocolate, or even a Grand Marnier Cheesecake.

2100 Spring Street and 404 South 20th; open 7 AM–7 PM Mon–Fri, 8 AM–7 PM Sat, 9 AM–5 PM Sun; www.darlingscheesecake.com

Also in Philadelphia

You might not think of going to a Mexican restaurant to sample Philly cheesecake, but local aficionados rate the pecan cheesecake at **Lolita** (www.lolitabyob.com; expensive) as one of the best desserts in the city. It's served with a goat-milk caramel sauce and has a crust of dark chocolate with a hint of ancho chili, adding some decidedly different flavors.

Also in the US

New York takes its own cheesecakes every bit as seriously as Philadelphia, and a recent panel of food experts voted the cheesecakes at the **Mona Lisa Pastry Shoppe and Café** (www.monalisabakery.com; inexpensive) in Brooklyn the best in the city. Their "marble swirl" cheesecake, using chocolate imported from Switzerland, is especially heavenly. You can dine at sidewalk tables or get a slice of cheesecake to go, and even order online if you live in the US.

Around the World

A Dublin café run by two sisters who trained as pastry chefs in New York has received all kinds of accolades, from the *Dubliner* magazine to the *New York Times*. The **Queen of Tarts** (www.queenoftarts.ie; inexpensive) has an old-world charm and serves a delicious New York-style cheesecake along with other exceptional desserts, Irish treats, and pastries such as chocolate scones.

Above A fruit vendor adds the finishing touches to his mouthwatering display in the Municipal Market, São Paolo, Brazil

South America

The Flavors of
South America

Few continents have been blessed with as varied a culinary heritage as South America, and this heritage is gaining wider international acclaim as more travelers start exploring the many different aspects of these nations. Rich stews and soups dominate the cooler mountain regions, while the long coastlines offer up fresh fish cured and cooked in unusual ways. Simply delicious beef is on the menu almost everywhere, but nowhere better than from the pampas of Argentina.

The indigenous peoples of South America, the conquering Spaniards and Portuguese, and a large influx of African slaves have all contributed their distinct cooking traditions and ingredients to the culinary mix in the continent. And as if these weren't enough, Chinese, Japanese, Jewish, Indian, Lebanese, German, French, Italian, and British gastronomical influences have followed in their wake, making South America a true foodie melting pot.

Many of the most popular foods enjoyed worldwide – potatoes, chili and sweet peppers, peanuts, corn, and the one with the highest "yummy factor" of all: chocolate – hail from South America. In an unofficial exchange, Europeans introduced chicken, pork, beef (along with dairy products), wheat, sugar, citrus trees, onions, and garlic, as well as certain herbs and spices such as oregano, parsley, and cloves, to South America, and also passed on their winemaking techniques, all of which changed the food culture forever.

The gastronomical centers of Lima, Buenos Aires, and Rio de Janeiro now boast world-class restaurants.

Today's cuisine has come a long way from its humble beginnings of often corn-based dishes, and the gastronomical centers of Lima, Buenos Aires, and Rio de Janeiro now boast world-class restaurants. Food festivals, such as Lima's Mistura and Medellín's Otro Sabor, also attract visitors from near and far. What's influenced South American cuisine more than any other feature is also what has inspired many a traveler – its wonderful variety of landscapes: desolate high plateaus, deeply cut ravines, snow-capped *cordilleras* (mountain ranges), endless rolling pasturelands, and the sheer immensity of the Amazon basin.

Coast-to-Coast Cuisines

In South America, food is often regional, rather than national, in character: warming stews and soups in the Andean region, good fish and seafood along the lengthy coastlines and mighty rivers, and superb beef in the cattle and farming areas. Peru's famous *ceviche* (lime-cured seafood with salt and perhaps a sprinkling of chili pepper) is popular along many parts of the Pacific and Caribbean coasts. In Colombia and Venezuela, as well as northern

Right One of the many vibrant street markets in Cusco, Peru
Below Harvesting coffee at a plantation near Cuidad Bolívar, Colombia

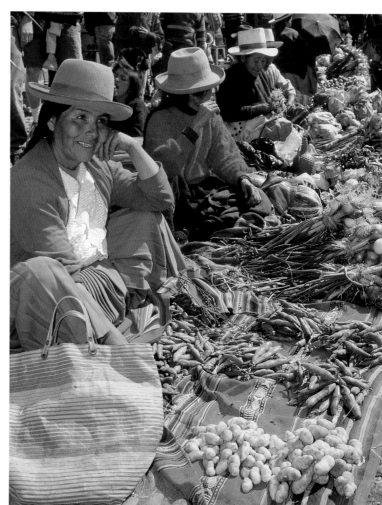

Brazil, the African influence remains strong, particularly in coastal communities. The Brazilian state of Bahia specializes in seafood dishes of African origin, such as *acarajé*. Brazil is blessed with a wide variety of culinary trends, and with a coastline of some 4,660 miles (7,500 km), it's no wonder fish and seafood feature heavily. The *moqueca capixaba*, a hearty fish stew flavored with annatto seeds, hot peppers, and cilantro looks as well as tastes fantastic, the annatto coloring the dish a bright orange.

South American Feasting

From the crashing waves of the vast Atlantic, it's a short hop to the evergreen, huge grassy plains of the Argentinian pampas, home of the gauchos, Argentina's own cowboys. These hardy souls, most often found on horseback, have the enviable responsibility of taking care of the country's most prized asset – its cattle. Argentinian meat is legendary, and there is nothing quite like a *parrillada* – a meat feast where all the best cuts, masterfully grilled and lightly seasoned, are served until diners can eat no more, all washed down with a fine local red wine.

In neighboring Chile, on the island of Chiloé, slow food is taken to dizzying heights in *curanto*, another form of feast, but one that's traditionally left to steam-cook in a hole in the ground. This far south in the Andean region, food goes with the climate and tends to be not just heart-warming, but body-warming as well.

Ecuador's *locro de papa* takes full advantage of the local ingredient *par excellence* – the potato. With 3,000 varieties found in the Andean countries alone, there's no shortage of choice, and the humble potato has rarely tasted better than in this creamy soup, with nothing but a sliver of garlic, some chopped onion, and a slice of bright green avocado to top it off.

The Andes climb farther north into Colombia and Venezuela, where they have devised different ways of keeping warm and well-nourished, choosing the one meat that is otherwise somewhat underrepresented elsewhere in South America – the humble pig. In Colombia, the *bandeja paisa*, originally from the center of the country but now found everywhere, is a celebration of all things porky. Ground pork, sausages, cracklings, and pork cuts all jostle for space in this dish, colorfully accompanied by rice, beans, salad, avocado, and fried potatoes, and topped off with a fried egg. Not for the cholesterol-conscious. Venezuela's *chicharrónes*, or pork cracklings, seem positively restrained by comparison. All across the continent there are vastly varied culinary adventures waiting to be enjoyed, with a mix of influences as unique as the continent itself.

> *With 3,000 varieties found in the Andean countries alone... the humble potato has rarely tasted better.*

Left Fresh fish landed from small fishing boats in Dalcahue Port, Chiloé Island, Chile
Below Cooking ribs and meat on an open fire, Buenos Aires, Argentina

A Day in Salvador

Salvador offers so much in a relatively small space – vibrant culture, fascinating history, and a string of lovely ocean and bay beaches.

MORNING Begin a wander through Salvador history on the **Terreiro de Jesus**, a square in the heart of the old city surrounded by a cluster of the best Baroque buildings in Brazil. These include the **Igreja e Convento do Sao Francisco**, whose interior is covered in almost a ton of gold. Afterward pay a visit to **MAfro**, the African museum also on the square, then have lunch in **Axego**.

AFTERNOON Wander downhill from Axego past the pastel-painted houses to **Pelourinho** for the best pictures of the colonial center. Visit the old African church of **Nossa Senhora do Rosário dos Pretos** at the foot of the main square, built by slaves in their precious free time during the late 18th century. Then take a taxi to the **Mercado Modelo,** a big open market crammed with souvenirs.

EVENING Take a taxi along the beaches, stopping off at **Barra** for a juice and finishing in **Rio Vermelho** for *acarajé* and local nightlife.

Essentials

GETTING THERE
Domestic and international airlines fly into Bahia's Salvador **airport;** there are **buses** and **taxis** to the historic center.

WHERE TO STAY
Albergue Hostel São Jorge (inexpensive) has backpacker bargain rooms in the heart of the historic center. *www.saojorgehostel.com*
Pousada do Boqueirão (moderate) offers boutique comfort in a renovated colonial building with wonderful views over the Bay of All Saints. *www.pousadaboqueirao.com.br*
Pestana Convento do Carmo (expensive) is Salvador's grandest hotel, housed in a converted Baroque convent in the picturesque district of Pelourinho. *www.pestana.com*

TOURIST INFORMATION
www.bahiatursa.ba.gov.br

Right A *baiana de acarajé* in traditional white clothing, with a necklace in the colors of her personal *orixa* (deity)
Below The main square in Pelourinho, the 16th-century heart of Salvador

SALVADOR BRAZIL

Crispy Acarajé in Salvador

Salvador's steep, sun-baked streets are lined with glorious Baroque churches and brightly painted 18th-century mansions. Music bursts from every other doorway, and in the coconut-palm-shaded squares, African Brazilians spin and swirl to the beats and claps of *capoeira*, a musical form of martial art. At street stands, women dressed in flowing white cook *acarajé*, a piquant patty.

Salvador feels like a rich slice of tropical Africa cut from a coconut coast and transposed to Brazil. It is a city of pearly beaches, lush tropical trees, and deep yellow light; of cobbled colonial streets lined with magnificent UNESCO heritage buildings, vibrant with rhythm and ritual. Pounding drum orchestras that parade at carnival troop through the narrow, Baroque-building-lined streets of the old center once a week. *Terreiros* – sacred temple grounds devoted to African-Brazilian Yoruba deities – dot the city, from the fervid *favelas* (shanty towns) to the affluent apartment blocks on the caramel-colored cliffs above the aquamarine Atlantic.

Under the European slave trade, more Africans were transported to Salvador and its state, Bahia, than to any other location in the Americas. They were mainly from the Yoruba nation (now Nigeria and the Republic of Benin) and, against all the odds, they largely kept their homeland culture – and its cooking. *Comida bahiana*, the food of Bahia, is celebrated throughout Brazil today for its full flavors, spiciness, and sauces.

The most famous dish is *acarajé*, a spicy, stuffed falafel-like fritter that has been sacred for centuries. West African Yoruba legend has it that the warrior goddess Iansã (also known as Oya) journeyed to find a potion that would enable her to spit fire; she is the goddess of lightning, winds, fire, and magic. Historically, the Yoruba people remembered her story through a fire-eating ritual in which they swallowed flaming balls of cotton soaked in *dendê* palm oil, which were called *àkàrà*. *Acarajé* means "to eat *àkàrà*" in Yoruba, and the food – also covered in *dendê* oil – is still strongly associated with the ritual.

The best *acarajé* is prepared by *baianas*, local women dressed in ritual white robes who can be found all over the city, but in the greatest numbers in Rio Vermelho, a neighborhood of higgledy-piggledy streets near the ocean. The *baianas* carefully mash black-eyed beans and green onions, sprinkle the mix with salt and chili pepper, and deep-fry it in a pan of sizzling *dendê* palm oil. The resulting patty is split and stuffed with salad and *vatapá*, a chili-pepper-laden shrimp, ginger, and peanut sauce. Truly the food of the gods.

What to Drink

You'll need to wash down your spicy *acarajé* with plenty of liquid, and there's no need for canned fizzy drinks in Salvador. The city has a wealth of tropical juices *(sucos)*, most of which are completely unknown outside Brazil and are brought to Bahia from all over the country – from the temperate south to the rain forests of the Amazon. Choose any fresh juice – you won't be disappointed. For something energy-inducing opt for purple **açaí**, which packs a powerful pick-up punch. For a healthy option buy a **camu-camu** – a 16-oz (half-liter) glass has almost a gram of vitamin C. For simple thirst-quenching, you can't beat **umbu**, made from the milky pulp of a medicinal semidesert fruit. **Caja**, a small fruit that tastes like a mixture of mango and peach, grows in Bahia and contains an amazing number of nutrients, including iron.

Above *Acarajé* stuffed with *camarão* – bright pink sun-dried shrimps – and *vatapá*

The Best Places to Eat Acarajé

Casa da Dinha inexpensive

The legendary Dinha has been making glorious Bahian food for over 20 years from what was originally her home kitchen in the bohemian district of Rio Vermelho. Her simple restaurant seats around 50 people over two floors, and serves the *acarajé* for which she became famous. They're rich and full of flavor, served with sumptuous *vatapá* and a host of other sauces (including *caruru*, made from okra and shrimp paste). The restaurant also offers a full menu of traditional Bahian dishes, a huge variety of delicious *moquecas* (see pp312–13), and the best fruit juices in Salvador. Be sure to try Dinha's *suco de pitanga* (cherry juice), whose tangy flavor perfectly complements *acarajé*.

Rua João Gomes 25, Largo de Santana, Salvador; open noon–4 PM & 6 PM–midnight Tue–Sat; www.casadadinhadoacaraje.com.br

Also in Salvador

Visitors have to clamber up steep stairs from the cobbled street of Rua João de Deus to find the delightful airy dining room of **Axego** *(+55 71 3242 7481; moderate)* in the heart of the historical center, Pelourinho. The *acarajé* is possibly the best in any establishment in central Salvador, but the restaurant is equally famous for its huge *moquecas* – such as *moqueca de peixe* (Bahian fish and coconut stew) – which serve at least two people.

Acarajé on the Street

Baianas sell *acarajé* throughout the city of Salvador. The most reliable stands are on and around the wide plaza of the **Terreiro de Jesus** in the old center of Pelourinho (which has good crafts fairs on weekends, too), on the waterfront in **Rio Vermelho**, and around the **Mercado Vermelho**, the market in Largo da Mariquita in Rio Vermelho.

Also in Brazil

Chef Ana Luisa Trajano spent several years traveling throughout Brazil, from the backwaters of the Amazon to the hinterlands of the northeastern desert, collecting recipes from local people. When she returned to São Paulo, she opened **Brasil A Gosto** *(www. brasilagosto.com.br; expensive)*, a cozy, bright restaurant on a quiet, leafy street in the upmarket neighborhood of Jardins. It serves gourmet versions of authentic, traditional Brazilian dishes, including excellent *acarajé*. In Rio de Janeiro's bohemian neighborhood of Santa Teresa, Bahian emigré Teresa Cristina Machado has been selling the city's finest *acarajé* for so long that she's become an institution. Try her perfect fritters at **Nega Teresa** *(www.negateresa.com; inexpensive)*; visit early, before the crowds get huge.

QUITO ECUADOR

Hearty Soup High in the Andes

Beneath towering snow-capped mountains, the highland Ecuadorians, living at some 10,000 ft (3,000 m) above sea level, have long cherished the restorative powers of their native crop, the potato. Amid the lower fertile valleys, herds of grazing cows provide fresh cheese and milk for the rich, creamy dish *locro de papa*, guaranteed to get you up and over the next hilltop.

The Ecuadorian Andes favor early risers. As the day warms, moisture condenses and gathers in the air, and by afternoon, more often than not, clouds have obscured the peaks of the world's longest mountain chain. But at dawn, the full glory of what 19th-century Prussian explorer Alexander von Humboldt named the "Avenue of the Volcanoes" is revealed, glacier-topped peaks puncturing the lush green, mountainous landscape.

The Andes run longitudinally through Ecuador, dividing the country into three separate realms. The rivers to the west feed the sweltering seaboard of the Pacific Ocean; those to the east forge their way to the great headwaters of the Amazon River, some 2,000 miles (3,200 km) distant. Down the center, the mountain chain is like a Titan's stepladder laid flat north to south, with the higher ground as the ladder's rungs and the populated valleys as the spaces in between.

These valleys and their surrounding hillsides are painstakingly cultivated by Andean families on their farmsteads, maintaining their close bond with their land and with Pachamama, the Earth Mother. Rising at dawn, they till and toil beneath the piercing rays of the equatorial sun and the constant gaze of their *apus*, local mountains personified as deities. Days are long. At lunch, there's no better dish to restore their energy than *locro de papa*, a thick, creamy soup made with the Andes' most important bequest to the world, the potato, combined with milk and fresh, crumbly white cheese and usually topped with slices of avocado.

The Incas, who came as conquerors from Peru and occupied these lands for around 50 years, were particularly fond of potatoes. They even used the time it took a certain variety to cook as a measurement of time – rather like a boiled egg. They were right to sing its praises: we now know that this tuber supplies every vital nutrient except calcium, vitamin A, and vitamin D. It grows fast, on very little land, almost anywhere.

And there are lots of varieties: wander through an Ecuadorian highland market and the color, shape, and size of the potatoes on sale is astonishing. In fact, the variety of all market produce here is amazing. Ecuador's varying altitudes and its position, right on the equator, allow it to produce just about every crop imaginable. On any one stand, you'll find blackberries next to bananas, avocados atop tree tomatoes, and corn cobs tumbling over sacks of rice. This cornucopia, crowned by the precious potato, is one of the delights of discovering this engaging, hardworking country.

Three Days in the Ecuadorian Highlands

The Ecuadorian highlands around the capital, Quito, are a tale of winding highways between valleys and mountains, rewarding the traveler with breathtaking scenery.

DAY ONE Head to **Quito's Old Town**, regarded as the largest, least-altered, and best-restored in the Americas. A World Heritage site since 1978, its colonial grid of streets is dominated by churches, chapels, convents, and monasteries, with enough museums and curiosities to keep inquiring minds happy for days.

DAY TWO Travel north to **Imbabura Province**, famed for flower-growing, haciendas-turned-inns, strong indigenous culture, and a daily craft market in **Otavalo**, which on Saturdays also features early-morning livestock trading and a fruit-and-veggie market.

DAY THREE Hop on the restored railway from Quito to chug south to **Cotopaxi Province**, overshadowed by the **Cotopaxi volcano** and a host of other craggy peaks. This is dairy and cowboy country *par excellence*, with comfortable haciendas making fine bases for hiking, mountain biking, or horseback riding.

Essentials

GETTING THERE
Quito **airport** has fair international connections. Due to the state of the roads and erratic driving, it's best to hire a **guide and driver** for touring.

WHERE TO STAY
Volcanoland (inexpensive) is well-located by the Cotopaxi volcano. *www.volcanoland.com*
Hacienda Cusín (moderate) north of Quito has airy, pretty rooms. *www.haciendacusin.com*
Casona de San Miguel (expensive) is a converted colonial mansion in Quito. *www.casonasanmiguel.com*

TOURIST INFORMATION
Quito Visitors' Bureau; *www.quito.com.ec*

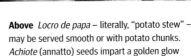

Above *Locro de papa* – literally, "potato stew" – may be served smooth or with potato chunks. *Achiote* (annatto) seeds impart a golden glow

Left The volcanic peak of Mount Cayambe looms over Quito, the world's second-highest capital city

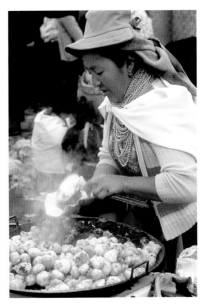

Above A vendor dishes up fried potatoes at the Thursday Saquisili market in Cotopaxi, south of Quito, one of the largest and busiest in Ecuador

What Else to Eat

A revelation for many, **hornado** might well change the way you regard roast pork. Slow-cooked, succulent, and tender, served with **ají hot sauce** or chopped red onions, potato patties, and fried corn, it's a must. The Plaza Grande Hotel in Quito serves a superb suckling pig version. A meal is not a meal in the highlands without a soup appetizer. Look for one with **quinoa**, another Andean wonder-ingredient. Hacienda Zuleta (*www.zuleta.com*) serves delicious soups made from organic ingredients. To warm the cockles on a cold Andean night, a swig of **canelazo** hits the spot. It's a hot toddy, usually made with naranjilla fruit and local liquor and spiced with cinnamon.

The Best Places to Eat Locro de Papa

Hacienda San Agustín de Callo
expensive

There's no better place to enjoy smooth, delicious, warming *locro de papa* than in the Inca-walled dining room of Hacienda San Agustín, in the shadow of the picture-postcard Cotopaxi volcano. The hacienda's walls are thought to have been part of an Incan temple, but even without them, this would be a fine place to dine. Its style is country-home-turned-inn, with individually painted rooms with quirky touches ringing a flower-filled central courtyard and fireplaces keeping the chill at bay at night. Service is personalized and, if you're staying here too, the living room with its comfy sofas and books soon feels like it could be your own.

The *locro* is rich and cheesy, topped with perfectly ripe avocados and with fresh, piquant *ají* sauce on the side for those who like a little zip in their soup. Also on the menu are quinoa soup and croquettes, *llapingachos* (potato cakes) with guacamole, and *fritada* of fried pork in cumin, and all the vegetables are harvested from its own gardens. Desserts are a treat too – guaranteed to have you waddling off to a nearby sofa or hammock for a well-deserved siesta.

Lasso, Cotopaxi Province; open 1–3 PM daily (reservations advisable); www.incahacienda.com

In Quito

The list of establishments serving *locro* is as long as the list of its variants, but in Quito, **La Choza** in the La Floresta neighborhood (*www.lachozaec.com; moderate*) is regarded by many as the best. It serves lots more fine traditional Ecuadorian dishes as well, such as *hornado* roast pork (*see* What Else to Eat, *left*), goat stew, soups, and ceviche.

Also in the Ecuadorian Andes

In the north, **Hacienda Zuleta** (*www.zuleta. com; expensive*) serves delicious soups made from organic ingredients; **Hacienda Cusín** (*see* Where to Stay*)* and historic **Hacienda Pinsaquí** (*www.haciendapinsaqui.com; expensive*) near Otavalo are also good options. South of Quito, **Estrella de Chimborazo** (*www.expediciones-andinas.com; inexpensive*) is a high-altitude mountain lodge with a spectacular setting beneath the Chimborazo volcano, while **Hostería Abraspungo** near Riobamba (*www. haciendaabraspungo.com; moderate*) has a nice rustic feel. In the southern highlands, try the **Posada Ingapirca** (*www.grupo-santaana.net; moderate*) close to the Inca ruins of the same name. In Ecuador's third-largest city, pretty Cuenca, **Hotel Santa Lucía** (*www. santaluciahotel.com; expensive*)*,* **Mansión Alcázar** (*www.mansionalcazar.com; expensive*) and the cheerful **Raymipampa** (*+593 7 283 4159; inexpensive*) shouldn't disappoint.

LIMA PERU

Spicy Ceviche in the City of Kings

Lima may not have the immediate allure of other Latin American cities, but this coastal capital isn't lacking in culture or cuisine. It boasts pre-Inca sites and colonial mansions, and some real gastronomic delights. An amazing assortment of ingredients alights in Lima from the Andes and the Amazon, but it's the fresh Pacific fish that everyone wants, transformed into *ceviche*.

More than 100 years ago, culinary revolutionary Auguste Escoffier ranked Peruvian cuisine third-best in the world, behind only French and Chinese. Some might scoff at the claim, but Peru has a rich cooking tradition, and the proof is in the pudding – or in this case, the fish.

Ask a Peruvian what their national dish is and more often than not the answer will be *ceviche*, small pieces of raw fish marinated, or "cooked," in lime juice mingled with sliced hot chili peppers *(ají limo)* and red onions. It's served up as soon as the fish has become firm and opaque on the outside (about five minutes), with a wedge of cooked sweet potato, a chunk of fresh-cooked corn cob, and a frill of lettuce. The spicy juice from the *ceviche* marinade, called *leche de tigre* (tiger's milk), is, locals say, the best hangover cure around.

The secret to a good *ceviche* is the combination of Peruvian lime, which has an unusually high acid content, with the freshest of fish. *Limeños* (the inhabitants of the city) insist, in fact, that *ceviche* be eaten only at lunchtime, when the fish is guaranteed to have come straight off the morning's boats.

There is a long tradition of eating marinated fish in Peru. The Incas were fond of fish steeped in home-made corn beer and fruit juices, and cultures before them marinated fish with a fruit known as "tumbo," a type of passion fruit. Later, the Spanish brought limes, lemons, and onions to the table, and Japanese immigrants introduced the sashimi sensibility. And it all comes together on the plate in Lima, the coastal city created by conquistadors in 1535.

Lima was the capital of the Spanish dominion in Latin America for almost 200 years. Remnants of this cultural boom-time remain in the centuries-old streets and buildings downtown, especially around Plaza Mayor, where it is obvious in the lavish carvings of enclosed wooden balconies, the ornate doorways, and the tranquil inner courtyards of the city's mansions. Farther afield, buzzing Barranco is dotted with the vacation villas of wealthy 19th-century Europeans, who flocked to the beaches here in summer. Peruvians have long had a love affair with the waters of the Pacific Ocean, and tourists can witness this both in the friezes of antique ruins and in the restaurants, where *ceviche* still reigns supreme.

Above The Cathedral commands the view over Plaza Mayor, where the city was founded in 1535, and down the pedestrian-friendly Passage Santa Rosa (above)

What Else to Eat

Lima's cuisine and restaurants are gaining a worldwide reputation for freshness and creativity, embracing Chinese, Italian, Japanese, African, and Andean influences. This is especially evident in **lomo saltado**, a stir-fry with a distinct Peruvian twist: alongside strips of beef, onion, tomatoes, chili peppers, and garlic come fried potatoes and rice. Try it at José Antonio *(www.joseantonio.com. pe)*. Another favorite is **causa**: cool, yellow mashed potato mixed with lime juice and chili paste and layered with avocado, mayonnaise, and tuna; Astrid & Gaston *(www.astridygaston. com)* makes a good one. **Papas rellenas**, potato croquettes stuffed with minced meat, hard-boiled egg, and olives are a Creole favorite. Brujas de Cachiche *(www.brujasdecachiche.com.pe)* serves them with a tangy, lime-infused *salsa criolla*.

A Day in Lima

Lima is a cosmopolitan city that has embraced its varied past with gusto. Andean and Spanish influences abound in city neighborhoods, peppered with traces of Africa and Asia, all united by an unmistakable Peruvian vibe.

MORNING Take a jaunt around the city's colonial center, visiting **San Francisco Monastery** with its religious art collection and bone-packed crypt. Loiter in front of the **Presidential Palace** around 11:45 AM to see the changing of the guard, then walk down Jirón de la Unión to French-influenced **Plaza Saint Martín.**

AFTERNOON Hightail it to **Miraflores** to walk the clifftop parks, past the black-and-white lighthouse to the **Parque del Amor** ("Love Park"), which has sinuous mosaic walls inlaid with love adages and a colossal sculpture of a couple kissing. Finish up in smart-bohemian **Barranco** at the showy **Museo Pedro de Osma**.

EVENING Catch a taxi down to **Cala**, the beachfront lounge bar-restaurant below the Barranco cliffs, and order a pisco sour – a cocktail of Peruvian brandy, lemon juice, egg white, and sugar syrup – and a *ceviche* scallop roll, then sit back and watch the Pacific waves ebb and flow.

Essentials

GETTING THERE
Lima's **Jorge Chavez International Airport** lies 10 miles (16 km) northwest of the city. Take an official, registered taxi from the airport to the city.

WHERE TO STAY
Hostal El Patio (inexpensive) is a basic but comfortable hotel in central Miraflores with a cool, leafy courtyard. *www.hostalelpatio.net*
Second Home Peru (moderate) is the Barranco home of Peruvian sculptor Victor Delfin, and now a stylish guesthouse with sea views and five airy bedrooms. *www.secondhomeperu.com*
Hotel Country Club (expensive) in upmarket San Isidro is a deluxe 1920s hacienda-style hotel. *www.hotelcountry.com*

FURTHER INFORMATION
www.peru.info

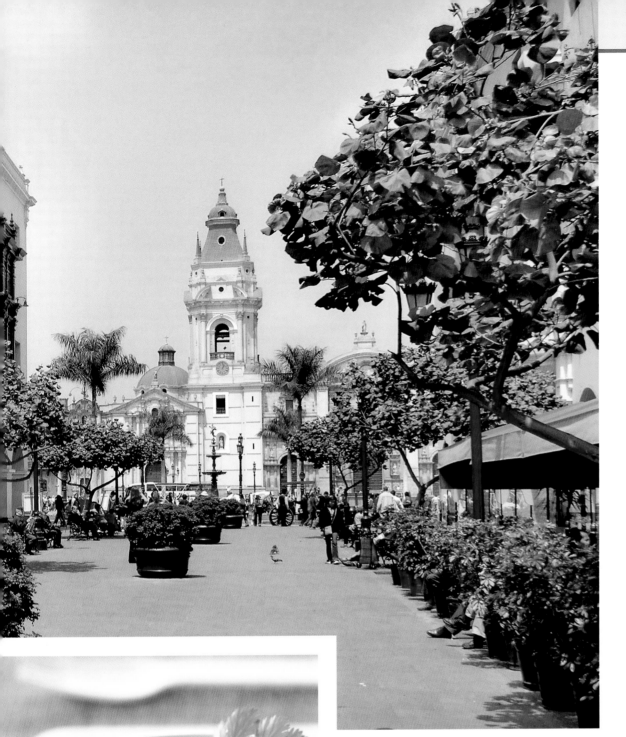

Above The Parque del Amor in Miraflores is lined with long, undulating mosaic benches covered in quotes from Peruvian poets

Left The fresh white fish meat of *ceviche* is "cooked" by being steeped briefly in a marinade of lime juice and chili peppers

The Best Places to Eat Ceviche

La Mar (moderate)

Part of the expanding empire of restaurants run by Peru's culinary ambassador and cordon-bleu-trained chef Gastón Acurio, La Mar is a lunch-only, seafood-focused destination, a *cebicheria peruano* (Peruvian *ceviche* restaurant). The restaurant doesn't take reservations and the best way to secure a table is to arrive around noon, otherwise you're likely to have a lengthy wait at the bar. Not that this is a bad thing, as they produce a great version of the pisco sour cocktail — fluffy, icy, and just a little bit addictive — as well as tempting snacks while you wait. There's a whole list of *ceviche* on the menu, from *clásico* with hot chili pepper, tiger's milk, and fresh fish, to *tumbes* — black scallops from the north of Peru, with octopus, mussels, calamari, and clams. Try the *degustación*: a selection of five *ceviche* to share, including *clásico*, *tumbes*, *nikei* (tuna), *elegante* (mixed fish), and *mistura* (shellfish, salmon, and fiercely hot green *rocoto* chili). There's also *tiradito*, which is like a cross between carpaccio and sashimi: paper-fine slices of raw fish dressed with lime and chili pepper.

Avenida La Mar 770, Miraflores, Lima; open noon–5 PM Mon–Thu, noon–5:30 PM Fri, 11:45 AM–5:30 PM Sat–Sun; www.lamarcebicheria.com

Also in Lima

Just down the road from La Mar, **Pescados Capitales** *(www.pescadoscapitales.com; moderate)* is another lunch-only seafood destination. The name is a pun on *pescados* (fish) and *pecados* (sins) and the menu plays up the "deadly fins" theme: *ceviche* comes under the heading *pecado original* (original sin), while main courses carry names such as "vanity," "envy," and "infidelity." *Ceviche* at the restaurant features *lenguado* (sole), octopus, mixed fish and shellfish, and deep-sea cachema fish.

Also in Peru

The improbably named **Big Ben** *(www. bigbenhuanchaco.com; inexpensive)* is the oldest restaurant in the beach resort-fishing village of Huanchaco on Peru's northern coast. Pick a table on the umbrella-covered terrace upstairs with a view over the ocean and order a fresh-off-the-boat *ceviche*.

Around the World

Not content with conquering Mexico, Chile, Brazil, Panama, Colombia, and Peru, chef Gastón Acurio has opened a **La Mar** *(www. lamarcebicheria.com; expensive)* in San Francisco. Located at the Embarcadero waterfront, it serves up *ceviche* with a local flavor: mahi-mahi, calamari, and octopus with cilantro and yellow chili pepper marinade; Californian halibut in a classic marinade; and ahi tuna with Japanese cucumber, daikon, and avocado in tamarind-flavored tiger's milk.

BUENOS AIRES ARGENTINA

Beefsteaks in Buenos Aires

Adorned with colorful plazas, *belle époque* palaces, and grand boulevards, Buenos Aires is the Paris of South America. Its hinterlands are lush alfalfa grasslands that roll out toward the Andes mountains, providing rich grazing for Argentina's prized beef cattle. Steak has long been the succulent staple of the gaucho and the centerpiece of the *asado*, an Argentinian barbecue feast.

From its location at the mouth of the Plate River, Buenos Aires rose to prominence at the end of the 19th century, when it became an important commercial capital and one of the world's richest cities. It embarked on a decadent Golden Age, modeling itself on Europe's great capitals, erecting palaces and monuments that recalled the splendors of Paris. Today, Buenos Aires is synonymous with the passions of tango and a thrilling restaurant scene, led by the city's fantastic steakhouses.

Echoes of Europe abound in Argentina's great capital. Walking south from Plaza de Mayo, its central plaza, visitors soon reach the city's romantic old quarters, where Spanish churches, sepia cafés, and colonial facades front cobbled lanes. North of the plaza, the glories of the *belle époque* unfold along broad, French-style avenues decorated with patriotic statuary and Parisian mansions adorned with cupolas and lavishly latticed balconies.

Visitors to Buenos Aires in the 21st century will discover these vintage architectural glories, but a new sense of style as well. The modern city buzzes with tourists and locals – *Porteños* – busily walking,

talking, shopping, and café-hopping. At night, visitors to the city are in search of two things: the tango and the eating ritual known as the *asado*. An ongoing barbecue of incredible meats, it is said to have developed from the rough-and-ready eating habits of the legendary gaucho, the Argentinian cowboy, who first roamed the pampas in the 17th century and is said to have slaughtered landowners' cows before roasting their carcasses over open fires.

In celebration of the gaucho, steakhouses today perform their own versions of this centuries-old ritual. Great slabs of red meat are thrown onto charcoal grills or hung from cross-poles over glowing pits of burning embers on the restaurant floor. Juicy beef cuts – sirloin, rib-eye, tenderloin, and more – are left to sizzle and smoke for hours until, beautifully tender, they are carved by an *asador* using long, glistening knives. A spectacle of dancing fires, bloody red meat, and razor-sharp blades, the Argentinian *asado* is a ritual steeped in masculinity and atavism. Delicious delicacies – tongue, sweetbreads, intestines, and blood sausages – wash the palate in rich, fatty flavors before the huge steaks arrive at table. The eating of every part of the animal is homage to the heroic gaucho, who left nothing of his kill for the vultures.

A Day in Buenos Aires

This city's historic central square, the Plaza de Mayo, is dominated by the Casa Rosada (Pink House), from whose balcony Eva Perón regaled the masses. This is the perfect place to start: *belle époque* wonders lie to the north, and colonial charms to the south.

MORNING From the **Plaza de Mayo**, go down Avenida de Mayo and have coffee at glorious **Café Tortoni**, the city's oldest café. Turn on to Avenida 9 de Julio, the city's greatest, patriotic thoroughfare, and admire the **Obelisco** and the **Teatro Colón** opera house. Take a taxi to the **Recoleta Cemetery**, where Eva Perón lies buried.

AFTERNOON Head back to **Plaza de Mayo** and walk south, into the old quarter. Stroll cobbled streets with colonial facades in **San Telmo**; enjoy an alfresco lunch in cobbled **Plaza Dorrego**; and go to **La Boca**, the colorful port district. Visit **La Bombonera**, the iconic stadium of Boca Juniors, Argentina's greatest soccer team.

EVENING Return to **San Telmo** for sizzling beefsteaks and a tango show at **El Viejo Almacén**, one of the oldest buildings in the city.

Essentials

GETTING THERE
International flights land at **Ezeiza Airport**, 35 miles (22 km) from downtown; use the official **taxi** service or a **shuttle bus**.

WHERE TO STAY
Abode Buenos Aires (inexpensive) is a modern B&B in Palermo. *www.abodebuenosaires.com*
Home Hotel (moderate) offers boutique rooms and apartments with spa, garden, and pool facilities. *www.homebuenosaires.com*
Sofitel Buenos Aires (expensive) is pure luxury in a 1929 Art Deco building. *www.sofitel.com*

TOURIST INFORMATION
www.turismo.gov.ar

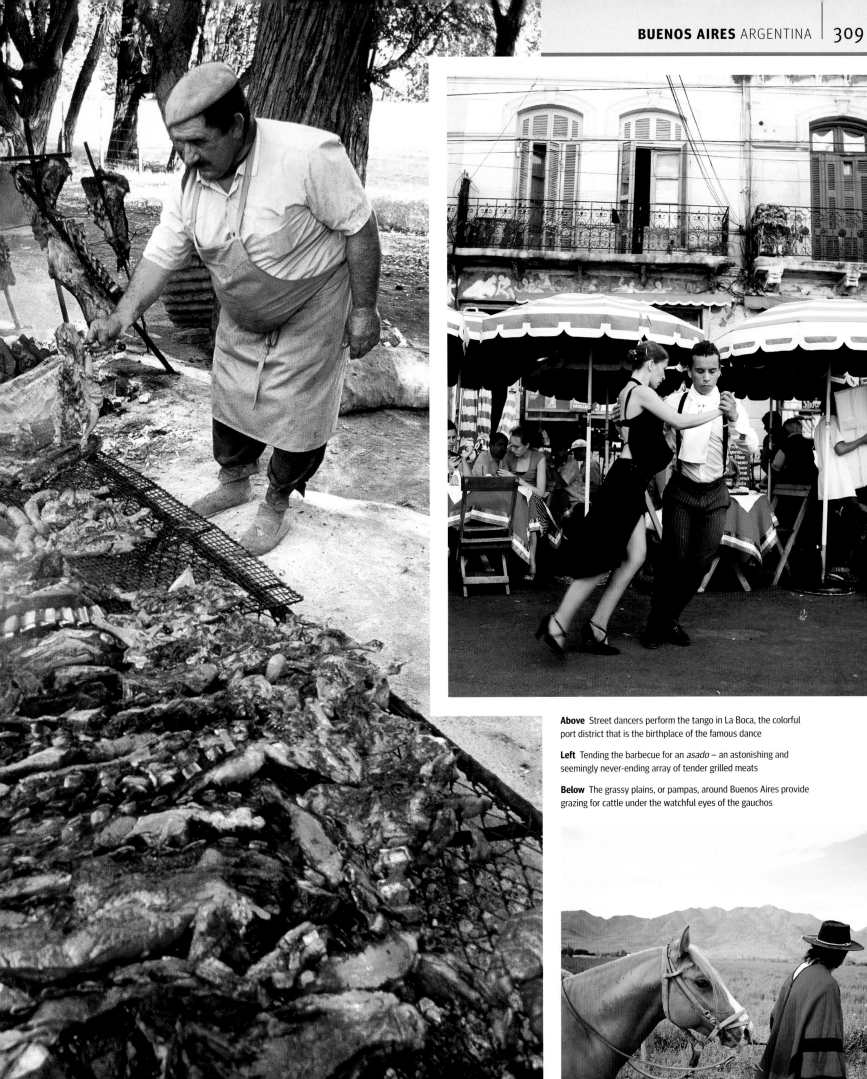

Above Street dancers perform the tango in La Boca, the colorful port district that is the birthplace of the famous dance

Left Tending the barbecue for an *asado* – an astonishing and seemingly never-ending array of tender grilled meats

Below The grassy plains, or pampas, around Buenos Aires provide grazing for cattle under the watchful eyes of the gauchos

Steak Around the World

Buenos Aires leads the world in the preparation of succulent, tender beefsteaks. But global travelers can enjoy great steaks at several other cities that lie close to lush, free-grazing grasslands and pride themselves on their beef-eating cultures.

BUENOS AIRES

Manolo inexpensive

Bolivar 1299, San Telmo;
www.restaurantmanolo.com.ar

Local Argentinians love this old-fashioned, cafeteria-style *parrilla* (restaurant serving grilled meats) for its delicious delicacies, which are incredible bargains. Chitterlings and sweetbreads, textured like melted butter and sprinkled with lemon juice, precede tender grilled steaks. Service is fast, the ambience loud, and walls feature soccer-themed memorabilia.

El Obrero moderate

Agustín R. Caffarena 64, La Boca; +54 11 4362 9912

U2's Bono, Francis Ford Coppola, and Robert Duvall are three celebrities that have been drawn to dine at this atmospheric steakhouse in the colorful La Boca portside district. It opened in 1954 and continues to serve some of the best, and biggest, steaks in town. Choose from the *parrilla* specials on the chalkboard and aim to arrive before the busiest time of 9:00 PM.

La Cabrera moderate

Cabrera 5099, Palermo Viejo;
www.parrillalacabrera.com.ar

A romantic steakhouse in one of the city's prettiest districts, La Cabrera comprises twin dining salons of mosaic flooring, timber furnishings, and stripped-bare walls. Its beefsteaks are huge and first-rate, and they come with around 12 side dishes, from Béarnaise sauce to roasted artichokes and mashed squash with raisins. Tables are candlelit; outdoor tables overlook a cobbled street.

Cabaña Las Lilas expensive

Alicia Moreau de Justo 516; www.laslilas.com

Situated on the waterfront in the Puerto Madero docklands district, this exclusive *parrilla* serves steaks from its own ranches. Ask for the superior rib-eye cut and accompany it with one of the 700 premium Argentinian wines offered.

MENDOZA, ARGENTINA

At restaurants in Argentina's wine capital, Mendoza, world-class red wines accompany Argentinian beefsteaks. Choose a downtown *parrilla* or dine at a wine estate, where vistas of vineyards and the snow-capped Andes form the backdrop to premium wines and prime beef.

Don Mario inexpensive

25 de Mayo 1324, Dorrego; www.donmario.com.ar

At this basic *parrilla*, Don Mario allows his cooking to do the talking. The sweetbreads are outstanding and the sirloin and tenderloin steaks are fit for gauchos. The mixed grill option of combined delicacies and beef cuts is excellent and economical.

Ocho Cepas moderate

Peru 1192; www.ochocepas.com

Ocho Cepas is a wine-and-gourmet-grill experience set within a beautifully refurbished colonial house, run by Argentine chef Max Casa. Choose alfresco dining beneath the Mendoza stars or opt for an intimate interior table amid colonial arches. Meat and wine options are both outstanding.

Cavas Wine Lodge expensive

Costaflores S/N; www.cavaswinelodge.com

This romantic restaurant is set in a luxury wine lodge and spa, situated within a 35-acre (14-hectare) vineyard. It emphasizes regional Mendoza cuisine, from appetizers such as goat cheese terrine with "wine caviar" to rib-eye steak with *chimichurri* – the spicy pesto-like sauce of choice for *asados*.

MONTEVIDEO, URUGUAY

Uruguay has the highest number of meat-eaters per capita in the world, outshining even its close neighbor, Argentina. Steakhouses in its capital city, Montevideo, overlook the Atlantic Ocean and serve classic beef cuts oozing with juices and flavors.

La Casa Violeta moderate

Rambla Armenia 3667; www.lacasavioleta.com

Choose a terrace table at gorgeous Violeta, which faces one of Montevideo's prettiest harbors. There are seven kinds of steak, from rib-eye and porterhouse to the restaurant's rib-chop specialty, and the fantastic meats are whisked to tables on long skewers in the local style.

Left (top to bottom) Tenderloin, the tenderest of cuts, should virtually melt in the mouth; a gaucho prepares steaks on the *parrilla* in Argentina; barbecue in the famous port market in Montevideo

Below (top to bottom) Peter Luger's famous half-pound burger is made of porterhouse trimmings; *bistecca alla fiorentina*, a juicy steak on the bone from the Chianina cattle of Tuscany

Los Leños expensive
San Jose; +598 2900 2285
A big rack of meat always roasts over the open fire at the casually chic *parrilla* of Los Leños. Start with a succulent seafood appetizer and follow with the signature tenderloin steak – *filet de lomo* – accompanied by mustard or the more exotic Roquefort or black-pepper sauces.

NEW YORK, NY
New York City is famously home of the tasty and tender New York strip steak (also known as Kansas City strip steak or strip loin steak). Eat it like the locals: rare, doused in sauces, and accompanied by a serving of truffle mac (macaroni) and cheese.

Angelo & Maxie's Steakhouse inexpensive
Park Avenue South at 19th Street; www.angelo-maxies.com
This inexpensive steakhouse serves juicy, oversized steaks (and some great fish dishes) in a splendid 1930s, Art Deco-style setting. Start with a seafood appetizer and order some onion rings or green salad to accompany your steaks. It's a romantic dining spot and has a great bar too.

Ottomanelli New York Grill moderate
1325 Fifth Avenue; www.nycotto.com
Savvy New Yorkers make a beeline to this grill, which has been run by the Ottomanelli family since 1900. Its specialty is enormous sirloin-steak burgers. Strip and hanger steaks, marinated in red wine and fresh herbs, are grilled to perfection as well.

Peter Luger Steakhouse expensive
178 Broadway, Brooklyn; www.peterluger.com
Open for over a century, Peter Luger is the Big Apple's finest traditional steakhouse, with luxurious wooden decor and chandeliers. It's a family business, and uses only the best US short-loin beef. Try its signature porterhouse steak, which the waiter cuts into filet and sirloin at the table, and douses with a superb wasabi-flavored or Merlot-based sauce.

Quality Meats expensive
57 W. 58th St.; www.qualitymeatsnyc.com
This upmarket steakhouse sizzles with sex appeal. Its industrial-chic decor features light installations fashioned from butchers' hooks and walls made from wine bottles. Its New American cuisine produces classic steaks marinated in inventive sauces. The clientele is young and hip.

TEXAS
Texas rivals Argentina for the crown of world's greatest steak-eating destination. The giant southern state is synonymous with grasslands, thundering cattle herds, and the iconic American cowboy. Houston, its biggest city, serves some of its most memorable beef.

Taste of Texas Restaurant moderate
10505 Katy Freeway, Houston; www.tasteoftexas.com
Having the air of an old-style cowboy joint, "T-O-T," as it is known, is a down-to-earth Texas steakhouse that emphasizes old-fashioned friendliness and uncomplicated dining, led by huge, juicy beefsteaks. Order the prime rib and you will exit smiling.

Pappas Bros. Steakhouse expensive
5839 Westheimer Rd., Houston; www.pappasbros.com
One of Houston's finest steakhouses, Pappas Bros. has an aged interior of red leather and polished wood furnishings. Its dry-aged steaks – from the filet mignon and rib-eye to a huge porterhouse – draw meat-lovers from across Texas. Its seafood starters are wonderful.

FLORENCE, ITALY
Florentines harvest their beef from the white Chianina cattle that graze the grasses of Tuscany's valleys. In Florentine kitchens, the tender, flavorful Chianina meat becomes the *bistecca alla fiorentina* – the Renaissance city's emblematic beefsteak.

Trattoria Mario inexpensive
Via Rosina 2R; www.trattoria-mario.com
Family-run Mario's has served the workers of Florence's Central Market since 1953. Diners share tables and the day's menu is attached to the wall with tape. Florentine steaks arrive big, bloody, and with hunks of bread on the side.

Ristorante Paoli moderate
Via de' Tavolini 12R; www.casatrattoria.com
A vaulted 14th-century ceiling painted with frescoes from the 1800s overlooks the tables at Paoli. It's an inspired setting, and the cuisine here is equally divine. Order succulent Florentine steak.

Buca Lapi expensive
Via del Trebbio 1R; www.bucalapi.com
Opened in 1880 in the cellars of Palazzo Antinori, this is an intimate trattoria set beneath vaulted, frescoed ceilings. Its *bistecca chianina* (Florentine porterhouse) steak is masterful, cooked over a charcoal grill and sprinkled with olive oil.

Right Humpbacks and other species can be seen on whale-watching trips off the Bahia coast from July to October

Below The creamy fish stew of *moqueca* includes tangy lime-marinated fish and fresh tomatoes

Three Days in Espírito Santo and Bahia

The pretty, unspoiled towns and villages of these regions sit against a backdrop of Atlantic coastal rain forests and border some of the finest beaches in Brazil.

DAY ONE Visit the rain forests of the **Monte Pascoal National Park**, which shroud the peak first sighted by the Portuguese and hide jaguars among the trees. Continue to **Alcobaça**, the region's festival capital, whose streets are lined with crumbling 19th-century houses.

DAY TWO Take a boat trip from **Caravelas** to whale-watch and snorkel in the **Abrolhos Archipelago**. These waters are home to some of the most extensive coral reefs in the South Atlantic and are one of the best places in the world to see humpback whales, who calf here between July and December. Stay the night in Caravelas.

DAY THREE Drive south to the relaxing little fishing resort of **Itaúnas**, which sits nestled in dunes behind a string of magnificent beaches visited by three species of marine turtles.

Essentials

GETTING THERE
The state's main international hub is Salvador-Deputado Luís Eduardo Magalhães **airport**; domestic airlines fly into the smaller **Porto Seguro airport**; both have **car rental** facilities.

WHERE TO STAY
Vila Morena (inexpensive) in Itaúnas offers colorful and friendly bargain accommodations a stroll from the sea. *www.vilamorena.com.br*
Brisa dos Abrolhos (moderate) in Alcobaça is great for families. *+55 73 3293 2022*
Marina Porto Abrolhos (expensive) in Caravelas is the best hotel in the region, right on the beach. *www.marinaportoabrolhos.com.br*

TOURIST INFORMATION
Bahia: *www.bahiatursa.ba.gov.br*;
Espírito Santo: *www.setur.es.gov.br*

ESPIRITO SANTO AND BAHIA BRAZIL

Moqueca on the Brazilian Coast

The coastline of the Espírito Santo and Bahia states is dotted with tiny fishing villages and glorious bays, where turtles nest in warm white sands and whales calf around the coral islands offshore. It was here that Europeans first set foot in Brazil, 500 years ago, and were doubtless offered a form of *moqueca*, a creamy seafood stew that is still the regional dish today.

Like Columbus before him, the Portuguese explorer Pedro Alvares Cabral was on his way to India in search of spices when he stumbled on Brazil on Easter Day in 1500. His coxswain sighted the spectacular verdant peak of Monte Pascoal, shrouded in rain forest and fringed with coral sand beaches. Instead of spices, Cabral found tantalizing tropical fruits and brilliantly colored berries, both of which were used in the rich cooking of the local Tupi-speaking peoples. The first Portuguese person to write about Tupi cooking was Padre Luís de Grã, who commented on the delicious way the locals prepared meat and fish – *carne* and *peixe* – as a *moquecada*, where the meat or fish is wrapped in a leaf or placed in a clay pot with Brazilian herbs, chili peppers, and root vegetables, then cooked over red-hot embers.

The dish was transformed by the Portuguese, who added European fruits and spices to the pot and served the dish with rice and green vegetables. Renamed *moqueca*, it quickly became one of the most popular dishes in the country. But in the 20th century it sparked a bitter rivalry between the two coastline states of Bahia and Espírito Santo, first sighted by Cabral – as both claimed the dish as their own.

The Bahian *moqueca* is certainly the most Brazilian, though it is a blend of Portuguese, Tupi, and African influences – the shrimp are cooked in *dendê* palm oil and creamy coconut (both introduced to Brazil from Africa). The people of Espírito Santo curl their lip; their *moqueca* – known as *moqueca capixaba* – is, they insist, far closer to the original. It is also preferred by cooking connoisseurs. Juicy shrimp or snookfish are marinated in lime juice and then pan-fried in olive oil in a clay pot. The chef then adds tomatoes, cilantro, and the blood-red juice of *urucum* (annatto) berries, before leaving it to simmer for an hour or so. The dish is served piping hot with a sprinkle of fresh parsley.

Regardless of who's right, it's hard to quarrel in such a peaceful region. The tiny, tranquil villages, forested mountains, and wildly beautiful coastline induce feelings of both awe and contentment, surely echoing Cabral's first impressions, 500 years ago.

What Else to Eat

Nowhere has a richer local cuisine than Espírito Santo, where pre-Columbian indigenous methods of cooking in clay pots have been spiced up with European and African influences and ingredients. **Muma de siri** is a spicy shrimp and crab dish simmered in a clay pot over a wood stove and served with rice and *farofa* (roasted or pan-fried manioc flour). **Torta capixaba** is a seafood tart that's crammed with oysterlike *sururus*, soft-shell crabs, shrimp, and salted codfish. Fruits are myriad and many are unknown outside Brazil. Most make wonderful juices, such as **acerola**, a tart tropical cherry; **umbu**, a berry that's pulped to make a milky liquid; piquant **pitanga** (the Brazilian cherry), and juicy **seriguela**.

Left A view over the Abrolhos Marine National Park, Bahia

The Best Places to Eat Moqueca

Restaurante Céu-Mar inexpensive

This brightly painted little restaurant overlooking the lush banks of the Itaúnas River has been a favorite with visiting Brazilians in the know for well over a decade. They come for the delicious seafood, which is as fresh as it gets – the restaurant's chef plucks the choicest catches of the day from local boats every evening. The menu is broad but the highlight is the seafood *moquecas capixabas*, served bubbling with bright red *urucum* berry juice in traditional clay pots. Portions are big enough for two and come with white rice and a green salad.

Av Bento Daher, Itaúnas, Espírito Santo; open 11:30 AM–midnight; +55 27 3762 5081

Also on the Coast

Maresia's *(+55 73 3293 2471; inexpensive)* is a modest, family-run restaurant on Avenida Atlântica, overlooking Alcobaça's beautiful beach. This is where the local Bahian people come for a great *moqueca*. The shrimp and snookfish are so fresh they are almost wriggling, and the huge Bahian *moquecas*, cooked in coconut and *dendê* palm oil, come in a simmering earthenware pot. Be sure to wash them down with a glass of tangy *mangaba* juice, made with fruits plucked from the trees that grow along the nearby river.

Also in Brazil

Bahian chef Neide Santos has created a mini-Bahia in Rio at **Yoruba** *(+55 21 2541 9387; moderate)*, a colorful little restaurant on Rua Arnaldo Quintela, near the Sugar Loaf mountain. The dining room is decorated with brightly colored Bahian ribbons and drapes and the menu consists almost entirely of Bahian dishes, including huge fish or shrimp *moquecas* big enough for two.

Around the World

Made in Brasil *(www.made-in-brasil-bar. co.uk; moderate)* in Camden, London, aims to re-create the relaxed feeling of a Brazilian beach café with its tables of unfinished driftwood, shuttered windows, and Latin American music. Its Brazilian chefs produce several types of *moqueca*, including the classic Bahian *moqueca de peixe*, as well as other Brazilian dishes such as *feijoada (see pp320–21)* and *bobo de camarao* (tiger shrimp in a creamy cassava and palm oil sauce).

In Cambridge, Massachusetts, the Brazilian-owned and run **Muqueca Restaurant** *(www.muquecarestaurant.com; moderate)* serves seven types of *moqueca*, including a plantain and tofu version for vegetarians. Dishes come accompanied by a range of uniquely Brazilian super-fruit juices, including açai *(see p303)*, tart Amazonian *cupuaçú*, and acerola, a vitamin-C super-fruit.

CHILOE CHILE

A Fine Feast in Southern Chile

An enchanted island archipelago, Chiloé is a bewitching place of silent forests and craggy peaks that tumble down to fishing villages and mist-shrouded bays. Once believed to be a place of demonic and benevolent spirits, its fishermen still look out for a beautiful mermaid, La Pincoya, who is said to ensure a bountiful catch – and fresh ingredients for *curanto*, an ancient feast.

Separated from mainland Chile by the narrow Chacao Channel, the Chiloé archipelago comprises one large island, Isla Grande, and several smaller ones. A magical, mystical world of emerald woods and silent fjords, its indigenous people, the Mapuche, lived here undiscovered for millennia until Spanish conquistadors arrived in the 1500s. Spain steered Chiloé on a historical course quite distinct from the mainland: the archipelago evolved its own culture, a unique cuisine, and a distinctive mythology rooted in Spanish Catholicism and Mapuche legend, with mythological figures like La Pincoya. In the 1600s, Jesuit missionaries built wooden churches across Chiloé to evangelize the Mapuche, and colorful towns grew around them.

On Isla Grande, Chiloé's capital city, Castro, is the archipelago's cultural heart. A small city of hilly lanes and fishermen's houses built on wooden stilts on the waters of the Castro Fjord, it was the beachhead for attempts to conquer the Mapuche. Nowadays, it is a springboard for inspirational road and ferry trips that travel through haunting waters, forest-cloaked mountains, and spooky fishermen's villages full of ghostly churches and tales of witchcraft.

Traditional customs still abound, and the steamy feast known as *curanto* seems to have sprung from the old fishermen's habit of adding fresh fish to long-life foods such as cured meats, which they kept on board in case the weather forced them to stay at sea for weeks at a time. *Curanto* still blends shellfish and fish with meats such as pork and chicken in a kind of ancient "clambake" that's unique to this southern archipelago.

Traditionally, islanders cook *curanto* by digging a wide pit in the ground in which they build a fire beneath smooth, round stones. Once these are hot, the flames are doused, and a blanketing layer of the huge native *nalca* leaves is spread over the stones. Layers of food are then piled on – fresh seafood, including baby mussels, clams, and fish, then meat and vegetables, including pork, chicken, potatoes, dumpling-like *chapaleles*, and *milacos*, a mix of fried raw potatoes, butter, and crackling. The food is covered with more *nalca* leaves, and then stones or chunks of sod to trap the heat, and the food is left to cook slowly over several hours. Today, restaurants prepare *curanto* "*a la olla*" – in huge cauldron-like pots, from which they serve small mountains of its many meats and vegetables. It's a magical concoction that's strangely perfect in these mystical islands.

Three Days on Chiloé

Frequent bus and ferry services connect the islands in the archipelago, but you'll need to rent a car to really explore the back-country roads and village life.

DAY ONE Visit **Castro**, Chiloé's capital. Tour **Iglesia San Francisco**, a UNESCO-protected Jesuit church; then descend hilly lanes to the **Castro Fjord**. Stroll along the waterfront, past the stilted, wooden fishermen's homes in the water. Go to the **Museo de Arte Moderno Chiloé**, where modern art examines Chiloé's island identity.

DAY TWO Rent a car and explore **Isla Grande**. Head north to **Ancud**, a historic fort settlement; then drive south to **Chonchi**, a village built into a vertiginous cliff overlooking a scenic bay. Visit **Iglesia de Chonchi**, a Jesuit church whose vanilla-and-powder-blue facade hides a vaulted interior painted with a thousand tiny white stars.

DAY THREE Hop on a ferry to small **Isla de Quinchao**, to walk the beaches and the gravel streets of old fishing village **Curaco de Vélez**. Back in **Castro**, round out your stay with a visit to a waterside restaurant for a dinner of steamy *curanto*.

Essentials

GETTING THERE
Fly to Santiago **international airport**, then take a **domestic flight** to the southern mainland city, Puerto Montt, where **ferries** cross to Chiloé.

WHERE TO STAY
Hotel Huildin (inexpensive) has garden cabins and rooms in Chonchi. www.hotelhuildin.cl
Hotel Unicornio Azul (moderate) is a restored 1910 building set on the Castro waterfront. www.hotelgaleonazul.cl
Hostería Ancud (expensive) overlooks the ocean and Ancud's historic fort. +56 65 622 340

TOURIST INFORMATION
www.visit-chile.org

Above A heaped bowl of *curanto*, demonstrating what a feast this is – slow-baked seafoods, meats, vegetables, and dumplings are piled high

Left The seemingly precarious but long-standing *palafitos*, or stilt houses, rise up from the water all over Chiloé, but most impressively in Castro

Above *Curanto* is cooked in an earthen pit; the food is protected from the fire-heated stones and sod layers between enormous *nalca* leaves

Festival Costumbrista

The Festival Costumbrista Chilote is Chiloé's biggest annual festival and a vibrant celebration of its island culture. It takes place at locations across the archipelago in January and February. Festival-goers take part in island activities including cooking *curanto* in traditional earthen pits (visitors take a hand in creating the pit and its food), as well as weaving, sheep-shearing, driving oxen, and making jelly. Food stands serve *curanto* and archipelago staples such as shellfish *empanadas* (savory pastry turnovers), *licor de oro* (a fermented cow-milk liqueur), and ulmo honey – a sweet honey made from the native ulmo tree.

The Best Places to Eat Curanto

Restaurant Octavio moderate

The setting for this restaurant is an old fisherman's house overlooking the glassy waters of the Castro Fjord. Built from native island wood, the house stands on tall stilts in the fjord's frigid waters and has an exterior painted in bright primary colors. On the inside, it is total rusticity and warmth. A wooden entrance door creaks inward, floorboards groan underfoot and, at the heart of the restaurant floor, an open fire crackles and roars. Choose a window table for its magical views across the Castro Fjord to mist-shrouded, forest-swathed mountains on the opposite shore.

The menu at Octavio brims with Chiloé specialties. Choose the *cochayuyo* (seaweed) soup appetizer and *curanto* main course. Prepared *a la olla*, in a cauldron, your *curanto* arrives steaming with clams and mussels plucked from the ocean at daybreak, and piled high with sausages and more. Servings are huge – you'll probably only need one portion to feed two. Round off your meal with Octavio's celestial papaya-fruit-and-cream dessert.

Avenida Pedro Montt 261, Castro; open noon–midnight daily; +56 65 632 855

Also in Chiloé

In Ancud, **Restaurant Kuranton** *(+56 65 623 090; moderate)* faces the sea and serves an inspired *curanto*. It has a snug ambience, with low ceilings and tangerine walls that are hung with carvings and aged artwork. All across the archipelago, colorful, family-run restaurants at fishermen's markets serve first-rate, and very cheap, *curanto*. **Ballena Sur** *(+56 99 414 354; inexpensive)*, over the waterfront and inside the market at Chonchi, is one of the very best, with beautiful views of Chonchi Bay. In Curaco de Vélez, on Isla de Quichao, **Restaurant Los Troncos** *(no telephone; inexpensive)* is a delight. A rustic garden restaurant with ocean vistas, it serves *curanto*, fresh salmon, and the house specialty: salty oysters, eaten raw with a hunk of lemon.

Also in Chile

On the mainland, Chiloé's gateway city, Puerto Montt, shares the *curanto* tradition. At its raucous Angelmó Fish Market, climb wooden stairs to **La Estrella de Angelmó** *(no telephone; inexpensive)*, which serves the dish amid a mind-boggling variety of ultra-fresh seafood specials, from stewed crabs to sea urchins. In the capital city, Santiago, **Restaurant El Galeón** *(www.elgaleon.cl; moderate)* is a seafood restaurant located within the capital's atmospheric Mercado Central (Central Market). It has dished up a fantastic *curanto* since 1935.

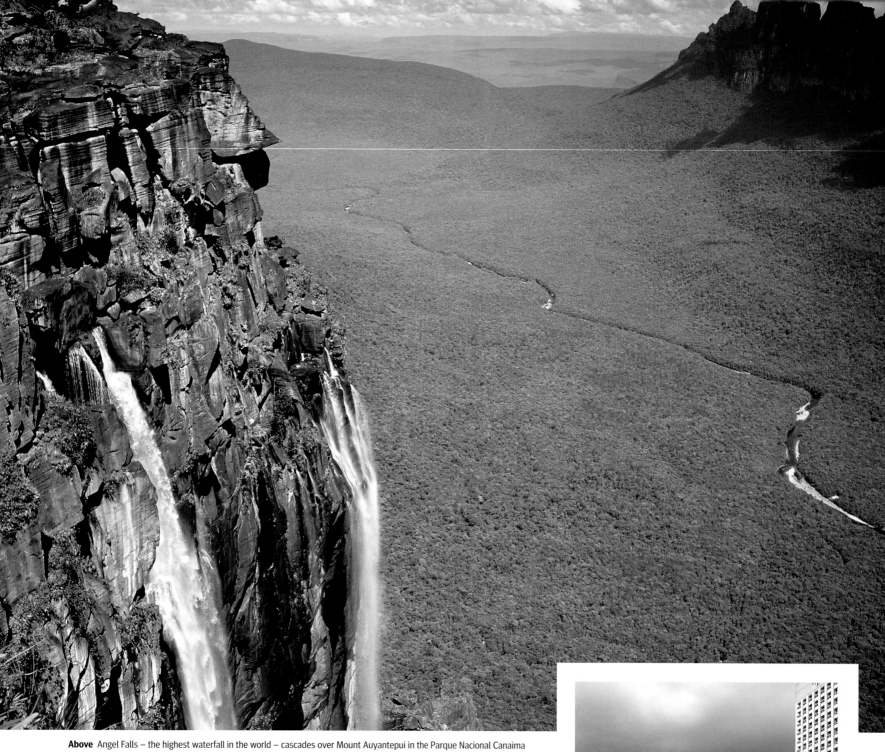

Above Angel Falls – the highest waterfall in the world – cascades over Mount Auyantepui in the Parque Nacional Canaima

Three Days in and around Caracas

The road from Caracas to Mérida in the Andean Mountains weaves between two mountain chains. To reach the grassy savannas of Los Llanos, you'll journey along roads hemmed by knots of ferns, palms, and vines before delving into the domain of the Venezuelan cowboy.

DAY ONE   Take a **city tour** of Caracas's challenging contemporary architecture, handsome ranchos, historic houses, and extensive slums of tin huts and cardboard boxes, all overlooked by Mount Avila, which rises from the beautiful **Parque Nacional El Avila**.

DAY TWO   Explore the sparsely populated **Los Llanos** countryside by driving across its picturesque rolling plains, punctuated by cattle farms and thousand-strong beef herds. Cook around an open fire on the banks of the **Orinoco**, South America's second-longest river.

DAY THREE   Trek the scenic, leafy trails that loop the Andean town of **Mérida**, nestled in a verdant valley close to the **Mucuy National Park** and its crystal-clear rivers. Mérida also boasts the longest cable-car ride in the world, to the top of **Bolívar Mountain**.

Essentials

GETTING THERE
Simón Bolívar International Airport in Maiquetia is 13 miles (20 km) from downtown Caracas. There are **car rentals** at the airport.

WHERE TO STAY
El Fundo de Pedernales (inexpensive) is a friendly lodge in the stunning Los Llanos plains offering guided tours. *+58 256 514 5070*
Hotel Plaza Mérida (moderate) is a charming 46-room hotel nestled in the mountain foothills that's packed with local art and crafts. *www.hotelplazamerida.com*
Embassy Suites by Hilton (expensive), in the business district of El Rosal, Caracas, has an outdoor swimming pool, gym, and business suites. *http://embassysuites1.hilton.com*

TOURIST INFORMATION
www.inatur.gob.ve

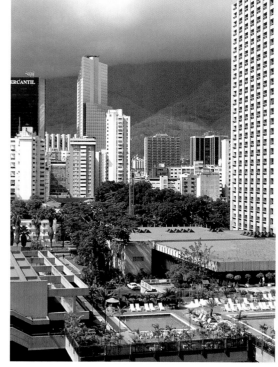

Above Caracas sits at the foot of the slopes of the vast Mount Avila

CARACAS VENEZUELA

Chicharrones in Venezuela

Venezuela is a dream road-trip destination. Drivers navigate against a dramatic backdrop of snow-capped Andean peaks and white-sand Caribbean beaches as they cruise through the lush Orinoco Basin, the skyscrapers of Caracas or the grassy savannas of Los Llanos. The savanna roads are lined with gaily painted food stands selling *chicharrones*, the nation's favorite travel snack.

Venezuela so inspired an awestruck Christopher Columbus during his third New World voyage that he described it as "paradise on earth." Today, its Angel Falls – the world's highest waterfall – still inspires plenty of hyperbole among travelers, as do the mighty Orinoco River and vast Lake Maracaibo. Elegant colonial towns steeped in whimsical nostalgia, such as the mountain settlement of Colonia Tovar, are easily reached by car from the valley-capital of Caracas via the rolling forests of the Cordillera de la Costa. Scenic shore-side roads reveal a palm-scattered, semitropical coast; the warm sands of the western coast roll out before emerald rain forest and resplendent cloud-topped mountain peaks.

Venezuela's maximum speed limit restricts every driver to a genteel 55 mph (80 km/h), so even hotheads settle into a relaxed, steady pace on the road. The highways have well-maintained surfaces that stretch out like asphalt tentacles to bird-filled rain forests, flooded meadows, and rustic mud-and-thatch villages, extending farther into ragged rural roadways, from dusty gravel to dirt tracks with potholes the size of minivans. Drivers need to keep their wits about them – all manner of farm animals and some extraordinary wildlife are prone to exploring Venezuelan roads too.

No road trip is complete without *chicharrones*, crunchy, deep-fried chunks of seasoned pork rind. Believed to have originated in Spain, they are plied by *buhoneros* (vendors) at virtually every street corner and highway rest stop of Venezuela's provinces and its capital, Caracas. Some rinds are heavily salted, slightly greasy, and slow-cooked to melt away the fat; others are peppered, fatty, and chewy. Cooked to a deep russet red, many still have bristles poking through the golden rind. Some are spicy and crinkled; others are shiny, dry, and smooth. All are frazzled until the rind puffs up into irregular curls and squiggles, some in great slabs, others in tiny popcorn-sized nibbles. There are dozens of *chicharrón* sellers in the capital's tree-lined Parque Central, each touting their own style of *chicharrones*, roasted to a recipe handed down through the generations that invariably still tastes good today.

What Else to Eat

In Venezuela's cool, crisp mountain region, age-old Andean cuisine dates back to ancient pre-Hispanic cultures when warming, high-protein foods were cooked over glowing embers. Dishes were filling and calorific, using root vegetables, grains, nuts, and plants with meat from **guinea pigs** *(cuy)* and llamas. Several types of edible clay, such as **pasa**, were used as a gloopy sauce. **Quinoa** remains an all-important Andean food staple in stews and soups. Meat and fish are still preserved by drying and salting. In Los Llanos, culinary traditions center on the region's grass-reared herds of cattle, with numerous recipes that celebrate a simple slab of **beef**. Steaks are man-sized, cut generously thick and hung over a smoky open fire for several hours. In Cowboy Country, very few green vegetables are consumed.

Above *Chicharrones*, roasted pork-skin snacks, are often eaten with coffee or aged rum

---

The Best Places to Eat Chicharrones

Sabana Grande Boulevard
inexpensive

Outdoor cooking on an open fire using the hottest fat helps to give *chicharrones* their salty, baconlike flavor and irresistible crunch. The best places to savor the flavors of Caracas's ultra-crunchy style of pork are the side streets of Sabana Grande Boulevard, where you can enjoy them sitting between groups of elderly chess and domino players hunched over wooden tables, amid the food and clothes-strewn market stands. Though different parts of the pig can be used, the skin of the belly strip is commonly the basis of Venezuelan pork rinds sold by sidewalk food stands in Caracas. Often touted by the owners of the carts that sell *arepas* (fried cornbread patties), *chicharrones* are offered as an alternative to the normal patty stuffings, such as *carne mechada* (shredded beef), *caraotas negras* (black beans), *pollo guisado* (stewed chicken), and *queso rallado* (grated cheese).

Sabana Grande Boulevard, Caracas; hours vary (stands operate virtually 24 hours a day, daily)

Also in Caracas

Both Sabana Grande Boulevard and Parque Central can be hectic; for a change of pace, venture into the city's atmospheric Spanish quarter of **La Candelaria** to find *chicharrón* sellers among its old cobblestone alleyways and handsome colonial plazas.

Also in Venezuela

You'll also find *chicharrones* along the road that crosses the Andes from Mérida to Barinas at the western edge of the Los Llanos region. At these welcome pit-stops, rosy-cheeked women in colorful aprons cut belly pork into ribbons on jagged rocks, chickens pecking greedily on the scraps, while black cauldrons of fat spit and pop. Car-weary travelers satisfy their rumbling stomachs, dipping into paper cones for chunks of the salt-encrusted crackling, washed down by fizzy drinks hawked by the local children.

Around the World

In New York, richly flavored homemade Venezuelan dishes are served up with considerable pride at the **Cocotero Restaurant** *(www.cocotero-restaurant.com; inexpensive)* on West 18th Street in Chelsea. An imaginative menu proves to New York gastronomes that Venezuelan fare extends well beyond griddle-cooked *arepas* without foregoing authentic simple recipes and homegrown produce. Yet it is the hole-in-the-wall joint **La Reina del Chicharron** *(212 304 1070; inexpensive)* that is the food temple in which fried pork scratchings are truly worshipped. Chef Elsa's *chicharrones* are crispy, crunchy, and served in a bag solo or in a dish of mashed plantains. It's strictly cash only.

Right The laid-back little town of Salento is a great base for exploring coffee country

Below Colombia's unofficial national dish, *bandeja paisa* is part mixed grill, part tortilla, and extremely filling

Three Days in Coffee Country

Good roads connect the cities with the smaller towns and rural attractions beyond. Though earthquakes have destroyed many historic areas and left the rebuilt cities with a modern face, you can still find old colonial buildings and cathedrals in this area.

DAY ONE Spend the day on a **coffee farm** such as Villa Nora *(see Where to Stay, right)*, touring the fields and processing sites and enjoying the beautiful rural scenery.

DAY TWO Visit the **Parque Nacional del Café** (National Coffee Park), just west of Armenia, offering a coffee museum, guided walks, cultural shows, a children's theme park, and an aerial cableway. Or visit **Panaca** in Quimbaya, an agricultural family attraction with farm animals, horseback riding, and an impressive stunt-riding show.

DAY THREE From the charming town of **Salento**, with its traditional central plaza, hike into the **Cocora Valley** with its lush vegetation and towering wax palms, or visit the **Acaime Natural Reserve** beyond.

Essentials

GETTING THERE
There are daily flights to Pereira's **Matecaña Airport** from Bogotá and other cities. **Taxis** are inexpensive and you can use them to tour the region if you don't want to rent a car.

WHERE TO STAY
Villa Nora (inexpensive) in Quimbaya has simple rooms and beautiful views on a working coffee farm. *+57 6 321 4424*

El Eden Country Inn (moderate), just outside Armenia, has spacious, well-furnished rooms with a pool, restaurant, and bar. *+57 6 749 5531*

El Delirio (expensive), near the National Coffee Park, has eight lovely rooms in a beautifully restored *finca*. *+57 6 745 0405*

TOURIST INFORMATION
www.turismocafeyquindio.com

ZONA CAFETERA COLOMBIA

Country Cooking in Colombia

Butting up against the rugged peaks of Colombia's Cordillera Central are rounded mountains in a dozen shades of green, their lush, forested slopes interspersed with wax palms, banana trees, and bamboo, and acre upon rolling acre of plantations. This is coffee country – perfect for touring, hiking, and all manner of outdoor recreation, with robust, rustic Andean cuisine to sustain you.

Colombia's Coffee Triangle, the Zona Cafetera, lies west of the capital Bogotá and south of Medellín. Apart from its spectacular natural beauty, it is a fascinating region to explore. Scenic roads between the three main cities – Pereira, Armenia, and Manizales – are lined with coffee fields and with flowers, from swaths of carnations grown for export to exotic heliconias. Bustling small towns such as Salento, which overlooks the beautiful Cocora Valley, offer glimpses of local life, from women cooking *arepas* (a kind of corn tortilla) on sidewalk grills to corner stands piled high with fruits and coconuts. National parks, hot springs, and nature preserves offer a variety of ways to enjoy the magnificent scenery, and adventure sports are popular here too: you can go riding, rafting, or "canopying" through the treetops on aerial cables.

But the coffee plantations themselves have the greatest appeal. Not only can you tour the farms and watch workers in broad-brimmed straw hats harvesting coffee beans by hand; many also offer simple but charming guest rooms in the brightly painted old haciendas and *fincas* (farmhouses), filled with antique furnishings and ringed with balconies on which to enjoy the views.

This is also the best place to eat a traditional *bandeja paisa*, the typical dish of Colombia's Andean region. *Paisa* is the name for the people of this region, while *bandeja* is the Spanish word for "platter" – and it takes an oversized plate to hold all 13 components of the dish. It includes minced beef, fried pork belly, spicy chorizo with lemon, and red kidney beans cooked with pork in an aromatic soup, as well as black pudding and a fried egg. Balancing the dish with color and texture are white rice, avocado, and crispy fried plantain. Last but not least are large, flat *arepas*, topped with *hogao*, a spicy sauce made with onions, tomatoes, and garlic.

Bandeja paisa is essentially a peasant dish, with enough protein and calories to keep the workers going through long days in the fields and treks over the mountains. An authentic *paisa* platter is hearty, tasty, sizzling South American fried food that has spread from the family kitchens of Colombia's coffee country to restaurant tables across the country.

What Else to Eat

Colombia has many other delicious regional dishes. In Bogotá and the surrounding Andean region, the most famous dish is **ajiaco**, a thick, tasty soup made with three kinds of potatoes, chicken, corn, and guasca, a fragrant local herb. It's served with dishes of cream, capers, and avocado, which you add to taste. On the north coast, another traditional soup is **sancocho**, made with various meats to which yucca, plantain, corn, potatoes, and spices are added. **Tolimenses** are a kind of corn tamale from the Tolima region, made with *lechona* (roast pig stuffed with rice and vegetables) wrapped in plantain leaves and boiled for several hours. **Ternera llanera**, a dish from the eastern Llanos cattle ranchlands, is veal spit-roasted over an open fire.

Left Coffee bushes blanket the slopes of the rolling Zona Cafetera

The Best Places to Eat Bandeja Paisa

Mama Flor moderate

Ask someone in the coffee region where to eat *bandeja paisa* and the first answer is always an enthusiastic one – Mama Flor! Located in a high-class residential area in one of Pereira's oldest neighborhoods, the restaurant is surrounded by green zones and has fine views of the city from its small balcony. It was founded by two local businessmen and named after one of the partners' mothers.

Built in the typical style of the coffee region from wood and *guadua* (the native bamboo), the restaurant has an airy, open dining room and rustic decor, which attracts international tourists as well as locals who come for the delicious grilled meats and traditional dishes. You can get a great *bandeja paisa*, known here as "bandeja Mama Flor." Other special dishes to try include Mama Flor pork (the haunch tip), *chunchurria* (pork belly), and Mama Flor soup, a traditional plantain recipe. The restaurant also offers some fish dishes, such as trout and sea bass.

Calle 11 No. 15–12, Los Alpes, Pereira; open noon–11 PM Mon–Sat, noon–5 PM Sun; +57 6 325 1713

Also in the Zona Cafetera

Another place in Pereira to try *bandeja paisa* is **La Piazzolla**, on Av. 30 de Agosto *(+57 6 326 5433; inexpensive)*. In Armenia, **La Fogata** *(+57 6 749 5980; moderate)* is a popular restaurant serving steaks and pork chops as well as typical *paisa* dishes.

Also in Colombia

In Medellín, **Hato Viejo** *(+57 4 268 6811; expensive)* is a beautiful hacienda with a flower-filled courtyard and fine views of the city. The Plato Montañero is their *bandeja paisa*; those with smaller appetites can order a half-portion. Another Medellín favorite is **El Rancherito** *(www.elrancherito.com.co; moderate)*, with a large airy dining room and open grill. In Bogotá, enjoy the best of traditional Colombian cuisine at **El Portal de La Antigua** *(www.portaldelaantigua.com; expensive)*, a classy restaurant with live music.

Around the World

In the US, Houston, Texas, has several Colombian restaurants; one of the best for *bandeja paisa* is **Gran Colombia** *(www.grancolombiarestaurante.com; inexpensive)*. The favorite place for London's Colombian community to enjoy *bandeja paisa* is **La Bodeguita** *(www.labodeguita.co.uk; inexpensive)*, tucked away in the hulking Elephant and Castle shopping center on the south side of the Thames River.

RIO DE JANEIRO

RIO DE JANEIRO BRAZIL

Feijoada in Rio de Janeiro

There is nothing that the people of Rio de Janeiro enjoy more than the beach. Unless it's a *feijoada*. Brazil's national dish is not so much food as the center of social celebration. After a swim off Ipanema Beach, a walk through Tijuca National Park, or a bit of shopping, families get together on Sunday lunchtimes over this hearty bean-and-meat stew to catch up and chew the fat.

Ipanema is the most famous beach in Brazil. This stunning sweep of pearly sand is sandwiched between towering headlands that twinkle with lights in the lilac dusk. A towering statue of Christ watches over it all, perched high on the rocky, rain forest covered mountain of Corcovado. The Atlantic Ocean is bottle-green and the weather eternally sunny.

Ipanema is also Rio's most fashionable neighborhood, packed with chic shops, swish restaurants, and cafés, and frequented by Brazil's beautiful people. Not far away, vast slum cities sprawl up the surrounding hillsides. The communities are a world apart, but united by the love of a few key things: samba, soccer, the beach, and the national dish, *feijoada*.

Feijoada is a black bean, pork, and sausage stew that is simmered for hours in a clay pot and served with rice, spring greens, *farofa* (pan-fried manioc flour), slices of orange, and strong *cachaça* rum. The dish is almost as old as Brazil itself: legend has it that *feijoada* evolved from stews cooked by Brazilian and African slaves on the sugar plantations in northeastern

Brazil, from leftovers given to them by the Portuguese and meager amounts of homegrown food. There was little time for preparation, but meat offcuts and beans could be quickly thrown in a pot to simmer over hot embers all day as the slaves worked the fields.

Like samba music, the dish spread from Brazil's poor communities to the rest of the country over the centuries. In the 19th century, a French traveler to Brazil, Augustin Saint-Hilaire, noted that black bean stew was as common at a rich man's table as it was in the wattle-and-daub houses of his slaves, and by 1833 a dish called *feijoada à la Brazilian* (beans Brazilian-style) was being served in high-society restaurants.

By the 20th century, eating *feijoada* every Friday had become a countrywide ritual to mark the end of the work week. Nowadays most Brazilians, rich or poor, get together for a Sunday *feijoada* lunch with family and friends. Visitors can enjoy the dish in a similar way – in good company and over several lunch-time hours – at one of Rio's traditional *feijoada* restaurants. The best *(see facing page)* sits just behind the beach in Ipanema, strategically positioned for diners to work up an appetite with a swim.

Above The statue of *Christ the Redeemer* overlooks Rio from the Corcovado mountain in the Tijuca National Park; it can be reached by cable car

Rio's Restaurant Street

Rua Dias Ferreira, a five-minute taxi ride from Ipanema, is one of South America's top foodie destinations. This 550-yd (500-m) street is lined with restaurants on both sides – from swanky São Paulo fusion establishments to nouvelle cuisine sushi, Brazilian Thai, and, of course, the inevitable spit-roast meat restaurants. This is the place for a leisurely stroll on a balmy evening, when you're in search of a restaurant. The most famous are **Carlota** (www.carlota.com.br), serving Brazilian food with an Asian and French twist; **Zuka** (www.zuka.com.br), with its fabulous beef; **Sushi Leblon** (www.sushileblon.com), where you can try slivers of fish with *pâté de foie gras*; and **Sawasdee** (www.sawasdee.com.br), with a Brazilian take on Southeast Asian cooking that is heavy on flavor and low on spice.

A Day in Rio de Janeiro

With breathtaking views at every turn, mountains covered in rain forest, and a myriad marvelous beaches, Rio de Janeiro is resolutely an outdoor city. *Cariocas*, as the locals are called, meet, greet, and eat outdoors.

MORNING Spend the morning on **Ipanema beach** – leave your valuables in the hotel and take nothing more than a *kanga* (shawl) and a *tanga* (bikini) or *sunga* (swimming briefs) with you to the beach. In the late morning, wander Ipanema's streets in search of a café or juice bar for lunch.

AFTERNOON Take a helicopter flight over the **Christ at Corcovado** for possibly the world's most unforgettable urban views. Land on the summit of the **Morro de Urca** mountain and spend the day walking around the forests here and the neighboring **Sugar Loaf** mountain (reachable by cable car).

EVENING Swing and sway to the samba beat in a bar, club, or just on the streets in **Lapa**, Rio's liveliest nightlife neighborhood, which is packed with party crowds at the weekend. Or opt for a more elegant evening spent sipping a cocktail in the super-chic 1920s **Copacabana Palace** or the Philippe Starck **Fasano** hotel.

Essentials

GETTING THERE
Domestic and international airlines fly into Rio's Tom Jobim international **airport**. The city can be reached by **bus** from all over Brazil. The best way to get around Rio is by **subway** or **taxi**.

WHERE TO STAY
Cama e Café (inexpensive) offers bargain homestays and the chance of *feijoada* with a local family. www.camaecafe.com.br
Arpoador Inn (moderate) sits in a modest block in a superb location overlooking the Atlantic. www.arpoadorinn.com.br
Fasano (expensive) is the most luxurious hotel in the city, situated right on the beach in Ipanema. www.fasano.com.br

TOURIST INFORMATION
www.rioguiaoficial.com.br

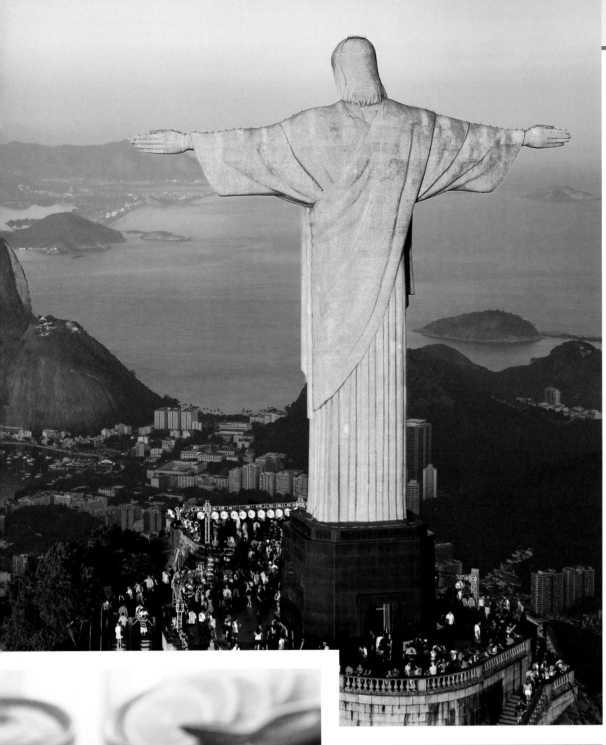

The Best Places to Eat Feijoada

A Casa da Feijoada moderate

This traditional restaurant, just a stroll away from the beach in Ipanema, has been serving *feijoada* to local families for decades. It's best to come with a very empty stomach for a full feast, which begins with a little bowl of rose coco (borlotti) bean soup. This is followed by a steaming tureen of *feijoada* (with extra bowls of meat so relentless carnivores can add to the stew at whim), and traditional accompaniments of spring greens pan-fried in garlic, fried manioc, rice, *farofa* (toasted manioc flour), and slices of succulent orange. Portions are large enough for two. Unlike most Rio restaurants, this one serves *feijoada* every day. Crowds get large on a Sunday, so be sure to make reservations.

Prudente de Morais 10, Ipanema, Rio de Janeiro; open noon–11 PM daily; +55 21 2247 2776

Also in Rio

The Casa da Feijoada vies with another fashionable alfresco restaurant and bar in nearby chic Leblon – **Academia da Cachaça** *(+55 21 2529 2680; expensive)*. Like its rival, the Academia serves a traditional *feijoada* daily (with smaller portions for kids on request). A meal here wouldn't be complete without a glass or two of fine Minas Gerais *cachaça* rum, from the most extensive *cachaça* menu in Rio.

Also in Brazil

In a poll conducted by São Paulo's prestigious *Folha* newspaper, **Veloso** *(+55 11 5572 0254; moderate)* was voted the best place in the city for *feijoada*. The lively bar and restaurant serves the classic stew with traditional trimmings. Drink it with a caipirinha cocktail (*cachaça* and plenty of lime) – barman Souza is said to serve one of the best in Brazil.

Around the World

The uber-trendy, arty Shoreditch bar and restaurant **Favela Chic** *(www.favelachic. com; moderate)* in London was inspired by the colorful bric-a-brac of a Rio *favela* slum and is famed for its exuberant atmosphere. Its daytime menu includes *feijoada* and the bar serves caipirinha cocktails, *cachaça* rum, and Portuguese Sagres beer. There's a branch of the restaurant in Paris too.

New Yorkers dine from a varied menu of Brazilian favorites at **Ipanema** *(www. ipanemanyc.com; moderate)*, a mid–West Side restaurant in the heart of a cluster of streets that have become known collectively as "Little Brazil." Prices are great for Manhattan, and the choice includes a huge *feijoada* big enough for at least two people.

Above Rio's Ipanema beach stretches for 2 miles (3 km); two mountains, the Dois Irmãos ("two brothers"), mark its western end

Left Traditionally made using pork offcuts, *feijoada* can encompass a range of different meats, from pork *choriço* to salted, cured beef

Food Festivals Around the World

No celebration is complete without good food and drink, but sometimes the food or drink itself is the reason for a party. It may be to welcome the coming of spring or harvest time; to rejoice in the arrival of seasonal produce; to pay tribute to a traditional local skill; or simply to celebrate a feast day handed down through the generations. Whatever the reason, the next eight pages give just a taster of the tens of thousands of food festivals that take place each year around the world – the best, the oldest, the most rustic, and the quirkiest. To take part in any one of them is to get a real sense of the place and the people, and is an opportunity not to be missed.

JANUARY

EUROPE

St-Antoni Abat, Andorra
Perched high in the Pyrenees between France and Spain, Andorra keeps out the cold on St. Anthony's Day with huge vats of its national dish, *escudilla*, a meaty stew cooked on an open fire and served in the terra-cotta dish of the same name. Everyone is welcome to join in the feast.

St-Vincent Tournante, Burgundy, France
At the end of January, when the vines are bare and snow is often on the ground, the villages of the Burgundy region take turns lauding the patron saint of winemakers with colorful processions, solemn ceremony, and a great deal of conviviality and fine wine. *www.st-vincent-tournante.fr*

Burns Night, Scotland
The birthday of Scotland's national poet, Robert Burns, on January 25 is enthusiastically celebrated across the country with readings of his verse, dishes of haggis *(see pp22–3)*, "neeps and tatties" (mashed rutabaga and potato), and, most importantly, a few drams of fine Scottish whiskey. *www.robertburns.org/suppers*

ASIA AND AUSTRALASIA

Auckland Seafood Festival, New Zealand
Auckland honors its fishing heritage with the biggest seafood festival in New Zealand. After a ceremonial blessing of the fleet, the harbor becomes a licensed market where visitors can sample the freshest seafood, matched with local wines and beers. *www.aucklandseafoodfestival.co.nz*

Blues, Brews and BBQs, Mount Maunganui, Hastings, and Blenheim, New Zealand
Celebrate the Kiwi summer in style at this community-oriented festival, held over three Saturdays in different towns. Top New Zealand blues bands entertain the ear, locally brewed beers, ciders, and wines amuse the palate, and gourmet chefs prepare barbecue to satisfy every taste. *www.bluesbrews.co.nz*

NORTH AMERICA

Niagara Icewine Festival, Canada
Over three weekends in January, Canada's vine-growing region celebrates its famous Ontario Icewine (produced from grapes left to freeze on the vine) with vineyard tours, tastings at alfresco ice bars, warming chestnut roasts, and Cellar Room dinners that pair award-winning wines with mouthwatering dishes and fine local cheeses. *www.niagarawinefestival.com*

Cayman Cookout, Grand Cayman, Cayman Islands
Not as rustic as it sounds, this festival of food and wine in the idyllic setting of the Cayman Islands is an exercise in contrasts – for example, when a "beach barbecue" is hosted by a world-renowned chef. A once-in-a-lifetime experience – heavenly cuisine in a tropical paradise. *www.caymanislands.ky*

Mendocino County Crab & Wine Days, California, USA
It's the height of the Dungeness crab season on Mendocino County's coastline, and these seven seafood-filled days feature everything from an all-you-can-eat Crab Feed to a Crab Cake Cookoff, with tastings to help match local wines to the food. *www.mendocino.com*

SOUTH AMERICA

Fiesta Nacional de Chivo, Mendoza, Argentina
The Feast of the Goat is Argentina's biggest food festival. Over 1,000 kid goats are roasted *asado*-style over open fires in a week-long extravaganza of meat, fire, and folk music. At daily gaucho shows, Argentinian cowboys display remarkable feats of horsemanship.

Costumbrista Chilote, Chiloé, Chile
On this misty, magical archipelago, legend and ceremony come together in the traditional dish *curanto (see pp314–5)*, and never more so than during Chiloé's annual celebration of island life and culture. The earth-oven-baked meat and fish sustained islanders against the lure of mermaids and trolls – folklore performances recount the tales.

EUROPE

Fête du Citron, Menton, France
After the Carnival of Nice, the biggest event on the Riviera is the spectacular Menton Citrus Festival. Over 150 tons of lemons, limes, and oranges are displayed as magnificent creations – from smiling Buddhas to marauding dinosaurs – on parades of gargantuan floats. *www.feteducitron.com*

Rye Bay Scallop Week, East Sussex, UK
The Cinque Port of Rye yields some of the finest scallops in the country, and this festival combines award-winning wines with music and eight days of events, from scallop-cutting, preparing, cooking, and tasting to the wheelbarrow-pushing "What a Load of Scallops" race. *www.ryebayscallops.co.uk*

Fiera del Cioccolato, Florence, Italy
The premier artisan chocolatiers of Tuscany come together once a year in Florence's historic and beautiful Piazza della Croce to display their skills and their wares. Visitors can watch these masters of their art at work and, of course, sample some of the finest chocolate creations in the world.

Brez'n Angeln, Oberammergau, Germany
Oberammergau is famed for spiritual sustenance in its Passion Play, but for food of a more earthly kind, it goes "Pretzel Fishing." Townsfolk in traditional dress, accompanied by a marching band, tour the town in a horse-drawn cart from which fresh-baked pretzels are dangled on rod and line. Everyone has to jump like fish to snatch a savory treat.

THE MIDDLE EAST AND AFRICA

Prickly Pear Festival, Port Elizabeth, South Africa
Strangely, on South Africa's famous Garden Route, they make a big fuss about a little fruit once considered an "alien undesirable." So much so that 16 tons of prickly pears are processed for the festival – into preserves, chutneys, candy, and *witblits*, a fiery spirit that is only legally distilled right here.

ASIA AND AUSTRALASIA

Setsubun, Japan

On the last day of winter, people flock to Buddhist temples and Shinto shrines to throw roasted soybeans and chant "Demons out, happiness in." It's considered lucky to catch and eat as many beans as your age. These events are supported by entertainers, celebrities, and sumo wrestlers.

Marlborough Wine Festival, New Zealand

The lovely Marlborough wine region of South Island is the largest in New Zealand, and was pivotal in introducing New World Sauvignon Blanc to a grateful Old World. Enjoy tastings and tutorials amid the vines of beautiful Brancott Estate. *www.wine-marlborough-festival.co.nz*

NORTH AMERICA

Feria del Alegría y el Olivo, Santiago Tulyehualco, Mexico City, Mexico

The sacred Aztec amaranth grain and the Spanish-introduced olive sit side by side in a festival that blends ancient culture with modern ideas. Visitors flock to this historic quarter of the city to taste olives and their oils, munch amaranth cakes and cookies, and watch displays of traditional dance and music.

Portland Seafood and Wine Festival, Oregon, USA

The finest Oregon seafood can be found at this family-oriented event, including lobster, crayfish, and the famous Dungeness crab. There's also an Oyster Shuck & Swallow Contest, a Celebrity Crab Cracking Contest, cooking demonstrations, and live music. Adults can sample from 50 local wines while the kids enjoy puppet shows and building sandcastles. *www.pdxseafoodandwinefestival.com*

SOUTH AMERICA

Pisco Sour Day, Lima, Peru

Some say that the pisco sour is as Peruvian as Machu Picchu. Those inclined to agree will lift a glass in Lima on the first Saturday in February and join in the celebrations for this pisco brandy, lime, egg white, and sugar cocktail, with bartender contests, music, and feasts of traditional Peruvian cuisine.

MARCH

EUROPE

Carnevale di Ivrea, Piedmont, Italy

Imagine thousands of brightly costumed combatants pelting each other with oranges, some in horse-drawn carts, others milling around them in the streets, up to their shins in citrus pulp. Or go to Ivrea on Shrove Tuesday and join in the fun. Huge pots of beans and sausages, cod, and polenta are all served free. Magnificent.

Beer Day, Reykjavík, Iceland

Prohibition in the US lasted 13 years; in Hungary it was only 133 days; but in Iceland beer was banned for 74 years, until March 1, 1989. Not surprisingly, that day became National Beer Day and is celebrated in style in pubs, clubs, and restaurants across the party town of Reykjavík.

Maslenitsa, Russia

Maslenitsa is a lively week-long festival that blends the pagan farewell to winter with the Orthodox preparation for Lent. The focus of the feast is the blini, a Russian pancake, round and golden like the sun, topped with sour cream, smoked salmon, honey, or caviar and washed down with vodka.

THE MIDDLE EAST AND AFRICA

Lamberts Bay Kreeffees, South Africa

Kreeffees is Afrikaans for "crayfish feast," and crayfish are in abundance at this festival in beautiful Lamberts Bay in the Western Cape. Match your tastings with a glass of Graça, South Africa's best-selling seafood wine, while watching stunning aerial displays and listening to live music. For the more energetic there is bungee-jumping and even a half-marathon. *www.kreeffees.com*

ASIA AND AUSTRALASIA

Melbourne Food & Wine Festival, Australia

Possibly the largest extravaganza of its kind, this event boasts more than 250 gastronomic and wine events over ten days, including "The World's Longest Lunch" and masterclasses from international chefs with more Michelin stars than you can shake a stick at. *www.melbournefoodandwine.com.au*

Wildfoods Festival, Hokitika, New Zealand

Judging by the crowds that flock here every year, it seems that everyone wants to try such delicacies as wasp larvae ice cream, huhu grubs, and beer-battered beetles. There's whitebait, venison sausages, and the like for the less adventurous, and a wide range of entertainment. Costumes are positively encouraged. *www.wildfoods.co.nz*

NORTH AMERICA

Vermont Maple Open House, Vermont, USA

"Sugar-on-Snow" – the pouring of boiling maple syrup onto a fresh snowfall to make taffy – is just the icing on the cake of this special weekend, when the region's "sugarhouses" open their doors for demonstrations, events, and tastings. *www.vermontmaple.org/events.php*

Yuma Lettuce Days, Arizona, USA

Yuma is the "Winter Lettuce Capital of the World," so it's no surprise that folks here make a bit of a song and dance about all things green and good, with culinary classes, food tastings, microbrew beers, and local wines, and fun events such as ice-carving and hayrides. *www.yumalettucedays.com*

SOUTH AMERICA

Fiesta de la Vendimia, Mendoza, Argentina

As befits the wine capital of Argentina, Mendoza hosts the biggest and most spectacular grape-harvest festival in the land, drawing tens of thousands to the party. They come for horseback gaucho parades, music-and-light shows, fireworks displays, and, of course, delicious, robust local red wine.

From left to right Piping in the haggis at a Burns Night dinner in Edinburgh, Scotland; children throwing beans during Setsubun in Tokyo, Japan; an impressive reconstruction of the Taj Mahal using citrus fruits at the Fête du Citron, Menton, France; the "World's Longest Lunch" at the Melbourne Food & Wine Festival

APRIL

EUROPE

Eel Day, Ely, UK

Ellie the Eel, a giant replica of the slippery fish that gave this Fenland city its name, leads a colorful procession from the 7th-century cathedral to the Jubilee Gardens, where everyone joins in the eel-tasting, beer-swilling, hog-roasting, and medieval jollity. There's even an eel-throwing contest – though these days they use socks!

Fiestas del Bollo, Avilés, Spain

On Easter Monday, Avilés' historic downtown pulsates with traditional music, decorated floats, folk dancers, and throngs of people in vivid costumes. Rows of tables, hundreds of place-settings long, are covered with a communal feast of mouthwatering Asturian dishes, the focus of which is the *bollo*, a multi-tiered, star-shaped extravaganza of an iced bun.

Fête de la Coquille, Côtes d'Armor, France

Three ancient fishing ports on the Côtes d'Armor take turns to host this celebration of the scallop. Up to 80,000 seafood-lovers come to see the boats unload their day's catch, watch the waterside auctions, and sample Brittany's legendary *coquilles St-Jacques* against a background of Celtic music.

THE MIDDLE EAST AND AFRICA

Ikeji, Arondizuogu, Nigeria

Ikeji isn't just a yam festival, it's a centuries-old veneration of the Aro tribal culture. The yam isn't just a vegetable, either: it is revered as the very essence of the Aro economy and way of life. As revelers enjoy a sumptuous feast, masked gods dance among them, dispelling evil spirits to the delirious rhythms of traditional drums, bells, and flutes.

Prince Albert Olive Festival, South Africa

High in the Swartbergs in the Western Cape, on the edge of the Great Karoo, the climate is perfect for growing olives. Village farms offer tastings of fresh and marinated olives and their oils, Karoo lamb stews, award-winning cheeses, and delicious local wines. Fire-dancers, folk music, fun runs, stargazing, ghost walks, and even a pit-spitting contest make this a great family experience. *www.patourism.co.za*

ASIA AND AUSTRALASIA

Hanshi, Xiamen, China

This festival dates to 2,500 years ago, when, once a year, cooking fires were extinguished and allowed to rest before relighting with new-season firewood. The custom is honored with cold food feasts of rice porridge, pickled vegetables, fish paste, bamboo shoots, tofu, date cakes, and preserved eggs.

World Gourmet Summit, Singapore

Singapore is always a gastronomic paradise, but never more so than in April, when some of the world's most renowned chefs come together to share their secrets with eager gourmets. Events include culinary masterclasses, intimate Chef's Table dinners, tutored tastings, and in-depth workshops. Every serious foodie should make the pilgrimage at least once. *www.worldgourmetsummit.com*

NORTH AMERICA

World Grits Festival, St. George, South Carolina, USA

It's over 25 years since St. George discovered it was the world's biggest consumer of grits – a dish made of coarsely ground corn – and the town hasn't stopped celebrating yet. Tens of thousands join in the fun and games – tossing corn cobs, rolling in vats of gooey grits, and chowing down in an all-you-can-eat contest.

Oistins Fish Festival, Barbados

Beautiful Barbados honors its fishermen and celebrates the spectacular harvest of its waters at this Easter event. Visitors can choose from a vast array of seafood and dine in the sunshine or under the stars to a calypso beat. If that's too laid-back, games and competitions include a fish-boning challenge and even a greasy pole contest.

Le Pince d'Or, Grand'Rivière, near Fort-de-France, Martinique

The tiny fishing village of Grand'Rivière brings together the island's French and Caribbean flavors in its Pince d'Or (Golden Pincer) competition, held each Easter Sunday. The aim is to cook the best *matoutou*, a rich crab stew flavored with lime, cinnamon, chili pepper, and garlic. Join the locals along the palm-fringed riverside for a day of feasting and music.

MAY

EUROPE

Spargelfest, Schwetzingen, Germany

Historic Schwetzingen is Europe's white asparagus capital. At the spring harvest festival, this "Royal Vegetable" is sold in the castle square, fresh or cooked in many different recipes. A favorite is with hollandaise sauce and smoked ham, but there's even asparagus ice cream. There are colorful parades, banquets, and the triumphant crowning of the festival's Asparagus King or Queen.

Fête des Fromages, Rocamadour, France

One of the most beautiful villages in France hosts the largest cheese festival in the south. It begins with a blessing of the herds of sheep and goats, which are then paraded through the streets, and continues with an outdoor festive lunch, a farmers' market, and performances of traditional regional music. Be sure to try Rocamadour's own esteemed Cabécou goat cheese. *http://fromages.rocamadour.free.fr*

Watercress Festival, Alresford, UK

Mineral-rich spring water is the secret behind Alresford's success as the UK's largest producer of this versatile and delectable superfood. The Watercress King and Queen lead a parade of jazz bands and morris dancers, handing out the new season's watercress to thousands of revelers. There's a huge street market, cooking demonstrations from celebrity chefs, and the World Watercress Eating Championship. *www.watercressfestival.org*

European Beer Festival, Copenhagen, Denmark

The best beer festival in the world? Who knows, but brewing giant Carlsberg opens its historic cellars and stables to host this intoxicating extravaganza that offers visitors the opportunity to taste hundreds of Danish and international beers, ales, and lagers. The festival is hosted in various venues across the city. Book events early to avoid disappointment.

THE MIDDLE EAST AND AFRICA

South African Cheese Festival, Stellenbosch

This is South Africa's biggest cheese festival, with over 200 palate-tingling varieties and a veritable cornucopia of accompaniments. Meander through the story of milk from the udder to the plate while the kids try their hand at milking, then relax by the waterfront with a tasting plate and unforgettable views of a Table Mountain sunset. *www.cheesefestival.co.za*

Taam Hair (A Taste of Tel Aviv), Israel

Indulge all of your senses at this explosion of sounds, sights, smells, and superb samplings from top Israeli chefs and vintners. Tour the culinary booths and take your pick of the tastes, eat while strolling through Hayarkon Park or sitting on the grass, or simply dance with thousands of party-goers.

ASIA AND AUSTRALASIA

Cheung Chau Bun Festival, Hong Kong

In one of the world's most exciting festivals, residents of Cheung Chau dress in colorful costumes and parade through the streets to commemorate the sea god Pak Tai. At midnight on the last day, teams race up 60-ft (18-m) towers to collect buns, which are then handed out to revelers.

NORTH AMERICA

Castroville Artichoke Festival, Monterey County, California, USA

In 1948, Marilyn Monroe was crowned Castroville's first Artichoke Queen – what finer pedigree could a festival have than that? Try this delicious edible bud fried, pickled, marinated, sautéed, griddled, or creamed, and sip silky California wines, all in this quaint little town at the heart of artichoke country. *www.artichoke-festival.org*

Maui Onion Festival, Lahaina, Hawaii, USA

Sweet, juicy Maui onions are prized by chefs and they're the star of the show here at Whaler's Village in a full day and evening of events, including chef demonstrations, a Best Onion Recipe contest, a Raw Onion Eating challenge, island music, and fine dining. *www.whalersvillage.com/onionfestival.htm*

Toledo Cacao-Fest, Belize

True chocoholics should make a pilgrimage to the land where cocoa ripens in the tropical sun, to see it being grown, harvested, and processed the traditional, handmade way into the food of the (Mayan) gods. It's all possible in this idyllic reef-and-rain forest setting, along with a gourmet Wine and Chocolate dinner, cultural events, and a spectacular festival finale of music and fireworks.

JUNE

EUROPE

Vlaggetjesdag, Scheveningen, Netherlands

"Flag Day" is named for the bright pennants that flutter from the rigging of the herring boats as they race the first of the new season's catch back to Scheveningen to be auctioned. Thousands line the quay to watch them arrive, listen to sea shanties, and, most importantly, eat herring – pickled, smoked, or even raw. *www.vlaggetjesdag.com*

La Grande Bufala, Eboli, Italy

Everyone agrees that buffalo-milk mozzarella is the best, and Eboli believes its Mozzarella di Bufala Campagna is the best of all. Leafy Piazza della Repubblica is the showcase for everything to do with this unctuously soft and milky cheese, offering tastings, workshops, and other events lauding all things deliciously Mediterranean.

Batalla del Vino, Haro, Spain

Every June 29, the normally sedate town of Haro, in La Rioja, goes wine-crazy. Revelers armed with buckets, bottles, and even water pistols full of wine launch into pitched battles during which everyone ends up soaking wet and purple from head to toe. It's all good-natured and ends with uproarious feasting and a lot more wine – quaffed, rather than thrown.

THE MIDDLE EAST AND AFRICA

V&A Waterfront Wine Affair, Cape Town, South Africa

Over 70 of the Western Cape's top wineries come together in this gorgeous water's-edge setting. Gourmet food is on hand as well, so visitors can match the perfect Pinotage to charcuterie or grilled ostrich fillet, or sip Sauvignon Blanc with ocean-fresh oysters. No need to fret over which wine route to drive – you can tour them all here in one place.

Feria Oramena, Taolagnaro, Madagascar

Beautiful Fort-Dauphin Bay is the backdrop to this culinary carnival in honor of the delicious and abundant seafood of Madagascar – notably the spiny lobster *(oramena)*, which is the heart of the banquet. Enjoy the best of the fun down on the Esplanade by the Town Hall.

Fête des Goyaviers, La Plaine des Palmistes, Réunion

Perched high on Réunion's lush slopes, La Plaine des Palmistes may be the smallest community but it has the biggest presence during this island-wide celebration of the fragrant and versatile guava. It's a lively time of tastings, music, dance, and stories, and it's almost impossible to come away without at least one jar of delicious guava jam.

ASIA AND AUSTRALASIA

Chanthaburi Fruit Festival, Thailand

An exotic and mouthwatering celebration of "the fruit bowl of Thailand." Pluck rambutan, mangosteen, and longan fresh from the trees. Taste the ripest mangos, zalaccas, and custard apples and savor the "king of fruits," the soft and creamy durian. Parades of multicolored fruit floats, regional music, and beauty pageants are all part of the experience.

A Taste of Manly, Sydney, Australia

Manly was once described as "seven miles from Sydney and a thousand miles from care." With stands serving high-quality Australian, Indian, Malaysian, Thai, African, and Mediterranean cuisine, supported by popular New South Wales wines, this seaside festival attracts over 30,000 visitors, with world music, jazz, street performers, and beach games for the whole family.

NORTH AMERICA

Taste of Chicago, Illinois, USA

Lovely lakeside Grant Park is the venue for the "World's Biggest Food Festival," a ten-day event that takes place in the run-up to Independence Day. All the city's top restaurants are represented, offering "taster" plates so that the 3-million-plus visitors can try as many dishes as possible, from classic Chicago deep-pan pizza to iconic Eli's cheesecake.

Arcata Main Street Oyster Festival, California, USA

Arcata Bay, a stunning, almost landlocked circle of blue water in northern California, provides 70 percent of the state's oysters. The citizens of Arcata are proud of their tasty mollusks and love to show them off at this friendly festival, when local chefs serve them every which way, from raw to barbecued, and fearless gourmets compete in the "Shuck and Swallow" contest. *www.oysterfestival.net*

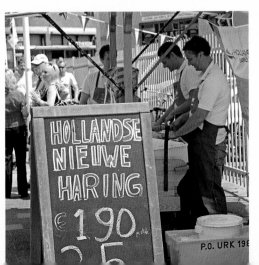

From left to right Crowds armed with "wine-pistols" at La Batalla del Vino in Haro, Spain; contestants scramble for buns up a 60-ft (18-m) tower at the Cheung Chau Bun Festival in Hong Kong; sidewalks are taken over by hundreds of food stands at the Taste of Chicago food festival; bunting decorates stands preparing and selling herring during Vlaggetjesdag in the Netherlands

JULY

EUROPE

Rapujuhlat, Finland

From late July for the next two months, Finland is simply smitten with the crayfish. Festivals and parties involve special plates, table linen, cutlery, bibs, lanterns, and even songs – and mounds of crayfish, of course. The feast is best enjoyed outdoors on a long summer evening, during which noisy, messy eating is actively encouraged.

Whitstable Oyster Festival, Kent, UK

Every aspect of Whitstable shouts tradition, and none more so than the oysters at the center of this exciting week-long festival. Entertainment abounds, with shanty singers, crab-catching, kite-flying, seashore safaris, and a very muddy tug-of-war. Don't miss the oyster-eating competition and the masked parade finale. *www.whitstableoysterfestival.com*

Pichelsteinerfest, Regen, Germany

This colorful festival is an encounter with all things Bavarian. Celebrating the delicious *Pichelsteiner* (a local stew of beef, pork, lamb, and vegetables in gravy), the whole town enjoys six days of marching bands, flag parades, music, dancing, giant fountains, fireworks, and lantern-lit boats on the Regen River.

Fête des Fruits Rouges, Noyon, France

Noyon's soft fruit has been renowned for 1,000 years and, for one day every July, the lovely cathedral square is filled with a mouthwatering aroma, as market stands are loaded with ripe, juicy currants, berries, and cherries. After a blessing of the harvest, the festivities begin, with cooking demonstrations and tastings, medieval games, and a huge communal feast.

THE MIDDLE EAST AND AFRICA

Knysna Oyster Festival, South Africa

They call it "the 10 best days of your winter" and, if you love oysters, they're probably right. Not even the South African Navy can stay away, sailing their huge minesweepers into Knysna's beautiful bay for the event. There are countless oyster stylings to sample, perfect with local microbrewery Mitchell's Raven Stout. *www.oysterfestival.co.za*

ASIA AND AUSTRALASIA

Singapore Food Festival

It's all about the delicious diversity of local cuisine at this month-long festival, which sees events all around the island, from tasting cruises and hands-on masterclasses to the lively Singapore River market. Best of all, Clarke Quay is transformed into Food Street, where street food and fine dining come together. *http://singaporefoodfestival.com.sg*

NORTH AMERICA

National Cherry Festival, Traverse City, Michigan, USA

For eight packed days in the heart of "Cherry Country" on the shores of Grand Traverse Bay, over half a million cherry-lovers gather for pie-eating, pit-spitting, road-racing, beach volleyball, and even Cherryopoly contests. And, if you can win the hole-in-one competition, the real cherry is the million-dollar prize! *http://visit.cherryfestival.org*

Copper River Wild! Salmon Festival, Cordova, Alaska, USA

Copper River salmon are prized the world over as simply the best you can eat. The unique flavor comes from extra oils they need to survive the freezing glacial waters of their spawning grounds. So it's worth the effort to seek out remote Cordova in Prince William Sound and join in the festivities with music, art fairs, road races, and plenty of tasty salmon.

Bagelfest, Mattoon, Illinois, USA

Americans love bagels so much that they have two national bagel days. The best way to celebrate this scrumptious twice-cooked Polish bread is in Mattoon, Illinois, where they bake a billion bagels a year. A giant Bagel Parade opens the festival, with a street market, pageants, dancing, a rock concert, and, best of all, free bagels. *www.mattoonbagelfest.com*

AUGUST

EUROPE

La Tomatina, Buñol, Spain

This is probably the most famous food festival of them all, and yet it's not about eating so much as painting the town red with tomatoes – around 100 tons of them. The battle only lasts an hour, but by the end, the 30,000 or so participants are soaked in scarlet juice and slipping and squelching in a sea of tomato pulp. *www.tomatina.net*

Isle of Wight Garlic Festival, Newchurch, UK

England's largest island, on the south coast, is perhaps more famous for its music festival held every June, but its annual celebration of "the stinking rose" draws equally enthusiastic crowds for garlic beer, garlic ice cream, and other fragrant delicacies. Non-garlic produce is also showcased. "Best of British" entertainment is on hand and visitors can be sure of a nice cup of (non-garlic) tea. *www.garlic-festival.co.uk*

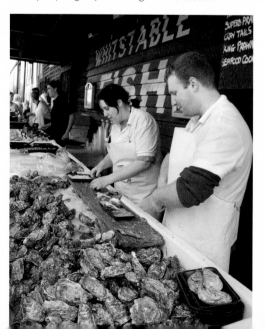

La Pourcailhade, Trie-sur-Baïse, France

Trie-sur-Baïse is in France's prime pork-producing region, so it should be no surprise that there is a Brotherhood of the Pig here. Competitions at their annual Pig Festival include piglet races, sausage-eating, best pig outfit, and the National Pig Squealing Competition (for people, not pigs). There is also music and dancing in the evening. *www.pourcailhade.com*

Skala Kalloni Sardine Festival, Lesvos, Greece

The stunning Gulf of Kalloni is almost an inland sea, and is famed for the quality of its sardines. The fishing port of Skala Kalloni gives thanks for its catch one weekend of the year with a feast of barbecued sardines and ouzo, along with traditional Greek music and dancing. It's an utterly charming experience.

THE MIDDLE EAST AND AFRICA

Imouzzer Honey Festival, Morocco

Jimi Hendrix reputedly named the "Paradise Valley" where Imouzzer sits, in the foothills of the Atlas Mountains. Here the Berbers keep bees in hives made of reeds and clay, and harvest exquisite honey flavored with mountain herbs and flowers. The Honey Festival celebrates this taste of paradise.

ASIA AND AUSTRALASIA

Yugambeh Corroboree, Southport, Queensland, Australia

What could be more Australian than a bush tucker feast after a walkabout? OK, the four-day Drumley Walk is optional, but the Yugambeh Corroboree Festival welcomes the walkers with traditional bush food, Aboriginal songs, arts and crafts exhibitions, and plenty of activities for jarjums (kids). *Yau yilnanbaugull* – or "yes, please!" *www.thedrumleywalk.com*

Onam, Kerala, India

For Kerala's Malayali people, and for this lovely state as a whole, the ten-day harvest festival of Onam is the most important event of the year. Featuring snake-boat races, traditional Kaikottikali story-dances, and intricate flower carpets, the festivities culminate with the Thiruonam feast of Onasadya, a nine-course banquet of exquisite vegetarian dishes, served on banana leaves. *www.onamfestival.org*

NORTH AMERICA

Howell Melon Festival, Michigan, USA

The delicious variety of cantaloupe melon found only in these parts was brought to Howell in seed form by a hobo during the Depression. His gift is honored every August with parades and parties, tastings of melon wine and ice cream, art exhibits and face painting (look like a melon!), and the sale of over 20,000 fine, ripe fruits. *www.howellmelonfestival.com*

Fête des Cuisinières, Point-à-Pitre, Guadeloupe

Where better for a festival of women cooks than this lovely French-Caribbean island? On the feast day of St-Laurent, the patron saint of chefs, over 200 *cuisinières* from all over the West Indies, in gorgeous Creole costumes, parade their dishes through the streets to the church to be blessed. The free five-hour gourmet banquet that follows is open to all.

Fête de la Poutine, Drummondville, Quebec, Canada

This lively weekend of music and family fun permits everyone to indulge in a little too much of the unofficial Quebecois national dish, *poutine* – a mushy but irresistible concoction of French fries, cheese curds, and rich brown gravy. Infinite varieties exist, many of which can be sampled here for as long as your appetite holds out. *www.festivaldelapoutine.com*

SOUTH AMERICA

Otro Sabor, Medellín, Colombia

In the beautiful setting of Medellín's Botanical Gardens, chefs and gourmets from Colombia, Latin America, and the world come together for this celebration of food and flavors. From the simple cornbread *arepa* to the 13-element *paisa* platter (ranging from avocado to pork rind), there's plenty to sample.

SEPTEMBER

EUROPE

Galway Oyster Fest, Ireland

Follow the colorful parade through the streets, then dig in to new-season oysters with smoked salmon, crab claws, seafood chowder, and chilled white wine. Not to mention the Guinness World Oyster Opening Championship finals, a gala ball, and the Saturday Oyster Trail, when 40 hostelries offer free oysters and live music. *www.galwayoysterfest.com*

Pizzafest, Naples, Italy

Naples' tantalizing ten-day festival honors their most famous culinary creation. But even before you get your hands on a pizza, the teasing aroma of freshly-baked marinara, Margherita, calzone, and *quattro stagioni*, wafting from wood-fired ovens all over the city, will have your mouth watering. Events include music, theater, and workshops.

Oktoberfest, Munich, Germany

Biggest? Oldest? Best? Superlatives can't describe this 200-year-old extravaganza, where over 6 million revelers consume 2 million gallons of beer. But don't forget the roast meats, fish, dumplings, pretzels, and, of course, sauerkraut and sausages, all served by energetic waiting staff wearing those famous dirndls and lederhosen. *www.oktoberfest.de*

Brick Lane Curry Festival, London, UK

Every year, Brick Lane, London's world-famous "Curry Mile," explodes with color and aromas as Bangla Town's fabulous feast inspires tens of thousands to savor every tongue-tingling spicy taste imaginable. Over 40 restaurants display their very best dishes to be tasted and enjoyed, to the vibrant sounds of the music festival. *www.curryfestival.co/*

THE MIDDLE EAST AND AFRICA

Soweto Wine Festival, Johannesburg, South Africa

What began in 2004 as a crazy dream around a braai in Pretoria has matured into South Africa's most up-and-coming,

trendsetting wine event. Three nights of tutored wine and food tastings, featuring over 800 wines, might sound like any other show, but this is Soweto-style, with spicy food and cool jazz. *www.sowetowinefestival.co.za*

ASIA AND AUSTRALASIA

Mooncake Festival, China

Also called the Mid-Autumn or Moon Festival, this nationwide event is honored with music, dancing, and mooncakes. These beautifully decorated pastry pies are on sale in every bakery. They're filled with a sweet bean or lotus seed paste, wrapped around a salted duck egg yolk representing the moon. Cut into small wedges, they're eaten while watching the full moon rise.

NORTH AMERICA

Posen Potato Festival, Michigan, USA

On the first weekend after Labor Day, the tiny town of Posen goes back to its Polish roots with traditional costumes, crafts, music, polka dancing, and potatoes. Entrants to the Potato Cooking Competition have no chance of beating Beatrice Richard's record – she notched up her 47th win with her Cheeseburger Soup recipe (secret ingredient: potatoes).

Feast of San Gennaro, New York City, USA

New York's Little Italy may be a shadow of its former self, but not when New York's biggest, oldest, and most revered festival bursts on to the streets. Processions, feasts, and festivities last 11 days, during which religious devotion and good eating go hand in hand. Don't miss the statue of San Gennaro being paraded through the streets – or the Cannoli Eating Competition. *www.sangennaro.org*

SOUTH AMERICA

Mistura, Lima, Peru

Mistura is a showcase for 7,000 years of Peruvian cuisine and produce. Hand-picked representatives, from street vendors and country cooks to gourmet chefs, demonstrate and serve every style of cooking. Adventurous diners can even sample roast *cuy* (guinea pig). Traditional and modern Peruvian music and a lively market and bazaar add to the unique flavor of the event. *www.mistura.pe*

From left to right New-season oysters on display at the Whitstable Oyster Festival, England; different varieties of mooncake eaten during China's Mooncake Festival in September; revelers getting messy during Spain's La Tomatina in August; crowds throng on Clarke Quay's Food Street during the Singapore Food Festival

OCTOBER

EUROPE

Fiera del Tartufo, Alba, Italy

Historic Alba's White Truffle Festival is an unforgettable experience for lovers of the "white diamond," with its truffle fair, market, and (for top chefs and gourmet millionaires only) auction. Many of Alba's restaurants have special menus, or will simply shave the truffle over risotto or pasta – perfect with a glass or two of delicious Barolo wine. *www.fieradeltartufo.org*

Fiesta de Exaltación del Marisco, O Grove, Spain

Over ten days of seafood heaven, the small fishing community of O Grove becomes an aromatic market teeming with mussels, oysters, scallops, crabs, clams, octopus, hake, sea bass, turbot, and sole. Sample them, fresh or cooked, with a glass of the local Rías Baixas wine, while enjoying Galician-Portuguese folk dancing and Celtic *gaita* bagpipes.

Fête des Vendanges de Montmartre, Paris, France

In 1933, the citizens of Montmartre resurrected a tiny vineyard only streets away from Sacré-Coeur. Ever since, they've rejoiced in the harvest and auctioned the wine off for charity. The festival is now so popular that hundreds of thousands of celebrants fill the streets to revel in the vintners' parades, live music, theater, and poetry, and buy wines from all over France.

Salone del Gusto, Turin, Italy

Showcase of the Slow Food Movement, the biennial Salon of Taste attracts exhibitors from around the world. Seasonality, locale, and quality are essential criteria for the cured meats, fish, vegetables, cheeses, fruits, and breads on display here. *www.salonedelgusto.it*

THE MIDDLE EAST AND AFRICA

Fête des Dattes, Erfoud, Morocco

With nearly a million date palms to harvest, it's not surprising that the people of Erfoud celebrate the year's sweet, sticky harvest with such zeal. For three days they feast and dance to traditional music; then comes the climax, a thrilling camel race into the dunes of the Sahara.

ASIA AND AUSTRALASIA

Crave Sydney, Australia

With a whole month of over 600 diverse gastronomic events across the city, Sydney is the place to be in October, with gourmet dinners, night noodle markets, pop-up barbecues, and bush tucker experiences. But the showpiece is Breakfast on the Bridge, when the traffic stops and the Harbour Bridge is grassed over for a grand picnic. *www.cravesydney.com*

Phuket Vegetarian Festival, Thailand

In this extraordinary but energetic and colorful festival, participants abstain from meat and other stimulants to expunge evil spirits and bring good luck. Vegetarian dishes are eaten, but not everyone will have the stomach for the fire-walking and outlandish body piercing displays by entranced Ma Song devotees. *www.phuketvegetarian.com*

NORTH AMERICA

American Royal Barbecue, Kansas City, Missouri, USA

Claiming to be the largest barbecue competition in the world, the American Royal attracts hundreds of tongs-bearing, apron-wearing, grill-firing teams from across the US. To the rhythms of live bands they cook brisket, pork ribs, pork, and chicken for the title, with a sauce competition as a bonus. Most important, though, it's all tastable. *www.arbbq.com*

World Championship Gumbo Cook-Off, New Iberia, Louisiana, USA

On the banks of the Bayou Teche, picturesque Bouligny Plaza is filled with makeshift kitchens, and tantalizing aromas waft into the sultry air. Saturday begins with traditional jambalaya, *étouffée*, boudin, and fried fish; then, on Sunday, the great Cook-Off gets under way. Around 12,000 lb (5,500 kg) of chicken and sausage, seafood, game, and even alligator gumbo make this a truly jumbo event.

New York City Wine and Food Festival, USA

To get an idea of the pace, excitement, and ground covered in this crammed foodie weekend, think "New York Marathon meets Woodstock meets Iron Chef." From meatballs to master chefs, fizzy drinks to finest New World wines, Blumenthal to Bourdain, there is something for everyone of every age. Book early. *www.nycwineandfoodfestival.com*

SOUTH AMERICA

Oktoberfest, Blumenau, Brazil

Founded in 1850 by Herman Otto Blumenau, his namesake city is a mini-Germany in the south of Brazil, but there's nothing small about their Oktoberfest. Over two weeks, a million party-lovers crowd the streets for the brightly costumed parades, marching bands, folk dancing, authentic German cuisine, and, of course, the local brews.

NOVEMBER

EUROPE

Les Trois Glorieuses, Beaune, France

It's been called "the greatest eating and drinking experience on the face of the planet," and certainly the Three Glorious Days, centered on Burgundy's famed charity wine auction, live up to their name. Tickets for Monday's eight-hour lunch at Château Meursault are beyond the reach of most, but everyone can enjoy the open-house tastings and the festive atmosphere that pervades noble Beaune and its vineyard villages.

Olioliva, Imperia, Liguria, Italy

Liguria's tiny purple Taggiasca olive is said to produce the finest olive oil in the world – mellow, woody, peppery, and utterly delicious. Imperia welcomes the new season's oil with a huge street market, and visitors from all over northern Italy and nearby Provence come to sample and buy – not just oils but Liguria's famed pesto, focaccia, and Cinque Terre wines too.

Ziebel Märit, Bern, Switzerland

Bern's medieval Onion Market begins as you would expect. Hundreds of stands are laden with every kind of allium – braided, bouqueted, decorated, and turned into all sorts of tasty onion-flavored products – as well as lots of other hearty winter food. Later, though, the carnival kicks off, with jesters, singers, onion-costumed locals, and wild confetti battles long into the winter night.

ASIA AND AUSTRALASIA

Guangzhou International Food Festival, China

Guangzhou is rightly proud of being said to have the best food in all of China. People flock from nearby Hong Kong and Macau to dine here, and never more so than during this annual exhibition of its culinary prowess. Lots of different cuisines are on display, but don't miss the Cantonese delicacies.

Nabanna, Dhaka, Bangladesh

The name Nabanna means "new food" and, in the Bangladeshi countryside, it's one of the most important events of the year. The rice harvest is celebrated with symbolic foods such as *payesh* (rice pudding) and *pitha* (rice flour cakes), as well as traditional music and dances, and offerings to the Hindu goddess of wealth, Lakshmi.

NORTH AMERICA

Kona Coffee Festival, Big Island, Hawaii, USA

Wake up and smell the coffee at Hawaii's oldest food festival. It's the rich volcanic soil that's said to give this pure arabica its rare depth of flavor and aroma, prized by connoisseurs the world over. No wonder the people of the Kona district choose to honor it with pageants, parades, competitions, cultural events, and plantation tastings. *www.konacoffeefest.com*

Chitlin' Strut, Salley, South Carolina, USA

Some say that, for a true taste of the south, nothing quite beats a chitlin'. Others prefer the fried chicken or barbecued ribs to deep-fried pig's intestines, but everyone's in agreement that a great time is to be had at the Salley Chitlin' Strut, with parades, a pancake breakfast, carnival rides, dancing, and the great Hawg Call competition. *www.chitlinstrut.com*

Festival Gourmet International, Puerto Vallarta, Riviera Nayarit, Mexico

Drawing culinary superstars from around the world to host events such as Chef's Table and Winemaker's Night dinners, Gourmet Safaris, and even a Chefs' Hell Raising Party, it's not difficult to see why this festival on Mexico's Pacific Riviera has made its mark. *www.festivalgourmet.com*

Cornucopia, Whistler, British Columbia, Canada

With snow already thick on the slopes, it's hard to imagine anyone is in town for anything else. But now's the time that serious foodies make a pilgrimage to Whistler for one of the most exciting and informative gastronomic events of the year – this is a wining and dining experience to beat any off-piste adventure. *www.whistlercornucopia.com*

DECEMBER

EUROPE

Les Glorieuses de Bresse, France

With its red comb, white body, and blue legs, the Bresse chicken is the *tricouleur* emblem of France – and rightly so, since it is often judged the finest poultry in the land. Four towns in this Burgundian region each host a day of this fête in its honor, with gourmet markets, tastings, culinary demonstrations, and dinners at which the *coq* is king. *www.glorieusesdebresse.com*

Sagra del Singhiale, Suvereto, Italy

The narrow streets, squares, and cloisters of this ancient Tuscan town take on a medieval flavor for the Wild Boar Festival. Pageants, archery, fencing, jesters, and even human chess games all contribute to the magical atmosphere. The focus of the feasting is, of course, roast wild boar, served with grilled polenta and wild mushrooms and plenty of local wine.

Christkindlesmarkt, Nuremberg, Germany

The Christmas Angel opens Nuremberg's magical old-world market, when the city square sparkles and the air is filled with the delicious aromas of mulled wine, hot chestnuts, roast sausages, gingerbread, fruit loaves, and marzipan candies. Hundreds of decorated stands form a "Little Town of Wood and Cloth." *www.christkindlesmarkt.de*

Fiera dia Castagna, Bocognano, Corsica, France

Corsicans call the chestnut the "tree of life," and its flour is used in bread, polenta, cakes, and even beer. Chestnut jelly, honey, and liqueurs are highly prized, as is charcuterie from the local boars that feed on the nuts. As the island's most important crop it truly deserves this annual celebration, which involves competitions, demonstrations, and market stands piled high with chestnut products.

THE MIDDLE EAST AND AFRICA

Franschhoek Cap Classique and Champagne Festival, South Africa

With a French heritage going back over 300 years, Franschhoek is understandably proud of its reputation as the gourmet capital of South Africa. Set in "the most beautiful wine valley in the world," it celebrates its good fortune, presenting its own Cap Classique bubbly alongside the great names of Champagne. Mouthwatering French delicacies are served to complement the wine. *www.franschhoek.org.za*

ASIA AND AUSTRALASIA

Taste Festival, Hobart, Tasmania, Australia

Charming Sullivan's Cove, in Tasmania's capital city, plays host to ten days of feasts and fun, culminating on New Year's Eve with a grand fireworks display over the tranquil harbor waters. Circus acts, buskers, stilt-walkers, and street theater entertain the kids, while the grown-ups can enjoy artisan beers, fine Tasmanian wines, and Tasting Tours of local gourmet cuisine.

NORTH AMERICA

Night of the Radishes, Oaxaca, Mexico

Leave radishes in the ground for months until they grow up to two feet long. Then dig them up and carve them into fantastic sculptures of Nativity scenes, dancers, warriors, folk heroes, trees, and buildings. Sounds crazy, but that's what happens at this extraordinary one-of-a-kind Christmas festival in Oaxaca.

Inn-to-Inn Cookie and Candy Tour, White Mountains, New Hampshire, USA

What better way to get into the holiday spirit than to make a snowy tour around the quaint inns of New Hampshire, all decked out in their Christmas finery? Visitors are welcomed with handmade cookies, candy canes, and other festive treats, and can vote on stunning gingerbread sculptures, collect family recipes, and depart with visions of sugarplums to last a lifetime.

SOUTH AMERICA

Santuranticuy, Cusco, Peru

Plaza del Armas becomes a vast, illuminated Nativity scene in the days before Christmas Eve's breathtaking Santuranticuy ("saints for sale") market. Country people flock into town with ceramic manger figures to sell, including the Andean baby Jesus, El Niño Manuelito. There's sweet rum punch, roast corn, and *panetón* cake for those who can afford it, while hot chocolate and fruited biscuits are given to the poor.

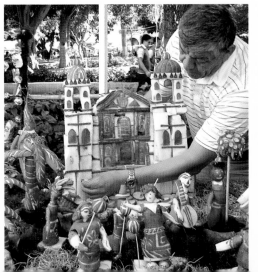

From left to right Blessing food at the Phuket Vegetarian Festival in October; stands lit up at night during Christkindlesmarkt, in Nuremburg's central square; singers and dancers perform in traditional dress at the Fête des Dattes in Erfoud, Morocco; a craftsman displays figures carved from radishes during Mexico's Night of the Radishes celebrations in December

Index

Acknowledgments

The publishers would like to thank the following for their text contributions:

Rudolf Abraham (pp40–1, 164–5, 178–9); Joshua Armstrong (pp212–5, 238–9); Brett Atkinson (pp240–3); Maryanne Blacker (pp 14–15, 34–5, 48–9, 58–9, 72–3, 88–9, 98–101, 114–5, 128–9, 142–3, 154–5, 216–7, 306–7); Michael Booth (pp196–7, 208–9, 218–9, 234–5, 246–7); Jonathan Bousfield (pp56–7, 108–9); James Brennan (pp172–3, 176–7); Philip Briggs (pp 166–7, 170–1, 182–3); Jules Brown (pp12–13, 42–3, 46–7, 84–7, 104–5, 126–7); Joe Cummings (pp244–5, 252–3); Donna Dailey (pp260–1, 272–283, 288–91, 296–7, 318–9); Nick Edwards (pp192–3, 210–1, 228–231, 250–1); Anna Maria Espsäter (The Flavors of South America; pp106–7, 116–7, 152–3); Steve Fallon (pp120–1); Fay Franklin (pp 322–9); Mike Gerrard (pp134–5, 150–1, 174–5); Frances Linzee Gordon (The Flavors of the Middle East and Africa; pp28–9, 50–3, 110–13, 162–3, 168–9, 180–1, 184–5); Dominic Hamilton (pp304–7); Patricia Harris and David Lyon (The Flavors of Europe; The Flavors of North America; pp18–21, 60–1, 68–71, 82–3, 102–3, 118–9, 136–7, 258–9, 286–7); Rachel Howard (pp32–3, 62–3, 140–1); David Leffman (The Flavors of Asia and Australasia; pp190–1, 198–9, 200–7, 220–3, 248–9); Sarina Lewis (pp194–5, 232–3); Gail Mangold-Vine (pp 44–5, 138–9); Anthony Mason (pp78–9, 96–7, 144–5);

Declan McGarvey (pp 308–11, 314–5); Norman Miller (pp22–3, 124–5); Jenny Myddleton (pp262–3, 284–5); Gillian Price (pp16–17, 30–1, 54–5, 66–7, 80–81, 90–91, 122–3, 146–9, 156–7); Dan Richardson (pp74–5, 94–5); Alex Robinson (pp302–3, 312–3, 320–1); Annelise Sorensen (pp264–9, 292–3); Christian Williams (pp26–7, 36–9, 64–5, 76–7, 93–3, 130–3); Dan White (pp224–5, 236–7); Matt Willis (pp24–5); Sarah Woods (pp270–1, 294–5, 316–7), and Martin Zatko (pp226–7).

General introduction by Patricia Harris and David Lyon: www.hungrytravelers.com

Dorling Kindersley would also like to thank Douglas Amrine, Georgina Small, Alexandra Whittleton, Louise Dick, Shahid Mahmood, Chloe Roberts, Rose-Innes Designs, and Kevin Gould for their part in the making of this book.

Cobaltid would like to thank Ellen Root and Marta Bescos for assistance with picture research, Hilary Bird for the index, Kati Dye for proofreading, and Christine Heilman for Americanization of the US edition.

Picture Credits

The publishers would like to thank the following for their kind permission to reproduce their photographs:

(Key: a–above; b–below/bottom; c–center; f–far; l–left; r–right; t–top)

Rudolf Abraham: 41tr, 165br.
Alamy Images: AA World Travel Library 120br; Hank Abernathy 258t; AllOver photography 56t; B.A.E. Inc. 1c; Pat Behnke 96t; Jeffrey Blackler 6b; Sam Bloomberg–Rissman 69br; Bluemagenta 272br; Bohi 196–197s; Bon Appetit 51br, 53t, 72tr, 95tr, 127bl, 142tr, 148c, 262bl, 280bl, 305tr; Terry Bruce 165tr; JS Callahan/Tropicalpix 327br; Franck Camhi 312t; Wendy Connett 189r, 212–213t, 226t, 246b; Dennis Cox 290br; CuboImages srl 111tr; Yaacov Dagan 310b; Jean–Dominique Dallet 112b; DBimages 112t, 118bl, 179tr, 266b, 270–271c; DC Premiumstock 65br; Danita Delimont 66t, 66cl; Gary Doak 322bl; Peter Eastland 18–19c; Susie M. Eising 16bl; EuroCreon Co.Ltd. 227br; Eye Ubiquitous 300r; F1online Digitale Bildagentur GmbH 73b; Kevin Foy 7b; Stephen French 133b; Gastromedia 27bl, 83bl, 105bl; Simon Hadley 42tl; David Hancock 241tr; Glenn Harper 58bl; Gavin Hellier 254–255c, 286–287b; Tim Hill 118tr, 167br, 182cl, 224l, 275tl; Hornbil Images 210–211c; Peter Horree 51tr; Ilianski 24br; Imagebroker 38t, 252–253tc, 262t; IMAGEMORE Co. Ltd. 191br; Islemount Images 193br; Itanistock 177bl; Jan Smith Photography 135cr; Graham Jepson 275br; John Warburton–Lee Photography 249br; Jon Arnold Images Ltd 15t, 29tr, 29cr, 288–289b; Tarek el Juan 31br; Paul Kingsley 52b, 328bl; Oliver Knight 78bl; Yadid Levy 20bl, 175tr, 175br, 303br.; Lightworks Media 214c; Lonely Planet Images 33tr; David Lyons 84–85c, 277br; Marka 317br; Martin Thomas Photography 36–37clb; Iain Masterton 132b; Tony McNicol 209bl; Mikecranephotography.com 208–209tr; Bildarchiv Monheim GmbH 92–93b; Eric Nathan 86b; Michael Neelon 286t; Niceartphoto 323bl; David Parker 200–201b, 218tr; Patrick/Sagaphoto.com 68–69bc; PCL 199b; Pegaz 120–121tc; PjrTravel 77br, 137br; Plinthpics 325br; Vova Pomortzeff 27br; Prisma Bildagentur AG 117b; Simon Reddy 47br, 113t, 139bl, 229br, 238tr, 253bl; Robert Harding Picture Library Ltd 329bl; Robert Preston Photography 178–179c; Roger Cracknell 01/Classic 22br; Pep Roig 230tr; Margaret S 182t; Pere Sanz 34–35c; Andre Seale 312–313b; Alex Segre 20tr; Neil Setchfield 75crb, 204r; Slick Shoots 87c; Michael Sparrow 315cr; Stock Italia 91bl; Stockfood Ltd 106cl, 170tr, 216cl; Jochen Tack 83br; Terry Harris Just Greece Photo Library 141tr; Domenico Tondini 184bl; Mikael Utterström 116t; Vario Images 306–307t; Michael Ventura 290tr; David Wall 242c; Graham Watts 70cr; Maximilian Weinzierl 146cr; Ken Welsh 19br, 106t; George Wilson 326bl; Gregory Wrona 21bl, 25l; Brian Yarvin 276bl.
Antica Focacceria San Francesco: 149b.
Bettys of Harrogate: 85t, 85bl, 86l.
Blue Pepper Restaurant: 125br.

Austin Bush: 212–213bl.
Choco–Story: 145tr.
Corbis: Peter Adams 10l, 167bl, 281bl; Piyal Adhikary 231bl; Alan Schein Photography 293bl; Abel Alonso 324bl; H.Amiard/Photocuisine 146–147cb; Arcaid 292bl; Art Bank 209br; Yann Arthus–Bertrand 32–33c; Astock 326br; Atlantide Phototravel 11r, 12–13ts, 122b, 188l; Olga Rosario Avendano 329bl; Youssef Badawi/epa 161r; Denis Balibouse 44tr; Morton Beebe 129tr; Neil Beer 71cl; Yannis Behrakis 141cr; Remi Benali 198bl; Bilic 48l; Blend Images/Inti St Clair 7b; Christophe Boisvieux 35crb; Massimo Borchi 16t; J Boyer 48tr, 78t ; Demetrio Carrasco 30bc; Roderick Chen 168l; Li Xu Cheng 207br; Romain Cintract 60b; David Clapp 82–83c; Jerry Cooke 101t; Pablo Corral V 304–305c; Creativ Studio Heinemann 74l, 107tl, 117tl, 239tl, 284bl; Richard Cummins 272–273t; Fridmar Damm 76b; Pascal Deloche/Godong 214t; P.Desgrieux 203bl; Nacho Doce 105br; Nacho Doce/Reuters 13bl, 13br; M.Duffas 155br; Envision 278–279tc, 289br; Robert Essel 234–235t; Macduff Everton 244br, 315tr; Neil Farrin/JAI 241br; Fleurent 283br; Owen Franken 10r, 54crb, 81cr, 100b, 115br, 243b, 310c; Stuart Freedman/In Pictures 146–147tc; Franz–Marc Frei 101b, 131br; Marc Garanger 95br; J.Garcia 80l; J.Garcia/Photocuisine 181tl; Bertrand Gardel 102tr; Sean Gardner 283tr; Hen Gongzheng/XinHua/Xinhua Press 185b; Philip Gould 74–75c, 256r; Tim Graham 100c, 216t; Darren Greenwood 274tr; Justin Guariglia 215b; Gyro Photography 235br; Paul Hardy 58t; Blaine Harrington III 6–7b, 196r, 246t; Martin Harvey 12l, 229tr; Chris Helgren 123br; Gavin Hellier 98–99c, 99br, 176–177tc, 180t; Jon Hicks 129br, 231tl, 232t, 232–233b, 258b, 250b; Olivier Hoslet 128–129c; Dave G. Houser 4t, 131tr, 267b; Xie Guang Hui/Redlink 190–191t; Image Source 245tr; Janet Jarman 285bl; Wolfgang Kaehler 271br, 280t, 305cr; Layne Kennedy 295bl; Kham/Reuters 239br; Reinhard Krause 206tr; Bob Krist 38b, 39t, 161l, 166–167cs, 296t; Kamil Krzaczynski 325bl; Zurab Kurtsikidze 41br; Last Refuge 316t; Last Refuge/Robert Harding World Imagery 134–135c; Graham Lawrence/Robert Harding World Imagery 94–95cs; Lester Lefkowitz 297bl; Danny Lehman 257l, 298–299c, 302b, 320–321t; Jean–Pierre Lescourret 142br; Leser/SoFood 89br; Yadid Levy 52r; Barry Lewis/In Pictures 11l; James Leynse 292t; Lisa Linder 204tr; Xiaoyang Liu 220–221b; Eduardo Longoni 308–309c; Steve Lupton 220l, 266c; Lo Mak/Redlink 226bl; Mascarucci 148bl; René Mattes 274cr; Stephanie Maze 291bl; Colin McPherson 23bl; A.Muriot 102br; Michael Nicholson 172–173tc; Morteza Nikoubazl 179br; Kazuyoshi Nomachi 164–165cs; Richard T. Nowitz 197l; Ocean 23tl, 109tr, 260tr, 270l, 306l; Pilar Olivares 307br; Othk 200–201t; Owaki/Kulla 282–283c; Douglas Pearson 22t, 39b, 152tl, 294–295t; Clay Perry 279bl; Photolibrary 126b; Radius Images 163br, 195b; Jose Fuste Raga 17bl, 138–139tl, 216–217b, 236t, 327bl; Steve Raymer/National Geographic Society 263bl; Redlink 220t; Carmen Redondo 67br;

Michael Reynolds 191bl; Jose Manuel Ribeiro 126tr; Riou 307bl; J.Riou 71tl; Riou/photocuisine 45br; Riou/SoFood 34l, 321bl; Riviere 169cr; Robert Holmes 269br; Martin Roe/Retna Ltd. 266t; Rosenfeld 97l; Guenter Rossenbach 62–63c, 64b; Hans Georg Roth 56–57b; Roulier/Turiot 19r, 35cra; Pablo Sanchez 61br; Michel Setboun 309tr; Hugh Sitton 309br; SoFood 81tr, 281l; Sylvain Sonnet 55cl, 72b; Brigitte Sporrer 122tr; Sprint 108l; Inti St Clair/Blend Images 7b; Klaus Stemmler 174l; Hans Strand 14–15c; Studio Eye 88l, 202tr; Keren Su 124–125tc; Jim Sugar 181br; David Sutherland 184t; Murat Taner 50–51c, 261br; Luca Tettoni 244t, 245br, 247br; Nico Tondini 312l; Onne van der Wal 314–315c; Niels van Gijn 170b; Jose Manuel VidaLepa 119br; Steven Vidler/Eurasia Press 2–5c; Westend61 130l; Nik Wheeler 155tr, 202br; Peter M. Wilson 46–47c, 284t; Michael S. Yamashita 301t; Bobby Yip 248–249tc; Bo Zaunders 63tr, 256l.
Dorling Kindersley: 17tl, 28l, 32l, 33cr, 59l, 61l, 62l, 84l, 98l, 114l, 119l, 134tl, 150l, 153l, 162tl, 222l, 225tl, 259l, 261l, 287t, 293l, 313tl, 314l; Philip Dowell 46l, 82l, 143l, 173br, 185tl, 248l Roger Dixon 18l, 40l, 54l, 127l, 278l, 282l, 308l, 319l; Andrew Downes 243t; Ben Fink 128l; John Freeman 317tl; Jill Fromer/iStock Exclusive © Getty 164l; Will Heap 93tl, 94l, 204l, 277l, 320l; John Heseltine 67tl; Dinesh Khanna 210l; Dave King 14l, 49l, 73tl, 166l, 178l, 183tl, 240l, 297l; David Murray 137l, 157cr, 247tl; David Murray and Jules Selmes 138l; Ian O'Leary 31tl, 77tl, 90l, 102l, 124l, 146tl, 195tl, 207l, 217tl, 221l, 227tl, 234l, 294l; Roger Phillips 303tl; Rob Reichenfeld 202cr; Tim Ridley 43t; Russell Sadur 110l; Helena Smith 242t; Simon Smith 140l, 193tr; Clive Streeter 63cr, 196l, 199t; Lorenzo Vecchia 171tl, 208l, 228l, 283tl, 285l, 304tl; Chris Villano 50l, 172l; Colin Walton 163tl; Linda Whitwam 140–141c.
Getty Images: 28–29c, 68–69c, 108–109c, 242b, 318t, 324br, 328br; A485 290cr; Peter Adams 110–111c, 162b, 228–229c, 240–241c; AFP 54–55t, 113b, 177br, 189l, 206b, 223br, 300l, 322br, 323br; Sang An 76tl; Bill Arce 53b; Klaus Arras 223bl, 232c; James Baigrie 125bl; Scott E Barbour 103l; Santiago Barrio 60tr; Meike Bergmann 269br; J Boyer 143br; Austin Bush 271tr; Rosemary Calvert 68l; Car Culture 257r; Stephen Caraccio 42l; Clive Champion – Champion Photography Ltd 21tl; Michael Coyne 5r; Creativ Studio Heinemann 65tl, 154l; Creative Crop 24l; Sebastian D'Souza/Stringer 192b; De Agostini 40–41c, 79bl; Bruno De Hogues 238b; Dea/M. Borchi 152b; Stuart Dee 59bl; Karen Desjardin 154–155cs; Joseph Devenney 5l; Digital Vision 13bl; Allison Dinner 180br; Dinodia Photos 211br; Jessica Dixon 274br; Shaun Egan 144–145cs; Luzia Ellert 26l; Anel Fernandez 136br; Dennis Flaherty 268–269r; Foodcollection 30tr, 38c, 57l, 157br, 212l, 296bl, 311b; FoodPhotography Eising 258l; Foodpicto 56cl; Franz Marc Frei 130–131cs; Lee Frost 171br; Eric Futran 310t; Gentl and Hyers 15c; Dennis Gottlieb 249bl; Tim Graham 87t; Sylvain Grandadam 198t; Jorg Greuel 36–37t; Andrew Gunners 301l; Gyro Photography/amanaimagesRF 200l;

Tim Hall 224t; Martin Harvey 5c; Will Heap 237tl; Katja Heinemann 271cr; Gavin Hellier 111br, 158–159cs; Peter Hendrie 222–223tc; Chris Hepburn 169tr; Jon Hicks 188r; Hiroshi Higuchi 92t; Andrew Holt 150–151c; Enamul Hoque 251tl; Simeone Huber 114–115cs; Hisham Ibrahim 316br; Image Source 47tr, 115tr; IMAGEMORE Co. Ltd. 219tl; Images of Africa 291tl; Spencer Jones 268l; Jupiterimages 87b, 192tr, 230bl, 318l; Ray Kachatorian 91br; Wolfgang Kaehler 173bl; Jonathan Kantor 288l; Kaveh Kazemi 160r; Wilfried Krecichwost 92cl; Kroeger/Gross 104l; Thomas Larsen 211t; Brian Lawrence 48–89c; Siegfried Layda 70br, 121cl; Brian Leatart 295br; Emma Lee/Life File 44b; Justin Lightley 194bl; Vincenzo Lombardo 147br; Sabine Lubenow 37br; Robin MacDougall 149t; MIB Pictures 52c; Alison Miksch 276tr; MIXA 219br; Camille Moirenc 89tr; Gareth Morgans 151tr; Ippei Naoi 218b; Neo Vision 100t; Karl Newedel 64tr, 231cl; NY Daily News 311t; Panoramic Images 42–43bl, 182–183bs; PhotoAlto/Laurence Mouton 252l; Photosindia 250tr; Andrea Pistolesi 112c, 214b; Nicholas Pitt 205l; Paul Poplis 109br; James Randklev 273br; Peter Richardson 139br; Anne Rippy 260b; Lew Robertson 272l; Michael Rosenfeld 233tl; Jeff Rotman 160l; Michael Runkel 213br; Joern Rynio 75tc; Tom Schierlitz 79l; Ralf Schultheiss 132c; Sandro Sciacca 123tl; Paule Seux 211tr; Pankaj Shah 251br; Martin Shields 66bl; Vladimir Shulevsky 120l; Camilla Sjodin 116bl; Slow Images 90–91t, 104–105cs, Otto Stadler 224–225b, 253br, 267t; Stefano Stefani 80–81c; Armstrong Studios 286c; Keren Su 174–175cs; Jean–Daniel Sudres 99tr; Jane Sweeney 318–319b; Tai Power Seeff 302tr; Murat Taner 48–49b; Tetra Images 288–289c; Teubner 36l, 153br; Tom Till 106–107b; Travelpix Ltd 136t, 203tl; Luca Trovato 156l; Ellen van Bodegom 156t; Heinrich van den Berg 133t; Guy Vanderelst 96–97b; VisionsofAmerica/Joe Sohm 258–259b; Matthew Wakem 236br; Anna Watson 148t; Brian Yarvin 71bl; H. & D. Zielske 26–27tc.
Glenn Grossman Photography: 276b.
© **Le Gruyère AOC:** 45tl.
David Hogan Junior: 237br.
Antony Mason: 96l.
Photodisc: felipedupouy.com 190l.
Photolibrary: Fabian von Poser 168–169c.
Rules Restaurant: 151br.
Vasse Felix Vineyard: 194t.
Marek Walisiewicz: 24tr, 135tr.
Zum Wenigemarkt 13: 132t.

Jacket images:
Front: **Corbis:** Judy Griesediec tl, JAI / Alan Copson tc, Daniella Nowitz tr; **Photolibrary:** Iconotec / Cali b; Back: **Corbis:** Jon Hicks r, Jean–Pierre Lescourret l; Spine: **Dorling Kindersley:** Suzanne Porter t

All other images © Dorling Kindersley
For further information see: www.dkimages.com

Ultimate Food Journeys:
Dishes Around Europe

NORWAY

SWEDE

Bergen
Gravadlax
p152

Bohuslan
Smorgasbord
p116

NORTH
SEA

DENMARK

Copenhagen
Smørrebrød
p106

Edinburgh
Haggis
p22

Whitby
Fish & chips
p42

York
Afternoon tea
p84

REPUBLIC OF
IRELAND

UNITED
KINGDOM

North Norfolk
Gastropub food
p134

NETHERLANDS

Amsterdam
Rijsttafel
p124

Berlin
Eisbein
p26

Bruges
Chocolate
p144

Brussels
Moules-frites
p78

GERMANY

London
Roast beef
p150

Ghent
Waterzooi
p96

BELGIUM

Aachen
Sauerbraten
p92

LUXEMBOURG

Nuremberg
Bratwurst
p130

CZECH REPU

Paris
Macarons
p58

Strasbourg
Choucroute garnie
p154

Ulm
Spätzle
p76

Munich
Knodel
p64

Brittany
Crepes
p34

Salzburg
Torten
p36

ATLANTIC

Loire Valley
Tarte Tatin
p114

Alsace
Tarte Flambée
p72

Zurich
Rösti
p138

OCEAN

Beaune
Boeuf Bourguignon
p14

AUSTRIA

FRANCE

Gruyères
Cheese fondue
p44

Treviso
Tiramisu
p90

SWITZERLAND

SLOVENIA

Lyon
Lyonnais bouchons
p48

Savoie
Cheese
p98

Milan
Risotto
p30

Kvarner
Scampi
p56

Liguria
Pesto
p156

Tortellini
Bologna
p146

San Sebastian
Modern Spanish cuisine
p60

Toulouse
Cassoulet
p142

Nice
Salade Niçoise
p88

Umbria
Truffles
p80

Marseille
Bouillabaisse
p128

ITALY

Rome
Carciofi
p54

Porto
Bacalhau
p46

SPAIN

Barcelona
Zarzuela
p102

Naples
Pizza
p16

PORTUGAL

Madrid
Churros, p68
Cocido, p136

Valencia
Paella
p82

Capri
Insalata Caprese
p122

Lisbon
Pasteis de Nata
p12

Evora
Porco à Alentejana
p126

Alicante
Tapas
p18

Algarve
Cataplana
p104

Seville
Gazpacho
p118

Noto
Gelati
p66

ALGERIA

TUNISIA

MEDITER

MOROCCO